MORAL THEORY
AT THE MOVIES

MORAL THEORY AT THE MOVIES

An Introduction to Ethics

DEAN A. KOWALSKI

ROWMAN & LITTLEFIELD PUBLISHERS, INC.

Lanham • Boulder • New York • Toronto • Plymouth, UK

Published by Rowman & Littlefield Publishers, Inc.
A wholly owned subsidiary of The Rowman & Littlefield Publishing Group, Inc.
4501 Forbes Boulevard, Suite 200, Lanham, Maryland 20706
http://www.rowmanlittlefield.com

Estover Road, Plymouth PL6 7PY, United Kingdom

British Library Cataloguing in Publication Information Available

Library of Congress Cataloging-in-Publication Data

Kowalski, Dean A.
  Moral theory at the movies : an introduction to ethics / Dean Kowalski.
    p. cm.
    ISBN 978-0-7425-4787-2 (pbk. : alk. paper) — ISBN 978-1-4422-1455-2 (electronic)
    1. Motion pictures—Moral and ethical aspects. 2. Motion pictures—Philosophy. I. Title.
  PN1995.5.K65 2012
  791.4301—dc23   2011031250

♾ ™ The paper used in this publication meets the minimum requirements of American
National Standard for Information Sciences—Permanence of Paper for Printed Library
Materials, ANSI/NISO Z39.48-1992.

Printed in the United States of America

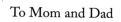

To Mom and Dad

Contents

Preface   xi

Acknowledgments   xiii

1 Rhetoric, Philosophy, and Moral Reasoning   1
Featured Film: *Thank You for Smoking* **(2005)**

   1.1   Thinking through the Movie   5

   1.2   Historical Setting: Plato, *Gorgias*   5

   1.3   Discussion and Analysis   12

   1.4   Two Additional Films: *Minority Report* (2002) and

       Dr. Horrible's Sing-Along Blog (2008)   29

   1.5   Reviewing through the Three Movies   33

PART I: METAETHICS

2 Simple Ethical Subjectivism   39
Featured Film: *Match Point* **(2005)**

   2.1   Thinking through the Movie   43

   2.2   Historical Setting: David Hume, *A Treatise of Human Nature*

       and *An Inquiry Concerning the Principles of Morals*   43

   2.3   Discussion and Analysis   46

   2.4   Two Additional Films: *The Emperor's New Groove* (2000)

       and *The Shape of Things* (2003)   57

   2.5   Reviewing through the Three Movies   62

3 Moral Relativism   65
Featured Film: *Hotel Rwanda* **(2004)**

   3.1   Thinking through the Movie   68

   3.2   Historical Setting: William Sumner, *Folkways*   69

   3.3   Discussion and Analysis   72

3.4   Two Additional Films: *The Joy Luck Club* (1993) and
       Do the Right Thing (1989)   84
3.5   Reviewing through the Three Movies   88

4   Divine Command Theory Ethics   89
Featured Film: *Frailty* (2001)
4.1   Thinking through the Movie   92
4.2   Historical Setting: Plato, *Euthyphro*   93
4.3   Discussion and Analysis   98
4.4   Two Additional Films: *Evan Almighty* (2007) and
       The Boondock Saints (1999)   108
4.5   Reviewing through the Three Movies   113

5   Ethical Objectivism   115
Featured Film: *The Cider House Rules* (1999)
5.1   Thinking through the Movie   118
5.2   Historical Setting: Thomas Reid, *Essays on the Active
       Powers of Man*   119
5.3   Discussion and Analysis   124
5.4   Two Additional Films: *Crimes and Misdemeanors* (1989)
       and *Schindler's List* (1993)   134
5.5   Reviewing through the Three Movies   139

PART II: WHAT OUGHT I TO DO?

6   Biology, Psychology, and Ethical Theory   143
Featured Film: *Cast Away* (2000)
6.1 Thinking through the Movie   146
6.2 Historical Setting: Thomas Aquinas, *Summa Theologica*   147
6.3 Discussion and Analysis   151
6.4 Two Additional Films: *Spider-Man 2* (2004) and *Boys Don't Cry* (1999)   166
6.5 Reviewing through the Three Movies   171

7   Utilitarianism   173
Featured Film: *Extreme Measures* (1996)
7.1   Thinking through the Movie   176
7.2   Historical Setting: John Stuart Mill, *Utilitarianism*   177
7.3   Discussion and Analysis   183
7.4   Two Additional Films: *Saving Private Ryan* (1998) and
       Eternal Sunshine of the Spotless Mind (2004)   197
7.5   Reviewing through the Three Movies   202

8   Kant and Respect for Persons Ethics   205
Featured Film: *Horton Hears a Who!* (2008)
8.1   Thinking through the Movie   208

8.2   Historical Setting: Immanuel Kant, *The Foundations of the
       Metaphysics of Morals*   209
8.3   Discussion and Analysis   214
8.4   Two Additional Films: *3:10 to Yuma* (2007) and *Amistad* (1997)   229
8.5   Reviewing through the Three Movies   233

9   Social Contract Theory: Hobbes, Locke, and Rawls   237
Featured Film: *V for Vendetta* (2006)
9.1   Thinking through the Movie   240
9.2   Historical Setting: Thomas Hobbes, *Leviathan*   240
9.3   Discussion and Analysis   245
9.4   Two Additional Films: *Lord of the Flies* (1990) and *Serenity* (2005)   259
9.5   Reviewing through the Three Movies   264

PART III: HOW OUGHT I TO BE?

10   Aristotle and Virtue Ethics   269
Featured Film: *Groundhog Day* (1993)
10.1   Thinking through the Movie   272
10.2   Historical Setting: Aristotle, *Nicomachean Ethics*   273
10.3   Discussion and Analysis   277
10.4   Two Additional Films: *The Last Samurai* (2003) and
        As Good As It Gets (1997)   289
10.5   Reviewing through the Three Movies   294

11   Care and Friendship   297
Featured Film: *Vera Drake* (2004)
11.1   Thinking through the Movie   300
11.2   Historical Setting: Nel Noddings, *Caring*   301
11.3   Discussion and Analysis   306
11.4   Two Additional Films: *The X-Files: I Want to Believe* (2008)
        and *Life Is Beautiful* (1997)   318
11.5   Reviewing through the Three Movies   323

12   Plato and Being Good   325
Featured Film: *The Emperor's Club* (2002)
12.1   Thinking through the Movie   328
12.2   Historical Setting: Plato, *Republic*   329
12.3   Discussion and Analysis   334
12.4   Two Additional Films: *GoodFellas* (1990) and
        The Man without a Face (1993)   347
12.5   Reviewing through the Three Movies   351

Index   353
About the Author   359

Preface

....

T he distinctive feature of the text is its implementation of film. Film is no longer the pedagogical novelty it once was. However, this text remains distinct in the extent to which it incorporates popular films. No other textbook (that I know of) does more with film than this one.

Each chapter opens with a lead film and each is anchored with two additional films. Each of the thirty-six films comes with a 1,000-1,500 word plot summary and subsequent discussion questions. The lead films have eight to ten questions each, many of which are time-coded to scenes within the film. Each of the two additional films has four to five questions, some of which are time-coded. Each chapter closes with a "reviewing through the three movies" section; it consists of chapter review questions that encourage students to synthesize the covered material by making connections between the films. Many of these could effectively serve as topics for short (formal) essays.

Thematic elements from the movies pervade much of the narrative within each chapter. The vast majority of the illustrative examples are taken from the three films, but sometimes the movies themselves (in a philosophy *of* film way) are employed to shed light on some ethically significant topic. Quotes from the films also appear throughout to emphasize some point being made in the surrounding paragraphs. And the last of the "reviewing through the three movies" questions invites students to consider how and why each quote appears where it does in the chapter.

Each chapter also contains three textboxes. The first box in each chapter provides detailed insights into how one can learn from the lead film. This information should be useful to both instructors and students. For instructors deciding to show parts of the film in class, this textbox offers suggestions about the segments most relevant to the topics covered in the chapter narrative. The segments are time-coded and also refer to scene numbers. Moreover, the starting and stopping points of the segments are described thematically to facilitate seamless classroom presentation. Yet this information should also be useful to students who are required to watch the film outside of class. As students watch, they should be particularly aware of the segments listed in the textbox; these are the philosophically richest of the movie.

The possibility of students watching the lead film outside of class also explains the second textbox in each chapter. It contains ten trivia questions from the movie that can only be successfully answered by watching it. Assigning these questions ensures that students watch the film prior to its being assigned, thereby facilitating class discussion of it at the appropriate time. (Of course, with extensive plot summaries for each movie, it is conceivable that watching the films, in part or in their entirety, in class or outside of it, might be supplemental.)

The third textbox in each chapter stipulates the relevant learning outcomes for assessment purposes. These are the pedagogical goals for the chapter. Instructors may utilize them in a pre-test/post-test fashion, as has become common in this current pedagogical age of assessment. Of course, they also could be implemented in some other way to gauge student comprehension of the material covered.

So, in some ways, this text is rather traditional. In addition to discussion questions, chapter review questions, and stipulated learning outcomes, each chapter contains a 3,000-word primary source selection that serves as a historical setting for the chapter. Students can benefit by the ethical insights of Plato, Aristotle, Aquinas, Mill, Kant, and Nel Noddings (among others). At the end of each historical setting selection, there are three review questions to gauge reading comprehension. The primary source selection is intended to complement the subsequent discussion and analysis of some classic issue in moral philosophy. That is, it is meant to be a tool for better understanding the themes of the chapter.

The text is broken up into three sections, with chapter 1 serving as a sort of introduction to them. Chapter 1 opens with a brief discussion of what philosophy is, what philosophers aim to do, and how philosophy differs from other disciplines. The chapter next delineates deductive and non-deductive argumentation, explaining how these tools are indispensible to (moral) philosophers. Finally, the chapter concludes with a very general discussion of terms like right, wrong, good, and bad. The idea here (again) is to provide a framework for the chapters to come. In these ways, the text is suitable for first or second courses in philosophy. This is beneficial because not all Ethics courses have prerequisites.

The focus of the text is moral theory. Chapter 6 offers an anatomy for moral theories and then suggests some very basic criteria by which they can be assessed for overall plausibility. Admittedly, there are some deep debates among philosophers about what a moral theory is, what it is supposed to do, and how competing moral theories are to be assessed. But the text is intended to be an *introduction* to moral philosophy. In this way, any conclusion reached about a theory is quite tentative. The goal is not to indoctrinate students to one theory over another, but to explain what its respective strengths and weaknesses are. This is to encourage students to investigate the matter more fully to see whether the strengths hold up to further criticism or whether the purported weaknesses might be somehow shored up on further review.

So, the driving motivation behind the text is to encourage you to keep doing (moral) philosophy! That you can do philosophy while enjoying your favorite films, I hope, only makes the invitation more appealing. Don't hesitate to share with me how your journey unfolds.

Acknowledgments

I must begin by thanking those at Rowman & Littlefield. Ross Miller courageously but enthusiastically contracted the book. When he left the company, Jon Sisk and Darcy Evans patiently but vigilantly nurtured its completion. The production team, led by Lynn Weber, was also tremendously supportive and cooperative in bringing the project to fruition.

I owe debts of gratitude to those who read and commented on earlier versions of the manuscript, including two insightful anonymous reviewers. I am grateful for the efforts of my UW-Colleges colleagues. Tim Dunn and Bill Schneider graciously offered their insights on a moment's notice. Joseph Foy, David Louzecky, Dale Murray, and Dan Putman kindly read and commented upon chapters 9, 8, 1, and 10 respectively. I am especially grateful to colleagues Stephen Schmid and Alan V. White for reading and commenting upon multiple chapters. And I am grateful to Tom Riley. Not only has he been a strong advocate of the project from the beginning, he also helped me frame chapter 11. I regret that he wasn't more involved, but his creative fingerprints can be found throughout the finished product. With all of this quality help, it goes without saying that any remaining infelicities are undoubtedly due to my inability to properly incorporate my colleagues' sage advice.

A project of this magnitude requires a diligent support team at home. I note Nicholas and Cassie, who waited patiently for daddy to finish yet another book. My wife, Patricia, has been incredibly patient, understanding, and kind. Without her, this book never gets finished.

Yet my largest debt of gratitude is certainly owed to my first teachers about right and wrong: my parents. Before I could spell "Kant" or "Aristotle"—before I could spell anything—they imparted to me the wisdom of doing the right thing and being a good person. With loving appreciation, I dedicate this book to them.

CHAPTER 1

Rhetoric, Philosophy, and Moral Reasoning

THANK YOU FOR SMOKING (2005)
Director and Screenwriter: Jason Reitman

PLOT SUMMARY

That's the beauty of argument; if you argue correctly, you're never wrong.

Nick Naylor, the vice president of the Academy of Tobacco Studies, informs the public about all the research performed in the investigation of the effects of tobacco. He regularly appears on television and often does newspaper and magazine interviews. But today, he appears before his son's grade school class to explain his job. He informs Joey's classmates that he is a bit like a movie star; he talks for a living—on behalf of cigarettes. A girl volunteers that her mommy believes cigarettes kill. Immediately, Nick retorts, "Really, is your mommy a doctor, or a scientific researcher of some kind?" When the blond-haired cherub answers "no," Nick quickly concludes, "Well, she doesn't exactly sound like a credible expert now, does she?" Nick clarifies that it's good to listen to parents, but "there will always be people trying to tell you what to do and what to think." He is merely pointing out "that when someone tries to act like some sort of an expert, you can respond, 'Who says?'" A puzzled little boy calls out, "So cigarettes *are* good for you?" The teacher jumps out of her chair: "No!" Nick further clarifies: "That's not what I'm getting at; my point is that you have to think for yourself." The children would never accept simply being told that chocolate was dangerous. So Nick suggests that they "should find out for themselves" about cigarettes.

After school, Nick and Joey spend the evening together, as they do almost every weekend since the divorce. Joey looks up and asks his dad for help with his homework, an essay to explain why America has the best government. Nick, after expressing some scorn about the assignment, indignantly asks whether America indeed has the best government in the world and what the phrase "best government" might mean in the first place. Joey initially rolls his eyes; however, he becomes intrigued when Nick claims that the question calls for a "B.S." answer. Nick reiterates, "Because even if America had the best government, there'd be no way to prove it, and definitely not in two pages." Nick assures Joey that he can write pretty much whatever he wants; any answer will be correct.

BOX 1A: INSIDE *THANK YOU FOR SMOKING*

Thank You for Smoking raises many interesting moral issues, including whether there are ethical constraints on how a person should employ arguments and rhetoric. It also vividly raises the issue of whether there should be any moral limits on behaviors that individuals know to be harmful (like smoking) and, in turn, what role the government or others generally should play in dissuading us from them. Along the way, it provides engaging (and sometimes humorous) examples of fallacious arguments and rhetorical devices. Being able to spot these allows one to be a better critical thinker and a more principled ethical decision maker.

To get a sense of how the movie portrays these issues, begin with scenes 2 and 3, continuing to 13:05 into scene 4. Scene 2 begins roughly at 5:50 into the film, with a white screen transitioning into a television studio audience. At 13:05 of scene 4, you'll see Joey falling asleep on his dad's lap. Then go to scene 9, which begins at 31:29. Here Joey has a discussion with his mother. Continue watching until 32:20, where Joey gets in the car with Nick, and Jill waves good-bye. Skip ahead to 35:20 in scene 9 to see Nick and Jeff Megall (Rob Lowe) discuss product placement. Continue watching into scene 10, which begins at 37:48 with a shot of the Santa Monica Yacht Harbor Cafe sign. Pay close attention to the conversation between Joey and Nick until 39:45, where Joey and Nick enjoy ice cream on a Ferris wheel. Next go to scene 12, beginning at 51:06. This scene opens with a white screen transitioning into Finistirre and his aide walking down some stairs; watch until 53:25, where you'll see a cutaway shot of an airplane in flight. At that point skip ahead to scene 13, which begins at 57:05 with Nick being abducted on the sidewalk. Continue watching until 59:23, where you'll see Nick losing consciousness and the screen becomes white. Finally, go to scene 18, and continue watching to 1:25:07 of scene 19. Scene 18 begins roughly at 1:15:37 with a shot of the Senate hearing room. At 1:25:07 of scene 19, you'll see BR's attempt to re-hire Nick, and Nick's response. Watching these scenes, along with reading the plot summary carefully, may give you a sufficient grasp of the movie.

Yet your instructor might show you the movie in its entirety or assign it to be watched outside of class. (If the latter, she might assign you to answer the "trivia" questions from Box 1B). Either way, a good way to proceed is to watch until scene 8, 30:55 into the film. (There is a fade to black here.) Stop to discuss or reflect on the movie. Skip ahead to scene 9 (thereby omitting the few R-rated shots of Nick and Heather alone together) and continue until scene 12, 53:25 into the film. Stop here for additional discussion or reflection on the movie. Skip ahead to scene 13 (again omitting some intimate moments between Nick and Heather), finish watching the film, and discuss or reflect on it as a whole.

Nick is summoned by the "Captain"—the last great man of tobacco and founder of the Academy of Tobacco Studies. The Captain is famous for introducing filters in 1952 after *Reader's Digest* slammed cigarettes for being unhealthy. The Captain wishes to speak to Nick about the idea of bribing Hollywood producers to show actors smoke on screen. (This was Nick's idea, but Nick's boss BR seems to have taken credit for it.) The Captain authorizes the Hollywood plan and Nick's (other) idea of promoting an anti-teen-smoking campaign to the tune of fifty million dollars (so long as it's not too persuasive, chuckles the Captain).

Nick meets weekly with his "colleagues" and kindred spirits Polly Bailey and Bobby Jay Bliss for lunch. The three jointly represent the chief spokespeople for the alcohol, tobacco, and firearms industries. Polly works for the Moderation Council and somehow managed to have the Pope endorse red wine. Bobby Jay works for SAFETY—the Society for the Advancement of Firearms and Effective Training for Youth. Bobby recounts his recent interview with the *Washington Post* regarding the latest "disgruntled postman." Bobby asked the reporter: "Now, if a plane crashes on account of pilot error, do you blame the Boeing Corporation?" Polly and Nick agree that this was a good response, but Polly and Bobby advise Nick not to meet with reporter Heather Holloway. Bobby Jay reminds Nick that beautiful, female reporters have ways of obtaining information.

Nick doesn't heed their advice. Upon meeting, Heather gets Nick's permission to tape their conversation. She begins: "Who is Nick Naylor?" Nick replies, "A mediator between two sects of society." Heather continues: "What motivates you?" Nick replies simply: "Everyone's got a mortgage to pay; ninety-nine percent of everything that happens is done to pay the mortgage." Nick calls this the "yuppie Nuremberg defense."

The next morning, Nick and Joey leave for California. Upon arriving, Nick and Joey meet Jeff Megall, an influential Hollywood agent. It's rumored that Megall invented product placement in movies. Nick asks Megall if he is concerned about the "health issue" associated with cigarettes. Megall reassures Nick: "I'm not a doctor. . . . Whatever information there is exists; it's out there. People will decide for themselves. . . . It's not my role to decide for them. It'd be morally presumptuous." But Megall also advises that the character seen smoking should be from the future, a time when the health thing has blown over and smoker and nonsmoker live in perfect harmony. Luckily, there is a science fiction picture (starring Brad Pitt and Catherine Zeta-Jones) looking for cofinancing. Perhaps Big Tobacco would be interested?

Nick's next stop is a guest spot on the Dennis Miller talk show. The other guest (via remote link) is Nick's nemesis, Senator Ortolan Finistirre, who is currently leading a crusade against Big Tobacco. They are to discuss Finistirre's proposal to place a skull and crossbones label on every pack of cigarettes sold in the United States. After opening volleys against each other's position, Miller interrupts them to hear from a caller. The caller asks Miller whether anyone's life has ever been threatened on his show. After reassuring the audience that this has never happened, the caller informs everyone that he will soon dispatch Nick Naylor from this earth for all of the pain and suffering he has caused as a lobbyist for Big Tobacco. Joey and Finistirre are alarmed; Miller breaks for commercial.

The threat was not idle. Back in DC, Nick is abducted by men in a white van. They slap dozens of nicotine patches on his bare skin and leave him for dead. Nick awakes in a hospital room. His friends and family are there, including the Captain via remote link. Nick's doctor frankly informs Nick: "No nonsmoker could have withstood the amount of nicotine in your bloodstream; I hate to say it, but cigarettes saved your life." Things only

---

BOX 1B: *THANK YOU FOR SMOKING* TRIVIA

If your instructor assigns the film to be watched outside of class, you should be able to answer the following questions:

1. On what television talk show does Nick appear at the very beginning of the film?
2. Who taught the Captain (Robert Duvall) the secret to making his favorite drink (mint julep)?
3. What is the name of the Captain's airplane?
4. Where do Nick and reporter Heather Holloway (Katie Holmes) first meet?
5. How much money do Brad Pitt and Catherine Zeta-Jones require to smoke together on screen?
6. When does Jeff Megall (Rob Lowe) sleep?
7. What brand of cigarette did Marlboro Man Lorne Lutch (Sam Elliott) smoke?
8. What color sport coat do the Captain's pallbearers wear?
9. What nickname (via *Newsweek*) does Joey call his dad?
10. Complete this sentence: The great state of Vermont will not apologize for _____.

---

get worse for Nick. Heather's article is published. It divulges a great deal of information, including things said while she and Nick were intimate. Nick asks her, "How can you do this to me?" and she answers, "For the mortgage." Nick is professionally ruined. BR tells him: "Your job relied on your ability to keep secrets and spin the truth." BR summarily fires Nick. The Academy of Tobacco Studies removes his belongings and the FBI discontinues its search for his kidnappers. He locks himself in his apartment.

After something of a pep talk from his son, Nick attempts a comeback. He regains popularity by discrediting Heather, explaining how she took advantage of his confidences through sexual relations. He is now ready to complete one last round with Senator Finistirre on Capitol Hill. Polly and Bobby Jay accompany him. Joey also attends the congressional proceedings. Finistirre begins by interviewing those sympathetic to his cause, but eventually Nick takes the stand.

Finistirre begins by asking who funds the Academy of Tobacco Studies. When Nick replies "conglomerated tobacco," Finistirre continues by asking whether that might affect the academy's priorities. Nick demurs, explaining that it accomplishes this no more than accepting campaign contributions affects the senator's priorities. When a different senator redirects, Nick (finally) admits to the dangers of cigarette smoking, but adds, "Sir, I just don't see the point of a warning label for something people already know." If a skull and crossbones is called for on items dangerous to the public's health, then they should also appear on airplanes, automobiles, and foods high in cholesterol—"the real demonstrated number one killer in America." Finistirre scoffs at the implication; the second senator again redirects. He reminds Nick that the warning imagery is really for those who don't know about cigarettes: the children. Nick pauses, but carefully explains that it is the job of teachers and especially parents to warn children about the dangers of cigarettes so that one day, they can choose for themselves. Finistirre becomes agitated. He inquires: On your son's eighteenth birthday, will you share a cigarette with him? Nick looks Finistirre in the eye: "If he really wants a cigarette, I'll buy him his first pack."

1.1. THINKING THROUGH THE MOVIE

Discussion Starter Questions

1. Is Nick a good father to Joey? If so, in what ways? If not, why not?
2. Should the government place a skull and crossbones poison label on every pack of cigarettes sold in this country? Defend your answer.
3. Does Heather Holloway do something morally wrong in securing the information for her article in the way that she did? Did she act wrongly in publishing the story? Explain.
4. Are some jobs (or careers) morally unacceptable? If so, does Nick have one of them? Explain your answers.
5. What seems to be the basic moral message of the film?

Questions for Further Thought

1. What does Nick seemingly mean by the "yuppie Nuremberg" defense (scene 8, roughly 30:10 into the film)? What is this apparently a defense of?
2. Near the end of the film, Nick (in a voice-over) states that some things are more important than just paying the mortgage (scene 19, roughly 1:25:00). What does he mean by this? How does this claim fit in with the "yuppie Nuremberg" defense?
3. Jeff Megall believes that it would be "morally presumptuous" of him to take a public stand on the "health issue" of cigarettes, claiming whatever information exists is out there for public access—people should decide for themselves (scene 9, roughly 35:45 to 36:05). Do your best to evaluate this (rather complex) position.
4. At the congressional hearing, Nick implicitly argues that, by putting poison labels on packs of cigarettes, the US government would be bound to put poison labels on all consumer goods dangerous to our health (scene 18, roughly 1:20:20 to 1:21:45). Senator Finistirre scoffs at this position. With whom do you agree and why?
5. At the very end of the film, Nick claims, "Michael Jordan plays ball, Charles Manson kills people, and I talk; everyone's got a talent" (scene 20, roughly 1:27:10). Is there something morally dubious (suspicious or suspect) about Nick's claim? Explain.

1.2. HISTORICAL SETTING

Gorgias (excerpt)[1]

Plato (427–347 BCE) is one the most important figures from the history of Western philosophy. It is widely held that his Academy served as the model for modern universities. His greatest work is the *Republic*, an extended treatise on justice (among many other topics). Here we read an excerpt from one of his earlier dialogues; as is often the case, his famed teacher Socrates is the main character.

Preparing to Read

A. In what ways would Nick Naylor from *Thank You for Smoking* agree with Gorgias about rhetoric?

B. Nick mentors his son, Joey Naylor, in the art of debate. How does this plot twist relate to the dialogue below?

Gorgias Defines Rhetoric

Socrates: Gorgias, what is the art which you profess?

Gorgias: Rhetoric, Socrates, is my art. . . .

Soc: And are we to say that you are able to make other men rhetoricians?

Gor: Yes, that is exactly what I profess to make them. . . .

Soc: Very good then; as you profess to be a rhetorician, and a maker of rhetoricians, let me ask you, with what is rhetoric concerned: I might ask with what is weaving concerned, and you would probably reply, with the making of garments?

Gor: Yes.

Soc: And music is concerned with the composition of melodies?

Gor: It is. . . .

Soc: Answer me in like manner about rhetoric: with what is rhetoric concerned?

Gor: With discourse.

Soc: What sort of discourse, Gorgias? Such discourse as would teach the sick under what treatment they might get well?

Gor: No.

Soc: Then rhetoric does not treat of all kinds of discourse?

Gor: Certainly not.

Soc: And yet rhetoric makes men able to speak?

Gor: Yes.

Soc: And to understand that about which they speak?

Gor: Of course. . . .

Soc: I am not sure whether I entirely understand you, but I dare say I shall soon know better; please answer me a question: you would allow that there are arts? . . .

Gor: Yes.

Soc: If rhetoric is one of those arts which works mainly by the use of words, and there are other arts which also use words, tell me what is that quality in words with which rhetoric is concerned. Suppose that a person asks me about some of the arts; he might say, "Socrates, what is arithmetic?" I should reply to him that arithmetic is one of those arts which take effect through words. And then he would proceed to ask: "Words about what?" and I should reply, Words about even and odd numbers, and how many there are of each. . . . And suppose, again, I were to say that astronomy is only words; he would ask, "Words about what, Socrates?" I should answer that astronomy tells us about the motions of the stars and sun and moon, and their relative swiftness.

Gor: You would be quite right, Socrates.

Soc: And now let us have from you, Gorgias, the truth about rhetoric. Would you admit it to be one of those arts which . . . fulfill all its ends through the medium of words?

Gor: True.

Soc: Words which do what? To what class of things do the words which rhetoric uses relate?

Gor: To the greatest, Socrates, and the best of human things.

Soc: But which are the greatest and best of human things? I dare say that you have heard men singing at feasts the old drinking song, in which the singers enumerate the goods of life, first health, beauty next, thirdly, as the writer of the song says, wealth honestly obtained.

Gor: Yes, I know the song; but what of it?

Soc: I mean to say that the producers of those things which the author of the song praises, that is to say, the physician, the trainer, the money-maker, will at once come to you, and first the physician will say: "O Socrates, Gorgias is deceiving you, for my art is concerned with the greatest good of men and not his." And when I ask, Who are you? he will reply, "I am a physician." And I shall say: do you mean that your art produces the greatest good? He will answer, "Certainly, for is not health the greatest good? What greater good can men have, Socrates?" And after him the trainer will come and say, "I too, Socrates, shall be greatly surprised if Gorgias can show more good of his art than I can show of mine." To him again I shall say, Who are you, honest friend, and what is your business? "I am a trainer," he will reply, "and my business is to make people beautiful and strong in body." When I am done with the trainer, there arrives the money-maker: "Consider Socrates," he will say, "whether Gorgias or anyone else can produce any greater good than wealth." And do you consider wealth to be the greatest good of man? "Of course," will be his reply. And we shall rejoin: Yes; but our friend Gorgias contends that his art produces a greater good than yours. And then he will be sure to go on and ask, "What good? Let Gorgias answer." Now I want you, Gorgias, to imagine that this question is asked of you by them and by me. What is that which, as you say, is the greatest good of man, and of which you are the creator? Answer us.

Gor: That good, Socrates, which is truly the greatest, being that which gives to men freedom in their own persons, and to individuals the power of ruling over others in their several states.

Soc: And what would you consider this to be?

Gor: What is there greater than the word which persuades the judges in the courts, or the senators in the council, or the citizens in the assembly, or at any other political meeting? If you have the power of uttering this word, you will have the physician your slave, and the trainer your slave, and the money-maker of whom you talk will be found to gather treasures, not for himself, but for you who are able to speak and to persuade the multitude.

Soc: Now I think, Gorgias, that you have very accurately explained what you conceive to be the art of rhetoric; and you mean to say, if I am not mistaken, that rhetoric is the artificer of persuasion, having this and no other business, and that this is her crown and end. Do you know any other effect of rhetoric over and above that of producing persuasion?

Gor: No: the definition seems to me very fair, Socrates; for persuasion is the chief end of rhetoric. . . . Rhetoric is the art of persuasion in courts of law and other assemblies, as I was just now saying. . . .

Persuasion and Knowledge

Soc: Then let me raise another question; is there such a thing as "having learned"?

Gor: Yes.

Soc: And there is also "having believed"?

Gor: Yes.

Soc: And is the "having learned" the same as "having believed," and are learning and belief the same things?

Gor: In my judgment, Socrates, they are not the same.

Soc: And your judgment is correct. If a person were to say to you, "Is there, Gorgias, a false belief as well as a true?" you would reply, if I am not mistaken, that there is.

Gor: Yes.

Soc: Well, but is there a false knowledge as well as a true?

Gor: No.

Soc: Indeed; this again proves that knowledge and belief differ.

Gor: Very true.

Soc: And yet those who have learned as well as those who have believed are persuaded?

Gor: Just so.

Soc: Shall we then assume two sorts of persuasion, one which is the source of belief without knowledge, as the other is of knowledge?

Gor: By all means.

Soc: And which sort of persuasion does rhetoric create in courts of law and other assemblies? The sort . . . which gives belief without knowledge, or that which gives knowledge?

Gor: Clearly, Socrates, that which only gives belief.

Soc: Then rhetoric, as would appear, is the artificer of a persuasion which creates belief . . . but gives no instruction [knowledge] . . . ?

Gor: True.

Soc: And the rhetorician does not instruct the courts of law or other assemblies . . . but he creates belief . . . ; for no one can be supposed to instruct such a vast multitude . . . in a short time?

Gor: Certainly not.

Soc: Come, then, and let us see what we really mean about rhetoric; for I do not know what my own meaning is as yet. When the assembly meets to elect a physician or a ship-wright or any other craftsman, will the rhetorician be taken into counsel? Surely not. For at every election he ought to be chosen who is most skilled; and, again, when walls have to be built or harbors or docks to be constructed, not the rhetorician but the master work-man will advise; or when generals have to be chosen and an order of battle arranged, . . . then the military will advise and not the rhetoricians: what do you say, Gorgias? . . .

Gor: Socrates, if you only knew how rhetoric comprehends and holds under her sway all the inferior arts! Let me offer you a striking example of this. On several occasions I have been with my brother Herodicus or some other physician to see one of his patients, who would not allow the physician to give him medicine, or apply a knife or hot iron to him; and I have persuaded him to do for me what he would not do for the physician just by the use of rhetoric. And I say that if a rhetorician and a physician were to go to any city, and had there to argue in the assembly as to which of them should be elected state-physician, the physician would have no chance; but he who could speak would be chosen if he wished. In a contest with a man of any other profession the rhetorician more than any one would have the power of getting himself chosen, for he can speak more persuasively to the multitude than any of them, and on any subject. Such is the nature and power of the art of rhetoric.

Yet, Socrates, rhetoric should be used like any other competitive art, not against every-body—the rhetorician ought not to abuse his strength any more than a boxer or wrestler because he has powers which are more than a match either for friend or enemy; he ought not therefore to strike, stab, or slay his friends. Suppose a man to have been trained in the gymnasium and becomes a prize fighter and, he in the fullness of his strength, goes and strikes his father or mother. . . . That is no reason why the trainers should be held in detestation or banished from the city. For they taught their art for a good purpose, to be used against enemies and evil-doers, in self-defense and not in aggression; others have perverted their instructions, and turned to a bad use their own strength and skill. But not on this account are the teachers bad, neither is the art in fault, or bad in itself; I should rather say that those who make a bad use of the art are to blame. And the same argument holds for rhetoric. For the rhetorician can speak against all men and upon any subject; he can persuade the multitude better than any other man of anything which he pleases, but he should not therefore seek to defraud the physician or any other artist of his reputation merely because he has the power. He ought to use rhetoric fairly, as he would also use his athletic powers. And if after having become a rhetorician he makes a bad use of his strength and skill, his instructor surely ought not on that account to be held in detestation or banished. For his teacher intended that he make good use of his instructions, but he abuses them. And therefore he is the person who ought to be held in detestation, ban-ished, and put to death, and not his instructor. . . .

Rhetoric, the Masses, and the Just Person

Soc: You say, Gorgias, that you can make any man, who will learn of you, a rhetorician?

Gor: Yes.

Soc: Do you mean that you will teach him to gain the ears of the multitude on any subject, and this not by instruction [knowledge] but by persuasion?

Gor: Quite so.

Soc: You were saying, in fact, that the rhetorician will have, greater powers of persuasion than the physician even in a matter of health?

Gor: Yes, with the multitude at least.

Soc: You mean to say, with the ignorant; for with those who know he cannot be supposed to have greater powers of persuasion.

Gor: Very true.

Soc: But if he is to have more power of persuasion than the physician, he will have greater power than he who knows?

Gor: Certainly.

Soc: Although he is not a physician, is he?

Gor: No.

Soc: And he who is not a physician must, obviously, be ignorant of what the physician knows.

Gor: Clearly.

Soc: Then, when the rhetorician is more persuasive than the physician, the ignorant is more persuasive with the ignorant than he who has knowledge? Is not that the inference?

Gor: In the case supposed, yes.

Soc: And the same holds of the relation of rhetoric to all the other arts. The rhetorician need not know the truth about things; he has only to discover some way of persuading the ignorant that he has more knowledge than those who know?

Gor: Yes, Socrates, and is not this a great comfort? Without learning the other arts, but the art of rhetoric only, and yet to be in no way inferior to the professors of them?

Soc: Whether the rhetorician is or not inferior on this account is a question which we will hereafter examine if the enquiry is likely to be of any service to us; but I would rather begin by asking, whether he is as ignorant of the just and unjust, base and honorable, good and evil, as he is of medicine and the other arts; I mean to say, does he really know anything of what is good and evil, base or honorable, just or unjust in them; or has he only a way with the ignorant of persuading them that he, not knowing, is to be esteemed to know more about these things than someone else who knows? Or must the pupil know these things and come to you knowing them before he can acquire the art of rhetoric? If he is ignorant, you who are the teacher of rhetoric will not teach him, this is not your business; but you will make him seem to the multitude to know them, when he does not know them and seem to be a good man when he is not. Or will you be unable to teach him rhetoric at all, unless he knows the truth of these things first?

Gor: Well, Socrates, I suppose that if the pupil does chance not to know them, he will have to learn of me these things as well.

Soc: Say no more, for there you are correct; and so he whom you make a rhetorician must either know the nature of the just and unjust already, or he must be taught by you.

Gor: Certainly.

Soc: Well, and is not he who has learned carpentering a carpenter?

Gor: Yes.

Soc: And he who has learned music a musician?

Gor: Yes.

Soc: And he who has learned medicine is a physician, in like manner? He who has learned anything whatever is that which his knowledge makes him.

Gor: Certainly.

Soc: And in the same way, he who has learned what is just is just?

Gor: To be sure.

Soc: And he who is just may be supposed to do what is just?

Gor: Yes.

Soc: And must not the just man always desire to do what is just?

Gor: That is clearly the inference.

Soc: Surely, then, the just man will never consent to do injustice?

Gor: Certainly not.

Soc: And according to the argument the rhetorician must be a just man?

Gor: Yes.

Soc: And will therefore never be willing to do injustice?

Gor: Clearly not.

Soc: But do you remember saying just now that the trainer is not to be accused or banished if the boxer makes a wrong use of his boxing skills; and in like manner, if the rhetorician makes a bad and unjust use of rhetoric, that is not to be laid to the charge of his teacher, who is not to be banished, but the wrong-doer himself who made a bad use of his rhetoric is to be banished, was not that said?

Gor: Yes, it was.

Soc: But now we are affirming that the aforesaid rhetorician will never have done injustice at all?

Gor: True.

Soc: And at the very outset, Gorgias, it was said that rhetoric treated of discourse, not [like arithmetic] about odd and even, but about just and unjust? Was not this said?

Gor: Yes.

Soc: I was thinking at the time, when I heard you saying so, that rhetoric, which is always discoursing about justice, could not possibly be an unjust thing. But when you added, shortly afterwards, that the rhetorician might make a bad use of rhetoric I noted with surprise the inconsistency into which you had fallen; . . .

Enter Polus: Rhetoric as a Talent

Polus: I will ask; and do you answer me, Socrates, the same question which Gorgias, as you suppose, is unable to answer: What is rhetoric?

Soc: Do you mean what sort of an art?

Pol: Yes.

Soc: To say the truth, Polus, it is not an art at all, in my opinion.

Pol: Then what, in your opinion, is rhetoric?

Soc: I should say a sort of experience [talent] . . .

Pol: An experience [talent] in what? . . .

Soc: In my opinion, the whole of which rhetoric is a part is not an art at all, but the habit of a bold and ready wit, which knows how to manage mankind.

Review Questions

1. What does Gorgias believe rhetoric is? Put his view into your own words.
2. According to Gorgias, to what extent are rhetoric instructors responsible for their students' misdeeds. Do you agree with him? Why?
3. What does Socrates believe rhetoric is? Put his view into your own words.

1.3. DISCUSSION AND ANALYSIS

Ethics is a primary branch of philosophy. Philosophy, classically conceived, is concerned with abstract or conceptual issues that are universally important. This isn't to say that empirical data is completely irrelevant to studying philosophy; for example, scientific inquiry may enrich our understanding of what constitutes the well-being of human persons, which certainly seems ethically significant. Yet the disciplines of science and philosophy remain vitally distinct. This is because philosophy "goes beyond" the empirical data—hoping to make sense of it—in its attempt to articulate basic conceptual categories that describe how things ultimately are. Furthermore, philosophy is concerned with articulating and defending good reasons for our nonempirical and universally important beliefs. Thus philosophy is also an enterprise. Philosophers endeavor to discover contradictions among nonempirical and universally important beliefs (by asking pertinent questions) and remove these contradictions through logical analysis (thinking critically and creatively). This process, if carefully conducted, results in bolstering one's reasons for thinking that some nonempirical and universally important belief is true. Therefore, philosophy is not merely something you have, but (more importantly) something you do. "Doing" philosophy can facilitate greater awareness of the world around you, a clearer understanding of yourself and your place within it, and optimally the wisdom thereby gained. Thus doing philosophy well can have the noblest of results. In this way, philosophers couldn't disagree more with Nick Naylor when he asserts that questions about justice, goodness, and truth are nothing but matters of "B.S."

Philosophy and Sophistry

Nick Naylor's comment to his son that "if you argue properly, you're never wrong" is not new. The belief that philosophy is merely "cleverly playing with words" goes back to the ancient Greeks. Socrates, Plato's famed mentor, denied such notions, striving to distance himself from sophistry and rhetoric at every turn. Socrates held that philosophers (unlike rhetoricians) pursue the *truth* of universally important nonempirical topics. He furthermore held that not all arguments are successful vehicles for this pursuit.

Philosophers obviously follow Socrates in his quest for truth. This often begins with achieving clarity about issues and concepts. Let's begin by getting clearer about "argument." Philosophers interpret "arguing properly" as employing true statements that follow the rules of logic. However, Nick regularly employs a broader interpretation of "arguing properly"—one that falls in line with the sophists (like Gorgias) of ancient Greece. He typically means properly implementing principles of rhetoric to *win* arguments. This is a skill (or talent), but not one that interested Socrates because "winning" an argument can involve nonrational processes and maneuvers. A rhetorician may conceivably "win" an argument even if the premises do not logically guarantee or prove the conclusion. However, philosophical arguments only employ rational processes; no philosophical argument is successful if the premises fail to prove the conclusion—regardless of how artful the philosopher is with her words.

Philosophers indeed engage in a kind of rhetoric, if by that is meant (roughly) the careful use of words. But philosophers are not *merely* rhetoricians. Sophists invariably employ rhetoric hoping to selfishly benefit from changing the attitudes of those hearing/reading their words. Philosophers only employ rhetoric to carefully seek the truth; they hope only to persuade with knowledge (unlike the sophists). Therefore, philosophers do not view rhetoric (argumentation) as good for its own sake. Argumentation is valuable because it proves to be an effective instrument in seeking the truth. Should the truth be found, there is no guarantee that one additionally benefits; sometimes the truth hurts. The end goal—discovering truth in nonempirical universally important matters—is

---

BOX 1C: LEARNING OUTCOMES

Upon carefully studying this chapter, students should better comprehend and be able to explain:

- The ways in which philosophy, following the example of Socrates, can be distinguished from mere rhetoric and sophistry.
- Different kinds of arguments to employ and fallacies to avoid in (moral) reasoning.
- How the ethically significant concepts of good, bad, right, wrong, just, and unjust can begin to be defined by their respective relationships to well-being, harms, and impartiality (or taking the "moral point of view").
- The roles played by ethically significant standards/principles, conceptual issues, and relevant facts in deriving a moral judgment.
- How *Thank You for Smoking*, *Minority Report*, and *Dr. Horrible's Sing-Along Blog* can be employed in initial attempts to think about ethics and moral reasoning.

intrinsically valuable. Finding the truth is its own reward and no additional selfish or self-centered motivations are involved. The differences between philosopher and sophist are thus important, even if sometimes subtle—which is why Socrates spent so much time distancing himself from them.

Arguments and Rational Persuasion

Philosophers attempt to rationally persuade one to accept a conclusion as true via logical argument. An argument in this sense consists of a group of propositions or statements. One of the statements is supposed to follow logically from the others. The truth of the proved statement follows necessarily or with a high degree of probability (depending on the type of argument) because of the preceding statements. The statement whose truth has been established is called the conclusion; the remaining statements—those providing rational support for the conclusion—are called premises. After careful questions have been asked and clarifications made, logical analysis proceeds by constructing an argument for some position or belief. This is how philosophers attempt to marshal reasoned beliefs.

> "You don't choose the things you believe in, they choose you." —*Minority Report*, scene 6

Some philosophical arguments successfully establish their conclusions, but others do not. This is determined by criteria germane to well-established standards of logic. Because there are two basic kinds of argument, deductive and non-deductive (inductive and abductive), the standards of success are different. For deductive arguments, the conclusion is to follow *necessarily* from the premises. There are two essential aspects to deductive arguments: validity and soundness. A valid argument is one in which the logical form of the argument guarantees that the conclusion must be true if the premises are true. If it is possible for the conclusion to be false if the premises are true, then the argument is invalid. Because validity tracks the form or structure of an argument, some deductive forms are always valid, while others are always invalid. After determining whether a deductive argument has a correct, valid form, then one can determine whether the argument is sound. A valid argument with only true premises is sound. If a valid argument contains a false premise, it is unsound (and all invalid arguments are unsound). If an argument is sound, its conclusion must be true.

A common example of a sound argument is: All men are mortal (first premise); Socrates is a man (second premise); thus, Socrates is mortal (conclusion). Some philosophers prefer to "stack" arguments, putting them in a sequential arrangement, with premises and conclusion numbered. That is, with the dividing line between statements (2) and (3) representing the word "therefore," the previous argument would appear:

1. All men are mortal.
2. <u>Socrates is a man.</u>
3. Socrates is mortal.

Some philosophers prefer this arrangement because it is easier for (many) students to see how the premises logically lead to the conclusion. In any event, if a deductive argument is sound, then it is a rationally persuasive argument—one must, on pain of being irrational and illogical, accept the conclusion of a sound argument.

Socrates serves as a point of departure for a more interesting example of a deductive argument. Socrates was very concerned with ideals and principles, including justice; he often sought out the essence of justice by interviewing other Athenians in the marketplace. Plato, his star pupil, once claimed that justice requires giving everyone his or her due. This seemingly entails that subjecting someone to treatment he doesn't deserve is inappropriate. The idea of justice plays a crucial role in Steven Spielberg's *Minority Report*. Based upon a short story by Philip K. Dick, Spielberg casts a futuristic, neo-noir yarn about genetically altered human beings—"precognitives"—who can foretell future criminal activity. The Precrime police team apprehends "future murderers" before they go through with their fatal deeds. The future murderer is summarily "haloed," convicted, and placed indefinitely in a stasis-tube.

Some philosophers have argued that *Minority Report* portrays an unjust system of punishment.[2] The deductive argument, grounded in worries about freedom, foreknowledge, and moral responsibility proceeds via the following six premises: (1) If the "precogs" know that a person will commit a future murder, then there are now truths about how the future will unfold; (2) if there are now truths about how the future will unfold, then the future must obtain in just that way; (3) if the "future murderer" must act as the precogs have foreseen, then that person cannot choose otherwise than as the precogs have foreseen; (4) if the future murderer cannot choose otherwise than as the precogs have foreseen, then his (future) act is not performed freely; (5) if a future act is not performed freely, then the person performing it is not morally responsible for its occurring; (6) if a person is not morally responsible for what he or she does, then that person is unjustly punished for those acts. Premises 1–6 deductively lead to the following conclusion: (7) if the precogs know that a person will commit a future murder, then that person is unjustly punished for it.

That arguments can become as involved as this one further explains why some philosophers prefer arguments to appear with numbered premises and conclusion in a "stacked" format. Nevertheless, if this argument is sound, then its conclusion must be true. But this entails that Precrime represents an unjust system, which ultimately serves as a reason to disband it. So, the question now becomes whether the premises of

> "We want to make absolutely certain that every American can bank on the utter infallibility of this system and to ensure that what makes us safe makes us free." — *Minority Report*, scene 3

this valid argument are indeed true. Are there reasons for thinking that some of the premises are false? Philosophers have more work to do in determining this. If we discover that at least one premise is false, then this valid argument is rendered unsound. And, if an argument is unsound, then there is no logical reason for one to be rationally persuaded by this argument. Philosophers caution that any judgment about an argument's success—its soundness—must be (rationally) justified. However, Naylor disagrees. He takes the sophist approach of persuasion *without* rational justification. But the philosopher's goal is not to (nonrationally) persuade you that her argument is sound merely through artful words or rhetorical flourish. She follows well-accepted rules of logic to establish the truth of her conclusion. This (again) highlights a significant difference between philosophers and sophists.

Not all philosophical arguments are deductive; some are nondeductive. Nondeductive arguments do not aspire to the ambitious standards of deductive arguments. Inductive arguments are one type of nondeductive argument (with abductive, or arguments to the best explanation, being the other). A successful inductive argument is one such that the premises, if true, make the conclusion more likely true than not. This is (more or less) a matter of probability. If the conclusion is more probably true than not, assuming the truth of the premises, then the argument is strong. If the conclusion is not so established, then the argument is weak. If a strong argument has only true premises, then it is cogent. If it has at least one false premise, it is uncogent (and all weak arguments are by definition uncogent). Sometimes it is difficult to definitively gauge a nondeductive argument's strength, but, unlike deductive arguments, the mere possibility that the conclusion is false is not sufficient to render it unsuccessful (uncogent).

Arguments by analogy are common inductive arguments. The basic idea of these arguments is that because two things (A and B) are so similar in various ways (and the more the better), and we independently know something, call it P, about A, we can (inductively) conclude that P also truly applies to B. So, because my friend's car is the same make, model, year, and engine type as the car I am considering buying, and my friend's car gets good gas mileage, it (inductively) follows that I will get good gas mileage with this car. Assuming all the premises are true, this seems to be a cogent argument by analogy. But, importantly, not all arguments by analogy are successful at achieving persuasion with knowledge. If an argument by analogy either fails to choose similarities relevant to the conclusion or fails to recognize an obvious and important dissimilarity between A and B, then the argument is weak.

An interesting argument by analogy is offered in *Thank You for Smoking*. During his congressional testimony, Senator Finistirre asks Nick whether the fact that the Academy of Tobacco Studies is funded primarily by Big Tobacco illicitly taints the academy's research findings due to a conflict of interests. Nick replies that this poses no more a conflict of interests than does Senator Finistirre's accepting campaign contributions from political interest groups. The argument seems to be something like this: It's not clear that Senator Finistirre's receiving funds from interest groups, although possessing their own interests, illicitly impinges on his adequately representing his public constituency—the great state of Vermont. The Academy of Tobacco Studies, similar to Senator Finistirre, receives funds from an interest group that possesses its own interests (Big Tobacco). Thus, it's not clear that the academy doesn't adequately represent its constituency—the general public regarding the effects of tobacco use. Whether this argument is cogent depends first on whether it's strong. This, in turn, depends on whether the similarity Nick employs between Senator Finistirre and the academy is relevant to establishing his conclusion and whether there are any obvious dissimilarities between them he overlooks. If neither is at issue, the argument's cogency depends on whether all of its premises are true. (It would be a good Socratic exercise to determine this for yourself.)

Logical Fallacies

Philosophy and sophistry can also be further distanced by becoming familiar with logical fallacies. If it can be shown that an argument is fallacious, then we have excellent reason to believe that it cannot be successful in securing truth. Detecting a fallacy signals that the person employing it has not "argued properly" regardless of how artful his words are or how frustrating it might be to "mount a comeback" (as witnessed by the difficulties Ron Goode or Senator Finistirre often had in responding to Nick's rhetorical ploys).

Thank You for Smoking, Fox Searchlight Pictures, 2005. Nick Naylor (Aaron Eckhart) argues for yet another point as the chief spokesperson for "Big Tobacco." (Moviegoods, Inc.)

There are formal and informal fallacies, roughly (although not perfectly) corresponding to deductive and nondeductive arguments. Formal fallacies are easier to spot, at least with a little practice. So first consider this *valid* argument:

1. If the precog previsions are infallible, then future murders are unjustly punished.
2. <u>Precog previsions are infallible.</u>
3. Future murderers are unjustly punished.

If the premises are true (and whether they are true is debatable), so must be the conclusion. The underlying logical form of this argument is: If P, then Q; P; thus, Q. Any argument with that form, regardless of content, is valid. But now consider this similar, but fallacious argument:

1. If the precog previsions are infallible, then future murders are unjustly punished.
2. <u>Precog previsions are not infallible.</u>
3. Future murderers are not unjustly punished.

Even if both premises are true, it doesn't necessarily follow that future murderers are not unjustly punished. After all, as Danny Witwer reminds the Precrime team, "We are arresting people who have committed no crime." Thus, Precrime could still be unjust but for reasons not directly related to the infallibility of previsions. The problem ultimately lies with the argument's underlying logical form: If P, then Q; not-P; thus, not-Q. Any deductive argument with this form is invalid; arguments with this logical structure commit the formal fallacy of "denying the antecedent."[3]

Informal fallacies are more difficult to spot because they can only be determined by carefully investigating the content and context of the relevant argument, but these differ for each argument. To begin grasping the significance of this, recall the deductive argument about Socrates's mortality: all humans are mortal; Socrates is human; thus, Socrates is mortal. The logical structure of this argument is the same as: all mammals are warm blooded; whales are mammals; thus, whales are warm blooded. Both arguments are valid. But now consider: all plants are chlorophyll producers; all factories are plants; thus, all factories are chlorophyll producers. Because this argument has the same underlying logical form as the previous two—All A are B; (All) C are A; thus, (All) C are B—it should also be valid, as validity is dependent on form. But it's false that all factories are chlorophyll producers, even if there is a sense in which both premises are true. Thus, this argument is unexpectedly *invalid*. Why? Careful inspection of the content shows that the term "plant" is used in two different senses.[4] This is to commit the (informal) fallacy of equivocation. Any argument that shifts the meanings of its terms is thereby fallacious and cannot rationally justify its conclusion.

Perhaps because they are not easily spotted, informal fallacies are regularly used by rhetorical virtuosos like Nick. And Nick is a charismatic speaker. Recall his aside, "Do you know the guy in school who could get any girl? I'm him, on crack." However, his persuasive successes are often partly due to his use of informal fallacies to "win" arguments. If you aren't paying careful attention to how Nick's argument proceeds given the context, it's easy to become flustered like Goode or Finistirre.

Consider that Nick sometimes employs the "red herring" fallacy to "win" arguments. He provides the viewer a clear example of it during a quiet conversation with his son. Nick and Joey rehearse a hypothetical argument between two people disagreeing about whether vanilla is better than chocolate. Nick informs Joey that he can't win that argument, so he subtly shifts the topic to the importance of being able to choose between vanilla and chocolate: "Well, I need more than chocolate, and for that matter more than vanilla. I believe we need freedom. And choice when it comes to our ice cream . . . is the definition of liberty." Joey immediately recognized that Nick didn't prove that vanilla was the best. Nick instructs his son, "I didn't have to. I proved that you're wrong, and if you're wrong than I'm right." This is a classic template for the red herring fallacy. Nick subtly changed the topic to something that, although not completely unrelated, isn't really at issue. However, by getting his discussion partner to agree to the new issue, he thereby fallaciously concludes that the original debate has been decided. To Joey's credit, he tells his dad, "But you still didn't convince me." Joey didn't fall for the rhetorical trick. Nick smiles and replies, "'Cause I'm not after you; I'm after them" and points to the unsuspecting passersby. Nick's sophistical colors are clear.

> "Hell, I was good at shooting VC, but I didn't make it my career." —*Thank You for Smoking*, scene 11

Another tactic that Nick regularly employs is an *ad hominem* fallacy. This fallacy occurs whenever someone critiques not the argument given, but the person who just gave it. For example, after listening to a brief lesson about the dangers of secondhand smoke—presented by Brad, a medical doctor currently dating Nick's ex-wife Jill—Naylor responds, "Brad, I'm Joey's dad; you're just a guy sleeping with his mom." But the fact that Brad is romantically involved with Joey's mother is irrelevant. It is very likely that Joey's health is endangered by his being subjected to secondhand smoke during his weekends with Nick, and Nick's mean-spirited quip does nothing to change that fact.

Sometimes Nick's *ad hominem* rebuttals take a slightly different form. Some of his responses attempt to make the person giving an argument seem hypocritical. Attempts to discredit an argument by putting its arguer in a bad light is to commit the *tu quoque* ("you too") fallacy. For example, during the *Dennis Miller Show*, Nick muses that Senator Finistirre called for the American tobacco fields to be slashed and burned on the same day that he appeared at Farm Aid bemoaning the downfall of the American farmer. But the senator's appearance at Farm Aid in no obvious way affects his argument that tobacco should no longer be produced in the United States. This is analogous to a congressman who, being known for advocating drunk driving legislation reform, gets arrested for drunk driving. The fact of the congressman's arrest doesn't thereby negate his arguments for reforming the law. Analogously, Nick is merely putting Finisterre in a bad light without directly addressing his arguments for tobacco reform.

The movie portrays other characters committing informal fallacies. At the congressional hearing, just before Naylor testifies, Finistirre subpoenas Señor Herera to speak on behalf of the Latino community. Herera argues that the "current use of words instead of imagery is an obvious move against the non-English-speaking population of the United States." Because the skull and crossbones symbol "speaks loudly in all languages," he concludes that those who oppose the new warning label (namely Big Tobacco) are ultimately saying "they want those who cannot read English to die." Herera's argument commits the "straw man" fallacy (which is similar to the red herring fallacy). This fallacy occurs when someone distorts an opposing argument or view so that it is easier to critique; once the distorted position is easily knocked down (hence the name "straw man"), it is fallaciously concluded that the original (stronger) argument or view has been discredited. It seems incredibly unlikely that dissent about the new warning label is grounded in blatant disregard for non-English-speaking Americans. Spotting this fallacy renders Señor Herera's testimony moot and uncovers his (thinly veiled) role as Finistirre's lackey.

But perhaps the most striking examples of fallacious reasoning are portrayed by Joey Naylor. Joey's sophistry is encouraged by his father, and Joey is a quick study. Nick distinguishes between arguments and negotiations, reminding his son that the former can always be successful even if the latter are not. The difference lies in how persuasion is achieved. Jill denies Nick's request that Joey accompany him on a California business trip. After Nick's negotiation attempt fails, Joey appeals to his mother's complicated emotional baggage regarding her ex-husband: "Mom, is it possible that you're taking the frustration of your failed marriage out on me?" Jill is stunned. After claiming that much good could come out of the trip, Joey sympathizes, "But if you think it's more important to use me to channel your frustration against the man you no longer love, I'll understand." We next see Jill waving good-bye to Joey as he piles into the car next to his father—bound for California. But Joey's ploy succeeds only because of its psychological relevance. This is a kind of fallacious appeal to pity. Joey plays with his mother's heartstrings rather than offering rational considerations for his accompanying his father.

Possessing an enriched understanding of how and when arguments are rationally persuasive—and how and why they are not—helps one distinguish philosophy from sophistry. In turn, this knowledge facilitates more informed positions about what is good and bad, right and wrong. And this can be very helpful given the fact that many classic ethical debates—abortion, euthanasia, and capital punishment—can become very emotionally charged. It thereby becomes easy to slide into *ad hominem* and straw man retorts rather than careful and considered logical analysis. In the pages that follow, you will find a *philosophical* (and not sophistical) approach to ethical explorations.

Well-Being, Harm, and the Nature of Ethical Judgments

Ethical issues are fairly easy to recognize, with abortion, euthanasia, and capital punishment quickly coming to mind. But providing a clear definition requires more than simply listing examples. So, what is it about abortion, euthanasia, and capital punishment that explain their being ethically significant topics? This is a difficult question, but any plausible answer begins by pointing out that all ethically significant situations are evaluative in distinctive sorts of ways. Different behaviors are judged better or worse, right or wrong. Ethically significant situations, then, are normative, calling for judgments about what ought or ought not to be done. Ought Dr. Horrible (from *Dr. Horrible's Sing-Along Blog*) assassinate Captain Hammer in order to gain entrance into the Evil League of Evil? Ought Anderton to kidnap the precog Agatha in his quest to prove his innocence? Answers to these questions are prescriptive; they indicate what one should do given the situation at hand.

That ethics is prescriptive immediately distinguishes it from science; the enterprise of science is descriptive. Scientists attempt to accurately describe how things actually are and predict how things will be. Ethicists attempt to delineate how things ought to be without making predictions about the future. As is well known, what ought to be and what actually happens often diverge. However, to say that ethics is *not* science only advances our understanding of the former so far. Positive characterizations of it—describing what ethics *is*—are required.

One plausible way to better understand the makings of an ethical issue stresses the idea of well-being.[5] That someone's well-being is at stake is evidence that the relevant situation is ethically significant. The concept of well-being is admittedly vague and requires further elucidation. For now, simply note that, plausibly, one's well-being can be positively or negatively affected in terms of benefits and harms. To positively affect (benefit) someone's well-being is to enhance or increase it; to negatively affect (harm) someone's well-being is to diminish or decrease it. The link to normativity initially presents itself with the plausible intuition that benefiting one's well-being is good (someone is "better off") but diminishing it is bad (someone is "worse off"). This proposed link is bolstered by the widely held intuition that inflicting harm unnecessarily is negligent or wrongful; thus diminishing one's well-being must be justified.

Accordingly, perhaps the account emerging here is clearest in terms of harm. But what does it mean to cause ethically significant harm? This is another difficult question, but it certainly seems that harms can be physical or psychological. The white van vigilantes who kidnapped Nick Naylor harmed him by violently abducting him and slapping an inordinate number of nicotine patches on his body. Nick's physical well-being was diminished by being poisoned; the nicotine patches shocked his system, inducing a coma. His psychological well-being was diminished by the dread and terror of being abducted. Furthermore, all of this was done against his will, which itself is a kind of harm. Having the ability to control one's own actions enhances well-being; having it taken away diminishes one's well-being and thereby counts as harm. So, generally, examples of physical harm are pain, disease, disability, and death (even if, perhaps, it is painless). Examples of psychological harm are fear, anxiety, sadness, and despair (even if, perhaps, one isn't completely aware of these maladies). Yet these lists are not meant to be exhaustive, as the example about Nick's loss of autonomy suggests, which begins to explain why a completely satisfying account of harm—especially ethically significant harm—is difficult to quickly achieve.

> "I cannot believe my eyes, how the world is full of filth and lies." —*Dr. Horrible's Sing-Along Blog*, act 2

If the discussion of ethically significant harms is roughly correct at least as far as it goes, then it seems that one's well-being is invariably enhanced by the removal of physical or psychological harm. One benefits by being freed of pain and suffering, disability, or despair, as Nick was after he recovered from his abduction (not to say that all such recoveries are instantaneous). These insights thus provide an initial account of ethically significant benefits; however, further examples of positively impacting well-being are a bit more controversial. One test is to ask whether the pending benefit would enhance the person's well-being—making him or her better off—in some nontrivial way. The difficulty lies in determining trivial benefits from nontrivial. But perhaps it could be said that enhancing physical health, emotional maturity, and intellectual abilities importantly benefit persons. This explains why it is important to keep healthy food and exercise habits, experience life fully in terms of its ups and downs, and receive a formal education while young. Furthermore, it might be claimed one's well-being is importantly enhanced by enjoying fulfilling work, being able to exercise one's freedom to make autonomous choices, possessing feelings of self-worth and self-esteem, and being happy generally.

Ethically significant situations also crucially involve the choices we make when well-being is at stake. Only moral agents can make ethically significant choices. Moral agents possess a sufficient level of awareness and understanding of a situation. They are able to grasp how situations could be made better (or worse) and are cognizant of how to make the world conform to their beliefs. They can also grasp the consequences of their pending behaviors, and form beliefs that subsequently influence their choices (or decisions) regarding them. That is, a moral agent can be aware of the fact that he is about to harm another and, in light of that knowledge, can decide to perform that act. Were the moral agent to refrain from that harmful act, he can ask what alternatives would be better or more acceptable for that situation. Thus moral agents possess high levels of belief formation and mental sophistication generally, including rich imagination and emotional depth.

This begins to explain why the harm animals cause each other isn't morally significant. For example, mallard ducks reproduce in ways that resemble rape. The male seemingly attacks the female, dragging her under the water to the point where she almost drowns. But we have no reason to believe that the male mallard is sufficiently cognizant of the situation. The male doesn't consciously decide to inflict this harm knowingly; he is simply instinctually driven to reproduce. Another example, although fictive, can be found in *Minority Report*. When John Anderton climbs over Dr. Iris Hineman's private wall, he is bitten by her Doll's eye plants. She genetically altered them to poison intruders, thereby protecting her and her property. They instinctively respond to Anderton's uninvited presence; they do not ponder whether there are better ways to detain Anderton (but still alert Hineman), consider how to consciously employ that more acceptable behavior, but decide to poison him anyway. They *react*, but do not *act*, and as such, like the male mallard, are not moral agents. But human persons are moral agents. When a man chooses to rape a woman he knowingly inflicts physical and psychological harm. When a woman chooses to knowingly poison her husband to benefit from his life insurance policy, she causes him harm. These acts are neither merely instinctual nor without awareness of consequence. This makes them ethically significant.

Accordingly, a moral or ethical issue is one in which a moral agent knowingly confronts choices that, if made, will nontrivially affect, positively or negatively, well-being. Some philosophers restrict moral issues to those choices that so affect the well-being of another; other philosophers are more inclusive, holding that moral issues may also arise when only the agent's own well-being is at stake. *Thank You for Smoking* is illustrative of this debate, especially with respect to secondhand smoke. Some argue that smoking cigarettes itself isn't a moral issue, but it becomes one when the smoker knowingly allows secondhand smoke to negatively affect the well-being of others (especially nonsmokers). However, the more inclusive view is not implausible. After all, it certainly seems that persons can make choices that nontrivially harm themselves, with suicide being a prime example. Moreover, John Anderton becomes a drug user in the wake of his son's abduction; this choice (assuming it was a choice) has harmed him in (arguably) nontrivial ways. Detractors of the inclusive view argue that suicide or Anderton's drug use is ethically significant only if it harms another (analogous to the smoking case). This is a difficult issue, but if your life could be nontrivially improved by some concerted effort of yours, then you can enhance your well-being. This is a moral agent knowingly enhancing her own well-being (by preventing a harm to herself), which accords with the more inclusive account of ethically significant well-being.

Bad and Wrong, Good and Right

Moral agents make choices that result in belief-guided behavior. Some of these choices, and thus behaviors, are better or worse than others. This requires evaluating choices and behaviors via normative judgments. Moral evaluation (as suggested in the previous subsection) plausibly begins with delineations of goodness and badness. Although care must be taken here, the fact that certain behaviors are good provides some evidence of their being morally acceptable, and the fact that certain behaviors are bad provides evidence of their being morally unacceptable. These evaluations, at least initially, can be made in reference to well-being. The fact that some behaviors (nontrivially) enhance well-being provides reason to believe that they are morally good (or desirable, commendable). The fact that some behaviors diminish well-being provides reason to believe that they are morally bad (or undesirable, blameworthy). If none of the behaviors contemplated in a given situation will nontrivially impact well-being, then the pending choice is not ethically significant.

Typically speaking, the terms "good" and "bad" have wide application in moral philosophy. They apply not only to individual acts, but also persons, character traits, intentions, and states of affairs generally. Furthermore, there are various levels or degrees of goodness and badness. We say that some things are best or excellent (and not just good), while other things are worst or tragic (and not just bad). However, the terms "right" and "wrong" have a rather limited application; they refer primarily (if not exclusively) to ethically significant actions. Furthermore, it seems that an act is either morally right or not right; therefore, right and wrong do not (easily) admit of degrees. Philosophers invariably delineate only three classifications of moral action: obligatory (morally required), permissible (merely morally acceptable), and impermissible (morally unacceptable). On one extreme, an act is obligatory if it is *the* thing (or among such things) to *do* given the situation and no other choice is morally acceptable. On the other extreme, an act is impermissible if it *the* thing (or among such things) *not* to do given the situation. In between, an act is permissible if it is neither obligatory nor impermissible given the situation; it is thus morally acceptable but not required.

Although the terms "good" and "bad" are not exactly synonymous with "right" and "wrong," informative connections arguably exist. Specifically, it seems that *some* good choices/actions are thereby right (obligatory), and *some* bad choices/actions are thereby wrong (impermissible). Such connections are easiest to see regarding bad and wrong. There seem to be situations such that there is one choice an agent could make that would be the worst in terms of diminishing the well-being of another. That action is not only bad, it is the worst harm that could be inflicted given the situation. Let's also assume that other choices are available that are not as bad. It intuitively seems that choosing the worst harm is impermissible; it is *the* one thing *not* to do. If so, then it ought not to be done, which is to say it is, or would be, morally wrong. However, it doesn't follow from this that all harmful acts are impermissible. Some harms, although bad, might be justifiable given the circumstances in that there aren't any better alternatives. Perhaps some harms are required in order to achieve a better benefit elsewhere. At this point, we could hazard the following definition: An act is morally wrong and, thus, impermissible if it unjustifiably diminishes well-being (or causes unjustified harm).

A unique kind of harm, one that does not easily fit the physical/psychological division, deserves special mention. It occurs when an agent, in deliberating what ought to be done, simply fails to (sufficiently) consider how the well-being (or nontrivial interests) of others will be affected by her act. This kind of negligence certainly seems contemptible. Some philosophers go so far as to claim that properly or sufficiently considering the well-being of all those involved is something of a precondition for morally permissible behavior. This is to affirm that impartiality has a special place in moral deliberation (although it's unclear if impartiality exhaustively describes moral deliberation).[6] In very important ways, your interests are no more—and no less—important than the interests of others. This explains why fairness and justice are inherently morally significant concepts. It is unfair and unjust, and, thus, impermissible not to consider another person (or sentient being) equally worthy of moral consideration.

Philosophers who stress this approach to understanding moral wrongness, which is sometimes called taking the "moral point of view," often develop it in the following way. Consider a stranger who, after casually but deliberately approaching you, strikes you firmly on the head with a blunt instrument, perhaps an oaken cudgel. Quite plausibly, you would complain that the stranger's act was unfounded; he had no right to harm you in this way. Furthermore, let's assume that he had no reason for striking you, perhaps apart from he "felt like it." Like anyone, you would quickly conclude that it was wrong (impermissible) of him to do what he did. But this situation can be generalized upon. Your interests, while just as important as the stranger's (or anyone else's), are no more important. All of us are deserving of equal consideration and treatment; none of us has any privileged moral standing or status (except, perhaps, those enjoined in close friend and family relationships). So, if it is wrong of the stranger to disregard your well-being by striking you without cause, then it is wrong for you to strike another without case. This account reinforces the plausible position that *any* instance of causing unjustified harm (to another) is morally impermissible.[7]

If impermissible acts can be defined in terms of causing unjustified harms, it seems intuitive that obligatory actions can be defined in terms of conferring nontrivial benefits. Unfortunately, the analogy is complicated by the problem of delineating the extent to which we are morally required to confer nontrivial benefits. Consider that donating all of your belongings and assets to fund a cause like Penny's Caring Hands Homeless Shelter (from *Dr. Horrible*) probably would nontrivially enhance the well-being of many people. In fact, this might be *the* best thing you could do for the homeless, and doing it would be morally good. However, giving away all that you own may not be obligatory because it's unclear whether you are morally required to sacrifice your well-being to such an extent. Actions, if any, that go beyond our moral requirements are call supererogatory. Nevertheless, sometimes an act is obligatory because it is *the* thing to do insofar as no other choice is justifiable *given the situation*. For example, you may be morally required to rescue a small child drowning in a shallow pool. The rescue presents no significant harm to you and the harm you prevent the child is obviously great. Furthermore, your providing aid to the child in no way requires you to harm anyone else. So, we might say that obligatory acts are those that confer nontrivial benefits (or prevent serious harms) in situations that pose no significant threat of harm to the agent (or others affected by the act). Conversely, failing to confer nontrivial benefits (or prevent serious harms) in situations that pose no significant threat of harm to the agent (or relevant others) is unjustifiable and, in this sense, is morally impermissible.[8]

Facts, Concepts, and Standards

Ethics is thus a discipline that concerns itself with explaining how moral agents ought to proceed in situations that unavoidably impact the (nontrivial) well-being of others (including, arguably, situations that impact only the agent's own well-being). Unfortunately, this definition remains a bit vague. Remedying this at least requires getting clearer about what counts as morally significant benefits and harms and what makes a harm justified or unjustified, both of which are among the goals for parts 2 and 3 of the text. But for now, and regardless of how harms and benefits are eventually understood, delineating moral judgments for any specific situation requires accomplishing three additional, interrelated tasks. The first is to get clear about the relevant facts. For example, it is sometimes believed that capital punishment is defensible on the grounds that it effectively deters violent crimes. Does it? What do studies show? The second task is to achieve sufficient clarity about the relevant concepts. For example, it is sometimes argued that abortion is wrong because it is murder. This view assumes that a fetus is a person, possessing moral standing. But is a fetus a person in this sense? How should "person" be defined in the first place? Or consider that even if bribes are morally suspect, are monies paid to foreign officials in business transactions bribes? If they are not bribes, then what are they? The third task is to articulate and properly apply a relevant, but plausible, value-laden principle. Such principles invoke moral standards by which individual actions of a certain type or kind can be evaluated. So, even after all the relevant facts and concepts have been properly investigated, the judgment that Dr. Horrible acted wrongly in stealing the Wonderflonium can only be made in reference to the following principle: Willfully taking what doesn't belong to you without permission is wrong. Given this principle, *any* instance of stealing is wrong (as it implies unjustified harm suffered by the owner). Upon identifying a principle, inquiries must be made into its alleged plausibility and relevance. Is it in need of revision or qualification? Is a different principle more relevant?

To better grasp how accomplishing these three tasks impacts moral judgments, reconsider an interesting, albeit fictional, example: Precrime ought to be disbanded. Substantiating this judgment requires investigation of the relevant facts, concepts, and principles. What facts (per the story) seem relevant? We might begin with noting that the Precrime team arrests citizens who have committed no actual crimes, that sometimes the precogs disagree about what an alleged future murderer will do (a fact that has been kept from the public), and that the accused doesn't receive any sort of recognizable due process. These facts seem to point to the issue of justice. Are so-called future murderers treated unjustly? Might issues of justice be relevant to whether Precrime ought to be disbanded?

> "The world's a mess and I just need . . . to rule it." — *Dr. Horrible's Sing-Along Blog*, act 1

Nina Rosenstand has also recognized the force of these questions. She writes: "The film *Minority Report*, where future crimes are punished before they take place—one might call it the ultimate forward-looking criminal justice system, but would we really label such a system 'just'?"[9] Rosenstand's query serves as a call for us to get clearer about the relevant conceptual usage of justice. First, note that Precrime might be unjust if moral responsibility requires a sort of (metaphysical) freedom that necessarily includes multiple, genuine alternatives.[10] This assumption drives the deductive argument introduced earlier in the chapter. The idea is that it is unjust to blame and punish someone for something that he could not have avoided, and foreknowledge of our choices makes it impossible for the agent to do otherwise than what is foreseen.[11] However, the relevant facts, and Rosenstand's question itself, suggest a different concern. Many philosophers follow Rosenstand

Minority Report, Dreamworks SKG, 2002. Anderton (Tom Cruise, left), Fletcher (Neal McDonough), and Witwer (Colin Farrell, right) rely on the "precognitives" to peer into the future and prevent crimes before they happen. (Moviegoods, Inc.)

by distinguishing between "forward-looking" and "backward-looking" theories of justice. How might this distinction be relevant to whether Precrime ought to be disbanded?

Forward-looking justice focuses on future states of affairs and attempts to determine what changes must be made from this point forward to level the playing field so that everyone, or as many as possible, attain the status of "equal." The primary concern or goal is to achieve the fairest system of distribution of social goods in the future. Thus, although we note where we are now, and we recognize that the current system or state of affairs includes disadvantaged or disenfranchised parties, the idea is to look to the future to achieve justice for everyone who exists in it. Forward-looking justice thus strives to achieve "social justice" by offering provisions to those with "special needs." The idea is that without such provisions, equality among citizens will not obtain, which seems unjust, especially given the fact that the "special needs" group has become disenfranchised through no fault of its own.

Backward-looking justice focuses on past states of affairs and attempts to determine how or why the current inequalities (including unfair distribution of social goods) or injustices have subsequently obtained. The next step is to determine how to make amends for them. This will invariably include identifying who has suffered the inequalities/injustices, and proposals for compensating those parties. The goal, then, is to rectify past transgressions by offering compensation to the appropriate parties, which often includes restitution from the offending parties. Whether this creates or accomplishes a system of fair (or fairer) distribution of social goods in the future isn't the issue. Rather, backward-looking justice strives to achieve "retributive justice" via restitution/compensation made by the parties responsible for past transgressions. This form of justice notes that some have made themselves unequal through their own doing and thus they must make amends.

Given a forward-looking approach, Precrime is not obviously unjust. Precrime does in a way identify disadvantaged individuals, targets them as special needs cases, and provides them extra privileges—at least in terms of their safety. The target group consists of those persons identified as victims of "future murders." They comprise a special needs group because their lives are in grave danger. The extra privileges provided to them are assistance from the Precrime team, which includes apprehending the relevant future murderer and (although this isn't very clear from the movie) providing psychological support to the "future-victim." In this way, the public good is obviously served insofar as citizens of Washington, DC, can walk the streets without fear of being murdered. Persons deemed "future murderers"—obvious threats to society—are removed. Citizens are more confident of receiving the basic, decent treatment all equals deserve. Peace of mind is greatly enhanced, resulting in (presumably) a more content and productive society.

What about Precrime and backward-looking justice? Immediately note that Precrime doesn't seem backward-looking at all. It peers into the future to locate transgressions (future murders) and the parties responsible for them (future murderers). Now Rosenstand's worry begins to materialize. Retributive justice requires that only the party responsible for the crime is appropriately punished. No one else deserves punishment for the committed crime. To punish anyone else for that crime is impermissible because doing so contravenes justice. Retributive justice is meted out when an individual appropriates privileges at the expense of others; he benefits by illicitly disadvantaging those around him. And by taking that to which he has no right, he thereby causes an improper inequality among his peers for which he must make amends. So-called future murderers have done nothing of the sort. They have committed no crime and no inequality has taken place calling for restitution.

This exploration of justice has led us to the relevant standard or principle to be applied: It is always wrong to punish someone for crimes he or she did not commit (or are not responsible for). To punish future murderers is to subject them to treatment they do not deserve. In this way, they are treated unjustly. Thus Witwer's worry—"the fundamental paradox of Precrime methodology"—seems well-founded. It is grounded in the factual reason that Precrime punishes citizens who have committed no crime and the conceptual reason that those convicted via previsions are thereby not deserving of punishment (or inappropriately required to make restitution); therefore, given the relevant principle that it is always wrong to administer undeserved punishment (insofar as this is an unjust practice), it does seem to follow that Precrime ought to be disbanded.[12]

Is this argument sound? If so, then its conclusion—Precrime ought to be disbanded—is true. Whether the argument holds up depends (in part) on whether we've gained sufficient clarity regarding the relevant facts and concepts. Have we overlooked any facts or conceptual issues? (What of Anderton's retort to Witwer that just because you prevent something from happening doesn't mean it wasn't going to happen?) Have we properly articulated the relevant morally significant principle? Is it open to counterexample or other calls for revision? (How could we bolster the assumption that forward-looking social justice benefits ought not to be secured by violating principles of retributive justice?) Therefore, as plausible as the argument now appears, moral philosophers (fledgling or professional) have more work to do to solidify its soundness. All of this, then, is to participate in the enterprise of moral reasoning.

Well-Being and Objectivity

Conceptual concerns are not limited to specific moral judgments. They arise in discussions of well-being, including the very attempt to define it at all. Recall it was argued that our moral obligations are a function of whether (nontrivial) harms and benefits regarding well-being are justifiable. But also recall the suggestion that morally significant benefits and harms aren't always easy to recognize (because some of them resist the straightforward physical/psychological division). Thus we must proceed very carefully when investigating the concept of well-being. Some remain unconvinced that this concept can be informatively explored at all. Exactly in what does well-being consist? What does it mean to say that someone's life can go better, best, or even worst? Even if informative insights about well-being can be gleaned, it is still left undetermined whose well-being matters. Must we, as moral agents, concern ourselves only with the well-being of (other) persons, or all sentient life?

To engage in issues pertaining to the meaning and application of basic moral concepts is to concern oneself with matters of metaethics. Studying metaethics doesn't provide one with guidance about what one ought to do in specific circumstances; rather, it better informs one about the meaning and implications of moral terms like "ought." A core metaethical issue explores the very notion of ethical truth. What ultimately makes some ethically significant claims true rather than false? This question arises given the fact that ethical statements are prescriptive and not descriptive. It's plainly true that water is two-parts hydrogen and one-part oxygen. Is it just as plain that terrorizing an innocent child is wrong? Many are initially inclined to believe that these examples are crucially different: the former is grounded in a descriptive *fact* about the world, but the latter, at best, is merely one's *opinion* because it is not grounded in any obvious descriptive fact about the world.

The metaethical issue about ethical truth emerging here can be alternatively under-stood via well-being. There are scientific facts that pertain universally. But are there any universally binding facts about well-being? If what makes someone's life go better is inherently subjective, won't our moral obligations be subjective and not universally bind-ing? At the very least, if what makes someone's life go well depends on the person, won't there be a great deal of disagreement about what is right or wrong? If so, can anything be "just plain wrong"?

The force of these questions suggests a lack of universal or necessary conditions regarding human well-being. At best, well-being is merely a matter of having one's desires fulfilled—getting whatever it is that you personally want. This might be the closest plau-sible candidate to anything remotely resembling a universally binding fact about well-being. However, some philosophers object that this desire-based theory of well-being suffers from a conceptual flaw, namely that, if the theory were true, it would be impossible to intentionally harm yourself. If you desire to harm yourself, then you're getting what you want, which is a benefit (and not a harm), according to this theory. Less abstractly, note how some people, after realizing their most considered and deepest desires, are nev-ertheless completely miserable. This certainly happened to Dr. Horrible (a.k.a. Billy the Laundry-buddy) at the end of *Dr. Horrible's Sing-Along Blog*. He finally received entrance into the Evil League of Evil, something he strived to accomplish for years. Yet when we last glimpse him, he is utterly lost, if not completely miserable. So, how can it be plausibly said that he is (nontrivially) better off? Examples like Horrible/Billy serve as a troubling counterexample to desire-based approaches to well-being.

Other philosophers understand well-being quite differently, contending that, gener-ally speaking, the welfare of a thing depends on what *kind* of thing it is. The well-being of a fish is impacted by whether it is forced to live on land and the well-being of an oak tree is impacted by the amount of sunlight it receives. Because human beings certainly seem to be rational, social animals—as Aristotle thought—perhaps our well-being is impacted by factors related to our rationality or sociability or both. Philosophers like Aquinas, Mill, and Kant, albeit in distinctive ways, follow Aristotle in grounding well-being in facts about the human condition. This, in turn, leads them to argue for differing concep-tions of morally significant benefits and harms. However, their conclusions, as we will see in parts 2 and 3 of the text, provide for universal application exactly because they are grounded in the human condition (assuming that their arguments are sound, of course).

For now, consider that, given our social nature, it would be a bad thing to be the last person alive on earth.[13] This solitary person would exist akin to the fish out of water or the oak tree in perpetual darkness. The fact that being alone for vast periods of time negatively impacts human well-being explains why solitary confinement (or exile) is so serious a punishment. Some philosophers argue that if one is harmed by being the last person on Earth, then it is bad to live like you are all alone. But if it is bad to lead your life completely separated from others, then one's well-being is enhanced by entering into meaningful relations with other people, connecting with them as equals. But so connecting with others requires recognizing that their welfare commands consideration equal to our own. This is to take the "moral point of view." Therefore, it seems to follow, contrary to subjectivist ruminations about well-being, that our well-being is enhanced by entering into the "moral point of view" and leading the moral life. (This may also explain, in part, why proceeding from a total disregard for the interests of others is a uniquely unfortunate harm.)

That entering into meaningful relationships with others is crucial to well-being (arguably) explains why Dr. Horrible *and* Captain Hammer, by the end of *Dr. Horrible's Sing-Along Blog*, found themselves in such dire straits. Both, albeit in different ways, led the vast part of their adult lives consciously separate from others. Horrible thought that everyone else was too stupid to recognize that humanity has been devoured by some sort of plague. The world has become a mess and he just needs to rule it. Hammer smugly believed that his superhero status drastically set him apart from everyone else; this explains his condescending tone and awkward social skills. Horrible becomes a miserable, hollow man surrounded by shallow, professional cohorts, "not feeling a thing." Hammer, the cowardly hero, eventually requires extensive psychotherapy in order to make sense of his twisted existence.[14]

> "There is nothing more destructive to the metaphysical fabric that binds us than the untimely murder of one human being by another." — *Minority Report,* scene 4

Nevertheless, subjectivist inclinations about value and ethics run deep, bolstered by the fact that there is so much disagreement about what it good, bad, right, wrong, just and unjust, and what constitutes our well-being. Anderton, at least initially, believed that Precrime was not a miscarriage of justice even if Witwer died being unsure of this. Dr. Horrible sees the world as getting worse, but Penny sees it as improving. Imagine all the controversy generated by someone like Senator Finistirre wishing to seriously curtail the livelihoods of many Americans—for what he sees as their own good! Thus, the idea that ethics is somehow merely a matter of human convention requires careful philosophical attention. This is the goal of part 1 of the text, to which we turn next.

1.4. TWO ADDITIONAL FILMS

Minority Report (2002)

Director: Steven Spielberg
Screenwriter: Scott Frank (based on a short story by Philip K. Dick)

Plot Summary

> Imagine a world without crime. . . . Within a year, Precrime has effectively stopped murder in our nation's capital. Now Precrime can work for you.

In 2046, the US homicide rate reaches epic proportions. But in the same year, the US government authorizes a federal grant to conduct experiments in "precrime." By 2049, the Precrime unit is operational. By 2054, the pilot Precrime unit in Washington, DC, runs so effectively that homicide, at least within a two-hundred-mile radius, has become a thing of the past. The program is a success, and Precrime is about to go national. If the pending national referendum vote is favorable, it will.

Precrime is the latest advance in criminal science. The police can now "see" homicides before they actually happen. In fact, the police "see" the homicides through the eyes of others, namely the "precognitives." The three "precogs," as they are commonly known, are accidents of genetic research and advancement. To some, however, the accidents were unfortunate at best. The precogs are the children of "neurorine" addicts, inflicted with a condition called Renning's syndrome as a result of their parents' addiction. The syndrome has grave effects upon a child's cerebral cortex. The world's top geneticists, in particular Dr. Iris Hineman, work to aid the children. However, for some of the children the "cure" afflicts them with a further unique condition, the ability to see the future—and more importantly, the ability to predict with seemingly absolute certainty homicides that are about to take place.

John Anderton is the chief of the Washington, DC, Precrime unit. Anderton's supervisor, Lamar Burgess, informs him that the Justice Department, in the person of Danny Witwer, will soon visit the Precrime division. Before Precrime goes national, the Justice Department wants to ensure that it runs as smoothly and effectively as possible. The primary concern is whether the system is infallible; if it is not, then the Precrime division could arrest innocent people—those who have committed no crime and will not commit a crime, at least not the one the precogs claim they will commit. Because Precrime police science is grounded in the idea that murders should be stopped before they happen, "previsions" are the only "evidence" the Precrime police have to make arrests; therefore, the precogs can never be wrong. If they are, then Precrime law enforcement seems unjust.

Fletcher, Anderton's lieutenant, informs Witwer about Precrime procedures. Skeptical, Witwer directs his response to the entire unit present: "I'm sure you've all grasped the legalistic drawback to Precrime methodology. Look, I'm not with the ACLU on this. . . . But let's not kid ourselves, we are arresting individuals who've broken no law." After some protestation from the unit, Witwer continues, "But it's not the future if you stop it. Isn't that a fundamental paradox?" Just then, Anderton enters the room and the discussion. After affirming that it does seem paradoxical, he announces to Witwer, "You're talking about predetermination, which happens all the time." Anderton takes a wooden egg out of Fletcher's hand and rolls it on a table toward Witwer. Just before it falls to the ground, Witwer catches it, prompting Anderton to ask why Witwer caught the egg. "It was going to fall," replies Witwer. "You're certain?" inquires Anderton, to which Witwer answers affirmatively. "But it didn't fall. You caught it," Anderton pauses, seemingly for effect, and concludes, "The fact that you prevented it from happening doesn't change the fact that it was going to happen."

Soon after, an alarm sounds, signaling that the precogs have foreseen another murder. The victim's name is Leo Crow. To Anderton's horror, the perpetrator is identified as "John Anderton." Will Anderton soon commit homicide—kill a man that he does not even know? Surely there has been some mistake. But the precogs are never wrong! Has someone tampered with the system and framed him for a crime that he will never commit? He quickly but quietly leaves Precrime headquarters. The quiet is soon broken. Alarms sound and Chief Anderton is now a wanted fugitive for the "future murder" of Leo Crow.

Anderton desperately makes his way to Dr. Hineman's residence. Now a recluse, perhaps the inventor of Precrime will be able to inform Anderton how someone could tamper with the system resulting in a false prevision. With great effort—including a run-in with her genetically altered (and poisonous) Doll's eye plants—he finds Hineman. She reminds Anderton of what he already knows—the precogs are never wrong. Hineman further informs him that she is not aware of any way to fake a prevision. Anderton is beyond despair. Hineman picks up her tea, and looking over the cup at Anderton, also informs him, "But occasionally they do disagree. . . . Once in a while, one will see things differently than the other two." Anderton is stunned. He was unaware of these "minority reports"; he, like everyone else, believed that the infallible precogs all "saw" the same murders in pretty much the same way. Anderton asks whether Burgess knows about these minority reports. Hineman admits that he does. Anderton despondently asks, "Are you saying that I've haloed innocent people?" Hineman replies, "I'm saying that every so often those accused of a precrime might—just might—have an alternative future. . . . But we felt their existence was an insignificant variable." Anderton quickly interjects, "Insignificant to you, maybe, but what about those people I put away with alternate futures? My God, if the country knew there was a chance . . ."

Of course, obtaining his minority report, if he has one, will be difficult. He must avoid retinal scans, or "eye-dents." He seeks the help of an ex-con surgeon who agrees to give him a new set of eyes, thereby avoiding the danger of retinal scans. But he must keep his old eyes in order to enter the temple. Concurrently, Anderton's old teammates employ all of their legal resources to apprehend their ex-chief. Most strikingly, they send their artificially intelligent, metal recon "spiders" into an apartment building in which they suspect Anderton is hiding. The spiders enter every apartment in order to "eye-dent" each person inside—man, woman, and child—regardless of whether they have reason to believe that Anderton is in that room. The "spiders" intrude on a single mother and her two children, interrupt a couple making love, and humiliate a man using the toilet. Anderton narrowly escapes (thanks to his new eyes). He must now use them to kidnap Agatha in order to determine whether he has a minority report.

Anderton does not know Leo Crow; he has never even met him. But just as Hineman told Anderton, "A series of events has started that will lead you, inexorably, to his murder." This series began with Anderton's visit with Hineman. It continues with his successful escape from the temple with Agatha. He must now keep her safe until he can access her memories. But how? Soon, Anderton begins to recognize some of the previsions from the Crow future murder. He looks at his watch; the time of the future murder draws near. Anderton—inexorably—drags Agatha up to the apartment where the future murder is about to happen. Agatha is desperate. She reminds Anderton that he can leave. She pleads with him, "You still have a choice! The others never saw their future. You still have a choice. . . . You can choose!"

Discussion Questions

1. Does Anderton act permissibly in removing Agatha from the "temple"?
2. Why is it so important that Precrime police "science" be infallible?
3. If Precrime is infallible and the precogs foresee someone committing murder tomorrow, is that person justly punished now for his (future) act? Explain. Is Anderton's explanation to Witwer any help in this regard? Explain.
4. Assume that the precogs are not infallible, but their previsions are correct 99.9 percent of the time. Is the elimination of homicide not important and beneficial enough to outweigh the statistical fact that previsions will be incorrect one time out of a thousand? Is the societal benefit great enough to enlist the services of the precognitives without their consent? Explain.
5. Which if any of the following are morally objectionable infringements on our basic rights: pervasive "eye-dents," the metallic recon spiders, Precrime itself? Explain. What does your answer show about the relationship between legality and morality?

Dr. Horrible's Sing-Along Blog (2008)

Director and Screenwriter: Joss Whedon

Plot Summary

> It's not about making money, but taking money—upsetting the status quo—
> because the status is not . . . quo.

Dr. Horrible, the neighborhood evil genius, believes that the world is a mess and he just needs to rule it. He also believes that (finally) gaining entrance into the Evil League of Evil will facilitate his quest. His application is strong this year, complete with a letter of condemnation from the deputy mayor. Yet Captain Hammer, the local superhero, thwarts Horrible at every turn; he has become the evil genius's nemesis. But the tides will turn with Horrible's nearly developed freeze ray. ("This is the one . . . stops time . . . tell your friends.") Captain Hammer, corporate tool, will thwart him no longer. Of course, we learn all of this on Horrible's video blog, which he updates regularly.

Dr. Horrible's other goal in life is to woo Penny, a girl that he sees at the local Laundromat (every Wednesday and Saturday, except twice last month she skipped the weekend). The problem here is not Captain Hammer, at least not right away, but the fact that Horrible is too nervous to speak to her. (Yet he believes that he is "so close to a real . . . audible connection.") But much to his surprise, he bumps into Penny on the street one day. Horrible, who introduces himself as Billy, is plotting a heist of Wonderflonium—the last necessary ingredient for his freeze ray. Penny is combing the neighborhood for petition signatures. She is lobbying the city to sign over a deserted building to her Caring Hands Homeless Shelter group. With the new building, her group can establish 250 new beds and begin implementing additional job training programs. Billy awkwardly replies that her efforts miss the mark because she is merely treating a symptom but the real problem rages on. A complete overhaul of the system is required; power must be put into different hands. He regains his composure (finally) long enough to sign Penny's petition, but then quickly ignores her to continue his heist. By the time he turns around again, Penny is gone. He is dejected, but the Wonderflonium will soon be his!

Captain Hammer (of course) bursts onto the scene in the attempt to prevent Dr. Horrible's larceny. He puts his fist through Horrible's transmitter (the one perched on top of the Wonderflonium currier van that allowed him to remotely control it). The van begins to veer wildly. Hammer jumps off to introduce himself to a young lady. Horrible sees the van careening directly toward an unsuspecting Penny. Horrible feverishly attempts to regain control of the van (the remote control is in his hand). Penny is stunned at the oncoming van. At the last second, Horrible stops the van. However, Penny believes that Captain Hammer saved her life; he pushed her out of the way, sending her airborne into bags of trash. She collects herself, thanks Hammer, and the two—very much to Billy's dismay—become smitten with each other. He bitterly walks away with the case of Wonderflonium, as Hammer and Penny gaze into each other's eyes.

This recent turn of events doesn't sit well with Horrible. His pessimistic view of humankind further sours. He's no longer sure that he'll upset the status quo if he puts poison in the water main; evidently humanity has become brain dead. But we learn more about Penny (because Billy follows—stalks—her and Hammer). She does not share Horrible's derogatory view of society. She believes that much can be made better if only we would be kinder to each other. We are not brain dead, but have simply turned a blind eye to the plight of our fellow human beings for too long. Both cannot believe their eyes. Horrible believes that evil is on the rise, but Penny believes that all of us are finally growing wise.

Penny and Billy become "laundry buddies," which Billy seems to enjoy, but it also requires him to hear about Penny's budding romance with Hammer. It also occasions a chance meeting between Hammer and Billy (Hammer claims Billy looks "horribly" familiar). Hammer now realizes that Billy has a crush on Penny. Hammer becomes crass, informing Horrible that he is taking his relationship with Penny to the next level simply because "he gets to have what Horrible wants." Hammer doesn't care about Penny; he only cares about hurting Horrible. Horrible is enraged by this.

Horrible's rage also inspires him. As it turns out, Horrible's first attempt using the freeze ray was a flop. By the time it warmed up, Hammer thwarted his plan to blow up a bridge. Hammer added insult to injury by subsequently throwing a car at Horrible's head. Bad Horse—the "thoroughbred of sin" and leader of the Evil League of Evil—witnessed the debacle and informed Horrible that "now assassination is the only way" to gain entrance into the league. Killing isn't Horrible's style; it isn't creative or elegant. But for Hammer, he would now make an exception; Horrible begins plotting Hammer's demise.

Horrible readies the freeze ray for the mayor's dedication of the Caring Hands Homeless Shelter. He also transforms his stun gun into a death ray. He'll stay hidden until Hammer's speech and then stop time long enough to do away with his nemesis for good. But the death ray misfires. Someone is killed, Horrible is blamed, he gains entrance to the league, but something is "horribly" amiss.

Discussion Questions

1. Is Dr. Horrible evil? Is Captain Hammer a hero? Explain your answers.
2. What does Horrible allegedly see about humanity that others don't? Would things be better if he ruled the world?
3. Is gaining entrance into the Evil League of Evil a worthy goal? Is Bad Horse every bit as much of an achiever as is (for example) Gandhi?
4. In what sense, if any, is it true that "everyone's a hero in their own way"? Why does this sound so unpalatable coming from Hammer?
5. What is the meaning of the very end of the short film?

1.5. REVIEWING THROUGH THE THREE MOVIES

1. Among Nick Naylor, John Anderton, and Dr. Horrible, which of the three characters would you be most likely to have dinner with? Why?
2. Among the three movies, which ethically significant choice or behavior was the worst? Which was the best? Was the worst also morally wrong/impermissible? Was the best morally required/obligatory? Defend your answers.
3. Among the three movies, which character was most morally commendable? Which was most morally undesirable? Explain.
4. Between the government placing stringent warning labels on cigarette cartons (per *Thank You for Smoking*) or the government shutting down Precrime (per *Minority Report*), which do you agree with more? Explain your answer.

5. Reconsider the six movie quotes from the chapter and explain whether each, given the adjacent paragraphs, *illustrates* a point the author is making, *supplements* (or extends) a point the author is making, or *contrasts* (for emphasis) a point the author is making. Explain your answers.

NOTES

1. Excerpted from *The Dialogues of Plato*, trans. Benjamin Jowlett (New York: Oxford University Press, 1920). Section headings and slight grammar emendations have been provided to aid reader comprehension.

2. Michael Huemer provides an accessible account of freedom and responsibility as it pertains to *Minority Report* in "Free Will and Determinism in the World of *Minority Report*," in *Science Fiction and Philosophy: From Time Travel to Superintelligence*, ed. Susan Schneider (New York: Blackwell, 2009), 103–12. For a more extensive (but still accessible) treatment of the issues as they pertain to *Minority Report*, see Dean A. Kowalski, "*Minority Report*, Molinism, and the Viability of Precrime," in *Steven Spielberg and Philosophy,* ed. Dean A. Kowalski (Lexington: University Press of Kentucky, 2008), 227–47.

3. The term "antecedent" refers to the first half of a conditional (or if-then) statement, that is, the "if" part. Any deductive argument that proceeds by negating or denying the antecedent is thereby invalid. Consider: If George Washington was killed in a plane crash, he is dead; George Washington wasn't killed in a plane crash; thus, George Washington is not dead. These true premises take us to an obviously false conclusion, which means that this argument breaks the very definition of a valid argument. Thus even though the premises are true, the argument is unsound.

4. Careful inspection thus reveals that, because the term "plant" has a different sense in premise one than it does in premise two, the chlorophyll argument actually has the form: All A are B; All C are D; thus, All C are B. This is an invalid deductive form, because valid syllogisms may only contain three (class) terms.

5. The present discussion of understanding ethical issues and judgments in terms of impacting well-being has been influenced by Emmett Barcalow, *Moral Philosophy: Theories and Issues*, 2nd ed. (Belmont, CA: Wadsworth, 1998), 6–8.

6. The exact role of impartiality in moral deliberation is complicated by the intuition that agents have special obligations to close friends and family members. If there are special obligations, then those close to the agent deserve considerations that strangers do not. For example, a parent may be obligated to help his or her child pay for college, but he or she is not obligated to help other children pay for college. This issue is explored in more detail in chapter 11.

7. Some philosophers afford the "moral point of view" preeminent status in moral deliberation, which partly explains why some argue that only (unjustifiable) harms done to *another* are ethically significant. As suggested earlier, other philosophers are inclined to interpret a harm-based approach in such a way that behavior that unjustifiably diminishes only your own well-being is not merely irrational or impractical, but morally significant. As we'll see, some philosophers hold that we have moral duties to ourselves (as persons) to account for this; others hold that the choices we make and the habits we develop regarding our own well-being can be morally better or worse (even if, not exactly obligatory or impermissible).

8. This discussion points to an ambiguity in the common usage of "morally right." Sometimes this refers to what is morally good or acceptable, including supererogatory acts. Such acts are commendable if you do them, but you are not blameworthy for not doing them. Other times, this refers to what is morally required or obligatory. For these acts, if you do not do them, you are morally blameworthy because you have failed some obligation. Thus, morally obligatory and impermissible can be straightforwardly defined in terms of one another in a way that morally obligatory and morally right cannot be.

9. Nina Rosenstand, *The Moral of the Story* (New York: McGraw-Hill, 2006), 339. Rosenstand doesn't answer the question she poses, but her ideas have influenced the current discussion of forward-looking and backward-looking theories of justice as they pertain to *Minority Report*.

10. Ethics is one of the primary branches or areas of philosophy, but there are others, including metaphysics. Metaphysics is the study of what ultimately or fundamentally exists. Metaphysical freedom, then, concerns whether moral agents—in some deep or fundamental sense—possess free will in a way similar (although not exactly so) to how circles possess roundness. Just as there are no nonround circles, there are no moral agents lacking genuine freedom of the will.

11. For the purposes of this text, it will be assumed that agents do indeed typically possess the sort of metaphysical freedom required for moral responsibility. However, it must be admitted that there are some circumstances in which our freedom and responsibility is diminished. In such cases, our agency is curtailed because we *react* more than we *act*. Such a possibility helps to justify the legal defense of "temporary insanity" and the like.

12. The relevant argument can be formally recast something like this: If person X is punished for a crime that he or she did not commit (or is not responsible for), then X is treated impermissibly. Persons labeled "future murderers" are convicted and punished via Precrime methodologies having committed no crime. Thus, so-called future murderers are treated impermissibly via Precrime methodologies. The argument continues: If so-called future murderers are treated impermissibly via Precrime methodologies, then Precrime ought to be disbanded; thus, Precrime ought to be disbanded.

13. The argument presented in this paragraph has been influenced by chapters 5 and 6 of Jean Kazez's *The Weight of Things: Philosophy and the Good Life* (Boston: Blackwell, 2007).

14. Indeed, Penny's life seemed to be going the best, exactly because of her deep connections with and concern about others. This interpretation arguably survives the potential counterpoint that Whedon ends his short film by killing off Penny. (Whedon is known to kill off his more sympathetic characters for dramatic effect.) For additional analysis of Joss Whedon's *Dr. Horrible's Sing-Along Blog* and its philosophically significant themes about well-being and the good life, see Dean A. Kowalski, "Plato, Aristotle, and Joss on Being Horrible," in *The Philosophy of Joss Whedon*, eds. Dean A. Kowalski and S. Evan Kreider (Lexington: University Press of Kentucky, 2011), 71–87.

PART I

METAETHICS

CHAPTER 2

Simple Ethical Subjectivism

MATCH POINT (2005)
Director and Screenwriter: Woody Allen

PLOT SUMMARY

There are moments in a match when the ball hits the top of the net and for a split second, it can go forward or fall back. With a little luck, it goes forward and you win. Or maybe it doesn't and you lose.

Chris Wilton, a young ex-professional tennis player, seeks employment as a tennis pro at a posh club in London. Among his first students is young Tom Hewett. They quickly become friends. Besides tennis, both have an interest in opera. Tom invites Chris to share in his family's reserved box at the local opera house. There Chris meets Tom's sister Chloe. Chloe seems smitten with Chris. Tom subsequently invites Chris to a party on Sunday at the family's country estate. Chris insists on expressing his gratitude by providing the Hewetts free lessons.

The Sunday soiree begins with Chris, Tom, and Chloe playing tennis. Chris seems grateful for being invited to the Hewett soiree. Tom soon excuses himself, but leaves Chloe behind. Chloe learns that she and Chris share a love of art and the theater. She insists on taking Chris to a local gallery. Chris offers to buy the tickets, but Chloe indicates that it won't be necessary. Chloe also suggests that they should meet for lunch beforehand. Chris immediately responds, "It's a date."

Chris, now showered and wearing a jacket, explores the lavish Hewett country home. He (politely) wanders the halls, but hears voices in one of the rooms and enters. He meets Nola Rice, a young American woman. Chris is immediately drawn to Nola, and she does not discourage his not-so-subtle advances. But Tom abruptly strolls in the room and quickly introduces Nola—his fiancée—to Chris.

BOX 2A: INSIDE *MATCH POINT*

Match Point is arguably Woody Allen's second attempt at exploring the issues of ethics and meaning through film (with *Crimes and Misdemeanors* being the first, but his films regularly touch on these interrelated issues). The movie might also be helpful to explore the issue of "moral luck," but it is used in this chapter as a way to explore the very nature of ethical truth. Unlike *Crimes and Misdemeanors*, Woody's implicit view in *Match Point* is more obvious: there is no moral structure implicit in the universe. If there were, Chris Wilton would have not "won" his "match" as the events of his life unfolded after his tennis career was over. At best, ethical truth is simply what people tend to believe or feel about it.

The most pertinent segments of *Match Point* regarding the issue of ethical truth begin early in the film, with Chris's voice-over at 1:35. Listening (and watching) this 40 second segment provides important context for much of the film. Additional important context can be gleaned by beginning at 19:48 (roughly the middle of scene 5), as Tom and Nola meet Chris and Chloe for dinner. Continue watching until the end of the scene (roughly 23:07), where you see a shot of a tall office building. Then go to the start of scene 15, beginning at 1:10:34. You're immediately informed about Chris and Nola's affair. Continue watching to 1:24:00 (roughly the middle of scene 17), where Chris comes to a quiet, nighttime revelation. Skip ahead into scene 18 at 1:28:28; you'll see Chris walking down a lane phoning Nola. Continue watching until 1:38:08 to learn the details of Chris's revelation. Next go to 1:43:32 (this is into scene 21), where you'll see a shot of Chloe's mother sitting on a couch. Continue watching until the end of scene 21 at 1:47:57; you'll see a barricade railing. This shot links up the opening voice-over to the main idea of the movie (pay close attention to what happens to the gold ring). Finally, skip ahead to scene 23 at 1:54:45; you'll see Chloe sleeping and Chris working late. Continue watching until 1:58:35, where the shot cuts away from Chris to the police detective. In this segment, Allen makes the point of his film explicit.

It is always best to watch the entire film. If you do, you should be able to answer the trivia questions from box 2B. But if time is limited, watching the specified segments after having carefully read the plot summary should provide you with a sufficient grasp of the film.

Chris and Chloe begin spending a great deal of time together. Chloe's parents notice this. Mrs. Hewett cautions Chloe about becoming involved with a tennis club pro. Mr. Hewett speaks up for Chris, announcing that he has had very interesting conversations with the young man, sometimes about Dostoyevsky. Chloe capitalizes on her father's goodwill. She asks him if there are any positions at his firm for Chris. Chris eventually agrees to begin working for Mr. Hewett. When Chloe discovers this, she insists that she and Chris open a nice bottle of wine and celebrate. But when Chris learns that Tom and Nola have also invited them to a movie, he suggests that they join them. After all, they can stay in any night.

Chris and Nola unexpectedly meet on the street one day. She is on her way to an audition, but she has become quite nervous about it. Her agent was supposed to accompany her, but he cancelled. Chris offers to walk with her. He waits outside the theater until Nola finishes. It didn't go well. Nola says that she would really like to get a drink. Chris leads her to a nearby pub. Nola begins drowning her sorrows and the two share their life stories. Nola's father left and her mother couldn't hold down a job; she drank too much. Nola had been briefly married once before she met Tom. Tom swept her off her feet, but Nola suggests that she is more attracted to the lifestyle Tom can provide her than Tom himself. Upon ordering another drink, Nola asks about Chris's situation with Chloe. He says that she is a very sweet person. Nola knowingly looks him in the eye. The conversation turns to Mrs. Hewett. Nola acknowledges that Mrs. Hewett doesn't care for her at all, but she goes on to say that things are different for Chris. She says, "You're being groomed. You're going to do very well for yourself unless you blow it." Chris slowly asks, "And how am I going to blow it?" Nola finishes her drink and confidently replies, "By making a pass at me."

The two couples spend another weekend at the Hewett country estate. But Chris seems more interested in Nola than Chloe. Mr. Hewett informs Chris that there is a new job at the firm that Chris would be perfect for, assuming that he would take a few business courses. Nola and Tom join Mr. and Mrs. Hewett in the library for a drink. Chloe and Chris retire to their room. Mrs. Hewett harps (again) on Nola and her struggling acting career. She wonders aloud, rather rudely, when the young American will try her hand at something else. Nola abruptly excuses herself; she makes her way to the courtyard. Chris glances out a window and sees Nola. It has begun to rain, but Nola doesn't seem to notice. Concerned, Chris follows Nola to the back garden. They embrace, fall to the ground, and make love.

The ill-advised tryst remains a secret, and Nola reminds Chris that nothing can come of it. They may become in-laws after all. Chris and Chloe are indeed soon married, but Tom and Nola break up. Nola disappears (much to Chris's dismay). Tom soon marries someone else; his new wife is already pregnant.

BOX 2B: *MATCH POINT* TRIVIA

If your instructor assigns the film to be watched outside of class, you should be able to answer the following questions:

1. When Chris first meets Nola, what is she doing?
2. Where do Chris and Chloe first kiss?
3. What is Nola's "dream car"?
4. Which is Nola's home state?
5. What movie do Tom, Chris, and Chloe see together?
6. After marrying Chloe, where is the first place Chris meets Nola?
7. What time does Nola get through with work?
8. What excuse does Chris use to enter Mrs. Eastby's apartment (Nola's neighbor)?
9. Where is detective Banner when he evidently "cracks the case"?
10. What is the name of Chris and Chloe's baby?

Months later, Chris fortuitously runs into Nola. He insists that she give him her new phone number. After reminding him that he is married, she relents. They soon meet for another tryst. Lying in bed, they chat about her new apartment. Nola admits that she was lucky to find it, even though it's far from perfect. The building has been burglarized recently and her shut-in elderly neighbor has mice.

Chris and Chloe strive to become pregnant. Chris continues his affair with Nola. On their way up to her apartment, they have a chance meeting with Nola's neighbor, Mrs. Eastby. Chris spends almost all of his free time with Nola. He and Chloe have yet to conceive, but Nola surprises Chris with news that *she* is pregnant. He wants Nola to have an abortion. She refuses. She doesn't feel comfortable doing that again. As Chris leaves to meet Chloe and her family, Nola pleads, "I expect you to do the right thing, okay?" Chris tries to tell Chloe, but he cannot. She immediately recognizes something is wrong. She asks whether he is having an affair. He denies it, but still murmurs, "I just feel so guilty, so terribly guilty." Is he talking about not getting Chloe pregnant? Chloe isn't sure.

Nola continues to pressure Chris "to do the right thing." He allows Nola to believe that he and Chloe's family will be away on holiday for a few weeks. Mr. Hewett informs Chris that a new, lucrative business opportunity is available. But soon Nola discovers that Chris lied to her about being away. She confronts Chris and threatens to make Chloe aware of the situation. Chris again reassures her, "Okay, okay, I'll do the right thing." That night, Chris lies awake with Chloe sleeping next to him. He abruptly sits up on the edge of the bed, seemingly having discovered what he ought to do. The next day, he visits Mr. Hewett's gun locker and pilfers a shotgun. He tells Nola that it will all be over tomorrow. She must meet him at her apartment right after work.

The next morning, news breaks that Nola's building was burglarized again. Chloe learns about it in the morning paper; she announces the terrible news to Chris. Tragically, Mrs. Eastby and Nola were killed. The police investigate, but what happened seems clear. Someone armed with a shotgun robbed Mrs. Eastby for her prescription medication and other valuables, unexpectedly met Nola in the stairwell, and also killed her in making his escape. The ensuing investigation uncovers Nola's diary; the police thereby learn of her affair with Chris. He is discreetly called in for questioning. On the way to the station, he throws Eastby's possessions into the river. Double-checking his pockets, he finds her wedding ring. He tosses it toward the river; it hits the railing, momentarily hangs in the air, but bounces back toward the sidewalk. At the station, he pleads for further discretion. He informs Detective Banner, "My wife is having a baby. This will devastate her. . . . Look, don't run irresponsibly roughshod over this and ruin innocent people's lives. I mean there is no case because I wouldn't harm anyone, much less Nola Rice." Banner replies, "We're not making any moral judgments, just investigating a crime."

Late that night, the apparitions of Nola and Eastby "visit" Chris in his kitchen. He tells Nola, "You can learn to push the guilt under the rug and go on. You have to—otherwise it overwhelms you." He tells Eastby, "The innocent are sometimes slain to make way for a greater scheme. You were collateral damage." Nola declares that Chris's actions were clumsy and that he should "prepare to pay the price." He replies, "It would be fitting if I were apprehended and punished. At least there would be some small sign of justice—some small . . . measure of hope for the possibility of meaning." But the next morning the police find Mrs. Eastby's wedding ring on the body of a drug addict killed in Nola's neighborhood.

2.1. THINKING THROUGH THE MOVIE

Discussion Starter Questions

1. Is Chris Wilton a good person? If not, why not?
2. Suppose Chris is never punished for his seeming misdeeds. Are they still morally bad or wrong? Explain.
3. Is it ever morally permissible to cheat on your spouse (or significant other)? Is it ever permissible to be dishonest? Was Chris's dishonesty permissible? Justify your answers.
4. What was the right thing for Chris to do with respect to Chloe and Nola once the latter became pregnant? Explain.
5. What seems to be the basic (moral) message of the film? Explain.

Questions for Further Thought

1. Is Chris correct (scene 5, roughly 23:00 into the film) that "all existence is here by blind chance" with no purpose or design? Either way, what might be the moral significance of your answer?
2. What role do guilt and conscience play in our moral judgments? Chris suggests that "guilt can be pushed under the rug." If so, is there any other reason (besides suffering a guilty conscience) for not acting immorally?
3. In the courtyard before they make love (scene 8, 38:50 into the film), Nola tells Chris, "We *can't* do this. This can't lead anywhere." What does she mean by this?
4. An important, recurring theme of the movie is that it's important to be lucky. Why? Does being lucky have any moral significance?
5. Banner tells Chris (scene 22, 1:52:22 into the film) that he isn't making a moral judgment about Chris's fidelity, but investigating a crime. Why are some presumably immoral acts not illegal?

2.2. HISTORICAL SETTING

A Treatise of Human Nature and *An Inquiry Concerning the Principles of Morals* (excerpts)[1]

David Hume is perhaps the most influential Scottish philosopher. He worked as a librarian and historian, but he never held a university position. Although he is perhaps best known for his positions in epistemology, logic, and the philosophy of religion, Hume wrote on many philosophical topics. His views are often subtle and complex. The subsequent passages convey some of his ideas about the nature of ethical truth.

Preparing to Read

A. Imagine that you watch *Match Point* with Hume. How would he react to the movie?

B. Note the difference between the following two claims: (1) Snow is white; (2) One ought to be honest. What makes (1) true? What makes (2) true? How would Hume answer these questions?

[Judgments about Good and Evil]

Some affirm that virtue is nothing but conformity to reason; that there are eternal fitnesses and unfitnesses of things, which are the same to every rational being that considers them; that the immutable measures of right and wrong impose an obligation, not only on human creatures, but also on the Deity himself. They concur in the opinion, that morality, like truth, is discerned merely by ideas, and by their combination and comparison. In order, therefore, to judge this position, we need only consider, whether it be possible, from reason alone, to distinguish between moral good and evil, or whether there must exist other principles to enable us to make that distinction.

[Ethics as Correlated with the Passions]

Philosophy is commonly divided into speculative and practical; and as morality is always comprehended under the latter division, it is supposed to influence our passions and actions, and to go beyond the calm and indolent judgments of the understanding. And this is confirmed by common experience, which informs us, that people are often governed by their duties, and are deterred from some actions by the opinion of injustice, and impelled to others by that of obligation.

Since morals, therefore, have an influence on the actions and affections, it follows, that they cannot be derived from reason; and that reason alone . . . can never have any such influence. Morals excite passions, and produce or prevent actions. Reason of itself is utterly impotent in this regard. The rules of morality, therefore, are not conclusions of our reason.

. . . Take any action deemed to be vicious: willful murder, for instance. Examine it in all lights, and see if you can find that matter of fact, or real existence, which you call vice. In whichever way you take it, you find only certain passions, motives, volitions and thoughts. There is no other matter of fact in the case. The vice entirely escapes you, as long as you consider the object. You never can find it, till you turn your reflection into your own breast, and find a sentiment of disapproval, which arises in you, towards this action. Here is a matter of fact; but it is the object of feeling, not of reason. It lies in yourself, not in the object. So that when you pronounce any action or character to be vicious, you mean nothing, but that from the constitution of your nature you have a feeling or sentiment of blame from the contemplation of it.

[The Difference between "Is Statements" and "Ought Statements"]

I cannot forbear adding to these arguments an observation, which may, perhaps, hold some importance. In every system of morality, which I have studied, I have always remarked, that the author proceeds for some time in the ordinary way of reasoning, and establishes the being of a God, or makes observations concerning human affairs; when all of a sudden I am surprised to find, that instead of the usual copulations [linking verbs] of propositions, *is*, and *is not*, I meet with no proposition that is not connected with an *ought*, or an ought *not*. This change is imperceptible; but is, however, of great consequence. For as this *ought*, or *ought not*, expresses some new relation or affirmation, it is necessary that it should be observed and explained; and at the same time that a reason should be given, for what seems altogether inconceivable, how this new relation can be a deduction from others, which are entirely different from it. But as authors do not commonly use this precaution, I shall presume to recommend it to the readers; and am persuaded, that this small attention would subvert all the common systems of morality, and shows that the distinction of vice and virtue is not founded merely on the relations of objects, nor is perceived by reason. . . .

Examine the crime of *ingratitude,* for instance, which has place wherever we observe good-will expressed and known, together with good offices [supportive deeds] performed, on the one side, and a return of ill-will or indifference with ill-offices [unkind deeds] or neglect on the other: anatomize all these circumstances and examine, by your reason alone, in what consists the demerit or blame. You never will come to any . . . conclusion.

Reason judges either of *matter* of fact or of *relations.* Inquire then, first, where is that matter of fact which we here call crime; point it out, determine the time of its existence, describe its essence or nature, explain the sense or faculty to which it discovers itself. It resides in the mind of the person who is ungrateful. He must, therefore, feel it and be conscious of it. But nothing is there, except the passion of ill-will or absolute indifference. You cannot say that these, of themselves, always and in all circumstances are crimes. No, they are only crimes when directed towards persons who have before expressed and displayed goodwill towards us. Consequently, we may infer that the crime of ingratitude is not any particular individual *fact,* but arises from . . . circumstances which, being presented to the spectator, excites the *sentiment* of blame by . . . his mind.

This representation, you say, is false. Crime, indeed, consists not in a particular *fact,* of whose reality we are assured by *reason,* but it consists in certain moral *relations,* discovered by reason, in the same manner as we discover by reason the truths of geometry or algebra. But what are the relations . . . ? In the case stated above, I see first good-will and good-offices in one person, then ill-will and ill-offices in the other. Between these, there is a relation of *contrariety.* Does the crime consist in that relation? But suppose a person bore me ill-will or did me ill-offices, and I, in return, were indifferent towards him, or did him good offices. Here is the same relation of *contrariety,* and yet my conduct is often highly laudable. Twist and turn this matter as much as you will, you can never rest the morality on relation, but must have recourse to the decisions of sentiment.

When it is affirmed that two and three are equal to the half of ten, this relation of equality I understand perfectly. . . . But when you then draw a comparison to moral relations, I admit that I am altogether at a loss to understand you. A moral action, a crime, such as ingratitude, is a complicated object. Does the morality consist in the relation of its parts to each other? How? After what manner? Specify the relation: be more explicit in your propositions, and you will easily see their falsehood.

[Not Metaphysical, but Emotional Foundations]

No, say you, the morality consists in the relation of actions to the rule of right; and they are deemed good or ill, according as they agree or disagree with it. What then is this rule of right? In what does it consist? How is it determined? By reason, you say, which examines the moral relations of actions. So that moral relations are determined by the comparison of action to a rule. And that rule is determined by considering the moral relations of objects. Is not this fine [circular] reasoning?

All this is metaphysics, you cry. That is enough; there needs nothing more to give a strong presumption of falsehood. Yes, reply I, here are metaphysics surely; but they are all on your side, who advance an abstruse hypothesis that can never be made intelligible, nor correspond with any particular instance or illustration. The hypothesis to embrace is plain. It maintains that morality is determined by sentiment. It defines virtue to be whatever mental action or quality gives *to a spectator the pleasing sentiment of approbation,* and vice the contrary. We then proceed to examine a plain matter of fact, to wit, what actions have this influence. We consider all the circumstances in which these actions agree, and then endeavor to extract some general observations with regard to these sentiments.

Review Questions

1. In what ways does Hume attempt to prove the conclusion that reason alone cannot sufficiently inform us about what is morally right or wrong? Put his reasoning in your own words.
2. What is Hume's view of "facts of the matter" about moral judgments?
3. What "hypothesis" does Hume "maintain" about what makes ethical judgments true? Put his position into your own words.

2.3. DISCUSSION AND ANALYSIS

Has anyone ever asked you to list all of your beliefs? Doing so proves to be surprisingly difficult. So, let's start with the easy ones, perhaps that each day lasts (about) twenty-four hours and that the earth has one natural satellite. We might describe ourselves. Perhaps you like the taste of chocolate ice cream better than vanilla, and your brother (incredibly) believes that hot dogs taste better without ketchup or mustard. And if we worked at this long enough, eventually the list would no doubt include moral beliefs, perhaps about marital infidelity and abortion. Perhaps you (like Chris Wilton's wife from *Match Point*) believe that marital infidelity is always wrong, while someone else (like Chris Wilton) believes that abortion is not always wrong.

Now let's ask a further question: What makes your beliefs—anyone's beliefs—true? When it comes to cases like the length of one day or how many moons orbit the earth, the answer seems straightforward. For these beliefs, there is a fact "out in the world" that matches up to your belief about it. The world apart from one determines whether a day is twenty-four rather than twenty-five hours long, and whether the earth has one moon or two moons.[2] But the situation seems crucially different for beliefs about which ice cream tastes best or whether condiments are worthy of hot dogs. It is the individual making the judgment, and *not* the "world out there," who ultimately serves as the final arbiter about whether vanilla tastes better than chocolate or hot dogs without mustard are preferable to those with mustard. These beliefs are true if and only if they accurately represent one's (personal) feelings or sentiments.

It is widely held that, among a person's true beliefs, some of them are ethically significant. Perhaps you judge (and thus believe) that 'Chris Wilton is a bad person' or 'Mrs. Eastby didn't deserve her fate'. Judgments like these certainly seem plausibly true. So, keeping with the assumption that moral judgments can be true, it can be asked: But what makes our *moral* beliefs (or judgments) true? Is there a fact (or set of facts) "out in the world" that makes our moral beliefs true? Is moral truth thus independent of moral belief? Or, do individuals themselves somehow provide the ultimate criteria for moral truth? Some people believe that marital infidelity is always wrong and some believe that abortion is sometimes morally acceptable. Assuming that truth is grounded in fact, is the only relevant fact of the matter how individuals feel about topics like infidelity or abortion? Metaethics, recall, is the philosophical subcategory that attempts to achieve greater clarity about the concepts inherent to ethical discourse. So when philosophers engage in the question of how ethical judgments (beliefs) are true (assuming that some are true), they are "doing" metaethics.[3]

Subjective and Objective Truths

The concept of truth is one of the most fundamental and difficult philosophical topics. Some philosophers may wince at any quick treatment of it, but introducing it now will aid our metaethical exploration into "truth-makers" for ethically significant statements. Philosophers call the things that can be true (or false) propositions, or statements. Statements are uttered in the attempt to describe how things are. Some statements are best understood as subjective truths—as we might say, they are "subjectively true"; however, others are best understood as objective truths (they are "objectively true"). Distinguishing statements in this way is primarily a matter of what kind of fact makes them true.

If a statement is subjectively true, then its being true is essentially grounded in some feature specific to the person or persons who utter or believe it. These statements invariably report or express the opinions, sentiments, preferences, or attitudes of the speaker. If the statement accurately represents the speaker's feelings about the topic, as it would unless the person was being dishonest, then the statement is true. (If the person is lying to us and the statement doesn't convey her actual feelings, then it is false.) And, again assuming honesty, these statements are believed exactly because they accurately represent the speaker's feelings. So, subjective truths are person-specific in distinctive sorts of ways.[4] In a manner of speaking, on this account, truth is invented or created whenever someone comes to hold a new belief based on alterations to her relevant sentiments.

Care must be taken in developing the discussion of subjectivity any further. The potential problem is that some of our subjective (or "inside") experiences are actually grounded in biological processes and responses to the world around us. Because human biology is largely uniform, so are many of our experiences, for example, the revulsion to

---

BOX 2C: LEARNING OUTCOMES

Upon carefully studying this chapter, students should better comprehend and be able to explain:

- The difference between subjectivity and objectivity as these concepts pertain to morally significant claims.
- Why and how the simple ethical subjectivist utilizes some of David Hume's ideas about metaethics.
- What simple ethical subjectivism is, and the reasons for and against its truth.
- How *Match Point*, *The Shape of Things*, and *The Emperor's New Groove* express ethical nonobjectivism themes.

rotting flesh. Some commentators stress the commonalities of our perceived experiences to argue that perceived experiences—and the sentiments arising from them—are not nearly as person-specific as the last paragraph suggests.[5] However, other commentators remind us of the remaining qualitative differences among our perceptions, especially when the environmental inputs are largely identical, for example, whether one prefers vanilla over chocolate, Chevy over Ford, or Beethoven over Bach (or, caring nothing for classical music, even Sammy Hagar over David Lee Roth). How should we interpret *these* opinions, sentiments, or preferences? It isn't implausible to assume that they have no obvious biological grounding. For the sake of the argument (and ease of discussion), the remainder of the chapter assumes that some personal preferences don't have convenient (or convincing) biological explanations, and, consequently, are person-specific.

In a manner of speaking, the relevant sort of person-specific claims (in part) define one's reality, occasioning the iconic "it's true for me that_____." So, assuming that there are such person-specific statements, nothing in addition to the speaker's personal feelings makes them true. Indeed, this might be their defining feature (thereby distinguishing them from the other subjective experiences introduced in the last paragraph). Furthermore, feelings or emotions are not the sorts of things that can be true or false in any impartial way. It may be (impartially) true that you feel positively about something, but your emotional reaction is not true in the same way that the earth has one moon or that two and two are four. There simply doesn't seem to be any person-neutral or impartial grounds for person-specific, subjective truths. There is no fact "out in the world" that makes these statements true. The

"It's not stupid if you feel it." — *The Shape of Things,* scene 8

only relevant fact of the matter is how you feel, but it is located completely "within" you. Thus, subjective truths tend to convey more about the speaker than about the subject matter being reported or discussed. Their truth (assuming honesty) is grounded *solely* in the sentiments of the speaker.

If a statement is objectively true, then its being true is essentially grounded in a feature of the world apart from the person who believes or utters it. Such statements are invariably uttered in the attempt to represent or report some fact "out in the world." If they successfully "match up" with the relevant facts, then they are true (and if they don't, then they are false). These truths are thus importantly person-neutral and not grounded in the individual feelings or attitudes of the speaker. Because the world simply is as it is, these truths are not dependent upon anyone knowing, believing, or feeling positively about them. Even if we are currently unaware of some objective truth, it remains true. In this sense, objective truth is better described as discovered than invented. Sometimes one's discovery is as easy as peering into the night sky. Other times it involves realizing that if it is true that Socrates is human and true that all human beings are mortal, then it must also be true that Socrates is mortal. But, importantly, how you feel about celestial bodies or ancient Greek philosophers doesn't change the truth value of 'The earth has one moon' or 'Socrates is mortal'.

An Initial Argument for Subjectivism in Ethics

The distinction between (person-specific) subjective and (person-neutral) objective truth leads some to argue that ethical statements cannot be objectively true. The argument has two parts. Let's call the first half the "baseline argument" for ethical nonobjectivism; it begins with the common belief that there is a direct correlation between objective truth and being proven by science. If being objectively true is synonymous with "being true for everyone" or "being plain true," it seems intuitive to equate objectivity with scientific fact. Everyone agrees that 'Objects fall at 9.8 m/s²'; 'Water is H_2O'; and 'The earth has one natural satellite'. What better candidates for "being true for everyone" than those statements about which *no one* disagrees? The baseline argument proceeds with a second premise that seems intuitively obvious to many: moral truths, should there be any, are nothing like scientific truths. Scientific claims are grounded in observation and experiment; moral judgments simply do not lend themselves to experimentation, at least not in the same way. Moreover, their being true does not seem to be a matter of empirical investigation. So, given the premise that objectivity requires empirical fact, the baseline argument concludes that ethical statements are not objectively true.

The second half of the initial argument for ethical subjectivism begins by noting that there seem to be only two kinds of truth, namely, (person-specific) subjective and (person-neutral) objective. Either truth is a matter of invention—a reality of one's own making—or it's not. But if it's not invented, then it must be discovered. If so, then these two alternatives are exhaustive. From this, and the conclusion from the baseline argument, it follows that ethical statements, if true at all, are subjectively true.

This sort of argument gets to the very heart of the debate about ethical foundations, a debate largely shaped by David Hume. Up to this point, the discussion has proceeded without directly relying on his ideas; however, consider the following argument heavily indebted to him. It begins simply with the observation that the world contains things like chairs, penguins, and beer mugs. That these things exist is a noncontroversial fact. Because it's an obvious fact that such things exist, we can plainly and truly assert such things as 'This chair is scratched' or 'Penguins lay eggs' or (tragically) 'My beer mug is empty'. If there were no chairs, penguins, or beer mugs, these claims couldn't be true. The argument then proceeds by examining ethical judgments; analogously, if 'Taking a mistress is wrong' or even 'Killing one's mistress with a shotgun is wrong' (like Chris Wilton from *Match Point*), then there is an object or fact that makes them true. But what? Can we point to the aftermath of Chris Wilton's violent act and confidently say, "There is the wrongness; it's right *there*!" Is it in Nola's broken body in the same way that Chris's unborn child is in her womb? We can say plainly that Nola's hair is blond, but where can we find any "wrongness" as she lies in the hallway bleeding to death? What could correspond to "the wrongness" of the situation? Because no candidates for "moral objects" or "moral facts" immediately present themselves, many people hold that ethical judgments cannot be true, at least not in the same objective way that other (empirical) statements are. With no fact of the matter out in the world for ethical judgments to match up with, it seems to follow that they cannot be objectively true; at best, they are subjectively true.

Hume and Allen on Ethical Nonobjectivism

No one doubts David Hume's credentials as a philosopher. The previous argument serves as testament to that. His ideas and arguments remain incredibly influential. Whether filmmaker Woody Allen is a philosopher is more controversial. There is an emerging debate among professional philosophers whether movie directors are doing philosophy (or being philosophical) in making a film. Without attempting to resolve that debate, it is plain that Woody Allen's films often convey philosophically stimulating issues. Indeed, a careful viewing of Allen's *Match Point* uncovers a distinctive (and interesting) metaethical view.[6]

Hume's metaethical views, at least their genesis, are well-known; he regularly appears in introductory ethics textbooks. Given Hume's view that "moral facts" do not exist "out in the world" in the way that other (empirical) facts do, his ideas provide an effective transition into the metaethical theory known as simple ethical subjectivism (which isn't to say that Hume thereby endorses the theory). Simple ethical subjectivism (SES) grounds the truth of ethical judgments in the person-specific feelings or sentiments of those making them. Each person, then, with his or her own unique approach to every situation, is the source of his or her own morality. This idea accords well with Evelyn's viewpoint throughout *The Shape of Things* and Emperor Kuzco from *The Emperor's New Groove* (at least at the beginning of the film). SES is indeed a popular view—not just among fictional characters—and represents a kind of hallmark of subjectivity in ethics. Its name captures the straightforward nature of the theory; it should not be construed to mean that the theory is silly or foolish. In the end, Hume doesn't advocate SES, but the simple ethical subjectivist borrows many of his arguments against ethical objectivism.

This simple ethical subjectivist might begin by borrowing Hume's celebrated "is/ought gap." Hume notes that there is a crucial distinction between descriptive claims and normative (or prescriptive) claims. Descriptive claims—"is statements"—describe some actual state of affairs, for example, 'Snow is white'. Normative claims represent how things ought to be; they regularly prescribe certain behaviors over others. They are thus "ought statements." Hume sees no problem in discerning the truth of "is statements." They either do or do not match up with the facts; if they do, they're true, if not, they're false. The problem is discerning the truth of "ought statements." As discussed in the previous subsection, Hume asks with what facts (out in the world) do they allegedly match up? At first glance, there simply doesn't seem to be any, which speaks against ethical objectivism. He argues that if ethical objectivism were true, then we would readily find the rightness or wrongness in morally significant situations (just as we readily find the whiteness in snow). But we do not readily find the rightness or wrongness in morally significant situations, and it's not at all clear exactly what to look for in the first place. Thus, ethical objectivism isn't true.

Furthermore, Hume doesn't understand how an "ought statement" could be derived from an "is statement." After all, it seems that descriptive statements are conceptually distinct from normative statements. They seem to assert different things. So, just because something is a certain way, it doesn't follow from that truth alone that it ought (or ought not) to be that way. It may be true that scientists are able to clone a dinosaur—or a human being—and it may be true that an emperor (like Kuzco from *The Emperor's New Groove*) has the power to build vacation homes wherever he pleases, but these descriptive facts (assuming they are facts) do not entail that these things should or should not happen. What is factually true is one thing, what ought to happen is something else: this is the "gap" Hume sees between "is statements" and "ought statements." According to Hume, it cannot be bridged. Analogously, then, Hume might argue that even though there are many true descriptive statements about Nola's broken body after the

"Tomorrow at my birthday celebration, I give the word and your town will be destroyed."
—*The Emperor's New Groove*, scene 6

shotgun blast (most of them too graphic to explicitly list), from those statements together, we cannot conclude that Chris ought not to have shot her.

The intuitions driving Hume's is/ought gap set up a further argument the simple ethical subjectivist can offer against ethical objectivism (even if it encapsulates many of Hume's more expansive philosophical views). It begins with the premise (sometimes called "Hume's fork") that if reason properly judges a statement, then that statement is either a matter of fact or expresses some logical relation. But recall that Hume has already argued that ethical statements do not correspond or match up with any fact out in the world. Furthermore, he believes he has proven that ethical judgments are importantly distinct from logical relations. The statements that two and two make four or the internal angles of a triangle equal 180 degrees are nothing like ethical judgments, and given Hume's is/ought gap, statements about descriptive logical relations cannot be used to derive ethical statements anyway. All of this allows Hume to conclude that reason does *not* properly judge ethical statements. But if reason does not properly judge ethical statements, then it seems that their truth is not a matter of being discovered out in the world. If so, then ethical statements are not objectively true.

It is therefore easy to see why the SES defender (at least initially) finds such an ally in David Hume. Both agree at least in that no fact of the matter about ethical statements can be found until, as Hume says, "you turn your reflection into your own breast." The only "truth-maker" for moral judgments are the personal sentiments that lie within each of us; no such truth-maker exists apart from that.[7]

Woody Allen's *Match Point* expresses a kind of ethical subjectivism from a cosmic perspective rather than the sentiments of individual persons. Nonobjectivist views can be gleaned from the very beginning of *Match Point* via Chris Wilton's voice-over. They are reinforced throughout the restaurant dinner table scene with Chris, Chloe, Nola, and Tom, the late night kitchen scene depicting Chris's visions of Nola and Mrs. Eastby, and the very end of the film when Banner and his partner locate Eastby's wedding ring.

Allen, through Chris, suggests that the most plausible source of value or meaning in the world would be a higher power; presumably God, or some supreme being, would somehow infuse these into the world. However, Chris believes that scientists have amassed sufficient data to confirm the belief that "all existence is here by blind chance." If we are here due to blind chance, then it seems that our existence is not due to a supreme being. And lacking a supreme being (like God) to serve as Creator, Allen seemingly believes that neither value nor meaning is infused into the world by a higher power. Consequently, the ideas of right and wrong have no real meaning. This position would also explain why Allen's script places such an emphasis on being lucky. Consider Chris's chat with his touring pro friend: "Isn't it amazing how much of life turns on whether the ball goes over the net or comes right back at you?" If there is no divine plan, then whether you receive good fortune—whether the ball goes over the net or falls back—is simply a matter of chance. This idea can be frightening. Chris shares, "Everyone is afraid to admit what a big part luck plays." Allen further suggests that this is one of the primary reasons many of us hang on to a religious worldview despite all of the startling scientific advances into understanding the universe.

Allen's other implicit argument for nonobjectivism is perhaps more subtle. His metaphor of whether the ball goes over the net or comes right back at you—itself a matter of chance—presupposes the well-established rules of tennis. The rules are not the products of mere chance. If the ball goes over, then it is likely that you will win the point. If the ball

Match Point, Dreamworks SKG, 2005. Chris Wilton (Jonathan Rhys Meyers) and Nola Rice (Scarlett Johansson) begin an illict tryst that comes to a tragic end. (Moviegoods, Inc.)

does not go over, then it is almost certain that you won't. Moreover, there are clear and obvious consequences for not following the rules of tennis or simply not playing well. If you do not play well or follow the rules, you will not succeed. Luck remains a part of the game perhaps, like whether the ball goes over or falls back after tipping the top of the net, but this nevertheless occurs within the confines of the rules: if the ball falls back, you lose the point.

Even if there isn't a supreme being to infuse value and meaning into the world, we might suppose that there are moral rules woven into the fabric of the universe analogous to the laws of nature. Perhaps Allen has in mind something like the law of karma, which is prevalent in (nonmonotheistic) Hindu and Buddhist traditions. In lawlike fashion, performing good deeds will bring you positive consequences, but performing evil deeds will bring negative consequences. Thus, the suggestion that there be a moral structure to things apart from (say) God erecting it seems coherent. This idea is nevertheless quite controversial to some; it invites the question, without a supreme being to write them, how did these rules come into existence? After all, the rules of tennis required someone to craft them. Similar things are often said about the laws of nature and ethics (should there be any). In any event, Allen's point is this: Even if there were unwritten, timeless moral rules—even if the moral structure of the universe comes "prepackaged" via karmic law or otherwise—there should be clear and obvious consequences for not following the rules. Rules work like this generally. If you miss-hit the ball, you lose the point. If you miss-hit the ball continually, you lose the match. But, in life, sometimes when the ball hits the top of the net and bounces back at you, you *still* win. This is exactly what happened to Chris. He threw Eastby's wedding ring toward the river but it hit the retainer wall railing. It bounced up into the air, fell back at him onto the sidewalk, but he still successfully got away with the crime. There were no (obvious) consequences of his actions.[8] In fact, once Nola was gone, only then did he and Chloe become pregnant, and only then did he and Chloe gain financial independence from her parents (in the form of the new business opportunity Mr. Hewett facilitated). In some sense, then, Chris was seemingly *rewarded* for breaking the moral rules. This leads Allen to (implicitly) conclude that there simply isn't any value, meaning, or moral structure to the world;

> "It would be fitting if I were apprehended. At least there would be some small sign of justice—some small . . . measure of hope for the possibility of meaning." —*Match Point*, scene 23

it is neither divinely infused from above, nor is it "woven" into it like the laws of nature. If there were, then people like Chris would face the appropriate consequences of their acts.

The Case for Simple Ethical Subjectivism

Simple ethical subjectivism (SES) is a metaethical theory. Recall that such theories often attempt to explain how moral judgments (if true at all) are generally true; they explore the nature of ethical "truth-makers." SES holds that the truth of any moral judgment depends upon the feelings or sentiments of the person making that judgment. So, when someone asserts 'X is wrong', her assertion is true just in case she indeed harbors negative feelings about X. Moreover, when someone asserts 'X is not wrong', his assertion is true just in case he does *not* in fact harbor negative feelings about X. Therefore, some moral judgment is true, at least for the person making the claim, just in case it accurately represents the speaker's current feelings or sentiments on the relevant issue. So, for SES, moral truth-makers simply are the current feelings or sentiments of those holding moral beliefs or making moral judgments. But moral judgments are only true for those making them; moral truth is completely individualized (or person-specific) on SES. No moral judgment is objectively true, or "true for everybody." In this way, SES can be summed up as the "it's true for me" theory of ethics.

> "So, all of it was a lie?" "Well, yeah, no wait. Uh, yeah. Yeah. It was all a lie. Toodles!" — *The Emperor's New Groove*, scene 18

In addition to arguments borrowed from Hume, proponents of SES attempt to justify their theory in a variety of ways. A common argument points to the widespread disagreement between individuals and their ethical views. The idea is that if moral judgments were objectively true, then there would be more agreement about what is right and what is wrong. Therefore, the argument concludes, moral judgments are not objectively true; they are, accordingly, subjectively true (if true at all). This sort of argument is sometimes bolstered by a second. Not only is there widespread ethical disagreement, there doesn't seem to be any (principled) way to rectify or resolve it. This is importantly unlike science. Scientists also enter into disagreement with each other, but eventually it is (invariably) resolved with further research, study, and experimentation. There are well-worn methods that scientists rely on to achieve consensus. Furthermore, even if current technology or data is insufficient to reach consensus, most scientists are readily agreed about what would be required to resolve the relevant debate. But it seems that ethical disputes will intractably remain, forever lacking any principled way to reach consensus. No hope for consensus, it is concluded, leaves us no hope for objectivity.

Other (less technical) arguments are also readily available. One variety stresses the uniqueness of persons, especially given our individual experiences. Each of us is special in this regard. But finding things to be morally correct or incorrect is one aspect of a person's experiences. So, just as each person is distinctively special, but not better or worse than any other person, so are that person's ethical views. All there is to ethics, on SES, is what *I* believe (based on my experiences) and if you believe something different, that is okay, too, because that is just what *you* believe (given your experiences). Nola believed that Chris should leave his wife; she felt that was morally correct. Chris didn't feel that way. He wasn't sure (and so didn't believe) that this was the best thing to do.

This kind of argument for SES stresses the deeply personal nature of making an ethical decision. We often hear: "You don't know what it's like to be in that situation; you weren't there, but I was and I had to do something!" Chris might give this sort of response when explaining his decision to murder Nola and her neighbor so he could get on with his life. Of course, since it

> "Sophocles said: 'To never have been born may be the greatest boon of all.'" — *Match Point,* scene 23

seems that each person's experiences are unique (because we are all different people), it seemingly follows that any morally significant situation one faces will be unique to him or her. Thus, the argument continues, a plausible view of ethics would capture the uniquely personal aspect of ethical decision making. But SES is just such a theory because it advocates that the individual and that individual alone is the person-specific basis of moral judgment.

The Case against Simple Ethical Subjectivism

For all of that, there are two rather well-known objections to SES. The first is that on this account we as human persons are morally infallible because we can never hold an incorrect moral judgment. Recall that ethical judgments on SES are true just in case they honestly represent the speaker's current feelings or sentiments; furthermore, this is the only measure of their truth. Thus moral truth changes whenever the speaker comes to have different feelings about a topic. If someone like Emperor Kuzco (from *The Emperor's New Groove*) has no negative feelings about displacing a village in order to construct his personal theme park and summer home, then it is not morally wrong for him to do so. Later, if his feelings change and he comes to believe that it would be wrong for him to do this, then his new moral judgment is also true. So, for a time, 'Displacing a village to erect a summer chalet is not wrong' is true, but later 'Displacing a village to erect a summer chalet is wrong' is true. Both moral judgments are correct, just at different times, because Kuzco's feelings have changed. This is why we can never have an incorrect moral belief if SES is true. But this entailment seems counterintuitive for (at least) two, interconnected reasons. On the one hand, we have little reason to think that we are infallible about anything. "To err is human," many people say, and this truism seems to apply here as well. On the other hand,

The Emperor's New Groove, Walt Disney Pictures, 2000. The young emperor Kuzco (David Spade voice, right) ecstatically informs the humble peasant Pacha (John Goodman voice) about "Kuzcotopia." (Moviegoods, Inc.)

how can it be that if a person holds *conflicting* views on a subject neither of her views is incorrect? These insights lead to the argument that if SES is true, then human persons are necessarily infallible in their ethical judgments, but human persons are not necessarily infallible in their ethical judgments. Thus, SES is not true.

How the SES defender would respond to this argument is not altogether clear. I suspect, however, that any rejoinder would involve the contention that ethics resists straightforward rational analysis. But since this seemingly entails that *any* ethical position is just as plausible as any other, many find this rejoinder highly counterintuitive. Can Chris Wilton's decision to kill his mistress in cold blood be just as commendable as Pacha's decision to stand up for his village in the face of the young emperor's startling and whimsical decision to destroy it? Are the moral views of Mother Teresa or Gandhi no better than the views of Hitler and Stalin? The rhetorical force of these questions lead many to conclude that (a) SES is conceptually flawed in other more telling respects and further investigation will show this, and/or (b) the search for more dependable ethical foundations must proceed in all earnestness.

The second common objection is that, according to SES, genuine moral disagreements are impossible. When Kuzco announces to Pacha that his village will be destroyed to build "Kuzcotopia" (the young emperor's summer chalet complete with waterslide), Pacha is initially confused. How can you displace so many families when there are other places Kuzcotopia could be built? Pacha thus believes that 'Displacing a village to erect a summer chalet is wrong' is obviously true, but Kuzco believes differently, namely that 'Displacing a village to erect a summer chalet is not wrong'. From *The Shape of Things*, Evelyn and Adam disagree about the permissibility of purposely misleading someone in order to craft him into an art project (without his consent). But if SES is true, these discussants are not actually disagreeing about the permissibility of mindlessly displacing a village or callously treating people as mere things. Each is *merely* reporting his or her likes or dislikes, analogous to a case where people report their favorite ice creams, one vanilla and the other chocolate. Given SES, then, when Kuzco and Pacha "disagree" about building the summer chalet, or the importance of shaking hands to seal an agreement, or making deals with peasants in the first place, they are not really discussing the finer points of morality; they are merely sharing their "favorites." The same can be said of Evelyn and her audience, on the one hand, and her subsequent discussion with Adam, on the other.

Furthermore, if SES is true, Kuzco and Pacha and Evelyn and Adam are actually talking about *different* things. The young emperor is referring to his inner, subjective feelings/sentiments and the kindly villager is referring to his inner, subjective feelings/sentiments, just as Evelyn shares her emotional ambivalence about her masters thesis but Adam shares his disgust and disappointment. But is this an accurate description of what happens in such discussions (debates)? If you were Adam, would you see yourself as morally wronged by Evelyn or merely the subject of her emotional ambivalence? Aren't Evelyn and Adam actually making reference to a distinctive course of action (perhaps the practice or concept of such) and disagreeing whether a certain characteristic appropriately applies to that practice or concept, namely, that it is impermissible? This is the most straightforward way to describe this scenario and seems to better capture the nature of morally significant disagreements.

These insights pertaining to moral disagreement lead to another argument against SES: If SES is true, then two conflicting ethical judgments are not actually in disagreement; however, two conflicting ethical judgments are actually in disagreement. Therefore, SES is not true.

> "Oh, I'm not sorry for what I've done." "You don't see this as wrong? You obviously have no concept here." —*The Shape of Things*, scene 16

The SES defender might respond that this argument assumes too much of what is at issue: only those who already believe that actual moral disagreement exists will agree with the argument's second premise. This rejoinder leaves philosophers (fledgling or professional) to rationally decide between the theoretical truth of SES or denying what seems intuitively and obviously true: people enter into genuine moral disagreements. Intuitions might differ here, but the obviousness of ethical disagreements is some reason for jettisoning SES in favor of other metaethical approaches.

A third argument focuses not on the nature of ethical truths so much as the importance of the feelings and sentiments that are supposed to make moral beliefs true. Note that if SES is true, facts about well-being cease to be ethically significant. That someone is harmed isn't the issue; rather, the emphasis is placed on how individuals feel about the well-being of others. Moreover, if SES is true, then *only* the speaker's (or agent's) feelings or sentiments are relevant to whether the choice or act in question is permissible. This importantly entails that the feelings or sentiments of the person about to receive the consequences of the pending act do *not* impact its permissibility. But why think only the speaker's (or agent's) feelings matter? Insofar as the pending act involves both the doer and the receiver of the action, shouldn't the feelings or sentiments of both matter?

Consider again Evelyn's choice to use Adam as her "nameless sculpture." If SES is true, Adam's sentiments about her choice are irrelevant. All that essentially matters is how Evelyn feels about conducting her graduate thesis. Because she has strong feelings that moralists have no place in an art gallery (or art period), it seems to follow on SES that her choice to treat Adam like a thing—regardless of how he feels about this—is permissible. Alternatively, why shouldn't the permissibility of Kuzco's choice to displace the hilltop village require us to include the feelings of Pacha and the other villagers? Why shouldn't the moral assessment of Chris Wilton's murderous choice require us to consider the feelings and sentiments of the two murdered women? Because the sentiments of those receiving moral acts certainly seem relevant, SES is rendered dubious.

This is *not* to say that feelings or sentiments are proper truth-makers for ethically significant statements. Rather SES relies on feelings and sentiments to determine which ethical judgments are true, but it discounts the feelings and sentiments of those receiving the agent's act. This is both paradoxical and arbitrary. But there is a further argument that seemingly shows that personal feelings or sentiments *cannot* be adequate moral truth-makers. Regardless of how a person feels about something, we can always ask, but should he act on that feeling? Moreover, we can ask if having that feeling is morally appropriate in the first place. If SES is true, these questions are incoherent or meaningless (because personal feelings are the sole truth-makers). Because these questions are neither incoherent nor meaningless, it follows that SES is false.

People often do not fully realize what they mean when asserting that ethics is *only* a matter of what individuals believe. Typically, we simply have in mind the morally significant differences, if any, between (say) becoming a teacher and a nurse. Because there does not appear to be any definitive answer to whether it is better (morally speaking) to dedicate your life to becoming one or the other, ethical judgments are simply "up to us." However, the theory implied by this kind of approach to ethics, namely SES, applies to much more than just choosing between being a teacher or a nurse. It applies (or would apply, if adopted) to any and all ethically significant situations, including those that seem clearly morally reprehensible. If you think SES is true, then it simply does not matter where anyone draws the line about what counts as morally acceptable behavior (assuming that person's sentiments/feelings are consistent with their behavior). On this view, hunting, killing, and eating young men is no better or worse, morally speaking, than becoming a teacher or nurse. Once this implication is uncovered, any initial intuitive support for SES begins to drain away. The problem is this: By making moral truth person-specific in the way that it does, SES does not only apply to the *already* acceptable choices/behaviors, it makes *all* choices/behaviors acceptable. And with this insight—that all choices or lifestyles are just as ethically worthwhile as any other is fully realized—it becomes clearer why SES does not effectively capture the nature of all moral judgments. If anything, it does away with ethics altogether.

2.4. TWO ADDITIONAL FILMS

The Emperor's New Groove (2000)

Directors: Mark Dindal
Screenwriters: Chris Williams and Mark Dindal

Plot Summary

When I give the word, your little town thingy will be bye-bye—okay, b-bye!

Young Emperor Kuzco lives the life of extreme luxury. He has never gone without satisfying his desires. He lives in a palace made of gold. He has personal chefs and barbers; attendants spoon-feed him his supper. But, not yet twenty, Kuzco greets us with a tale of woe. He tells that three people are responsible for ruining his life: Pacha, the unassuming local village leader; Yzma, his scheming advisor; and Kronk, Yzma's brawny but clueless assistant.

His sad story begins the day he is scheduled to meet Pacha. Just before the villager arrives, Kuzco again finds Yzma trying to run the empire behind his back. She acts like she is the emperor (or empress). Kuzco has had enough. He fires her on the spot. As she marches away fuming and muttering something about revenge, Pacha slowly enters Kuzco's throne room. Pacha is surprised to hear Kuzco announce, "Word on the street is that you're the man to fix my problem!" Pacha is a lowly peasant. How can he fix something for the emperor? Kuzco reassures him that his hilltop village is incredibly important to the empire. Pacha is speechless as they walk over to a scale model of the hill. He merely responds, "My family has lived on that hilltop for the last six generations." Kuzco mindlessly nods, but then quickly asks of the villager, "So, tell me, where do you find the most sun?" Confused, Pacha points to the place on Kuzco's scale model. Kuzco thanks him for his "insider's opinion" and announces that he will okay that spot for his new pool. Now Pacha is really confused: "What pool?" "Welcome to Kuzcotopia!" The emperor continues to explain that it will be the ultimate summer getaway, complete with waterslide. Kuzco can't contain his excitement any longer: "It's my birthday present to me! Ha! I'm so happy!" Pacha's confusion is now mixed with shock: "I don't understand how this could happen." Kuzco is unfazed by the peasant's reaction. "Well, let me explain it to you," he begins. "Tomorrow at my birthday celebration, I give the word and your town will be destroyed." In its place will be Kuzcotopia!" "But where will we live?" Without hesitation, but again mindlessly, Kuzco responds, "Hmm . . . don't know, don't care. How's that?"

Kronk meets Yzma in her secret laboratory to plot her revenge. They prepare a poison for Kuzco. Under the pretense of "burying the hatchet," Yzma invites Kuzco over for dinner. Kronk has prepared his famous spinach puffs appetizer. Yzma offers Kuzco some wine. Kronk (clumsily) poisons Kuzco's cup. The emperor heartily gulps it down. Kuzco's head immediately hits the table, and almost as fast he begins to transform into a llama. Kronk's abilities at mixing potions pales in comparison to his culinary skills! Yzma orders him to take the "llama emperor" outside and "finish the job" properly this time. Kronk puts Kuzco into a large sack and carries him to a canal that ends with a very high waterfall. But Kronk hesitates. He is visited by his "shoulder angel," an apparition complete with harp and white robe, and "shoulder devil," a second apparition complete with pitchfork and red horns. In trying to decide what to do, Kronk falls down a flight of steps and loses the sack. It falls onto the back of Pacha's cart as the peasant dejectedly makes his way back to the village.

Once atop the hill again, Chicha, Pacha's wife, asks him what the emperor wanted. Still not knowing how to tell his pregnant wife the news, Pacha claims that the emperor was too busy to see him today. Chicha is outraged: "Emperor or no emperor, it's called common courtesy. That kind of behavior is just—just—uhh." Pacha cannot make out the last words as his wife heads into the house to check on their two children. He yells to Chicha that he will put the llama away—the family's llama that pulled his cart up the hill. He sits down on a bench near the small barn. But he looks up long enough to see the unfamiliar sack on the end of his cart move. As Pacha inspects it, the llama emperor jumps out! Kuzco yells, "No touchy!" Pacha has never seen a talking llama before, let alone one that sounds exactly like the emperor. It doesn't take long for the two to realize that Yzma has turned Kuzco into a llama.

Kuzco demands the Pacha take him back to the palace. Pacha refuses, unless the emperor decides to build Kuzcotopia somewhere else. "I don't make deals with peasants!" the emperor llama retorts. Kuzco chooses to find his own way back to the palace. Pacha tries to stop him, informing him about the panthers and snakes he must avoid. Kuzco ignores him. Pacha sighs, but quickly mutters to himself, "No Kuzco, no Kuzcotopia—takes care of my problem." But the peasant almost as quickly changes his mind again, and begins to follow Kuzco.

After narrowly escaping a den of panthers, Pacha and Kuzco rest by a river bank. As he starts a fire, Pacha shares with Kuzco, "I just think that if you really thought about it, you'd decide to build your home on a different hilltop." "And why would I do that?" the emperor asks in response. "Because, deep down, I think that you'll realize that you're forcing an entire village out of their homes just for you," the peasant explains. "And . . . that's . . . bad." "Well, yeah. Nobody is that heartless." "Hmm . . . now take me back!" "Unless you change your mind, I'm not taking you back," Pacha reaffirms. The next morning, Kuzco announces that he has had a change of heart. Once they get back to the city, he might change his mind and pick a different hilltop. Pacha remains wary of the young emperor. He requests that they shake on it—like men—but warns him, "Don't shake unless you mean it." They clasp hand and hoof and begin their journey back to the palace.

At his first chance, however, Kuzco shows his true colors. With Pacha in grave danger, he leaves the villager hanging—literally, on a dilapidated rope bridge—and moves to travel the rest of the way alone. Before he crosses the remainder of the bridge, Kuzco also falls through, precariously hanging by some loose strands above a treacherous gorge. Pacha turns to the llama emperor and scoffs, "Why did I risk my life for a selfish brat like you? I was always taught that there was some good in everyone, but, ooh, you proved me wrong!" "Oh, boohoo, now I feel really bad. Bad llama!" Pacha is furious: "I could have let you die out there in that jungle, and then all my problems would be over!" "Well, that makes you ugly and stupid!" But before Pacha can return the insult, the final strands give way and he and Kuzco fall into the gorge, hurtling toward its alligator infested waters. If they are to survive this one, they must do so together.

Discussion Questions

1. If you were the emperor, would you build a summer home on top of Pacha's hilltop village? Why or why not?
2. Is Pacha a better man than Kuzco? If so, how? If not, why not?
3. What do Kronk's "shoulder angel" and "shoulder devil" represent (roughly 19:00 and again at 1:03:15 into the movie)? What function do these apparitions apparently serve?

4. During scene 18 (roughly 39:45 into the movie), Pacha shares his belief that "there is a little good in everyone." Is his belief correct? Of what exactly would this goodness consist?
5. Why is the movie called *The Emperor's New Groove*?

The Shape of Things (2003)

Director and Screenwriter: Neil LaBute

Plot Summary

> All that stuff we did was real to you; therefore, it was real. It wasn't for me; there-fore, it wasn't. It's all subjective, Adam—everything.

She is completing her master's degree in art. He is an undergraduate finishing up his English degree. She is confident and fiercely independent. He is demur and self-effacing. They meet in the Mercy College museum. She is about to lodge a controversial protest to how a sculpture is being displayed. It is his work-study job to prevent anyone from defacing the artwork. As he attempts to convince her to step away from the sculpture, she exclaims, "You're cute! But I don't like your hair." His shift is about finished. Her resolve remains. She spray paints her number inside his corduroy jacket. As he punches out, she prepares her can of spray paint. Her name is Evelyn. His name is Adam. They begin dating (of course).

Evelyn and Adam wait to meet his friends Jenny and Phillip. Evelyn bets Adam that Jenny and Phillip will notice the weight he's lost. Adam intimates that they should take their relationship to the "next level." She passionately kisses him in agreement, but he is uncomfortable. He murmurs "PDA." She is confused. He explains, "public display of affection." He remains unsure of why she likes him. She reminds him that his insecurities are the only things she doesn't like about him. Jenny and Phillip stroll up behind them as Evelyn and Adam kiss again. Jenny playfully announces, "PDA." Phil asks Adam if he's lost some weight. Jenny asks whether Adam is wearing his hair differently. Evelyn beams. She subtly puts her hand out to Adam so that he can pay up on their bet.

The four later retire to Phillip's apartment for a drink and conversation. Phillip and Adam were dorm roommates. Adam and Jenny had freshman class together. Jenny had a crush on Adam, but Adam was too shy to ask her out. Phillip swooped in and now he and Jenny are engaged. Evelyn listens intently, keen to learn more about her new boyfriend Adam. Phillip asks if anyone has heard anything new about the "stunt" at the museum. Immediately Evelyn questions whether it was merely a prank. Perhaps somebody was trying to make a statement. Phillip and Jenny refuse to accept this possibility. To spray-paint a penis on a marble statue is pornography at best and vandalism at worst. Phillip and Evelyn soon begin arguing and she storms out of the apartment. Adam sheepishly follows her.

After an evening out on the town, Evelyn and Adam spend some quiet time in her apartment. She asks if he enjoyed himself tonight. "Dinner was great. The trip into the city— that was fun. I like your car." She smiles, but further asks, "I meant the perfor-mance." He hesitates for a moment, but shakes his head no. No longer smiling, Evelyn asks, "You didn't think it was amazing?" "I thought it was amazing that the cops didn't bust in and stop her." He sarcastically adds, "I usually love it when a woman removes her tampon in front of me." Evelyn is appalled. She believes it was completely vanguard. "You simply didn't get it," she scoffs. "Maybe because she was finger-painting portraits of her daddy using menstrual blood!" he quickly replies, and continues, "To me it was nasty, it was private, and I felt like it was something that I wasn't supposed to be seeing." Evelyn retorts, "She allowed you into her world, into her work, but in a highly theatrical way." Evelyn storms off into the bathroom. But before long, she returns and they begin to make up.

Adam's relationship with Evelyn becomes more serious by the day. Phillip and Jenny continue to make wedding plans. Jenny gets cold feet and turns to Adam for advice and comfort. They meet in the park. When they greet each other, Jenny immediately notices that Adam now wears contact lenses. He has also stopped biting his fingernails. He claims that it's "no biggie," and he feels much better about himself lately. Jenny replies that she's known him for three years and hasn't gone longer than a month without biting his nails. She quickly adds, "You're, like, this totally hot guy now."

Evelyn and Adam meet at a doctor's office. Adam is considering having plastic surgery on his nose. She supportively confides that she had her nose done at sixteen, and reminds him, "cosmetic doesn't mean corrective." Adam has another surprise for her. He pulls her over to a secluded corner, admits that what he is about to show her is a "religious no-no," and then presents his new tattoo "E.A.T."—her initials—on his inner thigh. We next see Adam with a bandage on his nose, speaking with Phillip just before class. When asked about his nose, Adam tells his old friend that he fell and bumped it on a doorknob. Phillip isn't convinced. After again commenting on Adam's new haircut, Phillip notices his friend's new Tommy Hilfiger–type jacket. The old brown corduroy is gone; this was akin to Adam's security blanket. Phillip accuses him, "Where is *your* jacket?! For years I pleaded with you to get rid of it; that thing cost us a lot of dates." Adam defensively responds, "She likes it. It's reversible." "Well, isn't that neat. What I want to know—do *you* like it? A scuffle ensues and Adam scurries away on his bike.

As Evelyn's public performance for her master's degree approaches, she and Adam have become very close in the past eighteen weeks. Evelyn becomes a bit jealous of Adam's friendship with Jenny, and her distaste for Phillip has grown. After an uncomfortable encounter with Jenny in a coffee shop, Evelyn voices her displeasure. Adam becomes scared. He assures her, "I'll do anything you want. . . . Just tell me what to do and I'll do it. I just—I don't want to lose you. I love you." Evelyn looks Adam in the eye, and without blinking, says, "Give them up, as friends, both of them. No explanation. Don't see them or speak to them again, not ever. That's what I want. That will prove to me how you feel." Adam is crestfallen: "And if I don't?" "Well, um, I pretty much let these things end."

The day of Evelyn's performance, Adam and Phillip meet in the lobby. Phil wants to know why Adam has disappeared. Adam is surprised to hear that Phil's engagement to Jenny has been postponed. Jenny strides past them and Phil tries to get her attention. Phil (smugly) suggests that he and Adam get a seat by the door. Adam uncomfortably demurs, saying he would like a seat up front. Evelyn prefaces her performance with the surprising announcement that she was given an engagement ring two days ago. Adam blushes. Her formal presentation begins with her motto: "Strive to make art by changing the world." She presents to the audience a "human sculpture that she has been working on these past eighteen weeks." Adam is confused. Jenny glares at Evelyn, and exits the theater. Evelyn continues, "This was not done out of love or caring or concern. This was a simple matter of can I instill X amount of change in this creature using only manipulation as my palette knife?" Adam's heart sinks. He continues to blush, but now for different reasons. Phil shouts an expletive at Evelyn, and exits the theater. Evelyn isn't fazed: "As for me, I have no regrets or feelings of remorse for the manufactured emotions. None of it. I have always stood by the single and simple conceit that I am an artist, only that. There is . . . only art."

Discussion Questions

1. Are graffiti-type markings always impermissible defacement? Explain.
2. Evelyn includes the statement "moralists have no place in an art gallery" in her thesis project (scene 16, about 1:25:00 into the film). What does this statement mean? Is it true? Explain.
3. To what extent, if any, is it permissible to change yourself to suit another? Are some requests for change, even from a loved one, impermissible?
4. Near the very end of the film Evelyn challenges Adam: "If you feel that way about me, tell me what I did wrong, if I did something wrong." Is what Evelyn did to Adam morally wrong? If so, how would you answer her charge? If not, why not?
5. Why is the film called *The Shape of Things*?

2.5. REVIEWING THROUGH THE THREE MOVIES

1. Kronk's "shoulder angel" asserts (in scene 26 roughly 1:04:00 into the movie), "From above the wicked shall receive their just reward." While this has a double meaning in the movie, does this sort of claim provide us sufficient moral reason to act more like Pacha than Kuzco? How would Woody Allen (perhaps through *Match Point* character Chris Wilton) answer this question?
2. The closing song of *The Emperor's New Groove* (sung by Sting) includes the line (about 1:13:00 into the film): "You reminded me that the world is not my playground. There are other things that matter." Assuming that this is true, what might these "other things that matter" be? How would the characters from *Match Point* and *The Shape of Things* respond?
3. Chicha from *The Emperor's New Groove* believes in "common courtesy" (scene 11, about 22:30 into the film) and further believes that acting contrary to it is morally deplorable. What is common courtesy exactly? Why is it morally deplorable to act contrary to it? How would Evelyn from *The Shape of Things* or Nola from *Match Point* respond?
4. If you believe that Evelyn treated Adam impermissibly or Chris's actions with respect to Chloe or Nola were morally objectionable, is this so on subjective or objective grounds? Explain.
5. Reconsider the six movie quotes from the chapter and explain whether each, given the adjacent paragraphs, *illustrates* a point the author is making, *supplements* (or extends) a point the author is making, or *contrasts* (for emphasis) a point the author is making. Explain your answers.

NOTES

1. Excerpted from *A Treatise of Human Nature* (1740) and *An Inquiry Concerning the Principles of Morals* (1751) both by David Hume. Section headings and slight grammar emendations have been provided to aid reader comprehension.

2. The relevant issues regarding statements, beliefs, facts, and truth are quite complex. The phrase "out there in the world" is a gloss for the idea that there are some mind-independent truths that remain so even if they are not believed. The world—objective reality—presents itself to us in various ways that we attempt to decipher, that is, come to know. Therefore, objective reality determines (as in it provides a standard for) truth in terms of expressing or providing mind-independent facts—facts that exist even if they are not known. Nevertheless, how we discuss and come to know those facts—via language—is often a matter of convention. Thus how we use the term "day" or even "hour" could have been different. But once our terms and their meanings have been made sufficiently clear, whether the statement 'A day is twenty-four-hours long' is true ultimately depends on how the world, in fact, is.

3. There is a metaethical school of thought known as emotivism that holds that our moral beliefs are not the sorts of things that can be true. Although a venerable metaethical view, it will not be directly addressed in this text. On the one hand, the vast majority of students believe that some of their moral beliefs are true, and, on the other, many of the objections raised against simple ethical subjectivism also (at least ultimately) apply to emotivism.

4. To anticipate both substantive and pedagogical objections from Hume scholars, it can be granted that Hume would balk at the idea that all subjectively true statements are person-specific, especially given his more involved positions about moral sense and universal human sympathy. However, it is also the case that Hume, in the end, is not a subjectivist about ethical truth, at least not in the more obvious way that a defender of simple ethical subjectivism is.

5. Indeed, Hume is among them, and he famously exploits the commonalities of our shared experiences to provide his empiricist-based approach to ethics. Hume's overall moral views will not be discussed in this chapter; however, some of his initial arguments about the nature of moral truth will be, at least insofar as they may be employed by simple ethical subjectivists.

6. That Allen is one of the more philosophical "Hollywood" filmmakers is undeniable. He often pens editorials for high profile magazines like the *New Yorker*, and these invariably express philosophical concerns and ideas. Furthermore, please see *Woody Allen and Philosophy: You Mean My Whole Fallacy Is Wrong?*, eds. Mark Conard and Aeon Skoble (Chicago: Open Court Press, 2004).

7. Again, Hume's overall metaethical position is complicated by his adding a third person spectator to the process of establishing moral truth, which arguably (at least eventually) drives Hume toward a quasi-utilitarian view.

8. To be fair, Hindus or Buddhists would remind us that receiving karmic consequences for one's actions may not occur immediately. Conceivably, this may occur during the agent's next lifetime. Analogously, monotheists might reply that people like Wilson may be judged in the next life. To this, Allen might respond that the fact that people like Wilson get away with their foul deeds even that long is evidence of God's nonexistence.

CHAPTER 3

Moral Relativism

....

HOTEL RWANDA (2004)
Director: Terry George
Screenwriters: Keir Pearson and Terry George

....

PLOT SUMMARY

Now they have come back, these Tutsi rebels. . . . Rwanda is our Hutu land. We are
the majority. They are a minority of traitors and invaders. . . . C'mon good Hutus—
the graves are not yet full!

Rwanda of 1994 is beset with political strife. The native Hutus compose the majority, but when the Belgians imperially occupied the land, they favored natives
known as Tutsi. The Tutsi received influential administrative positions. They
were also socially preferred over the Hutu, as the Belgians saw (most) Tutsi as physically
more elegant. But the designations of "Hutu" and "Tutsi" were fluid, grounded largely
in whether a native owned cattle, and not in ethnic or racial factors. The Belgians made
the Hutu/Tutsi distinction permanent in 1935, albeit artificially so, with the help of an
institutionalized identification card. When the Belgians ceased occupying Rwanda in
(roughly) 1960, they left the Hutu, the majority, in power. This history fueled decades of
Hutu/Tutsi tension, which culminated in the political and social strife of 1994. The Hutus,
seeking revenge for years of repression (and Tutsi rebel uprisings post-Belgian occupation,
it seems), now view the once elitist Tutsi as "cockroaches," a pest to be exterminated; the
Tutsi strive to avoid Hutu persecution, including striking a peace accord with the current
Hutu Rwandan president. This maneuver only fans the political flames.

Paul Rusesabagina is a manager of the prestigious Mille Collines hotel in Kigali,
Rwanda. He is intelligent, eloquent, and refined. A superlative employee, he strives to
make his hotel an oasis of calm. He regularly relies on George Rutaganda to supply him
with top-shelf food, drink, and sundries. Paul is a good customer; he even "gifts" George

Cuban cigars on the side. This allows Paul to include fresh lobster on the dinner menu and pamper VIP guests like General Bizimungu (commander of the Rwandan army). The general, in turn, provides security for the hotel to further insulate it from the surrounding upheaval. The leader of the UN Peacekeeping forces, Col. Oliver, is also a regular guest. When we first meet the two military men, they are discussing the Hutu Interhamwe militia forces, which are growing dangerously strong. Bizimungu reassures Oliver—and everyone else who asks—that the Rwandan army is not training the militia. He is adamant that the president, in seeking Hutu-Tusti peace, has the full support of the army.

Paul is Hutu, but his wife, Tatiana ("Tatsi") is Tutsi. In their neighborhood, Hutus make regular sweeps looking for alleged Tutsi rebels and spies. Their Tutsi neighbors often seek Paul's help; he is the only Hutu they can trust. But the peace treaty has now been signed. Paul thus believes that things will begin to improve. Tatsi's brother, Thomas, and his wife, are unconvinced. They meet Paul at the hotel one evening, offering to take Tatsi and the Rusesabagina children to a safer place. Paul declines. Thomas respects Paul's wishes, but asks him to take great care; there will soon be a public announcement, signaling the beginning of outward militia aggression. Paul drives home that night very late. The streets are uncharacteristically dark. A bottle hits his van. He notices a house on fire. The police drive by announcing that everyone should stay inside. Paul becomes more alarmed when he arrives home; the house is completely dark. His children are not in their beds. He finds his wife, the children, and most of the neighbors huddled together in the master bedroom. They have heard reports that the Rwandan president has been killed. They fear that the country is on the brink of civil war.

BOX 3A: INSIDE *HOTEL RWANDA*

Hotel Rwanda tells a story based on actual events in Africa. The opening voice-over provides some historical background, but doing a bit of additional research might be wise. The main character, Paul Rusesabagina, is played by Don Cheadle, but Rusesabagina was also a consultant on the film.

The film is philosophically rich in many ways, but this chapter uses it to explore how cultural moorings impact, if at all, ethical truth. If time permits, it might be a good idea to view scene 1, that is, the first six minutes of the film. Then go to the start of scene 10, beginning at 41:24; you'll see Paul enter a guest room. This scene begins to convey how the conflict between the Hutu and Tutsi has escalated. Continue watching through scene 12, until 56:55. (Scene 13 begins with Paul and his wife lying in bed.) Skip ahead to the start of scene 15, which is 1:10:21; you see Paul riding in a van at night. Continue watching through scene 16, which ends 1:19:08, after a discussion between Paul and Dube on a bench. (Scene 17 begins with a shot of Tatsi in a room at night with the children.) Be forewarned that, because the film is based on actual events, these segments contain some disturbing (although not gratuitous) images and language.

The film is quite good, and deserving of a full viewing. Having done so, you should be able to answer the trivia questions in box 3B. But if time doesn't permit this, watching the specified segments, after carefully reading the plot summary, should give you a sufficient grasp of the film.

The next morning, the president's tragic death is confirmed. The Hutu blame the Tutsi rebels. The army takes immediate action; all Tutsi are being arrested, some are simply shot where they stand. A squad ransacks Paul's home. He handsomely bribes the commanding officer not to execute his Tutsi overnight "guests." The officer takes Paul's money, but calls him a traitor. Arriving at the Mille Collines, Paul secures guest rooms for some and staff rooms for others; however, all of his "guests" receive safe haven. Their safety is enhanced when the United Nations makes the Mille Collines one of its base camps; it is off-limits to the surrounding conflict. But Paul's situation becomes more complicated as the general manager (a Belgian) must immediately travel to another hotel. This leaves Paul solely in charge of all operations. He becomes ultimately responsible for the premises and its patrons (paying or not).

Interhamwe forces now surround Kigali and the carnage in Rwanda escalates. Col. Oliver desperately asks Paul to accept more "guests." Oliver simply cannot handle all the refugees piling into his UN compound. Paul protests; the Mille Collines is a five-star hotel, not a refugee camp. When Oliver promises more men to guard the hotel gate, Paul reluctantly agrees. Madame Archer, a local Red Cross coordinator, calls on Paul to house a group of orphans. He agrees, but asks Archer to locate Thomas and his family. Finding them will be difficult. She shares a story about the Interhamwe at the St. Frances orphanage: "They've started killing children. . . . There was a girl with her little sister wrapped on her back. As they were about to machete chop her, she cried out, 'I promise not to be Tutsi anymore.'" Archer explains that Tutsi children are being targeted to wipe out the next generation, thereby ensuring future Hutu dominance.

A UN-sponsored intervention force finally arrives, but Oliver is irate that the new troops are merely authorized to evacuate the Europeans and Americans. They are ordered not to intercede in the Rwandan conflict; no aid is being offered to native Africans, including the St. Frances orphans. The next morning, Paul awakes to a gun in his face. An officer tells Paul that everyone must leave the hotel. There are currently one hundred staff and eight hundred "guests." When Paul cannot reach Bizimungu for an explanation, he calls Belgium to speak with the Sabena company that owns the hotel. He reaches the vice president of Sabena, who is shocked by Paul's news. He quickly works to alleviate Paul's immediate situation, but fails to convince the Western "superpowers" to provide any overt aid to Rwanda. Paul meets with the staff and "guests," informing them that they must save themselves. If they have influential friends, call now to secure exit visas. Bizimungu finally arrives to take stock of the Mille Collines situation. He notes that "Paul's white friends" have gone, and thereby (paternalistically) promises to take care of the hotel (assuming proper compensation, of course).

Paul does his best to maintain the hotel's reputation. When supplies run low, he and a staff member risk the journey to visit George. George welcomes Paul's business; however, George quickly apprises him of the political situation: "Soon, all the Tutsi will be dead. . . . We are halfway there already." On the return trip, Paul and his driver compete with early morning fog. The van unexpectedly and suddenly begins driving erratically. They stop, only to realize that the van is driving over hundreds—perhaps thousands—of Rwandan corpses. Soon after, we hear on a radio that five hundred thousand victims are reported dead in the conflict; forty thousand bodies have been removed from Lake Victoria alone. We also hear the Western powers debate the difference between genocide and "acts of genocide" in Rwanda. How many acts of genocide does it take before there is genocide?

BOX 3B: *HOTEL RWANDA* TRIVIA

If your instructor assigns the film to be watched outside of class, you should be able to answer the following questions:

1. How much did Paul pay for the Cohiba cigar?
2. What does Paul offer the children when he returns home from the hotel?
3. What is the Hutu radio signal to begin the conflict (against the Tutsis)?
4. In which hotel room does Paul find his employee Gregoire?
5. How many UN troops does Col. Oliver have left after the intervention force leaves?
6. What is General Bizimungu's favorite beverage?
7. What kind of premium beer does Paul often secure from George?
8. What color is Paul's tie in the scene after he and Gregoire attempt to travel the river road?
9. What did Paul bribe the minister of health with to bring Tatiana (his wife) to Kigali?
10. What kind of vehicle are Paul and his family about to board at the very end of the film?

Genocide or no, Paul, his family, and his "guests" persevere. Exit visas arrive for some of them, including the Rusesabaginas, and Oliver arranges for their transfer to the airport. As Paul is about to board the transport truck, he rashly breaks a promise to never leave his wife. Tatsi is horrified, but Paul cannot leave his guests behind. This choice almost turns disastrous, as the truck is intercepted by the militia. Tatsi and the children barely make it back to the hotel alive. She is furious and shoves her wedding ring into his hand. Paul's difficulties grow worse when the general arrives looking for his "supplies." Paul has none. Bizimungu subsequently pulls all of his protection. But the Tutsi rebels are growing stronger. Many Hutu refugees flee into the Congo. The Hutu generals are willing to make a prisoner exchange; the Mille Collines guests are included in the bargain. But no one controls the militia. Bizimungu now calls them "the crazy people." Can Paul and his guests avoid the machete one last time?

3.1. THINKING THROUGH THE MOVIE

Discussion Starter Questions

1. Paul conducts his business affairs by including elements of bribery. Is bribery morally wrong? Explain.
2. Is it ever morally permissible for one country to imperially occupy another? Was it permissible of Belgium to imperially occupy Africa? Explain your answers.
3. Does Paul, a Hutu, do anything morally wrong by protecting Tutsi refugees at the hotel? Explain.
4. The Hutus attempt genocide upon the Tutsi. Is that permissible? Is genocide ever morally permissible?

Questions for Further Thought

1. What goals does the United Nations pursue? When, if at all, is UN intervention or involvement morally permissible? Explain.
2. Tatsi tells her husband (scene 17, roughly 1:20:24 into the film): "You are a good man, Paul Rusesabagina." Does she mean he is a good Hutu? If not (or if not *merely* that), what does it mean to be a (morally) good person?
3. Paul is sometimes dishonest with General Bizimungu (see scene 14, roughly 1:07:00–1:09:20); he also tells his guests to shame their friends into sending help (roughly 1:04:40–1:05:25). Is this behavior morally permissible? That is, is this something a "good man" would do? Explain.
4. How should we define a culture? How should we define societal norms about a topic? How do questions like these impact the prospects for directly linking ethical truth to cultural belief?

3.2. HISTORICAL SETTING

Folkways (excerpt)[1]

William Graham Sumner (1840–1910) was a professor of sociology at Yale University. Greatly influenced by the work of Charles Darwin, Sumner argued that ethics is grounded in social adaptation and natural selection. Thus, it makes little sense to claim that ethical judgments are "true" or "false" (in the typical sense) because these concepts do not properly apply to practical issues associated with Darwin's idea of "fitness."

Preparing to Read

A. What scenes from *Hotel Rwanda* most effectively portray Sumner's thesis?

B. What is ethnocentrism? How does Sumner utilize it to support his view?

[The Meaning of "True," "Right," and "Rights"]

If a savage puts his hand too near the fire, he suffers pain and draws it back. He knows nothing of the laws of the radiation of heat, but his instinctive action conforms to that law as if he did know it. If he wants to catch an animal for food, he must study its habits and prepare a device adjusted to those habits. If it fails, he must try again, until his observation is "true" and his device is "right." All the practical and direct elements in the folkways seem to be due to common sense, natural reason, intuition, or some other original mental endowment. It seems rational (or rationalistic) and utilitarian. Often in the mythologies this ultimate rational element was ascribed to the teaching of a god or a culture hero. In modern mythology it is accounted for as "natural." Although the ways adopted must always be really "true" and "right" in relation to facts, for otherwise they could not answer their purpose, such is not the primitive notion of true and right.

The folkways are the "right" ways to satisfy all interests, because they are traditional, and exist, in fact. They extend over the whole of life. There is a right way to catch game, to win a wife, to make one's self appear, to cure disease, to honor ghosts, to treat comrades or strangers, to behave when a child is born, on the warpath, in council, and so on in all cases which can arise. The ways are defined on the negative side, that is, by taboos. The "right" way is that which the ancestors used and which has been handed down. The tradition is its own warrant. It is not held subject to verification by experience. The notion of right is in the folkways. It is not outside of them, of independent origin, and brought to them to test them. In the folkways, whatever is, is right. This is because they are traditional, and therefore contain in themselves the authority of the ancestral ghosts. When we come to the folkways we are at the end of our analysis. The notion of right and ought is the same in regard to all the folkways, but the degree of it varies with the importance of the interest at stake. The obligation of conformable and cooperative action is far greater under ghost fear and war than in other matters, and the social sanctions are severer, because group interests are supposed to be at stake. . . . It may well be believed that notions of right and duty, and of social welfare, were first developed in connection with ghost fear and other-worldliness, and therefore that, in that field also, folkways were first raised to morés. "Rights" are the rules of mutual give and take in the competition of life that are imposed on comrades in the in-group, in order that the peace may prevail, which is essential to the group strength. Therefore rights can never be "natural" or "God-given," or absolute in any sense. The morality of a group at a time is the sum of the taboos and prescriptions in the folkways by which right conduct is defined. Therefore morals can never be intuitive. They are historical, institutional, and empirical.

World philosophy, life policy, right, rights, and morality are all products of the folkways. They are reflections on, and generalizations from, the experience of pleasure and pain that is won in efforts to carry on the struggle for existence under actual life conditions. The generalizations are very crude and vague in their germinal forms. They are all embodied in folklore, and all our philosophy and science have been developed out of them. . . .

[Ethnocentrism and Its Illustrations]

Ethnocentrism is the technical name for the view that one's own group is the center of everything, and all others are scaled and rated with reference to it. Folkways correspond to it to cover both the inner and the outer relation. Each group nourishes its own pride and vanity, boasts itself superior, exalts its own divinities, and looks with contempt on outsiders. Each group thinks its own folkways the only right ones, and if it observes that other groups have other folkways, these excite its scorn. . . . For our present purpose the most important fact is that ethnocentrism leads a people to exaggerate and intensify everything in their own folkways that differentiates them from others. It therefore strengthens the folkways.

The Papuans on New Guinea are broken up into village units that are kept separate by hostility, cannibalism, head hunting, and divergences of language and religion. Each village is integrated by its own language, religion, and interests. A group of villages is sometimes united into a limited unity by marriage rites. A wife taken inside of this group unit has full status; one taken outside of it has not. The group units are peace groups within and are hostile to all outsiders. The Mbayas of South America believed that their deity had bidden them live by making war on others, taking their wives and property, and killing their men. . . . The Greenland Eskimo think that Europeans have been sent to Greenland to learn virtue and good manners from the Greenlanders. Their highest form of praise for a European is that he is, or soon will be, as good as a Greenlander. . . . Amongst the most remarkable people in the world for ethnocentrism are the Seri of Lower California. They observe an attitude of suspicion and hostility to all outsiders, and strictly forbid marriage with outsiders. . . . These are all cases of ethnocentrism. . . .

[Morés, Morals, and Social Codes]

When the elements of truth and right are developed into doctrines of welfare, the folk-ways are raised to another plane. They then become capable of producing inferences, developing into new forms, and extending their constructive influence over men and society. Then we call them the morés. The morés are the folkways, including the philosophical and ethical generalizations as to societal welfare that are suggested by them, and inherent in them, as they grow.

The morés give the notion of what ought to be. This includes the notion of what ought to be done, for all should cooperate to bring to pass, in the order of life, what ought to be. All notions of propriety, decency, chastity, politeness, order, duty, right, rights, discipline, respect, reverence, cooperation, anti-fellowship . . . are in the morés. The morés can make things seem right and good to one group or one age that to another seem antagonistic to every instinct of human nature. The thirteenth century bred in every heart such a sentiment in regard to heretics that inquisitors had no more misgivings in their proceedings than men would have now if they should attempt to exterminate rattlesnakes. The sixteenth century gave to all such notions about witches that witch persecutors thought they were waging war on enemies of God and man. Of course the inquisitors and witch persecutors constantly developed the notions of heretics and witches. They exaggerated the notions and then gave them back again to the morés, in their expanded form, to inflame the hearts of men with terror and hate and to become, in the next stage, so much more fantastic and ferocious motives. Such is the reaction between the morés and the acts of the living generation.

The world philosophy of the age is never anything but the reflection on the mental horizon, which is formed out of the morés, of the ruling ideas that are in the morés themselves. It is from a failure to recognize this reaction that the current notion arises that morés are produced by doctrines. The "morals" of an age are never anything but the consonance between what is done and what the morés of the age require. The whole revolves on itself. . . . Every attempt to win an outside standpoint from which to reduce the whole to an absolute philosophy of truth and right, based on an unalterable principle, is a delusion. New elements are brought in only by new conquests of nature through science and art. The new conquests change the conditions of life and the interests of the members of the society. Then the morés change by adaptation to new conditions and interests. The philosophy and ethics then follow to account for and justify the changes in the morés, to claim that they have caused the changes. They never do anything but draw new lines of bearing between the parts of the morés and the horizon of thought within which they are enclosed, and which is a deduction from the morés. The horizon is widened by more knowledge, but for one age it is just as much a generalization from the morés as for another. It is always unreal. It is only a product of thought. The ethical philosophers select points on this horizon from which to take their bearings, and they think that they have won some authority for their systems when they travel back again from the generalization to the specific custom out of which it was deduced. The cases of the inquisitors and witch persecutors who toiled arduously and continually for their chosen ends, for little or no reward, show us the relation between morés on the one side and philosophy, ethics, and religion on the other. . . .

[Meaning of "Immoral"]

When, therefore, ethnographers [cultural anthropologists] apply condemnatory or depreciatory adjectives to the people whom they study, they beg the most important question that we want to investigate; that is, what are standards, codes, and ideas of chastity, decency, propriety, modesty, etc., and whence do they arise? The ethnographical facts contain the answer to this question. . . . "Immoral" never means anything but contrary to the morés of the time and place. Therefore, the morés and the morality may move together, and there is no permanent or universal standard by which right and truth in regard to these matters can be established and different folkways compared and criticized.

Review Questions

1. Explain, according to Sumner, the process and significance of going from folkways, to morés, and finally to definitions of "moral" and "immoral."
2. What does Sumner mean by "ethnocentrism" and how to does it impact his overall view?
3. What would Sumner say about the moral propriety of United Nations involvement in the activities of a culture?

3.3. DISCUSSION AND ANALYSIS

As the primary source reading suggests, it is tempting to somehow ground ethical truth in the evolutionary history of one's cultural perspective. Some cultures function perfectly well by including forms of bribery in their business practices and thus condone it. Paul regularly interacted in this way with General Bizimungu in *Hotel Rwanda*. But other cultures do not condone bribery. Some cultures, as seen in *The Joy Luck Club*, condone self-deprecation about culinary talents; however, not every culture appreciates this practice, as demonstrated by the American future son-in-law Rich as he doused Lindo's prized dish in soy sauce. Different practices have come to "work" for different cultures. This insight leads some scholars to defend the metaethical theory known as moral relativism (MR). According to MR, current cultural consensus is the sole "truth-maker" for any morally significant statement. If current cultural consensus is positive about a topic, then the corresponding behavior is permissible, if not obligatory, for its members. If current cultural consensus is negative about a topic, then the corresponding behavior is impermissible for its members. MR thus entails that moral judgments are binding upon everyone within the same culture. If someone in Rwanda (at least as it was in 1994) believes that bribery is morally wrong, then that person holds a false belief exactly because her belief is contrary to current cultural consensus about it. And if someone in China (at least as it was during the flashback sequences in *The Joy Luck Club*) disagreed with the practice of arranged marriages or wives being completely subservient to husbands and mothers-in-law, then that person likewise held a false belief. Therefore, MR allows for genuine moral disagreement, at least between individuals belonging to the same culture.

Moral relativists nevertheless disavow a universal or objective moral standard that applies to everyone for all times and locations. In specifying current cultural consensus as the sole ethical truth-maker, no cross-culturally binding moral judgments are possible. With no universal moral standard by which the various cultures can be evaluated, each culture becomes its unique standard for moral truth. Therefore, each culture or society is on equal moral footing with every other. Belgium is no morally better or worse than Rwanda, and China is no morally better or worse than America. The different cultures are merely that, different. Each has evolved with its unique perspective on the world, and each has found different practices that "work" for it. The uniqueness of each culture should be respected or at least appreciated, but not judged as superior or inferior. Were this attitude of tolerance more widely adopted, moral relativists often stress, the world would be a much better place to live.

> "It was an old tradition. Only the most dutiful of daughters would put her own flesh in a soup to save her mother's life. . . . This is how a daughter honors her mother." —*The Joy Luck Club,* scene 6

The Argument from Ethnocentricism

Initial considerations for MR stem from the implausibility of ethnocentrism. Ethnocentrism is the idea that your culture is morally superior to others just because it's yours. This entails that other cultures are morally inferior just because they are not yours. Not many people are openly ethnocentric anymore, but its shadow persists. Some argue that, despite its good intentions, the United Nations remains ethnocentric. Ethnocentrism was prevalent in the era of cultural expansion and imperialism. The British famously (infamously?) imperially occupied India, and countries like Belgium did the same in Africa (administrating lands previously occupied by Germany). Ethnocentric-type thinking may have initially motivated European expansion into Africa, but that imperialism only intensified (if not created) animosity between the Hutu and Tutsi. And we cannot forget that some Africans were forced to leave their native soil in a different kind of cultural imperialism: the slave trade. It is difficult to imagine the kind of cultural clashes Spike Lee portrays in *Do the Right Thing* without the African slave trade. The unfortunate instances of racial tension depicted in *Hotel Rwanda* or *Do the Right Thing* spur the rhetorical question: By what right does one country imperially occupy or otherwise interfere with another? To safeguard against cultural imperialism and the ethnocentric thinking that fuels it, many hold that one culture is no better or worse than another. External interference into another culture is therefore never justified. All cultures are uniquely special, but none are superior or inferior to another. This also applies to their moral codes. Thus, one culture's moral code is no better or worse than another, which is to affirm MR.

Ethnocentrism is indeed to be avoided. This way of thinking is flawed in that it assumes any belief you don't share is thereby dubious or simply false. Ethnocentrism thus entails that all of your beliefs are true or justified simply because you hold them. Some attempt to bolster this entailment with the further claim that "it's always been that way for me/us." But nothing in this establishes that your positions are true or best; after all, none of us is perfect and perhaps there is a better way of doing things if only we would investigate. Moreover, ethnocentrism fallaciously assumes that simply coming to have a belief thereby makes it true.

But the crucial point is that the failure of ethnocentrism does not logically establish MR. Any such attempt rests on a false premise. An ethnocentric outlook is most certainly myopic and ignorant; however, this only says something about the ethnocentric person (or culture), namely, he (or it) ought not to be that way. So Sal from *Do the Right Thing* can be blamed for being ethnocentric (if he is), and the kind of ethnocentric thinking that seemingly spurred European imperialism into Africa can be denounced *without* embracing MR. So, at best, the moral relativist offers the dilemma that one must accept the truth of either ethnocentrism or moral relativism. But, the argument continues, ethnocentrism is to be avoided; therefore, MR must be accepted. But this argument fails because the proffered dilemma is false; there are other metaethical positions to consider. We could, for example, hold that our moral beliefs are possibly incorrect or in need of further revision without disavowing a universal moral standard.

> "Who told you to buy a brownstone on my block, in my neighborhood, on my side of the street? Yo, what you wanna live in a Black neighborhood for, anyway?" —*Do the Right Thing*, scene 12

The Cultural Differences Argument

Twentieth-century social science scholars like Sumner and Ruth Benedict (1887–1948) were able to travel the globe in ways their predecessors could not. They made many novel anthropological and sociological discoveries. Their findings rejuvenated the social science thesis of cultural relativism. This venerable theory simply holds that, descriptively speaking, different cultures disagree about appropriate behavior. The obvious truth of cultural relativism drives the cultural differences argument. This argument begins with the claim that if there were any universal or cross-culturally binding moral truths, there wouldn't be widespread cultural disagreement about ethics. But because there is widespread cultural disagreement, or so it seems per cultural relativism, it follows that there are no universal or cross-culturally binding moral truths. Furthermore, the argument continues, if there

---

BOX 3C: LEARNING OUTCOMES

Upon carefully studying this chapter, students should better comprehend and be able to explain:

- What moral relativism is, and the reasons for and against its truth.
- How the ideas of ethnocentrism and (especially) tolerance seem paradoxically problematic for the moral relativist.
- How moral relativism is distinct from but also similar to simple ethical subjectivism.
- How *Hotel Rwanda*, *The Joy Luck Club*, and *Do the Right Thing* are conducive to learning about moral relativism.

are no universal cross-culturally binding moral truths, but some ethical statements are true, then either they are made true by the beliefs of individual persons or current cultural consensus. Because there are ethical disagreements, beliefs of individual persons are inadequate moral "truth-makers" (per the previous chapter). Therefore, ethical statements are made true by current cultural consensus. So, the failure of simple ethical subjectivism (SES) coupled with cultural relativism is supposed to provide adequate reason for adopting MR.

Accordingly, the cultural differences argument moves from the truth of cultural relativism to the truth of moral relativism. From the fact that Rwandans include bribes in their business dealings and Chinese revere their ancestors but other cultures do not, it is concluded that ethically significant statements, if true at all, are made true by current cultural consensus. This move assumes that disagreement about a topic is sufficient to establish the lack of universal or objective truth about the debated topic. This is supposed to hold for any topic; that it allegedly does anchors the cultural differences argument. If this underlying assumption is false, then the cultural differences argument fails. To that end, consider debates about the shape of the earth. Throughout time, some cultures have believed it to be flat, others perfectly spherical, and still others to be spherical but not perfectly so. Even today, there is some debate about this from the Flat Earth Society. However, it seems completely fantastical to hold that there is no (objective) truth to the shape of the earth that applies universally to all cultures. Thus there is one counterexample to the assumption that disagreement about a topic entails a lack of objective truth about it, which leads to the failure of the cultural differences argument.

Admittedly, the shape of the earth is an empirical issue, which spurs some students to wonder whether the cultural differences argument has been critiqued unfairly. The debate is not about empirical matters like the shape of the earth but nonempirical ethical matters. However, this objection doubly misses the mark. On the one hand, the cultural differences argument (as typically stated) *only* goes through if the deeper assumption about the logic of disagreement holds. So, in successfully critiquing the underlying assumption, it does indeed (deductively) follow that the cultural differences argument fails. On the other hand, the objection might uncover a bias toward objective truth requiring empirical topics or methods. If so, note that *cultural* disagreement becomes irrelevant; any debate about ethically significant judgments is sufficient to conclude that there are no universal cross-culturally binding moral truths (which is akin to the baseline argument discussed in the previous chapter).

But it's not at all clear that nonempirical matters necessarily lack objectivity. Do the basic laws of logic or math depend on current cultural consensus for their truth? Furthermore, there appear to be nonempirical cases where mere disagreement doesn't entail a lack of objective truth about the debated topic. Consider that many cultures disagree about God's existence; Muslims are theists, but Buddhists (invariably) are not. Does it follow from this that there is no universal (or cross-cultural) truth to the matter about God? This seems highly counterintuitive. If it did follow, then the Creator's existence depends upon what creatures believe. If all of us agree to be (or become) theists, then God is made to exist by our coming to believe in him. If some subsequently become atheists, then God is made not to exist by our lack of consensus about him. But this gets the relationship between creature and creator backward. If God exists, our existence depends on him and not vice versa. Moreover, beliefs about the world don't have this sort of causal power. Our beliefs about the world (even if true) are conceptually distinct from how it actually is.

Therefore, we have excellent reason for thinking that God's existence is logically distinct from our (conflicting) beliefs about it. This truism applies generally: just because people disagree about something is not sufficient reason for thinking that there is no (objective) truth to the topic being debated. Therefore, the proffered critique of the cultural differences argument stands. Even if cultural relativism is true, the move to moral relativism remains unjustified.

The Argument from Tolerance

The argument from tolerance is almost as popular as the cultural differences argument. It's driven by the fact that many are too quick to judge the practices of those in other cultures. However, perhaps we should first try to understand, for example, the positions of *The Joy Luck Club*'s "Aunties" in war ravaged China before we judge them for their acts. Indeed, perhaps we should better appreciate China and its customs generally before passing ethical judgment on any of its people. This requires tolerance. But it's widely believed that practicing tolerance requires us to resist positions that posit the existence of universal or cross-culturally binding moral truths. This is the conclusion that the argument from tolerance attempts to justify.

The argument from tolerance, accordingly, begins with (and hinges on) the premise that if there were universal or cross-culturally binding moral truths, then we ought to practice intolerance. After all, it's tempting to believe that the existence of universal or cross-culturally binding moral truths entails that the moral codes of some cultures would be morally inferior to others. Presumably, those codes that best approximate the universally binding moral truths would be morally superior to those that failed to approximate them. But this seemingly leads us to be intolerant of the morally inferior cultures. Why tolerate the practices of a morally inferior culture? However, being intolerant of other cultures should be avoided. Tolerance, not intolerance, is to be prized and valued. With this, given its first premise, the conclusion of the argument from tolerance falls into place: we should avoid (reject) the position that there are universal or cross-culturally binding moral truths. From here, the argument from tolerance concludes just as the cultural differences argument. If there are no universally binding moral truths, yet some ethical statements are true, then we are led to the conclusion that ethical statements are made true by current cultural consensus.

The argument from tolerance gains strength from the intuition that the world would be a (morally) better place if everyone practiced more tolerance. We would better appreciate and understand other cultures if we did. There is certainly some truth to this. Consider Sal's "Wall of Fame" from *Do the Right Thing*. Sal dogmatically refused to consider placing Africans (or African Americans) on the wall, even the likes of Nelson Mandela, Malcolm X, Martin Luther King, Jr., and Michael Jordan were forbidden to appear with Sal's personal Italian American heroes. Is it plausible to believe that neither Mandela, Brother Malcolm, Dr. King, nor Jordan is as famous or heroic as some that graced Sal's wall? A more plausible answer is simply that Sal is Italian American and not African American. True, Sal owns the establishment and it is thus his prerogative to display the pictures of whomever he wishes. However, Sal's antagonism and utter inflexibility about Buggin' Out's request is also (arguably) indicative of dogmatic and myopic attitudes about other cultures; bringing these attitudes about race to the foreground was one of Spike Lee's motivations for making *Do the Right Thing*. Consider Lee's very controversial "Some

Thoughts on Ethnicity" scene (scene 16 in the Criterion Collection edition). The camera first focuses on Mookie, who slurs Italians, but the camera then turns to Pino who slurs Africans. Lee moves his camera to other neighbors: a Puerto Rican slurs Koreans, and the Korean grocer slurs affluent Caucasians, including the Jews (and Mayor Ed Koch). Each cut shows one person alone speaking into the camera, as if we (the audience) were hearing his thoughts. What would the contents of your mind reveal? How tolerant are Americans? Lee would have us consider the extent to which each and every one of us is racist. But racism is the hallmark of intolerance. Surely Señor Love Daddy's words ring true: "Together, are we gonna live?" The moral relativist believes that living together harmoniously requires genuine tolerance, and this is only possible if we disavow a universal or cross-culturally binding moral standard. All cultures are morally equal and tolerance is the path for recognizing this.

> "I don't like being around them, Pop. They're animals. . . . I don't want to be here. They don't want us here. We should stay in our own neighborhood."
> —*Do the Right Thing*, scene 19

Accordingly, the argument from tolerance is importantly grounded in two interesting ideas. The first idea is that if some cultures are morally inferior, then they ought to be treated as such. The second idea is that tolerance is to be valued (and intolerance ought to be avoided). These two ideas serve as crucial premises for the argument. If either is problematic, the argument fails.

Regarding the first idea, the proper response to cultures that conduct themselves in behaviors that seem morally dubious is a difficult issue. Great care must be taken when assessing foreign cultural practices; careful investigation of the facts must precede moral judgment. Moreover, the existence of universal cross-culturally binding moral truths (if any) may permit alternatives about how to respond to cultures that fail to uphold them. So, it is far from clear that such cultures should be treated as inferior, childlike, or with extreme prejudice (or the like). In fact, if being tolerant is valuable, then tolerance might be our initial moral guide. However, practicing tolerance might not always be appropriate, especially for cultural behavior that has every indication of being especially morally egregious. The best example of this is probably genocide. Is cultural bias the only explanation for deeming the extermination of an entire race by another a moral atrocity? Are all such judgments merely the result of ethnocentrism? The rhetorical nature of these questions lead many to believe that for cases like Germany of the 1940s or Rwanda of 1994 direct intervention may be morally appropriate. Nevertheless, working to end (or prevent) genocide is not obviously the same as treating another culture as inferior. Thus the first idea—and the crucial premise it represents—is far from obviously true.

The second idea—tolerance as an ethical ideal—is ironically problematic for the moral relativist. If tolerance is an inherent feature of MR, then moral relativists like Sumner or Benedict catch themselves in a contradiction. If tolerance were an ethical ideal, then it would seemingly apply to all cultures. It would become a universal cross-culturally binding moral truth. However, if MR is true, then there are no universal cross-culturally binding moral truths. Thus, if tolerance is a necessary feature of MR, it follows that MR cannot be true because the view becomes self-contradictory. The moral relativist, in response, could deny that tolerance is a necessary feature of her theory, and hold that the value of tolerance is culture specific. If your culture practices it, then it is good (or right) for you, but it need not be good (or right) for those in cultures that don't currently condone it. But this rejoinder is doubly problematic. On the one hand, it entails that cultures practicing intolerance are not any morally better or worse than cultures that practice tolerance, which is a far cry from the idea that tolerance is the key to making the world a better place to live. On the other hand, it entails that the argument from tolerance has a false premise because the argument requires that intolerance is inherently bad—for all cultures. Therefore, moral relativists are left with a choice. Either practicing tolerance is a universal cross-cultural value or it's not. If it is, then MR becomes self-contradictory: for *all* cultures, it is good to be tolerant and bad to be intolerant. If the value of practicing tolerance is merely cultural specific, then MR avoids internal contradiction but at the price of giving up the argument from tolerance as a way to establish her theory. Neither result is welcome for the moral relativist.

Culture and Multiculturalism

It therefore seems that each of the three most popular arguments for moral relativism—the argument from ethnocentrism, the cultural differences argument, and the argument from tolerance—must overcome damaging criticism. Even if none of those criticisms can be overcome, it doesn't follow that moral relativism is false. This would only show that the most popular reasons for thinking it to be true fail. However, there are other more direct criticisms of moral relativism that, if successful, would demonstrate its implausibility.

Moral relativists often proceed as if there are noncontroversial ways to define culture. This is far from clear. Should we define culture by geographical boundaries? What about defining culture via shared religion or secular common ideology? Perhaps race or ethnicity would serve as plausible candidates? The task of defining culture quickly becomes exceedingly difficult. But if cultural delineations cannot be clearly made, MR is rendered unworkable because we then have no way to determine current cultural consensus.

"As they were about to chop her, she cried out to me, 'Please don't let them kill me. I promise I won't be Tutsi anymore!'" —*Hotel Rwanda*, scene 11

Hotel Rwanda serves as a particularly enlightening (historical) example of how cultural delineations are problematic for moral relativists. The Rusesabagina children have a Hutu father but a Tutsi mother. With which heritage should they identify? What should their (legally required) identification card read? Should they be allowed to simply choose whether they shall be Hutu or Tutsi? Remember that even the Rwandan army was forced to check identification cards so as to determine who to arrest. Presumably, the Interhamwe also depended on them in determining who should receive the machete. Therefore, these are not idle questions.

Moral relativists like Sumner or Benedict tend to assume that cultural "folkways" or "patterns" of behaviors and corresponding attitudes result from generations, if not centuries, of effort. The result of this effort is supposed to provide a proper conceptual basis for a culture's moral outlook. And rightly so, because moral judgments invariably signify foundational beliefs about what kind of life is best or what constitutes evil. But *Hotel Rwanda*, and the relevant African history of the area generally, show how a culture's moral judgments can nevertheless be couched in ultimately arbitrary or artificial machinations.

Hotel Rwanda, MGM/United Artists, 2004. Paul Rusesabagina (Don Cheadle) and his wife Tatiana (Sophie Okonedo) attempt to protect their children from social and political upheaval in 1994 Rwanda. (Moviegoods, Inc.)

Why believe that ethical statements can be made true by how one draws lines on a map? Can ethical statements go from true to false by simply redrawing those lines? (And recall that there was no such thing as Rwanda before the Europeans arrived.) The goal here is *not* to undermine or belittle the seriousness of Rwandan genocide or Hutu/Tutsi interactions in any way, but to raise theoretical questions about moral relativism itself. That is, the fact that cultural moorings can have artificial or arbitrary bases, coupled with the inherent difficulties in properly defining culture in the first place, seems to cast serious doubt on the very idea of moral relativism as a metaethical theory.

Even if cultural moorings could be plausibly delineated, MR suffers from other implausible entailments. Consider that if the Hutus composed the Rwandan majority in 1994, it seems that any Rwandan who aided the Tutsi acted impermissibly. If MR is true, it follows that Paul acted impermissibly in protecting his Tutsi hotel "guests," including his wife. Moreover, it follows that Gregoire simply upheld his moral obligations as a good Hutu in his efforts to thwart Paul's plans. But, of course, the movie is most plausibly interpreted as conveying the opposite message: Paul was the hero and Gregoire one of the antagonists.

> "If people see this footage, I think they'll say, 'Oh my God, that's horrible' and then they'll go on eating their dinners." — *Hotel Rwanda*, scene 10

Furthermore, it also seems to follow that the Tutsi acted impermissibly by not subjecting *themselves* to genocide. This conclusion seems to follow assuming that, because the Hutus were the Rwandan majority, the 1994 cultural consensus in Rwanda favored exterminating Tutsi "cockroaches." But can you ever be morally obligated to aid in the genocide of your own kind? But this (rhetorical?) question only leads to those more metaethically fundamental: Why think that "majority rule" is a proper "truth-maker" for ethical statements? Is the majority necessarily correct in its judgments just because it represents consensus? Why believe that cultural consensus is morally infallible when it comprises individuals who are not? These questions must be answered before moral relativism can be plausibly embraced.

Hotel Rwanda thus reminds us of another obvious (historical) fact: cultures are no longer homogeneous. The United States is a prime example of this. As *Do the Right Thing* poignantly portrays, there are African Americans, Italian Americans, Asian Americans, Puerto Rican Americans, among other subcultures populating the United States. Mister Señor Love Daddy would have us "live together" with genuine togetherness. But is this truly possible in a multicultural society? What should we do in cases where values clash? Should Mookie identify with the predominantly Caucasion population of the United States or with his African heritage? Is Buggin' Out's charge to "Stay black, Mookie!" appropriate or not? Should Mookie "fight the power" or not? These (again) are not idle questions (and Lee would certainly agree given the ending of *Do the Right Thing*). Moreover, consider that many young women find themselves in situations similar to Tina's, Mookie's girlfriend. Let's assume that, rather than giving birth to Hector, she and Mookie decide to abort the unexpected pregnancy. Assuming MR, because Tina is an American woman, it seems that an early-term abortion would be permissible. But as a Puerto Rican woman, plausibly assuming she was raised Roman Catholic, an early-term abortion would not be permissible. From this, given MR, it seemingly follows that having an early-term abortion is both permissible and impermissible for Tina. Therefore, MR leads to contradictory results for individuals from multicultural societies. But theories that entail contradictions cannot be true; it therefore follows that MR cannot be true. Thus, MR seems to be unworkable given the realities of multiculturalism.

This criticism could be deflected if there was a way to remove Tina's contradiction, and all others generated by MR in multicultural societies. However, no plausible strategy seems available. Perhaps the larger or more dominant culture should always prevail. But this leads back to "majority rule" at best and "might makes right" at worst. Why believe that majority opinion about an ethical issue is necessarily true? Alternatively, perhaps individual choice should prevail. Tina's decision could then be determined by whether she sees herself attached to one cultural perspective more than the other. But how would she justify such a distinction? Perhaps she simply finds herself equally attached to conflicting perspectives. It's tempting to say that she simply should rely upon her sentiments or feelings about this topic at a particular time. But this is tantamount to accepting SES, which (recall) leads to a view of morality "where anything goes." However, as previously argued (in chapter 2), if SES is true, ethics is all but done away with. At best, ethics becomes merely a matter of person-specific feelings, tastes, and sentiments. But (again) such things appear to be implausible truth-makers for ethical statements.

Moral Progress and Reform

Multiculturalism also presents the moral relativist with difficulties concerning moral progress and reform. Consider the Aunties from *The Joy Luck Club*. They lived in China for the first part of their lives, but spent the latter parts in America. Interestingly, the movie

The Joy Luck Club, Buena Vista Pictures, 1993. Prior to her life in America, Suyuan Woo (Kieu Chinh) is tragically compelled to leave her infant daughters along the roadside in China. (Moviegoods, Inc.)

is plausibly interpreted as the Aunties wanting a better life for themselves and especially their daughters in America. But if MR is true, this is impossible. Life in America or anywhere else cannot be better than life in China, at least not in any morally significant sense because MR disallows any morally significant cross-cultural judgments.

In fact, it seems that any plausible interpretation of *The Joy Luck Club* serves as a counterexample to MR. Recall some of the tribulations the Aunties faced. Lindo's marriage was arranged by the local matchmaker when she was just a small girl. Ying-Ying at least chose her own husband, but he was cruel and openly unfaithful. Both were completely subservient to their husbands (and his family) with little or no recourse. An-Mei's mother serves as a particularly interesting case. Chinese custom dictated that she mourn her husband's death for a significant period of time. This included avoiding relations with other men. However, because she was duped by another woman, An-Mei's mother unwillingly becomes pregnant. With her family disowning her, she has no choice but to become this man's fourth wife. As the fourth wife, An-Mei's mother is little more than a concubine; when her son is born, the second wife (the woman who duped her) is allowed to claim him as her own, thereby becoming the most revered wife (because the first wife produced no male heirs). The important point is this: If MR is true, subservient domestic existence in China cannot be any better or worse than the greater autonomy (now) enjoyed by American wives. Assuming MR, Chinese women cannot consistently look toward America as an example of how women receive morally better treatment. China has uniquely found methods that work for it, while America has uniquely found different methods. In fact, no culture can look to another as a moral model of any behavior if MR is true. Furthermore, if MR is true, the idea that the Aunties work to make the lives of their daughters better than what they suffered in China is incoherent because it assumes the existence of a universal cross-cultural ethical standard by which their respective lives can be evaluated. Yet the very message of the film is that the lives of the Aunties and their daughters have improved in some ethically significant sense. Moreover, this message is not implausible; it certainly seems that the lives of the women depicted in the film have relevantly improved. In this way, *The Joy Luck Club* serves as a counterexample to MR.

> "In America, I will have a daughter just like me. But over there, nobody will say her worth is measured by the loudness of her husband's belch. . . . And over there, she will be too full to swallow any sorrow." —*The Joy Luck Club*, scene 1

The argument from moral progress against moral relativism can be furthered by assessing the norms of one culture over time. The problem is grounded in the fact that, according to MR, the ideals a culture currently holds are no morally better or worse than those it held in the past. This is so because (recall) the *only* ethical standard of morality on MR is *current* cultural consensus. Just as there is no universal moral standard by which individual cultures can be evaluated as morally superior or inferior to another, there is no universal moral standard to which any "time slice" of one culture can be deemed morally superior or inferior to another. So, it follows on MR that Mookie's life in contemporary America as a pizza deliveryman in New York is no morally better or worse than it would have been 250 years ago as a slave in Georgia.[2] This seems incredibly implausible; the abolishment of slavery is evidence of real moral reform in this country. Moreover, perhaps Spike Lee (as he is sometimes interpreted) is correct in that Mookie's life as Sal's pizza deliveryman remains a bit too much like being a slave. Despite strides at moral progress, Americans very well may have a long way to go to achieve the kind of peace, love, and togetherness Mister Señor Love Daddy advocates. However, if there is moral reform that still needs to be made, it follows that there is a standard with which this judgment is made. The existence of a moral standard that transcends current cultural consensus is inconsistent with MR. So, if there has been real moral reform in this country, then there is a universal moral standard by which to gauge it. And if there is such a standard, MR is false.

Furthermore, the fact that cultural consensus changes over time is problematic for MR generally. If MR is true, *any* member of a culture who makes an ethical judgment contrary to the established norm holds a false belief. Recall that Paul Rusesabagina is an example of this; he broke with cultural consensus about exterminating Tutsi "cockroaches." But note that some historical individuals attempted to *significantly* alter a culture's established moral code. Martin Luther King, Jr., is a good contemporary American example (and explains, in part, why Lee chooses to include Dr. King's ideas at the end of *Do the Right Thing*). Other examples throughout history include the Buddha and Jesus. Assuming MR, these people are akin to "moral monsters" because they not only disagreed with current cultural consensus, they attempted to overthrow their (dominant) culture's value system.

This entailment of MR strikes many as highly counterintuitive. How can it be that Martin Luther King, Jr., was a moral monster, but the Ku Klux Klan were the moral heroes of the American South in the 1950s? Perhaps the MR defender might respond as

SES defenders did when various objections were leveled at their view: this argument (and others like it) assumes too much of what is at issue. Again, this type of rejoinder leaves philosophers (fledgling or professional) to rationally decide between the theoretical truth of MR or deny what seems intuitively and obviously true: genuine moral progress/reform occurs and people like Martin Luther King, Jr., are not moral monsters. And, again, intuitions might differ here, but the obviousness of, say, moral progress/reform is some reason for jettisoning MR in favor of other metaethical approaches.

MR and SES Compared

That MR has conceptual difficulties in dealing with clashing cultural perspectives within multicultural society suggests that MR and simple ethical subjectivism (SES) are actually more alike than different. This intuition is reinforced by interpreting the various cultures themselves as individuals. So, on this hypothesis, we can understand culture A as one individual and culture B as another and culture C as yet another. Now, according to MR, the only binding moral judgments are those that represent current consensus within the culture itself. There are no universally true, cross-culturally binding moral truths or judgments. So, now the question arises, how are we to resolve moral disputes among the individual cultures? If culture A attacks B and affirms that the attack is somehow justified by its own heritage and corresponding current beliefs, what grounds culture B's reaction/judgment that it was wronged? If MR is true, the answer must be nothing, apart from perhaps B's heritage and corresponding current beliefs. But this is simply a case of one individual holding one set of moral beliefs and another individual holding a different set, with no principled way to adjudicate between the two. Just as there is no principled way to resolve disputes between individual persons on SES (per the previous chapter), there is no principled way to resolve disputes between individual cultures on MR. If one signals the end of ethics, so does the other. Since we have good reason to think that SES more or less does away with ethics (again, per the previous chapter), so does MR.

Perhaps there is a final analogy in assessing SES and MR. When affirming that morality is merely a matter of one's cultural perspective or how one was raised, we typically have in mind only the "nice" cultures or upbringings. But, according to MR, *all* cultures are morally equal—none are morally superior to another. Thus, the discussion is not actually limited to the "nice" cultures. MR, as a theory that attempts to most effectively capture the nature of all moral judgments, must also include Nazi Germany. Hitler's Germany is just as "nice" as any other culture. But this seems counterintuitive. How can Nazi Germany be morally equivalent to Buddhist Tibet? Because MR has no way to consistently draw the line between the moral practices of the various cultures. But it seems intuitive that the line must be drawn somewhere (lest Adolph Hitler and the Dalai Lama be moral equals); we have reason to think that MR does not provide a plausible theory for grounding the truth of moral statements. In fact, current cultural consensus is no more effective a truth-maker for moral statements than is the current sentiments or feelings of individual persons. If there is little reason to think that moral truth can be constructed (invented) by one individual's current preferences, there is little reason to think that it can be constructed (invented) by the current preferences of a group of individuals. This conclusion leads many scholars to seek alternative ethical truth-makers.

3.4. TWO ADDITIONAL FILMS

The Joy Luck Club (1993)

Director: Wayne Wang
Screenwriter: Amy Tan

Plot Summary

> I was raised the Chinese way. I was taught to desire nothing, swallow other people's misery and to eat my own bitterness.

Four women, Suyuan, Lindo, Ying-Ying, and An-Mei, all originally from China, meet at church. This begins a very close, lifelong friendship among the four. The women become like sisters, sharing each other's hopes, dreams, fears, and joys. Their children, all women themselves, call the other three "Auntie." But Suyuan has recently died, well before her time; her daughter, June, is to take her place among the four.

The story begins on the night before June is to meet, for the first time, her older half-sisters—twins—in China. The whole "family" attends a dinner in June's honor, wishing her "good luck" for her pending voyage. The dinner is also to honor Suyuan. Tragically separated from her twin baby girls, surely she is making the trip as well, at least in spirit. But through June's narration and that of her "Aunties," we learn that the story is much longer than just one dinner party. It takes place over many years and multiple continents.

What June does not know is that Auntie Lindo, in helping to organize the dinner party, has not been completely honest with her. Lindo, on Suyuan's behalf, led the twins to believe that their mother, and not June, would visit them. We find out that this is not the first time Lindo thought it best to be dishonest. When she was a very young girl of four in China, she was promised to another family. At fifteen, she is to leave her family—never to see them again—and marry into her new family in the hope of providing them many sons. The marriage does not go well. Her mother-in-law is domineering and her husband is too immature. Relying upon the Chinese tradition of respecting family elders, she spins a tale where an elder came to her in a dream. In the dream, she is warned that there will be terrible consequences for the mother-in-law and her family if Lindo's marriage is not dissolved. The mother-in-law believes the yarn and Lindo immediately leaves for Shanghai. She eventually makes her way to the United States.

We discover more secrets about the Aunties at the dinner party, including one terrible secret that only one of them knows. Ying-Ying became enamored of a young, handsome Chinese man when she was a teenager in China. At first, their relationship was passionate and loving; they exchanged wedding vows. Soon after the birth of their son, however, her husband becomes promiscuous. His indiscretions are many, and eventually not so indiscreet. He also becomes abusive and cruel; he would "forget" to come home for days and when he did come home, it was often with another woman. Ying-Ying became unstable. After her husband (again) comes home with another woman—this time a prostitute—she narrates, "Had I killed him, or left him that night, I would not have lost the thing that mattered most. He had taken everything from me; so, I took the only thing of his I could, his son." Tragically, Ying-Ying lets her infant son drown in the bath. She eventually moved to the United States, remarried and had a daughter. But the horror of killing her own son has never left her.

An-Mei is June's third Auntie. An-Mei's life in China was equally challenging. Her father died when she was a young girl. Her mother grieved his death. One day when An-Mei's mother was honoring his memory, she meets another woman who befriends her. But there are ulterior motives. This new "friend" invites An-Mei's mother into her home, only to have the man of the house rape her. An-Mei's mother is now pregnant. Her family does not believe her story and disowns her. Consequently, An-Mei's grandmother, uncles, and aunts raise her. But the grandmother becomes gravely ill. Dutifully, and to the surprise of the family, An-Mei's mother returns home to honor her mother. She performs the "blood soup" ritual where she reveres her mother by bleeding into a bowl, prepares a soup with her blood, and feeds it to her mother. They reconcile. However, against the family's wishes, An-Mei takes advantage of the situation and leaves with her mother.

An-Mei arrives at the beautiful home of Wu-Ching. He is An-Mei's stepfather. He is also the man who raped her mother. An-Mei discovers that Wu-Ching has four wives and her mother is the last. The other three rank above her. Furthermore, An-Mei discovers that the woman who "befriended" her mother is Wu-Ching's second wife. "Second Wife" has given Wu-Ching a son, thereby becoming matriarch of the family and now ranking above Wu-Ching's first wife. But An-Mei also discovers that Second Wife did not give birth to the boy. Actually, the boy is her brother; however, Second Wife claimed him as her own. In despair and for the sake of her two children, An-Mei's mother eventually commits suicide.

Lindo, Ying-Ying, and An-Mei, respectively, advise their own daughters by relying upon their experiences in China. However, Suyuan and June never reached this stage. In fact, June believed that she never really knew her mother; there was always a barrier between them. The barrier, June discovers that night from her father, was Suyuan's decision to leave her infant twin girls at the roadside. As June's father tells the story, Suyuan suffered from terrible dysentery. In wartime China, antibiotics were difficult to find. Suyuan believed that she would soon die. But she also believed that it would be "bad luck" for her daughters if she died next to them because no one would be willing to care for her children "with a ghost-mother following them around." She left all of her possessions with the children and a note promising more if the children were returned to their father, Suyuan's first husband, in the nearby village. Suyuan's luck turned worse as she was later rescued and, receiving proper medical care, survived her bout of dysentery only to find that her babies were gone. June's father ends the touching story by telling June that because Suyuan thought it unforgivable to give up hope for one's children, she transferred all of her hope to June. This is what June never understood; it was the ever-present barrier between mother and daughter. June now takes her mother's hopes to China.

Discussion Questions

1. Did fifteen-year-old Lindo act impermissibly by lying to her in-laws? Explain.
2. By what standard, if any, could the Aunties gauge whether their daughters have a better life in American than they had in China?
3. A recurring theme of the movie is discovering one's self-worth. What is the moral significance of this idea? Why might this be more pertinent for women? Justify your answers.

Do the Right Thing (1989)

Director and Screenwriter: Spike Lee

Plot Summary

> Are we gonna live together? Together, are we gonna live? . . . And that's the triple truth, Ruth!

Matriarchal Mother Sister, pseudopatriarchal Da Mayor, volatile Buggin' Out, radio DJ Mister Señor Love Daddy, mentally challenged Smiley, indignant Radio Raheem, beautiful Jade, the Korean grocers, pizzeria owner Sal and his sons, Pino and Vito, and the rest of a small Brooklyn neighborhood (Bedford-Stuyvesant) prepare for the hottest day of the year. But the block seemingly revolves around Mookie (Jade's brother and apartment mate). Mookie is a handsome, smart, and amiable young African American man. Everyone greets him as he makes his way to work. Mother Sister tells him to take care in this heat and Da Mayor admonishes him to always "do the right thing." He is also Sal's pizza deliveryman. Sal treats him more like family than an employee, even if Sal wishes that Mookie would work harder.

Buggin' Out, one of Mookie's friends, saunters into Sal's for his daily slice. After another disagreement with Sal about the price, Buggin' calls Sal cheap but quickly finds an empty booth. Devouring Sal's delectable pizza, he glances at Sal's "Wall of Fame." It contains pictures of only Italian Americans: Frank Sinatra, Al Pacino, and Joe DiMaggio, among others. Scanning Sal's patrons, he sees only African Americans. He publicly demands that Sal's wall include the likes of Malcolm X, Nelson Mandela, or Michael Jordan. Sal quickly retorts that Buggin' should get his own place; in Sal's Famous Pizzeria, there are only Italian Americans on the wall, which only further annoys Buggin'. He makes a scene, which only further annoys Sal. Sal angrily orders Mookie to "escort" his friend to the curb, which spurs Buggin' to plan a neighborhood boycott of Sal's Famous. As he walks away, he charges Mookie to "stay black."

Radio Raheem, another of Mookie's friends, confidently strolls up and down the block with his blaring boom box. He seeks out a group of Puerto Ricans blasting their own radio. Raheem glares at them. They curse at him in Spanish, and order him to take his music somewhere else. He only turns up the volume of his Public Enemy song. They recognize the challenge. However, their attempt to drown out Raheem's music only results in shame. Raheem's box still reigns supreme in the neighborhood. He abruptly walks away, fist defiantly raised in the air.

As Mookie crisscrosses the neighborhood, we get to better know its residents. We meet the Korean family that owns the corner grocery store. Da Mayor complains when they stop carrying his favorite brand of beer. Mother Sister continues to disapprove of Da Mayor's drinking habits, but compliments his bravery for saving a young boy from being hit by a car. Mister Señor Love Daddy continues to publicize the "quintessential truth, Ruth" about love and togetherness. Jade strolls into Sal's for a slice, and Sal lavishes her with attention and affection (which she doesn't discourage), unnerving Mookie, Pino, and Vito. And we meet Tina, Mookie's girlfriend with whom he has fathered a child (but hasn't seen in a week).

But if the neighborhood revolves around Mookie, Sal's Famous is its anchor. Pino, the oldest, continually pleads with his father to sell the pizzeria and open a new one in their own neighborhood of Bensonhurst. Although most of Pino's sports and entertainment heroes are black, he tells his dad that he hates these people. Sal sighs and reminds Pino that he's been making pizza in Bedford-Stuyvesant for twenty-five years. Most of the neighborhood likes him and his pizza (even if a few don't). These people have grown up on *his* food. Sal takes this as a badge of honor. Vito is more accepting of the neighborhood. He often confides in Mookie. But Pino discourages Vito from befriending Mookie and the neighborhood, reminding him about family and "where he comes from." Mookie advises Vito to defend himself when Pino verbally and physically assaults him.

As night falls, Buggin' meets Raheem. Buggin' slyly asks whether Raheem owns any music other than Public Enemy. But soon they commiserate about their experiences at Sal's Famous. Raheem entered Sal's and ordered two slices, but Sal wouldn't serve him until he silenced his music. Raheem doesn't shut down his box for anyone. But Sal was adamant, "no music, no rap, no music" in his pizzeria! Raheem's love for Sal's pizza (although not for Sal) won out. He grabbed his two slices and directly walked out Sal's door, with Public Enemy echoing back into Sal's Famous.

Buggin' seizes the opportunity to further his plan to boycott Sal's Famous. With Raheem at his side, the two kindred spirits march into Sal's at closing time demanding that Sal include African Americans on the Wall of Fame. The two are resolute, taking threatening postures. At the end of a scorching day, Sal is quick to return their animosity; he shouts at Raheem to turn off his "jungle music." This time Raheem refuses. Sal retrieves his baseball bat and bashes Raheem's radio. A fight ensues and the police arrive. The cops haul Buggin' and Raheem outside. Buggin' is quickly handcuffed, but the physically imposing Raheem resists (although not a lot). A white policeman uses his nightstick to restrain Raheem, but begins choking him in the process. Raheem begins gasping for air, but the policeman doesn't relent. A second policeman warns his partner, but the nightstick remains pinned to Raheem's neck. He dies. The police quickly drag away his body.

The neighborhood is ready to explode. Da Mayor emphatically declares that if anyone is to blame, it is the police—not Sal. Mookie takes a deep breath, but cannot heed Da Mayor's words. Mookie's friend is dead, at the hands of New York's finest. He finds a trashcan and tosses it through Sal's front window. This ignites a riot. Sal's Famous is quickly set ablaze. Raheem's radio and Sal's pictures begin to melt.

The crowd turns toward the adjacent Korean corner store. One of the older black men warn them, "You're next!" The Korean proprietor stands before his store, pathetically waving his broom like a lance. He screams, "I no white! I no white! I black! You, me, same!" This confuses the older black man, but his friends oddly concur. The Koreans thus avoid the fate of Sal's Famous. The police again arrive, this time with the fire department. But the officers are just as interested in squelching the riot as they are the fire. Many of the hoses are turned on the crowd. Later, as the building still smolders, Smiley sneaks in and pins a picture of Martin Luther King, Jr., and Malcolm X to Sal's charred wall.

Discussion Questions

1. Does Mookie "do the right thing" at the end of the film? Does he ever do the right thing? Does anyone? Why does Spike Lee entitle the film "Do the Right Thing"?

2. Is Sal a racist? Is anyone in the film not racist? (You may wish to review scene 16 when answering this question.) What, if anything, is morally objectionable about being a racist?
3. Consider the scene about the Koreans facing the angry mob (scene 29). What seems to be the moral message here?
4. Consider the passages by Martin Luther King, Jr., and Malcolm X at the very end of the film. Why might Lee include these?

3.5. REVIEWING THROUGH THE THREE MOVIES

1. In what ways do *Hotel Rwanda*, *The Joy Luck Club*, and/or *Do the Right Thing* (jointly or respectively) exemplify moral relativism or convey relativistic themes? In what ways, if any, can they be interpreted as providing counterexamples to moral relativism?
2. How might it be argued that Paul, An-Mei, and Mookie, respectively, serve as heroic characters? Is their heroism established because of, or in spite of, moral relativism? What is the moral significance of your answer?
3. All three films portray harms (of varying degrees) done to children: the Interhamwe machete, Ying-Ying's spiteful disregard of her son, and Mookie's conscious neglect of Hector. Are these acts impermissible *merely* because cultures generally have prohibitions against them? Explain.
4. Of the three films, which character seems to be most morally commendable and which seems the most morally deplorable? Justify your answers. What do you thereby conclude about moral relativism?
5. Reconsider the six movie quotes from the chapter and explain whether each, given the adjacent paragraphs, *illustrates* a point the author is making, *supplements* (or extends) a point the author is making, or *contrasts* (for emphasis) a point the author is making. Explain your answers.

NOTES

1. From *Folkways*, William Graham Sumner (Ginn and Company, 1907). Section headings and slight grammar emendations have been provided to aid reading comprehension.

2. It might be objected that this illicitly compares two subcultures (the American North and South). But this objection is easily answered. Simply imagine that Mookie currently works in Macon rather than New York. It then follows, on MR, that Mookie's life in Georgia *now* is no better or worse than it would be *then*.

CHAPTER 4

Divine Command Theory Ethics

FRAILTY (2001)

Director: Bill Paxton
Screenwriter: Brent Hanley

PLOT SUMMARY

God has willed this and you must obey God!

A twentysomething man named Meiks gains admittance to the FBI headquarters in Dallas, Texas. The agent in charge of the unresolved God's Hand serial murder case is called back into work. Agent Wesley Doyle greets his late-night visitor and they speak in his office. Meiks claims that he has pertinent information about the God's Hand investigation. But the story is at least twenty years old; Meiks begins to tell Doyle of his childhood in the nearby city of Thurman.

In 1979, the Meiks family consisted of two brothers, Fenton and Adam, and their father. Their mother died giving birth to Adam. They lived in a house next to a rose garden. Mr. Meiks worked as a mechanic in Jupiter. He'd get home about 5:30 every day and the three would have supper together, a meal that the boys typically prepared. They had only each other, as the extended family members had either died or moved away. They were like any loving, close-knit family. But one night that all changed.

Mr. Meiks barges into the boys' bedroom, quickly flicking on the light switch. He solemnly tells his sons that God sent an angel to tell him "the truth of this world" and God's purpose for his family. The father tells his sons that the end of the world is near. A war is going on between God's faithful and demons. God has chosen the Meiks family to destroy the demons, "pitching them out of this world." Mr. Meiks claims that they can see the demons, but other people can't. To everyone else, the demons look like normal people. Mr. Meiks continues by telling his sons that God will send three magical weapons to aid them. He finishes his surprising speech by chiding the boys: they cannot tell anyone about their mission. If they do, they put themselves and others in great danger.

BOX 4A: INSIDE *FRAILTY*

Frailty is a dark tale about a man and his two young sons. Don't overlook the opening credits; the still photos are contextually important for understanding the story. Furthermore, the movie is filmed in a series of "flashback" sequences, with one of the Meiks brothers (Matthew McConaughey) narrating his story to an FBI agent (Powers Boothe). Be on the lookout for the movie expressing a distinctive relationship between ethics and religion, heavily relying on God's causal activity as the truth-maker for ethically significant statements (moral judgments).

The most relevant segments for this message are scenes 4 to the end of scene 7. Scene 4 begins at 13:36 with a shot of Fenton lying awake in bed; Mr. Meiks soon enters the boys' bedroom. Scene 7 ends at 31:30, with Mr. Meiks saying, "Don't be afraid, son." Yet it might be worthwhile to continue viewing, if you can, through scene 8, which ends at 35:18, with Mr. Meiks saying, "Do you understand?" The movie progresses to reveal intriguing plot twists and familiar analogies. Skip ahead to the start of scene 20, beginning at 1:20:11; you'll see a car driving down a dark path. Continue viewing through scene 21, which ends at 1:27:22, signaled by a cutaway shot back to McConaughey in the present day. However, if possible, simply proceed to the end of the movie (1:35:30). Note, however, that scene 22 contains some disturbingly violent images between 1:30:00 and 1:30:15.

The film is very suspenseful and worthy of a full viewing. If you view all of it, you should be able to answer the trivia questions from box 4B. If you cannot view all of it, viewing the specified segments, along with carefully reading the plot summary, should provide you with a sufficient grasp of the film.

Weeks go by, but driving home from work one day, Mr. Meiks is drawn to a dilapidated barn in a desolate field. Inside, he finds an axe and a pair of work gloves; each seems to be bathed in divine light. Mr. Meiks surmises that these are magical weapons. He takes the axe and the gloves, and heads for home to show the boys. On a subsequent day, he comes home with a steel pipe. This is the third and final magical weapon. The Meiks family now waits for God to send them their first list of demons. They are ready to do battle, instruments of God's will.

Or, at least two of them are ready. The older son, Fenton, has his doubts. He wonders whether his father is "right in the head." His dismay intensifies when his father arrives from work with the first list of names. While repairing a car, the angel appeared wielding a flaming sword. Although the angel said nothing, Mr. Meiks quickly emerged from under the car, and began writing names on his notepad. Fenton peruses the list, stating, "These are people's names." His father assures him that they are not people, but actually demons. Adam subsequently appears with his own list of names. He announces that, he, too, had a divine vision. Mr. Meiks reads the list, but one of them is a boy who teases Adam at school. Adam admits that he fabricated the list. Mr. Meiks admonishes his younger son, "Destroying demons is a good thing, but killing people is bad." Fenton, witnessing the exchange, again looks at his father with accusing eyes. Perhaps Mr. Meiks also fabricated *his* list?

Mr. Meiks arrives home very late one night. He drops a young woman, bound and gagged, in his toolshed. Fenton, flashlight in hand, stumbles outside to discover the source of the racket. Adam soon follows. Fenton is horrified, but his father attempts to explain by saying that God came to him again and told him it was time to collect and destroy the first demon on the list. Fenton nevertheless pleads with his father to stop. Mr. Meiks vehemently replies, "But we are God's servants and his will must be served! Don't be afraid, son." Mr. Meiks turns back to the woman. He lays (ungloved) hands on the woman; this produces in him some sort of violent reaction, as if he were electrocuted. Shaken, he resolutely retrieves his axe, and "destroys" the "demon" before him. Adam looks on solemnly; Fenton is mortified. Mr. Meiks and his sons take the body to the rose garden and begin burying it. Fenton is sobbing. The father buries the body in a peculiar way, telling his boys that "the angel was very specific" about how to dispose of the body. Each demon must be buried in exactly this way. When Adam asks why they must bury the bodies in the rose garden in this strange way, Mr. Meiks admits that he isn't sure. His only answer is, "God chose it, just like he chose us I suppose." However, Fenton has become indignant. Mr. Meiks addresses him, "This is our job now, son. You got to accept that. . . . You can't stop it. We are doing God's work here."

A month goes by without any further killings. The family doesn't speak of their "work" during that time. But one day, the boys walk home from school only to find a new cargo van parked in the driveway. Their father informs them that he purchased the van in order to make their "work" easier. They take it to find the next demon. In broad daylight, they abduct a sixtysomething man. They take him back to the toolshed. When Mr. Meiks lays his (ungloved) hands on the man, another violent reaction ensues. He grabs his axe, informing the man, "God saw you, and you cannot escape God's wrath!" The boys bury the body in the rose garden just so.

Mr. Meiks senses Fenton's growing disbelief and anger. He wakes the boy early one morning. Mr. Meiks tells Fenton that the angel visited him again last night with disturbing news. Without disclosing the news to Fenton, Mr. Meiks commands that Fenton dig a hole in the backyard—one large enough to serve as a cellar for the toolshed. Mr. Meiks presents his son a shovel and then heads to work. As he leaves, he tells Fenton, "You just don't have any faith. That's why you can't see the truth. But we're gonna change that."

BOX 4B: *FRAILTY* TRIVIA

If your instructor assigns the film to be watched outside of class, you should be able to answer the following questions:

1. What movie does Adam want to see again?
2. Fenton has difficulty with which school subject?
3. What is the name of the first "demon" the father finds?
4. What color is the van the father buys?
5. Where does the Meiks family capture "demon" Edward March in broad daylight?
6. What is the name written on the axe?
7. What does Adam bring Fenton when Fenton is locked in the cellar?
8. Who kills Mr. Meiks?
9. Who killed the FBI agent's mother?
10. Of what county is Adam (as an adult) the sheriff?

Fenton is also told to pray to God for faith. Fenton dug the hole, but he did not pray. The three move the toolshed—again by hand—over the newly dug cellar. Mr. Meiks congratulates his sons, saying, "You boys did good, especially you, Fenton." Dejected, Fenton answers, "No. I just did what I was told."

Fenton finally musters the courage to tell the Thurman sheriff about his father's murderous behavior. The sheriff is very skeptical, but he eventually accompanies Fenton home and chats with Mr. Meiks. Fenton drags the sheriff to the toolshed and shows him the cellar. Still not convinced, the sheriff heads for his truck; Fenton desperately shouts up from the cellar that he can show him where the bodies are buried, in the rose garden. There is a moment of silence and then an ominous thud. The sheriff tumbles back down the cellar steps. Mr. Meiks slowly follows, axe in hand, and delivers a second, fatal blow. The Meiks family buries the sheriff in the same manner as the demons. Mr. Meiks is very remorseful, mumbling, "I had to protect the mission." He turns to Fenton and reassures his son, "Before tonight, I never killed a man." Fenton quickly replies, "I've seen you kill plenty." The father corrects him, "Those were demons. Why can't you see that!"

Mr. Meiks subsequently locks Fenton in the toolshed cellar. Again, he tells Fenton to pray to God. After seven days of being in the cellar, he has some sort of vision. His father and Adam unlock the trapdoor and take him into the house. Fenton eats heartily. In between ravenous bites, he tells the other two that he now better understands about demons. His father beams. Adam smiles. A week later, the three of them go to capture another demon. They find their man (demon) and with the use of the steel pipe, knock him unconscious. In the toolshed cellar, Mr. Meiks lays (ungloved) hands on the man; he assures his sons that it is a demon. He gives the axe to Fenton. Grasping it with both hands, Fenton is about to strike.

4.1. THINKING THROUGH THE MOVIE

Discussion Starter Questions

1. If you were young Fenton, how would you react to your father's sudden change in behavior?
2. What is the significance of the fact that the "magical weapons" are ordinary, everyday objects?
3. Mr. Meiks claims: "God has willed this and you must obey God!" Why might this claim be true? Do you agree? Explain.
4. What, if anything, morally justified Mr. Meiks's choice to kill the Thurman sheriff?
5. Why is the movie called "Frailty"?

Questions for Further Thought

1. The McConaughey character is clear that divine permission must be explicitly granted before demons are permissibly destroyed (scene 20, 1:25:23). Why was it necessary for the Meiks family to wait for God's order to destroy a demon? Why not simply lay ungloved hands on everyone they meet?
2. When Adam asks about burying demons in the rose garden (scene 8, 34:25), Mr. Meiks replies, "I don't know, son; God chose it, like God chose us." What does Mr.

Meiks's response imply about God's choices? Must God have reasons for the commands he makes? How are these questions metaethically significant?

3. After digging the cellar and moving the shed (scene 13, 55:20), Mr. Meiks announces, "You boys did good, especially you, Fenton." Fenton replies, "No. I just did what I was told." What is the difference, if any, between "doing what is right/good" and "doing what you're told?"

4. After spending a week in the cellar (scene 17, 1:10:13), Fenton claims, "God sent me a vision. It was then that I understood my destiny." How could Fenton distinguish a divine vision from hallucination? How could we, as third parties, distinguish Fenton's "vision" from those had by the father? How are these questions metaethically significant?

5. Note the affinities between the biblical story of Abraham and Isaac and Mr. Meiks and Fenton (see scene 20, 1:24:45). Compare and contrast these, highlighting their metaethical significance.

4.2. HISTORICAL SETTING

Euthyphro (excerpt)[1]

In this dialogue, Plato recounts a chance meeting between Euthyphro—a self-proclaimed expert on piety—and Socrates (for bibliographical information on Plato, please see chapter 1). Euthyphro confidently argues that he piously and, so, righteously, prosecutes his father for negligent homicide (the father allowed a murderous servant to die of exposure). Socrates beseeches Euthyphro to share his alleged knowledge of righteousness so that he can better defend himself against Meletus's (infamous) charges that he doesn't believe in the gods and corrupts the youth.

Preparing to Read

A. What are some relevantly important similarities and differences between the metaethical messages of *Frailty* and Plato's dialogue?

B. When critiquing a position, why is it most effective to retain the beliefs and assumptions of the opposing side? How does this relate to Socrates's critique of Euthyphro's views on piety (i.e., goodness)?

[Socrates Poses the Question]

Socrates: And I, my dear friend . . . am desirous of becoming your pupil. For I observe that no one appears to notice you, not even this Meletus; but his sharp eyes have found me out at once, and he has indicted me for impiety. And therefore, I implore you to tell me the nature of piety and impiety, which you said that you knew so well, and of murder, and of other offenses against the gods. What are they? Is not piety in every action always the same? And impiety, again, is it not always the opposite of piety, and also the same with itself, having, as impiety, one notion which includes whatever is impious?

Euthyphro: To be sure, Socrates.

Soc: And what is piety, and what is impiety? . . .

[Euthyphro's First Definition]

Euth: Piety, then, is that which is dear to the gods, and impiety is that which is not dear to them.

Soc: Very good, Euthyphro. . . . But whether what you say is true or not I cannot as yet tell, although I make no doubt that you will prove the truth of your words.

Euth: Of course.

Soc: Come, then, and let us examine what we are saying. That thing or person that is dear to the gods is pious, and that thing or person that is hateful to the gods is impious, these two being the extreme opposites of one another. Was not that said?

Euth: It was.

Soc: And well said?

Euth: Yes, Socrates, I thought so; it was certainly said.

Soc: And further, Euthyphro, the gods were admitted to have hostilities, hatreds, and differences?

Euth: Yes, that was also said.

Soc: And what sort of difference creates hostility and anger? Suppose for example that you and I, my good friend, differ about number; do differences of this sort make us quarrel . . . ? Do we not go at once to arithmetic, and put an end to them by a sum?

Euth: True.

Soc: Or suppose that we differ about magnitudes, do we not quickly end the differences by measuring?

Euth: Very true.

Soc: And we end a controversy about heavy and light by resorting to a weighing machine?

Euth: To be sure.

Soc: But what differences are there that cannot be thus decided, and which therefore make us angry . . . with one another? . . . I suggest that these hostilities arise when the matters of difference are the just and unjust, good and evil, honorable and dishonorable. Are not these the points about which men differ, and about which when we are unable satisfactorily to decide our differences, you and I and all of us quarrel, when we do quarrel?

Euth: Yes.

Soc: And the quarrels of the gods, noble Euthyphro, when they occur, are of a like nature?

Euth: Certainly.

Soc: They have differences of opinion, as you say, about good and evil, just and unjust, honorable and dishonorable: there would have been no quarrels among them, if there had been no such differences—would there now? . . .

Euth: Very true.

Soc: But, as you say, people regard the same things, some as just and others as unjust— about these they dispute; and so there arise wars and squabbles among them.

Euth: Very true.

Soc: Then the same things are hated by the gods and loved by the gods, and are both hateful and dear to them?

Euth: True.

Soc: And upon this view the same things, Euthyphro, will be pious and also impious?

Euth: So I should suppose.

Soc: Then, my friend, I remark with surprise that you have not answered the question that I asked. For I certainly did not ask you to tell me what action is both pious and impious: but now it would seem that what is loved by the gods is also hated by them. And therefore, Euthyphro, in thus prosecuting your father you may very likely be doing what is agreeable to Zeus but disagreeable to Athena, and what is acceptable to Hephaestus but unacceptable to Hera, and there may be other gods who have similar differences of opinion.

[Euthyphro's Initial Rejoinder]

Euth: But I believe, Socrates, that all the gods would be agreed as to the appropriateness of punishing a murderer: there would be no difference of opinion about that.

Soc: Well, but speaking of men, Euthyphro, did you ever hear any one arguing that a murderer or any sort of evil-doer ought to be let off?

Euth: I should rather say that these are the questions that they are always arguing, especially in courts of law: they commit all sorts of crimes, and there is nothing that they will not do or say in their own defense.

Soc: But do they admit their guilt, Euthyphro, and yet say that they ought not to be punished?

Euth: No; they do not.

Soc: Then there are some things which they do not venture to say and do: for they do not venture to argue that the guilty are to be unpunished, but they deny their guilt, do they not?

Euth: Yes.

Soc: Then they do not argue that the evil-doer should not be punished, but they argue about the fact of who the evil-doer is, and what he did and when?

Euth: True.

Soc: And the gods are in the same case, if as you assert they quarrel about just and unjust, and some of them say while others deny that injustice is done among them. For surely neither god nor man will ever venture to say that the doer of injustice is not to be punished?

Euth: That is true, Socrates, in the main.

Soc: But they join issue about the particulars—gods and men alike; and, if they dispute at all, they dispute about some act which is called in question, and which by some is affirmed to be just, by others to be unjust. Is not that true?

Euth: Quite true.

Soc: Well then, my dear friend Euthyphro, do tell me, for my better instruction and information, what proof have you that in the opinion of all the gods about a servant who is guilty of murder, and is put in chains by the master of the dead man, and dies because he is put in chains before he who bound him can learn from the interpreters of the gods what he ought to do with him, dies unjustly; and on behalf of the dead man a son ought to proceed against his father and accuse him of murder. How would you show that all the gods absolutely agree in approving of his act?

Euth: It will be a difficult task; but I could make the matter very clear indeed to you.

Soc: I understand; you mean to say that I am not so quick of apprehension as the judges: for to them you will be sure to prove that the act is unjust, and hateful to the gods.

Euth: Yes indeed, Socrates; at least if they will listen to me.

Soc: But they will be sure to listen if they find that you are a good speaker. There was a notion that came into my mind while you were speaking; I said to myself: "Well, what if Euthyphro does prove to me that all the gods regarded the death of the servant as unjust, how do I know anything more of the nature of piety and impiety? For granting that this action may be hateful to the gods, still piety and impiety are not adequately defined by these distinctions, for that which is hateful to the gods has been shown to be also pleasing and dear to them." And therefore, Euthyphro, I do not ask you to prove this; I will suppose, if you like, that all the gods condemn and abominate such an action. But I will amend the definition so far as to say that what all the gods hate is impious, and what they love pious or holy; and what some of them love and others hate is both or neither. Shall this be our definition of piety and impiety?

Euth: Why not, Socrates?

Soc: Why not! Certainly, as far as I am concerned, Euthyphro, there is no reason why not. But whether this admission will greatly assist you in the task of instructing me as you promised, is a matter for you to consider.

[The Second Definition]

Euth: Yes, I should say that what all the gods love is pious and holy, and the opposite which they all hate, impious.

Soc: Ought we to inquire into the truth of this, Euthyphro, or simply to accept the mere statement on our own authority and that of others?

Euth: We should inquire; and I believe that the statement will stand the test of enquiry.

Soc: We shall know better, my good friend, in a little while. The point that I should first wish to understand is whether the pious or holy is beloved by the gods because it is holy, or holy because it is beloved of the gods.

Euth: I do not understand your meaning, Socrates.

Soc: I will endeavor to explain: we speak of carrying and we speak of being carried, of leading and being led, seeing and being seen. You know that in all such cases there is a difference, and you know also in what the difference lies?

Euth: I think that I understand.

Soc: And is not that which is beloved distinct from that which [or who] loves?

Euth: Certainly.

Soc: Well, and now tell me, is that which is carried in this state of carrying because it is carried, or for some other reason?

Euth: No; that is the reason.

Soc: And the same is true of what is led and of what is seen?

Euth: True. . . .

Soc: And the same holds as in the previous instances; the state of being loved follows the act of loving.

Euth: Certainly.

Soc: And what do you say of piety, Euthyphro: is not piety, according to your definition, loved by all the gods?

Euth: Yes.

Soc: Because it is pious or holy, or for some other reason?

Euth: No, that is the reason.

Soc: It is loved because it is holy, not holy because it is loved?

Euth: Yes.

Soc: And that which is dear to the gods is loved by them, and is in a state to be loved of them because it is loved of them?

Euth: Certainly.

Soc: Then that which is dear to the gods, Euthyphro, is not holy, nor is that which is holy loved of the gods, as you affirm; but they are two different things.

Euth: How do you mean, Socrates?

Soc: I mean to say that the holy has been acknowledged (by us) to be loved of the gods because it is holy, not to be holy because it is loved.

Euth: Yes.

Soc: But that which is dear to the gods is dear to them because it is loved by them, not loved by them because it is dear to them.

Euth: True.

Soc: But, friend Euthyphro, if that which is holy is the same with that which is dear to the gods, and is loved because it is holy, then that which is dear to the gods would have been loved as being dear to the gods; but if that which is dear to the gods is dear to them because loved by them, then that which is holy would have been holy because loved by them. But now you see that the reverse is the case, and that they are quite different from one another. For one is of a kind to be loved because it is loved, and the other is loved because it is of a kind to be loved. Thus you appear to me, Euthyphro, when I ask you what is the essence of piety, to offer an attribute only, and not the essence—the attribute of being loved by all the gods. But you still refuse to explain to me the nature of piety. And therefore, if you please, I will ask you not to hide your treasure, but to tell me once more what piety really is, whether dear to the gods or not (for that is a matter about which we will not quarrel); and what is impiety?

Euth: I really do not know, Socrates, how to express what I mean. For somehow or other our arguments, on whatever ground we rest them, seem to turn round and walk away from us.

Review Questions

1. What is Socrates's criticism of Euthyphro's proposal to define piety/goodness as that which the gods hold dear? Put this into your own words.
2. How does Euthyphro attempt to save his proposal from Socrates's critique? Explain.
3. Regarding Euthyphro's second proposed definition, what is the point of Socrates asking why all the gods would love something?

4.3. DISCUSSION AND ANALYSIS

Debates about an ethics of divine command famously begin with Plato's recounting of the discussion between Socrates and Euthyphro. Ancient Athenians tended to believe that morally appropriate action was directly linked to divine approval. Religious piety was more or less identical to righteousness, which is to say morally right or good, and impiety was similarly equated with morally wrong or bad. Socrates was among the apparent minority of Athenians who critically explored the relationship between piety and moral permissibility.

From Polytheism to Monotheism

It's tempting to argue that the source of Euthyphro's philosophical difficulties stem from the fact that ancient Greece was *polytheistic*. After all, it is a staple of Greek mythology that the gods disagree about what is just or unjust. It was widely believed, for example, that Hera cherishes marital fidelity but Zeus doesn't, and that Athena cherishes wisdom over beauty, but Aphrodite seems to cherish beauty over wisdom. Socrates argues that if the gods disagree about cherishing the same thing (as do Zeus and Hera about marital fidelity), then, if Euthyphro's first definition is correct, it follows that the same thing (marital fidelity) can be both pious and impious at the same time. But it seems clear that nothing can be both pious and impious at the same time, just as no person can be both six feet tall and not six feet tall at the same time. It therefore follows that Euthyphro's first definition (per the excerpt) entails a contradiction and cannot be correct.

BOX 4C: LEARNING OUTCOMES

Upon carefully studying this chapter, students should better comprehend and be able to explain:

- What divine command theory (DCT) is, and the (philosophical and theological) reasons for and against its truth.
- How studying DCT in its original polytheistic form via Plato's *Euthyphro* is useful for better understanding contemporary forms of DCT.
- How DCT can be compared and contrasted to its competitors SES and MR.
- How the films *Frailty*, *Evan Almighty*, and *The Boondock Saints*, respectively and jointly, are expressive of themes relevant to DCT.

But what if an ethics of divine command is placed in a *monotheistic* setting? No opportunity for divine disagreement arises because only one God—the One God—exists. This would also seemingly make Euthyphro's second definition (per the excerpt) irrelevant. We would no longer need to worry about what *all* the gods cherish or why they *uniformly* decide to cherish those things. In turn, this arguably seems to circumvent the implicit criticism of Socrates's celebrated question posed to Euthyphro: whether something is pious (righteous) because it is worthy of their uniform approval or merely because all the gods, perhaps arbitrarily, agree to cherish it. Furthermore, the all-powerful, all-knowing, all-loving Creator of heaven and earth seems to be a much better candidate for handing down the moral law than are the various Greek gods with their petty jealousies and idiosyncrasies, including Zeus. Finally, the Decalogue (Ten Commandments) itself seems supportive of the idea that right and wrong is directly linked to God's commands. The idea is that ethical judgments are made true by God's will, as expressed in authoritative religious texts (and not epic tales by Homer), or revealed in authentic, personal religious experiences (should there be any—with Mr. Meiks or Evan Baxter from *Evan Almighty* serving as hypothetical examples). Thus monotheism (and not polytheism) provides the proper foundation for linking ethics and religion. These ideas are expressive of a metaethical theory known as divine command theory (DCT).

Contemporary Divine Command Theory

It seems to be an essential feature of DCT that ethical judgments are made true *solely* by divine decree or command. That God's will is the only truth-maker for ethically significant judgments entails that there are no moral truths prior to divine decree. This entails that some act is obligatory or forbidden merely because—and for no other reason than—God deems it so. This also entails that whatever God commands (forbids), indeed whatever God *would* command (forbid), is thereby—and for that reason alone—morally obligatory (impermissible). Furthermore, moral

> "I put evil men behind bars, but the law has miles of red tape and loopholes. . . . I found out there are two guys who fix the situation with an iron fist, as if they had God's permission." —*The Boondock Saints*, scene 13

goodness is also derivative upon the divine will. Something is morally good only if God approves of it and God's approval is expressive of his will. Someone is morally good only if God approves of her. God's approval in this case may mean that the person regularly follows God's commands, but it may (again) simply be expressive of divine fiat. In any event, just as moral rightness (wrongness) is simply whatever God commands (forbids), moral goodness is nothing over or above God's approbation.

If DCT is true, then God's decrees are binding on everyone, regardless of one's faith—including atheists. This appears to be politically incorrect, but it achieves what simple ethical subjectivism (SES) and moral relativism (MR) could not: a basis for moral truth and genuine moral disagreement, each of which spans all persons and cultures. It thereby makes significant strides toward ethical objectivity. Ethics becomes objective or universal in the sense that it is not a human construction. We don't create or invent moral truth by coming to have certain beliefs; we must discover it through a source external to us.

Frailty, Lions Gate Films, 2001. Mr. Meiks (Bill Paxon, right) enlists the help of his two young sons in his divinely inspired quest to rid the world of demons. (Moviegoods, Inc.)

That source is God and only God, via his commands of us. All moral truths are at God's discretion. Consider in *Frailty* that the one (adult) Meiks brother did not "come for" the other until God put the second on the list, even though the first knew that he was a demon. As the grown Meiks brother told the FBI agent, "But I had to wait until God put him on my list. To come before that would be murder." Recall that the Meiks family was chosen by God to be his "hands" on earth. Their solemn task is to "destroy" demons. However, God alone evidently decides who is a demon and when any demon should be destroyed. For the Meiks family to act without God's explicit approbation—even though God has charged them to destroy demons on other occasions—would be morally wrong.

> "God commanded me to build an ark. We have to prepare ourselves!"—*Evan Almighty*, scene 12

This fictive example reminds us of an important entailment of DCT: an act is morally right (obligatory) or wrong (impermissible) *only* because God deems it. Adultery is wrong because—and only because—God says so. Being honest is good because—and only because—God approves of it. There is nothing inherently wrong about adultery and nothing inherently good about honesty. If God were to command us to commit adultery on every third Friday of the month, then we are obligated to act accordingly, and practicing fidelity (on that day) would be morally wrong. If God were to forbid honesty—either completely or to only a few—then practicing honesty would be morally wrong (for those whom God had specified).

DCT may seem initially plausible because it provides straightforward answers to two difficult questions pertaining to ethics. The first asks: What is my guide in moral matters? The DCT-defender answers: authoritative scripture. Thus the Bible or Qur'an, as representative of God's word, serves as a source for discovering moral truth. Scripture can be consulted analogous to how a health care professional consults the *Physicians' Desk Reference* guide. The second question asks: Why should I do the right thing? To this question, the DCT-defender answers: Out of concern for your eternal soul. This all but eliminates any apathy about keeping one's obligations. The DCT-defender can thereby echo Mr. Meiks's statement, "God has willed this and you must obey God!" Furthermore, on standard accounts, God is omniscient, which means (roughly) that God knows all truths and believes none that are false. So, if you act contrary to his will, he knows it. Those who disobey are liable to meet up with

> "You thought no one saw you. But God saw you, and you cannot escape God's wrath!"
> —*Frailty*, scene 11

the likes of the Meiks family or the MacManus brothers from *The Boondock Saints*. The latter swiftly enact the biblical credo, "Destroy all that is evil so that which is good can flourish." Thus all transgressors are punished, either immediately from God's chosen—or by God himself at the time of final judgment.

Some DCT-defenders appeal to God's causal role as the omnipotent Creator to further support their theory. Omnipotence is difficult to define quickly, but it at least includes being able to accomplish all tasks that can be done (without incurring an obvious logical contradiction). It is often thought that God's omnipotence allows him to create *ex nihilo*, that is, from nothing. Consider the physical world and its covering laws of physics, chemistry, and biology. Theists (those who believe in the One God) invariably hold that any complete explanation of the natural world must include the Creator. Indeed, theists believe that the natural world exists (as it does) only because of God's causal activity. But just like the natural world, the "moral world" had to come from somewhere. Therefore, DCT-defenders believe that any complete account of the "moral world" must also include the Creator's causal input. And just as the natural world, and its subsequent covering laws, originated solely with the Creator *ex nihilo*, so, too, does the "moral world" and it subsequent laws. Furthermore, just as God can suspend or alter the laws of nature (causing a miracle) even though they are objective and universal, God can suspend or alter the moral law even though it applies objectively or universally to all creatures; thus, the shape of the natural *and* moral worlds is completely at God's discretion. But only an omnipotent being can accomplish these causally creative tasks, which makes God the only serious candidate for being the Creator (and sustainer) of the moral world. Hence, DCT.

> "I remember creating this valley. . . . I wanted you to see the original design." —*Evan Almighty*, scene 7

DCT-defenders bolster the argument from God's causal activity by further claiming that the preexistence of moral truth is inconsistent with God's sovereignty. If moral truths existed independent of God's causal activity, then God is presumably bound by the same moral standards as we are; however, this impinges upon God's unique status as Creator, radically different from creatures. God is "first cause" among all things—physical and ethical—and any position that denigrates his exalted metaphysical status should be rejected. Therefore, there cannot be any moral truths apart from God's causal activity, which affirms DCT.

Apart from these theologically based arguments, some attempt to defend DCT by examining the philosophical nature or essence of a law. This examination begins with the intuition that any binding law without a lawgiver—someone bringing the law into existence—is incredibly suspicious. Any moral law without a moral lawgiver is thereby also dubious. Consider the nature of civil law (or legal codes). Imagine that you are driving down the highway in excess of the legal speed limit and you are subsequently pulled over by a law enforcement official. Were you to ask about the origins of the legal limit in this locale and the officer said, "No one decided that you cannot drive faster than fifteen miles an hour on this road—that's just the way it is," you would be suspicious indeed. How can there by a speed limit law without a legislative body mandating it? Analogously, if one were to inquire about the origins of an objective or universal moral law—one that allegedly applies to *all* locales—and you were subsequently informed, "that's just the way it is," you would be equally suspicious. An initially plausible response would be: Well, *someone*, and a very special someone at that, had to mandate such a law! So, if there are no binding moral laws without a lawgiver, and the goal is to establish the existence of moral truths that apply cross-culturally in lawlike fashion, there can be no better candidate than God. But, again, this is tantamount to accepting DCT.

Contra Divine Command Theory

An obvious reaction to the arguments for DCT is to simply deny God's existence. If God doesn't exist, God can't command anything. But remember Socrates. He teaches that criticisms of another's belief set are much more effective if you work within it rather than infusing it with foreign beliefs. His discussion with Euthyphro about piety is a prime example of this. So, without flatly denying God's existence, or the possibility of genuine religious experience, or the eventuality that religion and ethics might be related in some way, the following paragraphs offer a critique of DCT that even the most devout theist must carefully consider.

The first objection begins by reminding us that if DCT is true, then no behavior is obligatory or impermissible lacking divine decree. Apart from God's explicit decree(s) all behavior is presumably morally neutral; no behavior is inherently good or evil. Therefore, nothing morally speaking constrains God's decrees. God's wishes on such things as rape, kindness, murder, and honesty always could have been the opposite of what we typically take them to be; the first and third could have been commanded by God and the second and fourth could have been forbidden by God. Furthermore, there does not seem to be anything preventing God from changing his wishes on these matters at some time in the future. If God is indeed the sole author of the moral law, then—like all authors—God could have had the "story" of ethics turn out differently and, for that matter, could still have it turn out differently.

Therefore, the objection from ethical arbitrariness stems from that fact that lacking any preexisting moral truths, an omnipotent God is at liberty to make anything he wishes obligatory. This means that if DCT is true, even such behaviors as raping a child and torturing for pleasure are possibly morally obligatory. But many hold that there is something—all by itself—about raping or torturing another person that makes it impermissible. If so, then rape or torture for pleasure is *inherently* impermissible, and it is impossible for it to be otherwise. This leads many to believe that the content of morality is *not* arbitrary; it is simply implausible that the moral wrongness of rape or torture be capriciously grounded. And if this is correct, it follows that DCT is false.

There are interesting historical and fictitious examples of how moral truth becomes objectionably arbitrary if DCT is true. The first is the famous (or infamous) story of Abraham and his son Isaac. According to the Old Testament, God commanded Abraham to sacrifice his (innocent) son Isaac. But God later presented Moses the Ten Commandments and among them is the prohibition of killing the innocent. We thus apparently have a case where God has (actually) offered different decrees about the same topic. A cursory study of the Old Testament also has God decreeing that the Israelites should "despoil" or "plunder" the Egyptians as they flee captivity (Ex. 3:20–22), and commanding Samuel to purposely deceive Saul (1 Sam. 16:1–3). But these decrees seemingly contravene the eighth and ninth commandments, respectively. On DCT, then, it indeed seems that the permissibility of murder, stealing, or dishonesty depends on nothing apart from divine decree; this solidifies the claim that DCT entails an objectionable ethical arbitrariness.[2]

> "Whosoever shed my blood, by man shall his blood be shed." — *The Boondock Saints*, scene 6

For a fictive example, consider at the end of *Evan Almighty* when Morgan Freeman—as God—proclaims an *eleventh* commandment: Thou shall do the dance. Of course this is "simply a movie," but the point remains: if DCT is true, God has the ability to bestow additional commandments, regardless of their content, and we must thereby obey them. If we don't, we act impermissibly (even if it is our refusal to do Steve Carell's silly dance). Therefore, we have further evidence that DCT is open to the charge of arbitrariness. If the theory is true, ethics is merely a matter of divine whim. The fact that examples like these are hypothetical or fictional does not detract from their force.

DCT-defenders invariably find this last objection dubious. They stress the point that we are worrying about *merely* hypothetical (or fictional) situations; God would never *actually* command us to rape a child or torture for pleasure. Such acts are just "plain wrong" and God would never require us to do them. Indeed, God would only command what is best for us (no doubt leaving Carrell's dance forever off the list). However, this rejoinder doesn't explain away the (alleged) historical examples about Abraham, the Egyptians, and Samuel. Nevertheless, it is conceptually flawed for other reasons. First, it seems to reinforce the intuition that moral truth is *not* arbitrary. Reconsider the attempted response: God would never command us to do acts that are "plain wrong," which is to say *inherently* evil acts. If some behaviors are inherently good or evil, then they are so apart from God's decree. But if DCT is true, no acts are obligatory (good) or impermissible (evil) apart from God's will. So, in making this sort of move, the DCT-defender actually falsifies her theory. Second, the claim that God only commands what is best for us presupposes a moral standard apart from God's decree, namely, whatever is in our overall best interests (regardless of what that notion entails). If DCT is true, then there is *no* moral standard apart from God's will.[3] The only reason, on DCT, that an act is obligatory or impermissible is God has so decreed. Thus, responses like these actually show how DCT is false rather than how it escapes the objection that ethics is illicitly arbitrary.

Some theists are initially willing to accept the position that ethics arbitrarily depends on divine whim, resolutely declaring that God's will be done, not unlike Mr. Meiks's

Evan Almighty, Universal Pictures, 2007. Morgan Freeman reprises his role as "God" in *Evan Almighty*, the sequel to *Bruce Almighty*. (Moviemarket, Inc.)

charge to his son. However, this resolution raises practical and conceptual concerns. The practical concerns begin with religious experience. Some theists claim that God has directly "spoken to them," perhaps in a way not unlike Evan Baxter from *Evan Almighty*. Other theists claim that they have had *some* sort of less explicit religious experience, perhaps analogously to Mr. Meiks from *Frailty* or the MacManus brothers from *The Boondock Saints*. In any event, such theists believe that God has uniquely divulged his wishes to them, spurring them to take action. And there are more traditional examples of this—from Moses and the burning bush to Mohammad's transmittal of the Qur'an. But the arbitrariness problem rears its head again for DCT. Recall that, if DCT is true, God is the sole author of the moral law; he is at complete liberty to construct or alter it as he pleases. But this entails that theists have no way to determine heavenly messages from demonic. If God can require anything of us, by what means could any religious person determine whether the voice he hears or vision he sees is actually Satan and not God? Let's call this the demonic voices objection to DCT.

For DCT to claim support from religious experience, there must be evidence that the relevant experiences are veridical. When God (Morgan Freeman) appears to Evan at the woodpile outside his house, the latter quickly seeks to substantiate the former's divine status. Evan asks him to provide information that no one else could know in order to somehow verify that the man speaking to him is indeed God. When Mr. Meiks presents the first list of demons to his sons, the oldest son reacts very suspiciously. He reminds his father that "these are people's names," and then bravely suggests that his father isn't "right in the head." The issue is driven home when Mr. Meiks disparages the younger son's list of alleged demons. From a third person perspective, like that of the older son, how could anyone distinguish a genuine "demon list" from a false one? The MacManus brothers merely undergo some sort of (alleged) quasi-baptism via the dripping water from the ceiling of their holding cell; they never question the validity of their shared, revelatory experience. But in order for the relevant experiences to have any merit whatsoever, there must be some sort of accessible evidence that substantiates its divine origins. At the *very* least, one might proceed by carefully examining the content of the message. If it commands us to perform reprehensible acts (as was seemingly the historical case with Son of

> "But we are God's servants and his will must be served!"
> —*Frailty,* scene 7

Sam in the 1970s), then this is evidence that the voice is demonic (or simply illusory) and not divine. But the DCT-defender cannot say this. If DCT is true, then the content of the message *cannot* be a reliable guide to its source. God is at complete liberty to command *anything* of us, even if it contravenes everything we currently believe about appropriate behavior. And, again, if some theists attempt to counter that God would never command us to do (inherently) detestable acts like rape, maiming, or torture, so the content of the message is reliable, then this is (again) actually evidence that DCT should be rejected. Therefore, even devout theists have good reason to resist DCT; if they don't, they forfeit the possibility of religious experience providing moral guidance.

The more conceptual concern with ethical arbitrariness serves as a third objection to DCT. Theists are deeply committed to the idea that God is supremely worthy of our loving worship and praise. After all, God is morally perfect and unsurpassably good (omnibenevolent), thus representing an ideal to which all human beings should strive. Therefore, theists invariably take the claim 'God is good' and, by implication, 'God's acts are good' to be significant truths. Because issuing a command is a kind of act, it also follows that theists are deeply committed to the truth of 'God's commands are good'. However, DCT impacts God's goodness in a surprising way.

Given DCT, there seem to be only two ways to define moral goodness with respect to (moral) agents. The first (plausibly) entails that someone is good if she regularly does what is morally right (and avoids what is morally wrong). But for DCT, recall that moral rightness is merely a matter of divine decree; an act is right if and only if (and for no other reason than) God commands it. Therefore, being a good person is merely a matter of regularly doing what God commands of you. So, it seems that Abraham was a good person because he regularly upheld God's will, and probably people like Mr. Meiks and the MacManus brothers would also qualify as morally good people for the very same reason. However, DCT is also committed to the possibility that God finds favor with those who don't follow his commands. This insight leads to the second strategy: someone is morally good simply if God approves of her. God's approval is *not* necessarily tied to a person's regularly upholding God's commands. If it were, then there would be morally significant truths that exist apart from divine decree. Therefore, who God approves of, analogous to which commands he makes, is a matter of divine whim. And this entails that the DCT-defender cannot take refuge in the more plausible first strategy for determining morally good persons because it is not necessarily those who regularly follow God's commands. This leaves DCT-defenders with no (practical) way to discern who is morally good.

But the conceptual difficulty truly manifests with *God's* (moral) goodness. Consider again the two ways DCT proffers to determine moral goodness. On the one hand, if being a good moral agent were a matter of regularly upholding God's will, then God's goodness would merely be a matter of regularly enacting what God wants. But God is omnipotent; God can do anything he wishes.[4] This means that God's goodness is merely a matter of acting as God does. It also means that God would be equally morally good had he decided to do the exact opposite of what he does. No matter what the omnipotent creator does is thereby right (or good). On this account, then, God's goodness becomes completely trivial and meaningless; the belief 'God is good' thereby ceases to be significantly important (as does the belief that God is perfect). As the famous German philosopher Gottfried Leibniz once remarked, "In saying, therefore, that things are not good according to any [preexisting] standard of goodness, but simply by the will of God, it seems to me that one destroys, without realizing it, all the love of God and all his glory; for why praise him for what he has done if he would be equally praiseworthy in doing the exact contrary?"[5] On the other hand, if being a good person is simply a matter of enjoying God's approval (which, recall, it seems to be if DCT is true), then God's goodness is merely a matter of God approving of himself. But being morally good certainly involves more than simply approving of yourself. After all, everyone presumably approves of his or her own (voluntary) actions, regardless of who one is or what one does. It's likely that Hitler and Stalin approved of their decisions and actions, but they were not thereby morally good people.

Accordingly, if moral truth becomes arbitrary, then God's goodness—his being morally perfect or unsurpassably good—becomes empty and insignificant on either DCT-friendly account of moral goodness. Note, however, that the objection is not that we, as human beings, have no way to fathom God's unsurpassable goodness. The issue is not merely a matter of the cognitive limitations of finite minds. It is rather that if DCT is true, it becomes simply impossible to intelligibly hold that God is good in any significant (nontrivial) sense. No theist can reasonably accept the idea that God's unsurpassable goodness is anything less than superlative; after all, this is why theists lovingly worship and praise God in the first place. Therefore, on grounds that it renders ethical truth arbitrary, provides an uninformative account of moral goodness, and deflates God's moral status, we now have ethical and religious reasons for rejecting DCT.

Recent Modifications and Enduring Concerns

Some have recognized the force of these interlocking objections and have recently offered "modified" versions of the DCT. The most popular modification is to ground God's goodness in God's loving nature or essence.[6] It is unthinkable, they believe, for God to command us to do anything that isn't loving. Therefore, on modified DCT, God's commands cannot be arbitrary. Moreover, because not even God can choose his essence, then God's goodness cannot merely be a function of enacting his will, keeping the significance of God's goodness conceptually intact. *Evan Almighty* manages to reflect modified divine command theories in at least one instructive way. God asks Evan to build an ark. When Evan asks why, God answers, "Let's just say whatever I do, I do because I love you." The movie is plausibly interpreted as conveying the idea that acts of random kindness are good because they express love; they are not good merely because God approves of them.

Modified divine command theorists would agree; all of God's commands are made from love, which is the supreme value.

Evan Almighty is also instructive in terms of distinguishing modified-DCT from classic (monotheistic) DCT in the following way. Recall from the movie that the term "ARK" also stands in for "acts of random kindness." In building the ark, Evan was also spreading kindness. But if classic DCT is true, then "ARK" is inherently no better or worse than "ARC": acts of random cruelty. Not only do the two terms sound the same, but classic DCT holds that, prior to God's approbation, they are morally equivalent (or the same). Furthermore, had God, per his omnipotence, commanded Evan to perform acts of random cruelty, then that is what he would be morally obligated to do. Modified accounts of DCT disagree. Its defenders hold that there is a significant and inherent difference between acts of kindness and cruelty. God's essential nature as loving makes it impossible for God to command acts of random cruelty.

However, it is not entirely clear that this sort of modification is successful in saving DCT. First, the modified account entails that, necessarily, it is morally good to be loving. But this entails that the source of moral goodness is independent of divine decree, which is inconsistent with (classic) DCT. Second, God's commands are (on the modified account) constrained by and merely expressive of the value of love. Therefore, modified theories reject the idea that God's will *and God's will alone* is the source of all true ethical statements, an essential feature of DCT. Modified theories see God's nature as foundational and God's will as merely expressive of the foundation. This entails that an essentially loving God cannot command us to perform cruel acts. Were the being we recognize as God to command us to perform cruel acts, then we would have reason to think that the being in question is not God after all, or we would be justified in not upholding the command (or both). Therefore, it's far from clear that modified DCT qualifies as a version of DCT.

Some modified DCT-defenders might quibble with this quick assessment. Nevertheless, modified theories ultimately raise a venerable problem for DCT-sympathizers, which harkens back to Plato's *Euthyphro*. Recall that Socrates asks Euthyphro: Is an act right or good (pious) because the gods approve of it, or do they approve of it because it is right or good (pious)? The same sort of question can be asked of DCT: Is an act right or good because God commands it, or does God command it because it is right or good? The classic (nonmodified) divine command theorist must answer that an act is right (or good) merely and only because God commands it. But the modified divine command theorist disagrees, as do most philosophers. The modified DCT-defender holds that God commands an act because it is already right or (more likely) good, with the good defined as (roughly) "that which is loving." Thus modified theories are importantly different from a traditional version of DCT.

Because Socrates's famous question of Euthyphro can also be asked of the monotheist, it seems that versions of DCT grounded in the One God do not substantively improve upon their pagan, polytheistic roots after all. To say an act is right (or good) merely and only because God commands it is to embrace ethical arbitrariness; furthermore, as Socrates might say, it doesn't even begin to capture the essence of rightness (or goodness). To say that God commands an act because it is expressive of love avoids ethical arbitrariness; as Socrates might say, it makes strides toward an essence of rightness or (at least) goodness. God would then have a reason justifying his command, but it is that *reason*—and not God's will itself—that ultimately grounds the moral truth in question. However, to embrace this horn of Euthyphro's dilemma—via a modified DCT or some other way—all but eliminates God's causal role as author of the moral law. And if God is not the sole author of the moral law, then (classic) DCT is false.[7]

Concluding Insights

Religiously speaking, DCT (especially in its classic, nonmodified form) seemingly offers a skewed picture of the divine nature. It has been argued (via the emptiness objection) that God's omnipotence swallows up God's omnibenevolence; however, DCT also renders God's omniscience irrelevant to moral matters. If it is impossible for God to have a moral reason for making one command over another—because on DCT moral truths only come into existence *after* divine decree—then there is nothing for God to know morally speaking about the situation that would aid him in making the command he does. Any relevant divine knowledge of the moral world threatens DCT because, as knowledge requires truth, it entails the preexistence of moral truths not dependent on divine decree. But fortunately for theists, an alternative account of God's activity exists. It doesn't overly emphasize omnipotence at the expense of omnibenevolence. It affirms that God's omniscience guarantees that he knows all moral truths and has no false beliefs about ethics; it also guarantees that God knows how to best share those truths with us when necessary. God's omnibenevolence, safely intact, guarantees that he indeed (somehow) shares this knowledge with us for our benefit because he loves us and wants what is best for us. God's omnipotence guarantees that no internal flaw (selfishness, apathy) or external source (another being) prevents God from sharing his knowledge with us. But (classic) DCT must ultimately reject this alternative picture of God, which only serves as further reason to reject the theory.[8]

Metaethically speaking, the kind of objectivism (classic) DCT offers remains tainted with elements of SES, coupled with the idea that "might makes right." God, as the omnipotent divine personage, invents moral truths by mere fiat and has the resources to exact complete compliance. But neither SES nor "might makes right"–based theories seem metaethically defensible. Therefore, although DCT makes important strides toward ethical objectivism, the search for a more satisfying account of it continues. Seemingly, the metaethical goal is to articulate and defend an account of moral truth that exists apart from divine decree.

4.4. TWO ADDITIONAL FILMS

Evan Almighty (2007)

Director: Tom Shadyac
Screenwriter: Steve Oedekerk

Plot Summary

Let's just say whatever I do, I do because I love you.

Evan Baxter is leaving his Buffalo television news anchor chair to become a US congressman. His campaign slogan was "change the world." Although not an overly religious man,

Baxter prays the night before his first day of work. He admits that "with great power comes great responsibility" and he asks God to help him wield his new political power to the best of his abilities.

Evan's alarm awakes him at 6:14 the next morning, but he can't remember setting it for that time. He saunters off to the bathroom regardless, whispering his mantra: "I'm successful, powerful, handsome, happy." He arrives at his office, and his top assistant informs him that he has been asked to cosponsor a new bill with a prestigious senior congressman. Although the bill involves opening fringes of national forest land to developers, Evan quickly agrees to this opportunity to further his political career.

The number 614 shows up frequently in the days to come. It becomes his new work extension and his governmental license plates include it. In fact, the plate reads "GEN 614." This cannot be mere coincidence. In the midst of this, a man appears to Evan claiming to be God, asking whether Evan received his messages. He no doubt refers to the number 614. Evan looks up Genesis 6:14; it reads, "So make yourself an ark of gopher wood." The stately, but modern-looking man claiming to be God tells Evan, you build it and I'll fill it. Soon, pairs of animals begin showing up on his doorstep and following Evan to work. Birds begin flying into his windows. God tells Evan, "And if anyone asks what you're doing, tell them that a flood is coming."

Evan begins astounding physical transformations. He begins growing a beard. If he shaves it, it grows back almost immediately. Moreover, his hair and beard begin growing in an unkempt fashion. He somehow manages to buy the next eight lots next to his in the subdivision. Soon, large trucks arrive and leave great piles of wood and rudimentary construction implements. Evan begins reading *Arks for Dummies* and begins building. But Evan's wife is confused and she confronts him. He finally admits to her that "God appeared to me and told me to build an ark." She replies that "the boys need their father and I need my husband back."

Evan has missed a great deal of work. But on the day the land use bill he is cosponsoring is being discussed before Congress he is required to attend. He does so, but when it is his time to speak, he rises from his seat mysteriously looking a lot like Noah with his robes, full beard, and long hair (even though he left for work wearing a suit). More mysteriously, pairs of animals enter the hearing room to gather around Evan. Submitting to his circumstances, Evan tells Congress that there's going to be a flood. Congressman Long, now embarrassed for his association with Evan, replies, "This is the hottest, driest summer on record; who told you there is going to be a flood?" Evan replies, "God." Long is flabbergasted. He informs Evan that his name is being removed from the bill because "the stresses of this office are becoming too much for you." Evan interrupts, "No. No. You don't understand. God has commanded me to build an ark. We have to prepare ourselves!"

The proceedings were televised. Evan announced to the whole televised world that he and God "hang out a little." Evan returns home just in time to watch his wife and children leave for her mother's house. Evan asks her to reconsider. She answers, "Does God know that he is destroying our lives? Does God know that he's going to get you fired?" Evan: "Ya! He's trying to get me fired! That way, I'll have more time to work on the ark!" She frowns. They walk outside. As his wife and the kids drive away, Evan looks up and mutters, "I know, I know, whatever you do, you do because you love me."

During a stop at a roadside grill, a stately looking man very much resembling the man who spoke to Evan about the ark approaches Evan's wife. Striking up a conversation with her, the man suggests that many interpret the ark story incorrectly. It is not necessarily about God's wrath; it's a love story because the animals arrived in pairs and stood by each other. He continues, "When somebody prays for courage, does God provide courage or the opportunity to be courageous? If a family prays to become closer, does he zap them with warm fuzzy feelings or the opportunity to love one another?" As she looks away to consider his words, the stately man disappears. Nevertheless, his words stick. She returns with the kids to see that Evan has finished much of the ark's frame. His hair is completely white. The kids agree to help, but plead, "Don't make us do the dance anymore." Evan's wife adds, "Side by side, we will get out of this."

With the ark almost complete, Evan's staff pays a visit. They have discovered that Congressman Long has been behind development projects before. In fact, he was the driving force behind the development of Evan's subdivision. They further discovered that Long has "cut corners" in the past, for example, skipping important building code checkpoints. Evan demurs. He can't oppose Long or his new land development bill. He must finish the ark. Dismayed, his top assistant asks, "God told you to build an ark?" Evan immediately replies, "Yes." A different assistant interjects, "But did he tell you to make your friends believe in you and follow you here [Washington, DC] so you can make us look stupid?" Evan reassures them that they simply must have faith. But they are skeptical. Faith will not stop this bill; it will not stop Long.

Ironically, Long also pays Evan a visit, albeit with the local police in tow. Long attempts to stop Evan from finishing the ark, and Evan attempts to convince Long that he should stop destroying our national parks merely for financial gain. Neither is successful. Long leaves and instructs the police force to demolish the ark; after all, Evan does not have a building permit for the ark. As the police approach, storm clouds gather and thunder claps. Rain falls as the wrecking ball fires up. The police and other bystanders become worried. Was Evan right about the flood? But as quick as the storm rolls in, it dissipates. Free of their paralysis, the police move in again, but in the distance the waters rise again.

Discussion Questions

1. What leads Evan to believe that the Morgan Freeman character is God? Would this also convince you? Why or why not?
2. Is Evan morally obligated to build the ark, even though it does harm to his family and career (scene 13, roughly 56:55 into the film)? Explain.
3. Regarding scene 7 (roughly 32:55), why do you think that changing the world begins with one act of random kindness?
4. Are acts of random kindness (morally) good merely and only because God approves of them?

The Boondock Saints (1999)

Director and Screenwriter: Troy Duffy

Plot Summary

> Do not kill, do not rape, do not steal. These are not polite suggestions. . . . And those of you that ignore them . . . we will send you to whatever God you wish!

Connor and Murphy MacManus are (fraternal) twin brothers from Boston. They are devout Catholics, attending mass regularly. On one particular Sunday, the sermon's message is clear: It is bad to be evil, but it is worse to be a good person and do nothing against evil people. Connor turns to his brother and says, "I do believe that the monsignor's finally getting the point." Murphy nods, "Aye."

It's Saint Patrick's Day and the brothers meet their friend Roc at their favorite pub. Roc is a messenger boy for the Italian mob. "Doc," the elderly, addled-brained pub owner, informs them that the Russian mob is moving into the neighborhood. The Russians won't renew Doc's lease; the pub must soon close its doors forever. The three friends are dismayed, and Roc offers to talk to his superiors about it. But it's too late; three Russian mob soldiers enter, and tell Doc he must close now, on St. Patty's Day of all things. A brawl ensues, with the Russians badly embarrassed. The Russians track down Connor and Murphy the next morning. In a stunning display of brotherly love, the brothers are forced to kill the Russians in self-defense.

An FBI agent named Smecker has been assigned to the case. Some Bostonians are calling those responsible for the dead Russians "angels"; Smecker quickly adds, "but angels don't kill." The MacManuses turn themselves in. Smecker interrogates them himself, and determines that the brothers were indeed acting in self-defense. Smecker, like most people, becomes immediately impressed with the two young men. He informs the brothers that they are free to leave, but they ask to spend the night in a holding cell so as to avoid their rising public notoriety. They have already become local media darlings; the newspaper calls them "saints," no doubt referencing their devout Catholicism. But the night in the holding cell is less than peaceful. They attempt to sleep through a violent and torrential thunder storm. Rainwater leaks through the ceiling of their cell, dropping down upon their foreheads, crucifixes, and otherwise naked torsos. The two awaken simultaneously to a nondescript voice loosely quoting Genesis 9:5–6: "Whoever shed my blood by man shall his blood be shed." Connor faces Murphy and announces, "Destroy all that which is evil." Murphy turns to Connor and immediately adds, "So that which is good may flourish." They share a knowing half-smile, dress, and leave their cell to begin (as Murphy later puts it) their "new job."

The brothers begin their new career by executing eight influential members of the Russian mob. They place gold coins on each of their victim's eyes. Smecker investigates the crime scene and immediately recognizes the religious connotations. The brothers attempt to explain their "new job" to Roc. Roc, in disbelief, asks, "Anybody *you* think is evil? Don't you think that's a little weird, a little psycho?" Connor leans in to explain, "You know what I think is psycho, Roc? It is decent men with loving families. They turn on the news, you know what they see? They see rapists and murderers and child molesters. . . . And everywhere, everyone thinks the same thing, that someone should just go . . . kill them all." Roc immediately wants to be recruited. He impatiently asks, "Well, what do you do?" Connor dispassionately responds, "We haven't really got a system of deciding who, Roc. It's . . ." Roc interjects, "Me! I'm the one! I know where they live." The brothers accept Roc's offer to become *their* messenger boy. Roc first informs them about his "scumbag" boss who regularly visits a strip club. The three friends gain entrance, find Roc's boss, and shoot him without hesitation. They also execute two other club patrons they meet. Smecker is becoming obsessed with the case.

The local don, "Papa Jo," becomes nervous. He turns to his father's confidante. The retired Mafioso reminds Papa Jo about "Il Duce"—the Duke. The Duke, the mob's "cleaner" killing machine, has only two rules: no women, and no children. Papa Jo arranges for the Duke's parole and hires him to whack Roc. Unaware of Duke, Connor, Murphy, and Roc strive to rid the world of more Mafioso scumbags. But the latest mission ends awkwardly, with Roc using a billiard ball to kill the last mark. They nevertheless exit quietly, but the Duke is there waiting for them. The silence is broken by a hailstorm of bullets. The three friends manage to escape the Duke's first attack, but each is wounded. Roc's finger is shot off, and Smecker finds it in the bushes. Rather than include it as official evidence, Smecker places it in his pocket and uses it to secretly discover Roc's identity. Smecker remembers Roc; Roc visited the MacManuses at the police station. Smecker is convinced the brothers are also involved.

Smecker, like everyone else, realizes that the MacManus brothers never harm good people. They target criminals and moral degenerates. This leads him to a personal and professional crisis. After a night of heavy drinking, Smecker finds himself in a Catholic church, incidentally one that the MacManus brothers frequent. Smecker mindlessly enters a confessional; never having confessed to a priest, he claims his problem is more ethical than religious. He seeks advice. He explains to the priest that he has become disillusioned with the law and can't help but condone the brazen actions of the MacManus brothers. By what right do they act? Does God approve? He asks: "What should I do? Because I am a man who is supposed to uphold the law." The priest doubts that the brothers have received the sort of divine permission Smecker suggests, but he reminds Smecker that "the laws of God are higher than the laws of man." This leads Smecker to decide to help the brothers in their quest.

The three friends plan to invade Papa Jo's private residence in New York, and inform Smecker of this. The brothers' raid on Papa Jo's house does not go well; the three friends are captured. Tied to chairs in the basement, Papa Jo interrogates them. He kills Roc and orders his henchman to finish off the brothers. Having freed themselves, the brothers avenge their friend. They quickly dispatch Papa Jo's henchman (with some bizarre help from Smecker) and then begin their family ritual over Roc. They place coins on his eyes and recite in unison, "Shepherds we shall be for Thee, my Lord, for Thee. Our feet may swiftly carry out Thy command . . ." Just then, the Duke enters the room with both guns aimed at the brothers. He listens, holsters his guns, and finishes the MacManus family prayer, "So we shall flow a river forth to Thee, and teeming with souls shall it ever be." Now it only remains to be seen whether Connor and Murphy possess the "depth of faith to go as far as needed."

Discussion Questions

1. Is it true that, while evil people are bad, good people who do nothing about them are worse? What should be done about evil people?
2. From no photos to spraying ammonia to contaminate their blood samples, why are the MacManus brothers so concerned about keeping their identity a secret?
3. What is the MacManus brothers' "new job" exactly?
4. Is Smecker correct (scene 13, roughly 1:26:45 into the film) that God gave the brothers permission to act as they do, or is the priest correct in this response that God doesn't grant such permission?
5. Does Smecker act permissibly in aiding the MacManus brothers at the end of the film?

4.5. REVIEWING THROUGH THE THREE MOVIES

1. Compare and contrast the Meiks brothers with the MacManus brothers and Mr. Meiks with Evan Baxter. What morally significant issues arise as a result of this exercise?
2. Do careful viewings of *The Boondock Saints* and *Evan Almighty*, respectively, lead you to think that they affirm or deny DCT? Explain carefully.
3. If you were interviewed about the MacManus brothers (per the very end of *The Boondock Saints*), what would you argue about them? Do your arguments affirm or deny DCT?
4. Which character of the three films is most morally reprehensible? Explain. What is thus your implicit view of DCT?
5. Reconsider the six movie quotes from the chapter and explain whether each, given the adjacent paragraphs, *illustrates* a point the author is making, *supplements* (or extends) a point the author is making, or *contrasts* (for emphasis) a point the author is making. Explain your answers.

NOTES

1. Excerpted from *The Dialogues of Plato*, trans. Benjamin Jowlett (New York: Oxford University Press, 1920). Section headings and slight grammar emendations provided to aid reader comprehension.

2. Although some scholars rely on scripturally based arguments to support DCT, doing so ironically becomes problematic for the theory. First, scriptural passages are notoriously open to multiple interpretations (as *Evan Almighty* nicely reminds us of in scene 13 with its version of the true message of Noah and the flood). The Abraham and Isaac story is invariably reinterpreted so as to deflect its murderous message (but this is only testament to the aversion most have to a DCT reading). Second, even if scripture can be definitively interpreted, the various sources do not always present consistent messages on ethical significant topics. The Old Testament and Qur'an allow a man to divorce his wife for various reasons (including merely finding her displeasing), but disagree about the permissibility of remarrying your divorced wife. (Compare Deut. 24:1–5 with Qur'an 227, 230–33.) Both advise violent retaliation against one's enemies. (Compare I Sam. 15:1–18 with Qur'an 2: 190–94 and 216–18.) However, the New Testament forbids divorce (except in the lone case of infidelity) and violent retaliation against those who have harmed you. (See Matt. 5:31–32 on the former topic and Matt. 5:38–40, 43–46 on the latter.) Which source provides God's definitive view on these matters? Third, if DCT is true, scripture cannot (ultimately) provide God's definitive view of anything anyway, as God is always at liberty to change his mind about any morally significant topic.

3. This commitment is also problematic for the DCT-defender. On the one hand, DCT seems committed to it in order to preserve God's unique metaphysical status as creator of the natural and moral worlds. On the other hand, if there are no moral standards apart from God's decrees, it's unclear whether we can have *moral* reason to follow God's commands in the first place. At best, God might command us to follow his commands, but this only pushes the question back by providing one more command. It seems that 'We are morally obligated to keep God's commands' (or 'It is morally wrong not to follow God's commands') requires a source of truth apart from God commanding it; however, this is something DCT cannot consistently allow.

4. Most theists qualify this a bit, holding that God can perform any task so long as doing it does not involve making a contradiction true.

5. Gottfried Leibniz, *Discourse on Metaphysics*, sec. 2, trans. George R. Montgomery (1902).

6. Robert M. Adams is typically credited with this revision; see his "A Modified Divine Command Theory of Ethical Wrongness," in *Religion and Morality*, eds. Gene Outka and John P. Reader (New York: Anchor Press, 1973), 318–47.

7. Some contemporary theists follow William Alston's suggestions about navigating safely through this new dilemma. See "What Euthyphro Should Have Said," in *Philosophy of Religion*, ed. William Lane Craig (New Brunswick, NJ: Rutgers University Press, 2002), 283–98. For a critique of Alston's suggested aid for DCT, please see Dean A. Kowalski, "Remembering Alston's 'Evaluative Particularism,'" *Religious Studies* 47, no. 3 (2011): 1–22.

8. All of this presupposes that God exists, of course.

CHAPTER 5

Ethical Objectivism

THE CIDER HOUSE RULES (1999)
Director: Lasse Hallström
Screenwriter: John Irving

PLOT SUMMARY

You know, they ain't our rules. . . . We didn't write 'em. . . . We are supposed to make our own rules.

D r. Wilbur Larch became the sole resident physician at St. Cloud's orphanage hoping to become a hero. He soon discovered that in "the lovely sordid world of lost children, there were no heroes to be found." He thus became a "caretaker of many, but father of none." Yet he cared for the children diligently, affirming, "With each rule I make or break, my first priority is an orphan's future." But Larch showered one boy—Homer Wells—with extra attention. Larch tutored the boy in medicine and surgery. Homer, although never a licensed physician, grew to possess near perfect gynecological and obstetrical procedures. He regularly assisted Dr. Larch with his medical duties.

Abortions were the exception. This was a source of tension between quasi-father and son. Larch would ask: "You know how to help these women. How can you not feel obligated to help them when they can't get help anywhere else?" Homer: "One, it's illegal. Two, I didn't ask how to do it, you just showed me." Their debate intensifies when a teenage girl is found unconscious on the orphanage grounds. When Larch examines her, he discovers that a "back alley" abortion was attempted. A broken crochet hook remains inside of her, causing extensive internal bleeding. Larch pointedly asks Homer what he would have done if the girl had approached him for the procedure. Larch answers for Homer: "Nothing!" Despite Larch's best efforts, the girl dies. Larch has the two oldest boys, Homer and Buster, assist him with the burial. At the gravesite, Larch continues, "Homer, if you expect people to be responsible for their children, you have to give them the right to decide

---

BOX 5A: INSIDE *THE CIDER HOUSE RULES*

The Cider House Rules is a morality tale on various levels. It portrays a slowly evolving debate between a physician and his quasi-adoptive son about the permissibility of abortion. It portrays the (moral) development of that same young man as he grows up in an orphanage and leaves its familiar confines only to return once his quasi-adoptive physician father dies. It portrays the value of commitment to friends and lovers over time, and the extent to which such commitments ought to be honored. Finally, it (implicitly) raises questions about the status of moral rules in the first place, whether we are bound to them apart from our wishes or whether we can rewrite or even ignore them whenever the personal need suits us.

It might be a good idea to view (listen) to Larch's voice-over from 1:45 to 6:05 (that is, from the "The Cider House Rules" banner to the "St. Cloud's, Maine, March 1943" subtitle). See scene 8 for a debate between Larch and Homer about abortion. This scene begins at 22:26 with a shot of a chimney and ends at 26:30 with Larch, Homer, and Buster being passed by Wally and Candy. For segments about the nature of moral rules, see scene 13. This scene begins at 46:10 with Homer placing books on his cider house bunk, and ends at 48:29 with a shot of Homer lying on his bunk, closing his eyes. See also scenes 31–34. Scene 31 begins at 1:36:52 with Homer stumbling on Mr. Rose and Rose Rose having an argument. Scene 34 ends at 1:49:55 with a shot of the migrant workers sitting on the roof. (These scenes also include Homer's evolving view about abortion.) However, just what these scenes—and the movie as a whole—implicitly convey about moral rules is rather ambiguous, making for intriguing discussion.

If you are able to view the entire film, then you should be able to answer the trivia questions from box 5B. If you are not able to view the film in its entirety, then watching the specified segments, in addition to carefully reading the plot summary, should give you a sufficient grasp of the film.

---

whether or not to have children." Homer, between shovels of dirt, replies, "How about expecting people to be responsible enough to control themselves to begin with?"

On the way back to the orphanage, two young adults pass Dr. Larch and the boys. When the three arrive, the very same car is parked in front of the orphanage. Candy Kendall and her fiancé Air Force Lieutenant Wally Worthington (each only slightly older than Homer) greet the children and Dr. Larch. Candy is unexpectedly pregnant and Wally is on leave from World War II. They seek an abortion. Larch fulfills their request, but as they prepare to leave, Homer asks for a ride. Homer wishes to see the world. Wally asks where he's headed. Unsure, Homer simply wants to go wherever he and Candy are going. As the whole orphanage (save an embittered Larch) sadly waves good-bye, Wally, Homer, and a still groggy Candy depart.

Needing a job for the first time in his life, Homer agrees to work for Wally's family as an apple picker. Wally introduces Homer to Mr. Rose, the crew leader of a group of migrant workers. Mr. Rose, a rather well-spoken but imposing figure, believes "they are making history" by having Homer (a young white man) becoming a part of the team, living with the other workers (African Americans) in the bunkhouse. After introducing his daughter, Ms. Rose Rose—the only female member of the team—Mr. Rose begins training Homer to become an expert apple picker. Homer soon sends a crate of apples to the orphanage. The nurses are grateful for the gift; Dr. Larch scoffs. Muttering, he rhetorically asks the nurses, "You don't find it depressing that Homer Wells is picking apples?"

The migrant workers quickly accept Homer and he reciprocates. By learning to be an apple picker and being a team member, he believes that he is following Larch's dictum, "In any life, you have to be of use." Wally concurs. The young lieutenant is called back to war, but he is reassured that Homer is staying on to look after things. Homer reads to the migrants, helps Wally's mom with the farm, and assists Candy's dad on the docks. He and Candy begin spending a great deal of time together. This leads Rose Rose to warn: "Now, don't be gettin' into any trouble with that Ms. Candy, Homer." Rose Rose clearly saw something Homer didn't. One day at a secluded beach, Candy and Homer spontaneously embrace, which leads to (unprotected) sex. Candy feels guilty for the infidelity; Homer is awestruck (and a bit confused).

Dr. Larch receives a letter from the board of directors. They (again) suggest that the orphanage could benefit by Larch taking on an assistant. Larch is convinced that they are trying to replace him. Larch agrees to meet with the board, but only after he has hatched a plan to have Homer succeed him as the resident physician at St. Cloud's. Larch forges a medical school diploma (Harvard M.D.). He crafts a bogus resume (residency in Boston). He invents a story about why Homer is currently unreachable (volunteering pediatric care in India). But at the meeting, Larch utilizes reverse psychology. He makes it known that he isn't happy about this meeting (which is true), but begins to disparage the only suitable candidate for the position, Homer Wells. Larch manages to have the board forget every other candidate but Homer. Finally, they "convince" Larch to interview Dr. Homer Wells (once he returns from India, that is).

Larch's success with the board is tempered by a loss at the orphanage. Fuzzy, one of the sickest and feeblest orphans, has always had problems breathing. His condition has worsened. He had been sleeping under a breathing hood designed by Larch. But one night, with Larch standing over him, Fuzzy dies. Larch and Buster assume the duty of

---

BOX 5B: *THE CIDER HOUSE RULES* TRIVIA

If your instructor assigns the film to be watched outside of class, you should be able to answer the following questions:

1. What seems to be the most common way to visit the St. Cloud's orphanage?
2. What name do Homer and Dr. Larch finally give the newborn baby boy?
3. Finish this sentence: "Good night you princes of Maine, you _____?
4. What film is repeatedly played at the St. Cloud's orphanage movie night?
5. What do Wally and Candy bring the children on their first visit to the orphanage?
6. What does Homer see for the first time the morning after leaving the orphanage?
7. Where does Candy take Homer after lobster dinner with her dad?
8. Mr. Rose insists that Jack "go fishin'" for what?
9. Where are the migrant workers *not* supposed to eat their lunch?
10. What does Homer give Curly at the end of the film?

burying the boy. Larch instructs Buster, "If the little ones want to know what happened, tell them that Fuzzy was adopted." Buster, appearing uncomfortable about the deception, asks, "Will they believe that, you think?" Larch solemnly replies, "They'll believe it because they want to believe it." That night, Buster "informs" the other boys what happened to Fuzzy; they knowingly nod to each other and Larch weeps outside the door.

Larch returns Homer's generous apple crate gift by sending his quasi-son a doctor's medical bag. This sparks a letter writing exchange. Homer thanks him for the bag, even though he's not a doctor. Homer admits that his current apprenticeship may not be as important as what he learned from Larch, but he is happy learning new things. He remains unsure about the practice of medicine, sharing with Larch, "I know what you have to do. You have to play God. Well, killing mice [to protect the orchard] is as close as I want to come to playing God." Larch responds, "I have been given the opportunity of playing God or leaving practically everything up to chance. Men and women of conscience should seize those moments when it's possible to play God. There won't be many." Larch shares his plan to have Homer succeed him; he laments, "The board of trustees is looking for my replacement." Homer sadly replies, "I'm not a doctor . . . I can't replace you. I'm sorry."

Mr. Rose's group of migrant workers returns for the new apple harvest season. But the team is short one member and Ms. Rose Rose is acting strangely. She separates herself from the group, is often tired, and nauseous (especially in the mornings). Candy immediately suspects her friend is pregnant. Candy confides that, if Rose Rose doesn't want to have the baby, there is a place nearby that performs safe abortions. Rose Rose replies that Mr. Rose won't allow her to go anywhere. When Candy inquires about the unborn baby's father, Rose Rose becomes dejected. She nods toward her father. Candy doesn't understand at first, but then realizes that Mr. Rose has conceived a child with Rose Rose. Candy runs to tell Homer. Homer confronts Mr. Rose: "You're having sex with your own daughter. . . . Aren't you ashamed of yourself?" Mr. Rose indignantly replies, "You're gonna talk to me about lies and shame?" Homer is stung by this comment about Candy; however, as he walks away, he tells Mr. Rose, "Rose is pregnant. Did you know that?"

The next night, Homer overhears Mr. Rose and Rose Rose having an argument. She wants to leave; Mr. Rose forbids it. Mr. Rose commands Homer, "You just go in the house. This ain't none of your concern." Homer tries to interject, but Mr. Rose is adamant, "Homer, this ain't your business. . . . What is your business?" Homer resolutely replies, "I'm in the doctor business. I can help. That's all I'm saying." Rose Rose wants Homer to do the procedure. Mr. Rose insists that he stay with his daughter. As Homer prepares for surgery, he tells Mr. Rose, "If you stay, you make yourself a use."

5.1. THINKING THROUGH THE MOVIE

Discussion Starter Questions

1. Is Dr. Larch a (morally) good person? Explain.
2. In America, orphanages have been replaced by foster care. Is foster care morally superior to orphanages? Explain.
3. Did Homer act permissibly in deciding to leave the orphanage? Explain.
4. Does Larch act permissibly in lying to the board of trustees? Does Buster act permissibly in lying to the other boys about Fuzzy? Is it ever permissible to lie? Justify your answers.

5. Was Candy's abortion permissible? Was Rose Rose's abortion permissible? Is it ever permissible to have an abortion? Justify your answers.

Questions for Further Thought

1. What is meant by the claim "In any life, you have to be of use" (scene 4, roughly 7:40)? Are there (morally) better or worse ways to "make yourself of use"? Explain.
2. Larch claims (scene 15, roughly 54:38), "And don't be holy to me about the law. What has the law ever done for anyone here?" Evaluate Larch's claim. What is the law supposed to accomplish, anyway?
3. Reconsider the exchange (scene 26, roughly 1:20:00) between Larch and Homer about "playing God." What does this mean and why do so many believe "playing God" is impermissible?
4. What message does the film (implicitly) portray about the permissibility of abortion? (Hint: compare Larch and Homer with respect to their words and deeds about it throughout the film.)
5. What message about metaethics, and moral rules in particular, does the film (implicitly) portray? (Hint: compare Larch and Mr. Rose with respect to their words and deeds about them.)

5.2. HISTORICAL SETTING

Essays on the Active Powers of Man (excerpt)

Thomas Reid (1710–1796) is arguably Hume's only serious competitor for the moniker of most influential Scottish philosopher of all time. He certainly was one of Hume's staunchest critics. Championing the role of common sense in philosophical inquiry, Reid eventually succeeded Adam Smith as the chair of moral philosophy at Old College in Glasgow.

Preparing to Read

A. What morally significant examples from *The Cider House Rules*—permissible or not— seem to be a matter of common sense?

B. How would Reid interpret Homer Wells's evolving view about performing abortions?

[First Principles and Common Sense]

Morals, like all other sciences, must have first principles, on which all moral reasoning is grounded. In every branch of knowledge where disputes have been raised, it is useful to distinguish the first principles from the superstructure. They are the foundation on which the whole fabric of the science leans; and whatever is not supported by this foundation can have no stability.

In all rational belief, the thing believed is either itself a first principle, or it is by just reasoning deduced from first principles. When men differ about deductions of reasoning, the appeal must be made to the rules of reasoning, which have been very unanimously fixed from the days of Aristotle. But when they differ about a first principle, the appeal is made to another tribunal; to that of common sense.

. . . As first principles differ from deductions of reasoning in the nature of their evidence, and must be tried by a different standard when they are called in question, it is of importance to know to which of these two classes a truth which we would examine belongs. When they are not distinguished, men are apt to demand proof for every thing they think fit to deny: And when we attempt to prove by direct argument, what is really self-evident, the reasoning will always be inconclusive; for it will either take for granted the thing to be proved, or something not more evident; and so, instead of giving strength to the conclusion, will rather tempt those to doubt of it, who never did so before. I propose, therefore, . . . to point out some of the first principles of morals, without pretending to a complete enumeration. . . .

1. There are some things in human conduct that merit approbation and praise, others that merit blame and punishment; and different degrees either of approbation or of blame, are due to different actions.

2. What is in no degree voluntary, can neither deserve moral approbation [praise] nor blame.

3. What is done from unavoidable necessity may be agreeable or disagreeable, useful or hurtful, but cannot be the object either of blame or of moral approbation.

4. Men may be highly culpable in omitting what they ought to have done, as well as in doing what they ought not.

5. We ought to use the best means we can to be well informed of our duty, by serious attention to moral instruction; by observing what we approve, and what we disapprove, in other men, whether our acquaintance, or those whose actions are recorded in history; by reflecting often, in a calm and dispassionate hour, on our own past conduct, that we may discern what was wrong, what was right, and what might have been better; by deliberating coolly and impartially upon our future conduct, as far as we can foresee the opportunities we may have of doing good, or the temptations to do wrong; and by having this principle deeply fixed in our minds, that as moral excellence is the true worth and glory of a man, so the knowledge of our duty is to every man, in every station of life, the most important of all knowledge.

6. It ought to be our most serious concern to do our duty as far as we know it, and to fortify our minds against every temptation to deviate from it; by maintaining a lively sense of the beauty of right conduct, and of its present and future reward, of the turpitude [wickedness] of vice, and of its bad consequences here and hereafter; by having always in our eye the noblest examples; by the habit of subjecting our passions to the government of reason; by firm purposes and resolutions with regard to our conduct; by avoiding occasions of temptation when we can. . . .

[First Principles of Virtue and Vice]

These principles [listed above] concerning virtue and vice in general, must appear self-evident to every man who hath a conscience, and who hath taken pains to exercise this natural power of his mind. I proceed to others that are more particular.

1. We ought to prefer a greater good, though more distant, to a less; and a less evil to a greater.

A regard to our own good, though we had no conscience, dictates this principle; and we cannot help disapproving of the man that acts contrary to it, as deserving to lose the good which he wantonly threw away, and to suffer the evil which he knowingly brought upon his own head.

We observed before, that the ancient moralists, and many among the modern, have deduced the whole of morals from this principle, and that when we make a right estimate of goods and evils according to their degree, their dignity, their duration, and according as they are more or less in our power, it leads to the practice of every virtue: More directly, indeed, to the virtues of self-government, to prudence, to temperance, and to fortitude; and, though more indirectly, even to justice, humanity, and all the social virtues, when their influence upon our happiness is well understood....

Let a man's moral judgment be ever so little improved by exercise, or ever so much corrupted by bad habits, he cannot be indifferent to his own happiness or misery. When he has become insensible to every nobler motive to right conduct, he cannot be insensible to this. And though to act from this motive solely may be called *prudence* rather than *virtue,* yet this prudence deserves some regard upon its own account, and much more as it is the friend and ally of virtue, and the enemy of all vice; and as it gives a favorable testimony of virtue to those who are deaf to every other recommendation.

If a man can be induced to do his duty even from a regard to his own happiness, he will soon find reason to love virtue for her own sake, and to act from motives less mercenary. I cannot therefore approve of those moralists, who would banish all persuasions to virtue taken from the consideration of private good. In the present state of human nature these are not useless to the best, and they are the only means left of reclaiming the abandoned.

2. As far as the intention of nature appears in the constitution of man, we ought to comply with that intention, and to act agreeably to it.

... From the constitution of every species of the inferior animals, and especially from the active principles which nature has given them, we easily perceive the manner of life for which nature intended them; and they uniformly act the part to which they are led by their constitution, without any reflection upon it, or intention of obeying its dictates. Man only, of the inhabitants of this world, is made capable of observing his own constitution, what kind of life it is made for, and of acting according to that intention, or contrary to it. He only is capable of yielding an intentional obedience to the dictates of his nature, or of rebelling against them....

The Stoics defined virtue to be a life according to nature. Some of them more accurately, a life according to the nature of man, in so far as it is superior to that of brutes. The life of a brute is according to the nature of the brute; but it is neither virtuous nor vicious. The life of a moral agent cannot be according to his nature....

The intention of nature, in the various active principles of man, in the desires of power, of knowledge, and of esteem, in the affection to children, to near relations, and to the communities to which we belong, in gratitude, in compassion, and even in resentment and emulation, is very obvious, and has been pointed out in treating of those principles. Nor is it less evident, that reason and conscience are given to us to regulate the inferior principles, so that they may conspire, in a regular and consistent plan of life, in pursuit of some worthy end.

3. No man is born for himself only. Every man, therefore, ought to consider himself as a member of the common society of mankind, and of those subordinate societies to which

he belongs, such as family, friends, neighborhood, country, and to do as much good as he can, and as little hurt to the societies of which he is a part. This axiom leads directly to the practice of every social virtue, and indirectly to the virtues of self-government, by which only we can be qualified for discharging the duty we owe to society.

4. In every case, we ought to act that part towards another, which we would judge to be right in him to act towards us, if we were in his circumstances and he in ours; or, more generally, what we approve in others, that we ought to practice in like circumstances, and what we condemn in others we ought not to do. If there be any such thing as right and wrong in the conduct of moral agents, it must be the same to all in the same circumstances.

... We stand in the same relation to one another as members of the great community of mankind. The duties consequent upon the different ranks and offices and relations of men are the same to all in the same circumstances. It is not want of judgment, but want of candor [honesty] and impartiality, that hinders men from discerning what they owe to others. They are quick-sighted enough in discerning what is due to themselves. When they are injured, or ill treated, they see it, and feel resentment. It is the want of candor that makes men use one measure for the duty they owe to others, and another measure for the duty that others owe to them in like circumstances. That men ought to judge with candor, as in all other cases, so especially in what concerns their moral conduct, is surely self-evident to every intelligent being. The man who takes offence when he is injured in his person, in his property, in his good name, pronounces judgment against himself if he acts so toward his neighbor.

The equity and obligation of this rule of conduct is self-evident to every man who hath a conscience; ... It comprehends every rule of justice without exception. It comprehends all the relative duties, arising either from the more permanent relations of parent and child, of master and servant, of magistrate and subject, of husband and wife, or from the more transient relations of rich and poor, of buyer and seller, of debtor and creditor, of benefactor and beneficiary, of friend and enemy. It comprehends every duty of charity and humanity, and even of courtesy and good manners. Nay, I think, that, without any force or straining, it extends even to the duties of self-government. For, as every man approves in others the virtues of prudence, temperance, self-command and fortitude, he must perceive, that what is right in others must be right in himself in like circumstances.

To sum up all, he who acts invariably by this rule will never deviate from the path of his duty, but from an error of judgment. And, as he feels the obligation that he and all men are under to use the best means in his power to have his judgment well informed in matters of duty, his errors will only be such as are invincible.

It may be observed, that this axiom supposes a faculty in man by which he can distinguish right conduct from wrong. It supposes also, that, by this faculty, we easily perceive the right and the wrong in other men that are indifferent to us, but are very apt to be blinded by the partiality of selfish passions when the case concerns ourselves. Every claim we have against others is apt to be magnified by self-love, when viewed directly. A change of persons removes this prejudice, and brings the claim to appear in its just magnitude.

5. ... There is another class of axioms in morals, by which, when there seems to be an opposition between the actions that different virtues lead to, we determine to which the preference is due.

Between the several virtues, as they are dispositions of mind, or determinations of will to act according to a certain general rule, there can be no opposition. They dwell together most amicably, and give mutual aid and ornament, without the possibility of hostility or opposition, and, taken altogether, make one uniform and consistent rule of conduct. But, between particular external actions, which different virtues would lead to, there may be an opposition. Thus, the same man may be in his heart, generous, grateful and just. These dispositions strengthen, but never can weaken one another. Yet it may happen, that an external action which generosity or gratitude solicits, justice may forbid.

That in all such cases, unmerited generosity should yield to gratitude, and both to justice, is self-evident. Nor is it less so, that unmerited beneficence to those who are at ease should yield to compassion to the miserable, and external acts of piety to works of mercy. . . .

At the same time, we perceive, that those acts of virtue which ought to yield in the case of a competition, have most intrinsic worth when there is no competition. Thus, it is evident that there is more worth in pure and unmerited benevolence than in compassion, more in compassion than in gratitude, and more in gratitude than in justice.

[Math and Biology Analogies]

I call these *first principles,* because they appear to me to have in themselves an intuitive evidence which I cannot resist. I find I can express them in other words. I can illustrate them by examples and authorities, and perhaps can deduce one of them from another; but I am not able to deduce them from other principles that are more evident. And I find the best moral reasonings of authors I am acquainted with . . . to be grounded upon one or more of them.

The evidence of mathematical axioms is not discerned till men come to a certain degree of maturity of understanding. One must have formed the general conception of *quantity,* and of *more* and *less* and *equal,* of *sum* and *difference;* and he must have been accustomed to judge of these relations in matters of common life, before he can perceive the evidence of the mathematical axiom, that equal quantities, added to equal quantities, make equal sums.

In like manner, our moral judgment, or conscience, grows to maturity. . . . When we are capable of contemplating the actions of other men, or of reflecting upon our own calmly and dispassionately, we begin to perceive in them the qualities of honest and dishonest, of honorable and base, of right and wrong, and to feel the sentiments of moral approbation and disapprobation.

These sentiments are at first feeble, easily warped by passions and prejudices, and apt to yield to authority. By use and time, the judgment, in morals as in other matters, gathers strength, and feels more vigor: We begin to distinguish the dictates of passion from those of cool reason, and to perceive, that it is not always safe to rely upon the judgment of others. By an impulse of nature, we venture to judge for ourselves, as we venture to walk by ourselves.

There is a strong analogy between the progress of the body from infancy to maturity, and the progress of all the powers of the mind. This progression in both is the work of nature, and in both may be greatly aided or hurt by proper education. It is natural to a man to be able to walk or run or leap; but if his limbs had been kept in fetters from his birth, he would have none of those powers. It is no less natural to a man trained in society, and accustomed to judge of his own actions and those of other men, to perceive a right and a wrong, an honorable and a base, in human conduct; and to such a man, I think, the principles of morals I have above mentioned will appear self-evident. Yet there may be individuals of the human species so little accustomed to think or judge of any thing, but of gratifying their animal appetites, as to have hardly any conception of right or wrong in conduct, or any moral judgment; as there certainly are some who have not the conceptions and the judgment necessary to understand the axioms of geometry.

From the principles above mentioned, the whole system of moral conduct follows so easily, and with so little aid of reasoning, that every man of common understanding, who wishes to know his duty, may know it. The path of duty is a plain path which the upright in heart can rarely mistake. Such it must be, since every man is bound to walk in it.

Review Questions

1. Reid argues that in any "branch of knowledge" there are "first principles" and the "superstructure" (built upon them). What make the principles true? What makes the superstructure claims true?
2. What, according to Reid, tends to cloud our moral faculties/judgments? How would he rectify or at least alleviate this?
3. What is Reid's basic metaethical position? How does he use examples from math and biology to support it?

5.3. DISCUSSION AND ANALYSIS

The Cider House Rules implicitly raises the issue of how moral rules apply to our daily lives. The film can be interpreted as expressing the metaethical idea that each of us regularly invents—and reinvents—our own moral rules. This seems to be Mr. Rose's message at the end of the movie. Arguably, it is also Larch's message at the beginning of the film, with his cavalier attitude toward the rules he makes and breaks at St. Cloud's orphanage. But inventing moral rules seems arbitrary, leaving it up to us whether to accept the moral point of view at all. This is consistent with Aunt Mae's view from *Crimes and Misdemeanors*: "Nothing is handed down in stone. For those who want morality, there's morality." Mae's words raise a thorny (but familiar) issue: If divine commands cannot secure a proper foundation for ethics, then ethics must be a matter of convention after all. This position is bolstered by a second common assumption: The fact of intractable or persistent moral disagreement renders ethical truth conventional. As conventional, we are at liberty to revise our moral ideals and principles whenever it suits us, including whether to be moral at all.

> "I'm just tryin' to put things straight. Sometimes, ya gotta break some rules, to put things straight." —*The Cider House Rules*, scene 34

The messages of the previous paragraph, however, clash with another entrenched metaethical idea: *some* behaviors are just plain wrong. The atrocities committed by the Nazis of World War II, some of which are artfully portrayed by Steven Spielberg in *Schindler's List*, were morally impermissible regardless of whether the Nazis disagreed or felt otherwise. Moreover, Amon Goeth is clearly a moral monster; however, Oskar Schindler becomes a better person by the end of the film. Furthermore, *The Cider House Rules* and *Crimes and Misdemeanors* can also be interpreted as affirming objectivist moral

---

BOX 5C: LEARNING OUTCOMES

Upon carefully studying this chapter, students should better comprehend and be able to explain:

- What ethical objectivism is, and the reasons for and against its truth.
- The existence of "truths of reason," the distinction between moral principles and moral facts, and how these can be used in a case to support ethical objectivism.
- Thomas Reid's ideas about metaethics.
- How themes expressed in *The Cider House Rules*, *Crimes and Misdemeanors*, and *Schindler's List* are conducive to better understanding the debate between objectivists and conventionalists about ethics.

---

themes. Coercing your daughter into incestuous relations, as does Mr. Rose, is morally pernicious (even before Candy and Homer found out); Dr. Judah Rosenthal acts wrongly in taking a mistress and orchestrating her murder (even if he is never found out). Genocide, incest, and marital infidelity are all classic examples of acts that are simply wrong. So, the question that remains is this: How can moral judgments be (objectively) true apart from a supreme lawgiver, especially in the face of intractable disagreement?

Ethical objectivists (also known as moral realists) have an answer. They hold that ethical truth is dependent on neither belief nor sentiment about ethically significant situations. Just as our beliefs or wishes about the physical world do not (and cannot) constitute physical reality, our moral beliefs or sentiments do not (and cannot) constitute ethical truth. Just as the physical world exists in its own right, so does the "ethical realm." Just as truths about the physical world are

> "We're all faced throughout our lives with agonizing decisions, moral choices. Some of these are on a grand scale, most of these choices are on lesser points." —*Crimes and Misdemeanors*, scene 16

discovered and not invented, so are ethical truths. The only difference is that the physical world is discovered through empirical methods. Discoveries about the ethical realm require more philosophical and, thus, nonempirical, investigations.

Ethical objectivism is further distinguished from other metaethical theories if we emphasize (again) the idea of truth-makers. For example, what makes an ethically significant statement true, on SES, is that the speaker's belief matches up with how she currently feels. To the SES-defender, it may be true that Candy Kendall acted impermissibly in having an abortion, but *only* if she felt negatively about undergoing the procedure. However, if SES is true, there is nothing about abortion *itself* that makes ethical statements about it true or false. The moral relativist similarly holds that abortion may be impermissible, but *only* if the speaker's judgment accords with current consensus of his or her culture. For the ethical objectivist, if Candy's abortion was impermissible, then there is something about *it*—the abortion in Candy's particular circumstances—that makes it so. Ethical objectivists thus hold that personal feelings, sentiments, or beliefs (including

God's decrees on DCT) about Candy's abortion, or abortion generally, are not essential to whether ethical judgments about the relevant surgical procedure are true or false.

> "The truth, Helen, is always the right answer." —*Schindler's List*, scene 22

Scientific and Ethical Discourse

Scientists sometimes disagree about the physical facts. However, no one assumes that scientific disputes are irreconcilable. The scientific community possesses well-worn methods for effectively determining (objective) truths about the physical world. Thus the lack of intractable disagreement about the empirical facts is explained by the scientific community's profound success in developing methods to accurately represent those facts. This, in turn, explains the convergence we often see among scientific theories. It also explains the widespread belief that science is getting us closer and closer to what the physical world is objectively like.

Some empirical questions cannot currently be definitively answered through scientific means. Nevertheless, we invariably understand what would be required to answer or resolve them. Consider the ongoing debate about extraterrestrial intelligent life. If space is infinitely large, this debate might remain unsolved (at least it may never reach a definitive resolution). Yet we can grasp how to solve it, at least in theory. With an agreed upon working definition of intelligence, we explore space with some sort of advanced craft, seeking out those who meet the agreed upon definition. Therefore, even in cases where science hasn't reached consensus, we can easily agree what kind (or kinds) of evidence would be required to begin closing the debate.

This terse discussion of science only highlights the disanalogy that many see between science and ethics. Unlike judgments about the physical world, moral judgments seem *widely* divergent and intractably so. *The Cider House Rules* reminds us of the debate between the so-called pro-life and pro-choice positions regarding abortion. Pro-life advocates believe that the value associated with human life is simply absolute, while the latter believe that this value must be balanced with a woman's right to autonomy over her own body. Furthermore, there doesn't seem to be any conceivable evidence that, once in our possession, would resolve entrenched controversies about abortion. Like Homer Wells, we can learn firsthand all the physical facts associated with abortions without (necessarily) coming any closer to resolving the pro-life and pro-choice debate. The same can seemingly be said for a host of other ethical debates—euthanasia, capital punishment, and stem cell research, just to name a few. Therefore, divergence in ethical judgments persists, with no hope of convergence or resolution in sight.

These considerations lead some to the following argument for ethical nonobjectivism; let's call it the argument from intractable disagreement. If ethical objectivism (moral realism) were true, then we would not expect widely divergent moral judgments mired in intractable disagreement, or there would be some sort of conceivable evidence that would, in principle, resolve moral debates. However, moral judgments are widely divergent and mired in intractable disagreement. Moreover, there doesn't seem to be any conceivable evidence available that could even begin to close these debates. Therefore, ethical objectivism (moral realism) isn't true. And this is to say that, in some way or another, if there are any ethical truths, they are somehow grounded in our preexisting beliefs or personal sentiments.[2]

The Cider House Rules, Miramax Films, 1999. The friendship between Homer Wells (Tobey Maguire) and Candy Kendall (Charlize Theron) blossoms into romance while Candy's fiancé is serving in World War II. (Moviegoods, Inc.)

Ethical Nonobjectivism and Self-Defeating Claims

The argument from intractable disagreement is most effectively critiqued by reconsidering the baseline argument for ethical nonobjectivism. Recall from chapter 2 it was argued that if a statement is objectively true, then it must be a piece of science (that is somehow empirically confirmed). But because ethical statements are not pieces of science, it follows that ethical statements cannot be objectively true. Because there are only two kinds of truth—objective and subjective—it follows that, if true at all, ethical statements are somehow (merely) subjectively true, which is to say their truth is a matter of convention.[3]

The baseline argument hinges on the truth of its first premise: if a statement is objectively true, then it is scientific in nature. The problem with the argument is that it seems its first premise cannot be true, exactly because *it* is not a scientific claim. This premise is ironically flawed in that it cannot meet its own requirement for being (objectively) true. Philosophers sometimes call such claims self-defeating; all self-defeating claims possess a similar ironic flaw. Consider the following example; let's call it (E):

(E) This sentence cannot be understood in English.

Note two important observations about (E). First, its intended meaning is readily graspable. Second, it is (obviously) expressed in the English language. Putting these two facts together entails that (E) cannot be true. It is self-defeating; any (initial) reason to think that (E) might be true actually results in (E) proving itself false.

The relevant premise of the baseline argument suffers from a similar ironic flaw. Because it's supposed to be an objectively true claim, but it's philosophical (and not scientific) in nature, it follows that it cannot be true. If the statement were true, it would then provide a criterion for objective truth that all statements—including itself—must meet; however, it fails to meet that criterion. That it fails the proposed criterion entails that it cannot be true. Therefore, this initial argument for ethical nonobjectivism ultimately fails.

The argument from intractable disagreement for ethical nonobjectivism rests on an assumption that drives its main (and first) premise. The assumption, (A), is this

(A) If a statement (or theory) is true, then it cannot be subject to persistent, intractable disagreement or (at least) there would be some sort of conceivable evidence that would resolve the debate surrounding it.

If the argument from intractable disagreement succeeds, then its main premise must be true; however, the main premise is true only if (A), the assumption driving it, is true. But (A) is itself a statement. So, if there is intractable disagreement about it and if there is no conceivable evidence that would resolve that debate, it follows that it cannot be (objectively) true.

Note that (A) is a philosophical statement; therein lies its ironic flaw. Some philosophers plausibly hold that intractable disagreement about a topic does not rule out objective truth about it. For example, atheists disagree with theists about God's existence. But it seems plain that whether 'God exists' is true or 'God does not exist' is true is not impacted by this debate. Either God exists or God doesn't; either way, there is a fact of the matter. Philosophers who think like this ultimately dispute (A). These philosophers thereby disagree with ethical nonobjectivists who affirm (A). However, there doesn't seem to be any conceivable evidence on the horizon to resolve the debate about (A). No empirical evidence seems forthcoming exactly because (A) is a philosophical claim. The fact of disagreement about (A) has grave ramifications for the argument from intractable disagreement. Note that (A) provides a criterion for objective truth that all statements—including itself—must meet; however, because (A) itself is subject to intractable disagreement, (A) fails to meet that criterion. Thus the argument from intractable disagreement fails because it contains a premise that rests on a self-defeating assumption.[4]

Truths of Reason

The discussion thus far highlights the significance of what could be called "truths of reason." However, some philosophers, including Hume, are suspicious of such statements. Roughly, Hume held that the truth of any (meaningful) statement is grounded in its being either a straightforward definition or a matter of empirical fact. 'All uncles have nieces or nephews' is an example of a true definitional statement. Those influenced by Hume invariably hold that this is the only sort of true statement not grounded in empirical considerations. There cannot be any statements that are true in their own right apart from how language users merely decide to employ words. But note that Hume's position about true statements is itself a statement; it makes a claim about what is required for truth. As such, it possesses (a now familiar) ironic flaw: because *it* is neither straightforwardly true by definition, nor a matter of empirical fact, it follows that it cannot true. This result has led many philosophers to reconsider the possibility that some statements are true in their own right, and are true in interesting or informative ways (and not merely because of how we decided to define our terms). These statements are known as "truths of reason."

So, let's say that a truth of reason is any statement that, although not expressive of a straightforward definition, seems (a) obviously true such that careful scrutiny shows denying it entails some sort of contradictory, incoherent, or otherwise absurd resulting position, (b) objective in that its truth, in some important sense, applies universally, and (c) its being objectively true is not merely a matter of its being grounded in empirical considerations. For example, consider the claim: 'Nothing can (simultaneously) have incompatible properties'. Insofar as it makes a claim about all (existing) things, if it is true, it applies universally. Furthermore, its truth, if it is true, can be discerned without the help of a laboratory. Thus conditions (b) and (c) are satisfied. What about the first condition? Does denying this claim lead to counterintuitive or absurd results? It does. If this claim is denied, then Amon Goeth can simultaneously be the commandant and not be the commandant of the Plaszow labor camp. Moreover, someone like Wilbur Larch could simultaneously die because of an ether overdose and not. Since neither of these (alleged) scenarios is possible, it follows that nothing can (simultaneously) have incompatible properties. Thus, condition (a) is also satisfied and we have convincing evidence to think that 'Nothing can have incompatible properties' is, indeed, a truth of reason.

It must be stressed that truths of reason seemingly exist without being thought up or written down by anyone. They simply are true (because they must be). In this way, they are analogous to logical or mathematical truths. The number 17 is prime because it must be. Moreover, that some conclusions logically follow (necessarily) from their premises or that some mathematical formulas must hold requires no grand logician or mathematician making it so. Necessarily, if it's true that either a counting number is odd or even, and it's also true that the number you're thinking of isn't odd, then, it's even. And for any right triangle, necessarily, if it's true that the hypotenuse is 5 units long, and one of its sides is 4 units long, then the other side is 3 units long. Note that these truths about counting numbers and right triangles are grounded in more general, lawlike principles (respectively): "either A or B; not-A; thus, B," and "a-squared plus b-squared equals c-squared." These more general principles hold simply given the kind of claims they intrinsically are, irrespective of anyone's feelings, sentiments, or beliefs about them. Their truth applies objectively, universally, and in informative ways. Therefore, it is not at all clear that all lawlike principle or statements require lawmakers.

> "I realize that you are not a person in the strictest sense of the word, but, um . . . 'Hath not the Jew eyes?' . . . No, I don't think so. You're a Jewish bitch." —*Schindler's List*, scene 22

Furthermore, it seems that some truths of reason carry (epistemic) normative force. If you believe that the counting number you're thinking of is either odd or even, and if you believe that it isn't odd, then there is something else that you *ought* to believe: the counting number you're thinking of is even. If you don't also believe this third statement, it appears that you are subject to some sort of self-deception or ignorance. Similar considerations apply to right triangles. Believing that the hypotenuse is 5 units and one of the sides is 4, you ought to also believe that the other side is 3. If you don't believe this, then perhaps you don't fully understand geometry or at least right triangles. Perhaps, for some odd reason, you don't want to believe this and so you get yourself to (nonrationally) deny the second side is 3 units long. Perhaps you vehemently disagree that the second side is 3 units long and refuse to be swayed from your opinion. Nevertheless, it remains that you ought to believe its length is 3 units. Any other alternative is illogical. Your refusal to believe this may divulge insights into your personal psychological situation; however, it doesn't negate the normative force of the relevant belief. Mere disagreement about a topic entails a lack of neither objective truth nor normative force (if any) about it. And all of this is so without the normative force of statements being legislated by a lawgiver.

What Would an Objective Ethical Truth Be Like?

The examples from the previous section convey what we (objectively) ought to believe given well-established standards of rationality or principles of evidence (which accounts for their carrying epistemic normative force). Thus, the question now becomes whether there are any ethically significant truths of reason—statements conveying *moral* normative force—thereby indicating how we (objectively) ought to behave. Following the example of Thomas Reid, let's begin by considering the claim: 'No one is accountable for things (totally) beyond his or her control'. This statement seems to qualify as a truth of reason. If true, it pertains to everyone and it is not a scientific claim. And consider what would follow if we attempt to deny this claim. If it were false, then it would be possible to hold Homer Wells accountable for things that his mother did on the night before he was conceived! But this is patently implausible. It thus seems that 'No one is accountable for things (totally) beyond his or her control' is indeed a truth of reason.

At this point, Reid would remind us that we cannot be morally praised or blamed for that which is totally beyond our control. After all, one way in which something may be beyond one's control is if it occurs "from unavoidable necessity." As he puts it, such things "may be agreeable or disagreeable, useful or hurtful," but they "cannot be the object of either blame or of moral approbation [praise]." This seems to be another truth of reason. After all, note what follows if this position is denied. If you could be morally blamed for the occurrence of something that was totally beyond your control to prevent, then you could be permissibly punished for its happening. But this is implausible. Being permissibly punished for something implies that you are (appropriately) accountable for its occurring.[5] So, if you are not accountable for the occurrence of something, you cannot be permissibly punished for it. If you are punished for it, then you are treated impermissibly. Therefore, punishing a person for something that is totally beyond his or her control to prevent is morally wrong. This is a morally significant statement and seems to be an example of an ethically significant truth of reason.

The driving intuition in the case being developed here is that the person has done nothing to deserve punishment. Punishing an innocent person, especially for events she could not prevent, is impermissible. This seems to be a matter of justice. If a person has done nothing to warrant punishment, then subjecting her to punishment is unfair or unjust. These intuitions may uncover another ethically significant truth of reason: It is impermissible to treat equals unequally. For example, if a person has done nothing to distinguish herself from others—if she has not done anything that warrants blame for an unfortunate situation—then it is unjust to treat her in an unequal way by subjecting her to punishment. Subjecting this innocent person to punishment is thus morally wrong. Arguably, then, the ethically significant truth of reason that equals ought to be treated equally lends credence to the truth of reason that it is impermissible to punish a person for events beyond her control.

These truths of reason, in turn, may be supplemented by another, namely, the wrongness of doing unjustified harm. When a person is punished, he is somehow harmed. A punishment that doesn't inflict some kind of harm isn't much of a punishment. But if the person being punished is innocent or was unable to prevent the event for which punishment is doled out, then the person receiving punishment is being harmed unjustifiably. All instances of unjustified harms are wrong. Thus, if the person being punished is innocent or was unable to prevent the event for which punishment is doled out, that person is treated impermissibly. Moreover, that it is impermissible to do unjustified harm to others thus provides logical support for two further statements we have reason to believe are ethically significant truths of reason. Logic dictates that if these two further claims are truths of reason, then it must be that 'It is impermissible to do unjustified harm' is itself a truth of reason. Consequently, each of these three statements must be true, regardless of what is (in fact) believed about them, as denying them entails contradictory or otherwise absurd results. Thus it's not clear that all objectively (and universally) true moral claims require a moral lawgiver, which is exactly what the ethical objectivist affirms.

> "It's pure evil, Jack. A man kills for money and doesn't even know his victims." —*Crimes and Misdemeanors*, scene 10

Moral Facts and Moral Principles

That truths of reason exist sheds light on the nature of moral facts. Moral facts result from exemplifying (instantiating) some ethically significant truth of reason. Recall Reid's example: 'If person S is blamed (punished) for event E, but S has absolutely no control over E, then S is treated impermissibly'. Let's next assume that, as a matter of fact, Mr. White is convicted for a crime that someone else committed, one that he didn't know about and couldn't have prevented if he did know about it. This set of descriptive facts, coupled with the relevant truth of reason results in a moral fact, namely, that Mr. White was treated impermissibly. It was, in fact, wrong that Mr. White was so treated. Thus, moral facts need not be relegated to our personal sentiments. They are the (logical) result of properly applying descriptive facts to a relevant truth of reason. But because worldly events and truths of reason obtain even if someone doesn't believe them, it follows that moral facts are objective features of the world.

In chapter 1, moral principles were introduced. These evaluative statements (along with the relevant facts and conceptual considerations), recall, provide the means by which to deem some acts morally acceptable but others unacceptable. It now seems that moral principles may be plausibly interpreted as ethically significant truths of reason. Some moral principles are very general, providing the fundamental criterion for right action. These are often called moral standards (to be discussed in more detail in chapter 6). Others are less general, for example, 'Inflicting unjustified harm is impermissible' and 'Treat equals equally'. Yet others are rather specific, approaching the status of moral rules; just two such examples might be: 'Incestuous rape is wrong' and 'Monogamous spouses ought not to participate in extramarital sex'. In any event, properly conceived, a moral principle is a conditional statement: If agent S performs action A, then S acts impermissibly.[6] When someone, in fact, acts in the way described in the if-clause of a moral principle, a moral fact (logically) obtains. Thus, ethical judgments about what is, or is not, permissible are factual in the sense that they are grounded in the objective truth of a moral principle. Moral principles are grounded in their being truths of reason, which is to say that, properly articulated, they could not have been false. But if a (meaningful) statement cannot possibly be false, it must be true. Thus, moral principles must be true. This process thus begins to capture what ethical objectivists mean by "ethical truth-makers."[7]

Nevertheless, it must be admitted that great care must be taken when relying on truths of reason to establish the plausibility of ethical objectivism. The problem is that, on some level, truths of reason are supposed to be self-evidently true (as Reid believes), at least insofar as their denials involve (logical) absurdity. But what constitutes being self-evidently true or even logical absurdity can be tricky business because what is self-evident or obviously absurd to some may not be so to others. Perhaps you find some of Reid's appeals to "common sense" dubious, or at least debatable. Furthermore, although it seems perfectly obvious that Jewish people are persons deserving of full moral status, this wasn't obvious to Nazis like Goeth. He affirmed that Jews were not "persons in the strictest sense of the term." Ethically significant disagreement is a reality. So, given the fact of persistent ethical disagreement, how can it be that moral facts are grounded in self-evident truths of reason?[8] Even if there are such facts, how can they be known in light of intractable disagreement? Which side of the debate is more justified in their claims to self-evidency?

Some philosophers respond by contending that the source of persistent ethical disputes may be more a matter of psychology than philosophy. As Reid notes, it is easy for us to overexaggerate the wrongs done to us, but be indignant about wronging others. Calls for justice are sometimes driven by a lust for revenge, but we sometimes shirk our obligations to others out of laziness or apathy. However, ethical discourse indeed requires us to take *all* the relevant facts of the matter *fully* into account thereby achieving a sufficient degree of impartiality (which represents another of Reid's self-evident truths). Ethical discourse also requires us to see ourselves as we actually are, but this kind of self-reflective honesty is difficult to achieve. Nazis aside, mundane examples of this abound. The exhilaration of his secret life with Dolores prevented Judah Rosenthal, an otherwise kind and generous man, from seeing himself as a deceptive spouse and the harm he would rain down on his family. The love Mr. Rose had for his youthful daughter Rose Rose clouded his vision as his affections turned lecherous when she blossomed into adulthood; he could not see the harm he caused her (literally) by his own hand.

But what if these psychological impediments were removed? What if, as Michael Smith suggests, we could achieve a cool, calm, and collected idealized condition of reflection regarding moral issues?[9] Furthermore, as Reid states, just as we must work to achieve mathematical knowledge, why not hold the same about moral knowledge? This proposed analogy helps to explain why being self-evidently true doesn't entail that such statements are immediately recognized as self-evident. Just as it took some familiarity with the basic concepts of geometry to grasp that the sum of a triangle's internal angles equals 180 degrees, it may take some familiarity with basic ethical concepts to grasp that it is impermissible to treat equals unequally. Moreover, mathematical errors occur just as ethical errors. But they can be corrected (and avoided in the future). Indeed, analogous to beliefs in math (or logic), we often attempt to change someone's moral beliefs by engaging them in rational argument. An important feature of such engagement is facilitating more

Crimes and Misdemeanors, Orion Pictures, 1989. Dr. Judah Rosenthal (Martin Landau, right) and his brother Jack (Jerry Orbach) contemplate the dire significance of their choice to keep Judah's affair a secret. (Moviegoods, Inc.)

idealized conditions of reflection. And as Smith reminds us, "Sometimes, we succeed."[10] In math (and logic) we have achieved convergence. So why hold that a convergence in our ethical judgments will forever remain unattainable? True, we haven't achieved it yet, but perhaps only time (and a great deal of effort) will tell.[11]

Summing Up and Moving Ahead

Ethical objectivists thus press forward. They agree with Itzhak Stern from *Schindler's List* when he affirms the existence of absolute goods—some behaviors are morally good, simply given what they are and apart from what anyone believes about them. They thereby take issue with Aunt Mae's approach to ethics. Ethics could still be a matter of discovery rather than convention, and in idealized conditions of reflection, our obligations are not so easily shirked. They also disagree with Mr. Rose; moral rules are not invented by us daily. Rather, we work to better understand and articulate preexisting moral principles given our daily experiences. And this is how they interpret Larch's "making" and "breaking" rules at the orphanage. Larch *refines* his understanding of the rules; he doesn't *invent* them. They also hold that the debate between Judah Rosenthal and his patient Rabbi Ben expresses a false dilemma. It's not the case that if ethics is not grounded squarely in God and religion, life becomes an ethically barren and valueless existence. Moral goodness and obligation might be grounded in the existence of ethically significant truths of reason that, properly articulated, apply universally but require no nonhuman author.

This isn't to say that all forms of moral realism rely so heavily on truths of reason in this way (even if the existence of truths of reason makes any such defense more plausible). Louis Pojman (with an assist from Bruce Russell), for example, argues that moral prin-
ciples are descriptive of behavior that, if adhered to, would be conducive to promoting the most significant interests of persons. But because not all moral principles secure these interests equally, there is a sense in which ethical objectivism is true (exactly because such principles promote these interests apart from what anyone believes or whether someone would disagree.[12] If nothing else, it might be argued that, among the four leading metaethical theories attempting to

> "What, Mae, you challenge the whole moral structure of everything? . . . Do you not find human impulses basically decent?" —*Crimes and Misdemeanors*, scene 11

explain how moral judgments are true (assuming that some are true), ethical objectivism seems most likely true, as each of the other three theories face damaging objections. This isn't to say, necessarily, that ethical objectivism is completely free of criticism, but it does seem to fare (at least) somewhat better than its competitors, which allows for further exploration into normative ethics.

Accordingly, in the pages ahead, you will become acquainted with notable thinkers from the history of philosophy and their attempts to extend our moral knowledge. Philosophers such as Aquinas, Mill, Kant, and Aristotle (among others) will do their part to articulate and defend consistent and coherent theories that more carefully inform our moral intuitions about good and bad, right and wrong. The remaining chapters, then, consist of an exploration into how ethical objectivists tend to do moral philosophy.

5.4. TWO ADDITIONAL FILMS

Crimes and Misdemeanors (1989)

Director and Screenwriter: Woody Allen

Plot Summary

> For those who want morality, there's morality. Nothing is handed down in stone. . . . And I say, if he can do it and get away with it and chooses not to be bothered by the ethics—then, he is home free.

Consider how the lives of two persons, who have never met, can be so similar that they seem destined to one day meet. *Crimes and Misdemeanors* is (in part) a story about two such persons, Judah Rosenthal and Cliff Stern.

Judah Rosenthal is a respected and admired ophthalmologist; however, he is also a troubled man. For two years, he has kept a terrible secret from his wife, Miriam, and the rest of his family: he has been having an affair. His lover, Dolores, now emotionally unbalanced, insists that Judah make good on a promise to his wife. She threatens Judah with confronting Mrs. Rosenthal if necessary.

Cliff Stern is a struggling documentary director in a loveless marriage. His wife's brother, Lester, is a successful but self-absorbed television producer. Lester (as a favor to his sister) asks Cliff to film his biography, which is to appear on public television as part of its *Creative Minds* series. In order to fund his own project, a documentary on an NYU philosophy professor, Cliff reluctantly agrees. This is how he meets Halley Reed. Halley is one of the producers for the series. Soon Cliff's interest in Halley becomes more than just professional.

Judah confides in one of his patients, Ben, a young rabbi afflicted with a rare disorder slowly robbing him of his sight. Judah discloses everything about his affair to Rabbi Ben. Ben advises him to confess and beg his wife's forgiveness because, as he sees it, there is a "moral order" to the world; given this moral order, anchored in his religious beliefs, Ben urges Judah to do the right thing and then leaves the office. Judah, the skeptic, is hesitant. He is concerned about the negative consequences of telling his wife. It seems advantageous not to tell, especially if he can convince Dolores not to confront Miriam. Under the guise of helping her make up lost business opportunities she has foregone for their relationship, Judah subtly bribes Dolores not to confront Miriam. Outraged, Dolores refuses to acquiesce, suggesting this proposition is reminiscent of his self-serving "under the table" business deals.

Cliff and Halley both share a love of old movies. Once they discover this about each other, they begin to spend quite a bit of time together. Cliff begins to pursue Halley subtly; however, before too long, he does so overtly. He assures Halley that his marriage will not last. Halley is hesitant and informs Cliff that she needs more time. She tells him that she has an opportunity to produce a show in London; she will be gone for three or four months.

Judah, distressed about his last visit with Dolores, visits his less than respectable brother, Jack. Jack has contacts even less respectable than he. Judah is hesitant, but Jack is direct: he will have someone "talk" to Dolores so that she "stays quiet." Jack promises, seemingly from brotherly love, that he is willing to do whatever it takes to help Judah and that Judah will not be involved in the matter in any way—if, that is, Judah is willing to part with some cash. The two depart, leaving their business to be settled for a later time.

Desperate, Dolores calls Judah at home on his birthday. She informs him that she is calling from a gas station only two blocks away. Again, she insists on confronting Miriam. Desperate himself, Judah agrees to meet her, telling his party guests that a patient has a medical emergency. In doing so, Judah again avoids disaster. Later that night and alone, Judah recounts his conversation with Rabbi Ben. It appears Ben has become Judah's conscience, helping him mull over the pending business with Jack. The rabbi is less than successful; Judah calls Jack, asking him "how much he needs" to make his problem "go away." While entertaining friends and family days later, Judah answers a call from Jack, who informs him that their business has been completed. Hanging up the phone, Judah replies, "God have mercy on our souls, Jack." Judah returns to the party, and visibly shaking, refills his cocktail. But he is too anxious about his "business transaction." Jack described it as a "robbery that went bad." What did that mean? Judah leaves the party and returns to the scene of the crime. Dolores is there, eyes open, lying next to the bed motionless with a pool of blood gathering behind her head. He removes some incriminating pictures and her date book and solemnly leaves the apartment.

Rabbi Ben, now nearly blind, asks Judah whether that personal matter was ever resolved. From behind his apparatus and matter-of-factly, Judah assures Ben that it has been. Ben is relieved. Still feeling guilty, and now having misled the rabbi, Judah goes for a drive. Unconsciously, he stops at his childhood home. The current owner is kind enough to let Judah relive some old memories. During his tour, he recollects a poignant dinner conversation between his father, himself a rabbi, his aunt, and other friends apparently from temple. Not surprisingly, the topic of discussion was whether there exists a moral order to things. It quickly became more of an argument, with Judah's father, Rabbi Saul, and his aunt, Mae, taking up opposing viewpoints. Mae asks Saul sarcastically, "Are you afraid that if you don't follow the rules, God will punish you?" "He won't punish me, Mae; he only punishes the wicked," Saul retorts. Mae responds, "Like who—Hitler!?"

Months pass, but the story, and its characters, come together to celebrate the wedding of Rabbi Ben's daughter. Even though their divorce is almost final, Ben's sister and her soon-to-be ex-husband Cliff attend. So does Ben's trusted ophthalmologist, Judah Rosenthal. Ben's brother, Lester, is also there with his new fiancée—Halley. This is more than Cliff can bear. He sulks alone, far away from the festivities in the banquet hall. Judah stumbles upon Cliff on his way home and introduces himself. Having learned from Ben that Cliff is a moviemaker, he begins the conversation with "I have a murder story for you with a great plot . . ."

Discussion Questions

1. The dinner guests at Rabbi Saul's table make various claims about ethics and/or being ethical. How many different claims can you identify?
2. Contrast Mae's and Saul's view of ethics. With whose view do you tend to agree? Why?
3. What is the fundamental difference between Rabbi Ben and Dr. Judah Rosenthal in how they see the world? Which of these views do you find most plausible? Explain.
4. Was Hitler an evil person? Attempt to defend your answer. How would Mae answer this question? How would Saul?
5. An important theme in the movie is being faithful: Judah cheats on his wife, but Cliff (narrowly) does not. Why shouldn't one cheat on a spouse?

Schindler's List (1993)

Director: Steven Spielberg
Screenwriter: Steven Zaillian (based on the Thomas Keneally book)

Plot Summary

The list is an absolute good. The list is life; all around its margins lie death.

It is 1939 and Nazi Germany overruns Poland in two weeks. Polish Jews are required to register in Krakow. Meanwhile, Nazi party member Oskar Schindler also arrives. He throws lavish dinner parties where high ranking Nazi officials are the guests of honor. They take photographs with Schindler and soon befriend him.

Two years pass and the Krakow Jews are now forced to enter the oldest part of the city known as the ghetto. Their homes and businesses are taken from them and their new accommodations are abysmal. Schindler contacts the Jewish Council, Judenrat, and makes a proposition. If a number of Jews will invest in his new enamelware business,

Schindler will return their monies in less than a year. But more importantly, since the factory is outside the ghetto and Schindler will bankroll his workers with items profitable on the black market, the Jews will have opportunities to acquire other goods. This according to Schindler is better than money, given their current situation. Begrudgingly, the Jews agree.

Itzhak Stern, a member of the Judenrat, becomes Schindler's production manager and accountant. A very bright man, he quickly realizes that hiring Jews to make Schindler's pots and pans will save many from being "deported" to another part of Europe. Stern has heard of others being "deported." Deportation really means being sent to Auschwitz and certain death. Stern hires a rabbi, a musician, a history professor, and even an elderly one-armed man because he (rightly) suspects that these will be the first to be evacuated from the ghetto. If you aren't needed for the Nazi war effort, then you simply are not needed, especially if you're Jewish.

With Stern busy managing the factory, Schindler begins keeping his part of the bargain. He again sends his new Nazi friends extravagant gifts. As it turns out, these Nazi officials oversee war contracts to private businesses. All of Schindler's bids are approved; his business booms and he quickly becomes a rich man.

In the winter of 1942 a new Nazi officer arrives in Krakow. His name is Amon Goeth. He has been deemed the commandant for Plaszow, the new labor camp to be built outside of Krakow. As a sign of things to come, Goeth's first official business as commandant is overseeing the construction of a barracks. The lead engineer, a highly educated Jewish woman, informs the guards and finally Goeth that the foundation must be refashioned; if it is not, the barracks will fall over. But Goeth does not like her tone—or the fact that she is educated—and orders one of his officers to immediately shoot her in the head. After her assassination, Goeth orders that her instructions are to be followed.

The following March, Goeth conducts the "liquidation of the ghetto." Nazi troops forcibly remove Jews from the ghetto. Those that are uncooperative are summarily shot. Some attempt to hide. Everyone else is marched to Plaszow. As darkness falls, the liquidation continues in the form of a "search and destroy" mission. Goeth sends in troops armed with stethoscopes and dogs. They are also armed with rifles, of course. No attempt is made to relocate the hiding Jews. Those that are discovered either by a careful ear, canine nose, or simply on accident, are all viciously shot.

Schindler's factory now lies dormant. To correct this, Schindler arranges a meeting with Goeth. As Schindler drives up to Goeth's villa overlooking the labor camp, we see Goeth shooting Jews with a high-powered rifle. Those not working efficiently—and even some that are—meet a bloody end. Schindler bribes Goeth into allowing his workers to leave the camp, thus reopening his factory. However, Goeth does not allow Stern to leave. Stern will oversee Goeth's end of the business—part of the bribe—from inside the camp.

Business is good again for Schindler. His Nazi contacts and other acquaintances throw him a birthday party. Two Jewish girls appear to present Schindler with a cake. They very nervously wish him a happy birthday from all of the workers. Schindler returns the sentiment by kissing the older girl—in front of the high-ranking Nazi contacts and officers. This gets Schindler thrown in prison. Soon after, however, he is freed by one of his contacts. The Nazi contact informs Schindler that he should not become too friendly with the Jews because "they have no future; that's not just good old Jew-hating talk—it's policy now."

New workers arrive at Plaszow. To make room for them, Goeth orders that all current workers be examined by doctors to assess their general health. In a most embarrassing display, the Jews—both men and women—are stripped naked and forced to run in circles in front of Nazi doctors. Those who are deemed unhealthy are either shot or "deported." Some of the Jewish women desperately prick their fingers and gently smear the blood on their cheeks in the hope of making them appear healthier than they really are. Meanwhile, however, the children are rounded up and placed on trucks. It seems that part of Goeth's ploy was to distract the adults so that the children could be removed from the camp without detection. Some children are lucky enough to escape—by hiding in floors, chimneys, and latrines—but most are not. The adult Jews shriek in terror when they realize that part of the examination was a ruse to "deport" the children.

In April 1944, Goeth is ordered to exhume and burn the bodies of the ten thousand Jews killed during his tenure in Krakow and Plaszow. The sky over Krakow is filled with ash; it falls like gray snowflakes. The remaining Jews are to be shipped to Auschwitz. Stern informs Schindler that he is coordinating the final evacuation, with himself on the final train. By this time, Schindler's only goal is the safety of his workers; he now cares nothing for profit. He arranges another meeting with Goeth where he "buys" his workers. If Schindler is willing to give Goeth enough money, Goeth is willing to hand over Jews to Schindler so that he can set up another factory in a different camp. Schindler and Stern type up a list of eleven hundred Jews; they are to arrive at Schindler's new factory near his hometown in Czechoslovakia. Although there is a clerical error and the women are sent to Auschwitz rather than Czechoslovakia, Schindler, after discovering the error, procures their safety by bribing a Nazi officer with diamonds—a precious commodity in postwar Europe.

With Nazi Germany's surrender in 1945, the war is over. Schindler must flee, for fear of being tried for war crimes along with other members of the Nazi party. The "Schindler Jews" see him off, presenting him with a document signed by each and every survivor that describes Schindler's commendable efforts on their behalf and a gold ring smelted from Jewish teeth. Schindler breaks down at this gesture, murmuring that he could have saved more people, if only he had sold his car or jewelry. Stern calmly assures him that he had done enough, reading to him the inscription on his ring: "Whoever saves one life saves the world entire."

Discussion Questions

1. Were the acts of the Nazis against the Jews morally wrong in some sort of objective or universal sense, or is this subjective or relative judgment? Explain.
2. Why did Stern refuse to have a drink with Schindler (or even look him in the eye) for most of the film?
3. How would you characterize Oskar Schindler at the beginning of the film? How, if at all, was his character different at the end of the film? What might account for this transformation (if any)?
4. Compare and contrast Stern, Schindler, and Goeth, and then offer a moral evaluation of their characters.
5. Spielberg is sometimes criticized for creating an engrossing Hollywood depiction of Holocaust survivors and the Holocaust generally. Are such criticisms warranted (that is, did he do anything morally wrong in making this film)? Explain.

5.5. REVIEWING THROUGH THE THREE MOVIES

1. In what ways do the three films featured in this chapter (respectively) express ethical objectivist themes, on the one hand, but nonobjectivist themes on the other? Are they (respectively) best interpreted as more objectivist or nonobjectivist overall? Explain carefully.

2. The narrator at the very end of *Crimes and Misdemeanors* explicitly states that how a person chooses to affect others (in terms of his or her relationships) directly impacts one's happiness. (And note how *The Cider House Rules* and *Schindler's List* implicitly affirm this via Homer and Goeth.) Is this to understand ethics objectively or nonobjectively? Explain.

3. Compare and contrast the moral characters of Dr. Wilbur Larch, Cliff Stern, and Oskar Schindler. What do you find most morally admirable about each? What do you find most morally deficient about each?

4. On some level, each of the three films is concerned with the search for value and meaning. Do you agree? If not, why not? If so, what is the moral significance of this search? (Is there any objectivist import to such searches?)

5. Reconsider the six movie quotes from the chapter and explain whether each, given the adjacent paragraphs, *illustrates* a point the author is making, *supplements* (or extends) a point the author is making, or *contrasts* (for emphasis) a point the author is making. Explain your answers.

NOTES

1. Excepted from Thomas Reid, *Essays on the Active Powers of Man*, essay V, chapter 1 (1788). Section headings and slight grammar emendations provided to aid reader comprehension.

2. This last critique of ethical objectivism has Humean roots, but has been sharpened by contemporary logical positivists such as Rudolph Carnap and A. J. Ayer. For more on logical positivism and moral judgments, including its turn toward emotivism, see Ayer's *Language, Truth, and Logic*, 2nd ed. (New York: Dover Press, 1952).

3. To be thorough, there are some philosophers (Hume, for example) who would resist the position that grounding ethical truths in human sentiment or psychology generally entails some form of ethical conventionalism.

4. Put another way, disagreement about ethical nonobjectivism itself stubbornly persists. Despite the ethical nonobjectivist's best efforts, ethical objectivists (moral realists) continue to disagree with them (and vice versa). Ethical objectivists believe that moral value and obligations are (in one way or another) objective features of the world and, thus, not merely mind dependent; ethical nonobjectivists believe just the opposite—that all moral value and obligation exist (if at all) only because of what is (psychologically) felt or believed. But the fact of this philosophical debate entails that the theory of ethical nonobjectivism cannot be true if (A) is true. Therefore, because (A) is either true or false, it follows that versions of ethical nonobjectivism relying on (A) fail.

5. Alan V. White perceptively points out (via correspondence) that there are potentially two relevant senses of "being accountable" for something. The first is causal. It very well may be that you played a causal role in bringing something about (or making something happen) even if you could not have prevented it. But this sense of being accountable doesn't entail moral responsibility, which is the second sense of "being accountable." It seems implausible to blame someone for something completely beyond his or her control to (in fact) prevent even if he or she played some (unpreventable) causal role in making it happen. In fact, that it couldn't be prevented is typically understood to serve as reason to excuse the agent from blame. The second sense of being accountable does entail

moral responsibility. The relevant examples discussed in this chapter assume the second sense of being accountable.

6. That is, any moral standard or moral rule is a moral principle, but not all moral principles are moral standards. Or put yet another way, "moral principle" will be employed as the blanket term covering all relevant ethically significant truths of reason. The more descript term "moral standard" or "moral rule" will be used when the context allows.

7. The discussion of moral principles and moral facts has been influenced by Russ Shafer-Landau, *Whatever Happened to Good and Evil?* (New York: Oxford University Press, 2005).

8. It must be admitted that nonrational factors play a role in belief formation. Recall Aunt Mae's contention that "history is written by the winners. And if the Nazis had won, future generations would understand the story of World War II quite differently." Perhaps she is correct in that what we currently believe is (at least partly) shaped by history; however, the ethical objectivist is resolute in holding that nonrational factors do not impact what is true. Finding the truth requires careful employment of rational processes (as described in chapter 1) that help circumvent nonrational processes of belief formation.

9. Michael Smith, "Realism," in *A Companion to Ethics*, ed. Peter Singer (Oxford: Blackwell, 1993), 399–410. To be fair, although Smith advocates moral realism, his conception of moral facts is not quite the same as the view being expressed in this chapter.

10. Michael Smith, "Realism," in *Ethical Theory*, ed. Russ Shafer-Landau (Malden, MA: Blackwell Publishing, 2007), 76.

11. The words of Elliot Sober ring true: "I am inclined to think that morality is one of the last frontiers that human knowledge can aspire to cross. . . . Powerful [nonrational] impulses disincline us to stare moral issues squarely in the face. No wonder it has taken humanity so long to traverse so modest a distance." See Elliot Sober, "Prospects for an Evolutionary Ethics," in *Ethical Theory: Classical and Contemporary Readings*, ed. Louis Pojman (Belmont, CA: Wadsworth, 1998), 139.

12. Louis Pojman, *Ethics: Discovering Right and Wrong*, 4th ed. (Belmont, CA: Wadsworth, 2002), 52–53. Furthermore, recall the argument from chapter 1 about how if it is wrong of someone else to harm or injure you for no good reason, then it is wrong of you to harm or injure anyone else without due reason. This insight serves as the basis for another approach to establishing ethical objectivism (moral realism). For more on this approach, see Thomas Nagel, *What Does It All Mean?* (New York: Oxford University Press, 1987), chap. 6.

PART II

WHAT OUGHT I TO DO?

CHAPTER 6

Biology, Psychology, and Ethical Theory

CAST AWAY (2000)
Director: Robert Zemeckis
Screenwriter: William Broyles, Jr.

PLOT SUMMARY

I gotta keep breathing. Because tomorrow the sun will rise. Who knows what the tide could bring?

Chuck Noland is an effective systems manager and engineer for FedEx. His job requires him to fly across the world at a moment's notice. This cuts into his committed and loving relationship with Kelly Frears. She is a PhD student finishing her dissertation, soon to defend it. Although Chuck loves Kelly very much, he is sometimes uncomfortable around his colleagues, preferring to discuss work rather than personal issues. In any event, Chuck's continued absences provide Kelly a lot of time to conduct her research.

Chuck has just returned to Memphis—and Kelly—after a stressful stint in Russia. It is Christmastime. Chuck and Kelly gather at a large table with friends and family for dinner. Before dessert is served, people around the table wonder whether, that is, when, Chuck and Kelly will wed. They knowingly look at each other as they absorb the wedding barbs and banter. But Chuck's beeper vibrates. Chuck and Kelly knowingly look at each other again, but in a different way: Chuck is being rushed off again for work. Chuck and Kelly quietly sit in another room trying to recoordinate their schedules around Chuck's pending trip to Malaysia. Kelly defends her dissertation in mid-January, but she is most concerned about New Year's Eve. For that matter, when will they celebrate Christmas? Chuck suggests that they exchange gifts in the car on the way to the airport.

BOX 6A: INSIDE *CAST AWAY*

Cast Away is a simple movie in many ways, centering on one man's personal journey, both geographical and spiritual. It conveys our inherent drive to survive, but also our deep need for others. It also raises the question of what, if anything, do we owe ourselves (and others) with respect to these features of the human condition. In these ways, among others, it is fitting for philosophical explorations into both ethical egoism and natural law.

Recalling how hectic Chuck's life was before the plane crash, watch a segment of Chuck's life on the island, beginning at scene 17 (1:04:30) or 18 (1:13:15), depending on how much time you have. Scene 17 opens with a shot of Chuck using ice skates to crack a coconut; scene 18 opens with a shot of a roaring fire. Either way, continue watching until 1:34:58, which is into scene 23, to watch Chuck launch his raft. (As you do, consider carefully Chuck's decision to attempt suicide and his "interactions" with "Wilson.") Skip ahead to the start of scene 28, beginning at 1:55:55; you'll see Chuck's taxi driving in the rain. This scene contains Chuck and Kelly's reunion. Continue viewing through the end of scene 31 (2:12:15) to learn Chuck's final estimation of their relationship. (Scene 32 begins with Chuck driving down a highway.)

The movie contains some powerful performances, especially by Tom Hanks. If you are able to view the entire film, then you should be able to answer the trivia questions from box 6B. If you are not able to view the film in its entirety, then watching the specified segments, in addition to carefully reading the plot summary, should give you a sufficient grasp of the film.

Kelly presents Chuck with a family heirloom pocket watch, once belonging to her grandfather. The gift is especially poignant, as Chuck constantly reminds those under his employ, "We live and die by time; we must never allow ourselves the sin of losing track of time." Chuck promises that he will always keep the watch on Memphis time, "Kelly-time." Chuck presents her with a few gifts not nearly as meaningful as the watch. He is about to board the FedEx plane, but abruptly returns. Under the guise of giving Kelly the keys, he presents her a wrapped, ring box. He admits that his other presents to her were "joke gifts," but this isn't one that should be opened in a car. They promise to open it on New Year's Eve. Chuck promises Kelly, "I'll be right back," and then boards the plane.

But Chuck does not return. His plane, already having diverted course in the hopes of avoiding the brunt of a terrible storm, explodes and crashes into the Pacific. Chuck is the sole survivor of the crash. His life raft washes up on the beach of a small, deserted island the next morning. He finds his pager and Kelly's watch. Both are broken, but the picture of Kelly, carefully placed inside the watch cover, is intact. Chuck finds FedEx packages washing up on shore. He collects them. He writes "HELP" in the sand, but the tide slowly washes it away. He struggles to open a few coconuts, and with the (fortunate) help of chipped stone, manages to drink some of the milk inside. He goes exploring and finds a cave. But his feet are bleeding; his shoes went down with the plane. He fashions some crude foot coverings from his slacks (which are now cut-off shorts). He makes his way to the summit to survey the island and his prospects.

That night, Chuck spies a light beyond the breakers. It must be a ship. He tries to signal it, but he goes unnoticed. He prepares the life raft and begins paddling toward the reef. But the waves are strong. He capsizes. In the process, both his raft and thigh are punctured by the sharp coral. Bleeding badly, Chuck retrieves what is left of the raft and begins to make more permanent arrangements on the island. He opens all but one of the FedEx boxes. He finds a pair of ice skates, which serve as his only cutting instruments. He finds a lacey dress, which he fashions into a net for fishing. In another, he finds a Wilson-brand volleyball. But a storm rolls in, and Chuck makes his way to the cave for shelter and much needed sleep.

The ice skates make opening coconuts much easier and they also allow him to make better spears. The art of spear fishing still eludes him, but he is now able to pierce beach crabs. Yet without fire, they are inedible. Making fire is his next project. His hands become raw rubbing sticks together. He savagely wounds himself as one of the sticks breaks in his hand. In a fit of rage, he begins throwing things around his makeshift campsite, including the volleyball. When he retrieves the ball, he notices that his bloody handprint has made a crude face-like marking. Chuck makes the face more distinct. He names the ball "Wilson" and begins taking him everywhere he goes. Yet Chuck soon starts a fire and dines on crabmeat, striking up a "conversation" with Wilson.

Chuck takes full advantage of his newfound companion Wilson. They have many "conversations," and Chuck begins to reevaluate his situation via the ruse of explaining his circumstances to Wilson. With all of this chatter, Chuck's abscessed tooth becomes serious. Chuck decides that he must extract it himself. He carefully places an ice skate inside his mouth, and—whimpering—slams one end with a rock. The rotten tooth is knocked free, but Chuck is knocked out. When we see Chuck again, it is four years later. He is much thinner. His hair has grown out and has become bleached by the sun. He is a master spear fisher, sometimes not bothering to cook his catch before he eats it. In all of this, Wilson remains a steadfast companion, always near his side.

BOX 6B: *CAST AWAY* TRIVIA

If your instructor assigns the film to be watched outside of class, you should be able to answer the following questions:

1. How many hours does it take the clock to travel from Memphis to Russia?
2. Kelly's ex-husband did what for a living?
3. What was Chuck's first spoken word on the island?
4. What is the (full) name of the deceased pilot that Chuck finds on the beach?
5. What does Chuck find in the first FedEx box he opens on the island?
6. How many days did Chuck spend on the island?
7. What is the first animal Chuck encounters at sea?
8. What soft drink does Chuck enjoy on the plane after being rescued?
9. What possession of Chuck's did Kelly keep and then return to him?
10. What color is the pickup truck at the end of the film?

One morning, Chuck is awakened by a strange sound. He initially yells at Wilson to be quiet, but quickly realizes that it is coming from the beach. He investigates. Two sides of a port-a-potty have washed up on shore. Chuck stares at it for a while. When the wind knocks it over, Chuck turns to Wilson and says, "This could work." Chuck begins crafting a raft. He chops down larger trees for the planks and small trees to make rope—lots of rope. There isn't much time; if he and Wilson are to leave the island, they must do so during the offshore spring winds. As if in response to Wilson, Chuck admits, "Yeah, I know where there is thirty feet of extra rope! But I'm not going back up there." Nevertheless, Chuck climbs to the summit and pulls up the thirty-foot piece of rope. At its end there is a noose around a log that looks suspiciously like a corpse. Chuck had entertained the idea of committing suicide one year ago, and this was his way to test the strength of the rope and the limb from which it hung. With those painful memories behind him, the departure day arrives. Chuck launches his craft and paddles toward the breakers. As he is about to capsize (again), he releases the port-a-potty walls, and they immediately act like a sail. Picking up the offshore winds, Chuck is able to make it over the last breaker; he and Wilson make it to the open sea.

Their journey is not easy. Storms ravage the raft. There is very little to eat. Wilson is lost at sea, becoming untethered after a storm. Chuck mourns the loss of his "friend"; he sobs uncontrollably. When it seems that all hope is lost, a large tanker sails past. Chuck is rescued and swiftly returned to the FedEx family. He is reacquainted with his colleagues, especially Stan; Stan arranges for Chuck to meet with Kelly. But Kelly is now married to someone else and she has a daughter. Kelly attempts a meeting, but sends her husband instead. Later that night, Chuck takes a taxi to Kelly's house. They warmly embrace, and do their best to get reacquainted. He returns her grandfather's watch (but keeps the picture), and asks why she isn't a professor. She shows him all of her clippings and documents about the search. As he is about to leave, she runs after him. They kiss passionately. She looks up and admits, "I love you. You're the love of my life." He replies, "I love you, too, Kelly. More than you'll ever know." They look knowingly into each other's eyes again, but Chuck slowly says, "You have to go home."

Later that night Chuck confides to Stan, "We had both done the math, and Kelly had added it all up. She knew that she had to let me go. I added it up, knew that I'd—I'd lost her. Because I was never gonna get off that island. I was gonna die there, totally alone. . . . And one day, all that logic was proved wrong because the tide . . . came in and gave me a sail. And now here I am. I'm back . . . and I've lost her all over again."

6.1. THINKING THROUGH THE MOVIE

Discussion Starter Questions

1. Why does Chuck regularly "interact" with Wilson? Is Chuck's behavior in this regard unexpected? Why or why not?
2. After three years on the island, Chuck contemplates suicide. Had he gone through with this, would he have acted impermissibly? Explain.
3. Would it have been impermissible for Kelly to leave with Chuck (the love of her life) that night he visits her house?
4. Why does Chuck choose to leave the last FedEx box unopened? How does this choice save his life, per his note at the end of the film?

Questions for Further Thought

1. Compare Chuck's choices to leave his plane seat to retrieve Kelly's watch (scene 7, 24:40), extract his tooth with the ice skate (scene 19, 1:17:35), and advise Kelly to remain with her family (scene 29, 2:05:33). Why did he choose to do these things? Are the reasons similar or importantly different?

2. Chuck decides to take the deceased pilot's shoes (scene 13, roughly 50:30) and open the FedEx boxes (scene 16, 1:02:03), all without permission. Are these actions permissible? How does your answer impact your understanding of what it means to steal?

3. Is it ever permissible to intentionally end your life? Defend your answer. Does your answer cohere or contrast with the overall message of *Cast Away*? Explain.

4. Compare and contrast Chuck's interactions with Stan in scene 3 (roughly 11:00) and scene 26 (roughly 1:50:00). Generalizing on this, in what ways is Chuck a different person after being rescued than before the plane crash (that is, by the end of the movie)? Are any of these ways morally significant? Explain.

6.2. HISTORICAL SETTING

Summa Theologica (excerpt)[1]

Thomas Aquinas (1224–1274) defied his father in becoming a Dominican monk. After studying with Albert the Great, he taught theology for a while at the University of Paris. He is widely considered the greatest religious philosopher in the Western tradition. Here we read an excerpt from his magnum opus, *Summa Theologica*.

Preparing to Read

A. Are you naturally inclined to do anything? If so, what? Do others share this inclination with you?

B. Would you act any differently than Chuck Noland if you were the sole castaway on a deserted, tropical island?

Whether There Is an Eternal Law?

I answer that . . . a law is nothing else but a dictate of practical reason emanating from the ruler who governs a perfect community. Now it is evident, granted that the world is ruled by Divine Providence . . . that the whole community of the universe is governed by Divine Reason. Wherefore the very idea of the government of things in God the ruler of the universe, has the nature of a law. And since the Divine Reason's conception of things is not subject to time but is eternal, . . . therefore it is that this kind of law must be called eternal.

Whether There Is in Us a Natural Law?

I answer that . . . law, being a rule and measure, can be in a person in two ways: in one way, as in him that rules and measures; in another way, as in that which is ruled and measured, since a thing is ruled and measured, in so far as it partakes of the rule or measure. Wherefore, since all things subject to Divine Providence are ruled and measured by the eternal law ... it is evident that all things partake somewhat of the eternal law, in so far as, namely, from its being imprinted on them, they derive their respective inclinations to their proper acts and ends. Now among all others, the rational creature is subject to Divine Providence in the most excellent way, in so far as it partakes of a share of providence, by being provident both for itself and for others. Wherefore it has a share of the Eternal Reason, whereby it has a natural inclination to its proper act and end: and this participation of the eternal law in the rational creature is called the natural law. Hence ... the light of natural reason, whereby we discern what is good and what is evil, which is the function of the natural law, is nothing else than an imprint on us of the Divine Light. It is therefore evident that the natural law is nothing else than the rational creature's participation of the eternal law.

Whether the Natural Law Contains Several Precepts, or Only One?

I answer that ... the precepts of the natural law are to the practical reason, what the first principles of demonstrations are to the speculative reason; because both are self-evident principles. Now a thing is said to be self-evident in two ways: first, in itself; secondly, in relation to us. Any proposition is said to be self-evident in itself, if its predicate is contained in the notion of the subject: although, to one who knows not the definition of the subject, it happens that such a proposition is not self-evident. For instance, this proposition, "Man is a rational being," is, in its very nature, self-evident, since who says "man," says "a rational being": and yet to one who knows not what a man is, this proposition is not self-evident. Hence it is that ... certain axioms or propositions are universally self-evident to all; and such are those propositions whose terms are known to all, as, "Every whole is greater than its part," and, "Things equal to one and the same are equal to one another." But some propositions are self-evident only to the wise, who understand the meaning of the terms of such propositions: thus to one who understands that an angel is not a body, it is self-evident that an angel is not circumscriptively in a place: but this is not evident to the unlearned, for they cannot grasp it.

Now a certain order is to be found in those things that are apprehended universally. For that which, before all else, falls under apprehension, is "being," the notion of which is included in all things whatsoever a man apprehends. Wherefore the first indemonstrable principle is that "the same thing cannot be affirmed and denied at the same time," which is based on the notion of "being" and "not-being": and on this principle all others are based. ... Now as "being" is the first thing that falls under the apprehension simply, so "good" is the first thing that falls under the apprehension of the practical reason, which is directed to action: since every agent acts for an end under the aspect of good. Consequently the first principle of practical reason is one founded on the notion of good, viz. that "good is that which all things seek after." Hence this is the first precept of law, that "good is to be done and pursued, and evil is to be avoided." All other precepts of the natural law are based upon this: so that whatever the practical reason naturally apprehends as man's good (or evil) belongs to the precepts of the natural law as something to be done or avoided.

Since, however, good has the nature of an end, and evil, the nature of a contrary, hence it is that all those things to which man has a natural inclination, are naturally apprehended by reason as being good, and consequently as objects of pursuit, and their contraries as evil, and objects of avoidance. Wherefore according to the order of natural inclinations, is the order of the precepts of the natural law. Because in man there is first of all an inclination to good in accordance with the nature which he has in common with all substances: inasmuch as every substance seeks the preservation of its own being, according to its nature: and by reason of this inclination, whatever is a means of preserving human life, and of warding off its obstacles, belongs to the natural law. Secondly, there is in man an inclination to things that pertain to him more specially, according to that nature which he has in common with other animals: and in virtue of this inclination, those things are said to belong to the natural law, . . . such as sexual intercourse, education of offspring and so forth. Thirdly, there is in man an inclination to good, according to the nature of his reason, which nature is proper to him: thus man has a natural inclination to know the truth about God, and to live in society: and in this respect, whatever pertains to this inclination belongs to the natural law; for instance, to shun ignorance, to avoid offending those among whom one has to live, and other such things regarding the above inclination.

Whether All Acts of Virtue Are Prescribed by the Natural Law?

I answer that . . . we may speak of virtuous acts in two ways: first, under the aspect of virtuous; secondly, as such and such acts considered in their proper species. If then we speak of acts of virtue, considered as virtuous, thus all virtuous acts belong to the natural law. For . . . the natural law belongs everything to which a man is inclined according to his nature. Now each thing is inclined naturally to an operation that is suitable to it according to its form: thus fire is inclined to give heat. Wherefore, since the rational soul is the proper form of man, there is in every man a natural inclination to act according to reason: and this is to act according to virtue. Consequently, considered thus, all acts of virtue are prescribed by the natural law: since each one's reason naturally dictates to him to act virtuously. But if we speak of virtuous acts, considered in themselves, i.e., in their proper species, thus not all virtuous acts are prescribed by the natural law: for many things are done virtuously, to which nature does not incline at first; but which, through the inquiry of reason, have been found by men to be conducive to well-living.

Whether the Natural Law Is the Same in All Men?

I answer that . . . to the natural law belongs those things to which a man is inclined naturally: and among these it is proper to man to be inclined to act according to reason. Now the process of reason is from the common to the proper. . . . The speculative reason, however, is differently situated in this matter, from the practical reason. For, since the speculative reason is busied chiefly with the necessary things, which cannot be otherwise than they are, its proper conclusions, like the universal principles, contain the truth without fail. The practical reason, on the other hand, is busied with contingent matters, about which human actions are concerned: and consequently, although there is necessity in the general principles, the more we descend to matters of detail, the more frequently we encounter defects. Accordingly then in speculative matters truth is the same in all men, both as to principles and as to conclusions: although the truth is not known to all as regards the conclusions, but only as regards the principles which are called common notions. But in matters of action, truth or practical rectitude is not the same for all, as to matters of detail, but only as to the general principles: and where there is the same rectitude in matters of detail, it is not equally known to all.

It is therefore evident that, as regards the general principles whether of speculative or of practical reason, truth or rectitude is the same for all, and is equally known by all. As to the proper conclusions of the speculative reason, the truth is the same for all, but is not equally known to all: thus it is true for all that the three angles of a triangle are together equal to two right angles, although it is not known to all. But as to the proper conclusions of the practical reason, neither is the truth or rectitude the same for all, nor, where it is the same, is it equally known by all. Thus it is right and true for all to act according to reason: and from this principle it follows as a proper conclusion, that goods entrusted to another should be restored to their owner. Now this is true for the majority of cases: but it may happen in a particular case that it would be injurious, and therefore unreasonable, to restore goods held in trust; for instance, if they are claimed for the purpose of fighting against one's country. And this principle will be found to fail the more, according as we descend further into detail, e.g., if one were to say that goods held in trust should be restored with such and such a guarantee, or in such and such a way; because the greater the number of conditions added, the greater the number of ways in which the principle may fail, so that it be not right to restore or not to restore.

Consequently we must say that the natural law, as to general principles, is the same for all, both as to rectitude and as to knowledge. But as to certain matters of detail, which are conclusions, as it were, of those general principles, it is the same for all in the majority of cases, both as to rectitude and as to knowledge; and yet in some few cases it may fail, both as to rectitude, by reason of certain obstacles (just as natures subject to generation and corruption fail in some few cases on account of some obstacle), and as to knowledge, since in some the reason is perverted by passion, or evil habit, or an evil disposition of nature . . . .

Whether the Law of Nature Can Be Abolished from the Heart of Man?

I answer that . . . there belong to the natural law, first, certain most general precepts, that are known to all; and secondly, certain secondary and more detailed precepts, which are, as it were, conclusions following closely from first principles. As to those general principles, the natural law, in the abstract, can nowise be blotted out from men's hearts. But it is blotted out in the case of a particular action, in so far as reason is hindered from applying the general principle to a particular point of practice, on account of concupiscence or some other passion. . . . But as to the other, i.e., the secondary precepts, the natural law can be blotted out from the human heart, either by evil persuasions, just as in speculative matters errors occur in respect of necessary conclusions; or by vicious customs and corrupt habits, as among some men, theft, and even unnatural vices . . . were not esteemed sinful.

Review Questions

1. What is the interrelationship between the eternal law and the natural law?
2. How does an agent act impermissibly, according to Aquinas?
3. Why is the natural law the same for each human moral agent?

6.3. DISCUSSION AND ANALYSIS

The theories discussed in part 1 of the text were first and foremost metaethical, explicating the nature of moral truth generally. The theories to be discussed in parts 2 and 3, each committed to some variety of ethical objectivism, are primarily normative. A normative theory attempts to spell out defensible moral judgments for specific situations. Normative theories are invariably called, simply, moral theories. A moral theory is analogous to other theories attempting to convey deep, systematized insights into their subject matter. Just as mathematical or scientific theories, if successful, articulate important, coherent truths about arithmetic or the natural world (respectively), a moral theory attempts to articulate important and universally binding ethically significant truths. Furthermore, just as theories in math or science aspire to establish results that are free from bias, lest their findings be illicitly tainted with subjectivity, moral theories strive to delineate positions that are impartial and free from arbitrary authority. The end result in math, science, or ethics is thus a matter of *discovery* about the subject and not merely one of invention (or convention) by those putting forth those theories.[2]

The Anatomy of Moral Theories

Did Chuck Noland do the right thing in advising Kelly Frears to stay with her family? Did Mary Jane Watson (from *Spider-Man 2*) do the right thing in leaving John Jameson at the altar? Did Brandon Teena (born Teena Brandon, from *Boys Don't Cry*) act permissibly in pursuing intimate relationships with women? Moral philosophers invariably aspire to provide a moral theory that systematizes plausible answers to these and, indeed, any ethically significant question. Generally, then, a moral theory attempts to articulate and defend certain specific views regarding the nature of right action or good living (or both). It delineates when it is appropriate to think in moral terms, specifying what things or situations are morally significant. It describes in some detail what we ought to do (or what kinds of lives we ought to lead) and offers plausible explanations for why we ought to do (or lead) them. Moreover, it conveys this for any morally significant situation, deeming actions either impermissible, obligatory, or merely permissible (including, perhaps, supererogatory). This includes conflict situations or so-called moral dilemmas—those occasions such that no matter what the agent chooses, something morally unfortunate or tragic will obtain. Even here, a moral theory must be sufficiently action-guiding.

Accordingly, a moral theory will specify what makes an action right or wrong and provide a defensible account of each. But it will also specify what makes an agent good (or excellent) or bad (or evil) and provide a defensible account of such assessments. These two specifications will be accomplished in terms of the other, with one taking precedence. If the former takes precedence, then the latter requirement is roughly accomplished: "a good person is defined as one who typically performs the right actions for the right reasons." If the latter takes precedence, then the former requirement is roughly accomplished: "a right action is defined as that which a good agent/person typically performs." Which task takes precedence will be informative as to whether actions or agents are more fundamental to the theory at hand. The former kind of theory is (unimaginatively) known as "action-based" and the latter kind is known as "agent-based."

Any proposed moral theory will contain a moral standard, which serves as its most fundamental moral principle. The moral standard will accordingly provide the very criterion

---

BOX 6C: LEARNING OUTCOMES

Upon carefully studying this chapter, students should better comprehend and be able to explain:

- The essential elements of a moral theory and some criteria by which such theories can be assessed.
- The essential elements of ethical egoism and natural law ethics (respectively) and how each moral theory can be assessed via the relevant criteria.
- How issues in psychology and biology can be relevant to articulating and defending morally significant positions.
- How themes expressed in *Cast Away*, *Spider-Man 2*, and *Boys Don't Cry* are conducive to better understanding the nature of moral theories generally and ethical egoism and natural law ethics specifically.

(albeit rather abstractly) for determining right actions from wrong and good agents from bad. In fact, any moral judgment will ultimately be some derivation of the moral standard. This also pertains to the derived moral rules. Moral rules are moral principles that specify types or kinds of action as impermissible, obligatory, or merely permissible; they result from initial attempts to apply a moral standard to instances or sets of circumstances. They thus represent an important intermediate link between specific moral judgments and more general or abstract moral standards. Specific moral judgments obtain once factual and conceptual considerations have been properly considered in light of a relevant moral rule.

Moral theories will invariably (implicitly or explicitly) specify intrinsic value.[3] Something has intrinsic value just in case it is good for its own sake; merely possessing the thing in question is its own unique reward. If something has morally significant intrinsic value, this represents the highest good that can be achieved by moral agents. A moral

> "Intelligence is not a privilege; it's a gift to be used for the benefit of all mankind." — *Spider-Man 2*, scene 8

standard will provide general strategies for living in accordance with the highest good. Accordingly, a moral theory (once fully articulated) will specify what is of ultimate importance in life and offer carefully developed strategies for living in accordance with that ideal. Furthermore, morally significant benefits and harms can also be understood via specifications of ethically significant intrinsic value. One nontrivially benefits whenever one's position with respect to the highest good is somehow improved; one is nontrivially harmed when one's position with respect to the highest good is somehow diminished. Consequently, moral theories will, invariably, provide strategies for improving (or maintaining) one's position with respect to the highest good and avoiding situations in which one's position is diminished. Acts that so improve one's position are right or good; acts that result in diminishing one's position are wrong or bad.

Evaluating Moral Theories

Recall from part 1 that there are multiple metaethical theories, each offering competing views about the nature of moral truth. Analogously, there are multiple moral theories, each offering competing accounts of right action or moral goodness. Further recall that the primary goal of part 1 was to assess the competing metaethical theories via careful conceptual analysis. Parts 2 and 3 intend to accomplish the same goal regarding competing moral theories. Philosophers are admittedly somewhat divided about how to conduct conceptual analysis on moral theories. However, some criteria for accomplishing the assessment of moral theories remain highly influential.

First, any defensible moral theory, indeed any theory, must be free from internal logical contradiction; we might call this the *contradiction test*. All theories are made up of statements or assertions—what philosophers tend to call propositions. Any proposition is either true or false, depending upon whether what it asserts is actually the case. So, when determining whether a moral theory passes the contradiction test, we take all the relevant propositions into consideration and assess whether any of them together amount to (or even lead to, that is, entail) a contradiction. For example, if the same theory entails that it is both permissible and impermissible for Kelly to leave her family to be with Chuck, then it fails the contradiction test. That a moral theory fails the contradiction test is the most powerful evidence that it requires revision. Just as it is difficult to accept a scientific theory that affirms the sun is and is not the center of the solar system, it is difficult to accept a moral theory that affirms the same action (in the same circumstances) is both wrong and not wrong.

Second, any theory that attempts to convey deep, systematized insights into its subject matter must be sufficiently illuminating about its intended subject. That is, just any set of true and mutually consistent statements does not qualify as a theory. For example, the following three propositions are mutually consistent: 'Spider-Man is a well-known fictional superhero'; 'Tom Hanks and Hilary Swank have (respectively) won two Academy Awards'; 'Sexual orientation is a controversial topic'. Although the joint truth of these statements involves no logical inconsistency, they do not provide any illuminating account of anything. They are random assertions lacking any real coherence. But a moral theory is supposed to provide a coherent and illuminating account of ethics. That is, it must offer an intelligible and sufficiently complete picture about ethically significant situations and what leading the ethical life involves. This might be called the *completeness test*. One common way in which a theory fails this test is that some of its crucial concepts are not sufficiently defined or clarified. That a moral theory fails the completeness test is strong evidence that it requires revision.

Third, any defensible moral theory must be sufficiently action-guiding. This criterion, which might be called the *action-guiding test*, often flows from the second. The most obvious way in which a moral theory suffers from incompleteness is that it does not offer clear guidance about what to do in some ethically significant situations. Perhaps it cannot resolve a moral dilemma or a conflict between two relevant moral rules. Perhaps the range of permissible acts is implausibly large. Perhaps too many kinds or types of action are not adequately classified as obligatory, permissible, or impermissible. That a moral theory fails the action-guiding test is strong evidence that it requires revision. The force of these two criteria is grounded in the very fact that a moral theory is supposed to help us answer the question: "How ought I (we) to live?" If it leaves too much of that question unanswered, it fails on its own terms.

Fourth, any defensible moral theory must adequately specify what things or situations are ethically significant. The relevant specification can be neither too stringent nor too lax. Regarding the first constraint, the theory should not rule out, by simple fiat, things or situations that just obviously seem morally significant. For example, consider a theory that discounts the moral significance of persons with first and last names beginning with the same letter (Peter Parker, Otto Octavius). Regarding the second constraint, the theory should not allow just any thing or situation to count as morally relevant. For example, consider a theory that declares it impermissible to own Wilson-brand volleyballs because this fails to recognize the inherent rights of volleyballs as unique individuals. Even if volleyballs are given names ("Wilson") or are (surprisingly) like snowflakes such that no two are exactly alike, this view still seems a bit extreme.

Sometimes this criterion is expressed in terms of the size of the "moral universe." To explore the universe is to inquire into what (actually) exists. To claim that unicorns are actual members of the universe but horses are not is doubly faulty. To claim that Wilson volleyballs are members of the moral universe but famed *X-Files* actor David Duchovny is not is analogously dubious on both accounts. So, a plausible moral theory should profess a moral universe that is intuitively neither too large nor too small. This might be called the *moral universe test*. Although intuitions sometimes differ, that a moral theory fails the moral universe test is rather strong evidence that it requires revision.

Fifth, any defensible moral theory must withstand counterexamples leveled at it. This criterion, which applies to all theories, might be called the *counterexample test*. This test proceeds by noting what would follow if the theory were true. If the derived entailment seems *plainly* false or otherwise *obviously* counterintuitive, then the alleged counterexample must be suitably addressed. Ideally, defenders of the theory can explain away the alleged counterexample by successfully arguing that the relevant entailment is not all that problematic. Consider an example from the history of science. Galileo's helio-centered view of the solar system (obviously) entailed that the earth went around the sun rather than the sun revolving around the earth, as was then commonly believed. Immediately, it encountered the following objection: "How can the helio-centric theory be correct, when it is so obvious that the sun revolves around the earth? After all, the sun rises in the east and sets in the west *every day*!" That is, if the helio-centered theory was true, observing the sun moving across the sky is unexpected. But this counterexample can be successfully explained away by appealing to the rotation of the earth on its axis. (To the further objection that it doesn't feel like we are spinning, one might appeal, in part, to the massive size of the earth relative to the observer.) But if the purported counterexample cannot be successfully explained away, then the theory fails the counterexample test. That a moral theory fails the counterexample test is evidence that it requires revision.

This last criterion for evaluating moral theories is admittedly sensitive to conflicting intuitions, which tends to sometimes curtail the force of the counterexample test. (In fact, this point also applies to the moral universe test in that it is effectively understood as one vivid instance of the counterexample test.) Crafting a counterexample to a moral theory invariably requires an argument to the effect that it has *morally* objectionable or absurd implications. But this conclusion cannot be made without referring to an independently held *moral* judgment or belief. But should the theory be revised in light of the prior belief or the belief revised in light of the theory? This is where intuitions can conflict. It's conceivable that the theory might be able to explain the alleged counterexample away on its own terms, analogous to Galileo's success in answering the "sunrise-sunset" objection. Yet some cases exist where the counterexample against the theory is plainly decisive. Consider a theory that entails men, but not women, are members of the moral universe. What could possibly justify this arbitrary and absurd entailment? Upon occasion, then, the absurdity of the entailment is so obvious that no serious debate about it can arise, leaving one to revise the relevant moral theory. One way to decide this issue is to investigate whether the counterexample runs contrary to our most deeply held and well-considered moral beliefs.[4] Such beliefs or judgments are neither the result of non-rational processes nor simple unreflective social convention. That a moral theory overturns *these* beliefs is at least some evidence that it requires revision.

For all of that, the overall importance of the counterexample test for doing conceptual analysis cannot be overlooked. Consider that moral principles, and hence moral standards, are (or are akin to) ethically significant truths of reason. Thus moral standards are supposed to be (in some sense) necessarily true, resistant to any alleged counterexample. A carefully crafted counterexample, if it cannot be suitably explained away, therefore shows how the moral standard is not true. But moral standards are foundation to a moral theory. Therefore, a carefully crafted counterexample ultimately shows (invariably) how a moral theory is flawed *at its core*, which is evidence that its insights into the ethical life are somehow faulty. This consequence remains even if one is suspicious of the idea that moral standards are ethically significant truths of reason. Regardless of their truth-status, moral standards are analogous to basic axioms of math or logic. Any theory rests on basic axioms; they provide the conceptual foundation for the resulting structure built upon them. A carefully crafted counterexample to that structure ultimately shows (invariably) that its basic axiom cannot bear the conceptual weight it must to succeed. That axiom (or axioms) must be revised if the theory is to accomplish its intended explanatory goal. Therefore, if a moral theory is open to a powerful counterexample, this is evidence that it does not accomplish its intended goal of articulating and systematizing plausible insights into the ethical life. This, in turn, is evidence that different or revised ethically significant axioms (principles or standards) should be sought.

A Brief Admission (or Two)

It seems unlikely that any moral theory will be completely free of alleged counterexamples, and highly unlikely that any moral theory will pass all of the proffered tests uncontested. Any interesting moral theory, like all interesting philosophy, is at least somewhat controversial. But it is also conceivable that some moral theories will fare better than others with respect to the five tests. Theories that fail the contradiction test are more dubious than those that do not. Theories that face serious difficulties regarding multiple tests are more dubious than those that do not. Making definitive conclusions about the plausibility of moral theories will not always be easy; however, by engaging in this process one does moral philosophy, and, as Socrates would remind us, this is no unimportant matter. In fact, what could be more important than gaining insights into how to live? The fundamental goal of this text is to help students achieve these insights *on their own* by offering initial explorations of the classic moral theories. Any conclusion it might offer about the plausibility of a moral theory is, at best, tentative, leaving the "fledgling philosopher" much opportunity for further study.

The discussion in the chapter thus far admittedly provides little by way of application of the proffered criteria for assessing moral theories. The next two sections will correct that, paving the way for further assessment in the chapters to come. But it is worthwhile to point out now that not only must a moral standard be (relatively) free of reasons not to believe it, there must be reasons to believe it. Different moral theories attempt to accomplish this in distinctive ways. However, any such attempt to support a moral standard will invariably be indirect. This is because to directly prove a moral standard requires making it the conclusion to a sound (or cogent) argument. But this, in turn, requires articulating premises more obviously true than is the moral standard they are trying to prove, which seems unlikely. In any event, to better appreciate how moral theories can be evaluated via the proffered criteria, consider the following assessments of ethical egoism and natural law ethics.

Introducing Ethical Egoism

The nefarious Cigarette Smoking Man from *The X-Files* once ominously commented: "No act is completely selfless." Some scholars take this fictional character's words as fact. They believe that self-regarding behavior is a deep psychological truth about human nature. This view is called psychological egoism. According to psychological egoism, it is psychologically impossible for a person to act contrary to his or her (perceived) best interest. No matter what human agents decide to do, it is necessarily done out of self-interested motives. Psychological egoism is a descriptive theory, not prescriptive. It asserts something about how human beings do (necessarily) act, not how we ought to act. The psychological egoist affirms that all human action is done either to gain some personal benefit or avoid some personal harm.

If psychological egoism were true, it would have significant ethical ramifications. Note that if it were true, then it would be psychologically impossible for any agent to put the interests of others on par with, let alone ahead of, the agent's interests. Thus altruistic behavior is impossible for us. But we cannot be morally required to accomplish the impossible. So, if psychological egoism is true, we cannot be morally required to act altruistically, placing the interests of others on par with or ahead of our own. Yet it certainly seems we should *sometimes* act altruistically, putting the interests of others ahead of our own. Moreover, taking the moral point of view from the start requires impartial consideration of others' interests. Psychological egoism flies in the face of these intuitions. Consequently, if psychological egoism were true, we could not be morally required to perform any other-regarding behavior. In fact, it would cause us to rethink the very idea of taking the moral point of view.

One common reason offered in support of psychological egoism is the widely held belief that human agents necessarily act on their strongest motive or desire. This belief is bolstered by personal reports. When we inquire into why someone did something, we often hear, "because it's what I most wanted to do at the time." This includes any alleged altruistic acts. Acting in that way was what the agent wanted to do most at the time. But, the argument continues, to perform actions merely because they represent one's strongest motive or desire at the time is to act self-interestedly. Therefore, the argument concludes, human agents necessarily act self-interestedly. This, in turn, seemingly entails that we can act only so as to pursue self-interest in terms of seeking some personal benefit or avoiding some personal harm, which is tantamount to accepting psychological egoism.

There is a different, but related argument that threatens traditional approaches to ethics. This second argument proceeds from the idea that any and all binding imperatives must be grounded in good reasons for keeping them. This, of course, also applies to our moral obligations: if you ought to do something, then there are sufficiently good reasons for doing it—you have good reasons for upholding the obligation. But, if *you* have good reasons for doing something, then doing it thereby serves (or satisfies) *your* personal interests. Therefore, if you morally ought to do something, then doing it thereby serves your interests.[5] This argument converges with the argument from psychological egoism in the following way: if doing something doesn't serve (or satisfy) your personal interests, then you cannot be morally obligated to do that thing. Therefore, you cannot be morally obligated to act altruistically.

These two arguments are typically interpreted as lending intuitive support for ethical egoism. Ethical egoism is a rather austere moral theory. According to the ethical egoist, taking the moral point of view is simply to perform those actions that will most benefit the agent. It is appropriate to think in moral terms whenever, but only when, *your* personal well-being or interests are at stake. The egoist would therefore undoubtedly disagree with Peter Parker's dictum that "sometimes, to do what is right, you must give up the thing we want most." The moral standard of this theory can be succinctly put as:

Everyone ought to promote his or her own self-interest (exclusively).

An agent is morally required to perform *only* those actions that best promote his or her self-interest for the situation at hand. An agent might permissibly work to promote the interests of others, but only if doing so ultimately best promotes his or her own interests. An agent acts impermissibly if she performs an action that doesn't best promote her interests. A morally good person is one who regularly acts in her own best interests, and a bad person is one who regularly fails to act in her own best interests. Plausible candidates for moral rules of ethical egoism include: do educate yourself (so that you make proper decisions regarding your self-interests); do stay healthy, practicing good-health habits. Two additional plausible candidates for moral rules are: do not openly break the law; do not make sacrifices for others or engage in dangerous activities (except perhaps in rare cases that actually work to serve your best interests). Brandon Teena often violated the former; Peter Parker often violated the latter. Even Spider-Man should give pause before running into a burning building or stopping a runaway train with his bare hands.

One of the interesting entailments of ethical egoism is that each of us has duties to ourselves. In *Cast Away*, Chuck Noland was marooned and alone on a tropical island; his friends and family believed him to be dead. No one expected him to return. Nevertheless, the ethical egoist would affirm that Chuck had a moral duty to keep himself alive and healthy insofar as he was able. After a few years of isolation on the island, Chuck considered committing suicide. Committing suicide is invariably impermissible on ethical egoism, not because it violates God's command or it causes emotional harm to others. Even if no one learns of the suicide, it is wrong because it fails to serve your best interests—being alive is a precondition to have any interests.[6] But it must be stressed that, on ethical egoism, *only* the agent's interests matter morally speaking. The ethical egoist is thus likely to argue that Peter Parker's uncle, Ben Parker, is nothing short of a moral monster. Ben lived his life for others and instilled that self-sacrificing approach in his nephew, urging him to give up his dreams—including Mary Jane—for the sake of heroically bringing "honesty, fairness, and justice out into the world" as Spider-Man. His iconic mantra to Peter was: "With great

> "Am I not supposed to have what I want? What I need? What am I supposed to do?"— *Spider-Man 2*, scene 34

Cast Away, Twentieth Century Fox, 2000. Chuck Noland (Tom Hanks) is marooned on a tropical island and must help himself to again reach civilization. (Moviegoods, Inc.)

power comes great responsibility." Yet it's clear that Peter has become miserable living Ben's dream, thereby failing to effectively serve his own interests.

Assessing Ethical Egoism

With the essential elements of ethical egoism in place, consider how it fares with respect to the criteria delineated earlier in this section. The ethical egoist must take care in properly defining "self-interest." Most egoists are sympathetic to hedonism, and consider morally significant benefits and harms straightforwardly in physical and psychological terms. Moreover, most distinguish between immediate and long-range interests. Sometimes an immediate benefit will have serious drawbacks in the long term and sometimes an immediate harm has significant long-term benefits. Is it in Chuck's best interest to extract his own tooth or not open the last FedEx package? Is it in his best interest to leave the island, adrift on a rickety raft? These are surprisingly difficult questions. However, this isn't to say that these pending issues about self-interest cannot be properly addressed, but it is to say that if the egoist does not address them, ethical egoism will suffer from incompleteness, potentially failing the completeness test.

Many critics almost immediately point out that ethical egoism requires us to overturn or suspend some of our most entrenched and considered moral beliefs, which serves as a sort of default counterexample to the theory. The argument is this: if ethical egoism is true, then it might be permissible to rape, murder, torture, or humiliate. It's not exactly clear how performing these terrible acts would be in the agent's best interests, but it's not inconceivable. If it is in Doc Ock's best interest to rebuild the reactor, then perhaps he is required to rob the bank. Moreover, if the only way he can get the precious tritium he needs is by kidnapping Mary Jane and delivering Spider-Man to Harry Osborn while killing innocent people in the process, then so be it. Yet it seems plain that these sorts of terrible acts are never permissible. Thus, ethical egoism is not true. Of course, those sympathetic to ethical egoism might counter that this argument, especially its second premise, merely represents conflicting moral intuitions. There might be some truth to this, which is why this is often called a "default" counterexample. Nevertheless, it seems that the ethical egoist is willing to jettison even the most entrenched and well-considered moral beliefs. It is this feature of the objection that must be suitably explained away, lest ethical egoism fall prey to the counterexample test.

Other critics of ethical egoism argue that the theory suffers from action-guiding issues. The problem arises due to conflict situations between two (or more) agents. It's conceivable that achieving the same goal best promotes the interests of agents A and B. However, it's also conceivable that only A or B, but not both, can accomplish the relevant goal at the present time. Arguably, it is in Brandon's overall best interest to testify against John and Tommy (thereby removing a primary obstacle regarding the blossoming relationship with Lana), but it is in John and Tommy's best interest that she doesn't (lest they go back to jail for a very long time). How should Brandon and John and Tommy proceed? What advice does ethical egoism offer to resolve the conflict? If this objection cannot be adequately addressed, ethical egoism will fail the action-guiding test.[7]

The two preceding worries about ethical egoism are driven by a more fundamental objection. Ethical egoism proffers an incredibly small moral universe: population one. Only the agent and her interests possess moral significance. The interests of others are not (in themselves) morally significant. But it's not at all clear how the ethical egoist could justify the position that the interests of others are not at all morally significant. True, the agent is a unique individual, but so is everyone else. True, the agent has special regard for her own interests, but this is true of every person. In fact, the egoist seems hard pressed to discover any relevant difference between the agent and others that might justify why only the agent's interests are morally significant. Thus, ethical egoism arbitrarily assigns preferential treatment to the agent, which serves as a deeply problematic counterexample to the theory via the moral universe test. Put another way, the egoist has no plausible defense for assigning intrinsic value to only the agent's interests. What makes the agent so ethically special? Any defensible consideration that might be offered will equally apply to any other person, which discounts the plausibility of only the agent's interests counting as intrinsically valuable. This (again) serves as a devastating counterexample to ethical egoism's moral standard and, thus, the theory itself. The plausibility of ethical egoism is seriously threatened if this counterexample cannot be suitably explained away.

Furthermore, it is far from clear that the arguments initially offered in support of ethical egoism and its moral standard are sound. Psychological egoism, in the end, seems problematic. The most popular argument for it, that we naturally pursue our self-interests insofar as we always act on our strongest motive, seems flawed. The issue is that people are motivated to act for all sorts of reasons, and not all of them are for personal gain. People act out of love, hatred, kindness, jealousy, generosity, and greed. Sometimes persons keep their promises or provide aid to others, like Peter Parker, even if they would rather be doing something else. Sometimes persons, like Harry Osborn, wish revenge on others even if it means harming themselves. Therefore, psychological egoism—a theory allegedly descriptive of human nature—doesn't cohere with the relevant data. Descriptive theories that don't cohere with the data are thereby implausible.

Some proponents of psychological egoism reply that any reports of non-self-regarding behavior are deceptive or illusory. Although people like Peter Parker claim that they have acted altruistically, perhaps spurred by the inspirational words of a loved one, proponents of psychological egoism are driven to hold that they deceive themselves; somewhere in their psyche lurks a self-regarding desire accounting for their choices. However, this rejoinder is problematic. The psychological egoist now twists any and all data via preconceived assumptions such that it is impossible to falsify the theory *regardless of what the data actually show*. This renders the theory empty. Put another way, the psychological egoist is now committed to the following two claims: (a) persons necessarily act in accordance with our strongest self-regarding desire; and (b) our strongest self-regarding desire is whichever motive we act on. From these two claims it follows that persons necessarily act in accordance with whichever motive we act on. This is true, but uninformative and empty of any interesting or meaningful content. In response to pressures from obvious disconfirming instances to his theory, the psychological egoist manages to define away any import to his theory. Therefore, psychological egoism poses no real threat to the possibility of other-regarding behavior or taking the moral point of view as traditionally understood.

Finally, the argument that any binding imperative requires that you have good reasons, which entails that you morally ought to do something only if it thereby serves your interests is not irresistible. Certainly, all moral obligations must be grounded in good reasons; however, it's not clear that they must be grounded in self-regarding reasons. If you see a child drowning in shallow water, you have perfectly good reason to rescue her insofar as you save her from harm. The fact that the child will suffer harm you could easily prevent is itself reason for acting on her behalf. Of course, this might be denied if your interests were intrinsically valuable and hers were not in any way significant, but this suggestion is difficult to defend. As argued earlier, this suggestion seems simply arbitrary and, thus, implausible. Perhaps persons are inclined to act in self-regarding ways. Perhaps we are not sensitive enough to the interests of others and the reasons for acting on their behalf. Even so, it seemingly remains true that we ought not to behave in these ways, even if such behavior seems natural. Thus, it seems that there is little reason to believe that ethical egoism (or its moral standard) is true, and powerful reasons for thinking that it is false. Unless it can be suitably revised or the objections against it explained away, there is thus reason to conclude ethical egoism is a flawed moral theory.

> "Kids . . . need a hero—courageous, self-sacrificing people—setting examples for all of us." —*Spider-Man 2*, scene 35

Introducing Natural Law

It seems obvious that there are different kinds of things. Things are grouped into kinds because of distinctive shared commonalities. Beagles, collies, and pugs are of the same kind known as "dog," and Persian, Siamese, and calico are of the same kind known as "cat." Furthermore, that there are distinctive shared commonalities of being human is not implausible. If Lassie, Benji, and Spuds MacKenzie possess commonalities resulting in their being dogs, then Tom Hanks, Toby McGuire, and Hilary Swank possess commonalities resulting in their being human.

Note that evaluative judgments about how a thing acts or behaves are often made in respect to its kind. It is good that a cheetah eats meat, but not good that an antelope does. It is good that fish live in water, but not good that a cat does. Furthermore, some domesticated dogs, such as German shepherds are well-suited to be guard dogs. A German shepherd that can regularly decipher friend from foe and swiftly alert its owner to territorial threats is a good guard dog, but one that fails to efficiently accomplish these tasks is a poor example of a guard dog. Undomesticated cats, cheetahs for example, are invariably adept at stalking, chasing down, and killing their prey. Indeed, it seems to be the very nature of cheetahs to hunt antelope. An alert and swift cheetah is better than a sluggish and hobbled one. The life of an alert and swift cheetah goes well, but the life of a hobbled and sluggish cheetah goes rather poorly.

Things of the same kind are often said to share an essence or nature. Natural behavior is invariably viewed as good and unnatural behavior is viewed as bad. Some moral philosophers, natural law theorists, stress this approach to ethics. They hold that truths about what persons ought and ought not to do are importantly grounded in human nature.[8] This is as it should be, contends the natural law theorist, because ethics is supposed to regulate human conduct. But the dictates of morality should also aim at the good of human beings. The basic, intuitive force of natural law ethics therefore materializes: because evaluative judgments of good and bad are invariably grounded in a thing's nature, and ethics should promote the fulfillment of human beings, proper human behavior must be consonant with human nature. Furthermore, given that human beings share a nature or essence, natural law ethicists plausibly hold that the dictates of proper moral conduct apply equally to everyone exactly because each of us is human. Thus natural law moral principles are grounded in objective truths about human nature. But it remains to be seen how truths about human nature are discovered. Many natural law theorists, including Thomas Aquinas, hold that these truths can be determined by observing our behavioral patterns. Aquinas believes that careful observation uncovers our "natural inclinations," which is indicative of human nature.

> "I knew, somehow, that I had to stay alive. Somehow I had to keep breathing. Even though there was no reason to hope."
> —*Cast Away*, scene 30

An exhaustive list of our natural inclinations is a monumental task. However, a few select tendencies have received a great deal of attention from natural law theorists. The first (influential) tendency is to preserve one's life. The second tendency is engaging in sexual intercourse and producing offspring. Natural law theorists tend to interpret these two tendencies as embodying the values of life, good health, self-defense, procreation, and raising children, respectively. Apart from these biologically driven inclinations, natural law theorists also find human tendencies to be inquisitive and live in community via concentric circles of care and concern. These inclinations are interpreted as (respectively) embodying the values of employing our rational faculties; gaining knowledge, love, and friendship; and establishing stable family units and societies.

Natural law theorists hold that our natural inclinations are indicative of goals or values that are common to the human experience. For example, no one would choose to lead the completely solitary existence that was forced upon Chuck in *Cast Away*. His only companionship for four years was a face drawn on a volleyball. When "Wilson" was lost at sea, Chuck agonized over the fact that he could not "rescue" his "friend." Thus, the human inclination to socialize and form close bonds is strong; it represents one of the values of being human. Manifesting the values implicit in our natural tendencies is conducive to the fulfillment of human nature, which is the highest good that human beings can achieve. Therefore, natural law theorists invariably hold that life, procreation, knowledge, and sociability are intrinsically valuable.

Accordingly, the essential elements of natural law theory begin with the dictum that it is wrong to knowingly or purposely act contrary to an agent's nature. This core position points to the following moral standard:

> Everyone (human agents) ought to promote the values embodied in our natural inclinations as human beings.

Human agents who knowingly or purposely act contrary to reason act contrary to their natural inclinations. Furthermore, it is contrary to reason for persons to knowingly act in ways that contravene the natural inclinations of being human. Actions that are (knowingly) contrary to the values embodied in our natural inclinations are contrary to reason and thus impermissible. Acting in such unnatural ways is to cause morally significant harm to oneself or another. Actions that are consonant with our natural inclinations are permissible, if not obligatory. A morally good person is one who regularly performs actions that are consonant with the values embodied in our natural inclinations; such persons regularly confer morally significant benefits upon themselves and others, which is conducive to human fulfillment. A morally bad person is one who regularly performs (unnatural) actions that are in direct violation of those values. Some moral rules of natural law are: Do not commit murder or suicide; do not use contraceptive devices; do not engage in same-sex, intimate relationships; do not slander; seek knowledge and educate yourself; practice honesty; abide by the (just) laws of the state.

Natural law theory is often interpreted as holding that the values implicit in our natural inclinations are inviolable. This commits natural law to a form of moral absolutism. Moral absolutism is the view that some moral rules hold without exception, which is to say that some kinds of acts are always impermissible (or obligatory) regardless of the consequences. A moral theory committed to absolutism invariably faces action-guiding difficulties in conflict situations. If one applicable moral rule requires an agent to do action A, but a second applicable rule requires that the agent refrain from A, what should the agent do? Natural law theorists have developed a rather sophisticated method—the doctrine of double effect—for addressing this potentially problematic action-guiding issue. The doctrine of double effect (in brief), distinguishes between direct (or intentional) and indirect (or unintentional) violations of our natural inclinations such that an unfortunate consequence of one's action might be foreseen without being intentional. So, if a dying pregnant woman can only cure herself by immediately taking a particular medication, she may do so even if she knows that a side effect will terminate her pregnancy. The idea is that because there is no necessary connection between ingesting the medication and having an abortion, terminating the pregnancy is unintended—an unfortunate accident of making herself well. However, if a married, heterosexual couple wishes to use condoms because one of the spouses unfortunately contracted HIV through a blood transfusion, they may not permissibly do so because there is a necessary connection between using condoms and preventing procreation. This is a direct or intentional violation of the value associated with procreation and not merely an unintended but foreseen violation. The doctrine of double effect deserves further exploration; it must suffice for now to simply note that scholars are divided over whether it can satisfactorily address all conflict situations; if it cannot, natural law runs afoul of the action-guiding test.[9]

Assessing Natural Law

Natural law theory's stringent perspective on sexuality is contentious generally. The theory is clear: sex is for producing offspring. Any and all sexual activity not done for the express purpose of procreating is impermissible. It is thus impermissible for heterosexual spouses to use contraception so as to secure the future well-being of the children they already have. It is also impermissible for homosexual partners to engage in sexual activity even if they enjoy a mutually loving and monogamous relationship. In the movie *Boys Don't Cry*, Lana and Brandon Teena (born Teena Brandon) are immediately attracted to one another and soon begin a sexual relationship. This relationship continues even after Lana discovers the truth about Brandon's biology. According to natural law, because Lana and Brandon are both biological females and cannot engage in reproductive sex, they act impermissibly by knowingly participating in a physical relationship. Their same-sex physical coupling is simply unnatural.

The debate about homosexuality is often employed as a microcosm of a more general and pervasive objection leveled at natural law. The problematic issue is the way natural law theorists rely on observed human behavioral patterns to derive judgments about permissible and impermissible actions. The optimal relevant goal, it seems, would be to discover human tendencies that are universal across the species. Consider that all water (at a certain atmosphere) freezes at the same temperature and turns to steam uniformly at another and these transformations are universal and lawlike. Can the same be said about human behaviors? Initially, the answer seems to be negative; humanity is simply too diverse for such lawlike regularities. Some people are extroverted, some are introverted. Some have a lust for life, others are lethargic and sedentary. Some people desire large families, others have no interest in children. Consequently, universal truths about human behavior aren't forthcoming.

> "I invite you into my home and you expose my daughter to your sickness!" —*Boys Don't Cry*, scene 18

Alternatively, perhaps it is sufficient to find statistically pervasive tendencies. On this interpretation, a behavior is natural if *most* human beings behave in a certain way in distinctive circumstances; thus, acting contrary to the statistical norm is impermissible. This interpretation better coheres with the idea of a tendency, and probably better fits what natural law theorists have in mind when discussing human inclinations. However, the problem is that this interpretation of natural human behavior proves too much. It is statistically unlikely that one write an ethics textbook, but it's far from clear that a textbook author acts impermissibly by writing one. It is statistically unlikely that a woman win a gold medal in figure skating or a man become a Super Bowl MVP. However, neither Kristi Yamaguchi nor Aaron Rodgers is to be condemned for their achievements. Therefore, even if this interpretation of acting naturally is more defensible than the previous, it remains open to devastating counterexamples. Unless these can be explained away, natural

Boys Don't Cry, Fox Searchlight Pictures, 1999. Brandon Teena (Hilary Swank, right), experiencing a sexual identity crisis, pursues a romance with Lana Tisdel (Chloë Sevigny). (Moviegoods, Inc.)

law fails the counterexample test due to implausible entailments regarding natural and unnatural behavior.

Some natural law theorists attempt one final interpretation of acting naturally, grounded in the idea that biological objects in nature have purposes. Although some are inclined to deny purposes in nature, natural law theorists point to internal organ examples. The purpose of the heart is to pump blood and the purpose of the eye is to see. Natural law theorists hold that the purpose of the sex organs is to produce offspring. So, if it is wrong to knowingly act in ways contrary to nature and things in nature have purposes, then it is wrong to use something in ways contrary to its natural purpose. Therefore, homosexual sex acts are impermissible because they involve behavior contrary to the natural purpose of the sex organs.

This third interpretation of acting naturally faces two objections. First, it is often construed as assuming things only have one natural purpose. Arguably, some human organs have multiple natural purposes. The ear, for example, is for hearing and maintaining balance, and the mouth is for chewing food, talking, kissing, and whistling (among other things). Besides procreation, it seems sex is particularly well-suited for deepening a couple's relationship, drawing them physically and psychologically as close as feasibly possible. This explains why sexual infidelity is so morally grave; it denigrates, and thereby ruptures, the most important of human bonds. Moreover, given the inordinate number of nerve endings in the genital area, one might plausibly argue that part of the natural purpose of these organs is to experience intense pleasure. Therefore—and to say nothing of expelling bodily waste—it seems that the genitals have (at least) three natural purposes. But if biological objects have multiple purposes, it's not clear that one necessarily acts impermissibly by fulfilling only some of them.[10] Second, it's not obvious that using something contrary to its natural purpose is necessarily wrong in the first place. Does a man act impermissibly by using his eye to wink? Does a woman act impermissibly by adorning her lobes with fashionable earrings? Does a teenager act impermissibly by opening a plastic wrapper with his teeth? What of a person who intentionally shuts his eyes or covers her ears when receiving troubling news? The rhetorical force of these questions leads many to doubt that it is necessarily impermissible to use something in ways contrary to its natural purpose. Therefore, this third interpretation of acting naturally also seemingly runs afoul of the counterexample test.

There are (at least) two substantial insights to be gleaned from the debate about natural and unnatural human action. The first one is practical or procedural. Because what we ostensibly call human nature is so complex and varied, it is easy to allow preconceived notions to cloud judgments about it. On the one hand, sometimes we see what might not be there. For example, Aquinas believed we have a natural inclination to seek God and knowledge about him (which seemingly makes atheism impermissible). Yet there are nearly a billion Hindus, Buddhists, Jains, Daoists, and followers of Shinto who apparently lack any inclination toward theism. Furthermore, seeking God and being religious in general seems to be largely a cultural artifact, not a natural one. This better explains why various religious traditions are closely tied to distinctive geographical locations. On the other hand, sometimes observers overlook rather obvious human tendencies. For example, men—and, indeed, males across many species—are prone to sexually harass females.[11] Recall John and Tommy's reaction to discovering that Brandon was a biological female; they asserted their dominance by raping her, which is the hallmark of unwanted sexual attention. Can John and Tommy plausibly argue that raping Brandon was permissible because they were simply acting naturally? Furthermore, even if psychological egoism is false, it certainly seems that human agents are prone to act egoistically. We tend to think of ourselves first. However, the standard view is that we ought not to do this, or at least we ought to do this much less than we do. But if human nature sets the standard of ethical behavior, it seems we act impermissibly by resisting our natural inclination toward egoism.[12]

> "Then I realized that I was just like a boy-girl. . . . Finally, everything felt right." —*Boys Don't Cry*, scene 21

The second insight is conceptual. Recall Hume's venerable is/ought gap. Truths about what ought or ought not to be done cannot be straightaway deduced from truths about what is the case. If so, it also follows that truths about what is permissible or impermissible cannot be derived from truths about what is regularly or typically the case. This point is reinforced by the very title of *Boys Don't Cry*. Just because human males may tend to hide their emotions (or have difficulty dealing with them), especially painful ones, it simply doesn't follow that they ought to (always) act in this way. But at the very core of natural law ethics is the claim that agents who knowingly act contrary to regular behavioral patterns act wrongly. Therefore, it seems that natural law runs contrary to a position with great intuitive force, which serves as a powerful counterexample to its being a plausible moral theory.

In the end, then, (and leaving action-guiding issues aside) it seems that natural law theory has difficulty with the completeness test with respect to defining "natural" and "unnatural" behavior. Attempts to offer a more complete account of what these terms entail invariably either encounter various counterexamples or notably run afoul of Hume's is/ought gap (or both). If natural law cannot be reconfigured so as to more plausibly meet the completeness and counterexample tests, its credibility as a moral theory seems seriously threatened.

The Human Condition

The idea that principles descriptive of normative behavior are somehow grounded in facets of the human condition is not implausible. In fact, it's probably true. But the greater lesson of exploring ethical egoism and natural law ethics is that grounding evaluative judgments in facts about the human condition must be undertaken with great care. First, we must have the relevant facts correct. Second, we must be confident that we are employing relevant concepts properly. And third, once the relevant facts and concepts are properly sorted, we must be wary of Hume's is/ought gap in formulating ideas about good and bad and right and wrong. The remainder of the text canvasses some (other) influential attempts to accomplish these three goals.

There might be even a larger lesson implicit in this chapter. It seems plain that ethical discourse and practice should facilitate human flourishing and ameliorate suffering (which includes helping us resolve disputes between interested parties in principled ways). It is good that we flourish and bad that we suffer and these judgments must be somehow grounded in relevant facts about us (or sentient life as a whole). Our knowledge of these facts can undoubtedly be enriched by the findings of biology, psychology, and sociobiology. These empirically based disciplines may provide significant insights about the nature of (human) well-being, especially in terms of morally significant harms and benefits. Moreover, these disciplines may indeed help us better appreciate and refine known moral principles, and perhaps spur us to discover those that are currently unknown or underappreciated. However, some scholars believe that the natural and social sciences can achieve a great deal more. They argue that careful scientific scrutiny of the human condition will supersede or render obsolete philosophical inquiry about moral principles. But such scholars seemingly go too far.[13] Due to the crucial conceptual difference between having a belief and its being true, on the one hand, and between how things are (behave) and how they ought to be (behave), on the other, the prospect of the sciences supplanting traditional moral philosophy seems dim. If so, then ethics will forever remain an autonomous discipline, resisting the reduction to the natural or social sciences. In the pages that follow, students will learn about the ideas of other notable moral philosophers and how they articulate and defend their (respective) systematic approaches to ethically significant situations.

6.4. TWO ADDITIONAL FILMS

Spider-Man 2 (2004)

Director: Sam Raimi
Screenwriter: Alvin Sargent

Plot Summary

> Sometimes, to do what's right, we have to be steady and give up the things we want most—even our dreams.

Peter Parker cannot hold down a job. Joe Aziz has just fired him for failing "Joe's twenty-nine-minute delivery guarantee." Newspaper editor Jonah Jameson threatens to fire him from his other job over his latest photos—no pictures of Spider-Man. He is regrettably late paying his rent, again. "Sorry" doesn't pay the rent, as his landlord reminds him. His college grades are slipping; he still owes Prof. Connors a paper on fusion. Connors calls him "brilliant but lazy." He rarely sees his Aunt May or his friends Harry Osborn or Mary Jane Watson, even though he very much wants to (and especially "MJ").

But things take a turn for the better when Harry introduces him to Dr. Otto Octavius, a leading expert on fusion. Harry's Oscorp Industries is funding Octavius's current research project. Octavius begins describing the project to Peter, and he invites Peter to the fusion demonstration he's conducting tomorrow for Oscorp. Eventually, Peter sits down for a personal chat with Octavius and his wife, Rosalie. Rosalie asks Peter if he is seeing anyone. Peter fumbles for an answer. Octavius interjects, "Love should never be a secret. If you keep something as complicated as love stored up inside, it's gonna make you sick."

Peter takes his advice to heart and vows to finally see the play in which MJ is starring. But he is sidetracked on his way to the play. He has disappointed MJ once again. Peter tries to apologize over the phone. She doesn't pick up; he leaves a message. He sounds sincere, and just as she is about to pick up, the operator breaks in and requires an additional fifty cents to continue the call. But Peter doesn't have fifty cents. The operator disconnects him and MJ is once again disappointed. Exasperated, Peter speaks into the receiver, feigning a conversation with Mary Jane: "I want to tell you the truth. Here it is. I'm Spider-Man. Now you know why I can't be with you. If my enemies ever found out about you, if you got hurt, I could never forgive myself."

Peter is present for Octavius's demonstration. Octavius begins explaining the fantastic benefits of fusion-based energy sources, calling it "the power of the sun in the palm of my hand." Octavius also explains his four unique research assistants, each impervious to heat and magnetism. They are four mechanical, artificially intelligent limbs—"smart arms"—that are frighteningly attached to his spinal cord. An inhibitor chip protects his higher brain functions, ensuring that he remains in control of their movements. Octavius, along with his research team, achieve a successful fusion reaction. But it quickly spirals out of control. The magnetic force of the reaction is overwhelming. Metal objects fly into the containment field. There is a breech. The lab begins to crumble. The room is evacuated. Spidey arrives just in time to save Harry's life, but he cannot save Rosalie. Octavius's "smart arms" protect him, but the inhibitor chip overloads before Spidey can (literally) pull the plug on the demonstration.

Octavius is rushed to the hospital. The mechanical limbs have become fused to his spinal cord. The surgeons attempt to remove them. But the smart arms see this as a threat. They defend themselves by attacking the surgical team. Octavius awakes and the limbs lead him to safety. They are now in control. They help Octavius find a new location to rebuild the containment field apparatus. Now communicating with the limbs, Octavius mumbles, "But we need money." Responding to a voice only he can hear, "Steal it? No, no, I am not a criminal." After a silent moment, Octavius replies, "That's right. The real crime would be not to finish what we started." Dr. Octavius —now called "Doc Ock" by Jonah and his newspaper—begins a crime spree to fund his research.

Peter's personal life remains rocky. His friendship with Harry bottoms out. Harry blames Spider-Man for his father's death, and he blames Peter Parker for not turning "the freak" over to the police. Worse still, Mary Jane is now engaged to John Jameson,

Jonah's son and American astronaut-hero. This is more than Peter can bear. He leaves the engagement party and begins swinging from building to building as Spider-Man. But his webs fail him. He savagely falls. He attempts to climb a building, but slips and hits his head (again). He must squint to read Jonah's fake news reports about Spidey and Doc Ock. Is he losing his Spidey powers? Confused, Peter visits his doctor. He checks out physically, but his doctor wonders if Peter is emotionally well. Peter informs his doctor about a "dream" he has where, in his dream, he's Spider-Man but he's losing his powers. The doctor suggests that this might mean Peter isn't supposed to be climbing walls: "You always have a choice, Peter." Peter chooses to be Spider-Man no more.

Peter's life immediately improves. He begins excelling at his studies. He attends MJ's play. He is beginning to like his life again, which explains the large smile on his face. But the city is a mess. Doc Ock continues his quest to rebuild. He needs tritium, the rare element that fuels his fusion reaction. He visits Harry. Harry initially refuses, but reconsiders when the smart arms hang him over the ledge of his penthouse office. Harry declares, "Kill Spider-Man and I'll give you all the tritium you need. On second thought, bring him to me." Ock climbs down the building, all eight limbs striding with purpose, to find the one man who knows Spider-Man: Peter Parker.

Peter visits Aunt May. She has decided to sell the house and move into an apartment. Peter hopes that he and she can make peace about what happened to Uncle Ben. May applauds Peter for his bravery; it couldn't have been easy to tell her the whole truth. Peter is also having second thoughts about leaving Spider-Man behind. He's wondered to himself: "Am I not supposed to have what I want? What I need? What am I supposed to do?" May, for her part, wonders where Spider-Man has gone. She muses, "Too few characters out there, flying around like that, saving old girls like me. . . . Everybody loves a hero. . . . I believe there's a hero in all of us, that keeps us honest, gives us strength." Peter takes her words to heart.

But Ock has also taken Harry's words to heart. He finds Peter and MJ having coffee. Ock decimates the coffee shop and snatches Mary Jane. Ock threatens to harm her if Peter doesn't produce Spider-Man. As Ock exits the scene, Peter feels his powers returning. Spidey and Ock tussle on top of a moving elevated train. Ock turns it into a runaway. Spidey, unmasked in the melee, stops the train with his bare hands (with an assist from some carefully placed webs). But Ock returns and absconds with an exhausted Spider-Man. Ock drops an unconscious Spidey at Harry's feet and leaves with the tritium. Harry discovers that Spider-Man is Peter Parker. When Harry learns that Ock still has MJ, he tells Peter where to find them.

Spidey arrives to once again pull the plug on Ock's operation. First, he must save Mary Jane. Yet the fusion reaction has become self-sustaining. The containment field must be drowned in the river, an end the smart arms are desperate to avoid. Once again unmasked, Peter takes a moment: "MJ, in case we die, I love you."

Discussion Questions

1. Does Jonah Jameson act impermissibly by publishing stories that he knows are unsubstantiated if not simply false? Explain.
2. Is Peter morally obligated to tell Aunt May the whole truth about Uncle Ben (May's deceased husband)? Is Peter morally obligated to tell Harry the truth about Norman Osborn (Harry's deceased father)? Explain.

3. Does Peter do something morally wrong by ceasing to be Spider-Man? Explain.
4. What might it mean to say, as Aunt May does, that "there is a hero inside all of us?"
5. Is it natural for a son to wish vengeance upon his father's murderer? Should Harry Osborn act on this desire? Should anyone?

Boys Don't Cry (1999)

Director: Kimberly Peirce
Screenwriters: Kimberly Peirce and Andy Bienen

Plot Summary

Did you ever think about Lana in all of this?—Yes . . . she's all I think about.

Brandon Teena and Lonny are cousins headed to a skating rink outside of Lincoln, Nebraska. Brandon meets a girl. At the end of the evening, they share a magical kiss goodnight. Brandon, holding the girl tenderly, tells her that he won't leave until she is safely inside her door. The girl swoons and Brandon smiles. But Brandon is not smiling as he makes his way back to Lonny's trailer. He is being chased by a group of young men. They throw barbs and rocks at Brandon as he narrowly escapes them and locks Lonny's door behind him. Brandon is exhilarated. Lonny is annoyed. As it turns out, Lonny's cousin was born Teena Brandon, a biological female. However, Brandon has always considered himself a man.

Brandon visits a local tavern and meets a pretty girl named Candace. But a burly man butts into their conversation and makes a pass at Candace in front of Brandon. Brandon takes offence and picks a fight with the man. Brandon is knocked to the floor, but refuses to stay down. A classic barroom brawl ensues and John Lotter, a friend of Candace's, comes to Brandon's aid. The three run out a back door, laughing. Brandon is again exhilarated. As the night is still young, the three decide to go on a road trip.

Brandon awakes in a strange place. Rubbing his bruised cheek, he begins to remember his night. Candace appears, holding a baby. The troop drove back to Falls City, the small Nebraska town Candace and John call home. Brandon decides to stay and Candace, a single mom, takes him in. That night, Brandon meets Lana Tisdel, another member of John and Candace's troop. Brandon is immediately smitten by Lana, and she does not discourage Brandon's attention. Brandon makes sure that Lana gets home safely, but is uncomfortable about sharing her unstable home life. Lana's mom drinks too much, and, like her daughter, often parties with John and his friend Tommy. Yet Lana's mom welcomes Brandon, officially making him one of the Falls City troop.

Brandon revels in his new life, but his troubled past in Lincoln looms. He—Teena Brandon, that is—must return for a court date, to be arraigned for grand theft auto and writing counterfeit checks. Further, Brandon discovers how volatile John and Tommy can be. Each is on parole and each has nearly uncontrollable tempers (although Tommy claims he is the only one who can handle John). One night out, Brandon is driving John's car. Another car challenges them to a race and John tells Brandon to punch it. Soon a police car, lights flashing and siren blaring, is chasing John's car. Brandon is petrified. John tells him to turn off the highway, dim the headlights, and drive in an open field. The ruse doesn't work. Brandon gets a ticket. John seethes.

Lana works the night shift at a local factory. Brandon surprises her with a visit. Lana skips out of work before her shift is over and the two lay together on a blanket on the far side of the river from the factory. They begin to kiss and their intimacy builds, leading to their first sexual encounter. During their coupling, Lana is able to see down Brandon's shirt and catches a glimpse of Brandon's wrapped-down breasts. She is momentarily alarmed, but soon revels again in Brandon's touch. Afterward, Lana euphorically informs Candace of the encounter with Brandon.

Brandon's past catches up with him when he attempts to pay his speeding fine. The local police learn of the Lincoln bench warrant for Teena Brandon and detain Brandon. Lana arrives to post bail. However, she is confused about why Brandon is being held in the women's side of the jail. Brandon is less than honest, telling Lana that he is a hermaphrodite, "a person with both girl and boy parts. See Brandon is not quite a he. Brandon is more like a she." Lana holds Brandon's hand and responds, "That's your business. I don't care if you're half monkey or half ape. I'm getting you out of here." The two run out of the courthouse, still holding hands. They sneak away to Candace's car. Lana tells Brandon, "I want to touch you the way you touch me. . . . I want you to feel what I feel."

The rest of the Falls City troop discover Brandon's birth name. They alert Lana's mother to the situation and begin looking for Lana. They don't need to search for long as she enters the trailer; Brandon enters a few minutes later. Lana's mother feels betrayed. John and Tommy carry Brandon into the bathroom to discover for themselves the biological truth about Brandon. They undress Brandon against his will. They force Lana to look. John and Tommy cannot understand why Lana calls Brandon a "he"—Lana's "little boyfriend" is a biological female. Lana's mother asks John and Tommy to leave, threatening to call the cops. They later find Brandon and take Brandon to a deserted location. Enraged, confused, and drunk, they violently rape Brandon. The three return to Tommy's house. Brandon escapes out the bathroom window. But they swore Brandon to secrecy, perhaps no one will be the wiser, especially the police.

When Brandon arrives beaten, bruised, and bloodied at Lana's, Lana and her mother convince Brandon to file a police report. The sheriff has difficulties believing all the details of Brandon's story. Brandon tries to explain that his (or her) condition is known as "sexual identity crisis"; the sheriff refers to Brandon as an "it." Later that day, Brandon asks Lana to return to Lincoln with him; Lana agrees. They make plans to leave that night. Meanwhile, the police call John and Tommy and ask the two men to visit the station in the morning for questioning. Brandon must have ratted them out. The two men again look for Brandon, this time with gun in hand. They find Brandon at Candace's house. As they leave, Brandon and Candace are dead and Lana and Candace's toddler are left crying over their loved ones.

Discussion Questions

1. Was Brandon's (or Teena's) sexual attraction toward women unnatural? On what assumptions does your answer depend?
2. Was it in Teena's best interests to have hormone treatments or a sex change operation? Did she do something wrong by not undergoing such procedures?
3. Was it wrong for Brandon to not be completely honest with Lana about his sexual identity crisis?

6.5. REVIEWING THROUGH THE THREE MOVIES

1. Compare and contrast the ethical egoist and natural law perspectives regarding Chuck's proposed suicide.
2. Both Kelly Frears and Mary Jane Watson had the opportunity to be with the love of their (respective) lives, but they made contrary decisions. Compare and contrast their situations and offer an ethical evaluation of each woman's decision.
3. Compare and contrast the decision Lana Tisdel made about moving to Lincoln with Brandon with the respective decisions of Kelly and Mary Jane. Was Lana's choice impermissible in any way that Kelly's or Mary Jane's was not? Defend your answer.
4. Can it be argued that Chuck Noland and Brandon Teena, although not Spider-Man, are respectively heroic in some way? If so, how? If not, why not?
5. Reconsider the six movie quotes from the chapter and explain whether each, given the adjacent paragraphs, *illustrates* a point the author is making, *supplements* (or extends) a point the author is making, or *contrasts* (for emphasis) a point the author is making. Explain your answers.

NOTES

1. Excerpted from Thomas Aquinas, *Summa Theologica*, trans. Lawrence Shapcote (Benzinger Brothers, 1911). The prose has been truncated, omitting Aquinas's objection and reply style, to aid readability and comprehension.

2. The discussion of moral theories and how they are evaluated in this chapter has been influenced (albeit in varying degrees) by C. H. Harris, *Applying Moral Theories*, 4th ed. (Belmont, CA: Wadsworth, 2002), 9–11, 54–60.

3. This is admittedly somewhat controversial, with deontologists such as staunch natural law theorists and strict followers of Kant probably voicing the strongest complaints. But consider the more neutral examples of moral relativism and classic divine command theory. Each can be interpreted as metaethical *and* normative theories; that is, MR and DCT, respectively, can be interpreted as theories about (a) what makes some moral judgments true (but not others) and (b) how to derive moral judgments in specific situations. Neither theory, however, possesses a conceptual commitment to intrinsic value or a "highest good" that its followers can achieve. Yet, note that each theory becomes subject to devastating critiques as a result. MR falls prey to objections from moral progress (among others) and DCT falls prey to objections from arbitrariness. That these theories become conceptually suspect in these ways is (at least some) evidence that any defensible moral theory must be at least implicitly committed to some conception of the highest good. If so, then any defensible moral rule (and, hence, moral standard) must be held in light of some intrinsic good (which begins to provide a rejoinder to those with strong deontologist sympathies).

4. An appeal to John Rawls's "considered moral judgments" might be helpful here. Considered moral judgments represent those beliefs held with the greatest confidence. They are to be contrasted with judgments "made with hesitation" or "those given when we are upset or frightened, or when we stand to gain one way or another." They begin to convey the importance of common-sense morality and the often-overlooked consensus that exists among some of our moral judgments. See John Rawls, *A Theory of Justice* (Cambridge, MA: Harvard University Press, 1971), 47.

5. This additional argument in support of ethical egoism is adapted from Russ Shafer-Landau, *The Fundamentals of Ethics* (New York: Oxford University Press, 2010), 106–8.

6. It's unclear whether ethical egoism is committed to holding that suicide is *always* wrong. Chuck's case at least raises the question of whether one's interests, in some extreme situations, aren't better served by ending one's life, even if this means that one will have no future (positive) interests.

7. Sometimes this sort of objection is crafted in terms of the contradiction test. Because ethical egoism is a moral theory, it seemingly follows that its proponents would advocate that each of us pursue his or her own best interests. However, in advocating this, the egoist threatens his or her own interests. After all, your interests will invariably clash with the interests of other egoists. Thus, it is and it is not in one's best interests to advocate ethical egoism, which results in ethical egoism failing the contradiction test.

8. Natural law ethics must be distinguished from the laws of nature. Natural law is a moral theory that provides prescriptive principles for human action; whether we choose to follow its guidelines is up to us. The laws of nature are descriptive, explaining how objects in nature do behave; objects must behave in the ways that physics, chemistry, and biology dictate (assuming that the relevant laws are true) and there is obviously no choice in the matter.

9. This only begins to explain natural law theory's elaborate doctrine of double effect. One of the best introductory discussions of it can be found in C. E. Harris's *Applying Moral Principles*, 4th ed. (Belmont, CA: Wadsworth, 2002), 95–110. Harris helpfully discusses the relevant abortion and condom cases in greater detail.

10. Some commentators interpret Aquinas as agreeing that sexual relations have three natural purposes; nevertheless, he still maintains that procreation is the most important or valuable of the three so that his basic position remains unaffected by this admission. But how he could substantiate this hierarchy in any non-question-begging way is unclear. Do all biological objects having multiple natural purposes also admit of this sort of hierarchical ranking among them?

11. Natalie Angier, "Sexual Harassment: Why Even Bees Do It," *New York Times*, October 10, 1995.

12. Aquinas, perhaps, anticipated this sort of objection. He did note that some people tend to become aggressive or angry, which could be interpreted as natural behavior. He countered by arguing that this behavior was contrary to reason. But with this, Aquinas begins to sever the link between "contrary to reason" and "unnatural behavior" because sexual harassment remains natural for males and egoism natural for humans despite the fact that such behaviors ought to be avoided. Later natural law theorists, for example, Francisco Suarez, simply take Aquinas's rejoinder to its logical conclusion: human behavioral tendencies, being largely animalistic, are a poor standard of moral behavior.

13. For example, see Michael Ruse and Edward O. Wilson, "Moral Philosophy as Applied Science," *Philosophy* 61 (1986): 173–92. For a persuasive argument that sociobiology can only inform but not supplant traditional moral philosophy, see Philip Kitcher, "Four Ways to 'Biologize' Ethics," in *Conceptual Issues in Evolutionary Biology*, ed. Elliot Sober (Cambridge, MA: MIT Press, 1993), 575–86. See also Elliot Sober, "Prospects for an Evolutionary Ethics," in *Ethical Theory*, ed. Louis Pojman (Belmont, CA: Wadsworth, 2004), 131–43.

CHAPTER 7

Utilitarianism

··

EXTREME MEASURES (1996)

Director: Michael Apted
Screenwriter: Tony Gilroy

··

PLOT SUMMARY

If you could cure cancer by killing one person, wouldn't you have to do that? Wouldn't that be the brave thing to do? One person and cancer's gone tomorrow.

D r. Guy Luthan is a successful neurosurgery resident transitioning into a promising fellowship with a prominent NYU neurology program. One night, while working as the attending physician in the Gramercy Hospital emergency room, Guy is brought two gunshot-wound victims, both of whom are in serious condition. One is a drug user (there is a crack pipe in his pocket) who was shot by a police officer while, apparently, trying to hold up a city bus. The other gunshot victim is the apprehending thirty-two-year-old officer. The drug user shot first and wounded the officer in the chest and leg; the officer returned fire to defend himself and the bus patrons, wounding the drug user in the neck and arm. Although both require surgery, Guy is informed that there is only one operating room currently available. Guy is forced into deciding whether to use the room to treat the drug user or the police officer. The drug user seems more seriously injured. Nevertheless, with the policeman's wife and colleagues looking on, Guy sends the policeman to the operating room.

Jodie, a nursing colleague and friend, is dismayed by Guy's choice. She later confides to him, "You made a moral choice and not a medical one; I guess I'm kind of surprised, that's all." He reminds Jodie that both were stable and goes on to explain, "On my right I see a cop with his wife in the corridor and pictures of his kids in his wallet, and on my left some guy who has taken out a gun on a city bus!" Reminding Jodie that he had to make a choice, he continues, "I hope I made the right one. I think I did . . . maybe I didn't . . . I don't know." She raises an eyebrow at him and walks away.

Later that night, Guy is brought another patient. The man is all but naked and in serious condition. His vital signs are in complete disarray; Guy has never seen a patient in such a state. Luckily, Guy and his team manage to stabilize the patient, if only briefly. The patient utters his name—Claude Minkins—and asks Guy to find his friend, who apparently saved his life. But Minkins takes a sudden and violent turn for the worse. Just before he dies, he mutters "Triphase."

Guy is disturbed by Minkins and his mysterious afflictions. As he begins to search for answers regarding Minkins's cause of death, Guy finds that the man's body has somehow disappeared; furthermore, there is no record of Minkins having been treated last night. Guy digs deeper, against the recommendation of his supervisor, and discovers that Minkins had been in the hospital several years ago for minor outpatient work. As he searches, Guy finds cases very similar to what happened to Minkins. Other patients have also mysteriously disappeared, with no record of their stays, and the common thread is that all had been in Gramercy for minor treatments.

BOX 7A: INSIDE *EXTREME MEASURES*

Extreme Measures is a story that conveys various ethically significant situations in medicine and medical research. The most obvious connection is to (act) utilitarianism, and consequentialism generally. However, it also expresses reasons for distinguishing between act and rule utilitarianism, and issues germane to the connection between emotion and reason in ethical decision making.

The first segment that effectively conveys these topics begins with scene 2, from 4:25 to 10:33. Scene 2 opens with a moving camera shot through a hospital and it ends with a bright white screen, signaling the beginning of scene 3. This scene depicts the moral dilemma Guy faces described in the opening paragraphs of the plot summary. Another interesting segment consists of scenes 28 and 29; this depicts the time Guy is led to believe he is paralyzed. Scene 28 begins at 1:22:27 with a bright white screen that transitions into a shot of a hospital room. Scene 29 ends at 1:30:12, with a transition away from Guy and onto a computer screen. This second segment portrays "ends justifying the means" type thinking and also implicit connections between emotion and reason in moral discourse (as does the exchange between Jodie and Guy in scene 30). The third, and perhaps most explicitly consequentialist segment, can be found in scenes 34–36. Scene 34 begins at 1:42:25 with a shot of elevator numbers transitioning into a shot of the elevator doors. Scene 36 ends at 1:49:45 with a shot transitioning away from Guy into a bright white screen. This segment depicts a very tense, but frank discussion between Guy and Myrick (context for which is provided in scene 31 from 1:35:32 to 1:37:00).

Watching these three segments after carefully reading the plot summary should provide you a sufficient grasp of the film, but if you are able, you might consider watching from scene 28 or 29 to the end of the film (about a 30 minute segment). If you are able to view the film in its entirety, then you should be able to answer the trivia questions from box 7B.

Guy's investigation does not go unnoticed. Someone begins to make life very difficult for him. His apartment is broken into, and his neighbors, fearing a burglary, call the police. While investigating the (alleged) crime scene, the police discover pharmaceutical cocaine. Since Guy does not use drugs, he now realizes that he's been framed. Consequently, and in speedy fashion, he loses his job at Gramercy—and his NYU fellowship—requiring his return to Great Britain. This also means that his career will end in disrepute, just as his father's had for administering euthanasia to a friend of the Luthan family.

With nothing to lose and his flight home only days away, Guy searches desperately for answers. He is convinced that "Triphase" is the missing piece of the puzzle. Guy discovers that the patients disappearing from Gramercy are invariably homeless men with no family. But as Guy gets closer to solving the riddle, those determined to prevent him from uncovering the truth get closer to Guy. He is chased through a subway tunnel and is shot in the arm trying to evade his assailants. Desperate, he shows up at Jodie's apartment. While attending his wound, Guy serendipitously notices a plastic bag with the word "Triphase" on it. Is Jodie somehow involved? Before he can inquire, however, Guy is savagely struck on the back of the neck.

Guy awakes in a hospital bed. He is paralyzed. A leading neurologist, Dr. Myrick, visits him. Myrick is known for his cutting-edge research. Guy asks Myrick for a merciful and painless death—an injection of potassium chloride. Myrick informs him that this is a common request. Myrick then asks, "What if there was hope? What would it be worth to be able to walk again?" But Guy cannot be placated; he pleads with Myrick that he can't live like this. Myrick reminds Guy that, with proper care, he can live twenty years "like this." Guy becomes angry, reminding Myrick of his broken spinal cord. Myrick asks, "What if I told you there was a chance you can be healed?" Myrick suggests that there is a procedure that could allow Guy to walk again, be a doctor again; he then asks, "What would you do to make that happen?" Slowly, Guy quietly responds, "Anything." As Myrick leaves the room, he ominously retorts, "Anything. You better think about that."

Guy soon learns that Myrick induced his paralysis to solicit his expertise in neurology. As Guy slowly regains the use of his limbs, he also discovers, with Jodie's help, that Myrick is responsible for the mysterious disappearing patients. He has been conducting illegal research programs on human subjects—local homeless men. Without disclosing his methods to his "patients," Myrick purposely severs the spinal cords of these otherwise healthy men and then attempts to heal them through a combination of surgery and medication. Myrick endeavors to regrow nerves. Although the results have become rather promising, no "patient" has yet fully recovered. Indeed, many of the "patients" have died. Yet, through this research, Dr. Myrick provides real hope of a cure to many of his long-term paralysis patients. He strongly believes that the possibility of a cure justifies the means by which he (literally) operates.

Guy finally confronts Dr. Myrick about the research and accuses him of killing his patients. Dr. Myrick responds, "People die every day. For what? For nothing. . . . Pick your tragedy. Sniper in a restaurant. Fifteen dead. Story at eleven. What do we do? . . . Change the channel." But Myrick proceeds by making the issue more personal, lecturing, "You take care of the ones you think you can save. Good doctors do the correct thing. Great doctors have the guts to do the right thing. Your father had those guts. So do you." Myrick thus approvingly reminds Guy of his father's decision to euthanize a family friend and Guy's decision to treat the gold shield cop before the maniac who pulled a gun on a bus.

BOX 7B: *EXTREME MEASURES* **TRIVIA**

If your instructor assigns the film to be watched outside of class, you should be able to answer the following questions:

1. Guy, per his discussion with Jodie, has how many seconds to make the choice between sending the cop or drug user to the operating room?
2. The ribbon of Dr. Myrick's Wainwright medal displays what two colors?
3. Guy is asked to participate in what extracurricular, outdoor hospital activity?
4. What is the answer to the math question Dr. Myrick asks Mr. Randall?
5. The cops find how much cocaine in Guy's apartment?
6. Those living in "The Room" are called what?
7. Upon being shot, Guy arrives at Jodie's apartment at what time?
8. Jodie informs Guy that he is on what floor of Triphase?
9. How long has it been since Helen (Myrick's paralyzed receptionist) has walked?
10. At the very end of the film, what color shirt is Guy wearing?

Myrick then rhetorically asks whether it's worth it to sacrifice one person to cure cancer forever. And he reminds Guy of what he would do to walk again: "Anything."

Guy solemnly responds to Dr. Myrick by admitting that perhaps the homeless men upstairs don't have a great deal to live for. Guy is also willing to admit that they are doing a great thing and maybe this makes them heroes. Yet he adamantly objects, "But they didn't choose to be. You chose for them . . . You didn't ask for volunteers . . . And you can't do that, because you're a doctor, and you took an oath. . . . So I don't care if you can do what you say you can. I don't care if you can find a cure for every disease on this planet. You tortured and murdered those men upstairs." Guy believes that Myrick's actions make him a disgrace to their profession, and he hopes Myrick is punished for his crimes.

The movie ends with Guy receiving all of Myrick's files through a well-meaning third party—Mrs. Ruth Myrick. She confides in Guy, "My husband was trying to do a good thing, but in the wrong way. Perhaps you can do it in the right way." He accepts the files, and begins studying them as he deliberately marches up the steps of the NYU neurology department.

7.1. THINKING THROUGH THE MOVIE

Discussion Starter Questions

1. If you were in Guy's position at the beginning of the film and had to choose between the police officer and the drug user, what would you have decided? Why?
2. Why does Jodie disapprove of Guy's choice? Why does Myrick approve? Explain.
3. How does Myrick attempt to justify his research methods to Guy? For what reasons does Guy object to Myrick's defense?
4. What would it mean for Guy to conduct Myrick's research program "in the right way," per Ruth Myrick's suggestion at the very end of the film?
5. Why is the film entitled "Extreme Measures?" What might be its moral significance?

Questions for Further Thought

1. Myrick distinguishes between doctors who do "the correct thing" and doctors who do "the right thing" (scene 34, 1:44:10–1:45:00). What is the supposed difference? Evaluate Myrick's implicit position.
2. What should be done with research results that were obtained via morally objectionable means (with Nazi exploratory surgery on concentration camp Jews being one vivid example)? What does *Extreme Measures* suggest about this?
3. The movie implies that there is a substantive morally significant difference between conducting (experimental) research on human beings and nonhuman animals (see, for example, scene 7 roughly 21:15–22:45 and scene 34 roughly 1:43:20–1:43:45). Is there a substantive difference? Defend your answer.
4. Many of those involved with Triphase, including Myrick and Jodie, have loved ones who are paralyzed and confined to wheelchairs (for example, see Jodie's explanation at scene 30, 1:31:00–1:32:10). Is this factor sufficient to justify their being complicit in Myrick's research program? Defend your answer.
5. In scene 8 (24:55–26:10), Guy informs Jodie that his father lost his medical license because he complied with the euthanasia request of an old friend who was suffering a great deal of pain due to terminal cancer. He asks Jodie: "So, where do you stand on that one?" How would Myrick answer this question? How would you answer Guy's question?

7.2. HISTORICAL SETTING

Utilitarianism (excerpt)[1]

John Stuart Mill (1806–1873) was one of the keenest minds of the nineteenth century. While employed by the East India Company, he made significant contributions to several areas of philosophy, including the philosophy of science and logic. However, he is most remembered for his contributions to ethics and social-political philosophy. Regarding the former, he revised and valiantly defended the ethical views of his teacher, Jeremy Bentham, and regarding the latter, he played an instrumental role in the suffrage movement in England.

Preparing to Read

A. What makes you truly happy? How might Mill help you explain your answer?

B. Would Mill find Dr. Myrick's research morally acceptable? Let's assume that he successfully keeps it a secret. What would Mill then conclude?

[Utilitarianism Defined]

The creed that accepts as the foundation of morals, Utility, or the Greatest Happiness Principle, holds that actions are right in proportion as they tend to promote happiness, wrong as they tend to produce the reverse of happiness. By happiness is intended pleasure, and the absence of pain; by unhappiness, pain, and the privation of pleasure. To give a clear view of the moral standard set up by the theory, much more requires to be said; in particular, what things it includes in the ideas of pain and pleasure; and to what extent this is left an open question. But these supplementary explanations do not affect the theory of life on which this theory of morality is grounded—namely, that pleasure, and freedom from pain, are the only things desirable as ends; and that all desirable things (which are as numerous in the utilitarian as in any other scheme) are desirable either for the pleasure inherent in themselves, or as means to the promotion of pleasure and the prevention of pain.

Now, such a theory of life excites in many minds, and among them in some of the most estimable in feeling and purpose, incurable dislike. To suppose that life has (as they express it) no higher end than pleasure—no better and nobler object of desire and pursuit—they designate as utterly mean and groveling; as a doctrine worthy only of swine. . . .

[Higher and Lower Pleasures]

. . . The accusation supposes human beings to be capable of no pleasures except those of which swine are capable. If this supposition were true, the charge could not be gainsaid, but would then be no longer an accusation; for if the sources of pleasure were precisely the same to human beings and to swine, the rule of life which is good enough for the one would be good enough for the other. The comparison . . . to that of beasts is felt as degrading, precisely because a beast's pleasures do not satisfy a human being's conceptions of happiness. Human beings have faculties more elevated than the animal appetites, and when once made conscious of them, do not regard anything as happiness that does not include their gratification. . . . It must be admitted, however, that utilitarian writers in general have placed the superiority of mental over bodily pleasures chiefly in the greater permanency, safety, uncostliness, etc., of the former—that is, in their circumstantial advantages rather than in their intrinsic nature. And on all these points utilitarians have fully proved their case; but they might have taken the other, and, as it may be called, higher ground, with entire consistency. It is quite compatible with the principle of utility to recognize the fact, that some *kinds* of pleasure are more desirable and more valuable than others. It would be absurd that while, in estimating all other things, quality is considered as well as quantity, the estimation of pleasures should be supposed to depend on quantity alone.

[Higher and Lower Pleasures Distinguished]

If I am asked, what I mean by difference of quality in pleasures, or what makes one pleasure more valuable than another, merely as a pleasure, except its being greater in amount, there is but one possible answer. Of two pleasures, if there be one to which all or almost all who have experience of both give a decided preference, irrespective of any feeling of moral obligation to prefer it, that is the more desirable pleasure. If one of the two is, by those who are competently acquainted with both, placed so far above the other that they prefer it, even though knowing it to be attended with a greater amount of discontent, and would not resign it for any quantity of the other pleasure which their nature is capable of, we are justified in ascribing to the preferred enjoyment a superiority in quality, so far outweighing quantity as to render it, in comparison, of small account.

Now it is an unquestionable fact that those who are equally acquainted with, and equally capable of appreciating and enjoying, both, do give a most marked preference to the manner of existence that employs their higher faculties. Few human creatures would consent to be changed into any of the lower animals, for a promise of the fullest allowance of a beast's pleasures; no intelligent human being would consent to be a fool, no instructed person would be an ignoramus, no person of feeling and conscience would be selfish and base, even though they should be persuaded that the fool, the dunce, or the rascal is better satisfied with his lot than they are with theirs. They would not resign what they possess more than he, for the most complete satisfaction of all the desires that they have in common with him. If they ever fancy they would, it is only in cases of unhappiness so extreme, that to escape from it they would exchange their lot for almost any other, however undesirable in their own eyes. . . . Whoever supposes that this preference takes place at a sacrifice of happiness—that the superior being, in anything like the equal circumstances, is not happier than the inferior—confounds the two very different ideas, of happiness, and content. It is indisputable that the being whose capacities of enjoyment are low, has the greatest chance of having them fully satisfied; and a highly-endowed being will always feel that any happiness that he can look for, as the world is constituted, is imperfect. But he can learn to bear its imperfections, if they are at all bearable; and they will not make him envy the being who is indeed unconscious of the imperfections, but only because he feels not at all the good which those imperfections qualify. It is better to be a human being dissatisfied than a pig satisfied; better to be Socrates dissatisfied than a fool satisfied. And if the fool, or the pig, is of a different opinion, it is because they only know their own side of the question. The other party to the comparison knows both sides.

[Why Some Opt for Lower Pleasures over Higher]

It may be objected, that many who are capable of the higher pleasures, occasionally, under the influence of temptation, postpone them to the lower. But this is quite compatible with a full appreciation of the intrinsic superiority of the higher. Men often, from infirmity of character, make their election for the nearer good, though they know it to be the less valuable; and this no less when the choice is between two bodily pleasures, than when it is between bodily and mental. They pursue sensual indulgences to the injury of health, though perfectly aware that health is the greater good. It may be further objected, that many who begin with youthful enthusiasm for everything noble, as they advance in years sink into indolence and selfishness. But I do not believe that those who undergo this very common change voluntarily choose the lower description of pleasures in preference to the higher. I believe that before they devote themselves exclusively to the one, they have already become incapable of the other. Capacity for the nobler feelings is in most natures a very tender plant, easily killed, not only by hostile influences, but by mere want of sustenance; and in the majority of young persons it speedily dies away if the occupations to which their position in life has devoted them, and the society into which it has thrown them, are not favorable to keeping that higher capacity in exercise. Men lose their high aspirations as they lose their intellectual tastes, because they have not time or opportunity for indulging them; and they addict themselves to inferior pleasures, not because they deliberately prefer them, but because they are either the only ones to which they have access, or the only ones which they are any longer capable of enjoying. It may be questioned whether anyone who has remained equally susceptible to both classes of pleasures, ever has knowingly and calmly preferred the lower, though many, in all ages, have broken down in an ineffectual attempt to combine both.

From this verdict of the only competent judges, I apprehend there can be no appeal. On a question which is the best worth having of two pleasures, or which of two modes of existence is the most grateful to the feelings, apart from its moral attributes and from its consequences, the judgment of those who are qualified by knowledge of both, or, if they differ, that of the majority among them, must be admitted as final.... When, therefore, those feelings and judgment declare the pleasures derived from the higher faculties to be preferable *in kind,* apart from the question of intensity, to those of which the animal nature, disjoined from the higher faculties, is susceptible, they are entitled on this subject to the same regard.

[Personal Happiness and the Happiness of Others]

I have dwelt on this point, as being a necessary part of a perfectly just conception of Utility or Happiness, considered as the directive rule of human conduct. But it is by no means an indispensable condition to the acceptance of the utilitarian standard; for that standard is not the agent's own greatest happiness, but the greatest amount of happiness altogether; and if it may possibly be doubted whether a noble character is always the happier for its nobleness, there can be no doubt that it makes other people happier, and that the world in general is immensely a gainer by it. Utilitarianism, therefore, could only attain its end by the general cultivation of nobleness of character, even if each individual were only benefited by the nobleness of others, and his own, so far as happiness is concerned, were a sheer deduction from the benefit. But the bare enunciation of such an absurdity as this last, renders refutation superfluous.

According to the Greatest Happiness Principle, as above explained, the ultimate end, with reference to and for the sake of which all other things are desirable (whether we are considering our own good or that of other people), is an existence exempt as far as possible from pain, and as rich as possible in enjoyments, both in point of quantity and quality; the test of quality, and the rule for measuring it against quantity, being the preference felt by those who, in their opportunities of experience, to which must be added their habits of self-consciousness and self-observation, are best furnished with the means of comparison. This, being, according to the utilitarian opinion, the end of human action, is necessarily also the standard of morality; which may accordingly be defined, the rules and precepts for human conduct, by the observance of which an existence such as has been described might be, to the greatest extent possible, secured to all mankind; and not to them only, but, so far as the nature of things admits, to the whole sentient creation. . . .

I must again repeat, what the assailants of utilitarianism seldom have the justice to acknowledge, that the happiness which forms the utilitarian standard of what is right in conduct, is not the agent's own happiness, but that of all concerned. As between his own happiness and that of others, utilitarianism requires him to be as strictly impartial as a disinterested and benevolent spectator. In the golden rule of Jesus of Nazareth, we read the complete spirit of the ethics of utility. To do as one would be done by, and to love one's neighbor as oneself, constitute the ideal perfection of utilitarian morality. As the means of making the nearest approach to this ideal, utility would enjoin, first, that laws and social arrangements should place the happiness, or (as speaking practically it may be called) the interest, of every individual, as nearly as possible in harmony with the interest of the whole; and secondly, that education and opinion, which have so vast a power over human character, should so use that power as to establish in the mind of every individual an indissoluble association between his own happiness and the good of the whole; especially between his own happiness and the practice of such modes of conduct, negative and positive, as regard for the universal happiness prescribes. . . .

[On Proving the Utility Principle]

It has already been remarked, that questions of ultimate ends do not admit of proof, in the ordinary acceptation of the term. To be incapable of proof by reasoning is common to all first principles; to the first premises of our knowledge, as well as to those of our conduct. But the former, being matters of fact, may be the subject of a direct appeal to the faculties that judge of fact—namely, our senses, and our internal consciousness. Can an appeal be made to the same faculties on questions of practical ends? Or what other faculty takes cognizance of them?

Questions about ends are, in other words, questions about what things are desirable. The utilitarian doctrine is, that happiness is desirable, and the only thing desirable, as an end; all other things being only desirable as means to that end. What ought to be required of this doctrine—what condition is it requisite that the doctrine should fulfill—to make good its claim to be believed?

The only proof capable of being given that an object is visible, is that people actually see it. The only proof that a sound is audible, is that people hear it: and so of the other sources of our experience. In like manner, I apprehend, the sole evidence it is possible to produce that anything is desirable, is that people do actually desire it. If the end that the utilitarian doctrine proposes to itself were not, in theory, and in practice, acknowledged to be an end, nothing could ever convince any person that it was so. No reason can be given why the general happiness is desirable, except that each person, so far as he believes it to be attainable, desires his own happiness. This, however, being a fact, we have not only all the proof which the case admits of, but all which it is possible to require, that happiness is a good: that each person's happiness is a good to that person, and the general happiness, therefore, a good to the aggregate of all persons. Happiness has made out its title as *one* of the ends of conduct, and consequently one of the criteria of morality.

But it has not, by this alone, proved itself to be the sole criterion. To do that, it would seem, by the same rule, necessary to show, not only that people desire happiness, but that they never desire anything else. Now it is palpable that they do desire things that, in common language, are decidedly distinguished from happiness. They desire, for example, virtue, and the absence of vice, no less really than pleasure and the absence of pain. The desire of virtue is not as universal, but it is as authentic a fact, as the desire of happiness. And hence the opponents of the utilitarian standard deem that they have a right to infer that there are other ends of human action besides happiness, and that happiness is not the standard of approbation and disapprobation.

[Happiness as Varied and Complex]

But does the utilitarian doctrine deny that people desire virtue, or maintain that virtue is not a thing to be desired? The very reverse. It maintains not only that virtue is to be desired, but that it is to be desired disinterestedly, for itself. Whatever may be the opinion of utilitarian moralists as to the original conditions by which virtue is made virtue; however they may believe (as they do) that actions and dispositions are only virtuous because they promote another end than virtue; yet this being granted, and it having been decided, from considerations of this description, what is virtuous, they not only place virtue at the very head of the things which are good as means to the ultimate end, but they also recognize as a psychological fact the possibility of its being, to the individual, a good in itself, without looking to any end beyond it; and hold, that the mind is not in a right state, not in a state comfortable to Utility, not in the state most conducive to the general happiness, unless it does love virtue in this manner—as a thing desirable in itself, even although, in the individual instance, it should not produce those other desirable consequences which it tends to produce, and on account of which it is held to be virtue. This opinion is not, in the smallest degree, a departure from the Happiness principle. The ingredients of happiness are very various, and each of them is desirable in itself, and not merely when considered as swelling an aggregate. The principle of utility does not mean that any given pleasure, as music, for instance, or any given exemption from pain, as for example health, are to be looked upon as a means to a collective something termed happiness, and to be desired on that account. They are desired and desirable in and for themselves; besides being means, they are a part of the end. Virtue, according to the utilitarian doctrine, is not naturally and originally part of the end, but it is capable of becoming so; and in those who love it disinterestedly it has become so, and is desired and cherished, not as a means to happiness, but as a part of their happiness.

. . . In these cases the means have become a part of the end, and a more important part of it than any of the things that they are means to. What was once desired as an instrument for the attainment of happiness has come to be desired for its own sake. In being desired for its own sake it is, however, desired as *part* of happiness. The person is made, or thinks he would be made, happy by its mere possession; and is made unhappy by failure to obtain it. The desire of it is not a different thing from the desire of happiness, any more than the love of music, or the desire of health. They are included in happiness. They are some of the elements of which the desire of happiness is made up. Happiness is not an abstract idea, but a concrete whole; and these are some of its parts. And the utilitarian standard sanctions and approves their being so. Life would be a poor thing, very ill provided with sources of happiness, if there were not this provision of nature, by which things originally indifferent, but conducive to, or otherwise associated with, the satisfaction of our primitive desires, become in themselves sources of pleasure more valuable than the primitive pleasures, both in permanency, in the space of human existence that they are capable of covering, and even in intensity.

Virtue, according to the utilitarian conception, is a good of this description. There was no original desire of it, or motive to it, save its conduciveness to pleasure, and especially to protection from pain. But through the association thus formed, it may be felt a good in itself, and desired as such with as great intensity as any other good; and with this difference between it and the love of money, of power, or of fame, that all of these may, and often do, render the individual noxious to the other members of the society to which he belongs, whereas there is nothing which makes him so much a blessing to them as the cultivation of the disinterested love of virtue. And consequently, the utilitarian standard, while it tolerates and approves those other acquired desires, up to the point beyond which they would be more injurious to the general happiness than conducive of it, enjoins and requires the cultivation of the love of virtue up to the greatest strength possible, as being above all things important to the general happiness.

It results from the preceding considerations, that there is in reality nothing desired except happiness. Whatever is desired otherwise than as a means to some end beyond itself, and ultimately to happiness, is desired as itself a part of happiness, and is not desired for itself until it has become so.

Review Questions

1. According to Mill, what has intrinsic value and, consequently, what fundamental moral principle does he advocate?
2. How does Mill generally distinguish the "higher" and "lower" pleasures? What specific criterion does he provide for distinguishing them?
3. According to Mill, why do we pursue the virtues? How does his answer fit into his overall view?

7.3. DISCUSSION AND ANALYSIS

"The needs of the many outweigh the needs of the few, or the one." This phrase, rasply uttered by Mr. Spock, is iconic science fiction lore. *Star Trek II: The Wrath of Khan* (alas) is not included among those featured in this chapter. However, consider Dr. Myrick's position about curing cancer. If it could be cured—forever—wouldn't accomplishing that expansively great good outweigh any harm suffered by only one person? Or consider the Allies' decision to invade Germany-controlled France (per the realistic portrayal in the opening scene of *Saving Private Ryan*). Fully expecting that thousands of troops would be lost in the beach landings, their deaths were considered acceptable given the greater good of defeating Nazi Germany and swiftly ending World War II. The common theme of these scenarios—fictional or historical—is that accomplishing extraordinarily good ends can justify any means required for them, at least if the beneficial result significantly outweighs the cost of achieving it. This idea is a staple of an ethical approach known as utilitarianism.

The Conceptual Framework

Utilitarian ethical systems are invariably consequentialist in nature. Consequentialism is the view that moral theories should stress the importance of results, or consequences, of actions. Consequentialists thereby hold that the rightness or wrongness of an action is judged in terms of the positive or negative results it brings about. Classic utilitarians, like John Stuart Mill and (more explicitly) his teacher and godfather Jeremy Bentham before him, evaluate positive and negative results straightforwardly in terms of pleasure and pain. This makes Mill and Bentham hedonists.[2] Hedonism is the view that *only* pleasure is intrinsically good (good for its own sake) and *only* pain is intrinsically bad. Other things beside pleasure and pain can be considered good or bad, but only instrumentally so. If something other than pleasure is deemed good—perhaps knowledge or friendship—it is so because it brings about an intrinsic good, namely, pleasure (or reduces pain or suffering). Mill and Bentham, then, believed moral agents should perform actions that tend to produce pleasurable or pleasant consequences and avoid those that produce painful consequences. On this score, the Lacuna memory-wipe technology from *Eternal Sunshine of the Spotless Mind* might be considered a good thing exactly because it eases pain and suffering, allowing its users to lead happier lives (assuming it does, indeed, accomplish those positive results).

Morally significant benefits are understood in terms of experienced pleasure and morally significant harms are understood in terms of experienced pain or suffering.[3] Whenever

---

BOX 7C: LEARNING OUTCOMES

Upon carefully studying this chapter, students should better comprehend and be able to explain:

- The distinctive themes of a utilitarian ethical perspective and its strengths and weaknesses as a moral theory.
- The alleged difference between act and rule utilitarianism, what motivates some moral philosophers to embrace the latter, and how others argue the former is the only consistent form of utilitarianism.
- How some philosophers argue that classic utilitarianism's commitment to hedonism leads to problematic issues regarding morally significant benefits and harms.
- How themes expressed in *Extreme Measures, Saving Private Ryan,* and *Eternal Sunshine of the Spotless Mind* are conducive to better understanding utilitarian approaches to ethics.

---

someone or something experiences pleasure or pain, that entity is having a sensation or feeling. One must be conscious—possessing mental states—in order to have sensations or feelings. Thus conscious states and only conscious states having specific qualitative content possess inherent moral worth. Mental states containing pleasurable content are inherently good and those possessing painful content are inherently bad. People and most animals have sensations and feelings. That nonhuman animals have conscious mental states entails that their pleasure or pain is morally significant; they can be harmed and, thus, mistreated like any other conscious entity. This position on animal suffering is often seen as one of the conceptual strengths of classic utilitarianism.

> "I could die right now, Clem. I'm just . . . happy. I've never felt that way before. I'm exactly where I want to be."—*Eternal Sunshine of the Spotless Mind*, scene 12

Some utilitarians follow Bentham in holding that pleasures differ only in degree (the more, the better) and that pains also differ only in degree (the more, the worse). Thus pleasure and pain are to be considered only in terms of *quantity*. No kind of pleasure is more valuable than any other, and no instance of pain is to be overlooked. Moreover, the pleasure or pain of every conscious entity must be taken into account equally. This leads to a kind of impartiality that ethical systems invariably strive to achieve. No one is morally special or privileged. All that matters is the amount of pleasure or pain experienced by each entity involved. In this regard, the fundamental question to ask about any course of action is: What are its foreseeable consequences regarding pleasure and pain? In detail, one is to ask: How intense will the pleasure be? How long will it last? How long will it be before the pleasure starts? Will it reduce capacity for future pleasure? Will it bring future pain? Will it be mixed with pain? Will others be affected by the pleasure and to what extent? And one is to ask similar questions concerning the pain that an action will foreseeably bring about. Once these questions are answered, according to classic utilitarians like Bentham, the agent can better determine what ought to be done in the situation at hand. (This process is often called the "hedonic calculus.")

Mill disagreed with his teacher about whether only the quantity of pleasure was morally significant. He famously argued that some pleasurable states are more valuable than others. Mill was thus also concerned with the *quality* of pleasures. In terms of evaluating pleasures, Mill held that the intellectual pleasures ranked ahead of the merely sensual. Mill makes this move in the hopes of deflecting the venerable objection that utilitarianism caters to pleasure-mongers and is "a doctrine worthy only of swine." But Mill counters that, because the intellectual pleasures are more valuable than the merely sensual, "it is better to be a human being dissatisfied than a pig satisfied; better to be Socrates dissatisfied than a fool satisfied." So, some, or even a little, high quality pleasures (the intellectual ones) may outweigh a lot more low quality pleasures (the merely sensual ones). For example, then, the pleasure Dr. Howard Mierzwiak receives from developing, refining, and implementing the Lacuna memory-wiping technology is to be prized ahead of Stan and Mary's nights of alcohol and marijuana infused sexual intercourse—regardless of how often or pleasurable their orgasms.

"Drink up, young man. It'll make the whole seduction part less repugnant." —*Eternal Sunshine of the Spotless Mind*, scene 3

Given the distinction between the higher and lower pleasures, Mill argues that utilitarianism does not merely pander to pleasure-mongers. Mill's utilitarianism advocates that we strive to exercise our capacities for poetry, math, art, and (of course) philosophy.[4] Yet Mill hoped to be as inclusive as possible about what counted as a higher pleasure. He believed that the "higher" and "lower" pleasures could be distinguished by a panel of competent judges—those experienced in all sorts of pleasurable activity. If the panel was agreed that one kind of pleasure was not to be sacrificed regardless of how much pleasure could be alternatively achieved via other means, then it was of a higher quality and should be valued accordingly. Nevertheless, it seems that Mill remains committed to the idea that pleasures, in terms of their kind and intensity can be ranked or compared even if the entities experiencing them are not relevantly similar.

Although Bentham and Mill did not always agree, their views seem similar enough to consider both classic utilitarians. Classic utilitarians are united in their adherence to an ethical view grounded in achieving pleasurable mental states and avoiding those that are painful. Bentham clearly states, "Nature has placed mankind under the governance of two sovereign masters, pain and pleasure. It is for them alone to point out what we ought to do."[5] This basic position can be expressed in a single moral standard:

Among the foreseeable consequences, one ought to always bring about the greatest good for the greatest number over the long run.

This principle—often simply called the "utility principle"—provides the fundamental criterion for rightness of action for (classic) utilitarians. Per Mill's eloquent recapitulation: "Actions are right in proportion as they tend to promote happiness, wrong as they tend to produce the reverse of happiness. By happiness is intended pleasure, and the absence of pain; by unhappiness, pain, and the privation of pleasure." That an action causes a great deal of pain and suffering is reason not to do it; actions that bring about happiness or pleasurable results (or the best ratio of pleasure over pain all things considered) ought to be performed. Thus classic utilitarians affirm that agents are morally obligated to perform actions that have optimal consequences—those that "maximize utility." Agents that regularly maximize utility are morally good, and those that regularly fail to maximize it are morally bad.

Utilitarianism captures many morally significant insights. First, it seems plain that if a course of action will bring about only pain and suffering and no positive results, then this is excellent reason to avoid it. When someone correctly says, "No good will come of this," she means that it ought not to be done. Moreover, when inquiring about what ought to be done, it seems intuitive to ask: What will produce the most good for everyone involved? Second, utilitarianism requires that *everyone's* pain/suffering and pleasure/happiness be taken into account when deciding upon a course of action. This intuition gets to the heart of taking the moral point of view in the first place. Recall from chapter 1 that taking the moral point of view requires that we impartially take into consideration the interests of everyone affected by our pending choices and actions. Utilitarianism provides us a straightforward way to accomplish that. This second intuition, furthermore, reminds us that not only human beings can suffer. Many nonhuman animals are also capable of experiencing pleasant and painful mental states. Thus, utilitarianism also works to safeguard the interests of nonhuman animals; it offers a strategy for explaining why they can be mistreated in ethically objectionable ways and how to avoid such treatment. Third, building on its prior intuitive strengths, utilitarianism strives to reduce suffering on a global scale—without regard to race, gender, geographical location, or even species, which is certainly a noble pursuit. Achieving this would indeed make the world a better place, which seems to be a staple for thinking ethically in the first place. And, finally, it attempts to accomplish all this through a straightforward, single principle applicable to any situation.

It is noteworthy that (classic) utilitarians offer two distinct strategies for accomplishing these goals. This is because utilitarians sometimes disagree about how to implement the utility principle. Some believe that it should be applied to each and every act an agent is about to perform. Others demur, holding that it should be applied to rules or policies that a society adopts. Moral philosophers of the former camp are called "act utilitarians"; those in the latter camp are invariably called "rule utilitarians." (Bentham is invariably classified as an act utilitarian; scholars are somewhat divided about whether Mill is best classified as an act or rule utilitarian.)

Act Utilitarianism

Act utilitarians, not surprisingly, hold that thinking in moral terms is confined to actions, and the results that flow from them. They believe that morally significant choices ultimately boil down to their pleasure and pain quotient. Many act utilitarians follow Bentham by referring to discrete units of pleasure or pain when deriving these quotients; a unit of pleasure or pain is called a "hedon." A "positive hedon" is a unit of pleasure or happiness, and a "negative hedon" is a discrete unit of pain or suffering. Thus act utilitarian moral reasoning applies only to actions, requires assigning positive and negative hedons accurately, and then doing proper arithmetic when adding up the positive hedons and subtracting negative hedons for that action.

Act utilitarians accordingly assess morally significant actions as obligatory, permissible, and impermissible in the following ways. An action is morally required just in case it, among all the alternatives open to the agent at the time, is the one that will bring about the greatest balance of positive hedons (pleasure/happiness) over negative hedons (pain/suffering) considering everyone affected and taking the long run into account. So, following Bentham's usage, if action A will bring about fifty positive hedons and action B results in ten positive hedons, then an agent acts impermissibly by choosing to do B instead of A. If choices A and B will produce an identical amount of positive hedons, then an agent may permissibly do either (assuming that no third alternative will produce more). If the agent is faced with a tragic situation such that no matter what she does, only negative hedons will be produced, then the agent ought to choose that action that has the least balance of negative hedons over positive hedons. That is, if an agent is faced with only doing A or B, and doing A brings about one hundred negative hedons and B results in two hundred negative

> "You wanna explain the math of this to me? I mean, where's the sense of riskin' the lives of the eight of us to save one guy?" —*Saving Private Ryan*, scene 6

hedons, then she is morally obligated to do A. Finally, if an agent must choose between A or B, and each produce the same number of negative hedons, then she may permissibly perform either option.

Two examples from *Extreme Measures* are noteworthy on an act utilitarian analysis. First, recall Guy's decision at the beginning of the movie. He was faced with a choice between sending the police officer or the drug user to the operating room. This appeared to be a moral dilemma; moral dilemmas are conflict situations such that no matter what one does given the operative circumstances, something morally unfortunate will obtain. Guy needed operating rooms for both men, but only one was available. No matter what Guy chooses, someone's life will be put at risk. Act utilitarians are not fazed by alleged conflict situations. They would offer Guy the advice they offer everyone: maximize utility. Removing Guy's "dilemma" is merely a matter of applying the utility principle to the case at hand. He would calculate all the positive hedons and subtract any negative hedons regarding his two alternatives. Treating the cop first, thereby putting the drug user at some risk, is likely to maximize utility. After all, the police officer is likely to serve and protect the public for years to come. Furthermore, he has a loving family that depends on him. The drug user seems neither to serve the public good, nor have anyone depending on him, except perhaps for the few people who buy drugs from him (assuming that he also deals). Even so, the long-term harm of drug addiction probably outweighs any short-term benefits of getting high. Thus, it seems likely that the act utilitarian will agree with Guy's choice (even if Jodie disagreed).

Second, consider how the act utilitarian assesses Dr. Myrick's decision to conduct his research on local homeless men. Because the homeless men don't have any families, no one depends on them. Furthermore, because they are more or less detached from society, no one will really miss them, apart from the other homeless persons with which they associate. Thus, the only negative hedons produced by Myrick's decision, assuming that he keeps his research mostly secretive, are those experienced by his test subjects (and perhaps a few of their friends). However, the potential benefits of curing paralysis forever are astonishingly great. Furthermore, Myrick will no doubt make other significant medical discoveries along the way, leading to cures for other maladies. As Myrick informs Guy, "I'm doing medicine here that no one has ever dreamed of, baseline neurochemistry." In

Extreme Measures, Castle Rock Entertainment, 1996. Dr. Guy Luthan (Hugh Grant, right) becomes embroiled in the unconventional and controversial research program of Dr. Lawrence Myrick (Gene Hackman). (Moviegoods, Inc.)

this way, it seems that the negatives associated with the pain and suffering experienced by a small group of homeless people are substantially outweighed by the expansive benefits of Myrick's research.

The only potential glitch for Myrick might be the question of why he is using human test subjects in the first place. Why not use nonhuman animals for his research? Might this incur reduced amounts of negative hedons? It may, but, keep firmly in mind that the issue for the act utilitarian is merely what will bring about the optimal happiness/suffering quotient. Thus, the choice between human subjects and nonhuman test subjects cannot be decided any other way, lest we fall into the error of "speciesism."[6] Moreover, as Myrick points out, experimenting on nonhuman animals would also jeopardize the

> "And most of them will die.
> . . . These men are heroes.
> Because of them, millions of
> people will walk again." —
> *Extreme Measures*, scene 31

significance of the benefits achieved. Recall his comment to Guy: "Growth factors only code to species; to do the work, you need human subjects." Moreover, Myrick is already of advanced age; in his own words, he "doesn't have much time." Assuming that no one else is able to properly conduct his program, there isn't time for nonhuman trials. True, Myrick's decision initially seems controversial, but act utilitarians affirm that moral flexibility is called for in some extreme situations, especially when the benefits clearly outweigh the costs. Therefore, even if further debate must be had about whether Myrick's situation is as extreme as, say, needing to invade Germany-controlled France to swiftly end World War II, and whether public knowledge of Myrick's program significantly alters the pleasure and pain quotient, it is conceivable that act utilitarians would also agree with Myrick's decision (even if Guy did not).

Act utilitarianism also provides an interesting lens for viewing *Saving Private Ryan*. Initially, General Marshall's order to locate and send home Private James Ryan from Iowa seems dubious, as witnessed by the objections leveled by Marshall's advisors. Marshall nevertheless remains steadfast. Capt. John Miller is ordered to select *seven* soldiers from his company to search the German-controlled French countryside for *one* conscripted paratrooper. Ryan is not an extraordinary soldier. He is neither an engineer about to invent something wonderful (like a longer-lasting light bulb), nor a scientist on the verge of curing some terrible malady (as is Myrick). Spielberg cleverly drives this point home with how Miller's squad reacts to the helicopter crash in scene 10 of *Saving Private Ryan*. The helicopter had been unusually reinforced with steel plating to protect General Amend from ground fire. This decision was undoubtedly made because of Amend's important role in the war effort. But the helicopter became unstable with the extra weight. Despite the pilot's best efforts, it crashed, killing Amend and twenty-two other soldiers. Miller surveys the gruesome scene and murmurs, "All that for a general?" The surviving pilot replies, "One man." Miller's squad echoes the pilot's estimation of the situation: "FUBAR." If Miller's squad concludes this about Amend's helicopter, what is the viewer to conclude about Marshall's decision to send Ryan home? True, Ryan's mother will be pleased about her son's safe return from Europe, but it's incredibly unlikely that her happiness alone justifies the effort and resources required to get him there. After all, as one of Miller's men points out, "I got a mother, all right? I mean, you got a mother. Sarge's got a mother. I bet even the Captain got a mother." If every soldier serving in World War II has a mother, what, then, makes Ryan so special or deserving? Because the pleasure over pain quotient certainly seems incredibly low, act utilitarians would probably not agree with General Marshall's decision (even if many of Spielberg's viewers might).

> "This Ryan better be worth it. He'd better go home and cure some disease or invent a longer-lasting light bulb or something. 'Cause the truth is, I wouldn't trade ten Ryans for one Vecchio or one Caparzo."
> —*Saving Private Ryan*, scene 9

The Debate about Act Utilitarianism

Despite utilitarianism's many strong points, it remains quite controversial. The controversy begins with its assumption that for any two things A and B, both of which have value, there is a measure or unit of value in terms of which the value of A and the value of B can be compared. This assumption manifests in that an action carrying ten positive hedons is more valuable than one carrying five positive hedons. However, it is not at all clear that there are such things as "hedons." They seem to be a convenient fiction. Even if there were such things as hedons, it is not at all clear how they should be accurately assigned with any precision. What value do we give a hot drink on a winter day or a cold drink on a summer day? Note the previous discussions of *Extreme Measures*. Recall that no hedons were assigned to the morally significant facts. Exactly how many negative hedons should be assigned to Claude Minkins as he attempts to function with a severed spinal cord? How does this effectively compare to the joy Myrick's team experiences upon learning that Minkins survived as long as he did, thereby demonstrating significant progress in Myrick's research? If accurate measures of pleasure (or happiness) against pain (or suffering) cannot be made, then act utilitarianism cannot offer definitive advice about what we ought to do. Unless this objection can be properly addressed, it seems act utilitarianism does poorly regarding the action-guiding test, thereby threatening its plausibility as a moral theory.

The typical response to this objection is that act utilitarianism doesn't crucially rely on the existence of hedons. Even without precise measurements of pleasure and pain, it seems intuitive that some options are far better candidates for maximizing utility than others. Rough estimates may suffice in terms of enacting the utility principle. Even so, it is worth noting that act utilitarians still require that we make roughly accurate predictions about the future, as we are to somehow evaluate all the foreseeable consequences of our alternative courses of action and then do the action that is in accordance with the utility principle. But because the future has not yet come to pass, we can never be certain whether or not our choices or actions are morally right when we make them. This issue presents difficulty for any moral agent. But what of Miller's decision to let the German POW go free? Was Miller in any position to determine whether dragging him along or even executing him wouldn't better serve the greater good? And what should we say about Dr. Myrick's research? As there are so many untested variables in experimental procedures, can he justifiably believe that he is maximizing utility? It thus seems that utilitarian approximations of what will maximize utility, be they in mundane or unusual circumstances, are *extremely* rough. This troubling result (again) provides evidence that act utilitarianism has difficulty with the action-guiding test. Unless this objection can be suitably addressed, its plausibility as a moral theory is threatened.[7]

Other critics object that act utilitarianism requires too much of us as moral agents. This objection invariably takes one of three forms. The first form is sometimes called the "no rest" objection. Recall that for every situation that I find myself, to guarantee that I act permissibly, I must constantly perform the hedonic calculus (as best I can). This seemingly requires the kind of effort from moral agents that is bound to have counterintuitive results. On the one hand, it eliminates supererogatory actions from act utilitarianism. A supererogatory act is one that is above and beyond the call of duty. But if act utilitarianism is true, no action is above and beyond the call of duty; regarding each and every situation, we are obligated to perform the action that will maximize utility, and that action, regardless of what it is, is required of us. On the other hand, the *constant* effort to maximize utility is bound to have the ironic effect that each and every moral agent will be miserable. If every moral agent suffers from the effort to constantly maximize utility, then utility will not be maximized. Therefore, the "no rest" objection shows how act utilitarianism is open to counterexample (by eliminating supererogatory acts) or falls prey to the contradiction test (by requiring moral agents to cause more harm than good). These criticisms must be addressed.

The second formulation of the objection that act utilitarianism is unduly demanding argues that it requires individuals to sacrifice any and all personal projects or ideals for the sake of maximizing utility. An agent might find that murdering an innocent person maximizes utility. Surely, the circumstances calling for this would be strange, but not inconceivable. Thus, the agent is morally required to commit murder if act utilitarianism is true. This remains so even if he is a pacifist, following the teachings of (say) Mohandas Gandhi.

Perhaps a doctor, like Guy Luthan, might find himself in a position such that purposely not curing a patient he could otherwise heal maximizes utility. Guy, like the pacifist, must eschew his personal ideals for the sake of the greater good. That a moral theory requires agents to straightaway act contrary to such noble ideals serves as a troubling objection.

This objection is actually a consequence of the extreme moral flexibility that act utilitarianism allows (and is similar to an objection leveled at ethical egoism in chapter 6). If act utilitarianism is true, no act is intrinsically or necessarily wrong (and no act is intrinsically or necessarily right). Actions are made impermissible or obligatory given their consequences. Thus, it is possible, however unlikely, that maiming or rape might be morally obligatory. In this regard, act utilitarians contravene commonsense morality, which invariably holds that some actions are inherently wrong. The second formulation of the objection that act utilitarianism is unduly demanding—in either of the two forms presented here—presents a counterexample that must be addressed. Perhaps (again similar to ethical egoism) this debate devolves into a battle of clashing intuitions, but the fact that act utilitarians are willing to require agents to perform *any* act (so long as it maximizes utility), including those contrary to our well-considered moral beliefs, seemingly serves as some evidence that it runs afoul of the counterexample test.

The third version of the objection that act utilitarianism is unduly demanding of moral agents is grounded in the entrenched commonsense belief that individuals have special obligations to close friends and family members. It certainly seems plain that a parent is required to care for his children in ways that other adults are not. It also seems permissible that a parent care for his children more than the children of others. These intuitions ground the commonsense belief that special obligations exist. However, act utilitarianism's strong commitment to impartiality threatens this belief. If a parent faces a choice between saving his own children or saving a group of children he has only known for five minutes (but not both groups), he must resolve this dilemma like any other: do that which maximizes utility. Therefore, it is possible that the parent is morally required to sacrifice his own children if saving the other group maximizes utility. Yet many would argue that the mere suggestion that a parent be required to perform such calculations—let alone be required to sacrifice his children—is evidence enough that act utilitarianism is flawed. That is, act utilitarianism falls prey to an intuitively powerful counterexample; it faces a serious challenge from the counterexample test because it denies what seems obviously true, namely, that special obligations exist.

The objection that act utilitarianism is overly demanding thereby raises problematic issues for the theory in various ways. However, act utilitarians tend to respond in the same basic way: so much the worse for commonsense morality. Why should commonsense beliefs always prove to be decisive, especially about complex matters like ethical discourse? Furthermore, it's probably true that many of us could be exerting more effort to ease the suffering of humankind. Act utilitarianism thus serves to shake up the status quo, waking us from our dogmatic (moral) slumber. That is, even if Myrick's research methods *seem* extreme, what ought we to do about the homeless problem? Certainly, something ought to be done. Are we doing enough? Act utilitarianism charges us to answer these questions honestly and follow through on our answers.

But detractors of act utilitarianism counter by arguing that it requires us to overturn even our most deeply held and well-considered moral beliefs, including those about justice and fairness. Recall how issues of justice and fairness lead Guy to disparage Myrick's research. Guy tells Myrick, "Maybe those men upstairs are heroes, but they didn't choose to be. You chose for them." Many would agree with Guy's brief assessment. It certainly seems unjust of Myrick to subject the local homeless men *he* chooses to such pain and suffering, exactly because they did not consent to it. They have done nothing to deserve the treatment they (literally) receive at Myrick's hands. So, to paraphrase Guy, whether Myrick can cure every disease on the planet cannot justify how he mistreats the homeless men. If so, then act utilitarianism is rendered implausible because it advocates unjust practices.

This objection is often crafted in terms of rights. It is argued that act utilitarianism can be rejected because it advocates ignoring the rights of individuals for the sake of maximizing utility. The issue is not whether persons, by acting impermissibly, *deserve* to have their rights curtailed or impeded. Rather, the issue is whether basic human rights can be ignored for the sake of the greater good. But to ignore basic human rights, especially when individuals have done nothing to deserve such treatment is to condone unjust practices. Thus act utilitarianism condones unjust practices. Because it seems odd, to say the least, that a plausible moral theory condones injustice, it follows that act utilitarianism is implausible. Moreover, although there might be some debate about whether our commonsense moral beliefs about special obligations are warranted, there is *very* little debate about whether our commonsense beliefs about rights, justice, and fairness are well-founded— they are among our most deeply held and well-considered beliefs. A sheriff that frames an innocent vagrant to bring about positive mental states within her county acts unjustly and, thus, impermissibly. Analogously, Myrick acts impermissibly when he authorizes his associates to frame Guy for drug possession, regardless of how beneficial his research program may—or even will—become to paralysis victims. If act utilitarianism cannot explain away this carefully crafted counterexample, then there is strong evidence that it must be revised lest its plausibility as a moral theory be seriously jeopardized.

The Move to Rule Utilitarianism

Some utilitarians favor rule utilitarianism over act utilitarianism. This isn't because act utilitarianism lacks moral rules. For act utilitarians, moral rules—keep your promises, do not murder—are the result of generalizing upon past experience. Typically, past experiences have shown that, for example, not keeping one's promises causes more harm than good. Act utilitarians advise to act in accordance with these established guidelines (or "rules of thumb"), especially when agents have no time to consider the consequences of alternative actions. Yet they are quick to point out that any such guideline can be superseded by careful utilitarian reasoning via the utility principle. Rule utilitarians, however, aspire to provide moral rules a more prominent conceptual status. They hope to accomplish this by applying the utility principle not to the foreseen consequences of particular actions, but by applying it to the foreseen consequences of enacting and following particular rules or social practices. Consequently, the rule utilitarian would have us consider competing policies that society could follow, envision what would happen if each of the competing policies were enacted over the other, and then advise us to adopt the one that most effectively maximizes utility (produces the most optimal results).

To better grasp the process the rule utilitarian advises, consider two competing policies relevant to *Extreme Measures*: "doctors give treatment priority to patients in most medical need" and "doctors give treatment priority to patients on a nonprofessional (personal preference) basis." Among these competing policies, it seems pretty clear that enacting the second would have significant detrimental results for various reasons. First, the quality of health care could only decline as doctors begin mixing professional with personal goals. Second, the general population would be filled with anxiety, wondering whether a friend or loved one rushed to the hospital will meet with the doctor's personal preferences. What if the doctor is racist, sexist, or simply a misanthrope (perhaps not unlike Dr. Gregory House from *House M.D.*)? Even if the attending physician attempted to decide between patients on a moral principled basis, as Guy arguably did, such decisions will invariably be made quickly without all the relevant facts sufficiently considered (if at all); this will almost certainly lead to questionable decisions, and can only lead to further public malaise about visiting the emergency room or urgent care. It therefore seems that the rule utilitarian would advise that the former policy be adopted by society.

This example also illustrates how actions are deemed obligatory, permissible, or impermissible on rule utilitarianism. Guy, recognizing that he is in a situation that falls under the former (and thus not the latter) policy, is morally required to send the drug-user to the operating room first. This action is obligatory because it falls under a rule that most effectively maximizes utility. Therefore, assuming that the police officer was in more stable condition, it seems that the rule utilitarian would claim that Guy acted impermissibly because he failed to follow the more optimal rule. Generally, then, rule utilitarians hold that an action is obligatory if it's required by an adopted social policy that, among all its relevant competitors, most effectively maximizes utility. Agents act impermissibly when they enact a rule that fails to produce optimific results. If an agent finds herself in a situation that falls under two competing social policies, for example, being kind or being honest regarding a friend's feathered mullet hairstyle (similar to the one worn by David Spade in *Joe Dirt*), but being honest means being unkind and being kind means being dishonest, then she may resort to act utilitarianism as a way to remove the conflict (dilemma). She should choose the act that, in those specific circumstances, will maximize utility (including, perhaps, saying nothing about the unfortunate 80s hairstyle). If the alternatives before her are all equal with respect to maximizing utility, then she may permissibly choose among them.

To better grasp the emerging differences between act and rule utilitarianism reconsider General Marshall's decision to risk eight soldiers to save one lowly private. Moreover, as it turns out, two of Miller's men lost their lives in the attempt to find Ryan, and only two of the squad members survived the battle at the bridge. Thus, Marshall decided to sacrifice six soldiers to save just one. Certainly Mrs. Ryan will be very happy and relieved to have her last remaining son at home with her; however, it is extremely unlikely that this outweighs the lives of those six men. Thus, the act utilitarian would probably disparage Marshall's choice. But the rule utilitarian is likely to view Marshall's decision differently.[8] The rule utilitarian might ask for the reasons America entered World War II in the first place. American soldiers were arguably sent into battle so that those at home could live in continued freedom. However, if there are no sons or daughter left at home as a result of the war, then all the sacrifices made for the greater good of the war effort are nullified. In this way, Ryan is not merely one lowly private; he is a symbol of the future—a future which must be protected and saved. Therefore, perhaps a rule or policy could be articulated that embodies these ideas. If so, it is plausible to interpret the decision to send Ryan home as resulting from Marshall recognizing that the rule in question needs to be enacted. If he doesn't enact the relevant rule, then he impermissibly chooses to put America's future at risk.

Saving Private Ryan, Dreamworks SKG, 1998. Captain John Miller (Tom Hanks) leads his company on a unique but dangerous mission to locate James Ryan of Iowa, lost somewhere in France during World War II. (Moviegoods, Inc.)

The differences between act and rule utilitarianism can also be gleaned in the way that the latter addresses the classic objections made to the former. Regarding the objection that utilitarianism is unduly demanding, recall the "no rest" and "no special obligations" variants. Regarding the first, the rule utilitarian would advise us to choose between two policies, one in which we never cease performing utilitarian calculations or one in which we include some time for personal considerations (yet always keeping an eye out for when a situation calls for more careful utilitarian analysis). It's pretty clear that the latter will produce more optimal results; enacting this rule thereby addresses the concern that utilitarianism is self-defeating in terms of making everyone miserable via incessant efforts to maximize utility. The rule utilitarian might also attempt to answer the second variant in a similar way. It might be that what maximizes utility is enacting the policy that everyone gives the interests of close friends and loved ones priority over those of complete strangers.

The rule utilitarian strategy being developed here can be generalized to address other objections leveled at act utilitarianism. Recall that no action is intrinsically wrong according to act utilitarianism. Consequently, in certain (perhaps unusual) circumstances, the act utilitarian is committed to the claim that slavery, torturing the innocent, using unwilling human research subjects, or framing innocent persons for social harmony is obligatory. But the rule utilitarian asks: What if the *practice* of enslaving a minority group, torturing the innocent for pleasure, doctors using human test subjects without consent, or law enforcement framing innocent persons was regularly followed? If any of these became a practice of a society, it seems that utility would not be maximized due to the mistrust and general ill-ease brought on it. But if these practices would not maximize utility, then there is solid utilitarian reason not to enact them. Thus, rule utilitarianism, unlike act utilitarianism, does not run afoul of our most entrenched (and well-considered) moral judgments; seemingly, it accomplishes this without sacrificing the core ideals of a utilitarian approach to ethics.

The Debate about Rule Utilitarianism

Although rule utilitarians believe that they can offer a more defensible brand of utilitarianism, it remains somewhat controversial. Some of the controversy is generated by concerns external to the theory. However, the most significant source of controversy (invariably) comes from act utilitarians, who offer concerns internal to utilitarianism.

Scholars are divided about whether rule utilitarians fare any better than act utilitarians with respect to anticipating positive and negative results of society adopting and enacting one policy over another. Attempting to calculate the (future) consequences of specific actions is a difficult task, but attempting to calculate the (future) consequences of general rules that cover a wide range of specific actions all occurring in slightly different yet similar circumstances seems impossible. This task is made more difficult with the realization that society adopts and enacts multiple rules and, ideally, a set that maximizes utility over competing sets of (consistent) rules. How might we accurately predict the ways in which agents will uphold or shirk from such a set of rules? The force of these questions raises doubt about how rule utilitarianism fares regarding the action-guiding test. However, to be fair, this issue and the questions that surround it, require additional exploration.

The internal criticism of rule utilitarianism is grounded in its strategy to prohibit specific actions that, if performed at the time, would maximize utility. Therefore, rule utilitarians require agents to knowingly perform actions that produce consequences that run contrary to the utilitarian ideal. In this way, it is argued that rule utilitarianism becomes internally inconsistent, failing the contradiction test.

A bit more carefully, assume for the sake of the argument that hedons exist, can be accurately assigned, and that the particular practice of not lying typically brings 100 positive hedons. Suppose further that in some specific circumstances lying to a friend so as to not needlessly hurt her feelings brings 125 positive hedons. In this case, the exception to the policy of being dishonest maximizes utility. In addressing this scenario, it seems that the rule utilitarian has one of two choices. First, she could hold firm to the established rule and accept the anti-utilitarian results. But it seems contradictory to require utilitarians to eschew the utilitarian ideal of maximizing utility. Second, she could agree that the rule should be modified and derive a new rule of the form "Do not lie except in these particular circumstances." Adopting this modified policy more effectively maximizes utility; enacting it thus fits the utilitarian ideal. But this is not anything different from what would cause the act utilitarian to break or modify one of her moral guidelines. Whatever would lead an act utilitarian to break or modify some guideline would also lead a rule utilitarian to modify a rule. Thus an internally consistent version of rule utilitarianism collapses into act utilitarianism. Either way, it seems that the rule utilitarian cannot consistently hold her distinctive brand of utilitarianism. Scholars typically find this argument to be decisive against rule utilitarianism. It's not exactly clear how the rule utilitarian answers this charge that it fails the contradiction test, but it's clear that it must be answered lest its plausibility as a moral theory be seriously curtailed.

A Question of Values

There is another problematic issue for both classic act and rule utilitarians, namely, their joint assertion that pleasurable (and painful) mental states are the *only* things that have inherent moral worth. Perhaps seeking pleasure is important to us, and perhaps it is typically rational for us to pursue it. However, it seems implausible that all of our *moral* values are merely a function of the pleasure/pain associated with various courses of action.

The emerging issue for classic utilitarians here is cleverly portrayed in *Eternal Sunshine of the Spotless Mind*.[9] The film depicts technology that allows its user to erase painful experiences from his or her memory. Clementine Kruczynski decides to erase her ex-boyfriend Joel Barish, who, in turn, decides to have her erased from his memories; however, the remainder of their memories is kept safely intact. Lacuna Inc. provides this service to all those who seek it (including those attempting to deal with dead pets or unsuccessful sporting events). Arguably, this procedure, if successfully implemented, would significantly decrease the amount of pain and suffering in the world. If so, it thus seems that classic utilitarians would advise its widespread use. Yet a careful viewing of the movie seems to convey reasons for not undergoing the procedure and, thus, by extension offers (implicit) objections to classic utilitarianism.

In various ways, the movie raises the issue of whether some things possess morally significant value apart from how they make us feel ("on the inside"). Does Clementine harm Joel in some way via her decision to completely erase him from her life? The answer may depend on whether we have a moral obligation not to intentionally misrepresent those we come into contact with, and whether completely erasing someone from memory is tantamount to misrepresentation. Does she harm herself in going through the process? She (and Joel, too) choose to live a lie rather than face the truth. Is there value in honestly leading your own life apart from considerations of pain and pleasure? At one point during the memory-wiping procedure, Joel becomes aware of it (analogous to how people incorporate reality into their dreams just before waking). He wishes to end the procedure, but Lacuna Inc. is unaware of this because Joel is (technically) unconscious. Is Joel harmed by not having his autonomous decision recognized? Might it be argued that Clementine and Joel are objectionably mutilating themselves? A piercing is

> "Our files are confidential, Mr. Barish. . . . Suffice it to say, Miss Kruczynski was not happy and she wanted to move on. We provide that possibility."
> —*Eternal Sunshine of the Spotless Mind*, scene 7

one thing, but radically altering how you (later) perceive the world is another. Finally, at the end of the movie, Clementine and Joel meet "again"; however, the receptionist at Lacuna, who discovers that she has also been a client, sends all of Lacuna's files to their (respective) clients. Clementine and Joel thus learn that their "first" relationship ended poorly with both of them quite miserable. Yet they decide to give romance another try. Is their choice easily interpreted on classic utilitarianism?[10]

In some ways, the memory-wiping procedure from *Eternal Sunshine of the Spotless Mind* reverses the famous "experience machine" thought-experiment offered by Robert Nozick. Lacuna's memory-wiping technology takes away painful mental states, but the experience machine allows us to add pleasant ones; both facilitate contemplating the plausibility of hedonism. The experience machine represents a sort of virtue reality that once "plugged in" to, provides users with whatever experiences they wish (complete with the false belief that your experiences correspond to how things actually are). Nozick asks: "Should you plug into this machine for life, preprogramming your life's desires?"[11] Nozick is convinced that many of us would turn down the opportunity because we, as agents, value doing things and becoming certain kinds of people as a result of our efforts. That is, there is an important difference between having the experiences of being a good person and *actually* becoming and being a good person. In this way, we value being the authors of our own lives. But all of this requires that we embrace reality as it is and come to grips with it through our own efforts. Plugging into the experience machine or using Lacuna's memory-wiping technology runs contrary to the value many of us put on truth and reality.

So it is far from obvious that pleasure alone is intrinsically good. Other things such as friendship, love, and integrity, for example, are equally plausible candidates. Yet classic utilitarianism holds that friendship, love, integrity, knowledge, and indeed anything whatever is only instrumentally valuable. But if X is Y's friend *only* for the sake of the pleasure that X gets from Y's company, then X is no real friend to Y; the same considerations apply to love. X and Y loving one another is different from and incompatible with X and Y simply using one another for the pleasure it gives. These results seem consistent with one of the underlying messages of *Eternal Sunshine of the Spotless Mind*: the value of close personal relationships, in crucial ways, seems somehow independent of hedonistic considerations. The movie thereby also solidifies the objection that classic utilitarianism offers an implausible account of personal relationships. Because it certainly seems to be the case that personal relationships are crucial to leading a full moral life, we have further reason to think that (classic) utilitarianism is in need of revision. If it cannot adequately explain away or accommodate this counterexample, its plausibility as a moral theory is threatened.

Perhaps revisions to utilitarianism in some form or another are forthcoming. This would be welcome, as a utilitarian approach to ethics has much going for it, not the least of which is the ideal of reducing suffering on a global scale. Whether the requisite revisions can be accomplished wholly from within, or whether utilitarianism must be bolstered with additional external approaches remains to be seen.

7.4. TWO ADDITIONAL FILMS

Saving Private Ryan (1998)

Director: Steven Spielberg
Screenwriter: Robert Rodat

Plot Summary

Except this time, the man is the mission.

Three days have passed since the gruesome D-Day Normandy landing. Although Omaha Beach was secured, scores upon scores of American soldiers lost their lives. Some never got off the boat, ripped apart by German machine gun fire as soon as the transport doors swung open. Others were only so lucky as to drown under the weight of their packs. Yet many survived and fought bravely. These soldiers await new orders.

Meanwhile, office secretaries at US Army General Headquarters are busy typing letters; they have the unenviable task of informing parents and spouses that their loved ones gave their lives for the war effort. One perceptive secretary alerts the officer in charge of a disconcerting fact regarding the Ryan family from Iowa. This news is passed on to Chief of Staff General George Marshall. General Marshall learns that three Ryan brothers have died in the span of only a few days. Their mother will receive all three letters at once. Marshall also learns that there is a fourth brother, the youngest, James Ryan. Ryan's exact whereabouts are unknown, as his paratroop unit missed their drop point. Marshall sighs deeply and walks to his desk. He produces a letter, written by Abraham Lincoln, and begins to read it aloud. The letter conveys Lincoln's most sincere condolences to a Boston woman who lost five sons in the Civil War. Marshall recites the last half of the letter from memory. Placing the letter back in the drawer, Marshall addresses his staff. Waving aside their counsel (and protestations), he solemnly orders, "That boy is alive. We are gonna send somebody to find him. And we are gonna get him the hell . . . outta there."

Captain John Miller reports to his commanding officer, Lt. Colonel Anderson. Anderson acknowledges the difficulty of the beach landing, but perfunctorily proceeds to give Miller his new orders sent "straight from the top": he is to take a squad of soldiers and find Pvt. James Ryan, ensuring his return to his mother in Iowa. Miller selects the best of his remaining men, including Sgt. Horvath, and they begin their quest to save Pvt. Ryan.

Miller's men bemoan their assignment. As they march into German-controlled French territory, Pvt. Reiben brazenly asks Miller why the eight of them were ordered to risk their lives to send one soldier home. Wade, the medic, answers, "Reiben, think of the poor bastard's mother." Reiben curtly responds, "Hey, doc, I got a mother all right. I mean, you got a mother." The squad continues to banter about their mission, but Miller soon interjects, "We all have orders, and we have to follow 'em. That supersedes everything, including your mothers." Reiben considers Miller's words, but then asks, "Even if you think the mission is FUBAR, sir?" Miller immediately responds, "Especially if you think the mission is FUBAR."

Miller and his men arrive near the location of Ryan's designated drop point. The American troops they meet there are taking heavy German fire. Initially, the only thing Miller's men find is trouble. A German sniper has a French family pinned down. Pvt. Caparzo moves to assist them, as the daughter reminds him of his young niece back home. Miller is furious: "Caparzo, get that kid back up there!" Caparzo does his best to dissuade Miller, replying, "Captain, the decent thing to do would be to take her over to the next town." Miller adamantly replies, "We're not here to do the decent thing; we're here to follow orders!" The sniper eyes Caparzo and a bullet pierces his chest. As Caparzo falls to the ground, the girl runs back to her parents. The squad takes cover. To rescue Caparzo is to become the sniper's next victim. Pvt. Jackson, the squad's sharpshooter, surmises the sniper's location and sends a single bullet through the German's riflescope. Miller points to Caparzo's corpse and derisively declares: "That's why we don't take children!"

Later that night, the squad rests in an abandoned church. Miller and Horvath commiserate privately. Horvath notices Miller's right hand shake uncontrollably and jests, "You need to find a different line of work; this one no longer agrees with you." Slightly embarrassed, Miller tries to laugh it off and clasps his hands together. He looks up at Horvath and shares, "You see, when you end up killing one of your men, you tell yourself it happened so you could save the lives of two, or three, or ten others—maybe a hundred others. . . . That's how you rationalize making the choice between the man and the mission. Miller pauses, but solemnly adds: "Ryan better be worth it."

The squad presses on. They learn of the army's recent attempt to reinforce a helicopter in the hopes of better protecting a general from ground fire. But the added weight of the metal plating made the helicopter dangerously unstable. Despite the pilot's best efforts, it crashed, killing twenty-two men, including the general. The squad deems this FUBAR. This chance occurrence, however, provides them some news about Ryan's current whereabouts. But in plotting their new course, the squad also learns about Miller's hand condition; it shakes as he holds his compass. This fully embarrasses Miller, leading him to take an (arguably) unnecessary risk on the final leg of their journey. He intended to regain his squad's respect, but Wade is killed in the process. This drives the squad to near mutiny. Reiben refuses to continue. Miller, realizing the seriousness of the situation, confides in his men, "I don't know anything about Ryan. I don't care. The man means nothing to me. It's just a name. But if going to Ramelle and finding him so that he can go home earns me the right to get back to my wife, then that's my mission."

They finally find Ryan. He is part of a hopelessly small unit defending a strategic bridge. He refuses to leave his post. He observes, "Hell, these guys deserve to go home as much as I do. They've fought just as hard." Miller is sympathetic, but only slightly. He replies, "Is that what I'm supposed to tell your mother when she gets another folded American flag?" To save Pvt. Ryan, the squad must now help him save the Ramelle bridge, at least until reinforcements and relief arrives. Miller and Horvath mull over their options; they are torn. Horvath speaks first: "Part of me thinks the kid is right. He asks what he's done to deserve this. . . . But then another part of me thinks, what if by some miracle we stay . . . and actually make it out of here. Someday we might look back on this and decide that saving Private Ryan was the one decent thing we were able to pull out of this whole godawful mess."

Decades later, James Francis Ryan from Iowa visits Arlington National Cemetery with his wife, children, and grandchildren. He stands before the grave of Captain John Miller. Falling to one knee, head nearly resting on the gravestone, he says, "I've tried to live my life the best I could. I hope that was enough. I hope that, at least in your eyes, I've earned what all of you have done for me."

Discussion Questions

1. What justified American involvement in World War II? Does this justification involve any salient ethical considerations?
2. Is it morally permissible to risk the lives of eight soldiers to save the life of one?
3. Why does General Marshall decide to send Pvt. James Ryan home? Was this decision ethically objectionable? Explain.

4. Miller tells Ryan, "Earn this, James, earn it" (scene 19, 2:36:24–2:36:50). What did he mean? What would be required of Ryan to meet Miller's dying request? (Note that he never cured a disease or invented a longer-lasting light bulb.)
5. How can soldiers act decently in times of war? What ought they to do when acting decently contravenes an order from a superior officer?

Eternal Sunshine of the Spotless Mind (2004)

Director: Michel Gondry
Screenwriter: Charlie Kaufman

Plot Summary

> Blessed are the forgetful, for they get the better even of their blunders.

Joel Barish and Clementine Kruczynski meet on Valentine's Day 2004. They wouldn't have except for the fact that Joel uncharacteristically ditched work that morning. He unexpectedly boarded the train for Montauk. Clementine isn't sure why she visited the beach that cold February morning, but, unlike Joel, she is a rather impulsive person. They spend the train ride back to Rockville Center getting to know each other. He sports a stocking hat; she models Blue Ruin hair dye. He's nice; she's exhilarating. Departing the train, Joel spies her on the sidewalk and offers to drive her home. Inexplicably drawn to each other, they have an evening picnic on the frozen St. Charles River the next night. He's afraid to stray too far from the shore; she daringly skids to the middle. They lie down on the ice and gaze at the stars. It's morning when they get back to town. Clementine has fallen asleep in Joel's car. Joel wakes her when they arrive at her apartment. She wishes to sleep at his place. He agrees.

But this isn't the first time Joel and Clementine have met. In fact, and although they no longer know it, they had been dating for two years. Two weeks ago, Joel and Clementine had a terrible fight. Their relationship was already crumbling. Clementine was unhappy and wished very much to move on with her life. Lacuna Inc. offered her that possibility. Lacuna, developed and managed by Dr. Howard Mierzwiak, offers clients the opportunity to selectively forget painful experiences. Clementine had Joel erased from her memory. Joel learns about Clementine's decision from his friends Rob and Carrie. Joel is confused. He immediately visits Lacuna. Mierzwiak is apologetic: "You should not have seen this." Joel refuses to believe it. Surely this is some sort of hoax. Mierzwiak, and his receptionist Mary, assure him it's not. Joel's confusion turns to grief. Carrie attempts to comfort him: "You know Clementine. She's like that. . . . She decided to erase you almost as a lark." Joel's grief turns to vengeful anger. He decides to erase Clementine from his memory. Although February is Mierzwiak's busiest time of the year, he provides Joel preferential treatment. Joel's procedure is scheduled for the evening of February 13, 2004.

Joel is instructed to go home, take a strong sedative, and simply fall asleep. Two Lacuna technicians, Stan and Patrick, subsequently arrive in Joel's apartment to conduct the procedure. The two men, neither of whom are medical professionals, place an electric-hairdryer-helmet-like apparatus over Joel's head, which is then linked to a computer that Stan operates. Stan uses the computer to locate Joel's memories of Clementine and eradicates them. (Mierzwiak warned Joel: "Technically speaking, the operation is brain damage, but it's on par with a night of heavy drinking. Nothing you'll miss.") Stan informs Patrick that he invited Mary to visit them. Patrick replies, "I like Mary. I like it when she visits." He continues, "Maybe I should invite my girlfriend over. I have a girlfriend now." Patrick opens two bottles of beer and asks Stan if he recalls the girl they memory-wiped last week. Stan does, noting that it was Joel's girl. Patrick confides, "I kinda fell in love with her that night. . . . I stole a pair of her panties, as well." Stan is horrified. Patrick introduced himself to Clementine the day after the procedure and they have seen each other every day since (with some help from Joel's journal and mementos, which Patrick stole from Clementine). Mary arrives as Patrick leaves to visit Clementine. Mary is profoundly impressed by Dr. Mierzwiak and the technology he pioneered. She tells Stan: "It's incredible, isn't it, what Howard gives to the world. To let people begin again. It's beautiful. You look at a baby, and, it's so pure and so free and so clean. And adults are like, this mess of sadness. . . . Howard just makes it all go away." Stan puts the computer on "autopilot," the couple get stoned, have sex in Joel's chair, and fall asleep.

The two are awoken by the buzzing of Stan's computer. During the drama going on around him, Joel somehow managed to realize—perhaps in a way that one incorporates reality into a dream just before waking—that he was being subjected to the Lacuna memory-wiping procedure. He hears Patrick telling Stan about Clementine, and hears Patrick calling Clementine on the phone even though, in his mind, Clementine is sitting next to him on the couch. Joel's memories of Clementine begin to fade; the most recent are the first to go. Slowly, Joel is reliving his relationship with Clem in reverse. He arrives at a particularly touching moment between the two; she whispers in his ear, "Joely, don't ever leave me." Joel pleads, "Mierzwiak, please let me keep this memory. Just this one." But it, too, begins to fade. Joel shouts, hoping someone in his apartment will hear him, "I want to call it off. . . . I don't want this anymore!" No one hears him. Joel laments, "You're erasing her from me. You're erasing me from her!"

Joel, still trapped in his own mind, somehow achieves conversations with Mierzwiak and later Clementine. The former is less than helpful: "I'm part of your imagination, too, Joel. How can I help you from there? Uh, I'm inside your head, too. I'm you." But Clem-inside-his-head is more helpful. Joel alters a memory of him and Clementine going for a hike. This allows Joel to complain about her choice to have him erased: "*You* erased me. . . . That's why I'm doing this in the first place." Clem-inside-his-head apologizes, reminding him (that is, himself) that she is impulsive. He knowingly looks at Clem-inside-his-head and responds, "That's what I love about you." Clem-inside-his-head suggests that Joel take her to unexpected places in his psyche. Infuse her into memories that she wasn't originally a part of. It works. This skews Joel's "memory-map" of Clementine, resulting in Stan's computer sounding an alarm.

Stan (at Mary's suggestion) calls Mierzwiak, alerting him to the situation. He arrives to correct it. He is surprised to see Mary, and asks about Patrick's whereabouts. Howard manages to locate Joel's memories (and quasi-memories) of Clementine. Slowly, they again begin to disappear from him. Joel and Clem-inside-his-head become desperate. They find themselves on the beach at Montauk in 2002, the actual very first time they met. As Clementine vanishes from Joel's mind, Clem-inside-his-head whispers, "Meet me in Montauk."

But the drama is not finished. After Stan leaves to get some air, Mary initiates intimacy with Howard. When Mrs. Mierzwiak unexpectedly arrives, Mary learns that she and Howard previously had an affair, and when he broke it off, she decided to have a memory-wipe to ease her pain. Mary returns to the Lacuna office to find her file hidden in Howard's desk. She listens to the audiotape that Howard requires all of his patients to record. She learns about the affair and how it affected her. She decides to return every patient's file to him or her, including Joel and Clementine.

On the morning of February 16, 2004 (that is, after their second first night at the Charles River), both Joel and Clementine hear their audiotapes, complete with all the reasons why their relationship fell apart. As Clementine runs out of Joel's apartment, embarrassed, confused, and angry, Joel runs after her. He yells, "Wait! . . . I can't see anything that I don't like about you." Clementine responds, "But you will. . . . I'll get bored with you and feel trapped, because that's what happens with me. Joel: "Okay." Clementine: "Okay." They laugh, cry, and begin "again."

Discussion Questions

1. Did Rob and Carrie act impermissibly by informing Joel of Clementine's decision to erase him? Explain.
2. Reconsider Mary's views about the memory-wiping procedure (scene 10, 48:55–49:24). Do you agree with her that it is a boon to humankind? Alternatively, is it somehow detrimental or morally objectionable?
3. Did Patrick do something wrong in stealing Clementine's underwear? Explain.
4. Upon learning about Lacuna Inc., Joel complains to Clem-inside-his-head, "I can't *believe* you did this to me" (scene 9, 38:35). What did Clementine do *to* Joel? Was her choice morally objectionable (as Joel suggests)?
5. Did Mary act permissibly in returning all the Lacuna client files? Explain.

7.5. REVIEWING THROUGH THE THREE MOVIES

1. Which of the three movies offers the most pro-utilitarian message? Which offers the most anti-utilitarian message? Defend your answers.
2. Explain how act and rule utilitarians offer alternative (and competing) interpretations of the events portrayed in *Extreme Measures* and *Saving Private Ryan*. How, if at all, might act and rule utilitarians differently interpret the events of *Eternal Sunshine of the Spotless Mind*? If they would not disagree (about the latter film), explain why.
3. Make a list of all the things that characters from the three movies value. Can each valued item be put into a utilitarian framework? Are there any that resist a utilitarian analysis?
4. Would you use Nozick's experience machine or Lacuna's memory-wiping technology? Explain your decision either way. What does your decision indicate about what you value?
5. Reconsider the six movie quotes from the chapter and explain whether each, given the adjacent paragraphs, *illustrates* a point the author is making, *supplements* (or extends) a point the author is making, or *contrasts* (for emphasis) a point the author is making. Explain your answers.

NOTES

1. Excerpted from John Stuart Mill, *Utilitarianism* (1861). Section headings and other emendations added to aid reader comprehension.

2. Spurred primarily by Mill's distinction between quantitative and qualitative pleasures (to be discussed below), scholars are divided about whether Mill actually is a classic hedonist. For a recent helpful discussion on this topic, see S. Evan Kreider, "Mill on Happiness," *Philosophical Papers* 39, no. 1 (March 2010): 53–68.

3. Arguably, the capacities for experiencing pleasure and pain might need to be included in this account insofar as losing the capacity to experience pleasant or pleasurable states is tantamount to suffering harm. Yet being harmed in this way, if it is a harm, is explained by the fact that one will no longer be able to experience pleasant or pleasurable states.

4. Mill is sometimes criticized for this position because it seems to cut against his hedonism. This arguably weakens his commitment to consequentialism, thereby threatening his commitment to (classic) utilitarianism. That is, once Mill distinguishes between the higher and lower pleasures, properly developing our intellectual capacities is valuable because it constitutes the realization of human nature. On a straightforward interpretation of this position, realizing our intellectual capacities is itself intrinsically valuable, which explains why the higher goods always supersede the lower. But, if so, then issues of the greater good (or maximizing utility) may become secondary to developing our latent, intellectual abilities. Whether this objection is damaging to Mill's overall view depends on the coherence of "eudaimonistic utilitarianism." Many (but not all) scholars argue that eudaimonistic utilitarianism is tantamount to a contradiction in terms, making the view untenable. For an attempt to stave off this sort of objection, see David O. Brink, "Mill's Deliberative Utilitarianism," *Philosophy & Public Affairs* 21 (1992): 67–103.

5. Jeremy Bentham, *An Introduction to the Principles of Morals and Legislation* (1789), chap. 1.

6. Peter Singer has seemingly coined this term. He is, perhaps, the leading advocate of taking utilitarian approaches to contemporary moral problems, including nonhuman animal experimental research practices. See his widely anthologized article, "All Animals Are Equal," *Annual Proceedings of the Center for Philosophical Exchange* 1, no. 5 (1974): 103–11.

7. In an effort to answer this charge, act utilitarians often distinguish between morally obligatory and (objectively) morally right actions. Most action (or rule) based theories do not distinguish between these concepts; however, because our knowledge of future consequences is quite limited, it might be that current beliefs about what will maximize utility are distinct from actions that actually will maximize utility. Thus, for act utilitarians, what we are obligated to do (as far as we can discern) and what is actually morally required of us does not always coincide.

8. The present discussion of exploring the differences between act and rule utilitarianism via *Saving Private Ryan* has been influenced by Nina Rosenstand's *The Moral of the Story*, 5th ed. (New York: McGraw-Hill, 2006), 255.

9. The present discussion of exploring classic (hedonistic) utilitarianism via *Eternal Sunshine of the Spotless Mind* has been influenced by Thomas E. Wartenberg's *Thinking on Screen: Film as Philosophy* (New York: Routledge, 2007), 85–93 and especially Christopher Grau's "*Eternal Sunshine of the Spotless Mind* and the Morality of Memory," in *Thinking through Cinema*, eds. Murray Smith and Thomas Wartenberg (Oxford: Blackwell, 2006), 119–33.

10. Admittedly—and unfortunately—the discussion of *Eternal Sunshine of the Spotless Mind* is left rather speculative. I strongly recommend Grau's article (in addition to viewing the film, of course) for further exploration.

11. Robert Nozick, *Anarchy, State, and Utopia* (New York: Basic, 1974), 43.

CHAPTER 8

Kant and Respect for Persons Ethics

HORTON HEARS A WHO! (2008)

Director: Jimmy Hayward and Steve Martino
Screenwriters: Cinco Paul and Ken Daurio
(based on the Dr. Seuss story)

PLOT SUMMARY

Let that be a lesson to one and to all; a person is a person, no matter how small.

We meet Horton the elephant on the 15th of May, in the Jungle of Nool. In the heat of the day, he was splashing in the cool of the pool and enjoying the jungle's great joys. When all of a sudden, he heard a small noise. It sounded like a faint yelp. Could it be a tiny person calling for help? Then he heard it again. All he could see was a speck, no bigger than a head of a pin, floating by on the breeze. But he thought that there must be someone—a family perhaps—on top of that small speck of dust. He had to investigate.

Suspending his class (the jungle children are learning so much from him), he went crashing through the jungle chasing the speck.[1] This draws the ire of the Wickershams. Narrowly escaping their dreaded banana-cannon, Horton races to catch up with the speck. As it is about to fall into a pond, he stretches out a pink clover, upon which the speck gently rests. He exhales slowly, affirming seemingly to no one, "Now, you're safe; I know I heard you say something." Bringing the speck close to his eye, he asks, "Where are you?"

Horton's antics have also drawn the ire of Sour Kangaroo, "the self-proclaimed head of the Jungle of Nool." (She makes every law and enforces every rule.) She not-so-politely asks Horton what he's doing. Horton nervously replies, "There was this speck. And it called out for help." Sour Kangaroo is annoyed. She wonders how a speck could call out for help. Horton clarifies: "No, there is a tiny *person* on that speck that needs my help."

She snickers, "There aren't people that small; it's absurd." Horton retorts that maybe he and she are big. In this way, the persons of the speck aren't that small. Kangaroo will have none of this. Why can't she hear Horton's little people? Why is Horton the only one? She perfunctorily lectures him, "If you can't see, hear, or feel something, it doesn't exist." She reminds him that believing in tiny imaginary "person-specks" won't be tolerated in the Jungle of Nool. She will not allow him to poison the minds of the children with his nonsense. Hopping away, she warns Horton, "This community has standards and if you wish to remain a part of it, I recommend you follow them."

Horton doesn't heed Kangaroo's words. He attempts to contact the tiny persons-of-the-speck. Surmising that their ears must be comparatively tiny, he yells, "Hello." The viewer travels on the sound wave (with the help of the narrator) to Whoville. The tiny speck-persons are called Whos. To them, they aren't tiny; they have houses, churches, and grocery stores. We meet Mayor McDodd, his wife, and their inordinately large family. We meet Jo-Jo, his oldest child, and next in line to become mayor of Whoville. Unfortunately, Jo-Jo doesn't really want the job. The Whos are quite unaware that their world is the size of a tiny speck; they thus don't know the potential dangers that lurk ahead.

BOX 8A: INSIDE *HORTON HEARS A WHO!*

Now more than fifty years old, Dr. Seuss's *Horton Hears a Who!* has become a classic children's story. The 2008 film adaption does nothing to tarnish its image. Like the original, it conveys intuitive insights into the moral significance of persons regardless of shape, color, or size. In this way, the story affords a novel platform from which to explore the work of Immanuel Kant, and an ethics of persons generally.

Scenes 4–8 (5:55 to 15:57 into the film) are helpful for learning about Horton and Mayor McDodd. Scene 4 begins with a shot of the speck floating by Horton's eyes. Scene 8 ends with the hallway pictures in McDodd's home going askew and quickly righting themselves. Scene 10 depicts McDodd's primary challenge to telling the truth: the council chairman. It begins at 18:58 with a shot of a puzzled McDodd spying a swirling cloud pattern and it ends at 21:06 with McDodd being escorted out of the council chamber. (Scene 11 begins with a shot of a large gold W.) Scene 15 depicts Horton's primary challenge to truth telling: Sour Kangaroo. It begins at 29:32 with a shot of Horton walking along a jungle path and ends at 32:02 with Horton running away from Sour Kangaroo and the Wickershams. Scene 15 also conveys the importance of helping persons. Scene 25 raises the issue of how far one might need to go to provide that help. It begins at 59:20 with a moving shot of a pink clover field and ends at 1:04:21 with Horton leaving the clover field impersonating John F. Kennedy. Scenes 26–30 implicitly raise the issue of whether our obligations toward others have limits. Scene 26 begins at 1:04:22 with Horton continuing down the jungle path, holding the clover. Scene 30 ends at 1:17:49 with Morton holding a cookie and calling Horton a "warrior poet."

If you cannot watch the film in its entirety, watching the specified segments along with carefully reading the plot summary, should provide a sufficient grasp of the film. If you do watch the film in its entirety, then you should be able to answer the trivia questions from box 8B.

But Mayor McDodd begins to suspect something is amiss in Whoville. He bravely approaches the city council about the possibility of postponing the Whoville Centennial. Nothing has gone wrong in Whoville for one hundred years! The council chairman, predictably, tells the mayor that he's being an idiot. In a fit of rage, the mayor screams out. His voice reaches through the Who heavens to Horton's inordinately sensitive ears. First contact! McDodd is skeptical. No sane person hears an invisible elephant from beyond the clouds. Horton calls it some sort of cosmic convergence. McDodd slowly begins to believe Horton that Whoville is floating on a speck in an unfathomably large universe. He (comically putting Horton on hold) runs to consult with Professor Larue—the "brainiest brain on the staff at Who-U." He nonchalantly asks her about the ramifications of living on a tiny, floating speck. She ominously reports that if the speck didn't eventually achieve some sort of stability, its world would eventually be destroyed! McDodd runs back to his office and asks for Horton's help to "achieve stability."

Horton quickly works to find the Whos a new, more permanent home. He spies a peaceful location at the top of Mt. Nool. The only problem is reaching its peak. But Horton is faithful, stalwart, and kind (especially in his own mind). He will succeed. But it won't be easy. His students catch up with him. They all have their own clovers with "worlds" on them. Indeed, news of Horton's eccentricities has reached Sour Kangaroo again. Even her son, Rudy (who is pouched-schooled, of course), has a clover with a "world" on it. It contains his new best friend, Thidwick. His mother scolds Rudy, reminding him that it's not possible for anyone to live on a speck. This is too much! Horton has become a menace! The other children run and hide in fear as she hops up to chide Horton again. He refuses to hand the speck over to her. He remains resolute in his belief that there are tiny persons on the speck and they need—deserve—his assistance, like any other person.

Kangaroo contracts the services of Vlad Vladikoff (the bad-Vlad) to, once and for all, dispose of Horton's clover "properly." Morton Mouse subsequently alerts Horton of the situation: "So unless you're cool with giant, razor-sharp claws ripping the flesh off your body, I'd get rid of the clover!" Horton refuses his friend's advice. He gave his word to the mayor. He reminds Morton of "his code, his motto": "I meant what I said and I said what I meant—an elephant is faithful one-hundred percent!" Morton is insistent: "Please, for me, just this once, be faithful ninety-nine percent of the time." Morton reminds Horton that he's never gotten as high as 99 percent on anything, but he's still awesome! Horton nevertheless thanks his friend for the advice. All Morton can do is to remind Horton to watch the skies.

Horton quickly relays the message to the mayor. His people are in danger! He must prepare Whoville for an aerial attack by a huge carnivorous bird! But how will the mayor get the Whos to believe him? Will anyone believe a story about an invisible elephant in the sky being chased by an invisible carnivorous bird even higher in the sky? But the mayor bravely announces: "Whoville is in terrible danger! Everyone must proceed to the underground storage area immediately!" The chairman interjects: "Fine. Fine. Let's do this democratically." He calls for a vote. The Whos resoundingly agree that the festivities of the Who Centennial should proceed as planned. The chairman chortles that no one believes the mayor, and no one supports him.

McDodd, in desperation, calls upon Horton to make himself known to the Whos. But he doesn't answer because, at that moment, Vlad snatches away the clover! Horton gives chase—up cliffs, through snow, over peaks. Vlad lets the clover drop in a great field

---

BOX 8B: *HORTON HEARS A WHO!* TRIVIA

If your instructor assigns the film to be watched outside of class, you should be able to answer the following questions:

1. Horton introduces his students to what "amazing jungle creature"?
2. How many daughters does Mayor McDodd have?
3. What does the mayor's friend Joe construct in Whoville?
4. When the mayor first hears Horton's voice, who does he think is playing a trick on him?
5. At the top of Mt. Nool, Horton intends to place Whoville on what object?
6. Horton suggests "A. S. A. P." is short for what phrase?
7. According to Horton, what is lighter than a feather?
8. How many bathrooms do the McDodds share?
9. What is the good Vlad (Vlad the bunny) known for?
10. Horton shares a treat with whom at the end of the movie?

---

of clover. But Horton remains steadfast by carefully searching the vast clover field. By noon, Horton, more dead than alive, had picked, searched, and piled up 9,005 clover heads. All day he looked on, until his hope was almost gone. But, at last, Horton had found them on the three-millionth flower. But things in Whoville are dire. Buildings have become rubble. Their world is all but upside down. Now all the Whos hear Horton. McDodd introduces various Whos to Horton (who manages to remember all their names—an elephant never forgets). They all survived the clover field crash. Horton presses on with his quest of reaching the top of Mt. Nool.

Word reaches Sour Kangaroo that Horton's quest continues. Vlad has let her down. She calls upon the denizens of Nool: "Our way of life is under attack. And who is leading that attack? Horton! Are we gonna let troublemakers like Horton poison the minds of our children?" The jungle animals are unified in their goal of stopping Horton by taking his clover. They stampede toward him. They rope and cage him. They prepare the boiling Beezle-Nut oil. Sour Kangaroo gives Horton one last chance. All he must do to avoid the roping, caging, and boiling oil is assert that there are no tiny people living on that speck, that he was wrong, and she was correct all along. If he admits these things, then things can go right back to the way they were. Nervously, Horton clarifies: "So, I just have to say it isn't true?" Horton will not relent. He is willing to accept the consequences. He must protect the tiny speck-persons. Horton desperately yells to the Whos, and instructs them to make noise. As the ropes tighten and the oil boils, the Whos shout: "We are here, we are here!"

8.1. THINKING THROUGH THE MOVIE

Discussion Starter Questions

1. Does Horton take an acceptable risk chasing after the speck at the beginning of the film, thereby drawing Kangaroo's ire?

2. Kangaroo is suspicious of Horton's choices (or abilities) as a teacher. What makes for a good teacher?

3. Describe the relationship between Mayor McDodd and his son Jo-Jo. What prevents them from connecting? How should fathers and sons (or parents and children generally) interact?

4. Is Morton being a good friend by suggesting to Horton that he give up his project of protecting the speck-on-the-clover? Explain.

5. When the animals of Nool finally hear the Whos, why do they immediately change their minds about what to do with the speck-on-the-clover?

Questions for Further Thought

1. In scene 5 (about 10 minutes into the movie), Kangaroo affirms that we have no reason to believe in things that we cannot see, hear, or feel. What are the ethical (or generally philosophical) ramifications of her assertion?

2. Scene 7 (about 12:35) informs us about the McDodd family; the mayor only has twelve seconds per child. Is there anything morally objectionable about having so many children? Explain.

3. Scene 10 (about 18:10) depicts Horton agreeing that his students may (permissibly) keep his secret by only telling one other person. Is enacting this rule advisable? Explain.

4. Sour Kangaroo argues that in teaching the children about worlds beyond the jungle, he teaches them defiance, which only leads to anarchy (scene 26, about 1:06:35). Evaluate this argument.   *Life beyond*

    questions

5. What might it mean to say (as Morton does in scene 21, roughly 50 minutes into the film) that Horton should be less than 100 percent faithful in keeping his word. Is it ever morally permissible (a good thing) to not be completely faithful to your word? Explain.   — *Self Preservation*   *questions in question parents*

8.2. HISTORICAL SETTING

The Foundations of the Metaphysics of Morals (excerpt)[2]

Immanuel Kant (1724–1804) was born, raised, and—after accepting a university position there—lived out his years in Konigsberg, Germany. He made significant contributions to almost all areas of philosophy—most notably, perhaps, in epistemology and ethics—and is consequently considered among the most influential philosophers of the Western tradition.

Preparing to Read

A. How is it that persons differ from things? How might these differences be morally significant?

B. Would Kant agree with Morton's advice that Horton not be 100 percent faithful to his word? Explain.

Preface

As my concern here is with moral philosophy, I limit the question suggested to this: Whether it is not of the utmost necessity to construct a pure moral philosophy, perfectly cleared of everything which is only empirical, and which belongs to anthropology? For that such a philosophy must be possible is evident from the common idea of duty and of the moral laws. Everyone must admit that if a law is to have moral force, i.e., to be the basis of an obligation, it must carry with it absolute necessity; that, for example, the precept, "Thou shall not lie," is not valid for men alone, as if other rational beings had no need to observe it; and so with all the other moral laws properly so called; that, therefore, the basis of obligation must not be sought in the nature of man, or in the circumstances in the world in which he is placed, but *a priori* simply in the conception of pure reason; and although any other precept which is founded on principles of mere experience may be in certain respects universal, yet in as far as it rests even in the least degree on an empirical basis, perhaps only as to a motive, such a precept, while it may be a practical rule, can never be called a moral law. . . .

[The Moral Significance of Duty]

To be beneficent when we can is a duty; and, besides this, there are many minds so sympathetically constituted that, without any other motive of vanity or self-interest, they find a pleasure in spreading joy around them, and can take delight in the satisfaction of others so far as it is their own work. But I maintain that in such a case an action of this kind, however proper, however amiable it may be, has nevertheless no true moral worth, but is on a level with other inclinations, e.g., the inclination to honor, which, if it is happily directed to that which is in fact of public utility and accordant with duty, and consequently honorable, deserves praise and encouragement, but not [moral] esteem. For the maxim [principle] lacks the moral import, namely, that such actions be done from dicta [duty]; not from inclination. Put the case that the mind of that philanthropist was clouded by sorrow of his own, extinguishing all sympathy with the lot of others, and that while he still has the power to benefit others in distress, he is not touched by their trouble because he is absorbed with his own; and now suppose that he tears himself out of this dead insensibility, and performs the action without any inclination to it, but simply from duty, then first has his action its genuine moral worth. Further still, if nature has put little sympathy in the heart of this or that man, if he, supposed to be an upright man, is by temperament cold and indifferent to the sufferings of others, perhaps because in respect of his own he is provided with the special gift of patience and fortitude, and supposes, or even requires, that others should have the same—and such a man would certainly not be the meanest product of nature—but if, nature had not specially trained him for a philanthropist, would he not still find in himself a source from whence to give himself a far higher worth than that of a good-natured temperament could be? Unquestionably. It is just in this that the moral worth of the character is brought out which is incomparably the highest of all, namely, that he is beneficent, not from inclination, but from duty.

[That Ethics Is "Universalizable"]

As I have deprived the will of every impulse which could arise to it from obedience to any law, there remains nothing but the universal conformity of its actions to law in general, which alone is to serve the will as a principle, that is, I am never to act otherwise than so *that I could also will that my maxim should become a universal law*. Here, now, it is the simple conformity to law in general, without assuming any particular law applicable to certain actions that serves the will as its principle, and must so serve it, if duty is not to be a vain delusion and a chimerical notion. The common reason of men in its practical judgments perfectly coincides with this, and always has in view the principle here suggested. Let the question be, for example: May I when in distress make a promise with the intention not to keep it? I readily distinguish here between the two significations which the question may have: Whether it is prudent, or whether it is right, to make a false promise? The former may undoubtedly often be the case. I see clearly indeed that it is not enough to extricate myself from a present difficulty by means of this subterfuge, but it must be well considered whether there may not hereafter spring from this lie much greater inconvenience than that from which I now free myself, and as, with all my supposed *cunning*, the consequences cannot be so easily foreseen but that credit once lost may be much more injurious to me than any mischief which I seek to avoid at present, it should be considered whether it would not be more *prudent* to act herein according to a universal maxim, and to make it a habit to promise nothing except with the intention of keeping it. But it is soon clear to me that such a maxim will still only be based on the fear of consequences. Now it is a wholly different thing to be truthful from duty, and to be so from apprehension of injurious consequences. In the first case, the very notion of the action already implies a law for me; in the second case, I must first look about elsewhere to see what results may be combined with it which would affect myself. For to deviate from the principle of duty is beyond all doubt wicked; but to be unfaithful to my maxim of prudence may often be very advantageous to me, although to abide by it is certainly safer. The shortest way, however, and an unerring one, to discover the answer to this question whether a lying promise is consistent with duty, is to ask myself: Should I be content that my maxim (to extricate myself from difficulty by a false promise) should hold good as a universal law, for myself as well as for others? And should I be able to say to myself, "Every one may make a deceitful promise when he finds himself in a difficulty from which he cannot otherwise extricate himself?" Then I presently become aware that while I can will the lie, I can by no means will that lying should be a universal law. For with such a law there would be no promises at all, since it would be in vain to allege my intention in regard to my future actions to those who would not believe this allegation, or if they over-hastily did so, would pay me back in my own coin. Hence my maxim, as soon as it should be made a universal law, would necessarily destroy itself.

I do not, therefore, need any far-reaching penetration to discern what I have to do in order that my will may be morally good. Inexperienced in the course of the world, incapable of being prepared for all its contingencies, I only ask myself: Can I also will that my maxim should be a universal law? If not, then it must be rejected, and that not because of a disadvantage accruing from myself or even to others, but because it cannot enter as a principle into a possible universal legislation, and reason extorts from me immediate respect for such legislation. I do not indeed as yet *discern* on what this respect is based (this the philosopher may inquire), but at least I understand this, that it is an estimation of the worth which far outweighs all worth of what is recommended by inclination, and that the necessity of acting from pure respect for the practical law is what constitutes duty, to which every other motive must give place, because it is the condition of a will being good in itself, and the worth of such a will is above everything.

Thus, then, without quitting the moral knowledge of common human reason, we have arrived at its principle. And, although, no doubt, common men do not conceive it in such an abstract and universal form, yet they always have it really before their eyes, and use it as the standard of their decision. . . .

[Hypothetical and Categorical Imperatives]

. . . The question, how the imperative of *morality* is possible, is undoubtedly one, the only one, demanding a solution, as this is not at all hypothetical, and the objective necessity which it presents cannot rest on any hypothesis, as is the case with the hypothetical imperatives. Only here we must never leave out of consideration that we *cannot* make out by *any example,* in other words empirically, whether there is such an imperative at all; but it is rather to be feared that all those which seem to be categorical may yet be at bottom hypothetical. For instance, when the precept is: You ought not promise deceitfully; and it is assumed that the necessity of this is not a mere counsel to avoid some other evil, so that it should mean: You ought not make a lying promise, lest if it become known you should destroy thy credit, but that an action of this kind must be regarded as evil in itself, so that the imperative of the prohibition is categorical; then we cannot show with certainty in any example that the will was determined merely by the law, without any other spring of action, although it may appear to be so. For it is always possible that fear of disgrace, perhaps also obscure dread of other dangers, may have a secret influence on the will. Who can prove by experience the nonexistence of a cause when all that experience tells us is that we do not perceive it? But in such a case the so-called moral imperative, which as such appears to be categorical and unconditional, would in reality be only a pragmatic precept, drawing our attention to our own interests, and merely teaching us to take these into consideration.

We shall therefore have to investigate *a priori* the possibility of a categorical imperative, as we have not in this case the advantage of its reality being given in experience, so that [the elucidation of] its possibility should be requisite only for its explanation, not for its establishment. In the meantime it may be discerned beforehand that the categorical imperative alone has the purport of a practical law: all the rest may indeed be called principles of the will but not laws, since whatever is only necessary for the attainment of some arbitrary purpose may be considered as in itself contingent, and we can at any time be free from the precept if we give up the purpose: on the contrary, the unconditional command leaves the will no liberty to choose the opposite; consequently it alone carries with it that necessity which we require in a law.

Secondly, in the case of this categorical imperative or law of morality, the difficulty (of discerning its possibility) is a very profound one. It is an *a priori* synthetical practical proposition; and as there is so much difficulty in discerning the possibility of speculative propositions of this kind, it may readily be supposed that the difficulty will be no less with the practical.

[The Categorical Imperative: Formulation One]

In this problem we will first inquire whether the mere conception of a categorical imperative may not perhaps supply us also with the formula of it, containing the proposition which alone can be a categorical imperative; for even if we know the tenor of such an absolute command, yet how it is possible will require further special and laborious study, which we postpone to the last section. When I conceive a hypothetical imperative, in general I do not know beforehand what it will contain until I am given the condition. But when I conceive a categorical imperative, I know at once what it contains. For as the imperative contains besides the law only the necessity that the maxims shall conform to this law, while the law contains no conditions restricting it, there remains nothing but the general statement that the maxim of the action should conform to a universal law, and it is this conformity alone that the imperative properly represents as necessary.

There is therefore but one categorical imperative, namely, this: *Act only on that maxim [principle] whereby you can at the same time will [intend, accept] that it become a universal law.*

Now if all imperatives of duty can be deduced from this one imperative as from their principle, then, although it should remain undecided whether what is called duty is not merely a vain notion, yet at least we shall be able to show what we understand by it and what this notion means.

Since the universality of the law according to which effects are produced constitutes what is properly called *nature* in the most general sense (as to form), that is the existence of things so far as it is determined by general laws, the imperative of duty may be expressed thus: *Act as if the maxim of your action were to become by your will [intention] a universal law of nature.*

[The Categorical Imperative: Formulation Two]

. . . Now, I say: man and generally any rational being exists as an end in himself, not merely as a *means* to be arbitrarily used by this or that will, but in all his actions, whether they concern himself or other rational beings, must be always be regarded at the same time as an end. All objects of the inclinations have only a conditional worth; for if the inclinations and the wants founded on them did not exist, then their object would be without value. But the inclinations themselves being sources of want are so far from having an absolute worth for which they should be desired, that, on the contrary, it must be the universal wish of every rational being to be wholly free from them. Thus the worth of any object which *is to be acquired* by our action is always conditional. Beings whose existence depends not on our will but on nature's, have nevertheless, if they are nonrational beings, only a relative value as means, and are therefore called *things*; rational beings, on the contrary, are called *persons*, because their very nature points them out as ends in themselves, that is as something which must not be used merely as means, and so far therefore restricts freedom of action (and is an object of respect). These, therefore, are not merely subjective ends whose existence has a worth for us as an effect of our action, but *objective ends*, that is, things whose existence is an end in itself, moreover, for which no other can be substituted, which they should subserve *merely* as means, for otherwise nothing whatever would possess *absolute worth*; but if all worth were conditioned and therefore contingent, then there would be no supreme practical principle of reason whatever.

If then there is a supreme practical principle or, in respect of the human will, a categorical imperative, it must be one which, being drawn from the conception of that which is necessarily an end for everyone because it is *an end in itself*, constitutes an *objective* principle of will, and can therefore serve as a universal practical law: The foundation of this principle is: *rational nature exists as an end in itself*. Man necessarily conceives his own existence as being so: so far then this is a *subjective* principle of human actions. But every other rational being regards its existence similarly, just on the same rational principle that holds for me: so that it is at the same time an objective principle, from which as a supreme practical law all laws of the will must be capable of being deduced. Accordingly the practical imperative will be as follows: *So act as to treat humanity; whether in your own person or in that of any other, in every case as an end and never as means only. . . .*

[Kingdom of Ends]

The conception of every rational being as one which must consider itself as giving in all the maxims of its will universal laws, so as to judge itself and its actions from this point of view—this conception leads to another which depends on it and is very fruitful, that of a *kingdom of ends*. By a *kingdom of ends* I understand the union of different rational beings in a system by common laws. Now since it is by laws that ends are determined as regards their universal validity, hence, if we abstract from the personal differences of rational beings, and likewise from all the content of their private ends, we shall be able to conceive all ends combined in a systematic whole (including both rational beings as ends in themselves, and also the special ends which each may propose to himself), that is to say, we can conceive a kingdom of ends, which on the preceding principles is possible.

For all rational beings come under the *law* that each of them must treat itself and all others *never merely as means*, but in every case *at the same time as ends in themselves*. Hence results a systematic union of rational beings by common objective laws, i.e., a kingdom which may be called a kingdom of ends, since what these laws have in view is just the relation of these beings to one another as ends and means. . . .

Review Questions

1. What is Kant's (first) formulation of the categorical imperative? How does he apply it to the case of making a "deceitful/false promise" to explain its impermissibility?
2. How does Kant distinguish "person" from "thing?" What is the ethical importance of this distinction?
3. Near the end of the passage, Kant offers a second version of the categorical imperative. How does he now describe it? Apply this new formulation to Kant's "deceitful/false promise" example and explain its impermissibility on this new formulation.

8.3. DISCUSSION AND ANALYSIS

Immanuel Kant is among those philosophers who hold that it is wrongheaded to ground ethics in the emotional states or psychological preferences of human beings. Such philosophers believe that utilitarianism is a nonstarter. Kant, for one, holds this (roughly) because (a) he believes our desires and preferences often get in the way of our upholding our duty and (b) human emotion and psychology admit of too many contingencies. He advises that the proper foundation of ethics will consist of fulfilling duties grounded in factors apart from positive mental states or psychology generally. He believes that only rationality—the careful use of one's reason—has the potential to corral our desires and be informative as to what, necessarily, we ought and ought not to do.

Philosophical discussions about the moral value of rationality and personhood cannot begin without Kant. His ideas in this regard have been seminal. However, few

3:10 to Yuma, Lions Gate Films, 2007. A posse is formed to bring the notorious bank robber Ben Wade (Russell Crowe, left) to justice. (Moviegoods, Inc.)

philosophers agree with all facets of his view, with his staunch commitment to moral absolutism being one notable example. For the past two centuries or so, philosophers have attempted to retain the intuitive heart of Kant's ethical ideas, but rework some of the details for the sake of overall plausibility. A careful examination of *Horton Hears a Who!* and *3:10 to Yuma* suggests one such revision. Thus, although the discussion that follows elucidates key Kantian themes, it should not be interpreted as a defense or historical exegesis of Kant's views.

"Acting from" or "According to" Duty

Another distinctive feature of Kant's moral philosophy is his insistence that full moral worth or esteem requires that agents do the right thing *only* because it is right. If you act in a way duty requires, but because it makes someone happy (or any other motive), then you act according to duty, but not from duty. Doing the right thing for selfish reasons or even to make someone happy is not as morally commendable as doing the right thing simply because it is right. So, *why* Horton saves the Whos, or Dan Evans puts Ben Wade on the prison train in *3:10 to Yuma*, or Roger Baldwin defends the Africans in *Amistad* matters, morally speaking. On a Kantian analysis, Horton probably is the best example of the three for acting from duty. Baldwin, at first, does the right thing only to develop his floundering law career. Later, perhaps, his defending the Africans is deserving of full

Kantian esteem. Evans's behavior remains dubious with respect to his intentions. In this way, it remains controversial whether Evans is deserving of full Kantian esteem, even though he acts bravely in walking Wade to the train station when no one else will and heroically sacrifices his life for that project. Acting bravely and heroically certainly seem worthy of moral praise. Kant nevertheless remains steadfast in his position. If personal circumstances constitute the sole motivations for acting, then removing them results in not doing the right thing. Only acting from duty will guarantee that you keep your moral obligations.

Distinguishing between acting from duty and in accordance with duty brings forth another anticonsequentialist aspect of Kant's moral philosophy. All that matters, ethically speaking, for Kant is that you uphold your obligations (because it is right). The consequences of keeping your obligations—in terms of harms or benefits to you or others—matters very little (if at all). The problem, seemingly, is that consequences admit of too many contingencies. Kant maintains that doing the right thing because it is right, despite any negative consequences you undergo as a result, is the hallmark of ethical praise. But again, to act in accordance with duty merely because of the positive consequences of doing so invites the question: Would you so act if those consequences didn't obtain? If the consequences are your sole motivating factor, then the answer must be no. Again, only acting from duty will guarantee that you keep your ethical obligations.

> "Give us the courage to do what is right. And if it means civil war, then let it come."
> —*Amistad*, scene 21

"I Said What I Meant, and Meant What I Said"

Kant held that persons, as inherently rational, possess the unique ability to provide reasons and ultimately principles for their (our) behaviors. Kant thought this fact was crucial because although you cannot help feeling certain ways about certain things, you are always in control of your own thoughts. Some action-guiding principles are (merely) pragmatic. If you wish to practice law like Baldwin, then you should attend law school. Kant called these sorts of principles "hypothetical imperatives" because they recommend or command a course of behavior assuming that the relevant hypothesis (say going to law school) applies to you. But Kant also held that there exists an action-guiding principle (or classification of principles) that is not merely pragmatic; this kind of principle represents the benchmark for all morally significant behavior. This he called the "categorical imperative." Operative categorical imperatives are not merely contingently binding on persons. This kind of principle is binding upon all persons insofar as we are rational.

The categorical imperative serves as Kant's fundamental moral principle. His preferred way of delineating it highlights the moral importance of keeping one's word. This accordingly dovetails with Horton's motto: "I meant what I said, and I said what I meant, an elephant is faithful one-hundred percent." No matter how much trouble Sour Kangaroo causes Horton, keeping his promise to the Whos—staying faithful to his word—is more important; it is something he simply must do.[3] Kant would agree. In its initial phrasing, known as the "universal law" formulation, Kant's categorical imperative reads:

> Act only according to that maxim [principle] by which you can at the same time will [intend, accept] that it should become a universal law.

Admittedly, it's not initially clear how this pertains to truth telling. But as a general moral principle, Kant intends to deduce more specific moral obligations from it. Kant believed that he could derive obligations against committing suicide, to develop one's latent but natural talents, and offering aid to those in need. But scholars agree that the moral force of the universal law formulation is most obvious in cases that involve making a lying promise. This serves as a good place to begin unpacking Kant's categorical imperative; this, in turn, will shed light on why Kant would approve of Horton's faithfulness to his word.

By the term, "maxim," Kant meant something like an implicit, general rule to be followed. So, with respect to any action we are about to undertake, we must be cognizant of its corresponding implicit rule (and the intention from which is it made). Articulating the implicit rule is merely a matter of generalizing or universalizing: whenever someone is in circumstances relevantly similar to mine, that person should act as I do (or am about to do).

Once the maxim is carefully articulated, Kant puts it to a kind of two-part test. This is captured by his phrase "will that it become a universal law." Kant's usage of "will" here implies that you, as a rational or reasonable person, would be willing to accept your rule upon its being universalized. So, the first part of the test comes in the form of a question: Could you reasonably or rationally accept that everyone follow the implicit rule that you are about to enact? Would you be willing that everyone do as you are about to do? Upon asking yourself this, the second part of the test is to answer it. The key to its answer (again) relies on the idea of reasonability or rationality. If there would be contradictory or self-defeating results were everyone to do as you are about to, then you cannot reasonably or rationally accept your implicit rule. You would not be willing that it become a universal law. In such cases, the answer to your question is no; a negative answer in the second part of Kant's test is definitive evidence that the act you intend is impermissible (morally wrong). You, as a rational agent, are about to perform an act that you would not be willing others do in that situation. In this, you are being inconsistent, or irrational, allowing an exception for yourself that you are not willing to grant others, even though they are exactly like you in every relevant way. This, concluded Kant, provides you reason not to perform that act.

How Kant's universal law formulation forbids making lying promises (and dishonesty generally) is now clearer. Kant used the example of securing a loan that you had no intention of repaying. For example, perhaps someone is in dire straits like Dan and Alice Evans, in desperate need of money just to make it through the winter; however, this person, unlike the Evanses, has no intention of repaying the money once loaned. Yet remember, the specifics of the situation matter very little. It could be a Wickersham looking to start his own banana farm or Vlad hoping to expand his "business." The crucial feature is the underlying maxim. Accordingly, were the proposed action to be universalized, then it would read: whenever a person (you, a Wickersham Cousin, Vlad) is in need of money, he or she should make a lying promise to secure the desired funds. It's pretty clear that this maxim has contradictory or self-defeating results. Dishonesty only achieves its intended goal in a culture that presumes truth telling (and cultures not proceeding on this assumption don't last very long). Were everyone to make lying promises whenever in need of money, then people would cease to lend money. So, if everyone were to act as you intend, you couldn't secure any funds, which entails that no reasonable or rational person could accept its implicit maxim. You would not be willing that everyone obtain a loan in the way you intend. So, if you proceed, you are making an exception for yourself that you are not willing to allow others, even though they are in your exact circumstances.

Sometimes the contradictory or self-defeating nature of the maxim lies in its intention. Consider the prospect of shirking your civil obligations. Perhaps you don't wish to pay your taxes. Perhaps a bit like Jo-Jo (the "young twerp" from the original story but not the movie), you do not wish to engage in civic responsibility simply because you don't feel like it. According to Kant, it's not the prospect of the Whos being dunked in hot Beezle-Nut oil that makes Jo-Jo's choice impermissible; it is simply that such a maxim cannot be universalized. Consider that if everyone were to act in your mindless "Jo-Jo yo-yo bouncing fashion," then society would no longer function smoothly. After all, no one really likes serving jury duty, not to mention paying taxes. But, presumably, the whole idea behind your intention—shirking your civic responsibilities—is to benefit from everyone else's conscientious efforts. *They* will keep society running smoothly, while *you* laze around as an anonymous freeloader. But if everyone were to act as you, then society would break down, thereby contravening your initial intention. You wouldn't benefit at all, but rather place yourself in great peril (Beezle-Nut oil or no). Thus, your maxim has contradictory or self-defeating consequences; no rational person could reasonably accept that everyone act on it. You intend to grant yourself an exception you would not be willing to allow others were they in your situation.

"An Elephant Is Faithful . . . One-Hundred Percent [?]"

Recall that Morton Mouse implores Horton to be less than 100 percent faithful. The little blue mammal asserts that he's never achieved 99 percent on anything, but he's still awesome! Maybe Horton should follow suit, especially with Vlad (and his razor sharp claws) flying about. Kant would disparage Morton for this advice. Kant believes that you should *always* be honest—that is, faithful to your word—regardless of any seemingly negative consequences. Moreover, Kant believes our moral obligations hold without exception, making him a moral absolutist. Because we have a moral duty to tell the truth (as the opposing maxim fails the universalization test), it follows that there are no circumstances in which we may permissibly break our word or practice dishonesty. This remains so even if our proposed dishonesty has no other goal than protecting innocent persons. In "On a Supposed Right to Lie from Altruistic Motives," Kant writes, "To be truthful (honest) in all deliberation, therefore, is a sacred and absolute commanding decree of reason, limited by no expediency."[4] The idea seems to be that just as there are no exceptions to the principle that the sum of the interior angles of a triangle is 180 degrees, there are no exceptions to the principle that making lying promises is (always) wrong. Both are grounded in rational or logical considerations, and principles so grounded hold without exception.

But many scholars find moral absolutism to be implausible. Kant was not unaware of such concerns. To bolster his position, he considers a dilemma involving a murderer looking for his next victim. Assume that a known murderer like Ben Wade approaches you and inquires about the location of his next intended victim, an innocent neighbor of yours. Only moments ago, you saw your neighbor frantically enter the front door of his home. What should you do? Assuming no viable third alternative, should you lie to Wade to protect the life of your innocent neighbor, or report your neighbor's location truthfully, knowing that this will undoubtedly get the innocent man killed? Kant was clear: morally speaking, you must answer Wade (or any murderer) truthfully, thereby disclosing the neighbor's location. Your duty to tell the truth is absolute.[5]

The debate emerging here is not whether it is ever permissible to lie for selfish or personal gain. Rather, worries about the moral absoluteness of honesty are grounded in situations when moral duties conflict. We have a duty to tell the truth and a duty to protect the lives of innocent people (insofar as we can), and in this Kant agrees. However, what should we do in situations where we must choose one over the other? All systems committed to moral absolutism, including Kant's, are conceptually precarious because they seem ill-equipped to reconcile such moral dilemmas.

After all, imagine the following alteration to the lying murderer case. Assume that you had promised the neighbor that you would not disclose his location to anyone, but especially the sociopath chasing him. When the murderer inquires about your neighbor's location, what should you do? Keep your promise to your neighbor or answer the murderer's question honestly? Alternatively,

> "What kind of place is this? Where you almost mean what you say? Where laws almost work? How can you live like that?" —*Amistad*, scene 16

let's say that your other next door neighbor performs a kindness to you and, out of gratitude, you promise to repay it whenever he needs it. Let's further say that he requests you to repay the kindness by assassinating his professional rival (something a person like Ben Wade might ask of you). Even if Horton is laudable for keeping his promise to the Whos, should you keep your promise in this case and assassinate the rival? Doesn't it seem just as plausible (if not more so) to break your word so as to not end the life your neighbor's rival?

The undeniable rhetorical force of these questions speaks against Kant's blanket insistence on truth telling. But it's not clear that Kant's absolutism is necessary to his overall larger project. It only requires grounding moral duties in what rational agents can consistently will. So long as the person pondering the exception to the rule can consistently accept that everyone act as he is considering, then his act is permissible. Nevertheless, this remains a bit contentious. It might be argued that qualified maxims about being honest except to save the life of innocent persons, if universalized, become self-defeating insofar as murderers may no longer believe those they question. (Would the inquiring murderer believe you regardless?) Yet, intuitively, the alleged self-defeating result isn't as obvious as lying to a bank manager to get a loan (that you never intend to pay back). *Would* the relevant (qualified) maxim, if universalized, negate the intended purpose of attempting to nonviolently protect the life of an innocent? Furthermore, note that the agent is not making an exception *for* herself, which seems to be a staple to deeming maxims impermissible.[6]

Without definitively resolving this debate, note that the interpretation proposed here highlights (or safeguards) the heroic nature of acts that agents undergo in the face of extreme adversity. The most natural view to take about Horton is that he is a hero. He kept his word to the Whos even though his life was threatened by the denizens of Nool. However, Kant seems committed to holding that Horton is morally required to keep his word in even extremely dangerous, life-threatening circumstances. But is this plausible? Can agents be seriously required to keep their word in each and every situation, even if doing so means giving up their lives? A more plausible approach is to label such choices heroic. But acting heroically invariably means going above and beyond what is required. In this way, perhaps Horton ought to be praised as a hero, but *not* (contra Kant) to be blamed should he not keep his obligations when

> "Now what you gotta figure is why you and your boy are gonna die. Because Butterfield's railroad lost some money?" —*3:10 to Yuma*, scene 19

his life is immanently threatened. No one can be blamed for not being a hero, even if she can be praised for being one.

This Kantian amendment does safeguard the commonsense notion of supererogatory acts, but it remains a bit controversial. Recall the decision made by the marshal and his two men when Wade's gang surrounds the Contention hotel. Having agreed to help Butterfield, they recant upon learning that every man in Contention is now looking to kill them. Although this decision is understandable—their lives are in imminent danger, and much more danger than Horton's—it's difficult to not judge these men as cowardly. This is reinforced when Evans tosses the gold star at the marshal. But are these lawmen doing something wrong by breaking their word to Butterfield? Labeling them as cowards and distinguishing Dan as a hero doesn't seem implausible. However, judgments like these invariably remain distinct from deeming acts impermissible or obligatory. Perhaps we should keep "cowardly" distinct from "impermissible" and "heroic" distinct from "obligatory" and simply conclude that even if the marshal and his men act more cowardly than expected for lawmen, they don't necessarily act impermissibly. This is reinforced with an analysis of Evans: because nonlawmen cannot be morally required to sacrifice their lives to bring criminals to justice, he acts heroically. His actions may be (and probably are) commendable, but not obligatory. Consequently, the actions of the Contention lawmen may be undesirable or shameful, but not necessarily impermissible.

In portraying Horton as a hero, then, Seuss invites us to rethink some of Kant's ethical ideas. However, perhaps the genius of Dr. Seuss is that he invites each of us to reexamine ourselves. Seuss agrees with Kant that keeping our promises is extremely important. If you knowingly give your word then you ought to keep it, even if doing so causes you some displeasing inconveniences. Furthermore, perhaps those who become police officers thereby accept the responsibility of responding to dangerous situations. However, Seuss can be interpreted as demurring from Kant's insistence that we must be faithful to our word 100 percent. Those who do so keep their word, at least if that means giving up their life like Dan Evans, are heroes. However, apart from the controversial decisions made by the Contention lawmen, so many of us become unfaithful to our word too soon. Far from facing a murderous mob, we often give up when the going gets even a little bit rough. This is a moral failing. We should be more like Horton.

"I ain't never been no hero, Wade. The only battle I seen, we was in retreat. My foot got shot off by one of my own men. You try telling that story to your boy. See how he looks at you then." —*3:10 to Yuma*, scene 22

"A Person Is a Person, No Matter How Small"

The next step is getting clearer about how exceptions to general (Kantian) moral rules might be crafted. What constitutes the difference between praising morally heroic behavior and blaming someone for (impermissibly) not doing enough? Answers to these questions begin to emerge upon further synthesizing *Horton Hears a Who!* and Kant's "ends in themselves" formulation of the categorical imperative, especially when the latter is interpreted via the former. The idea of human dignity or personhood holds the key. In fact, Kant believed that this idea resides at the very core of all ethical behavior; his "ends in themselves" formulation reads:

> Act so that you treat humanity, whether in your own person or in that of another, always as an end and never as a means only.

This version of the categorical imperative clearly conveys—in a way that the "universal law" formulation doesn't—the idea that persons themselves possess a certain kind of unique worth or value. Kant labeled nonpersons "things." Roughly, it is always impermissible to treat a person as if he or she were a mere thing.

Accordingly, the conceptual differences between a person and a thing are crucial. Things are objects that have purposes or goals put upon them. They are used as a means to achieve some project. Persons, however, are sources of value insofar as they (we) independently implement purposes or goals into (or onto) the world. Persons, but not things, possess the ability to universalize and contemplate implicit maxims, recognize the difference between right and wrong, and grasp the significance of that difference. Persons, but not things, can perform actions because they are right and refrain from actions because they are wrong (not that we always do). Persons, but not things, are appropriately praised or blamed given how they choose with respect to the moral knowledge they possess. Persons are therefore sources of moral behavior, and, in a way, of morality itself. Kant labels these morally significant features of personhood "being autonomous." For Kant, the fact that persons are autonomous—rational agents, possessed of volition (free will) and foresight—is the crux of all moral value and ethically significant judgments.

This also begins to explain why Kant believes that persons possess unconditional and intrinsic moral worth. Persons possess a kind of inherent dignity that is beyond or above any price. This dignity may not permissibly be sacrificed or traded for any (other nonmoral) goal or project exactly because it is beyond or above any such goal or project. When a person's dignity is so sacrificed, implicitly the person who fails to recognize the dignity of the other implicitly affirms, "You, fellow person, are not as important or deserving as

Horton Hears a Who, Twentieth Century Fox, 2008. Horton (Jim Carrey voice, left) and Jane Kangaroo (Carol Burnett voice) "discuss" the possibility of tiny persons living on a speck. (Moviegoods, Inc.)

me; I am more deserving or important than you and thus am at liberty to treat you as a mere tool (means) to achieve my personal projects." Such affirmations implicitly condone treating persons like mere things. Failing to treat persons with the dignity they inherently possess—and the respect they thereby deserve—is to make the gravest of moral errors.[7]

Because persons are not things and deserving of full moral respect, it is simply impermissible to consider them property. But note that exactly this occurs in Steven Spielberg's *Amistad*. When the "cargo" of the *La Amistad* rise up against their captors, their success is short-lived. Rather than reaching the shores of Africa, they only get as far as Connecticut. At first, it seems that the Africans will be tried in criminal court for murdering members of the *Amistad* crew. However, an incredibly convoluted legal battle quickly ensues over who has proper claim of ownership of them. The Africans are simply consider property. It is noteworthy that their status as property is crucial to Baldwin's defense. He believes that Joadson and Tappan's case is not as complicated as it seems. If the Africans are property, then they are no more due a criminal trial than a bookcase or plow. Consequently, they cannot be rightly tried in criminal court. If the Africans are not property (because they were not born on a plantation), then it is more appropriate to consider them illegally acquired. But if they were illegally acquired, then no one has proper claim to ownership over them. Either way, Baldwin believes that Joadson and Tappan's abolitionist project is affirmed and furthered. If the Africans are property, then they ought not to be hanged. If they were acquired illegally, they ought to be returned to their homeland. Baldwin will take the case for two dollars a day.

Tappan meets Baldwin's stratagem with scorn. This case should be waged on the battlefield of righteousness, not the vagaries of property law. Kant would countenance this reply. Only things can be property and persons are not things; thus persons are not property. Because persons are not property, they should not be treated as such. This leads Tappan to believe that Baldwin's legal counsel is radically confused. However, Baldwin believes his approach will succeed in a court of law, which makes it pragmatically justified. Tappan believes it degrades the Africans. It is an unfortunate historical fact that abolitionists like Tappan were ever faced with such difficult decisions.

The historical drama surrounding the *La Amistad* only emphasizes the keen moral insight of the fictional character Horton the elephant. He clearly saw the difference between persons and things, thus perfectly exemplifying this important Kantian distinction. Horton surmised that the floating dust speck, even though as small as the head of a pin, somehow contained persons; it commanded his attention and respect. But the clover that he placed the speck on is a mere thing. It is perfectly acceptable for him to use or implement the clover for his purposes exactly because it is not a person. But the speck was unusual; he had "never heard tell of a small speck of dust that is able to yell." Nevertheless, Horton was perceptive enough—with his inordinately large and sensitive moral ears—to realize that the inhabitants of that speck were very small persons requiring his assistance. Horton learns that the speck denizens are called "Whos," living in Whoville. They have houses, churches, and grocery stores. The

> "Give us, us free! Give us, us free!" —*Amistad*, scene 13

mayor of Whoville, on behalf of all the Whos, expresses his gratitude to Horton for the elephant's careful assistance. Furthermore, that the Whos are persons entails that Horton cannot put a price on their well-being—this is beyond all price. Regardless of how much trouble Sour Kangaroo and the Wickershams cause him, recognizing the Whos' inherent moral worth—respecting their dignity as persons—is more important. In fact, nothing could be more important than protecting persons in serious need, especially if providing aid presents no serious harm to you. Horton indeed affirms, "I can't let my very small persons get drowned! I've *got* to protect them. I'm bigger than they."

For Kant, anyone who willingly fails to observe the respect due to a person acts impermissibly. Moreover, the moral duties owed to persons entail that we must not treat others as a mere means even if upholding those duties is inconvenient or bothersome. And sometimes this can be downright difficult. After all, it would have been much easier for Horton to ignore the speck's faint yelp on that 15th of May. He could have gone back to his splashing in the cool of the pool, and his enjoying the jungle's great joys. He wouldn't have had to suffer Sour Kangaroo's disparaging "humpfs" and other verbal assaults. His reputation would not have suffered. The Wickersham Uncles and the Wickersham Cousins would have left him alone. But Dr. Seuss provides the reader with someone—Horton—who does the right thing despite all the troubles it causes him. Horton goes so far as to spend all day searching three million flowers to relocate the Whos. Indeed Horton is willing to sacrifice his personal safety to the extent of being lassoed (with ten miles of rope) and caged by Sour Kangaroo and her cronies. Such is the extent of our obligations to our fellow autonomous persons (no matter how small).

"I'll Stick By You Small Folks through Thin and through Thick!"

It seems intuitive that we cannot be morally required to sacrifice our own life for another. This contention is supported by the "ends in themselves" formulation. We are to respect humanity, including that of our own person. Each of us is due equal respect insofar as each of us is autonomous. This entails that no person can be morally required to sacrifice himself or herself for another. Taking action that sacrifices your life, like a parent for a child, is invariably heroic. The lengths to which Horton goes to protect the Whos also borders on heroic sacrifice. He might be suffocated by the ten miles of rope or find himself in the Beezle-Nut stew! But remember that heroic behavior is above and beyond the call to duty. Heroic acts are thus not morally required. This suggests the revisionist position that, regarding respecting persons, the ends in themselves formula takes moral precedence over the universal law formulation.

This interpretation of Kant has at least three interesting implications.[8] First, it provides insights into how Kantian rules might be recrafted generally. Consider again the inquiring murderer. The dilemma is that you are duty bound to protect the life of your innocent neighbor, but also duty bound to answer the murderer's question honestly. No matter what you do (assuming no third alternative and that your beliefs regarding the inquirer's murderous intentions are well justified), something morally unfortunate will result. Here, Kant advises you to tell the murderer the truth; he requires you to disclose your neighbor's whereabouts so as to allow the murderer to make his own autonomous decision, about which you are absolved of the consequences. However, this leaves us with no principled way to deal with conflicts of duties generally.[9] On the interpretation proffered here, and even if Kant would disagree, it seems that you should allow the "ends in themselves" formulation to trump the "universal law" formulation. So, the rule of thumb here might be: whenever faced with two conflicting (Kantian) duties, always perform that action that disrespects persons the least. Telling a solitary lie to the murderer is not as serious as giving up the life of your innocent neighbor. Furthermore, you might now derive a new maxim, one more sensitive to the circumstances: whenever someone can tell a small, isolated lie to save the life of an innocent person (especially if you are quite certain that you will be believed), then one ought to tell the lie. Not only does this revision pass the "end in themselves" requirement, but it also (arguably) passes the maxim test because it doesn't obviously have the self-defeating ramifications of a more expansive policy of dishonesty (at least in terms of making an exception for yourself that you wouldn't be willing to grant others).[10]

Second, it helps to clarify the thorny issue of determining the extent to which we are duty bound to provide assistance to others in their attempt to lead autonomous lives. Our negative duties—what we ought not to do—are rather well-defined in Kant's system; however, our positive duties—what we ought to do—are not. What lengths are we required to go in offering aid? Reconsider Horton. Surely he is obligated to find the speck a safe resting place as he splashes in the pool. His obligation is not obviated by the mere fact that some gossipy denizens of Nool find him eccentric for carrying around a speck. None of this presents any great danger to Horton. However, as we just saw, it is not clear whether he is obligated to protect the speck if it requires him to be tortured to death with hot Beezle-Nut oil. Thus, the rule of thumb is that you, as an autonomous person, cannot be obligated to become a mere tool or means to another person's autonomous projects. Your autonomous projects are just as important as theirs. Help someone move when you are not doing anything? Yes. Donate a kidney to your brother when both of his are failing and you can live with one? Probably. Subsequently donating your only remaining kidney to your sister? No.

Third, this interpretation interestingly conveys the conceptual benefits of combining Kant's two categorical imperatives. Recall the maxim test from the universal law formulation: if an implicit maxim, once universalized, has contradictory or self-defeating ramifications, you may not do the action you are considering. Also recall the only explanation for why you would be willing to employ such a maxim: you must allow an exception for yourself that you would not be willing to grant others. If you allowed the relevant exception generally, your maxim becomes unworkable. This uncovers the irrationality of your proposal. But the core *moral* reason why you ought not to proceed with your act is solidified once we supplement the universal law formulation with the ends in themselves formulation. By allowing the exception only for yourself, you are implicitly saying that you are more important than anyone else. You are deserving of the exception, but no one else. But what makes you *alone* morally deserving of this benefit? Aren't you simply one autonomous person among many? Aren't you just as, but no more so, deserving as anyone else? The relevant rational error you make is that you are placing yourself morally above others, even though you have absolutely no good reason for doing so.

On this interpretation, furthermore, note that the deeper maxim—whenever a person wishes to selfishly gain by treating others as mere things, he or she ought to do that—cannot be universalized due to its self-defeating ramifications. After all, the very reason why you contemplate this sort of behavior is to benefit by the moral rectitude of others. You are seeking to become a moral freeloader, gaining selfishly from the fact that others generally uphold their moral obligations. But if everyone were to act as you are considering, it would be impossible for you to benefit. If persons generally ignored their moral obligations for selfish gain, then the moral community breaks down and no one benefits. This is how your deeper maxim becomes self-defeating.

Horton's example also conveys the insight that we often fail to offer aid to others in need simply because we are lazy or apathetic. Many of us hide behind the excuse that keeping this promise or doing that chore is asking too much. At best, this is mere self-deception. At worst, this is an implicit affirmation of selfishness. Too often we falsely believe that our (nonmoral) projects are more important than those of others. Consequently, Horton's (moral) heroism lies not explicitly in the fact that he was willing to become an ingredient in the Beezle-Nut stew, but rather in the fact that he was not quick to shirk his responsibilities. In *this* sense, Seuss and Kant agree. Horton was willing and able to keep his word insofar as he could. If that is all it takes to be a hero, Dr. Seuss implicitly argues, then all of us can be *that* sort of hero. We should be more like Horton.

"We Are Here!"—"Give Us Free!"

It's true that Horton's heroism causes unrest in Nool, at least temporarily. However, Horton's neighbors are to blame for the disruption. They are the ones who have failed to properly investigate the facts. Indeed, note why we see Sour Kangaroo as the antagonist: by single-mindedly valuing her personal project—even one that brings general harmony to Nool—over the Whos' well-being, she fails to respect their inherent worth as persons. She thereby affirms that the denizens of Nool and the contentment they enjoy are more important than the Whos and their livelihoods and, indeed, their very lives. Therefore, although hers is not a completely selfish project, she still commits the gravest of Kantian moral errors. However, upon realizing her error, she quickly makes amends, immediately exclaiming to Horton "from now on, I'm going to protect them with you!" ("And the young kangaroo in her pouch said, ME TOO!"). Sour Kangaroo instantaneously changes her ways exactly because of the obviousness that "a person is a person, no matter how small."

That the temporary civil unrest in Nool was caused by willful ignorance highlights an important feature of doing moral philosophy: one must be sufficiently informed by getting the relevant facts straight. Note that Horton and Sour Kangaroo disagreed about what ought to be done with the speck, but only because they disagreed about whether it contained persons. ("On that speck—as small as a head of a pin—persons never have been!") But once the Whos "yopped" loud enough and Sour Kangaroo was sufficiently attentive, her disagreement with Horton disappeared. Ethically speaking, they didn't disagree. Both agree with Kant that persons are of utmost moral value and deserving of respect.

Unfortunately, civil unrest caused by disagreements about the facts is not reserved to Dr. Seuss stories alone. The dignity of actual persons has not always been respected, as *Amistad* poignantly reminds us. Blind (and willful) ignorance is often the root cause of the injustices associated with not respecting the inherent worth of persons. True, those in the Jungle of Nool were blind to the Whos; however, this was due to the obvious fact that Whos can't be seen with the naked eye. We must remember that Dr. Seuss originally published this story in 1954, in the midst of the controversies of the civil rights movement. Although African American civil rights activists like Martin Luther King, Jr., did their best (like the Whoville mayor) to organize chants akin to "We are here! We are here!" and all other nonviolent "yopps" to achieve social recognition, many Americans remained "blind" to the plight of African Americans. Cinque and his fellow Africans "yopped" before the entire courtroom: "Give us, us free! Give us, us free!" At least Sour Kangaroo couldn't see the Whos standing in front of her. But people in this country—for hundreds of years—could obviously see African Americans and the injustices they faced. Horton pleaded with Sour Kangaroo to try just a little harder—listen just a little more carefully—if her eyes failed her. Perhaps Dr. Seuss was pleading with his audience: just look and listen a little more carefully to what is going on right in front of you. So perhaps the real beauty of *Horton Hears a Who!*—perhaps the deepest message Seuss was attempting to convey (one echoed by Spielberg in *Amistad*)—is that once you realize that Whos are persons, you can better see that persons are "Whos." As "Whos" and not "Whats" or "Its," persons are deserving of your respect because they possess inherent worth. When "Whos" are treated like things, this is the gravest of moral errors.

Accordingly, what grounds the importance of human dignity is that human beings are *persons*. What Seuss recognized so clearly is that being a person—being a "Who"—is not merely a biological category. It is a moral category. In this sense, all the inhabitants of Nool are persons. Yes, they look like animals and insofar as they are kangaroos, monkeys, elephants, and eagles, they are animals. But they are also persons because they represent creatures who are autonomous—rational agents possessed of volition and foresight. In ways that only Dr. Seuss can, he was reminding us that persons come in all shapes, colors, and sizes. It doesn't matter whether a person has male or female shape. It doesn't matter whether persons are white, black, red, or yellow. It doesn't matter whether persons are large or small—even if they are small enough to live on a speck. And, of course, it doesn't matter whether persons hail from Africa, Asia, Europe, or America. Claiming that color, shape, size, or geographical origins does morally matter is to fail to recognize that persons are "Whos." Horton recognized that the Whos are persons. He listened, he heard, and he acted—bravely. In doing so, he hears me and he hears you. We, too, are "Whos." We, once again, should be more like Horton the elephant.

Assessing Respect for Persons

Moral theories best categorized as "respect for persons" are invariably Kantian based but depart from Kant in affording the ends in themselves categorical imperative preeminent status. As autonomy (or being autonomous in the senses described in the chapter) is intrinsically valuable, morally significant harms are interpreted as anything that results in curtailing autonomy, which explains why treating a person like a thing is so morally egregious. The moral standard for a respect for persons approach can be articulated:

> Everyone ought to respect persons (including oneself) as autonomous agents, ends onto themselves and not merely as a means to an end.

Examples of "negative" moral rules might be: "don't make lying promises" and "don't steal." Examples of "positive" moral rules might be: "do offer aid to others when doing so does not seriously threaten your own person" and "do make informed, uncoerced decisions."[11] Whenever an agent is faced with a tragic (or conflict) situation such that autonomy will be infringed upon regardless of what she chooses, she should perform that action (enact the rule) that fails to respect persons the least (or that which represents the lesser of two evils regarding infringements upon autonomy). An act is wrong if it fails to respect autonomy and is not made permissible by the "lesser of two evils" qualifying principle. A good person is one who regularly performs actions that respect the autonomy of persons (primarily because that is the right thing to do, and not for self-serving reasons). A bad person is one who regularly fails to perform actions that respect the autonomy of persons.

A Kantian respect for persons ethic has many intuitive strengths. However, it also has its weaknesses. In affording persons central ethical importance, many argue that it saddles itself with counterintuitive entailments regarding nonpersons. Kant, for one, was clear: we have *no* ethical obligations to animals. Thus, it is impossible to treat a dog, horse, or cow impermissibly. But this seems contrary to commonsense morality; if you cause an animal pain or suffering for no reason, you have acted wrongly. A respect for persons ethic also has some difficulty, it seems, in adequately dealing with beginning of human life issues (and perhaps end of human life issues) and issues involving (permanently) mentally challenged human beings. The difficulty in all these cases is the same: How should we understand the moral status of beings that have significantly attenuated rationality (or autonomy)? Because no easy answer presents itself, many are led to believe that Kantian ethics does poorly regarding the moral universe test. Unless this counterexample can be suitably addressed, its plausibility as moral theory is jeopardized.

Apart from an illicitly small or restrictive moral universe, other scholars object to how Kantians so heavily rely on moral principles in shaping the ethical life. This objection manifests in various ways. Some, influenced by Aristotle, contend that ethics is far too complex or "messy" to admit of stringent rules logically derived from a single abstract standard; if ethical decision making does not merely consist of deriving rules because it resists the precision of disciplines like math, then Kantian ethics is seriously flawed.[12] That Kantian ethics requires such precision in ethical decision making when none (allegedly) exists serves as a counterexample that must be adequately addressed. Other scholars argue that Kantian ethics becomes implausible due to unfortunate vagueness of what it means to respect persons in various circumstances. If the idea of affording persons respect is inherently vague, the prospect of articulating informative Kantian moral rules is dim. This version of the objection, therefore, alleges that Kantian ethics does poorly with respect to the completeness test for moral theories, threatening its plausibility as a moral theory.

Other detractors of Kantian-based systems of ethics grant that perhaps formulating rules is necessary to taking the moral point of view. However, these detractors argue that moral rules cannot be adequately derived given certain constraints upon which Kantians insist. Typically, this objection is targeted at Kant's insistence on ethical absolutism. Kant offers no plausible guidance about what to do when moral rules conflict; therefore, Kantian moral theories fail the action-guiding test. But even if some sort of strategy is offered for resolving such conflicts (as was argued for in this chapter), then the objection becomes that working out all the qualifications to general rules is cumbersome and impractical; this is to argue that Kantian ethics still runs afoul of the action-guiding test even in its nonabsolutist forms. After all, how likely is it that we can articulate informative rules and *all* of their exceptions? (That this doesn't seem likely perhaps led Aristotle to discount rules-based approaches.) Other scholars argue that even if informative rules and their exceptions (or revisions) can be derived, moral behavior includes more than simply following rules. Kantian ethics seems open to the charge that moral goodness (or morally commendable behavior) is achieved by merely robotically following the categorical imperative (acting from duty); however, moral goodness seems to involve more than robotic behavior. Issues of character are also important, but Kantian approaches overlook this point, threatening to render them illicitly incomplete as a moral theory.

The charge of incompleteness with respect to moral goodness takes either of two forms. On the first version, suppose a friend of yours visits you in the hospital while you recover from an operation. However, if you discover that he visits only because he believes it is his Kantian duty, you might disparage his actions. True, he is visiting you, but not because he cares for you, or wishes you a speedy recovery and he is doing what he can to help. Rather, his decision is grounded exclusively in his enacting a Kantian moral rule, derived from the categorical imperative, and performed *simply* from duty. But this seems entirely too cold and calculated, which is evidence that there is something morally lacking in his Kantian approach.[13]

The second version is a converse of the first, and it can be witnessed in *Horton Hears a Who!*. When Jane Kangaroo approaches Vlad to do her dirty work, he pauses to consider what his fee might be for services rendered. Initially, he requests that Jane hand over the tasty morsel in her pouch—her son, Rudy. Jane seems to deliberate about this. It's tempting to interpret her as pondering whether this could be made permissible by some sort of unusual exception to a general Kantian rule. Perhaps she is thinking: "Well, generally, it would be impermissible for me to sacrifice my son, but does this situation fall under some sort of plausible qualification?" Whether she is actually doing this (or simply acting to psychologically manipulate Vlad) doesn't really matter. The basic point is that those who must consult rules all the time before making morally significant decisions are less morally desirable persons

"Quiet, Rudy, mommy is thinking . . ." —*Horton Hears a Who!*, scene 19

than those who have developed distinctive kinds of characters where morally appropriate action becomes second nature. So, again, due to the strong emphasis Kantian approaches place on deriving moral rules and their exceptions, there is something radically incomplete about them. Unless Kantian-based respect for persons approaches can be suitably supplemented, there is evidence that they fail the completeness test for moral theories.

These objections, some of them venerable, must be suitably addressed before Kantian ethical systems can prevail. Perhaps some of them can be answered within the confines of a basic Kantian approach (with worries about Kant's insistence on absolutism being one example). But even if some are not easily answered, it might be that Kantian approaches could be melded with other ethical systems in ways that deflect their force but still retain Kant's more significant ethical insights. This possibility is worth exploring, and deserving of the effort.

8.4. TWO ADDITIONAL FILMS

3:10 to Yuma (2007)

Director: James Mangold
Screenwriters: Halsted Welles and Michael Brandt

Plot Summary

> He's a killer, Daniel. —Then someone ought to have the decency to bring him to justice.

"Dan, maybe it's the wind," Alice Evans whispers as her husband gets up from bed. Dan Evans, a Civil War veteran who lost the lower part of his leg defending Washington, DC, cocks his rifle and looks out the window. He sees his barn ablaze. He hobbles outside only to find Glen Hollander's men echo their boss's fiery warning: "You have a week, Evans, and then we burn the house." Dan's fourteen-year-old son, William, runs out of the house as Hollander's men ride away. Dan and William save the horses and a few saddles before the barn collapses.

Dan rides into Bisbee to confront Hollander, but the Evanses are behind on their loan payments—money they owe to Hollander—because they had to buy feed for the livestock, tuberculosis medicine for their younger son, Mark, and three months' worth of water. Hollander reminds Dan: "You've borrowed a good deal of money and I got rights to recompense." Evans immediately replies: "But you damned up my creek. You shut off my water. How do you expect me to pay off my debts if you can't . . ." Hollander rudely interrupts: "Before that water touches your land, it resides and flows on mine!" Desperate, Dan offers Hollander his wife's family-heirloom brooch in lieu of payment. Hollander refuses, claiming that with the railroad coming, the property is worth more with the Evanses off of it.

But earlier that day, Dan and his sons experienced a chance meeting with the notorious outlaw Ben Wade. Wade and his gang robbed their twenty-second Southern Pacific Railroad payroll stagecoach near the Evans ranch. Wade allowed Dan and his sons to go free (although he did hide their horses to ensure that they wouldn't follow). But as fate would have it, Wade and his gang also traveled to Bisbee after the robbery. When Dan chases after Hollander to continue their "discussion," he instead finds Wade. He also finds the Bisbee marshal and his men. Wade is surrounded. The local Southern Pacific Railroad agent, Mr. Butterfield, hires a posse to escort Wade to Contention where he will board the prison train to Yuma Prison. At the prison, he will receive a perfunctory trial and be hanged until dead. Dan volunteers to be a part of the posse—for two hundred dollars, which is exactly what he owes Hollander.

Wade's gang soon finds out that their boss has been arrested. The coach transporting Wade stops in front of Dan's house outside of Bisbee. Charlie Prince, Wade's second in command, carefully studies the situation. But from a distance, Charlie doesn't recognize that the marshal sneaks Wade into the Evans's home, putting a member of the posse in the coach. Prince follows the coach; Alice prepares dinner for the marshal's posse. After dinner, Dan and Alice have a quiet moment: "You can change your mind, Dan; no one will think less of you." Dan slowly turns to face his wife: "No one can think less of me. . . . I've been standing on one leg for three damn years waiting for God to do me a favor. And he ain't listening." After a few words to his sons, Dan solemnly departs with the posse. They head for Contention to make the 3:10 train to Yuma.

Around a campfire, Wade brazenly asks: "What are you doing out here, Dan? You got a family to protect. You're not a lawman. You don't work for the railroad." Dan nonchalantly replies, "Maybe I don't like the idea of men like you on the loose." Unconvinced, Wade replies, "You must be hurtin' bad for money to take this job." A scuffle ensues when the conversation turns to Alice. Dan peels himself away from Wade to get some sleep. The next posse member takes watch. The others wake to Wade, still handcuffed, stabbing that man to death with a fork Wade stole from the Evans's dinner table.

Wade almost escapes the next morning, but fortuitously William, disobeying his father, was following the posse. William pulls a gun on Wade, who surrenders. That night, the posse is attacked by Apache snipers. Wade kills the Apache warriors with his bare hands, saving Dan's life in the process. Wade slips away. But in the morning, he stumbles upon a railroad construction encampment. He is identified by one of the railroad men; Wade killed his brother. The railroad men accost Wade and begin torturing him—simply to cause him pain. Dan's posse catches up and spies the scene. One of them asserts, "You can't do that. That's immoral." A torturer mindlessly replies, "Moral ain't got a damn thing to do with it." Dan steps forward: "I need to collect my two hundred dollar reward for that man." The torturer responds: "Need it bad enough to die?" The posse rescues Wade, thereby returning his favor from the night before, and all of them narrowly escape the encampment.

Wade's gang, uncovering the marshal's ruse (and having tortured the lawman in the coach), make their way to Contention. But Dan's posse arrives first. Mr. Butterfield leaves Dan with Wade in a Contention hotel room while he finds the local marshal. Wade tries bribing Dan; Wade will pay him a thousand dollars for his freedom. Dan refuses. Butterfield returns with the marshal and two of his best men. Wade asks how much Butterfield paid them for such a dangerous mission. William runs to the room. He has spied Wade's gang riding into town. Prince announces that he will pay two hundred dollars to anyone who shoots dead any man detaining Ben Wade. Prince has thus hired his own posse—thirty or forty armed men with murderous intentions. The marshal, looking upon the mob forming below, quickly reneges. He confesses to Butterfield, "Look, if it's a fair fight, well, sure. I'd stay for that. That's a man's duty. But there's only five of us." He then apologizes to Dan: "Sorry mister, but I'm not going to die here today. And neither are my men." Dan flings a gold star at him as he walks out the door. Butterfield chases him down the stairs, pleading that he will double the marshal's money. One deputy announces that they all have families; they will not die here today. But that is just what they do; Wade's gang executes them as they walk out of the hotel unarmed.

Butterfield reenters the room. He pays Dan his money and absolves Evans of any further obligation to him or the railroad. But it is Butterfield who walks away. This leaves only Dan and William to bring Wade to justice. Dan remains steadfast. He has Butterfield escort William back to Bisbee and pay his wife one thousand dollars. Further, Dan requests that Butterfield work to keep Hollander off his land and ensure that his water always flows. Dan turns to his son and presents Alice's brooch. Dan asks William to return it and inform her that it helped him to "find what was right." Should something happen to Dan, William becomes the man of the house. They shake hands, and Dan says, "And you just remember that your old man walked Ben Wade to that station when nobody else would." Butterfield and William prepare their return to Bisbee. Dan and Wade prepare for their trip to the station.

Discussion Questions

1. Does Hollander do something wrong by damning up the river on his land?
2. Did the railroad men act impermissibly in torturing Wade as they did? What is morally controversial about torture anyway? Are there any circumstances in which it is not morally dubious?
3. Evaluate the decision made by the Contention lawmen to not escort Wade to the train station after giving their word that they would. Was their choice morally objectionable? Explain.
4. What might have Dan meant when he said that carrying his wife's brooch helped him to "find what was right?"
5. Does it matter morally speaking whether Dan brings Wade to justice simply because it is the right thing to do rather than some other reason, for example, for payment or the admiration of his son?

Amistad (1997)

Director: Steven Spielberg
Screenwriter: David Franzoni

Plot Summary

> I disagree with the minds of the South. . . . The natural state of mankind is instead—and I know that this is a controversial idea—is freedom.

It is 1839 and the Spanish ship *La Amistad* suffers insurrection near Cuba. But the mutineers are not sailors or soldiers—they are its cargo. They wish to return to Africa. However, the two remaining white sailors manage to dupe the Africans. They do not sail east, but mostly north. The *Amistad* is soon intercepted by an American survey brig. The Africans are moved from their dark wooden cell to a dank metal one in New Haven, Connecticut, awaiting their day in court for murdering the crew of the *Amistad*.

The major political players line up to be heard. The preteen Isabella II, Queen of Spain, immediately sends her American ambassador with a 1795 treaty in hand to collect her property. In a reelection year, President Martin Van Buren initially sees the whole matter as an inconvenience. He sends Secretary of State John Forsyth to appease Spain, thereby making the whole matter (literally) go away. Two leading abolitionists, Misters Tappan and Joadson, neither of whom are lawyers, (improperly) present the court a writ of habeas corpus so as to buy time to arrange proper defense for the Africans. Two American naval officers argue that because they salvaged the *Amistad*, they have a right to its cargo. An attorney representing the two white Spanish sailors presents a bill of sale (receipt) executed June 26 in Havana, Cuba; the Africans, thus, literally belong to them.

Roger S. Baldwin, attorney at law, fortuitously introduces himself and offers his services to the two abolitionists. Baldwin is a real estate and property lawyer, exactly what the abolitionists seemingly need. However, they (and especially Tappan) smugly smile at Baldwin, and inform him what they really need is a criminal attorney, a trial lawyer. Tappan and Joadson travel to Washington, DC, requesting an audience with former president John Quincy Adams. Now a congressman from Massachusetts, Adams has a reputation of being sympathetic to the abolitionist movement—much like his father before him, President John Adams. The younger Adams agrees to see Tappan and Joadson, but inexplicably declines to aid them. Joadson, an ex-slave from Georgia but now a free and learned historian of American politics, objects. He reminds the former president that, while in office, he consistently sided with abolitionists. Adams warns Joadson that erudition is useless unless it is accompanied by a modicum of grace and then departs.

Joadson and Tappan subsequently meet with Baldwin to discuss strategy. Baldwin believes that the case is not as difficult as it might appear. He begins by asking the two whether the Africans were born slaves, as on a plantation. If they were, then they are possessions and "no more deserving of a criminal trial than a bookcase or plow." If they are not born slaves, then "they were illegally acquired" and their situation is a matter of "wrongful transfer of stolen property." Either way, Baldwin believes that the case is won. Tappan indignantly demurs, saying, "Sir, this war must be waged on the battlefield of righteousness. . . . It would be against everything I stand for to let this deteriorate into an exercise in the vagaries of legal minutiae. . . . These are people, Mr. Baldwin." Baldwin is unsure of Tappan's convictions, but nevertheless requests a "two and one-half dollars a day" retainer. The two abolitionists warily agree.

The trial does not go nearly as smoothly as Baldwin envisioned. The problem is that he has some difficulty convincing the court that the defendants aren't from Cuba, born on a Cuban plantation. Baldwin must therefore somehow prove that the defendants are indeed Africans. Baldwin and Joadson subsequently work very hard to connect with the Africans (that is, the defendants, who they hope are from Africa). They hire a linguist, but he is not familiar with their dialect. They receive a warrant to inspect the *Amistad*. Baldwin discovers a hidden manifest. It seems to indicate that the *Amistad*'s cargo was purchased from another ship, the *Tecora*—a notorious cross-Atlantic slave transport ship. This is the break Baldwin needs. The manifest seems to indicate that the *Amistad*'s cargo originated from the Ivory Coast, most likely Sierra Leone. These African locales are under the protectorate of Great Britain, a country that has already outlawed slavery. It thus indeed seems that the defendants are Africans taken illegally.

Meanwhile, Isabella puts more pressure on President Van Buren. The Southern states do the same—most notably in the person of Senator John Calhoun—intimating the case will spur civil war. Van Buren's advisors remind (inform?) him that he has the power to disband the jury and have the judge removed. A new judge could be handpicked. The trial could reconvene without a jury. Baldwin is furious when he hears about the executive branch's involvement. Joadson again calls on former president Adams. Adams is more receptive this time. He advises that Baldwin and Joadson discover the Africans' story, to truly know who they are. After all, quips Adams, if he has learned anything about the law, it is that "in a courtroom, whoever tells the best story wins." The two subsequently find someone who speaks Mende, thereby discovering that the African leader is named Cinque. Cinque saved his village from a man-eating lion; this is why the others look up to him. Baldwin corrects him: Cinque has slain two lions, the second being the *Amistad*.

Cinque recounts the horrific events of their capture and cross-Atlantic voyage. The two come to know the Africans' story indeed.

Baldwin puts Cinque on the stand; opposing counsel attempts to discredit Cinque's testimony. Baldwin calls a British naval officer to substantiate Cinque's testimony. Listening and watching the proceedings now from his defendant's chair, Cinque becomes emotionally charged. He stands and shouts, "Give us, us free!" Give us, us free!" Baldwin's arguments and Cinque's testimony is persuasive. Van Buren and his advisors are shocked to hear that the new judge rules in the Africans' favor.

Calhoun puts more pressure on the president. Van Buren acquiesces and appeals the decision to the Supreme Court—currently stocked with seven judges from Southern states. Baldwin is forced to inform Cinque that they must argue the case one last time. Cinque is at first confused. Enraged, he shouts, "What kind of place is this? Where you almost mean what you say? Where laws almost work? How can you live like that?" Baldwin desperately writes Adams, pleading for assistance with the Supreme Court case. The former president finally agrees. He, too, begins to know Cinque and the Africans. By knowing their story, Adams better remembers his story—America's story—and this proves to be the key to finally securing the Africans' freedom.

Discussion Questions

1. Compare and contrast Baldwin's and Tappan's basic arguments in approaching the case (paragraph 4 of the plot summary). Which seems like the stronger argument? Explain carefully.
2. What should be done about state-sanctioned laws, like slavery, that seem obviously unjust?
3. Is Adams correct that in the courtroom what really matters is who tells the best story? If not, why not? If so, what does this say about the judicial system?
4. Reconsider Cinque's dismay (see last paragraph of plot summary) upon learning the case must be presented to the Supreme Court. Is Cinque's disillusionment justified?
5. Evaluate the following argument espoused in *Amistad* (scene 19): "There has never existed a civilized society in which a segment did not thrive on the labor of another. . . . In Eden where only two were created, even there one was pronounced subordinate to the other. Slavery has always been with us and is neither sinful nor immoral. . . . Slavery is as natural as it is inevitable."

8.5. REVIEWING THROUGH THE THREE MOVIES

1. Compare the characters of Horton, Dan Evans, and Cinque; in what does their heroism consist? Which is most heroic? Explain.
2. Compare and contrast the interactions between Mayor McDodd and Jo-Jo with those of Dan and William Evans; evaluate their interactions in Kantian terms.
3. According to Kant, at what point, if any, do Baldwin's actions (in *Amistad*) on behalf of the Africans achieve full moral praise? Do you agree? What is Kant's analogous position about Dan Evans's actions (in *3:10 to Yuma*) about bringing Ben Wade to justice? Do you agree? Explain your answers.
4. Are there any definitive examples in the three movies of persons being treated with respect? If so, which? If you cannot find any definitive examples, explain why.

5. Reconsider the six movie quotes from the chapter and explain whether each, given the adjacent paragraphs, *illustrates* a point the author is making, *supplements* (or extends) a point the author is making, or *contrasts* (for emphasis) a point the author is making. Explain your answers.

NOTES

1. The 2008 motion picture is a faithful rendering of the original Dr. Seuss story, but there are interesting thematic differences. For example, the movie portrays Horton as a sort of grade school teacher, charged with teaching children of different species about life in the Jungle of Nool. Consequently, this plot summary will no doubt remind readers of the classic 1954 story (originally published by Random House and adapted for television in 1970), but it must diverge from it in places to tell the 2008 film version of the story.

2. Excerpted from *The Foundations of the Metaphysics of Morals*, T. K. Abbott translation (1873). Section headings and other stylistic emendations have been added to aid reader comprehension.

3. Much of the discussion linking *Horton Hears a Who!* with Kantian ethics is adapted from Dean A. Kowalski, "Horton Hears You, Too!: Seuss and Kant on Respecting Persons," in *Dr. Seuss and Philosophy*, ed. Jacob Held (Lanham, MD: Rowman & Littlefield, 2011), 119–132.

4. Immanuel Kant, "On a Supposed Right to Lie from Altruistic Motives," in *Critique of Practical Reason and Other Writings in Moral Philosophy*, trans. Lewis White Beck (Chicago: University of Chicago Press, 1949), 348. ("On a Supposed Right to Lie from Altruistic Motives" originally published in 1797.)

5. This sort of dilemma is sometimes expressed via an actual historical situation. Dutch fishermen attempted to smuggle Jews to England during World War II. Sometimes Dutch fishing boats would be stopped by a Nazi patrol boat. A Nazi officer would inquire of the Dutch fisherman where he was headed and who was on board. If you were the fisherman (and assuming no third alternative), what would you do? Should you lie to the officer to protect the life of innocent people, or answer the question honestly, knowing that the innocents in your cargo hold will undoubtedly die a horrible death at Auschwitz?

6. Kant, of course, would balk at qualifying maxims. He might remind us that each and every person is responsible for his or her own actions. This important fact must be respected in ways that preserve everyone's dignity, including the inquiring murderer. You are not responsible for the murderer's actions, or what subsequently occurs upon your informing him truthfully (even if he goes ahead with his ghastly deed). To quell worries that this seems unduly harsh, Kant would no doubt appeal to God's existence as a necessary postulate for guaranteeing the happiness of the virtuous (and victimized) and the punishment of the wicked. That is, Kant believed that God played the role of infallible judge and enforcer in a way that (allegedly) conceptually underwrites his moral absolutism.

7. There is also a sense in which persons, by willfully choosing to not uphold their ethical obligations, fail to respect their own inherent dignity. This entails (among other things) that we have moral duties to ourselves and not merely to other persons, which (some argue) is another controversial feature of Kant's view.

8. It may have a fourth, namely, that it affords a strategy for addressing maxims that can be universalized but nevertheless seem impermissible. For example, the maxim that all persons of a certain blood type should be enslaved for a period of ten years and then executed doesn't seem self-defeating, especially if the person formulating it is willing to have himself subjected to such treatment if he discovers that he possesses the relevant blood type. On the revisionist interpretation offered here, this maxim is impermissible because it fails to respect the personhood of those possessing the relevant blood type.

9. That is, unless complete honesty is *always* the course of action an agent should take. If so, then the alleged dilemma here isn't actually a dilemma at all. But on this account, it also seems to follow that you should keep your promise to your other neighbor and kill his professional rival. But is this plausible? Also, note that some purported dilemmas won't involve honesty. Assume that you have the opportunity to save either one child on one end of a burning building or two on the other, but not both (that is, all three children). Who should you rescue? Furthermore, the relevant interpretation provides a unifying and intuitively satisfying solution to the inquiring murderer, repaying the kindness, *and* the burning building children dilemmas: do that action that disrespects persons the least (or values autonomous personhood the most). It also provides a strategy for bolstering Kant's claims about suicide, developing one's talents, and offering aid to others (insofar as one can). Finally, it achieves all of this without any (obvious) appeals to God as a postulate for the "complete good."

10. Any lingering contention is no doubt grounded in Kant's insistence that human dignity should *never* be sacrificed or traded away. Kant seems correct in that trading your dignity away for a nonmoral (selfish) project is impermissible. However, Kant's position is not nearly as forceful with respect to conflict situations such that agents must choose between two morally significant (and nonselfish) projects. Morally speaking, why must I sacrifice the life of the innocent person? Isn't her autonomy deserving of my consideration?

11. The classifications of "negative" and "positive" moral rules correspond to negative and positive duties, per the discussion of this chapter. However, these classifications are not merely limited to Kantian ethics. Natural law also admits of positive and negative moral rules.

12. An often cited passage from Aristotle is: "We should not, after all, seek the same precision in all discussions. . . . It is to be welcomed, then, when discussions . . . can indicate the truth roughly and in outline . . . [and] things that hold only 'for the most part' can also reach conclusions of that sort. . . . For it is the mark of an educated person to seek as much precision in each kind of study as the nature of the thing permits. Accepting probable reasoning from a mathematician is apparently just as silly as demanding demonstrative proofs from an orator," *Nicomachean Ethics*, bk 3, trans. J. F. Heil, quoted in *Living Well*, ed. Steven Luper (Orlando, FL: Harcourt Brace Publishers, 2000), 30.

13. This type of objection is often attributed to Michael Stocker. See his "The Schizophrenia of Modern Ethical Theories," *Journal of Philosophy*, 73 (1976): 453–66. This kind of objection might have relevance to the movie *Amistad* in that there seems to be a difference between defending the Africans and striving for abolition, on the one hand, and caring for Cinque and the Africans—as people ripped from their distant homeland—on the other. This might help to explain Adams's advice to Joadson and Baldwin (scene 9) to know *who* they are rather than merely learning *where* they're from.

CHAPTER 9

Social Contract Theory

Hobbes, Locke, and Rawls

PLOT SUMMARY

People should not fear their governments; governments should fear their people.

Evey Hammond is a young production assistant at the BTN—British Television Network—the only remaining station in England. Evey is late for a rendezvous with talk show host Gordon Deitrich. It is after 11:00 p.m., past the citywide curfew. She nervously but carefully winds her way through back alleys and side streets in the attempt to avoid the "Fingermen," London's special police force led by party leader Creedy, but to no avail. She is apprehended and about to be harassed, when a cloaked, masked man intervenes. Wielding assassin's knives, the Guy Fawkes–looking vigilante incapacitates the Fingermen and memorably ("a humble vaudevillian veteran cast vicariously as both victim and villain by the vicissitudes of fate") introduces himself to Evey (not surprisingly) as "V."

Evey's fate becomes intertwined with V's. She rather inexplicably accompanies V to witness the spectacular but unexpected demolition of the Old Bailey justice building. V synchronized its violent destruction with fireworks and classical music blaring over each street corner loudspeaker. This is quickly dubbed a terrorist act by High Chancellor Sutler and his ultraconservative Norsefire political regime. Evey crosses paths with V only hours later at the BTN. V forces his way in to BTN headquarters in Jordan Tower; he threatens to blow it up unless he is granted airtime. BTN officials reluctantly agree, and V's message is broadcast across London on the emergency channel.

V politely greets Britain by asserting that there is something terribly wrong with this country, but reminds them "where once you had the freedom to object, to think and speak as you saw fit, you now have censors and surveillance coercing your conformity and soliciting submission." He acknowledges that Britain faced difficult times worrying about war abroad and terrorist acts at home, but Sutler now rules mercilessly. In any event, V blames his fellow citizens for Sutler's oppressive, police state. He calls for revolution by announcing, "If you see what I see, if you feel as I feel, and if you would seek as I seek, then I ask you to stand beside me, one year from tonight outside the gates of Parliament. And together, we shall give them a 5th of November . . . that shall never, ever be forgot."

V exits Jordan Tower through swarms of police officers, only to find Evey fortuitously aiding his escape. She is hurt in the process, knocked unconscious. V hesitates only for an instant and takes Evey with him back to his lair, the Shadow Gallery.

V informs (or politely demands of) Evey that she cannot leave his home (the Shadow Gallery) until his greater plan for Britain comes to fruition. Their relationship thus becomes complicated and strained, but amicable. V decides to enlist Evey's help on one of his violent escapades, this time to a local abbey to "visit" a member of the cloth V once knew. But she takes advantage of the situation to free herself from V's dominion, fleeing to Gordon's house. She stays with Gordon, but on the evening of Gordon's most controversial show—one that draws Sutler's ire—the Fingermen barge into the house. During

BOX 9A: INSIDE *V FOR VENDETTA*

V for Vendetta effectively portrays the ideas of Hobbes and Locke, especially as they pertain to social contract theory. The most pertinent segments begin with scenes 3–5. Scene 3 starts at 9:07 with Evey and V on a rooftop looking at the Justice Building. Scene 5 ends at 21:53 with Evey seeing a red V on a television screen after V finishes his broadcast message. The second segment is short, portraying a brief discussion between V and Evey. It begins at the start of Scene 8 (30:08) with a shot of a frying pan on a stove; it ends at 32:48 with a shot of Prothero's BTN show. The third segment is longer, scenes 23–33. Scene 23 starts at 1:29:15 with a shot of Sutler on a large screen; he and his undersecretaries are preparing for November 5. Scene 33 takes you to the end of the movie (2:04:00). If you are really pressed for time, the third segment can be trimmed. Begin at scene 23 and continue viewing through scene 24, which ends at 1:36:14, with a shot of V in disguise walking away from Finch. Skip ahead to view scene 28, which begins at 1:48:43 with Finch and his lieutenant in a car, and ends at 1:51:56 with V walking down a tunnel away from Evey. Then skip to scene 31, which begins at 1:57:44 with a shot of Evey sitting next to the subway cars, and continue watching until the end of the film.

If you cannot enjoy the entire movie, you might be able to glean enough about Hobbes, Locke, and social contract theory from reading the plot summary carefully and stopping to watch the first segment and then some combination of segments two and (especially) three. If you are able to view the entire film, then you should be able to answer the trivia questions from box 9B. (Also look for wider ethical issues regarding V's character, whether his dishonesty to Evey is permissible, and how Norsefire fares on a consequentialist analysis.)

the raid, the Fingermen find some of his more incriminating possessions, not the least of which is a fourteenth-century Qur'an. He is viciously beaten and hauled away in one of Creedy's "black bags." Much as she did when her mother was arrested many years before, Evey hides under the bed. When the Fingermen leave the room, Evey jumps out of a window, but is caught outside of Gordon's residence. She is "processed" (like many other political "criminals") and soon tortured so as to disclose the whereabouts of the terrorist V. Spurred by the serendipitous example of an earlier prisoner, a woman named Valerie, Evey does not succumb. Eventually, she is freed without disclosing any information about V. Upon being freed, she seems to be a changed woman—transformed in some important way—unafraid for herself or her future.

We quickly find out that V had a hand in Evey's release from prison. But in the meantime, V has managed to exact his revenge on many of the key players that caused him harm years ago, including Lewis Prothero, BTN's acerbic, conservative "Voice of London." Police chief Finch discovers terrible truths about V's past, dating back to the Reclamation (Norsefire's rise to power) and specifically the detention center at Larkhill. We thus better understand V's character and his motivations for vengeance. It seems his vendetta is first and foremost personal. But simultaneously, he facilitates political revolution for Britain. Each act of revenge weakens Sutler's control over the country. The high chancellor responds by ordering his undersecretaries to increase surveillance measures and arrests for sedition and treason. But Sutler's undersecretaries begin to mistrust each other and lose faith in the high chancellor. The populace no longer sees him as a savior. The next November 5th is drawing near.

On the eve of V's revolution, Evey somewhat unexpectedly arrives at the Shadow Gallery. The two had been estranged for months, since Evey's release from prison. V requests that she accompany him one last time, not to a rooftop, but underground—to a closed "tube station" (subway). V spent a great deal of time, money, and effort to secretly refurbish this line. It runs directly underneath the Parliament building. Evey is impressed, but confused. V asks her to play one last part in bringing about a 5th of November that will never be forgot.

BOX 9B: *V FOR VENDETTA* **TRIVIA**

If your instructor assigns the film to be watched outside of class, you should be able to answer the following questions:

1. What famous piece of music does V play over the loudspeakers as he blows up the Old Bailey?
2. How long must Evey stay in V's home once he takes her there?
3. What is V's favorite movie?
4. What is the number of V's cell at Larkhill?
5. Who is the special guest star on "the best show Gordon has ever done"?
6. What is the first thing that happens to Evey when she is "processed"?
7. Where is Evey to be executed by "the detail of six men"?
8. Who does V pretend to be when he meets Finch at the closed St. Mary's school?
9. What do Evey and V do in his house on "the eve of his revolution"?
10. Who rides the underground train at the end of the film?

The British people, donning V-type costumes, march en masse toward the Parliament building. The military police cannot reach anyone at Norsefire for instruction. They—and not the people—begin to panic. The military stands down; the people peacefully march by them toward Parliament. The streets are filled with smiling Guy Fawkes personas, waiting for the stroke of midnight: "Remember, remember the 5th of November . . ."

9.1. THINKING THROUGH THE MOVIE

Discussion Starter Questions

1. Is V correct that "there is something terribly wrong" in *Vendetta*'s Britain? If so, what? Why does V believe that British citizens are ultimately to blame?
2. V is quickly labeled a terrorist by the British government. Are there any circumstances in which terrorism is morally permissible? Explain.
3. What kind of a governmental leader is Adam Sutler? Is Britain better off under his leadership? Explain.
4. Evaluate the credo "Strength through unity, unity through faith"; is it permissibly enacted?
5. Explain the meaning of the opening quote (uttered by V in scene 8, 32:20) of the plot summary. What is its philosophical significance?

Questions for Further Thought

1. Is V's declaration (scene 9, 38:35), "Violence can be used for good" true? Explain.
2. Connecting the "VTV" and "All of Us" scenes (5, beginning at 16:25 and 32, beginning 1:59:27, respectively), what is the philosophical significance of V allowing Evey, and British citizens generally, to ultimately decide Britain's political future?
3. Sutler (scene 29, 1:52:22) declares, "Our enemy is an insidious one, seeking to divide us and destroy the very foundation of our great nation. . . . But most of all we must remain united!" Is V the enemy of Britain? Explain.
4. Does Gordon act impermissibly (scene 17, beginning 1:04:42) by airing a national television show in which the high chancellor is made fun of? What does Gordon imply at the end of this controversial episode? Is broadcasting *this* message impermissible?
5. BTN executive Dascomb states (scene 4, 13:15), "Our job is to report the news, not fabricate it. That's the government's job." Why might the government and/or the media be under a moral obligation to disseminate the truth? If they are so obligated, are there any circumstances in which it might be overridden?

9.2. HISTORICAL SETTING

Leviathan (excerpt)[1]

Thomas Hobbes (1588–1679) was educated at Oxford University and tutored British royal family members, including King Charles II. This allowed him time to correspond with other great minds of his day, including Galileo, Descartes, and Francis Bacon. The following passage is from his greatest work, *Leviathan*, where he explicates his ideas about the just state.

Preparing to Read

A. In what ways are Hobbes's ideas about human nature and government represented in *V for Vendetta* (and *Lord of the Flies*)?

B. In what ways does High Chancellor Sutler embody a Hobbesian sovereign?

Of the Natural Condition of Mankind as Concerning Their Felicity and Misery

Nature has made men so equal in the faculties of body and mind as that, though there be found one man sometimes manifestly stronger in body or of quicker mind than another, yet when all is considered together the difference between them is not so considerable that one man can claim to himself any benefit to which another may not pretend as well. For as to the strength of body, the weakest has strength enough to kill the strongest, either by secret machination or by confederacy with others.

And as to the faculties of the mind, setting aside the arts grounded upon words, and especially that skill of proceeding upon general and infallible rules, called science . . . I find yet a greater equality among men than that of strength. . . . That which may perhaps make such equality incredible is but a vain conceit of one's own wisdom, which almost all men think they have in a greater degree than the vulgar; that is, than all men but themselves, and a few others, whom by fame, or for concurring with themselves, they approve. For such is the nature of men that however they may acknowledge many others to be more witty, or more eloquent or more learned, yet they will hardly believe there be many so wise as themselves; for they see their own wit at hand, and other men's at a distance. But this proves that men are in that point equal rather than unequal. . . .

From this equality of ability arises equality of hope in the attaining of our ends. And therefore if any two men desire the same thing, which nevertheless they cannot both enjoy, they become enemies; and in the way to their end endeavor to destroy or subdue one another. And from hence it comes to pass that where an invader has no more to fear than another man's single power, if one plant, sow, build, or possess a convenient position, others may probably be expected to come prepared with forces united to dispossess and deprive him, not only of the fruit of his labor, but also of his life or liberty. And the invader again is in the like danger of another.

. . . Again, men have no pleasure (rather a great deal of grief) in keeping company where there is no power able to overawe them all. Every man believes that his companion should value him at the same rate he sets upon himself, and upon any sign of contempt or undervaluing by others naturally strives, as far as he dares to extort a greater value from his associates, by damage, and from others, by the example.

[On the Meaning and Causes of War]

So that in the nature of man, we find three principal causes of quarrel. First, competition; secondly, diffidence [mistrust]; thirdly, glory.

The first makes men invade for gain, the second for safety, and the third for reputation. The first use violence, to make themselves masters of other men's persons, wives, children, and cattle; the second to defend them; the third, for any other sign of undervalue, either direct in their persons or by reflection in their kindred, their friends, their nation, their profession, or their name.

Hereby it is manifest that during the time men live without a common power to keep them all in awe, they are in that condition which is called war; and such a war as is of every man against every man. For war consists not in battle only, or the act of fighting, but anytime the will to contend by battle is sufficiently known: and therefore the notion of time is to be considered in the nature of war. . . . So the nature of war consists not in actual fighting, but in the known disposition during all the time there is no assurance to the contrary. . . . In such condition there is no place for industry, because the fruit thereof is uncertain: and consequently no culture of the earth; . . . no commodious [suitable] building; . . . no knowledge of the face of the earth; no account of time; no arts; no letters; no society; and which is worst of all, continual fear, and danger of violent death; and the life of man, solitary, poor, nasty, brutish, and short.

. . . This is confirmed by experience. Consider: when taking a journey, man arms himself and seeks to go well accompanied; when going to sleep, he locks his doors; when even in his house he locks his chests; and this when he knows there be laws and public officers, armed, to revenge all injuries done to him; what opinion he has of his fellow subjects, when he rides armed; of his fellow citizens, when he locks his doors; and of his children, and servants, when he locks his chests. Does he not thereby accuse mankind by his actions as I do by my words? . . .

It may be thought there was never such a time nor condition of war as this; and I believe it was never generally so, over all the world: but there are many places where they live so now. For the savage people in many places of America, except the government of small families live at this day in that brutish manner. Nevertheless, it may be perceived what manner of life there would be, were there no common power to fear, by the manner of life which men that have formerly lived under a peaceful government use to degenerate into a civil war. Further, in all times kings and persons of sovereign authority, because of their independency, are in continual jealousies, and in the state and posture of gladiators, having their weapons pointing, and their eyes fixed on one another, and continual spies upon their neighbors, which is a posture of war. . . .

To this war of every man against every man, this also is consequent: nothing can be unjust. The notions of right and wrong, justice and injustice, have there no place. Where there is no common power, there is no law; where no law, no injustice. Force and fraud are in war the two cardinal virtues. . . . It is consequent also to the same condition that there be no propriety, no dominion, no mine and thine [yours] distinct; but only that to be every man's that he can get, and for so long as he can keep it. . . .

The passions that incline men to peace are: fear of death; desire of such things as are necessary to commodious living; and a hope by their industry to obtain them. And reason suggests convenient articles of peace upon which men may be drawn to agreement. These articles are called the laws of nature, whereof I shall speak more particularly in the two following chapters.

Of the First and Second Natural Laws, and of Contracts

The right of nature, which writers commonly call *jus naturale*, is the liberty each man has to use his own power as he will himself for the preservation of his own nature; that is to say, of his own life; and consequently, of doing anything which, in his own judgement and reason, he shall conceive to accomplish this. By liberty is understood, according to the proper signification of the word, the absence of external impediments; which impediments may often limit a man's power to do what he would, but cannot hinder him from using the power left him according as his judgement and reason shall dictate to him. A law of nature is a precept, or general rule, found out by reason, by which a man is forbidden to do that which is destructive of his life, or takes away the means of preserving the same, and to omit that by which he thinks it may be best preserved. . . .

And because the condition of man (as has been declared in the previous section) is a condition of war of every one against every one, in which case every one is governed by his own reason, and there is nothing he can make use of that may not be a help unto him in preserving his life against his enemies, it follows that in such a condition every man has a right to every thing, even to one another's body. And therefore, as long as this natural right of every man to every thing endures, there can be no security to any man, no matter how strong or wise he be, of living out the time which nature ordinarily allows men to live. And consequently it is a precept, or general rule of reason: that every man ought to endeavor [seek] peace, as far as he has hope of obtaining it; and when he cannot obtain it, that he may seek and use all helps and advantages of war. The first branch of this rule contains the first and fundamental law of nature, which is: to seek peace and follow it. The second, the sum of the right of nature, which is: by all means we can to defend ourselves.

From this fundamental law of nature, by which men are commanded to seek peace, is derived a second law: that a man be willing, when others are so too, as far forth as for peace and defense of himself he shall think it necessary, to lay down this right to all things; and be contented with so much liberty against other men as he would allow other men against himself. For as long as every man holds this right, of doing anything he likes; so long are all men in the condition of war. But if other men will not lay down their right, as well as he, then there is no reason for anyone to divest himself of his: for that would expose himself to prey, which no man is bound to, rather than to dispose himself to peace. . . .

[Of Contracts]

Right is laid aside, either by simply renouncing it, or by transferring it to another. By simply renouncing, when he cares not to whom the benefit thereof accrues. By transferring, when he intends the benefit thereof to some certain person or persons. And when a man has in either manner abandoned or granted away his right, then is he said to be obliged, or bound, not to hinder those to whom such right is granted, and that he ought, and it is duty, not to make void that voluntary act of his own: and that such hindrance is injustice, and injury. . . . The way by which a man either simply renounces or transfers his right is a declaration, or signification, by some voluntary and sufficient sign, or signs, that he does so renounce or transfer, or has so renounced or transferred the same, to him that accepts it. And these signs are either words only, or actions only; or, as it happens most often, both words and actions. And the same are the bonds, by which men are bound and obliged: bonds that have their strength, not from their own nature (for nothing is more easily broken than a man's word), but from fear of some evil consequence upon the rupture.

When a man transfers his right, or renounces it, it is either in consideration of some right reciprocally transferred to himself, or for some other good he hopes for thereby. For it is a voluntary act: and of the voluntary acts of every man, the object is some good to himself. . . . The motive and end for which this renouncing and transferring of right is introduced is nothing else but the security of a man's person, in his life, and in the means of so preserving life as not to be weary of it. And therefore if a man by words, or other signs, seems to despoil himself of the end for which those signs were intended, he is not to be understood as if he meant it, or that it was his will, but that he was ignorant of how such words and actions were to be interpreted.

The mutual transferring of right is that which men call contract. . . . One of the contractors may deliver the thing contracted for on his part, and leave the other to perform his part at some determinate time after, and in the meantime be trusted; and then the contract on his part is called pact, or covenant. . . .

If a covenant be made wherein neither of the parties perform presently, but trust one another, in the condition of mere nature (which is a condition of war of every man against every man) upon any reasonable suspicion, it is void: but if there be a common power set over them both, with right and force sufficient to compel performance, it is not void. For he that performs first has no assurance the other will perform after, because the bonds of words are too weak to bridle men's ambition, avarice, anger, and other passions, without the fear of some coercive power; which in the condition of mere nature, where all men are equal, and judges of the justness of their own fears, cannot possibly be supposed. . . . But in a civil estate, where there is a power set up to constrain those that would otherwise violate their faith, that fear is no more reasonable; and for that cause, he which by the covenant is to perform first is obliged so to do. . . .

Of Other Laws of Nature

From that law of nature by which we are obliged to transfer to another such rights as, being retained, hinder the peace of mankind, there follows a third, which is this: that men perform their covenants made; without which covenants are in vain, and but empty words; and the right of all men to all things remaining, we are still in the condition of war.

And in this law of nature consists the fountain and origins of justice. For where no covenant has preceded, no right been transferred, and every man has right to everything and consequently, no action can be unjust. But when a covenant is made, then to break it is unjust and the definition of injustice is no other than the not performance of covenant. And whatsoever is not unjust is just.

. . . Therefore before the names of just and unjust can have place, there must be some coercive power to compel men equally to the performance of their covenants, by the terror of some punishment greater than the benefit they expect by the breach of their covenant, and to make good that propriety which by mutual contract men acquire in recompense of the universal right they abandon: and such power there is none before the erection of a Commonwealth. And this is also to be gathered out of the ordinary definition of justice in the Schools, for they say that justice is the constant will of giving to every man his own. And therefore where there is no own, that is, no propriety, there is no injustice; and where there is no coercive power erected, that is, where there is no Commonwealth, there is no propriety, all men having right to all things: therefore where there is no Commonwealth, there nothing is unjust. So that the nature of justice consists in keeping of valid covenants, but the validity of covenants requires the constitution of a civil power sufficient to compel men to keep them: and then it is also that propriety begins. . . .

. . . The only way to erect such a common power, as may be able to defend them from the invasion of foreigners, and the injuries of one another, and thereby to secure them in such sort as that by their own industry and by the fruits of the earth they may nourish themselves and live contentedly, is to confer all their power and strength upon one man, or upon one assembly of men, that may reduce all their wills, by plurality of voices, unto one will: which is as much as to say, to appoint one man, or assembly of men, to bear their person; and every one to own and acknowledge himself to be author of whatsoever he that so bears their person shall act, or cause to be acted, in those things which concern the common peace and safety; and therein to submit their wills, every one to his will, and their judgements to his judgement. This is more than consent, or concord; it is a real unity of them all in one and the same person, made by covenant of every man with every man, in such manner as if every man should say to every man: I authorize and give up my right of governing myself to this man, or to this assembly of men, on this condition; that you give up, your right to him, and authorize all his actions in like manner. This done, the multitude so united in one person is called a Commonwealth; in Latin, *civitas*. This is the generation of that great Leviathan, or rather, to speak more reverently, of that mortal god to which we owe, under the immortal God, our peace and defense. For by this authority, given him by every particular man in the Commonwealth, he has the use of so much power and strength conferred on him that, by terror thereof, he is enabled to form the wills of them all, to peace at home, and mutual aid against their enemies abroad. And in him consists the essence of the Commonwealth; which, to define it, is: one person, of whose acts a great multitude, by mutual covenants one with another, have made themselves every one the author, to the end he may use the strength and means of them all as he shall think expedient for their peace and common defense.

And he that carries this station is called sovereign, and said to have sovereign power; and every one besides, his subject.

Review Questions

1. What does Hobbes mean by a "state of war" and what are its causes?
2. According to Hobbes, by what means do we (eventually) escape from a state of war?
3. According to Hobbes, what must obtain to make the terms "just" and "unjust" meaningful?

9.3. DISCUSSION AND ANALYSIS

Hobbes lived through troubling times in England, including the English civil war, which began in 1642. His experiences of these unfortunate times seemingly influenced his views on political philosophy. It's thereby fitting that Hobbes is best remembered for providing social contract theory its modern formulation.

The State of Nature

V for Vendetta begins with Lewis Prothero, the politically charged "Voice of London," providing the viewer his rousing account of world events, including the demise of the *former* United States.[2] Prothero's commentary leads one to wonder what it might be like to live in a world without *any* established governments. The classic tale *Lord of the Flies* (1990 film version) provides another opportunity to imagine life without government. Philosophers of the Enlightenment were preoccupied with the idea of pregovernment existence, hypothetical or not. They called it the "state of nature."

Hobbes's depiction of the state of nature is particularly striking. He believes that, lacking a strong government to deter our inherently egoistic impulses, the state of nature would be a constant struggle. Fueling our adversarial interactions are the facts that resources are limited and that we combatants are more or less equal in ability regarding the "faculties of body and mind." This doesn't mean that individuals don't have particular talents or strengths. In terms of the characters from *Lord of the Flies*, for instance, Roger is the strongest, Jack the most cunning, Ralph the most diplomatic, and Piggy the most intelligent. But Hobbes believes that these differences tend to balance out in ways such that no one is obviously superior to another. Although Piggy is overweight and asthmatic, he still has the potential to kill Roger either by himself (perhaps as Roger sleeps) or in allegiance with Ralph and the twins Samneric. Although Piggy is clearly the most intellectually gifted of the cadets, Jack is certainly able to successfully plot Piggy's demise (as he probably did in the story, with Roger's help).

Such parity creates the genuine hope of subduing our competitors, which further embroils us in our struggle to gain the upper hand. But any advantage one person may achieve in the state of nature ultimately makes him (or her) a target. Others will soon conspire against the one holding advantage (as was the case with Piggy

> "You're not going to get away with this." "Oh yeah, what are you going to do about it!?" — *Lord of the Flies*, scene 14

regarding his eye glasses).[3] Thus retaliation and re-retaliation is a never ending cycle that breeds fear, contempt, revenge, mistrust, and more fear. Hobbes seems correct that, in these conditions, "the life of man is solitary, poor, nasty, brutish, and short." Clearly, living in Hobbes's state of nature is to be avoided at all costs.

V for Vendetta paints a bleak picture of the near fictive future. War, terrorism, and general chaos surround England, apparently triggered by American foreign policy. Britain was not completely immune to terrorist attacks. A subway station (tube station) was bombed, killing innocent people. The death toll spiked dramatically when St. Mary's grammar school, the Three Waters water treatment facility, and a (different) tube station were

---

BOX 9C: LEARNING OUTCOMES

Upon carefully studying this chapter, students should better comprehend and be able to explain:

- What philosophers mean by a state of nature and the important role this idea plays in social, political, and moral philosophy.
- Social contract theory via Hobbes and Locke and the role it plays in justifying governmental authority.
- The ethically significant differences between Hobbes and Locke, and how the later attempts to defend the possession of natural, human rights.
- How the ideas of John Rawls compare and contrast to earlier social contract theorists such as Hobbes and Locke.
- How *V for Vendetta*, *Lord of the Flies*, and *Serenity*, respectively and jointly, convey important messages about society, rights, and justice.

simultaneous targets of biological terrorism. The unleashed virus caused eighty thousand deaths. England took appropriate action, all for the sake of not devolving into a Hobbesian state of nature. Prothero might say that England "did what it had to do," and thereby, in his mind, avoided divine judgment and wrath (unlike the United States). Britain closed the subways, and took the further measures of expelling foreigners and subduing political activists. It evacuated its Muslim constituency (and presumably other marginalized faiths). It began quarantining "social undesirables," including homosexuals and those suffering from various diseases. Britain sealed off its borders and approached homogeneity in the hopes of protecting itself from the rest of the world. As a result, British society remained stable. As Prothero might say, "Good guys win, bad guys lose, and England prevails."

Hobbes's Two Laws of Nature

It's not entirely clear whether Hobbes believed that the state of nature was merely a hypothetical construct. Nevertheless, he believed that those existing in it, not being subject to any governmental influence, soon come to realize that forming contracts (compacts, covenants) with one another is the key to well-being. The crucial first step is to seek out others who also desire peace, safety, and prosperity. Among the cadets, Piggy and Ralph most clearly understood this, which begins to explain the strong alliance between Piggy and Ralph. Making the sort of first step Piggy and Ralph did represent Hobbes's self-proclaimed first law of nature. To secure our best interests, we must seek peace. Hobbes believed that rational people should—and inexorably will—come together for everyone's mutual benefit. Piggy attempted to explain this benefit to Jack and his gang: "We might have to live here a long time, maybe the rest of our lives. We can't go on acting like kids. We need to be sensible and make things work." Although Piggy was not successful (to say the least), Hobbes maintains that the group of peace seekers will eventually embody his second law of nature by forming contracts with one another. The contracts that we form should be such that individuals agree to refrain from certain (especially hostile or threatening) behaviors so long as others also agree to avoid such behaviors. The contract is in effect a promise not to harm others on the condition that others promise not to harm you. Entering into such agreements is the second necessary step in avoiding the state of nature.[4]

Even granting Hobbes's assumption that rational people will eventually enter into contracts vowing to limit hostile behavior, he nevertheless believes that we will continue to act from self-interested motives. Hobbes thus thought that we would never pass up a chance to violate our contracts, so long as we benefited (more) from doing so and we were reasonably sure that our violation would go undetected. Hobbes in effect held that the contract entered into *all by itself* was nothing but empty words. Recall that Jack's gang and Ralph's gang agreed to segregate, but détente didn't last long. Jack's gang wanted Piggy's glasses for the technological (fire-making) advantage they represented and they simply took them one night during a raiding party. The problem, it seems, was that nothing forced Jack's compliance. According to Hobbes, for any contract to be operatively binding, it had to include allegiance to a governing body Hobbes called a "sovereign." Hobbes believed that allegiance to a politically powerful sovereign was necessary for stability, which, in turn, is necessary for justice. The sovereign, as the political head of state, is to deter any and all instances of injustice, which is to say contractual violations. His successfully doing so will ensure the state's stability and integrity; the alternative is to return to the state of nature. But because leaving the state of nature was the goal of entering into the contract in the first place, the sovereign must be allowed any means necessary to keep contracts intact.[5] Because we cannot trust ourselves to keep our agreements, we must transfer our will to the

> "That's what governments are for, to get in a man's way," — *Firefly*, episode "Serenity"

sovereign. He now speaks for us. According to Hobbes, affirming allegiance to a sovereign was the only way for Ralph and especially the vulnerable Piggy to establish the peace they sought, and what is true of Ralph and Piggy applies generally: each of us must exchange freedom for security. Once delivered from ourselves, only then can we enjoy the benefits of security and peace of mind of living in a stable society.

The Hobbesian Sovereign

It certainly seems that the chaos suffered on the island in *Lord of the Flies* was due (at least in part) to the lack of a politically strong leader—a Hobbesian sovereign. The conch shell agreements the boys made lacked a sufficiently powerful person to deter violators; all Ralph could initially think of was doling out meaningless demerits. Jack repeatedly exploited this situation, often targeting the physically vulnerable and socially awkward Piggy.

In many ways, the boys on the island (and especially Piggy) could have benefited by the presence of someone like *V for Vendetta*'s Adam Sutler. He began his political career as England's undersecretary of defense, making it his job to protect British citizens. He also became a stalwart of the ultraconservative Norsefire party. The British people, fearful of the consequences of America's war and the threat of further biological attacks, sought security and peace of mind and thus someone with the resolve to provide it. That year, Sutler was the Norsefire candidate for prime minister. The staple of his platform was the newly penned Articles of Allegiance. Electing him and pledging to these articles were the sole tickets to quashing further threats to British soil. He won in a landslide victory. Soon after, a cure for the St. Mary's virus was developed in British laboratories. Many British citizens saw this as a sign from God. The Almighty had confirmed their decision to elect Sutler, and he was thus duly anointed Britain's savior. A new political office was created for him: high chancellor. His new office provided him with limitless political power.

Upon being appointed high chancellor, Sutler expeditiously wielded his new extensive powers. He established a citywide curfew in London for minors and adults. He erected security cameras throughout the city. These facilitate near complete video surveillance of London and presumably all of Britain. This technology was soon upgraded to include retinal scanning for immediate identification of anyone deemed suspicious. Similar audio surveillance was established by tapping phone lines and implementing constant radio sweeps of the city. Such monitoring technology soon included the "Interlink" and personal e-mail exchanges. Sutler can thus eavesdrop on any audible or electronic conversation in the country. Furthermore, Sutler created a special, covert police force—the Fingermen. They are charged with controlling the more insidious threats to England's future. Sutler also took control of media outlets, most notably the British Television Network (BTN). He authorizes what is broadcasted to the public. In fact, the BTN seems to be the only remaining broadcasting station in the country. It is clearly the only station that may carry emergency broadcasts. These interrupt whatever program viewers are currently watching.

V for Vendetta, Warner Brothers Pictures, 2006. Adam Sutler (John Hurt, center) rises to political power as the leader of the ultra-conservative Norsefire party. (Moviegoods, Inc.)

(If citizens are not watching the "telly," the audio of the emergency broadcast is provided via the public loudspeaker system.) Of course, all of these new machinations were deemed necessary for national security. They were the price of security and peace of mind in a chaotic, terrorism-infected world.

Hobbes wouldn't object to Sutler's political station. Making Sutler high chancellor solidified Britain's new political turn and ensured that everyone would abide by the new articles. Britain's goal was reestablishing stability and peace of mind, thereby avoiding a return to the state of nature (and Piggy's fate). With constant and extensive surveillance by the government, the likelihood of someone breaking a contract undetected is nil. By reducing the modes of public transportation and the hours at which people may travel freely, governmental surveillance is that much more effective. With a sovereign inclined to zealotry and mercilessness, punishments for noncompliance are swift and harsh. Thus the common good is tightly secured. Whether this approaches tyranny wouldn't bother Hobbes. He believed that nothing else would suffice. Tyranny is better than anarchy, he believed, and without a Hobbesian sovereign securely in place, anarchy is exactly what we face.

Hobbes thus holds that any definitive sense of moral permissibility or impermissibility comes into existence only when his two laws of nature are enacted and presided over by a powerful sovereign. This is to understand Hobbes as giving us a rudimentary ethical theory grounded exclusively in his brand of social contract theory. John Locke offers us an important alternative to Hobbes's version of social contract theory. The most telling difference lies with natural rights and justice.

John Locke (and *Vendetta*'s Valerie) on Natural Rights

BTN employee Evey Hammond is apprehended and interrogated due to her involvement with the terrorist V. A prisoner seemingly in an adjoining cell clandestinely contacts Evey with a letter written on toilet paper. The author's name is Valerie, and the letter is her autobiography. Valerie fears that she may die in this awful place and hopes that Evey does not. Evey learns that young Valerie was unlike most other girls. Rather than chasing boys, she was more fascinated with girls. As a young adult, she "came out" to her parents. They disowned her. Valerie recounts, "But I only told the truth. Was that so selfish? Our integrity sells for so little, but it is all we really have. It is the very last inch of us. But within that inch, we are free." Valerie soon starred in *The Salt Flats*. She shares with Evey that "it was the most important role of my life, not because of my career, but because that is how I met Ruth. The first time we kissed, I knew that I never wanted to kiss any other lips but hers again." The two lovers moved to a small flat in London together. Ruth grew Scarlet Carsons for Valerie in their window box, and thus their apartment always smelled of roses. Those were the best years of her life.

But Valerie's makeshift autobiography becomes foreboding as she recounts how America's war came to London. She wistfully reports, "After that, there were no roses anymore, not for anyone." She never quite understood why the British government and its new Articles of Allegiance hated people like her so much. Valerie shares with Evey how the Fingermen abducted her and Ruth, and hauled them away to a detention facility. Valerie admits that it is strange her life should end in this terrible place, but "for three years, she had roses and apologized to no one." She accepts that she will die here; every inch of her shall perish— every inch but one. This inch is "small and fragile, and it is the only thing in the world worth having. We must never lose it or give it away, and we must never let them take it away from us."

> "Take my love, take my land . . . I don't care 'cause I'm still free; you can't take the sky from me." —*Firefly* theme song

Evey never knew Valerie apart from the words on the tissue paper. They never met. John Locke never knew or met Valerie either (obviously), but the fictional character and the historical philosopher agree on one thing: the value and importance of humanity. The fact of human existence is so important that each of us possesses natural or basic moral rights merely in virtue of being human. Locke writes:

> The state of Nature has a law of Nature to govern it, which obliges everyone, and reason, which is that law, teaches all mankind who will but consult it, that being all equal and independent, no one ought to harm another in his life, health, liberty or possessions. . . . Everyone as he is bound to preserve himself, and not quit his station wilfully, so by the like reason, when his own preservation comes not into competition, ought he as much as he can to preserve the rest of mankind, and not unless it be to do justice on an offender, take away or impair the life, or what tends to be the preservation of life, the liberty, health, limb, or goods of another.[6]

So, Locke believes in (normative) laws of nature, but, unlike Hobbes, holds that they are binding in the state of nature, that is, prior to any established government. The operative moral law here is something like "Mankind ought to be preserved and co-exist in peaceful interactions with one another" (ch. 2, sec. 7). This law is grounded partly in our rationality—our unique ability to recognize the dictates of the moral law and recognize why it's important to do so. It is also grounded in our equality (ch. 2, sec. 4). Because we are naturally rational and (roughly) equal in status and ability, each of us is bound by the moral obligation not to impinge on the life and liberty of another.

Because of our ability to understand the moral law, we grasp the supreme significance of respecting our equality and independence. We are thus bound not to harm another person's life, liberty, or possessions because by choosing to harm others in this way, we fail to act in accordance with what is supremely valuable in life. This moral obligation grounds our basic human rights. Possessing a moral right is a justified claim against others to respect some moral obligation. We can thus justifiably demand, as is our (natural) right, that others respect our equality and independence. In fact, our ability to articulate this idea further grounds our unique status as (natural) moral rights possessors. For Valerie, what grounds our uniqueness is our integrity as individuals. Our integrity is our very humanness; it underlies who we are and the projects we undergo. It is supremely valuable. This is why she believes that it is the only thing truly worth having and the only thing that we should never give away. To give it away is to give up being the independent human person each of us is; this would fail to respect our equal status with others. For others to take it from us is for them to fail to respect our equality. Thus, each of us has a right to have our integrity—our humanness—respected. Locke (more or less) calls it being created as rational with the capability to grasp the natural (moral) law; Valerie calls it integrity. However, these terms are merely different ways to articulate the same idea.

Insofar as Locke holds that we ought not to harm another in terms of his or her life, health, limb, liberty, or possessions, it seems he also holds that we ought not to (unjustifiably) impinge on another's happiness. Thus you have a basic right not to have your happiness infringed upon. Valerie clearly had her happiness infringed upon. She was living quietly with Ruth in a loving, consensual, adult relationship. She and her projects posed no real threat to others. But the newly elected Norsefire political regime imposed its agenda on Valerie, Ruth, and others who were deemed "different" and thus dangerous. Under the blanket of national security, people like Valerie were taken to detention facilities and used as research for advancing England's biological weapons program (of course without consent), which led to many tragic deaths, including Valerie's. Sutler and his new Articles of Allegiance indeed unjustifiably infringed on the happiness of many, if not all, of England's citizenry. The extensive and constant surveillance, the strict curfews for mature adults, the restriction of public transportation, the blacklisting of arts and literature (including statues of the Buddha and copies of the Qur'an) all work to objectionably curtail the happiness of British citizens. But, for Locke, our happiness is merely a matter of not having our basic human rights unnecessarily infringed upon. Thus, Locke (as does Valerie) would conclude that the nature of the social contract after Sutler violates basic human rights. As we will soon see, this is reason to doubt the genuineness of Sutler's political authority in England.[7]

The so-called terrorist V also finds Sutler's authority dubious. But V's motives are two-pronged. With almost classic flair, he exacts his revenge against those who harmed him. This helps to explain the title of the film (and graphic novel). But once vengeance is satisfied, V places a single Scarlet Carson on each of his casualities. Each of his "victims" was directly responsible for the atrocities performed on Valerie and other "social undesirables" (like V himself, as we later learn, which begins to explain his resolve). The Scarlet Carsons thus embody something greater than merely V's vendetta. They symbolize happiness. As it was taken from Britain, V takes the life of those responsible. The rose is thus a symbol of what is lost. This is why Valerie claims that once Sutler came to power, there were no roses for anyone. And this is why V makes his vendetta public. He works to demonstrate the inherent tyranny of the Sutler regime.

> "Symbols are given power by people; alone a symbol is meaningless, but with enough people, blowing up a building can change the world." —*V for Vendetta*, scene 8

Sutler as Lockean Tyrant

Locke thus differs with Hobbes about the necessity of subjecting ourselves to tyranny in order to preserve our best interests. He believes that Hobbes, by stressing examples similar to Piggy, offers us a false dilemma: either subject ourselves to complete tyranny or suffer the ordeals of chaos and anarchy in the state of nature.[8] It is not necessary for us to fear our government; there is a third alternative, one that still preserves safety and stability. Furthermore, Locke denies that the state of nature would be an unbearable constant struggle of everyone against everyone. He believes that persons are basically decent and that we regularly will consult the moral law and respect each other's basic rights. But Locke isn't naive. He realizes that a few people in the state of nature, like Jack, will invariably choose not to uphold the moral law. Because of this, our interests are better served if we enter into a social contract with others and erect a stable government.

Locke believes that our interests are better secured by the government because of three interlocking facts about human persons and our relationship to the moral law. First, understanding the (normative) laws of nature require time, effort, and skill, but not everyone is able or willing to commit to grasping them. Second, people are often clouded by self-interest in applying the law and meting out appropriate punishments for infractions of it. Third, even if some individuals accomplish fair and impartial application of the law, not everyone will be able (for various reasons) to execute retribution. These three facts make life in the state of nature unstable and uneasy (although not nasty, brutish, and short). Thus we soon form governments in order to better protect our basic rights (ch. 9, secs. 123–27). Doing so is clearly in our best interest. We benefit by the establishment of publicized common law, the machinery to settle disputes among interested parties, the elevation of impartial judges to rule over such disputes, and the political means by which to enforce the judges' decisions.

By entering into the social contract, individuals agree not to punish infractions of the moral law themselves; we transfer that power to the state. We thereby agree to uphold the laws of the state generally. However, we are bound to this agreement on the condition that the state works to preserve our liberty and property, which is the common good (ch. 9, sec. 131). Locke interprets "property" in a broad sense. This includes all that we have a right to—our lives, health, limbs, liberty, and estates. Therefore, when the government extends its power beyond the common good, which is the joint preservation of our basic rights, and begins to infringe on our property (and thus happiness), our duty to recognize the government's authority is rendered null and void.

Cases where the government becomes tyrannical provide the best examples of how our obligation to the state is nullified. Tyranny occurs when governments, under the pretense of political authority, purposively act to violate our basic rights to life, health, limb, and liberty. As Locke puts it:

> Tyranny is the exercise of power beyond right, which nobody can have a right to; and this is making use of the power anyone has in his hands, not for the good of those who are under it, but for his own private, separate advantage. When the governor, however entitled, makes not the laws, but his will, the rule, and his commands and actions are not directed at the preservation of the properties of his people, but the satisfaction of his own ambition, revenge, covetousness, or any other irregular passion [tyranny obtains]. (ch. 18, sec. 199)

When tyranny begins, true government ends. The social contract is effectively dissolved, and the magistrate thereby (in principle) surrenders authority. Acting without authority, the magistrate ceases to be such and may be justifiably resisted, like any other transgressor of human rights.

Sutler's rule certainly seems tyrannical. It is infused with ambition for money and especially power. Sutler and the Norsefire party leaders were responsible for developing and unleashing the St. Mary's virus. These men became obscenely rich and powerful once the cure was made public. Norsefire was also responsible for the "social cleansing" that resulted in the persecution and death of further English citizens. People who are deemed "different" and thus dangerous continue to live in fear, if they live at all. Sutler spins the news and limits the flow of information pertinent to the public good. He has made various "decadent" commodities—like butter—illegal, but he continues to enjoy them. The number of blacklisted items ballooned so quickly that Sutler instituted the Ministry of Objectionable Materials, from which V relies on to furnish his Shadow Gallery. Whenever Sutler's authority is challenged, he responds with vitriol, quick to exact revenge (and not merely retribution) for any affront. When V's timetable for a second terrorist outburst draws near, Sutler charges his undersecretaries "to make everyone remember why they need us!" Because Sutler exerts political power that he is no longer entitled to, V seems justified in spurring the citizens of Britain to oppose him.

Voracious Villain . . . Virtuous Vanguard . . . Vox Populi?

One can now see how V is more of a patriot or freedom fighter than a terrorist (even if his overall character remains morally ambiguous). His attempt to spur a revolution begins with his blowing up the Old Bailey justice building. Just before the (literal) fireworks begin, V tells Evey, "It is to Madame Justice that I dedicate this concerto in honor of the holiday she seems to have taken from these parts, and in recognition of the imposter that stands in her stead." The imposter is most certainly Sutler. By making his will the law, he operates above it. Only hours after destroying the Bailey, V hacks his way into the emergency broadcasting channel to urge his fellow countrymen to join him a year from now to free themselves from Sutler's tyranny. But, of course, the citizenry must decide for themselves whether they should enact their right to rise up against the Sutler establishment.

Locke would concur with V's call for immo-bilization. Governmental authority, for Locke, is ultimately grounded in trust. Citizens entrust their government to protect their rights and thus their interests. When it violates this trust, politi-cal authority reverts back to the people and they are at liberty to dissolve the government (ch. 19, secs. 221–22). Sutler's cartel grasped for themselves an absolute power over the lives, lib-erties, and fortunes of the British people. Sutler and Norsefire operate by instilling fear, which allowed them to accomplish their greater, ultraconservative agenda at the expense of their fellow countrymen. Even someone like Piggy would no doubt agree that living in the state of nature with individuals like Jack is no worse than life under the institutional-ized terror of Norsefire; revolt is called for despite the specter of the state of nature. Locke would thus agree with V that revolution is appropriate; Sutler's administration clearly violated its trust with the citizenry. That revolution is morally called for is exactly why V believes that governments should fear their people.[9]

> "Beneath this mask there is an idea . . . and ideas are bul-letproof." —*V for Vendetta,* scene 31

The revolution that V attempted to spur was violent and explosive. But Joss Whedon's *Serenity* conveys a different kind of revolt, one more suited for the informa-tion age. Unlike Sutler's Norsefire cabal, the futuristic Alliance offers a faceless totali-tarian regime. But this doesn't make its total disregard for individual rights any less egregious. When Malcolm ("Mal") Reynolds and his motley crew of the spaceship *Serenity* discover the atrocities the Alliance perpetrated on the settlers of Miranda, and how the Alli-ance tried to cover it up, they decide to take action. Mal's words are inspirational: "Sure as I know anything . . . they will try again. . . . A year from now, ten, they'll swing back to the belief that they can make people . . . better. And I do not hold to that." Mal and his crew, at great personal risk, attempt to broadcast the Miranda file on the Cortext (interstellar Internet). Analogous to V, Mal, according to the specifics of Alliance law, becomes something of a terrorist. But unlike V, Mal does so exclusively for the common good. With the Miranda file broadcasted, the Alliance's authority is weakened, spurring dem-ocratic ideals in the 'verse.[10]

> "Shepherd Book used to tell me: If you can't do something smart, do something right." —*Serenity,* scene 14

Hobbes and Locke Reassessed

Hobbes is probably correct that a stable society is necessary for leading the good life. However, Hobbes also believed that much, if not all, of ethical discourse is *defined* by his version of social contract reasoning. This position seems difficult to defend. If Hobbes were correct that ethics simply is his version of the social contract, then anything not expressly forbidden by some state-sanctioned contract (or civil code) cannot be morally wrong. But many morally undesirable choices and character traits are not expressly forbid-den by a civil code, for example, being cruel to strangers or becoming malicious. Further-more, the possibility of unjust laws as conveyed in *V for Vendetta* and covert governmental programs in *Serenity* also speak against Hobbes's view. Therefore, Hobbes's position that all of ethics is captured by social contract reasoning seems dubious.

This sort of objection becomes more forceful once we remember that not all of our interactions with others fall under a state-sanctioned contract. Consider two prominent examples. First, because the sovereign is required to solidify all contracts but is not included in any, it follows that none of the sovereign's acts can be unjust (or morally inappropriate). However, it seems plain that there are morally better and worse ways for a sovereign to enforce contracts. Furthermore, there seem to be better and worse ways for a sovereign to conduct all of his affairs. But Hobbes must deny both of these points, which makes his position implausible. Second, Hobbes's view also entails that if you encounter someone from a different commonwealth led by a different sovereign, there is no way for either of you to treat the other unjustly (or impermissibly). But (again) it seems plain that there are morally better and worse ways for you to treat each other: all things being equal it is better to politely greet each other rather than acting cruelly or rudely. For the reasons stipulated in this paragraph and the previous one, it seems that Hobbes's implicit moral theory fails the completeness test. Unless it can be suitably revised or supplemented, its plausibility as a moral theory is substantially jeopardized.

Locke of course would object to Hobbes's view about natural rights. Locke holds that we possess them even in the state of nature, contrary to Hobbes's view that ownership can only exist once the politically empowered commonwealth is formed. So Locke would agree with Piggy's complaint to Jack that he has no right to take his eye glasses. However, Locke's view about rights and justice is not completely unproblematic. For Locke, the people (ultimately) decide upon which laws the commonwealth enact. Furthermore, the people decide when revolution, in its various forms, is appropriate. Because Locke advocates democracy, when he speaks of the people, what he apparently really means is the *majority* of the people. Locke writes: "Every man, by consenting with others to make . . . one government, puts himself under an obligation . . . to submit to the determination of the majority" (ch. 8, sec. 97). So it is the majority who decides which laws will be enacted and when, if ever, revolution is appropriate.

The problem, as movies like *Serenity* demonstrate, is that some majorities can be just as oppressive or tyrannical as any monarchy (even if not maliciously so).[11] Thus Locke's political theory is susceptible to the same objection that Locke leveled at Hobbes's position, namely, that it would allow for those within the commonwealth to be exploited. With Hobbes, it was possible that the sovereign exploit all the commonwealth's subjects. With Locke, it is possible that the majority exploit minority voices within the commonwealth. Put another way, although Locke holds that the laws enacted must be always for the good of the people, it is not entirely clear whether he means the majority of the people or each and every member of the commonwealth. Since it is the majority who ultimately decides which laws become enacted, it can be argued that Locke intends the former and overlooks that this allows for the possibility of exploiting the latter.

Earth-That-Was and the Original Position

The film *Serenity*—and its short-lived television series precursor *Firefly*—depict a futuristic but still rustic world. Whedon's characters refer to earth as the mythical Earth-That-Was because it is little more than a dream to them. In Whedon's fictive universe (the 'verse), Earth-That-Was, natural resources depleted, could no longer sustain its numbers. Its denizens sought a new solar system. Eventually, one was found; its planets and moons were terra-formed, making them suitable for human life. Reminiscent of the Old West and the ideals of Manifest Destiny, settlers eventually arrived, but only after a long journey via spaceship. So, in a very real sense, this provided denizens of Earth the opportunity to rethink the political and social arrangements. This harkens back to the ideas of John Rawls—including his "original position" and "veil of ignorance"—but especially his views about social justice and liberalism.

Imagine that the settlers had a meeting before departure to discuss what sort of social and political arrangements to enact. According to Rawls, the most effective way for them to proceed probably wouldn't be too far from the truth: with very little knowledge of what their future life in a distant solar system will be like. The settlers have no (definite) knowledge about whether they will be an owner or a worker or healthy or sick. But Rawls would (ideally) extend their ignorance even further. He argues that each settler should imagine that he or she has no knowledge of his or her personal situation, including facts about wealth, station, creed, color, or gender. Moreover, each is to assume ignorance about natural abilities like intelligence, strength, or physical constitution. Because no one, behind the "veil of ignorance" in this "original position," is able (hypothetically speaking) to make self-serving arrangements, the settlers would agree to arrangements that were fair to everyone. After all, he or she doesn't know who he or she will turn out to be; adopting arrangements that favor one group over another very well may only work to harm oneself (because you might not be a member of the preferred group).[12] Consequently, the agreed upon arrangements will exemplify fairness, securing justice for all.

According to Rawls's "justice as fairness" approach, he believes those in the original position will agree to two basic principles: first, everyone in society must have equal political rights and duties; second, the only justifiable economic inequalities are those required to make everyone in society better off. Rawls writes:

> I shall maintain that the persons in the initial situation would choose two . . . principles: the first requires equality in the assignment of basic rights and duties, while the second holds that social and economic inequalities, for example, inequalities of wealth and authority, are just only if they result in compensating benefits for everyone, and in particular the least advantaged members of society.[13]

That is, everyone is due political equality; however, justice need not entail economic equality. Although everyone should be accorded equal opportunities to improve one's station, and not be subjected to undue governmental interference, it might be that some enjoy economic benefits that others do not. However, this is not unjust, assuming that everyone benefits. The idea is that those who work harder or better or produce more should receive their economic due. But the wealth resulting from this should also provide assurances to the least advantaged, perhaps in terms of welfare programs.

Rawls's "justice as fairness" brand of social contract theory arguably provides the basis for an ethical system. Any enacted arrangement that was unfair or unjust seems morally impermissible. Furthermore, at least in principle, other moral principles might be agreed upon by rational agents behind the veil of ignorance. It seems incredibly likely that they would agree to prohibitions against murder, rape, theft, and mandates to be respectful and keep one's word, among others. Generalizing on this, it could be claimed that moral rules are derived and justified by the mutual consent of rational persons working to cooperate with one another in ways such that everyone benefits (and no one is intentionally

Firefly, Twentieth Century Fox, 2002. Former Browncoat Malcolm Reynolds (Nathan Fillion, right) is the captain of spaceship *Serenity* and, with the help of his crew, does everything he can to keep flyin'. (Moviegoods, Inc.)

discriminated against). The arrangements those behind the veil of ignorance would agree to simply are the moral rules. This is sometimes called contractarianism.

It is thus easier to see how, upon careful analysis, Joss Whedon's *Firefly* and *Serenity* represent an *illiberal* society. The Alliance, having begun between the Core planets, sought unification in the new solar system. The Core planets enjoy considerable wealth, which allowed them to put pressure on the outer rim planets to join the Alliance. Those on the Rim—the Browncoats—fought for their political independence. They lost. But after Unification, the Alliance immediately ignored the outer rim planets. Thus the wealth enjoyed by the Core planets does not benefit the least advantaged in any clear way, violating the second of Rawls's two basic principles. Because in the original position, individuals wouldn't know whether they would live on a core planet or an outer rim world, it seems incredibly unlikely that everyone would agree to an arrangement where Unification would result in loss of political autonomy and financial hardship.

Furthermore, although the Alliance is not as nefarious as the Norsefire regime, it remains totalitarian, hegemonic, and expansive. This combination causes an interesting tension for Lockean liberalism. Locke (unlike Hobbes) believed that one is always free to leave a commonwealth, presumably because one is sufficiently disillusioned with the terms of the operative social contract. All one needs to do is sell his or her property and begin a new life elsewhere, under a morally suitable social contract. By not doing this, one provides the state tacit consent to abide by the terms of the contract; one thus becomes bound to follow the laws of the land. However, in the 'verse, and as the result of Unification in light of the Alliance's politically expansive programs, there are no other operative commonwealths. Thus Browncoats like Mal and Zoe have nowhere else to go, except perhaps farther and farther out into the "black" of space. But the farther they go, the more likely they are to encounter the Reavers, symbolizing the state of nature in Whedon's science fiction world. This, of course, is to be avoided, but what viable choices do they have? Apart from the interesting issues this raises regarding interpretations of Whedon's work, it also reminds philosophers of a more classic problem regarding social contract theory: if it is not viable for an individual to leave a commonwealth, especially if he or she didn't choose to become a part of it in the first place, how should he or she proceed if his or her rights are being unnecessarily infringed upon? Thus Whedon's science fiction example raises real-world issues regarding civil disobedience, and whether leaving a commonwealth should be the first or last option for a citizen.

Because the Browncoats fought against Unification, it is difficult to see how they ever agreed to any binding contract with the Alliance in the first place. Because they have nowhere else to go, their remaining in Alliance-controlled space is no indication of tacit consent. This, perhaps, explains why Mal bought the spaceship *Serenity* after the Unification War. By continually flying, and by hiring a crew "of those that feel the need to be free" like him, he is able to form a sort of miniature commonwealth and "not be under the heel of nobody ever again." Spaceship *Serenity* itself, then, becomes a moving commonwealth comprising free and equal individuals. They may leave the ship at any time (and Inara and Book eventually do), but if they stay, they thereby agree to respect each other's rights and pursuit of happiness.[14] Of course, the Alliance doesn't recognize spaceship *Serenity* as a (mobile) sovereign nation, which is why its crew are considered brigands, thieves, and pirates. It also explains why most of the jobs they accept are illegal. However, because the Alliance doesn't (obviously) provide financial assurances for its economically disadvantaged citizens, it again seems that Mal and his crew have little choice. They may risk Alliance involvement by operating outside the law (but still under its radar, whenever possible) or kowtow to a regime that proliferates unsuitable social and political arrangements.

Finally, *Serenity* and Whedon's corpus generally suggest (at least implicitly) a problematic issue for contractarianism with respect to establishing moral principles. According to contractarianism, each rational agent behind the veil of ignorance must agree to a rule or arrangement before it becomes morally binding. But what if there is disagreement among those in the original position? Presumably, there won't be disagreement about basic moral rules, for example, prohibitions against murder, but what about more specific or complex issues like euthanasia, abortion, or the exact nature of welfare policies? Disagreement seems much more likely in such cases. It seems, assuming contractarianism, that disagreement about a rule, arrangement, or policy entails that it is morally neutral. Disagreement about abortion, for example, entails that it is neither obligatory nor impermissible. But this entailment seems to significantly dim contractarianism's prospects of providing an adequate basis for moral truth. In effect, contractarianism seems to run afoul of the completeness test for moral theories.

Rawls seemingly intended to avoid this entailment by conceptually stripping everyone behind the veil of ignorance of anything that might cause disagreement. We are more or less clones of each other. Because we are exactly similar in terms of being rational and interested in mutual cooperation, possessing no other distinguishing marks, there is nothing to disagree about. However, why think ethical truth can be properly established by the wishes of such antiseptic agents? The connection to Whedon's corpus manifests at this point; it is filled with interestingly complex and vibrant characters. They have very relatable strengths and foibles. Simply put, they seem real. Mal, Book, Inara, and Jayne almost never agree on anything, but they somehow must come to compromises and agreements. Here art mirrors life. Ethical disputes involve real persons enmeshed in complex social webs. Resolving our disputes is complicated. It is thus objected that even if Rawls is correct and disagreement wouldn't arise among the insipid in the original position, why should real-world persons be bound by their agreements? After all, those in Rawls's original position are nothing like the persons we encounter and interact with on a daily basis. Russ Shafer-Landau succinctly puts this objection via a (rhetorical) question: "Why should I live according to the rules set by some person who isn't at all like the real me?"[15]

So, the objection being developed here can be seemingly put in the novel terms of the Earth-That-Was settlers. The argument driving it assumes that persons are bound to the agreements they make, which seems to be a core tenet of social contract theory. If the settlers put themselves completely behind Rawls's veil of ignorance when contemplating social arrangements, then perhaps some morally significant principles would achieve universal assent, but it's unclear whether this hypothetical process results in binding obligations for the settlers such as they (actually) are. If the setters do not put themselves completely behind Rawls's veil of ignorance when contemplating social arrangements, then they would be obligated to follow the agreements made, but it's not at all clear whether very many morally significant principles would indeed achieve universal assent. But if very few moral principles achieve universal assent, then the settlers are bound by very few moral obligations. Either way, it's not clear whether Rawls's view provides a suitable system for deriving moral obligations. On the one hand, being committed to the agreements of another person seems to serve as a counterexample to contractarianism (and it may provide evidence of its failing the contradiction test). On the other hand, action-based moral theories that establish very few moral obligations seem unworkable due to incompleteness. Therefore, even if Rawls's version of social contract theory is preferable to other versions (most notably Hobbes's), there certainly seems to be some problematic issues yet to be suitably resolved, at least if it is to serve as a platform for a thoroughgoing contractarian approach to ethics.

9.4. TWO ADDITIONAL FILMS

Lord of the Flies (1990)

Director: Harry Hook
Screenwriter: Sara Schiff (based on the William Golding novel)

Plot Summary

> We did everything just the way grown-ups would have. Why didn't it work?

A group of military cadets—children—are marooned on a tropical island in the middle of the ocean. The boys are thirsty, hungry, and frightened. They sleep unsure of their future. One of the quieter cadets, Simon, awakes before the others and finds fresh water. He alerts his comrades and all drink heartily. The cadets next scout the island. They soon discover that they are all alone, save an ailing airplane pilot. The boys spend their first day on the island in full military dress.

A husky and spectacled cadet nicknamed "Piggy" finds a conch in the surf. He and Ralph, the ranking cadet, employ the shell to symbolize the order and stability enjoyed during military school. When the conch is blown, the cadets are to appear for "assembly." Ralph asserts, "Whoever has the conch gets to speak at assembly." He further decrees that a signal fire should be kept to ensure rescue; turns will be taken on fire watch so that the fire constantly burns.

With these new rules, some of the boys wonder about who is actually in command. One asks, "Who's the leader?" Another quickly echoes, "Jack is the oldest, but Ralph is the colonel." The boys soon arrive at a consensus that Ralph should be the leader. To this, Ralph replies, "It doesn't matter who is in charge—we just have to work together. First we build a camp." With the camp nearly complete, some of the boys are shirtless in the tropical sun. They march up a hill to light the signal fire. Ralph quickly realizes that the only way to light the fire is with Piggy's eyeglasses; however, the fire blazes out of control, scorching a nearby tree.

Days pass, and almost all the boys go shirtless and some of them go without trousers. Personal hygiene becomes an issue as some of the boys eat too much fruit. Ralph urges the boys to stay focused. One of the boys announces that someone stole his pocketknife. Another reaffirms that things are disappearing all over the place. This leads another to ask: "What are we to do with thieves when we catch them?" A little unsure of himself, Ralph announces, "We can't have kids stealing and running wild; we'll have to have stricter rules, and hand out demerits—I guess." Many of the boys laugh at this suggestion, with Jack appearing to laugh the loudest.

Some heed Ralph. Their common goal is being rescued; they must stay healthy until then. But others, influenced by Jack's pessimism, now believe that they are never going home again. The island is their new, permanent home. Jack's "group" begins to chastise the other boys, and especially those loyal to Ralph.

Jack laments that they lack "real food." He and his group intend to kill a wild boar; they sharpen sticks in preparation for "the hunt." They also begin painting each other's faces in warrior-type fashion. Soon, Jack's group spends entire days hunting. This causes lapses in the fire watch and a squandered opportunity to be spotted by a passing rescue helicopter. When confronted about this, Jack demonstrates little remorse or concern. Rather, he jubilantly announces that his group has killed its first pig. He also declares the existence of his "hunter-group" and roughly half the boys leave the original base camp with him. Over his shoulder, Jack sarcastically remarks, "When you other brats get older or get hungry enough, you can come, too."

Meanwhile, one of Jack's group discovers a cave and claims that a monster lives inside. Jack is skeptical, but he and Roger, his lieutenant, investigate. Jack and Roger hear the "monster's" growl. They run back to the "hunter's camp" and report, "Whatever it is, it's in there." Next appearing atop the fire hill, Jack informs Ralph's fire-watchers about the monster and takes some fire back to his hunters.

A hunter appears at the base camp, now "Ralph's camp," and proclaims, "Jack wants the survival knife!" Ralph refuses to give up the knife. Although the hunter leaves without the knife, two of Ralph's gang leave with him to join Jack's group. That night, Jack's group returns to base camp, this time fully camouflaged. They assault the camp, stealing the knife. Ralph protests, "What do you think you're doing? You have no right—come back here!" In the melee Piggy's eyeglasses are broken. Piggy is distraught.

Jack's hunters again charge the base camp, but this time during broad daylight. Jack announces that his gang has killed another pig and will host a feast. Ralph and his gang may attend, if they wish. Prompting his hunters, they chant: "The chief has spoken!" Jack adds mockingly, "See you tonight, girls." Two more defect to Jack's gang. Later that night, Ralph, Piggy, and three others make their way to Jack's feast.

Nearly naked, Jack's gang circles a large bonfire near the shore. The scene is primal and ghastly. All the boys have sticks sharpened at one end and many re-create the last successful hunt. Wildly, they jab their weapons into the air and at each other. After exploring the cave and discovering the "monster's" true identity, Simon rushes upon the boys around the bonfire. As Ralph and Piggy look on in horror, Jack's gang mistakes Simon for the monster and they brutally stab him to death. Jack utilizes the idea of the monster to keep his troops in line. The monster is still out there he tells them. He brutally punishes a hunter because the boy stole. Jack's methods are clear. As his gang grows in number, he must retain order. Only Ralph and Piggy are not part of Jack's group now.

Jack's gang again tramples the base camp, harassing the two dissenters. The goal this time is stealing Piggy's glasses. Jack and his gang leave successful; Piggy is now all but blind. The next morning, Ralph and Piggy visit Jack's camp. Piggy is carrying the conch. Ralph demands that Piggy's glasses be returned. Jack refuses and a fight breaks out between the two. Piggy blows the conch. All the boys freeze. Piggy proclaims: "We might have to live here a long time, maybe the rest of our lives. We can't go on acting like kids. We need to be sensible and make things work." Clearly tired of hearing Piggy's proclamations, Roger pushes a boulder off the rock ledge above Piggy. He is instantly killed. Jack is not fazed.

Dawn breaks. Fearing for his life, Ralph hides in the jungle. Jack and his gang hunt him as they would a boar. They use Piggy's glasses to burn the jungle and in the hopes of "smoking out" Ralph toward the beach. The island burns, the hunters savagely shriek, and Ralph weeps.

Discussion Questions

1. In what ways do the boys on the island embody Hobbes's "state of nature?"
2. Would people actually behave as the boys did in the story? Justify your answer.
3. Does Jack act in his own best interests by burning the island to eliminate Ralph, his only remaining competitor? If not, what is in Jack's best interests?
4. Ralph attempts (scene 6, roughly 27:30) to rectify poor behavior by suggesting that they have stricter rules with demerits. Why do the other boys laugh at him?
5. Piggy claims (scene 14, roughly 1:16:25) that they must stop acting like kids and be sensible to make things work. How might this be accomplished? What are the chances of success?

Serenity (2005)

Director and Screenwriter: Joss Whedon

Plot Summary

> So, me and mine gotta lie down and die for you and yours so you can live in your better world?

Earth-That-Was could no longer sustain its inhabitants. A new solar system was found. Its planets and moons were "terra-formed," to be as earth-like as possible. The process took decades. But soon colonists arrived. That was five hundred years ago.

The Central planets—Londoninium and Shinon, formed the Alliance under parliamentary rule. The Parliament decided that all the newly settled worlds should be under the Alliance. The "outer rim" settlements—those farthest from the Core worlds—disagreed. They organized, and calling themselves the "Browncoats," fought for their independence. Some, like Malcolm "Mal" Reynolds, volunteered to serve in the cause for independence. Others, like Zoe Washburne, were regular military. At the battle of Serenity Valley, Browncoats like Mal and Zoe bravely made their last stand. They lost.

Everyone fell under Alliance rule. The defrocked Browncoats tended to stay as far from the Alliance as they could. Mal, for one, bought a dilapidated Firefly-class transport ship. So, no matter how far Alliance control extended, he could always get a little farther away. Zoe became (that is, remained) his second-in-command. They called their ship *Serenity*. They took jobs when they could—not all of them legal.

Slowly, they acquired a crew. They hired Wash, a pilot, who later married Zoe. Kaylee left her father's farm to become the mechanic. Mal and Zoe hired Jayne away from another crew; he is a hired (gun) hand without much of a conscience. Later, Inara, a registered, guild-trained Companion agreed to rent one of the ship's shuttles. This provides *Serenity* a modicum of respectability, which also allows Mal to port in locales that he otherwise couldn't. One fateful day, they took on passengers to help cover expenses. Shepherd Book, a monk from the Southdown Abbey, wanted to walk in the world for a while and bring the Word to those who need it. (He was surprised to find Inara, and even more surprised when Mal wouldn't allow him to say grace out loud at the dinner table.) Simon and River Tam also boarded that day, even though the former kept the latter's presence a secret. He was a skilled surgeon; she was an eccentric but psychologically troubled young girl. They were siblings. They all were looking for serenity.

Life on the border planets remains difficult, not unlike the Old West on Earth-That-Was. The Alliance, despite fighting a bloody war for interplanetary control, mostly ignores citizens on the Rim. Not only are jobs hard to find, but so are health care and education. The goal is to get by as best you can without any Alliance help, not that they would offer much—even if you did ask.

Mal and Zoe are tipped off to a store of cash. The Alliance is making a payment to a local company contracted to provide security and police services on the Rim. The Alliance apparently lacks the resources or interest (or both) to provide this service to its citizens. Mal and Zoe intend to abscond with the Alliance funds (holed up in a train station vault of all places) and leave town as quickly as they arrived. But the job "goes south" when the Reavers unexpectedly descend. "Reavers" is the name given to men who "forgot how to be." They act savagely. As Zoe once shared with Simon (who wasn't initially sure that they actually existed): "If they take the ship, they'll rape us to death, eat our flesh, and sew our skin into their clothing. And if we're very, very lucky, they'll do it in that order." Not even menacing Jayne (who Simon once called "the ape-man gone wrong thing") will go anywhere near Reaver territory, even with "Vera, his very best gun." Luckily or intuitively (or both), Mal brings River along on the job, suspecting that her psychic abilities will be of use. River indeed provides the crew advanced notice of the Reavers' arrival. With some fancy flying by Wash, they narrowly escape, with Alliance funds in tow.

But the robbery and Reaver involvement made the Cortex (what they called the Internet on Earth-That-Was). This re-alerts the Alliance to Simon and River. The younger Tam, a child prodigy, was chosen for the Academy. But the school for the ultragifted was merely a front for an Alliance-sponsored covert and clandestine military intelligence program. The government, without the consent of the students or their parents, hoped to reprogram the Core's best and brightest into assassins and spies. Simon, deciphering code River ingeniously placed in her letters to home, finally managed to break her out. The Alliance, fearing what a gifted psychic may have learned while high-level governmental officials roamed the hallways, wants River back. They send in an agent known only as the Operative. This officer of the Parliament has neither name nor rank. He kills without remorse, emboldened by his conviction that the Alliance is making a better world—"all of them, better worlds."

The Operative methodically but surgically pursues spaceship *Serenity*. He holds Inara—now back at the Companion training house—hostage. The ploy works. Mal arrives; however, he successfully rescues her. The Operative becomes more aggressive. He attacks the mining colony, Haven. Because Shepherd Book now runs it (and because of its inconspicuous size and location), Mal and crew often visit. Spaceship *Serenity* arrives to find the colony decimated by Alliance forces. Children are killed. Shepherd Book lies dying. Mal holds him as he breathes his last, but not before he raspingly chides Mal to "just believe in something." Mal is devastated. Mal has lost so much at the hands of the Alliance: his way of life, his faith in God and humanity, and now the only man left he turned to for counsel.

River had recently informed the crew of a planet called Miranda. It doesn't appear on the Cortex or in any history book. Its existence seems to be part of what the Alliance fears she knows. Why is the Alliance so desperate to keep it a secret? Mal is determined to find out; however, to get there, they must go through the heart of Reaver space. For some reason, Reaver ships tend to surround the planet. Mal does the unthinkable: he turns their "home into an abomination" (as Zoe complains) by disguising it as a Reaver ship. The ruse works. The crew lands on Miranda to find all its inhabitants dead. They simply laid down and died. By retrieving an old data tape, the crew discovers that the Alliance secretly placed a chemical, G-23 Paxilon Hydrochlorate ("The Pax"), in the air processors. This was supposed to calm the population and weed out aggression so the planet could flourish. It doubly failed. In addition to killing over 90 percent of the population, it caused a small fraction to become ultraviolent and savage. Wash gasps, "Reavers. They made them!"

This knowledge consumes and transforms Mal. In a stirring speech, he requests the crew's consent to accompany him. He intends to make this information—"the secret that burned up River Tam's brain"—public. Gaining access to a proper broadcast location requires tangling with the Alliance—something Mal has constantly avoided for the last six years. The broadcasting location is well guarded. The Operative is waiting for them. Mal tells him that people must know what's on this tape. "Are you ready to die for that belief?" the Operative asks. "I surely am," Mal replies.

Discussion Questions

1. Do Mal and Zoe take the money from the train station permissibly? Explain.
2. Does Simon take River out of the Academy permissibly? Explain.
3. Is it ever permissible to break the law? If you disagree with a law or the basic principles upon which a government operates, what should you do? What should Mal and Zoe do?
4. What kind of government should have been established in the new solar system? How and when should this had been decided?

9.5. REVIEWING THROUGH THE THREE MOVIES

1. How would Hobbes evaluate Sutler (*V for Vendetta*), Jack (*Lord of the Flies*), and the Parliament (*Serenity*) as political leaders?
2. How do *V for Vendetta*, *Lord of the Flies*, and *Serenity* (respectively or jointly) express the common belief that government is necessary to secure our best interests? How would Locke evaluate their messages?
3. How is the difference between a legal and moral right expressed in the three films?
4. Compare and contrast how *V for Vendetta* and *Serenity* portray V's and Mal's respective decision to violate the law and then assess those characters on a Hobbesian, Lockean, and Rawlsian perspective (respectively).
5. Reconsider the six movie quotes from the chapter and explain whether each, given the adjacent paragraphs, *illustrates* a point the author is making, *supplements* (or extends) a point the author is making, or *contrasts* (for emphasis) a point the author is making. Explain your answers.

NOTES

1. Excerpted from Thomas Hobbes, *Leviathan* (1651). Some section headings appear in the original, but others have been provided, along with slight grammatical emendations, to aid reading comprehension.

2. Some of the discussion of Hobbes and Locke that follows has been adapted from Dean A. Kowalski, "R for Revolution: Hobbes and Locke on Social Contracts and Scarlet Carsons," in *Homer Simpson Goes to Washington*, ed. Joseph Foy (Lexington: University Press of Kentucky, 2008), 19–40.

3. The examples here are all from the immensely influential *Lord of the Flies*. But examples from Joss Whedon's *Serenity*, and its lead-in but short-lived television series *Firefly*, would serve equally well. Malcolm Reynolds, former army sergeant and now captain of the Firefly-class spaceship *Serenity*, was the most cunning and charismatic, Jayne the strongest, Saffron the most ruthless, Zoe the best at arms combat, Inara the most refined and educated, and Shepherd Book the most resourceful. Despite these interesting individual differences, Hobbes would nevertheless argue that each is roughly equivalent in "the faculties of body and mind" with respect to gaining advantage over the other. Any remaining differences of ability could be compensated for by making alliances between the characters, as was the case with Mal's crew coming together to subdue Saffron in the episodes "Our Mrs. Reynolds" and "Trash."

4. Hobbes's two laws of nature interestingly trade on an ambiguity between descriptive and normative states of affairs. Typically, laws of nature are merely descriptive. But Hobbes's two laws

of nature seemingly include both descriptive and normative elements. The reason for this is that he was describing the behavior of *rational* animals. Acting on his two "laws," Hobbes believes, is actually in our best interest and because we are rational creatures, we will eventually abide by them to the best of our abilities.

5. Hobbes holds that the sovereign's political power is nearly limitless. The sovereign did not have the authority to act in (irrational) ways that undermined his power. What sorts of acts Hobbes had in mind wasn't always clear, but presumably a sovereign cannot rule the commonwealth if he commits suicide. Thus, the sovereign did not have the authority to take his own life (even if he might have the authority to ask for yours).

6. John Locke, *The Second Treatise of Government* (New York: Barnes & Noble, 2004), chap. 2, sec. 6. The first and third segments of section 6 are excerpted here. In the middle section, Locke buttresses his account of basic human rights and moral obligations with an argument grounded in God's role in creating us. The extent to which Locke's moral and political views require religious grounding is controversial. Some scholars believe that Locke offers two distinct defenses of human rights and moral obligation making his arguments "overdetermined." Others believe that Locke's theistic and more naturalistic arguments can be integrated to offer one, unified theory to ground his ethical and political views. In any event, future references to Locke's *Second Treatise* shall be cited in text parenthetically by chapter and section.

7. A similar story applies to River Tam from *Firefly* and *Serenity*. River was a child prodigy. As her brother Simon once said, "She wasn't just gifted, she was a gift." Her wealthy parents sent River, at her request, to a new governmentally sponsored school for gifted children called the Academy. But the Alliance and its governing body, the Parliament—a totalitarian regime in its own right—trampled on River's rights by performing unauthorized medical experiments on her in the hope of enhancing her psychic abilities. The Alliance, against her will, had hoped to turn her into a spy or assassin. These procedures caused River a tremendous amount of psychological harm.

8. To be fair, the kind of anarchy that Hobbes and Locke (more or less) intend is different from what can be called philosophical anarchy. For this latter view, see Robert Paul Wolff, *In Defense of Anarchism* (New York: Harper and Row, 1970).

9. Put another way, the people are the true shareholders in the corporation of society. Like any other corporation, the shareholders empower its executives conditionally. If the executives do not run the company with the best interests of the shareholders in mind, the shareholders retain the right to remove them. Therefore, regardless of what we might think about a man who painstakingly and surgically exacts cold-blooded revenge—and by his own admission it consumed him for twenty years—he is on firm Lockean grounds for rousing the British people to revolt against the tyranny of the Sutler regime.

10. For more on how *Firefly* and *Serenity* connect with classic social contract theory, see Joseph J. Foy, "The State of Nature and Social Contracts on Spaceship *Serenity*," in *The Philosophy of Joss Whedon*, eds. Dean A. Kowalski and S. Evan Kreider (Lexington: University Press of Kentucky, 2011), 39–54. I am indebted to Professor Foy for many stimulating and informative discussions about Joss Whedon; Foy's ideas of how the spaceship *Serenity* embodies Lockean ideals have influenced my own.

11. For more on this, see Foy, "Social Contracts on Spaceship *Serenity*."

12. See John Rawls, *A Theory of Justice* (Cambridge, MA: Harvard University Press, 1971), 11–13.

13. Rawls, *Theory of Justice*, 14–15.

14. I am again indebted to Joe Foy for this interpretation of spaceship *Serenity*, and the television show *Firefly* and motion picture *Serenity* generally.

15. Russ Shafer-Landau, *The Fundamentals of Ethics* (New York: Oxford University Press, 2010), 197.

PART III

HOW OUGHT I TO BE?

CHAPTER 10

Aristotle and Virtue Ethics

....

GROUNDHOG DAY (1993)
Director: Harold Ramis
Screenwriter: Danny Rubin

....

PLOT SUMMARY

I think you're the kindest . . . person I've ever met in my life. I've never met a person who is nicer than you are. I don't deserve someone like you.

P hil Connors is a TV weatherman for WPBH 8, Pittsburgh. He is also pretentious, abrasive, impatient, vain, condescending, and egocentric. He again attempts to skirt his annual duties of covering Groundhog Day in Punxsutawney. He reluctantly acquiesces only after discovering that Rita, with whom Phil is smitten, is producing this year's remote segment. Rita seems to be the antithesis of Phil; she is kind, caring, genuine, and thoughtful. Maybe a few days in bucolic Pennsylvania is just what Phil needs to finally win Rita over.

On the morning of February 2, Phil awakes at 6:00 a.m. to a clock radio; two radio DJs are bantering about the day's activities. Before leaving the Punxsutawney bed and breakfast, Phil rudely greets two people and briskly heads for the town square, where Rita and Larry, the cameraman, are waiting for him. On his way, he meets Ned Ryerson—a high school classmate. Although Ned briefly dated Phil's sister, Phil has no recollection of him. Obviously annoyed, Phil briskly takes his leave of Ned.

"So, did you sleep all right without me—you tossed and turned, didn't you?" Phil asks Rita upon finding his colleagues in the town square. Upon the prediction of six more weeks of winter, Phil sarcastically reports into the camera, "This is one time where television really fails to capture the true excitement of a large squirrel predicting the weather; I, for one, am very grateful for being here." Rita requests another take without the sarcasm; Phil hurries toward the truck and Pittsburgh. But they don't get very far. The blizzard that

269

Phil predicted would miss Punxsutawney arrives in full force. The roads are closed. The telephone lines are down. Phil has no access to the outside—"real"—world until tomorrow. Much to his chagrin, he is forced to spend another night in Punxsutawney. As Rita is not at all charmed by him, Phil believes this is a fate worse than death.

He awakes the next morning again at 6:00 a.m. and again to a clock radio. Coincidentally the same song, "I Got You Babe," rouses him. Incredibly, the DJs again banter about the Groundhog Day's activities—verbatim. Phil, from the bathroom mutters, "Nice goin' boys—you're playing yesterday's tape." He looks out his window only to find people scurrying toward the town square as if it were Groundhog Day all over again! Phil is greeted by the same portly man he insulted yesterday. The man asks, "Good morning—off to see the groundhog?" Phil replies, "Don't mess with me pork chop—what day is this?!" Phil descends to the lobby only to find everyone there (again) preparing for the Groundhog Festival outside. He stops one of the passersby and hesitantly asks, "Where is everybody going?" She answers, "To the town square—it's Groundhog Day!" Phil retorts: "It's still just once a year, isn't it?!"

Phil's dismay continues as he (again) meets Ned Ryerson. But this time, of course, Phil remembers Ned (after all, Phil just met him "yesterday"). This time Phil runs from his classmate to confer with Rita about the strange goings-on. But Rita, along with everyone else is unaware and the ceremony continues, exactly as Phil had remembered it. Later, Phil finds himself (again) speaking with the operator about outside phone lines. He is (again) informed that none are available until tomorrow. He retorts, "What if there is no tomorrow? There wasn't one today." Before he retires, he breaks a pencil and places it on the nightstand. When he finds the pencil unbroken in the morning, he confides in Rita, but she cannot believe his story.

Phil soon sees his predicament as license to do whatever he wants. He punches Ned. He practices gluttony and takes up smoking. Rita asks, "Aren't you worried about high cholesterol, love handles, or lung cancer?" He replies, "I don't worry about anything." Phil resets his sights on Rita. He spends the day with her on a fact-finding mission about her likes and dislikes, and most importantly what she is looking for in a man. Rita shares that her "perfect man" is too humble to know he's perfect; nevertheless, he is also intelligent, funny, romantic, courageous, kind, sensitive, gentle, likes animals and children, plays an instrument, and loves his mother. Phil meets Rita for a drink to learn more about her. After a few "days" Phil begins to exhibit all the traits Rita is looking for in a man. But she seems to see past Phil's exterior; at least a "week" passes and Phil remains unsuccessful with Rita.

Depression sets in. But after a while, Phil's depression turns to resignation. He seemingly accepts his fate of repeating the same day over and over. Rita notices the change. Phil finally convinces her of his predicament. She tells him, "Well, sometimes, I wish I had a thousand lifetimes. I don't know Phil; maybe it's not a curse. It depends upon how you look at it." They spend the day together talking, sharing, and learning about each other with no ulterior motives. Phil again wakes up at 6:00 a.m., but this time jumps out of bed impatient for the day to begin.

Phil now warmly greets everyone he meets. He ice sculpts and has taken up the piano. Phil meets Ned again and showers him with affection, so much that Ned hurries away, embarrassed and confused. Phil finds a homeless man, calls him "father," and provides him shelter and a hot meal. But the elderly man is quite sick; he dies before daybreak even though Phil has taken him to the hospital. Phil is visibly shaken and upset—he refuses to accept the old man's death. We immediately see Phil sitting with the old man at the

---

BOX 10A: INSIDE *GROUNDHOG DAY*

You might be able glean enough about Aristotle and virtue ethics from reading the plot summary carefully (reminding yourself of how rotten of a character Phil is at the beginning of the movie) and start watching the film at scene 22, which begins at 1:06:03 with a shot of Rita and Phil at the café. If you're really pressed for time, start watching at scene 23, which begins at 1:15:20 with a shot of Phil walking toward the homeless man. Either way, watch until the end of the film (1:38:15). If you do view the whole film, you should be able to answer the trivia questions from box 10B.

Watching the entire film provides a deeper appreciation for Phil's character transformation. The first important segment is scene 11; it conveys Phil's confusion and initial reaction to being trapped in Punxsutawney. This scene begins at 28:25 with a shot of an X-ray and ends at 34:28 with Phil being thrown in jail. The second segment consists of scenes 18–21; it conveys the depths of Phil's depression. Scene 18 begins at 44:14 with Phil approaching the café; scene 21 ends at 1:06:02 with a coroner placing a sheet over Phil's body. The third segment is scene 22; it conveys the start of Phil's transformation. Scene 22 (recall) begins at 1:06:03 and ends at 1:15:19 with Phil waking up after his day with Rita. The fourth segment is scene 30; it begins at 1:29:57 with a shot of a band and ends at 1:32:42 with Rita and Phil meeting Ned Ryerson. Compare and contrast Phil's interaction with Ned in this scene with earlier encounters. This scene also signals the culmination of Phil's transformation, symbolized by the bachelor auction.

---

diner—it must be the next "day." Phil's "father" is now clean-shaven and bathed; he is wearing a new winter coat, presumably bought by Phil. Nevertheless, Phil is soon giving the man CPR in an alleyway; Phil is urging him to breathe, beating on the man's chest. Phil looks toward the heavens in bewilderment.

Phil undertakes other altruistic acts. Walking down the sidewalk, he checks his watch and then quickens his pace to an all-out sprint. He stretches out his arms to catch a boy who is falling out of a tree. As the boy scurries away, Phil cries out, "What do you say? What do you say? You have never thanked me; I'll see you tomorrow—maybe!" Clearly Phil has rescued the boy before. Breathing heavily and discovering a pulled muscle in his back, Phil returns to town. Phil changes a tire for three elderly ladies—they don't even have time to exit the car. Phil strolls into a restaurant, just in time to free a piece of food from a choking man's windpipe.

During the evening of February 2, everyone attends the Groundhog Day's dance. Many people thank Phil and greet him eagerly. Rita is confused; she asks Phil how all of these people know him. The music stops and a bachelor's auction begins. Phil is ushered up first. Competitive bidding ensues; however, Rita trumps all bids by donating the entire content of her checking account. Leaving the dance, Phil and Rita run into Ned. Ned is also happy to see Phil and is very grateful for his generosity. Phil introduces Ned to Rita by informing her that Ned is his new insurance agent. After Phil has purchased more insurance than he will probably ever need, Ned tells Rita, "This is the best day of my life." Both Phil and Rita reply, "Mine, too." Under the winter's night sky, Phil shares with Rita, "No matter what happens tomorrow or the rest of my life, I'm happy now because I love you." "I think I'm happy, too," she replies as they gently kiss and walk off.

BOX 10B: *GROUNDHOG DAY* TRIVIA

If your instructor assigns the film to be watched outside of class, you should be able to answer the following questions:

1. At the beginning of the movie, Phil predicts that the oncoming blizzard will miss Pittsburgh, but hit where?
2. What is the name of the menswear store in the background as Phil meets Ned on the street?
3. Who is the author of the poem Rita quotes to Phil in the café?
4. What movie does Phil, a.k.a. "Bronco," see with his date the French maid?
5. What is Rita's favorite drink?
6. What is Rita's favorite ice cream?
7. What TV game show does Phil watch with a group of elderly people?
8. What is Phil's first (failed) attempt at committing suicide?
9. How much does Rita bid for an evening with Phil at the bachelor auction?
10. What is Phil's last line of the movie?

It's morning . . . 6 o'clock—again. Sonny and Cher—again. Phil awakes, but it's a new day. Rita is there; she awakes next to Phil. He is as giddy as a young boy on Christmas morning. Phil nuzzles Rita lovingly and quietly asks, "Is there anything I can do for *you* today?"

10.1. THINKING THROUGH THE MOVIE

Discussion Starter Questions

1. What was the worst thing Phil did in the movie? What was the best?
2. Phil develops various talents over the course of the movie. Which talents would you like to develop? Why?
3. Consider the best person, morally speaking, that you know. How would you describe him or her? Do any of the characters in *Groundhog Day* compare to this person?
4. How, if at all, are Phil's interactions with Rita significant to his character transformation?
5. Why does Phil become appealing to Rita only by movie's end?

Questions for Further Thought

1. At the bowling alley, Phil tells us (scene 11, roughly 30 minutes into the film), about a day he spent in the Virgin Islands with a beautiful woman, reminiscing, "*That* was a pretty good day." He then asks, "Why couldn't I live *that* day over and over?" Why does Phil pick that day? What day would you pick? What might this say about Phil (or you) as a person?
2. Phil asks Rita (scene 18, 44 minutes in), "What is your perfect guy?" Rita answers, providing a lengthy list of psychological and physical traits (see plot summary). In

what sense does Rita's description represent the "perfect man?" Is the idea of a "perfect person" completely subjective (or culturally relative)? If not, why not?

3. We see Phil running down a sidewalk so as to catch a young boy about to fall out of a tree (scene 27, 83 minutes in). If the boy never thanks Phil and if Phil must go out of his way to catch the boy, why does Phil continually catch the boy (each "day")?

4. Note Phil's interactions with Ned Ryerson and classify them as morally appropriate or inappropriate taking care to justify or explain your answers.

5. Philosophers often distinguish between pleasure and happiness (or between that which makes us feel happy and *true* happiness). What might account for this distinction? How is it portrayed in the movie?

10.2. HISTORICAL SETTING

Nicomachean Ethics (excerpt)[1]

Aristotle (384–323 BCE) was Plato's famed pupil and rivals his teacher as one of the greatest thinkers who has ever lived. Aristotle offered significant contributions in many disciplines, including (among others) logic, physics, psychology, biology, and aesthetics. He is also noteworthy for having tutored the young Alexander the Great.

Preparing to Read

A. How would Aristotle interpret Phil Connor's evolving interactions with the insurance salesman Ned Ryerson throughout the film?

B. How would Aristotle explain Phil's character transformation and Rita's role in it?

[Aristotle's Conception of Happiness]

We think happiness the most desirable of all things, and that not merely as one good thing among others. If it were only that, the addition of the smallest more good would increase its desirableness; for the addition would make an increase of goods, and the greater of two goods is always the more desirable. Happiness is something final and self-sufficient and the end of all action.

Perhaps, however, it seems commonplace to say that happiness is the supreme good; what is wanted is to define its nature a little more clearly. The best way of arriving at such a definition will probably be to ascertain the function of man. For, as with a flute player, a sculptor, or any artist, or in fact anybody who has a special function or activity, his goodness and excellence seem to lie in his function, so it would seem to be with man, if indeed he has a special function. Can it be said that, while a carpenter and a cobbler have special functions and activities, man, unlike them, is naturally functionless? Or, as the eye, the hand, the foot, and similarly each part of the body has a special function, so may man be regarded as having a special function apart from all these? What, then, can this function be? It is not life; for life is apparently something that man shares with plants; and we are looking for something peculiar to him. We must exclude therefore the life of nutrition and growth. There is next what may be called the life of sensation. But this too, apparently, is shared by man with horses, cattle, and all other animals. There remains what I may call the active life of the rational part of man's being. Now this rational part is twofold; one part is rational in the sense of being obedient to reason, and the other in the sense of possessing and exercising reason and intelligence. The active life too may be conceived of in two ways, either as a state of character, or as an activity; but we mean by it the life of activity, as this seems to be the truer form of the conception.

The function of man then is activity of soul [psyche] in accordance with reason, or not apart from reason. Now, the function of a man of a certain kind, and of a man who is good of that kind, for example, of a harpist and a good harpist are in our view the same in kind. This is true of all people of all kinds without exception, the superior excellence being only an addition to the function; for it is the function of a harpist to play the harp, and of a good harpist to play the harp well. This being so, if we define the function of man as a kind of life, and this life as an activity of the soul or a course of action in accordance with reason, and if the function of a good man is such activity of a good and noble kind, and if everything is well done when it is done in accordance with its proper excellence, it follows that the good of man is activity of soul in accordance with virtue, or, if there are more virtues than one, in accordance with the best and most complete virtue. But we must add the words "in a complete life." For as one swallow or one day does not make a spring, so one day or a short time does not make a man blessed or happy. . . .

Inasmuch as happiness is an activity of soul in accordance with perfect virtue, we must now consider virtue, as this will perhaps be the best way of studying happiness. . . . Clearly it is human virtue we have to consider; for the good of which we are in search is, as we said, human good, and the happiness, human happiness. By human virtue or excellence we mean not that of the body, but that of the soul, and by happiness we mean an activity of the soul. . . .

[Virtue Is Best Acquired through Practice and Habit]

Virtue then is twofold, partly intellectual and partly moral, and intellectual virtue is originated and fostered mainly by teaching; it demands therefore experience and time. Moral virtue on the other hand is the outcome of habit, and accordingly its name, *ethike*, is derived by a slight variation from *ethos*; habit. From this fact it is clear that moral virtue is not implanted in us by nature; for nothing that exists by nature can be transformed by habit. Thus a stone, that naturally tends to fall downwards, cannot be habituated or trained to rise upwards, even if we tried to train it by throwing it up ten thousand times. Nor again can fire be trained to sink downwards, nor anything else that follows one natural law be habituated or trained to follow another. It is neither by nature then nor in defiance of nature that virtues grow in us. Nature gives us the capacity to receive them, and that capacity is perfected by habit.

. . . But the virtues we get by first practicing them, as we do in the arts. For it is by doing what we ought to do when we study the arts that we learn the arts themselves; we become builders by building and harpists by playing the harp. Similarly, it is by doing just acts that we become just, by doing temperate acts that we become temperate, by doing brave acts that we become brave. . . .

Again, the causes and means by which any virtue is produced and destroyed are the same and equally so in any part. For it is by playing the harp that both good and bad harpists are produced; and the case of builders and others is similar, for it is by building well that they become good builders and by building badly that they become bad builders. If it were not so, there would be no need of anybody to teach them; they would all be born good or bad in their several crafts. The case of the virtues is the same. It is by our actions in dealings between man and man that we become either just or unjust. It is by our actions in the face of danger and by our training ourselves to fear or to courage that we become either cowardly or courageous. It is much the same with our appetites and angry passions. People become temperate and gentle, others licentious and passionate, by behaving in one or the other way in particular circumstances. In a word, moral states are the results of activities like the states themselves. It is our duty therefore to keep a certain character in our activities since our moral states depend on the differences in our activities. So the difference between one and another training in habits in our childhood is not a light matter, but important, or rather, all-important.

[Extreme Behavior Is to Be Avoided]

In the matters we are now considering deficiency and excess are both fatal. It is so, we see, in questions of health and strength. (We must judge of what we cannot see by the evidence of what we do see.) Too much or too little gymnastic exercise is fatal to strength. Similarly, too much or too little meat and drink is fatal to health, whereas a suitable amount produces, increases, and sustains it. It is the same with temperance, courage, and other moral virtues. A person who avoids and is afraid of everything and faces nothing becomes a coward; a person who is not afraid of anything but is ready to face everything becomes foolhardy. Similarly, he who enjoys every pleasure and abstains from none is licentious; he who refuses all pleasures, like a boor, is an insensible sort of person. For temperance and courage are destroyed by excess and deficiency but preserved by the mean.

Again, not only are the causes and agencies of production, increase, and destruction in moral states the same, but the field of their activity is the same also. It is so in other more obvious instances, as, for example, strength; for strength is produced by taking a great deal of food and undergoing a great deal of exertion, and it is the strong man who is able to take most food and undergo most exertion. So too with the virtues. By abstaining from pleasures we become temperate, and, when we have become temperate, we are best able to abstain from them. So again with courage; it is by training ourselves to despise and face terrifying things that we become brave, and when we have become brave, we shall be best able to face them.

The pleasure or pain that accompanies actions may be regarded as a test of a person's moral state. He who abstains from physical pleasures and feels pleasure in so doing is temperate but he who feels pain at so doing is licentious. He who faces dangers with pleasure, or at least without pain, is brave; but he who feels pain at facing them is a coward. For moral virtue is concerned with pleasures and pains. It is pleasure that makes us do what is base, and pain that makes us abstain from doing what is noble. Hence the importance of having a certain training from very early days, as Plato says, so that we may feel pleasure and pain at the right objects; for this is true education. . . .

[The Importance of a Virtuous Character]

But we may be asked what we mean by saying that people must become just by doing what is just and temperate by doing what is temperate. For, it will be said, if they do what is just and temperate they are already just and temperate themselves. . . . But acts in accordance with virtue are not justly or temperately performed simply because they are in themselves just or temperate. The doer at the time of performing them must satisfy certain conditions; in the first place, he must know what he is doing; secondly, he must deliberately choose to do it and do it for his own sake; and thirdly, he must do it as part of his own firm and immutable character. If it be a question of art, these conditions, except only the condition of knowledge, are not raised; but if it be a question of virtue, mere knowledge is of little or no avail; it is the other conditions, which are the results of frequently performing just and temperate acts, that are not slightly but all-important. Accordingly, deeds are called just and temperate when they are such as a just and temperate person would do; and a just and temperate person is not merely one who does these deeds but one who does them in the spirit of the just and the temperate.

It may fairly be said that a just man becomes just by doing what is just, and a temperate man becomes temperate by doing what is temperate, and if a man did not so act, he would not have much chance of becoming good. But most people, instead of acting, take refuge in theorizing; they imagine that they are philosophers and that philosophy will make them virtuous; in fact, they behave like people who listen attentively to their doctors but never do anything that their doctors tell them. But a healthy state of the soul will no more be produced by this kind of philosophizing than a healthy state of the body by this kind of medical treatment.

[The "Golden Mean" and Virtue Defined]

Now of everything, whether it be continuous or divisible, it is possible to take a greater, a smaller, or an equal amount, and this either in terms of the thing itself or in relation to ourselves, the equal being a mean between too much and too little. By the mean in terms of the thing itself, I understand that which is equally distinct from both its extremes, which is one and the same for every man. By the mean relatively to ourselves, I understand that which is neither too much nor too little for us; but this is neither one nor the same for everybody. Thus if 10 be too much and 2 too little, we take 6 as a means in terms of the thing itself; for 6 is as much greater than 2 as it is less than 10, and this is a mean in arithmetical proportion. But the mean considered relatively to ourselves may not be ascertained in that way. It does not follow that if 10 pounds of meat is too much and 2 too little for a man to eat, the trainer will order him 6 pounds, since this also may be too much or too little for him who is to take it; it will be too little, for example, for Milo but too much for a beginner in gymnastics. The same with running and wrestling; the right amount will vary with the individual. This being so, the skillful in any art avoids alike excess and deficiency; he seeks and chooses the mean, not the absolute mean, but the mean considered relatively to himself.

Every art then does its work well, if it regards the mean and judges the works it produces by the mean. For this reason we often say of successful works of art that it is impossible to take anything from them or to add anything to them, which implies that excess or deficiency is fatal to excellence but that the mean state ensures it. Good artists too, as we say, have an eye to the mean in their works. Now virtue; like Nature herself, is more accurate and better than any art; virtue, therefore, will aim at the mean. I speak of moral virtue, since it is moral virtue that is concerned with emotions and actions, and it is in these we have excess and deficiency and the mean. Thus it is possible to go too far, or not far enough in fear, pride, desire, anger, pity, and pleasure and pain generally, and the excess and the deficiency are alike wrong; but to feel these emotions at the right times, for the right objects, towards the right persons, for the right motives, and in the right manner, is the mean or the best good, which signifies virtue. Similarly, there may be excess, deficiency, or the mean, in acts. Virtue is concerned with both emotions and actions, wherein excess is all error and deficiency a fault, while the mean is successful and praised, and success and praise are both characteristics of virtue. . . .

Virtue then is a state of deliberate moral purpose, consisting in a mean relative to ourselves, the mean being determined by reason, or as a prudent [wise] man would determine it. It is a mean, firstly, as lying between two vices, the vice of excess on the one hand, the vice of deficiency on the other, and, secondly, because, whereas the vices either fall short of or go beyond what is right in emotion and action, virtue discovers and chooses the mean. Accordingly, virtue, if regarded in its essence or theoretical definition, is a mean, though, if regarded from the point of view of what is best and most excellent, it is an extreme.

[Becoming Virtuous Is Admittedly Difficult]

. . . That is why it is so hard to be good; for it is always hard to find the mean in anything; it is not everyone but only a man of science who can find the mean or center of a circle. So too anybody can get angry—that is easy—and anybody can give or spend money, but to give it to the right person, to give the right amount of it, at the right time, for the right cause and in the right way, this is not what anybody can do, nor is it easy. That is why goodness is rare and praise worthy and noble. One then who aims at a mean must begin by departing from the extreme that is more contrary to the mean . . . for of the two extremes one is more wrong than the other. As it is difficult to hit the mean exactly, we should take the second best course, as the saying is, and choose the lesser of two evils. This we shall best do in the way described—steering clear of the evil that is further from the mean. We must also note the weaknesses to which we are ourselves particularly prone, since different natures tend in different ways; and we may ascertain what our tendency is by observing our feelings of pleasure and pain. Then we must drag ourselves away towards the opposite extreme; for by pulling ourselves as far as possible from what is wrong we shall arrive at the mean, as we do when we pull a crooked stick straight. . . .

Undoubtedly this is a difficult task, especially in individual cases. It is not easy to determine the right manner, objects, occasion and duration of anger. Sometimes we praise people who are deficient in anger, and call them gentle, and at other times we praise people who exhibit a fierce temper as high-spirited. It is not however a man who deviates a little from goodness, but one who deviates a great deal, whether on the side of excess or of deficiency, that is blamed.

Review Questions

1. What does Aristotle mean by happiness, and how does it compare and contrast with hedonistic accounts?
2. What important role does habit play in Aristotle's account of moral goodness?
3. What important role does "the mean" play in Aristotle's account of moral rightness?

10.3. DISCUSSION AND ANALYSIS

At the beginning of *Groundhog Day*, Phil Connors seems far from virtuous. He is condescending and crass. Rita seems to be the opposite of Phil. She is kind, warm, and genuine.

We (the audience) hope that Phil doesn't succeed in his romantic overtures toward her. From *The Last Samurai,* Katsumoto is brave, honorable, humble (but not overly so), and wise, but Captain Nathan Algren is bitter, hollow, depressed, and angry. We wonder whether Katsumoto can reinspire the fallen US army hero. From *As Good As It Gets,* Carol Connelly is caring and loyal, Simon Bishop is empathetic and compassionate, but Melvin Udall is rude, insensitive, and mean-spirited.

We sympathize with Carol and Simon in their respective familial hardships, but cheer with the restaurant patrons when Melvin is finally banned from the establishment. It is easy to distinguish morally good people from bad; the former possess desirable character traits that invite emula-

> "Katsumoto is an extraordinary man, is he not?" *The Last Samurai,* scene 4

tion, but the latter possess undesirable traits that invariably cause scorn or disdain. Some philosophers hold that the character traits we develop—and thus the kind of person we become—is crucial to a proper conception of ethics. Aristotle is at the foreground of this approach.

Excellence and Happiness

Exploring Aristotle's moral philosophy profitably begins with his belief that each thing invariably has a primary function. Something's primary function is that which makes it unique from every other thing, and this can be determined by observing its behavior. The primary function of a knife is to cut and that of an eye is to see. Furthermore, different types of trade or profession also possess primary functions. The primary function of a doctor is to heal and that of a carpenter is to build. Aristotle believes that excellence is achieved when a primary function is performed well. But excellence of function is not accidental or occasional; it is regular or habitual. Thus an excellent doctor is one who heals well *regularly,* as a matter of course or "second nature." When a doctor achieves this state of being (i.e., professional character), she has become "virtuous." Thus "being virtuous" for Aristotle is akin to "being a virtuoso." Aristotle believes that doctors or carpenters become virtuosos when they have actualized an ideal state of (professional) being.

Aristotle holds that human beings have a primary function. He observed, plausibly, that we distinctively have the capacity to reason. So, being rational is our primary function.

BOX 10C: LEARNING OUTCOMES

Upon carefully studying this chapter, students should better comprehend and be able to explain:

- What Aristotle meant by becoming virtuous and enjoying or approaching *eudaimonia.*
- Why many find virtue ethics to be so intuitively plausible.
- The unique way in which virtue ethics defines "right action" and why some find virtue ethics problematic as a result.
- How *Groundhog Day, The Last Samurai,* and *As Good As It Gets* effectively convey insights relative to virtue ethics.

Aristotle thus believes that an excellent human being is one who reasons well habitually. This leads to developing and possessing a distinctive sort of character, which in turn, leads to being virtuous *as a human person*—a human "virtuoso." By reasoning habitually well, the virtuous person achieves a certain kind of (morally) desirable character, thereby actualizing an ideal state of being and thriving in the good (human) life.

There seems to be a distinctive relationship between a thing's achieving excellence and its possessing certain traits or characteristics conducive to its flourishing. For example, a knife must be constructed so as to hold its edge without chipping or cracking and it must be resistant to rust and corrosion. Note that a knife has no choice in the matter about whether it possesses these traits; whether it has them or not is completely beyond its control. Aristotle plausibly assumes that persons must first have sufficient food, water, clothes, shelter, and live in a stable community complete with at least a few friends in order to have any realistic hope of achieving human excellence. Whether a person enjoys all of these basic necessities is at least somewhat beyond his or her control. But achieving human excellence requires more than the basic necessities; we must choose to become excellent in ways conducive to human flourishing.

Consider again Captain Algren from *The Last Samurai*. Once he was nursed back to health by Katsumoto's sister (something not within his control), he wished to become an able swordsman. This required a great deal of physical and mental effort. He practiced regularly. It was fairly clear that the samurai soldiers, and especially the sword master, encouraged Algren to develop distinctive traits so as to better accomplish his chosen goal. Algren was thus on his way to becoming a virtuoso swordsman. But all of this began with his choice to improve himself. Yet Aristotle's favorite example was excellence among doctors. This minimally requires extensive knowledge of anatomy, practice at diagnosis, dexterity of hand, and confidence in one's healing abilities. But the important insight here is that the swordsman or doctor must do something—usually through an incredible amount of effort—to acquire the relevant excellence-making characteristics. But such efforts must be calculated, the outcome of careful planning and reasoning. Habitual proper reasoning leads to acquiring distinctive character traits that are conducive to achieving excellence in one's (professional) endeavors.

Aristotle further held that a person can likewise achieve excellence and thus flourish *as a human being*. The key to this goal, once the basic necessities are met, is reasoning well habitually in *all* that one does, and not merely at one's profession, trade, or hobby. Aristotle holds that accomplishing this is tantamount to achieving true happiness. This doesn't mean that achieving excellence as a human being necessarily includes enjoying sensations of pleasure or some sort of perennial euphoria (even if achieving excellence is typically associated with experiencing a sort of contentment). Rather, Aristotle would remind us that the ultimate goal in life generally is achieving a certain sort of character. True happiness is first and foremost a way to be for Aristotle and not a way to feel. This is a crucial distinction for Aristotle. We become excellent for its own sake, thereby achieving true happiness and hopefully contentment as a result; we do not become excellent for the feelings of contentment or quasi-euphoria

"I was in the Virgin Islands once. I met a girl. We ate lobster, drank piña coladas. At sunset, we made love like sea otters. *That* was a pretty good day. Why couldn't I get *that* day over, and over, and over . . ."
—*Groundhog Day*, scene 11

often associated with being virtuous. Our achieving the ideal human state of being is the pinnacle of existence and, thus, ought to be the true goal (and becomes one way to distinguish Aristotelian from utilitarian conceptions of happiness).

Consider again Phil Connors. When he realized that he was repeatedly living the same day, he was first frightened. However, he soon concluded that he could do whatever he wanted without repercussion. Once he further realized that only he retained memories of the previous February 2, his fright was replaced by schemes to fulfill his baser desires. Because each day is exactly the same, although not quite for Phil, he eventually gathers sufficient information to effortlessly steal money from an armored car and seduce beautiful women. But the irony is that the happiness Phil experiences is fleeting. In fact, he soon becomes miserable. His schemes turn to suicide attempts, which all fail. He continually awakes at 6:00 a.m. to the famous Sonny and Cher song. It is only after Phil begins to explore behaviors for their own sake—ice sculpting, playing the piano, trying to save a homeless man's life—that Phil starts to experience more genuine or lasting happiness. At the very least, he becomes content with himself in ways that he wasn't when he pursued his baser desires. Phil ironically found a deeper or more significant kind of happiness by not directly seeking it. This begins to capture the sort of true happiness—what Aristotle called *eudaimonia*—operative in the Aristotelian pursuit of human excellence.

The Golden Mean and Becoming Virtuous

Aristotle held that human excellence is achieved in conjunction with acquiring desirable characteristics. That is, one becomes a human virtuoso because desirable character traits are developed by habitually reasoning well. Reasoning well leads one to (generally) avoid extreme courses of behavior that err neither on the side of excess nor deficiency.[2]

For example, a person facing a dangerous situation calling for bravery will not act foolhardily or recklessly (vices of excess) and she will not act cowardly (vice of deficiency). Acting from either extreme is to not use one's reason, or rather, not to act from one's reason. However, acting courageously only occasionally is not to reason well habitually and, so, is not constitutive of excellence. One must, like Katsumoto, act courageously as a matter of course; this is a mark of

> "His name was Custer. . . . He was arrogant and foolhardy. . . . He was a murderer who fell in love with his own legend. And his troopers died for it."——
> *The Last Samurai*, scene 14

virtue. Thus, Aristotle believed that individual actions, even if they seem virtuous, lack full or genuine moral worth unless they proceed from a virtuous character. So, performing acts that are truly courageous (in the full moral sense) is possible only if one is a courageous person and, in turn, being courageous seems to be one of the characteristics persons acquire in their pursuit of achieving excellence. But, certainly *eudaimonia* requires one to reason habitually well about any situation. Consequently, the truly virtuous person—a human virtuoso—will habitually and appropriately be honest (rather than boastful or deceptive), generous (rather than extravagant or stingy), loyal (rather than fawning or duplicitous), and temperate (rather than hot-headed or meek). And, so, in performing our primary function habitually well, we thereby acquire a morally desirable character. We thus become virtuous and approach the highest (intrinsic) good—*eudaimonia.*

Groundhog Day, Columbia Pictures, 1993. By living the same day over and over, Phil Connors (Bill Murray) has many attempts to woo his co-worker Rita (Andie MacDowell) at a bed and breakfast in Punxsutawney. (Moviegoods, Inc.)

Achieving excellence in our primary function requires us to "act from reason." Doing so involves taking full account of our current situation. This guideline is sometimes called the "doctrine of the golden mean"; it advises us to follow the "middle path" given the circumstances at hand. A bit more carefully, it calls for us to act appropriately in any situation we may find ourselves, with an eye to avoid over or under reacting (unless a situation uniquely calls for unusual or extreme behavior). Admittedly, then, appropriate action will vary somewhat from person to person given his or her current situation, as Aristotle points out with his example about food intake for various athletes. We see Phil Connors grasping at Aristotle's golden mean in various ways, but perhaps most notably in Phil's interactions with the insurance salesman Ned Ryerson. The first time they meet, Phil is smarmy, and he feigns ignorance of Ned even though Ned briefly dated Phil's sister. The second time, Phil runs away from Ned, dreading another meeting. These behaviors represent vices of deficiency; Phil underreacts in these situations. The third time, Phil punches Ned in the face and then calmly walks away. The fourth time, Phil approaches Ned, hugs him tenderly, and deviously feigns romantic longing for him resulting in Ned's quick and uncomfortable departure. These latter two behaviors represent vices of excess; Phil overreacts in these situations. At the end of the movie, with Phil's character transformed, he is genuinely pleased to bump into Ned. Phil tells Rita that Ned is his new insurance agent and that Phil has recently bought a great deal of insurance from him. However, both Phil and Rita decline any further personal involvement with Ned and depart without hurting his feelings.[3]

In the movie, Phil had many opportunities to live the same situation with Ned. We are not so lucky. We get one shot at each situation. But Aristotle would remind us that, although finding the golden mean is difficult, we must learn from our trials, being fully aware of ourselves in those situations. People like Melvin Udall who are (or have become) mean-spirited, must recognize this fact when finding themselves in situations calling for kindness or generosity. Algren must take full account of his dour and bitter demeanor when facing situations calling for honor and loyalty. Achieving this kind of honesty about ourselves is difficult. Self-deception becomes habitual, and indeed a way of life. Note what happened to these two men once each interrupted his typical behavior patterns. The former gained insight into his character by taking in Simon's dog; by caring for the dog, he became more aware of who he was and thus more conscious of his instances of inappropriate behavior. The latter gained insight into his character by traveling to Japan and being captured by Katsumoto; when immersed in completely different surroundings, Algren had the opportunity to reflect on his former life. These men also serve as painful examples of how hard finding the appropriate response can be, especially at first. Sometimes we underreact, as Melvin did rushing to his therapist looking for answers. Sometimes we will overreact, as Algren did in foolhardily challenging the sword master to a duel. We must remember and learn from those mistakes so that, in similar circumstances in the future, we will act appropriately. Eventually, with sufficient effort, acting appropriately in that kind of situation will become second nature, as it did for Algren and Phil (and even though it seems that Melvin's transformation is not yet complete).

Aristotle's doctrine of the golden mean therefore requires us to take proper stock of ourselves, in terms of the kind of person we currently are. We must recall how we tend to react in our current circumstances. This kind of self-knowledge is crucial to being fully aware of a situation. This also means that it might be appropriate for us to "overshoot" the mean for a time, in exactly the same way that you must "over-bend" a crooked stick in order to straighten it. That is, if you currently anger quickly, you might need to act deferentially a bit more than is typically expected of one so that this "kink" in your character is eventually ironed out. If you are self-absorbed like Melvin, you need to behave more altruistically than is typically expected of one so as to correct this character flaw. Indeed, procuring a personal physician for Carol's son, although initially done for less than completely noble reasons, nevertheless played an important role in transforming his character. (And had Melvin not first cared for Simon's dog, it's unclear whether providing Spencer medical care would have occurred to him.) If you are like Algren, prone to overindulge in alcohol, you should (at least for a while) completely abstain. With the virtues of temperance and courage in place, perhaps later you could resume imbibing (appropriately) in social settings. Going back to Phil, in order to correct his smugness and egotistical tendencies, he regularly found himself using his wit and humor to be the butt of his own jokes. Phil's self-deprecating humor became an effective tool for him to become more humble. Thus, not only is Aristotelian appropriate behavior "the mean relative to us as the wise person determines it," but it is also a difficult process involving a great deal of trial,

> "From the moment they [the Samurai's camp] wake, they devote themselves to the perfection of whatever they pursue. I have never seen such discipline." —*The Last Samurai*, scene 18

error, and learning from our mistakes. But the rewards of our success are great—nothing less than human excellence.[4]

By way of summary, Aristotle held that human beings are of a certain kind; we are essentially rational, social animals. This is the key to understanding Aristotle's ideas about human well-being, which, in turn, is linked to possessing basic necessities and developing character traits. Once our basic necessities are met, we must take an active, self-directed role in our development. If we develop virtuous (excellent) character traits—courage, honesty, loyalty, generosity, temperance—those that allow us to flourish as human in community with others, then we approach *eudaimonia*. Achieving *eudaimonia* is intrinsically valuable; it represents the highest good we can attain. Approaching this high level of well-being is impossible without the careful use of reason (or presumably living in complete seclusion). If our basic necessities are not met or we develop vicious (deficient) character traits, then our well-being is negatively affected; these eventualities constitute morally significant harms either done onto us or that we do onto others (even if only harms resulting from human free choice are fully morally significant). Therefore, although Aristotle's approach is grounded in biological and psychological facts about human nature, it remains distinct from natural law theory because it does not advocate the status quo or argue that what people regularly do constitutes the moral norm. Rather, Aristotle offers us an ideal to which we humans ought to aspire. Should we develop in ways conducive to human flourishing, then we are to be morally commended (especially as this will invariably include helping others to approach *eudaimonia* as well).

The Strengths of Virtue Ethics

According to Aristotle's virtue ethics, *eudaimonia*—the flourishing or excellence of persons insofar as they acquire a virtuous character—represents the highest morally significant good that can be achieved. Possessing a virtuous character is a matter of developing certain character traits that are conducive to leading a rich, full, and distinctively human life. Becoming excellent or virtuous in this (human virtuoso) sense is to improve one's well-being; it is how you are benefited, morally speaking. One suffers morally significant harm when excellence, or its pursuit, is frustrated. Consequently, the moral standard is

> Everyone ought to act in ways that promote the flourishing of human persons.

Virtue ethics is unique among other moral theories in that it grounds or defines "right action" simply as a function of what good (virtuous) agents do. That is, virtue ethicists offer the following definition: an action is right if, in those circumstances, it is what a good (virtuous) person would do (assuming she is acting in character). Moral rules are grounded in Aristotle's doctrine of the golden mean: act in accordance with reason, such that one responds appropriately (virtuously) given the particular situation. Typically (although not always) this involves habitually avoiding extreme behaviors such that appropriate action becomes a part of one's character. A virtue ethicist faces a conflict situation (or moral dilemma) when one must choose between acting in accordance with two virtues, but the agent cannot do both. In such cases, we are to do as the virtuous person would.

The intuitive strengths of virtue ethics run deep. The first is how it coheres with commonsense intuitions about acting properly. It seems rather obvious that one acts inappropriately when one overreacts (or underreacts) in a morally significant situation. We often say, "You didn't need to do that!" or "That was unnecessary!" or "You should take this situation more seriously!" In each case, it seems that the speaker is admonishing someone for not acting appropriately. Conversely, however, we also praise those individuals—moral sages—who, regardless of the circumstances, always speak or act appropriately. They effortlessly approach situations, even difficult ones, with wisdom, creativity, amiability, and sensitivity. Aristotle's virtue-based approach plausibly explains why moral sages are so highly regarded *as exemplars*. They do not merely meet their moral obligations; they have attained a kind of moral excellence that the rest of us should aspire to achieve.

The second strength of virtue ethics operates at the level of moral motivation. A common complaint about moral theories that exclusively focus upon right action is that the moral principles driving them is external to the agent. Action-based theories like utilitarianism, respect for persons ethics, or (for the most part) natural law ethics, require one to discover true abstract moral principles and then psychologically internalize them. We must personally adopt it before a moral principle can guide our lives. Some remain skeptical about the existence of such abstract, (presumably) necessarily true principles. But even if there are such truths, they remain importantly distinct from who or what we are. Consequently, action-based theories face the perennial question: Why ought I to do the right thing (as Spike Lee advises)? Why should I act upon the moral standard once I discover it? However, by emphasizing the conceptual role of reflective human agents and character development, virtue ethics has an immediate and plausible response to these questions: No one truly desires something that is not in his or her best interests, but not being virtuous is not in anyone's best interests. Thus everyone desires to be virtuous (that is, become excellent). Simply, we are "better off" if we actualize our full potential as human persons. This was certainly true of Phil Connors and Nathan Algren. Furthermore, virtue ethicists invariably add that we cannot begin formulating moral principles without first knowing what virtuous agents would do anyway. Thus, relying on general, abstract principles to determine morally proper behavior is doubly wrongheaded.

> "You make me want to be a better man." —*As Good As It Gets*, scene 21

The third strength highlights another difference between virtue ethics and action-based moral theories. Many scholars point out that one can fulfill every moral rule or obligation without fail very robotically. On action-based theories, one is thereby leading a sufficiently worthy ethical life. Kant was clear about this: our acts become fully morally significant only when they are done from duty. We do them merely for duty's sake and not out of care or concern for others. But it seems obvious to many that robotically performing obligatory actions, even if it is without fail, is not to lead a sufficiently worthy ethical life. Kant seemed to overlook this point. There is more to ethics than discovering true principles, making inferences, deriving true moral judgments, and acting on them merely for duty's sake. If so, then there seems to be an important difference between following rules and being a morally good person. Action-based moral theories (Kant is not alone) seemingly cannot effectively make this distinction. If so, then action-based moral theories are incomplete because they cannot capture the ethical significance of being a good person—one who is caring, kind, generous, loyal, and cultivates significant relationships.

In a very important sense, then, it seems that leading a sufficiently rich moral life should include being—or better yet *becoming*—a better all-around person. Any moral theory that doesn't properly accord with the intuition that ethics is about agents making

The Last Samurai, Warner Brothers Films, 2003. Initially his enemy and prisoner, Nathan Algren (Tom Cruise, right) slowly transforms himself into Katsumoto's (Ken Watanabe) friend and ally. (Moviegoods, Inc.)

moral improvement is thereby deficient. Reconsider the three main characters from each of the three movies for this chapter. Phil Connors was smug, condescending, egotistical, and short-sided. He was also miserable. By the end of the movie, however, he is kind, generous, altruistic, sensitive, and polite. Nathan Algren was a broken and tortured man. He was crass, rude, and insensitive. He drinks whiskey excessively, which helps him cope with his day and sleep at night. When sober, he wishes for death to provide him release from his personal demons. But by the end of the movie, he is honorable, centered, and appreciative. Algren offers to end his own life, if the emperor wishes it; he does so, not for selfish reasons, but for a purpose greater than he—the good of Japan. Melvin Udall was obnoxiously rude, self-centered, and uncaring. He was also lonely and sad (even if not completely aware of this). By the end of the movie, he is warmer, kinder, and more generous. Each of these men accomplished his transformation to a more morally desirable character by changing his habitual behaviors. In requiring that we regularly or habitually become honest, kind, generous, and brave through regular proper use of our reason given the situation at hand, Aristotle's virtue ethics seems a highly plausible moral theory. In fact, of all moral theories virtue ethics (arguably) most effectively secures the importance of character and character development.

Action-Guiding Worries

The action-based moral theories, not surprisingly, define "good person" as someone who regularly performs right actions (for the proper reasons). The virtue ethicist, recall, objects that this affords an illicitly thin or incomplete conception of moral goodness. However, virtue ethics invariably faces objections about its account of right action. Initially, such objections are grounded in the widely held intuition that moral theories are to be action-guiding. Even in conflict situations (moral dilemmas), a moral theory must inform agents about what to do. However, some critics argue that virtue ethics offers insufficient guidance in such situations.

Suppose that you must choose between two actions, A and B. The first, A, represents a scenario where you can be honest but unkind, while the second, B, represents a scenario where you can be kind but dishonest. An example might be your being honest about your friend's horrendous new (Joe Dirt mullet) haircut, as he or she (proudly) asks: How does it look? Assuming that there is no third course of action, it seems we have a conflict of virtues. But what ought you to do? Even more pressing, perhaps, is the situation where your new boyfriend, someone you are very much in love with, asks what your parents think of him. You know that they disapprove. What should you do here? The natural law theorist and Kantian would probably recommend honesty; the utilitarian would require that one first determine which option leads to the best consequences. But for the virtue ethicist, the question is: Which virtue should you act upon and which vice should you accept? Of course, Aristotle might remind us that we ought to do what the virtuous person would do in this situation. However, the advice of any virtuous person would seemingly only be relevant in a very indirect way: you must use your reason properly in deciding what to do. But we already knew *that*. What is presumably needed is some way to rank the virtues in a hierarchy of importance, one sensitive to the specifics of various situations. This would provide guidance about how to resolve operative dilemmas. But it is unclear which virtues take precedence simply from within the theory itself.

Perhaps this last objection can be met by simply requiring agents to act in accordance with one or the other of the virtues. If so, then perhaps the vicious act would be not acting at all. But then, again, perhaps it would not be. Conceivably, some virtuous persons might justifiably come to the conclusion that it is not vicious to do nothing in the relevant circumstances. If so, then it seems that some virtuous persons could justifiably act according to honesty and (gently) share the relevant disheartening news, others could justifiably act according to kindness and answer the question with a "white lie," and others could justifiably take no action whatsoever. Moreover, it seems as if no matter what you did, so long as you (as a virtuous agent) did something, you would do the virtuous thing. But how plausible is that? Can it really be that all of these logically incompatible alternatives are equally morally acceptable?

Other critics argue that, intuitions about the degree to which a theory must resolve all conflict issues aside, the very way that virtue ethicists define right action is problematic. Consider that virtue ethicists often point to moral exemplars as models of morally correct behavior. This isn't surprising because (recall) virtue ethics defines morally right action as that which the virtuous (excellent) person does when acting in character. Because moral exemplars never (or almost never) act out of character, they provide highly reliable moral guidance. However, intuitively, there are various or multiple moral exemplars: Socrates, Buddha, Gandhi, Martin Luther King, Jr., Mother Teresa, just to name a few. But that multiple moral exemplars exist raises the distinct possibility that they would act differently in relevantly similar circumstances. In *The Last Samurai*, some samurai warriors, like General Hasegawa, followed the emperor in his quest to modernize Japan, but some, like Katsumoto, resisted. Both samurais were of similar age, ability, and knowledge. Both believed that they were acting honorably, and both were well-respected by those around them. There is no evidence that either was acting out of character. Yet the fact of their disagreement seemingly leads to the following paradoxical result: It is and is not morally acceptable to follow the emperor in his modernization of Japan. This quasi-historical example is analogous to the actual debate between Plato and Aristotle with respect to allowing women to serve in important political offices. Plato thought this was appropriate, assuming the woman was suitably qualified, but Aristotle thought that it was never appropriate because no women could be suitably qualified. The fact of disagreement between the two Greek sages yields: it is and it is not appropriate that women hold political office. The problem for virtue ethics, then, is that it defines right action in a way that seemingly admits of contradictory results; the same act performed by suitably similar agents can be (simultaneously) right and not right. This is evidence that virtue ethics runs afoul of the contradiction test for moral theories.

The virtue ethicist might reply to this objection by further clarifying the role moral exemplars play in defining right action in the following way. Performing action A in circumstance C is obligatory if moral exemplars universally agree about doing A in C. Performing action A in C is impermissible if moral exemplars universally agree about refraining from A in C (that is, if no moral exemplar would perform A in C). Performing action A in C is permissible if some, but not all, moral exemplars would perform action A in C. Therefore, disagreement is not evidence that virtue ethics entails the truth of a contradiction, but rather that some choices are difficult, leaving room for alternative, permissible responses. Going back to *The Last Samurai*, the choice facing Hasegawa and Katsumoto was obviously difficult. Should Japan move ahead or hold dear to old values? On the revised account of moral rightness, either choice is permissible in the relevant circumstances. And, arguably, this strategy could appropriately deal with any or all moral conflict situations (including those pertaining to unfortunate hairstyles from the 1980s).

Yet two interlocking worries about this move remain. First, it's intuitively doubtful that universal agreement would be achieved about very many topics. If so, then virtue ethics still fares rather poorly regarding the completeness test, as an inordinate number of choices (or actions) will be left merely morally permissible. Second, and more importantly, it can be asked what explains universal agreement among moral exemplars in the first place. Why would they all agree that some action is (or is not) to be performed in the relevant circumstances?

This last question harkens back to the question Socrates posed of Euthyphro: Is an act pious (right or good) merely because all the gods agree to cherish it, or do all the gods cherish it because it is of a nature deserving of their approval? Analogously, it can be asked of the virtue ethicist: Is an act right (obligatory) in the relevant circumstances merely because all the moral exemplars agree to do it, or do all the moral exemplars agree to do it because it is right (morally required) given those circumstances? Insofar as the virtue ethicist offers a version of ethical objectivism, she must avoid the specter of arbitrariness; therefore, moral rightness cannot be determined merely by universal assent. But if universal agreement among exemplars is explained by right action, then moral rightness is explanatorily prior to virtuous behavior. If moral rightness is explanatorily prior to virtuous behavior, then the virtue ethicist's account of right action is mistaken, serving as a counterexample to her theory.[5]

Accordingly, assuming universal assent among exemplars acting in character, it can be asked: Do exemplars have reasons for acting as they do in those circumstances or not?

If no, then their choices, although uniform, are ultimately arbitrary; however, this sort of arbitrariness is inconsistent with ethical objectivism. If yes, then it seems that the operative reasons—and not merely the exemplars' choices (even if they do flow from virtuous characters)—provide the grounds for moral rightness. But morally significant reasons, by their very nature, can be universalized. Universalizing on morally significant reasons leads to moral principles. Therefore, it seems virtue ethics, insofar as it offers a version of ethical objectivism, is committed to the existence of moral principles that ultimately serve as the grounds for moral rightness.[6] So, to avoid the specter of arbitrariness, it seems that the virtue ethicist must jettison the position that acts are morally right just because virtuous persons would (uniformly) perform them in the relevant circumstances. Therefore, to preserve the integrity, imaginativeness, wisdom, and, ultimately, goodness of moral exemplars, it seems that the virtue ethicist must revise his core tenet about right action.

This divine command theory based critique of virtue ethics highlights Aristotle's admission that not every moral or immoral action admits of analysis via the golden mean. This admission is puzzling because proper application (or embodiment, perhaps) of the golden mean serves as Aristotle's only plausible criterion for generating moral rules and, by extension, moral rightness.[7] Aristotle writes:

> But not every action admits of a mean. There are some whose very name implies wickedness, as, for example . . . adultery, theft and murder. . . . All these and others like them are marked as intrinsically wicked, not merely the excess or deficiencies of them. . . . Right or wrong in such acts as adultery does not depend on our committing it with the right [wo]man, at the right time, or in the right manner; on the contrary, it is wrong to do it at all. (*NE,* 1107a 9–17)

It seems that some acts simply are wrong apart from the doctrine of the golden mean, which is de facto evidence for concluding that virtue ethics suffers from incompleteness with respect to defining moral rightness. Note that the problematic issue is not that there are some ethically significant situations that any theory will have difficulty assessing. The issue for virtue ethics is that it has difficulty properly accounting for the impermissibility of something as obvious as murder. This worry can be remedied with an appeal to general moral principles, thereby bolstering the position suggested in the previous paragraph. To have an intuitively satisfying account of right action, one that is sufficiently action guiding, we must appeal to moral principles that are informative about what virtuous agents (will) do. That is, no virtuous agent commits adultery, theft, or (especially) murder *because* these acts are wrong; that they are (already) wrong most effectively explains why virtuous agents universally avoid them. Furthermore, any genuinely virtuous person would know the relevant rules and follow them in exemplary ways. On this account, then, virtuous agency most effectively describes the manner in which agents have internalized and effortlessly enacted moral principles; it is not constitutive of moral rightness itself. Therefore, there is indeed evidence that virtue ethics fails the completeness test with respect to issues of moral rightness; furthermore, attempts at correcting this shortcoming seemingly leads to jettisoning her distinctive position regarding moral goodness defining moral rightness.

This is not to say that virtue ethics should be discarded altogether. The incompleteness objection cuts deep because it affects a particularly distinctive feature of virtue ethics, but it leaves most of the theory otherwise untouched. Furthermore, it might be argued that even if virtue-based approaches suffer incompleteness with respect to moral rightness, no action-based theory can succeed without the aid of a virtue-based approach. This seems so for at least three reasons. First, moral goodness is not merely about minimally meeting moral obligations; it consists of forming one's character is distinctive ways, making one a better person. Second, within the range of permissible actions, it's intuitive that some are better than others; virtuous agents invariably opt for the more commendable over the merely acceptable actions and inspire the rest of us to do the same. Third, when generally accepted moral rules conflict and it is not initially clear what one ought to do, it seems

> "I might be the only one who appreciates how amazing you are in every single thing that you do . . . and how you almost always mean something that's all about being . . . good. . . . And the fact that I get it makes me feel good, about me." —*As Good As It Gets*, scene 28

virtuous persons are in a better situation to resolve such situations; it seems that relying on the integrity, imaginativeness, empathy, and wisdom of moral exemplars will invariably provide insightful guidance into how a new rule might be discovered and properly derived. Moreover, it seems that moral exemplars, predominantly free of undue biases or egoistic tendencies, are in optimal positions for discerning moral knowledge in the first place. Therefore, it appears that virtue ethics can be blended or combined with another moral theory (or theories) such that its conceptual weaknesses are suitably addressed but its commonsense strengths—especially those regarding character development—are retained.

10.4. TWO ADDITIONAL FILMS

The Last Samurai (2003)

Director: Edward Zwick
Screenwriter: John Logan

Plot Summary

> And I say Japan was made by a handful of brave men, warriors willing to give their lives, for what seems to be a forgotten word: honor.

Captain Nathan Algren is a highly decorated Civil War hero and expert on Native American Indian military tactics. But by 1876, he is a troubled soul. To help him sleep at night, he's turned to whiskey. To afford his whiskey, he has further tarnished his image by peddling rifles for Winchester. Sgt. Zeb Gant surprises Algren in an alley after a "Winchester performance" to tell him of a new job opportunity. They meet their old commanding officer, Col. Bagley, and a contingent of Japanese diplomats he is hosting. Algren glowers and quickly orders two glasses of whiskey. The Japanese diplomats wish to hire Algren to train their new nationalist army. They will pay him handsomely for his efforts to put down a tribal rebellion led by the samurai Katsumoto. It's an offer Algren cannot refuse. Algren, Gant, and Bagley soon leave for Japan.

Simon Graham is America's liaison and translator. Graham informs Algren that Japan, at the behest of the new, young Emperor Meiji and his chief minister Omura, wish to become a modernized country. Graham also states that not everyone in Japan is happy about the modernization, including the emperor's former teacher, Katsumoto. As Graham puts it, "The ancient and modern are at war for the soul of Japan," and this explains why Katsumoto has taken action. After receiving a rare audience with the emperor (believed to be of divine lineage according to Shinto tradition), Algren addresses his new troops. Most are peasant conscripts. With Gant's help, and that of General Hasegawa—leader of the nationalist Japanese army and respected samurai warrior, Algren moves toward his goal.

When Katsumoto attacks a train, Bagley and Omura order Algren to mobilize the army. Algren protests that the nationalist troops aren't ready to engage Katsumoto. He proves this by ordering one of the Japanese soldiers to fire at him. The soldier is obviously confused and nervous. Algren whispers to himself, "Shoot me, damn it." Algren wishes to die. Finally, the young soldier shoots, but wildly misses his mark—Algren's chest. Nevertheless, Bagley—technically Algren's superior officer again—orders the regiment to leave at dawn.

Mist and fog cover the wooded battlefield. Algren disobeys Bagley's direct order to move to the rear; Gant disobeys Algren's similar order. Katsumoto and his warriors fight with ancient weapons; many nationalist soldiers are killed. Gant dies via spear and sword wounds. Others die at the skillful hands of Katsumoto's archers on horseback. Algren is seriously injured. He desperately attempts to defend himself against three warriors. He manages to kill one of them before Katsumoto—remembering a dream he had about a white tiger—intervenes and spares Algren's life. Algren is taken prisoner.

The samurai orders his sister to nurse Algren back to health. Katsumoto's sword master disagrees. Algren should take his own life rather than live with the shame of defeat. Katsumoto reminds him that Americans do not share this belief. The sword master then requests permission to kill Algren. Katsumoto demurs, saying, "There will be plenty of killing to come. For now, we will learn from our new enemy." A guard is posted outside of Taka's house as Algren begins to go through withdrawal. He calls for sake (presumably American whiskey is sparse in Japan), but is forced to face his demons sober. He slips in and out of consciousness remembering the terrible actions he took against the Indians, many of which were innocent women and children. We learn of Algren's hatred for men like Bagley (and Custer). While Algren suffers, Katsumoto meditates and prays to Lord Buddha. He also reads from his enemy's journal.

Algren is finally well enough to explore the village. His guard follows closely. Algren sees men training for battle. He stumbles upon the samurai's temple. Katsumoto greets him honorably and wishes to have conversations in English with Algren (if he will honor him in return). The samurai asks if "captain" is a high rank in the army. Algren replies that it is a middle rank. Katsumoto inquires about Algren's "general" or superior officer. Algren informs him that it was a man named "Custer." Algren is adamant: "Custer wasn't a good general. He was arrogant and foolhardy. He got massacred. . . . He was a murderer who fell in love with his own legend, and his troopers died for it." The English conversation ends as abruptly as it began.

One night there is a play, a comedy, and the samurai participates. The warriors laugh and morale is high. However, the nationalist army takes this opportunity to conduct an assassination attempt on Katsumoto. The warriors strive to protect the samurai. Algren comes to his aid and the aid of Taka's family. The attempt is thwarted. Katsumoto wishes to have another conversation with Algren the next morning. As Algren approaches, the samurai points at the trees, "The perfect blossom is a rare thing. You could spend your whole life looking for one and it would not be a wasted life." Algren is unsure of his meaning. Katsumoto knows of Algren's nightmares; they linger because the one who dreams them is ashamed of what he has done. Katsumoto also knows that Algren does not fear death, but sometimes wishes for it. Katsumoto reminds Algren that such things are not uncommon with warriors. But he then instructs Algren, "And then I come to this place of my ancestors, and I remember: like these blossoms, we are all dying. To know life in every breath, every cup of tea, every life we take. The way of the warrior." Algren looks up at the trees, and slowly repeats, "Life in every breath." The samurai returns Algren's journal and other belongings, saying, "When I took these, you were my enemy."

The emperor guarantees Katsumoto safe passage for a meeting, and the samurai agrees. The emperor informs him, "I need advisors who know the modern world." Katsumoto immediately presents Meiji his sword and answers, "If I am no longer useful, I will happily end my life." Omura and Bagley meet with Algren, but the captain does not divulge any details. He is now loyal to Katsumoto, like so many others. Omura approaches Algren privately and offers him a glass of American whiskey. To his surprise, Algren declines. Omura then surprises Katsumoto: It is now illegal to bear swords inside Tokyo city limits. Katsumoto must remove his sword or be imprisoned. The samurai looks toward the emperor, but the divine one does not contravene Omura's edict. Katsumoto is jailed; Algren conspires (successfully) to free him. Outside of Tokyo, Katsumoto and Algren share a quiet moment. The samurai speaks, "For nine hundred years my ancestors have protected our people. I have failed." Algren thoughtfully interjects, "So, you will take your own life—in shame. Shame for a life of service? Discipline? Compassion?" But Katsumoto interjects, "The way of the samurai isn't necessary anymore," to which Algren questions, "What could be more necessary?"

Algren is by Katsumoto's side as they ride into one last battle against Japan's modernity. They face Omura, Bagley, cannons, Howitzers, a well-trained Japanese army, and fate itself.

Discussion Questions

1. Was Katsumoto wrong (or perhaps unwise) to resist Japan's modernization, at least as it is portrayed in the movie?
2. Which character in the movie has the most morally *undesirable* character? Why?
3. What were some important transformations in Algren's character as the movie progressed? How did Katsumoto and the way of the samurai impact it?
4. Is Algren correct that the way of the samurai is now (in modernity) more necessary than ever? Explain.

As Good As It Gets (1997)

Director: James L. Brooks
Screenwriters: Mark Andrus and James L. Brooks

Plot Summary

> You don't love anything. . . . You absolute horror of a human being.

Melvin Udall contently lives alone in his posh penthouse apartment crafting romance novels. His sixty-second novel is nearly complete. He dislikes everyone, including his neighbor's dog, Verdell. After another episode of trying to "help" Verdell get into the elevator, Udall opts to send the little dog down the trash shoot. Verdell's owner is Simon Bishop, a gay artist who also works at home. Simon summons up the courage to confront "Mr. Udall." Udall flings his door open. Simon swallows hard and asks Melvin if he knows how Verdell "found" the basement. Ignoring Simon's query, Udall blusters, "I work at home. So, never, never interrupt me, okay? . . . Not even if you hear the sound of a thud from my home and a week later there's a smell coming from there that can only be a decaying human body. . . . Even then don't come knocking. . . . Not on this door. . . . Do you get me, sweetheart?" Simon meekly confirms that it's not a subtle point "Mr. Udall" is making.

After washing his hands with near scalding water and tossing the new bar of soap, Melvin leaves for his favorite lunch restaurant. He walks, but refuses to step on any sidewalk cracks and avoids all human contact. "Don't touch," he screams to passersby. Arriving at the diner, a young couple is sitting at "his" table. Udall hovers over them. He is close enough to crudely eavesdrop on their conversation, and callously states: "People who talk in metaphors should shampoo my crotch!" The couple attempts to ignore him. Melvin complains to Carol, his regular waitress. Carol tells him that he'll have to wait for them to leave, or sit in another waitress's station. Her coworkers gasp, but Udall slinks back to wait for "his" table. After hurling a not-so-subtle racial slur their way, the couple finally leaves; Udall sits down and gets out his plastic tableware (evidently the restaurant's silverware isn't suitable). He places his regular order with Carol, and she responds, "You know, you'll die soon with that diet." Udall effortlessly replies, "We're all going to die soon. I will, you will, and it sure sounds like your son will."

Simon asks one of his associates to find him a model. A young man named Vincent arrives the next day. Simon incorrectly assumes that he is a professional model. In fact, Simon's associate found him on a street corner. After a week or two of posing for a portrait, Vincent arranges it so that his friends rob Simon while artist and model reminisce about the sitting. But Simon unexpectedly leaves the studio and walks in on the burglary. Vincent's friends beat Simon terribly and steal many of his valuables. Simon is hospitalized, and without any medical insurance, he incurs hospital bills he cannot afford.

Simon's friends, Frank, his art dealer, and Jackie Simpson, his agent, attempt to comfort him. Frank somehow convinces Melvin to care for Verdell while Simon is healing. Udall is initially terrified, but slowly warms to the cuddly little dog. Melvin feeds him bacon and plays the piano at mealtime. Melvin soon brings Verdell with him to the restaurant. Surprisingly, he leaves "his" table so that he can better watch Verdell (who is tied up on the sidewalk). Melvin smiles as he sees children playing with the dog. But Simon soon returns home signaling Verdell's return to his owner. Udall is clearly upset, indeed sad, that the dog is leaving. Melvin marches down to his therapist's office—without making an appointment—barges in, and exclaims, "I changed just one pattern as you said I always should!" The therapist refuses to see Melvin without an appointment. Disgruntled, Melvin leaves the office, but not before he poses a question to those in the waiting room: "What if this is as good as it gets?"

Udall heads for the restaurant and consolation. "His" table is available, but "his" waitress is not. To Melvin's horror, the new girl informs him that Carol might not come back. Udall bribes a busboy for Carol's last name and makes his way to her apartment. Carol sees his visit as an intrusion. She asks him to leave, but not before he demands that she return to work. He finally departs and hails a taxi, but Carol and her son Spencer rush toward the cab. Spencer has another high fever (104.9) and must get to the hospital quickly. Melvin "offers" to share the cab. Now better realizing just how ill Spencer is, he uniquely arranges (through his publisher) for Spencer's healthcare. (His publisher is married to a medical doctor; if she wants another book, she'll convince her husband to make house calls on Spencer.)

Carol and her mother are grateful for the personal medical attention, but Carol fears the ramifications. Melvin is unsure of his new association with Simon (via Verdell). The uneasy relationships become a triad when Simon is forced to ask his parents for help with his financial hardship. He will almost certainly lose his apartment if he doesn't. But his parents live in Baltimore, which requires someone to make the road trip with Simon. Frank lends his car, but cannot accompany Simon. Frank again "convinces" Melvin to go. Melvin then convinces Carol to accompany them. With Melvin's curt introduction, "Carol the waitress, meet Simon the fag," they depart for Maryland.

The journey is a bit awkward (unsurprisingly), and made more awkward by Simon's parents' refusal to offer their son any money (or indeed even see him). There is more awkwardness as Melvin and Carol decide to go out for fresh seafood. Carol admits to Melvin: "When you first entered the restaurant, I thought you were handsome—but, then, of course, you spoke." Nevertheless, there is some sort of connection between Melvin and Carol. After tripping over his tongue a few times, Melvin finally admits to Carol, "You make me want to be a better man." Carol replies that she has been paid no nicer compliment. When the three arrive back in New York, we learn that Melvin has arranged for Simon (and Verdell, of course) to cheaply rent his spare room. Simon returns the kindness by convincing Melvin to visit Carol again, to make it work. Udall is hesitant, but finally (at 3:00 a.m.) gathers enough courage to make his affections known. When he arrives, she wonders why she can't have a "normal boyfriend" (ever), but the two leave for a walk to an early morning bakery. Melvin, ignoring the sidewalk cracks, pays her another compliment, albeit in a way only he can: "I might be the only one who appreciates how amazing you are in every single thing that you do . . . and in every single thought that you have, and how you say what you mean, and how you almost always mean something that's all about being straight and good. I think most people miss that about you, and I watch them, wondering how they can watch you bring their food, and clear their tables and never get that they just met the greatest woman alive." Melvin assures her that he can "do better"— become a better person like Carol—and the two kiss.

Discussion Questions

1. Compare and contrast Melvin's character at the beginning and at the end of the movie. What changes have taken place? Would you say that Melvin is a good person by the movie's end?
2. What accounts for the changes in Melvin's character? How might have Verdell been the catalyst for this?
3. How would you describe Carol's character? How is it different from Melvin's? Are there any ways in which their characters are similar?
4. Who would you say is Simon's closest friend(s) by the end of the movie: his mother, Frank, Carol, or Melvin? Explain your answer.

10.5. REVIEWING THROUGH THE THREE MOVIES

1. How were the characters of Phil Connors, Nathan Algren, and Melvin Udall alike? How were they different?
2. How were the characters of Rita, Katsumoto, and Carol alike? How were they different?
3. View again the last time Phil meets Ned at the end of the film. Recalling all of Phil's previous interactions with Ned, explain how Phil finally achieves Aristotle's elusive "golden mean" in dealing with Ned.
4. Is it reasonable to assume that characters like Melvin Udall (or even Phil Connors) would make the sorts of changes to their characters as displayed in *As Good As It Gets* (or *Groundhog Day*)? What does your answer imply about motivations to act morally?
5. Reconsider the six movie quotes from the chapter and explain whether each, given the adjacent paragraphs, *illustrates* a point the author is making, *supplements* (or extends) a point the author is making, or *contrasts* (for emphasis) a point the author is making. Explain your answers.

NOTES

1. Excerpted from Aristotle's *Nicomachean Ethics*, trans. James Weldon (Macmillan Press, 1897). Section headings and slight grammar emendations have been provided to aid reader comprehension. Future citations to the *Nicomachean Ethics* will be made parenthetically (via standard margin number) in the text.

2. The "generally" qualifier is necessary because Aristotle allowed for some extreme sorts of behavior, but only if the situation called for it. For example, it seems to be appropriate to be outraged if a loved one is senselessly murdered. In fact, Aristotle might say that *not* being outraged at such tragedies might be evidence of a flawed character.

3. Nevertheless, other people might virtuously interact with Ned in other ways. Although this fact introduces some subjectivity into Aristotle's system, the underlying principle or guideline applies universally—aim for appropriate behavior, tending to avoid extremes, given your situation.

4. Achieving *eudaimonia* for Aristotle also seemingly includes an element of good fortune. Aristotle seemingly held that becoming truly happy requires one to be born into an affluent family with some political influence, as well as being physically attractive with dedicated children (*Nicomachean Ethics*, bk 1, chap. 8). Perhaps we can agree with Aristotle up to a point. Because no one can live well when struggling to meet the basic needs of food, water, shelter, and clothing, it seems that Aristotle is on firm ground to require these fundamental external goods. However, it is far from clear that it is *necessary* for one to enjoy all the external goods he cites in order to become truly virtuous, because, seemingly, we do not prize all the same moral and societal values he did. As times change, so do emphases upon the individual virtues; nevertheless, Aristotle holds that it is timelessly true that we should all endeavor to flourish as human persons taking full account of the situation in which we find ourselves.

5. The present discussion connecting action-guiding concerns about virtue ethics with arbitrariness concerns about divine command theory has been influenced by Russ Shafer-Landau, *Fundamentals of Ethics* (New York: Oxford University Press, 2010), 256–58. Dan Putman, however, doubts (via correspondence) that the analogy to divine command theory is all that strong, because there exists, he argues, a great deal of psychological and biological data about human flourishing. Therefore, worries about arbitrariness never really arise. Even so, the relevant data is most effectively interpreted as undergirding the morally significant reasons exemplars have for making the decisions

they do. Therefore, in the end, this rejoinder may only serve to reinforce the arguments of the next paragraph about the primacy of moral principles.

6. Those sympathetic to a virtue-based approach (for example, those sympathetic to an ethics of care) might attempt to deny that moral reasons can be universalized, thereby adopting some form of moral particularism; however, moral particularism itself is quite controversial. This issue will receive more attention in the next chapter.

7. A bit more carefully, a virtuous person, in Aristotle's sense of the term, habitually enacts or invokes the golden mean in masterful and natural ways. Therefore, although what the virtuous person does (acting in character) serves to define moral rightness, proper invocation of the golden mean further elucidates how the virtuous agent comes to her decisions.

CHAPTER 11

Care and Friendship

VERA DRAKE (2004)

Director: Mike Leigh
Screenwriter: Mike Leigh

PLOT SUMMARY

Oh, that's not right is it, Lily?—Well, I don't think so.—Still gotta help them out, ain't you?

It is 1950 in London, England, and the British are still feeling the aftereffects of World War II. Vera Drake lives in a small flat with her husband, Stan, and their grown children, Sid and Ethel. The family is not rich, but their combined incomes make for a reasonable life. Vera is a domestic worker cleaning local houses of affluent families; Stan is a mechanic working in a garage owned by his brother Frank; Ethel works in a light bulb factory; and Sid is an upstart tailor. The family's interactions with one another are comfortable and familiar. Thus the Drakes are contented, relying on each other for sources of strength and support. Yet, Vera, as wife and mother, is the anchor.

Not only does Vera tirelessly care for her family, she constantly helps those outside her home. Caring for others is simply a part of her day. In fact it looks as though Vera lives to serve, and aiding others makes her happy. She sings to herself as she runs her errands. Vera's mother, seemingly suffering from some kind of dementia, still lives on her own but only because of Vera's constant help. But her care extends to nonfamily members, too. She regularly visits one sick neighbor, George, and his depressed wife, Ivy. She makes them tea and helps with meals, especially on Ivy's "bad days." She keeps tabs on Reg, a bachelor in her building. When Vera discovers he isn't eating well, she invites him to dinner. (The fact that she suspects he would make a good husband for Ethel and she a wife for him may also partly explain the invitation.)

Stan and Frank have an open and affirming relationship at the shop. Frank is the owner, even though he is younger. Frank also seems a bit more affluent than Stan, even

---

BOX 11A: INSIDE *VERA DRAKE*

Vera Drake portrays a kindly British woman in the title role who gives of her time and efforts selflessly. Her days are regularly filled with serving and caring for others. That she lives her life in this way explains why *Vera Drake* is used to explore an ethics of care.

Even if you cannot watch all of the movie, start at the beginning and continue viewing through scene 2. Scene 2 ends at 7:57 with a shot of Vera dusting a piano. Note the stark contrast between the Drakes and how Susan Wells and her mother interact. Skip ahead to scene 5, which begins at 13:58 with Vera polishing a piece of furniture. Note the brief exchange between Vera's husband Stan and his brother Frank at 17:07. Continue watching through scene 6, which ends at 26:02 with a shot a Vera walking down a narrow alleyway. This segment provides insight into Frank's home life with his wife, Joycie. More importantly, the viewer witnesses Vera performing one of her "procedures." Skip ahead to scene 15; it conveys the police's initial questioning of Vera. This scene begins at 1:10:11 with a shot of a detective entering Vera's bedroom, and ends at 1:18:48 with a shot of the police taking Vera to the station as Frank looks on. Next view scene 19; it portrays Stan informing Sid and Ethel about why Vera has been arrested. This scene begins at 1:36:00 with a shot of Sid and Ethel sitting at the dining room table, and ends at 1:41:15 with a shot of Frank witnessing Vera being led out of the courtroom. Note how Vera seems so out of place in the criminal justice system (and it may be profitable to ask why the filmmakers portray her this way).

If you are able to watch the entire film, then you should be able to answer the trivia questions from box 11B. Also note the differences with which Lily and Vera tend to conduct their daily affairs (notably scene 11 from 46:19 to 48:49), on the one hand, and the differences between Stan and Vera and Frank and Joyce, on the other (especially the beginning of scenes 13 and 14, respectively). Finally, note how Stan and Frank are portrayed as brothers who have also become friends. See particularly scene 13, 54:30 to 55:30, and scene 18, 1:32:29 to 1:34:45.

---

though Stan and Vera helped fund Frank's apprenticeship, which paved the way for his financial success. But Stan is neither jealous of nor begrudges his younger brother. In fact, if anything, Frank is envious of Stan, especially in terms of his older brother's family. Frank regularly attests his fondness for Vera, once telling Stan, "She's got a heart of gold that woman. . . . You're a lucky man." Furthermore, Frank's approach toward his brother's family is made more poignant given his own. His wife, Joycie, is a young attractive woman, but she is also somewhat emotionally detached and more interested in climbing the social ladder than ingratiating herself to her extended family. But she is interested—even insistent—on starting her own family, even though Frank is unsure whether this is the right time. This might be her way of telling Frank that he spends too much time with his brother's family. Joyce responds to Frank's admiration of Vera—especially to Vera's compassion toward those who are lonely—with contempt. "She wants to mind her own business . . . she's a little busybody, bless her. She's going to get herself in trouble one of these days."

One day, Vera turns down a back alley to visit a house that is much shabbier than those of her employers. A distressed young woman is waiting. The woman nervously unlocks the door and they go upstairs. Vera puts a kettle on the stove and asks for a towel.

BOX 11B: *VERA DRAKE* TRIVIA

If your instructor assigns the film to be watched outside of class, you should be able to answer the following questions:

1. What is Vera polishing near the beginning of the film?
2. What is the Drakes' house (or flat) number?
3. Where does Reg's brother live?
4. What does Ethel do at the light bulb factory?
5. What is Sid trying to sell to his friends in the pub?
6. Vera performs an abortion on Nora; Nora already has how many children?
7. At the police station, the female officer requires Vera to surrender what personal item?
8. What does Frank's wife, Joyce, keep badgering him to buy for her?
9. What food do Vera and her family share at Christmas?
10. What is the length of Vera's prison sentence?

The young woman, still beside herself, remains disorientated. Towel in hand, Vera leads the girl to the bedroom and instructs her to lie down on her back over the towel. Vera offers her kind words of reassurance and then walks back to the kitchen and removes various items from her bag: a bar of heavy-duty pink soap, a cheese grater, a bottle of disinfectant oil, and a rubber syringe tube. She grates some soap into a bowl, covers the shreds with disinfectant and pours hot water over the concoction. She reenters the bedroom, inserts the tube, and begins pumping the solution into the young woman, saying, "We'll stop when you feel full." Vera soon removes the tube, informing the woman, "In a day or two, you'll have a pain down below. Get yourself to the toilet. You'll start bleeding and it will all come away. Then you'll be right as rain, dear." Vera smiles gently and then the young woman walks her out (only to quickly lock the door again).

It becomes clear that Vera offers women this kind of help regularly. On multiple occasions, we see the perennially cheerful and compassionate Vera going about her business, visiting women only to prepare and administer the soapy solution. Many of the women are young, but not all. Most are not married, but some are. Many are frightened and alone (including some of the married women), but not all. Meeting women who are in trouble is part of Vera's routine. But it remains a secret to her family; she has never discussed it with them, not even Stan, to say nothing of her children. They are totally unaware of her activities, which were, of course, illegal in England of 1950 (and remained so until much later).

Her appointments are made through Lily, whom she has known since they were children, and who now operates a black market service for items such as tea and sugar, which are still in short supply in postwar England. Lily, again in sharp contrast to Vera, is all business, and her interactions with prospective clients are often judgmental and sometimes downright nasty. Lily charges the women a fee for arranging Vera's visits. Lily keeps this a secret from Vera. Vera collects no money for the procedures, and would most certainly decline if any payment was offered.

Vera's home life continues on happily. Reg quickly becomes part of the family, and starts to court the extremely shy Ethel. Eventually, he proposes marriage, and she accepts, much to everybody's delight. As Vera and Stan reflect together on their good fortune and contentment, we discover that both Vera and Stan come from broken families and desperate poverty. In fact, Vera's mother was in the same situation as some of her clients—alone, with no husband to support her family.

One weekend, a girl whom Vera has "helped" is suddenly taken ill, and is rushed to the hospital. It is obvious to the doctor what has happened, and the girl's mother reluctantly admits the truth when the police get involved. Unfortunately for Vera, the mother of Vera's client recognized her from before the war. The reluctant mother has no choice but to identify Vera as the person who performed the abortion.

Frank and Joyce go to Vera and Stan's flat one Sunday to celebrate Ethel and Reg's engagement, and to announce their own news—that Joyce is expecting their first child.

They have barely broken this news when there is a knock on the door. Stan opens it, to discover the police, who enter and ask to see Vera. They will not reveal to the family the reason for their intrusion. The detective inspector, his detective sergeant, and the uniformed policewoman accompany a stunned Vera into the bedroom. She knows why they have come. Barely able to speak, she admits everything, and, at their request, produces her abortion kit from a cupboard. Detective Inspector Webster is sympathetic and patient, but persistent in his questioning of Vera: "What is it that you do, Mrs. Drake?" "I help young girls out, dear." "How do you help them out?" Vera, still mindful of her guests, pleads: "I don't want to spoil it for my family. Can't you come back tomorrow?" Webster responds, "I'm sorry, Mrs. Drake, we need to deal with this matter today." Vera: "Do you?"

Without informing the family, the police abruptly escort Vera to the station. Webster tells Stan that he may follow in a separate car. At the station, Vera is processed. Webster again questions Vera, inquiring into how she helps girls. Vera begins answering: "When they can't manage." Webster continues: "You mean when they are pregnant. So, how do you help them out?" Vera answers: "I help them to start their bleeding again." Webster: "You help them get rid of the baby? You perform an abortion. You perform abortions, don't you, Mrs. Drake?" Vera solemnly but compassionately replies: "That's not what I do, dear. That's what you call it, but they need help. Who else are they gonna turn to? They got no one. I help them out."

Vera is formally charged with her crime, and Inspector Webster suggests that since Stan is inevitably going to find out the truth anyway, why doesn't she tell him herself? The inspector brings in the bewildered Stan, and Vera confesses all. Vera is traumatized and clearly very confused by what has happened. What will happen at her trial, and what is to become of her family?

11.1. THINKING THROUGH THE MOVIE

Discussion Starter Questions

1. Which characters are portrayed sympathetically in the film? Which are portrayed unsympathetically? What accounts for the differences?
2. Which of Vera's actions are morally commendable? Which, if any, are morally blameworthy? What accounts for the difference?
3. Vera believes she is helping the young girls she visits. Is she? Explain.
4. Is Vera is a good person? Justify your answer.
5. Are Vera and Stan happy? What makes for a happy marriage anyway?

Questions for Further Thought

1. When Frank informs Joyce of Vera's situation (scene 20, 1:43:30 into the film), she disparages her sister-in-law: "Stupid cow. How can she be so selfish?" Was Vera selfish rather than caring? Explain.
2. Is it morally significant that Vera decides not to tell her family that she performs these procedures? Is this another example of Vera caring for her family or not?
3. Stan (scene 18, roughly 1:34:00 into the film) confides in Frank about Vera's activities and her request that he not tell the kids. Frank replies: "You got to tell them the truth." Is Stan morally required to inform his children about this? Justify your answer.
4. Sid has a difficult time accepting the truth about his mother (scenes 19 and 20). Stan (about 1:36:00 into the film) tries to explain to his son, "Whatever she done, she's done it out of the kindness of her heart." Can acting from kindness mitigate or even obviate moral censure?
5. Reg is the most sympathetic about Vera's decision to "help out girls who can't manage" (especially scene 21, 1:45:30 into the film). Evaluate Reg's position against that of Sid's. With whom do you agree with more and why?

11.2. HISTORICAL SETTING

Caring (excerpt)[1]

Nel Noddings is Lee L. Jacks Professor of Education, emerita, at Stanford University. She is past president of the Philosophy of Education Society and of the John Dewey Society, and the author of a very large number of articles, contributed chapters, and books— including the very influential *Caring: A Feminine Approach to Ethics and Moral Education*, from which this excerpt is taken.

Preparing to Read

A. What would Noddings think of the character of Vera Drake and the choices she makes?

B. In what ways is Noddings's ethics of care approach similar to an Aristotelian virtue ethics zx approach?

[Caring as Ethical Ideal]

We shall discuss the ethical ideal, that vision of best self, in some depth. When we commit ourselves to obey the "I must" even at its weakest and most fleeting, we are under the guidance of this ideal. It is not just any picture. Rather, it is our best picture of ourselves caring and being cared for. It may even be colored by acquaintance with one superior to us in caring, but, as I shall describe it, it is both constrained and attainable. It is limited by what we have already done and by what we are capable of, and it does not idealize the impossible so that we may escape into ideal abstraction.

Now, clearly, in pointing to . . . an ethical ideal as the source of ethical behavior, I seem to be advocating an ethic of virtue. This is certainly true in part. Many philosophers recognize the need for a discussion of virtue as the energizing factor in moral behavior, even when they have given their best intellectual effort to a careful explication of their positions on obligation and justification. When we discuss the ethical ideal, we shall be talking about "virtue," but we shall not let "virtue" dissipate into "the virtues" described in abstract categories. The holy man living abstemiously on top of the mountain, praying thrice daily, and denying himself human intercourse may display "virtues," but they are not the virtues of one-caring. . . .

I am obliged, then, to accept the initial "I must" when it occurs and even to fetch it out of recalcitrant slumber when it fails to awake spontaneously. The source of my obligation is the value I place on the relatedness of caring. This value itself arises as a product of actual caring and being cared-for and my reflection on the goodness of these concrete caring situations. . . .

Let me say here, however, why it seems preferable to place an ethical ideal above principle as a guide to moral action. It has been traditional in moral philosophy to insist that moral principles must be, by their very nature as moral principles, universifiable. If I am obligated to do X under certain conditions, then under sufficiently similar conditions you also are obligated to do X. But the principle of universifiability seems to depend . . . on a concept of "sameness." In order to accept the principle, we should have to establish that human predicaments exhibit sufficient sameness, and this we cannot do without abstracting away from concrete situations those qualities that seem to reveal the sameness. In doing this, we often lose the very qualities or factors that gave rise to the moral question in the situation. That condition which makes the situation different and thereby induces genuine moral puzzlement cannot be satisfied by the application of principles developed in situations of sameness.

This does not mean that we cannot receive any guidance from an attempt to discover principles that seem to be universifiable. We can, under this sort of plan, arrive at the doctrine of "prima facie duty" described by W. D. Ross. Ross himself, however, admits that this doctrine yields no real guidance for moral conduct in concrete situations. It guides us in abstract moral thinking; it tells us, theoretically, what to do, "all other things being equal." But other things are rarely if ever equal. A and B, struggling with a moral decision, are two different persons with different factual histories, different projects and aspirations, and different ideals. It may indeed be right, morally right, for A to do X and B to do not-X. We may, that is, connect "right" and "wrong" to faithfulness to the ethical ideal. This does not cast us into relativism, because the ideal contains at its heart a component that is universal: Maintenance of the caring relation. . . .

[Determining Moral Obligation]

Our obligation is limited and delimited by relation. We are never free, in the human domain, to abandon our preparedness to care; but, practically, if we are meeting those in our inner circles adequately as ones-caring and receiving those linked to our inner circles by formal chains of relation, we shall limit the calls upon our obligation quite naturally. We are not obliged to summon the "I must" if there is no possibility of completion in the other. I am not obliged to care for starving children in Africa, because there is no way for this caring to be completed in the other unless I abandon the caring to which I am obligated. I may still choose to do something in the direction of caring, but I am not obliged to do so. When we discuss our obligation to animals, we shall see that this is even more sharply limited by relation. We cannot refuse obligation in human affairs by merely refusing to enter relation; we are, by virtue of our mutual humanity, already and perpetually in potential relation. Instead, we limit our obligation by examining the possibility of completion. In connection with animals, however, we may find it possible to refuse relation itself on the grounds of a species-specific impossibility of any form of reciprocity in caring. . . .

I am working deliberately toward criteria that will preserve our deepest and most tender human feelings. The caring of mother for child, of human adult for human infant, elicits the tenderest feelings in most of us. Indeed, for many women, this feeling of nurturance lies at the very heart of what we assess as good. A philosophical position that has difficulty distinguishing between our obligation to human infants and, say, pigs is in some difficulty straight off. It violates our most deeply cherished feeling about human goodness. This violation does not, of course, make the position logically wrong, but it suggests that especially strong grounds will be needed to support it. In the absence of such strong grounds . . . we might prefer to establish a position that captures rather than denies our basic feelings. We might observe that man (in contrast to woman) has continually turned away from his inner self and feeling in pursuit of both science and ethics. With respect to strict science, this turning outward may be defensible; with respect to ethics, it has been disastrous.

[The Example of Abortion]

. . . Operating under the guidance of an ethic of caring, we are not likely to find abortion in general either right or wrong. We shall have to inquire into individual cases. An incipient embryo is an information speck—a set of controlling instructions for a future human being. Many of these specks are created and flushed away without their creators' awareness. From the view developed here, the information speck is an information speck; it has no given sanctity. There should be no concern over the waste of "human tissue," since nature herself is wildly prolific, even profligate. The one-caring is concerned not with human tissue but with human consciousness—with pain, delight, hope, fear, entreaty, and response.

But suppose the information speck is mine, and I am aware of it. This child-to-be is the product of love between a man deeply cared-for and me. Will the child have his eyes or mine? His stature or mine? Our joint love of mathematics or his love of mechanics or my love of language? This is not just an information speck; it is endowed with prior love and current knowledge. It is sacred, but I—humbly, not presumptuously—confer sacredness upon it. I cannot, will not destroy it. It is joined to loved others through formal chains of caring. It is linked to the inner circle in a clearly defined way. I might wish that I were not pregnant, but I cannot destroy this known and potentially loved person-to-be. There is already relation albeit indirect and formal. My decision is an ethical one born of natural caring.

But suppose, now, that my beloved child has grown up; it is she who is pregnant and considering abortion. She is not sure of the love between herself and the man. She is miserably worried about her economic and emotional future. I might like to convey sanctity on this information speck; but I am not God—only mother to this suffering cared-for. It is she who is conscious and in pain, and I as one-caring move to relieve the pain. This information speck is an information speck and that is all. There is no formal relation, given the breakdown between husband and wife, and with the embryo, there is no present relation; the possibility of future relation—while not absent, surely—is uncertain. But what of this possibility for growing response? Must we not consider it? We must indeed. As the embryo becomes a fetus and, growing daily, becomes more nearly capable of response as cared-for, our obligation grows from a nagging uncertainty—an "I must if I wish"—to an utter conviction that we must meet this small other as one-caring.

If we try to formalize what has been expressed in the concrete situations described so far, we arrive at a legal approach to abortion very like that of the Supreme Court: abortions should be freely available in the first trimester, subject to medical determination in the second trimester, and banned in the third, when the fetus is viable. A woman under the guidance of our ethic would be likely to recognize the growing possibility of relation; the potential is clearly dynamic. Further, many women recognize the relation as established when the fetus begins to move about. It is not a question of when life begins but of when relation begins.

But what if relation is never established? Suppose the child is born and the mother admits no sense of relatedness. May she commit infanticide? One who asks such questions misinterprets the concept of relatedness that I have been struggling to describe. Since the infant, even the near-natal fetus, is capable of relation—of the sweetest and most unselfconscious reciprocity—one who encounters the infant is obligated to meet it as one-caring. Both parts of this claim are essential; it is not only the child's capability to respond but also the encounter that induces obligation. There must exist the possibility for our caring to be completed in the other. If the mother does not care naturally, then she must summon ethical caring to support her as one-caring. She may not ethically ignore the child's cry to live.

The one-caring, in considering abortion as in all other matters, cares first for the one in immediate pain or peril. She might suggest a brief and direct form of counseling in which a young expectant mother could come to grips with her feelings. If the incipient child has been sanctified by its mother, every effort must be made to help the two to achieve a stable and hopeful life together; if it has not, it should be removed swiftly and mercifully with all loving attention to the woman, the conscious patient. Between these two clear reactions is a possible confused one: the young woman is not sure how she feels. The one-caring probes gently to see what has been considered, raising questions and retreating when the questions obviously have been considered and are now causing great pain. Is such a view "unprincipled"? If it is, it is boldly so; it is at least connected with the world as it is, at its best and at its worst, and it requires that we—in espousing a "best"—stand ready to actualize that preferred condition. The decision for or against abortion must be made by those directly involved in the concrete situation, but it need not be made alone. The one-caring cannot require everyone to behave as she would in a particular situation. Rather, when she dares to say, "I think you should do X," she adds, also, "Can I help you?" The one under her gaze is under her support and not her judgment. . . .

[Ethics and Justification]

For an ethic of caring, the problem of justification is not concentrated upon justified action in general. We are not "justified"—we are *obligated*—to do what is required to maintain and enhance caring. We must "justify" not-caring; that is, we must explain why, in the interest of caring for ourselves as ethical selves or in the interest of others for whom we care, we may behave as ones-not-caring toward this particular other. In a related problem, we must justify doing what this other would not have us do to him as part of our

genuine effort to care for him. But even in these cases, an ethic of caring does not emphasize justification. As one-caring, I am not seeking justification for my action; I am not
standing alone before some tribunal. What I seek is completion in the other—the sense
of being cared-for and, I hope, the renewed commitment of the cared-for to turn about
and act as one-caring in the circles and chains within which he is defined. Thus, I am not
justified but somehow fulfilled and completed in my own life and in the lives of those I
have thus influenced. . . .

It should be clear that my description of an ethic of caring as a feminine ethic does
not imply a claim to speak for all women nor to exclude men. As we shall see in the next
chapter, there is reason to believe that women are somewhat better equipped for caring
than men are. This is partly a result of the construction of psychological deep structures
in the mother-child relationship. A girl can identify with the one caring for her and thus
maintain relation while establishing identity. A boy must, however, find his identity with
the absent one—the father—and thus disengage himself from the intimate relation of
caring. . . .

[Applications and Ramifications]

[Caring] will not allow us to be distracted by visions of universal love, perfect justice, or
a world unified under principle. It does not say, "Thou shalt not kill," and then seek other
principles under which killing is, after all, justified. If the other is a clear and immediate
danger to me or to my cared-fors, I must stop him, and I might need to kill him. But
I cannot kill in the name of principle or justice. I must meet this other—even this evil
other—as one-caring so long as caring itself is not endangered by my doing so. I must,
for example, oppose capital punishment. I do not begin by saying, "Capital punishment is
wrong." Thus I do not fall into the trap of having to supply reasons for its wrongness that
will be endlessly disputed at a logical level. I do not say, "Life is sacred," for I cannot name
a source of sacredness. I may point to the irrevocability of the decision, but this is not in
itself decisive, even for me, because in many cases the decision would be just and I could
not regret the demise of the condemned. (I have, after all, confessed my own ferocity; in
the heat of emotion, I might have torn him to shreds if I had caught him molesting my
child.)

My concern is for the ethical ideal, for my own ethical ideal and for whatever part
of it others in my community may share. Ideally, another human being should be able to
request, with expectation of positive response, my help and comfort. If I am not blinded
by fear, or rage, or hatred, I should reach out as one-caring to the proximate stranger
who entreats my help. This is the ideal one-caring creates. I should be able to respond to
the condemned man's entreaty, "Help me." We must ask, then, after the effects of capital
punishment on jurors, on judges, on jailers, on wardens, on newspersons "covering" the
execution, on ministers visiting the condemned, on citizens affirming the sentence, on
doctors certifying first that the condemned is well enough to be executed and second that
he is dead. What effects have capital punishment on the ethical ideals of the participants?
For me, if I had to participate, the ethical ideal would be diminished. Diminished. The
ideal itself would be diminished. My act would either be wrong or barely right—right in
a depleted sense. I might, indeed, participate ethically—rightly—in an execution but only
at the cost of revising my ethical ideal downward. If I do not revise it and still participate,

then my act is wrong, and I am a hypocrite and unethical. It is the difference between "I don't believe in killing, but . . ." and "I did not believe in killing cold-bloodedly, but now I see that I must and for these reasons." In the latter case, I may retain my ethicality, but at considerable cost. My ideal must forever carry with it not only what I would be but what I am and have been. There is no unbridgeable chasm between what I am and what I will be. I build the bridge to my future self, and this is why I oppose capital punishment. I do not want to kill if other options are open to me, and I do not want to ask others in the community to do what may diminish their own ethical ideals.

While I must not kill in obedience to law or principle, I may not, either, refuse to kill in obedience to principle. To remain one-caring, I might have to kill. Consider the case of a woman who kills her sleeping husband. Under most circumstances, the one-caring would judge such an act wrong. It violates the very possibility of caring for the husband. But as she hears how the husband abused his wife and children, about the fear with which the woman lived, about the past efforts to solve the problem legally, the one-caring revises her judgment. The jury finds the woman not guilty by reason of an extenuated self-defense. The one-caring finds her ethical, but under the guidance of a sadly diminished ethical ideal. The woman has behaved in the only way she found open to protect herself and her children and, thus, she has behaved in accord with the current vision of herself as one-caring. But what a horrible vision! She is now one-who-has-killed once and who would not kill again, and never again simply one who would not kill. The test of ultimate blame or blamelessness, under an ethic of caring, lies in how the ethical ideal was diminished. Did the agent choose the degraded vision out of greed, cruelty, or personal interest? Or was she driven to it by unscrupulous others who made caring impossible to sustain?

Review Questions

1. What is Noddings's position on universalizable moral principles?
2. Noddings says "To remain one-caring, I might have to kill." Explain.
3. Is abortion wrong, according to Noddings? Craft your response with Vera Drake in mind.

11.3. DISCUSSION AND ANALYSIS

There are different ways to approach the world. Scientists and philosophers tend to do so rationally (some might say "hyperrationally"), the former via empirical methods and the latter via nonempirical methods. This is understandable, as humankind seems to be essentially rational. However, following Aristotle, we might say that we are rational *and* social, biological beings. Some scholars, then, advocate approaching the world by emphasizing the social aspect of our nature. One incontrovertible aspect of our social nature is our propensity to care, especially among those in close, personal circles. This approach goes back at least as far as the Chinese philosopher Mencius.[2] Yet it must be admitted that a rational approach has been dominant in the history of philosophy. Some contemporary philosophers in the West, most notably feminists, have argued that a singularly rational approach to ethics—one grounded in articulating, deriving, and applying moral principles—radically misconstrues moral philosophy. Room must be made for an ethics of care (and friendship) based approach.

Reexamining Autonomy and Impartiality

Taking a rational (or hyperrational) approach to the world invariably emphasizes one's individuality and atomic status as a knowledge-seeker. This is reminiscent of Rene Descartes and his *Meditations*. By reexamining his basic approach to the world in terms of his belief-acquisition process, Descartes single-handedly attempted to reground the sciences, making them finally secure from skeptical attacks.

Interpreting knowledge-seekers (regarding the empirical or nonempirical) as isolated, atomic individuals also emphasizes personal autonomy, and, indeed, prizes it. Seeking requires the personal space to do so; thus, one is impermissibly treated when his or her personal space is infringed upon. This implication harkens back to Kant, and a respect for persons approach. Each of us possesses autonomy—being rational, with a grasp of the moral law and the ability to act on that knowledge. Each of us, insofar as we are autonomous, possess intrinsic worth, eminently deserving of respect; to treat a person as a mere thing (invariably invading his or her "moral space") is to commit the gravest of moral errors.

An ethics of care approach questions this Kantian starting point to moral discourse. We are not nearly as atomic or autonomous as it may initially appear. All of us are enmeshed in various social relationships or associations. We are not atomic units separate from everyone else. We are parents and children (like Dora, Guido, and Joshua), spouses (like Stan and Vera), brothers and sisters (like Frank and Stan, and Sid and Ethel), friends and lovers (like Mulder and Scully), doctors and patients (like Scully and Christian), and teachers and students (like Dora and her pupils). Furthermore, we tend to make sense of who we are in terms these relationships, and our connectedness tends to limit our autonomous behavior. There are some things children don't do with respect to their parents, and there are some things parents only do for their children. Thus, what is or isn't permissible must take into account how we are enmeshed with others.

According to an ethics of care approach, then, our moral obligations are primarily derivative upon our connectedness with others. This explains why parents have special or

---

BOX 11C: LEARNING OUTCOMES

Upon carefully studying this chapter, students should better comprehend and be able to explain:

- How an ethics of care offers a distinctive approach to ethics, and, so, how it differs with more venerable theories like Kantian-based systems and utilitarianism
- How contemporary philosophers, particularly Nel Noddings, articulate and defend an ethics of care.
- How aspects of Aristotle's virtue ethics, particularly his ideas about friendship, are consonant with an ethics of care (even if some aspects are not).
- How themes expressed in *Vera Drake*, *Life Is Beautiful*, and *The X-Files: I Want to Believe* are conducive to better understanding ethical issues associated with care and friendship.

Life Is Beautiful, Miramax Films, 1997. Guido (Roberto Benigni, center) and Dora (Nicoletta Braschi) do everything they can to keep their son safe as World War II looms in Europe. (Moviegoods, Inc.)

unique obligations only to their children. Guido is obligated to care for Joshua in the concentration camp in ways other adults are not, and Dora's demand (recall she is not Jewish) that she be put on the train headed for the concentration camp is morally dubious made by a complete stranger. Moreover, consider how ill-fitted a Kantian approach is to morally significant interactions between parents and children, spouses, and close friends. People who approach their ethical dealings with their children merely "from duty" are bad parents because acting in this way can only harm the children and the parent-child bond. Furthermore, parents simply don't stand behind their rights when interacting with their children. Rather than make rights-based claims,

> "My husband and son are on that train. I want to get on that train. Did you hear me!" —*Life Is Beautiful*, scene 18

the parent-child relationship seems to proceed most effectively when love, empathy, and concern are the primary motivational factors. So, while justice is not completely absent in parent-child relationships, justice is notoriously difficult to square with love. Entering into a loving relationship with children, friends, or spouses, and the closeness required to foster such relationships, is not easily reconciled with the notion of inviolable moral space of autonomous agents. That a Kantian approach fails to adequately capture some of our most important ethical relationships lends intuitive support for care-based ethics.

A vivid example of this is Guido's tendency to spin falsehoods (he impersonates a government official, for example), and particularly his unwavering decision to deceive his son

Joshua about the horrors of World War II, especially the notorious "Jewish Solution." Kant is just as unwavering in his condemnation of dishonesty: it is always impermissible to tell a lie. Even on a modified Kantian approach, one must determine whether being honest with Joshua constitutes a conflict situation, and whether it would be disrespecting the boy more to tell him the truth. On an ethics of care, what Guido is actually doing is his best to make life beautiful for his son (and others close to Guido, most notably Dora). Perhaps the most uncaring thing Guido could do in this situation is be honest with the boy; this would cause him the most harm. For Guido to tell the boy the truth simply because it is right (and for no other reason) is thus incredibly counterintuitive. In this way, then, an ethics of care argues that issues of moral autonomy are not nearly as central to ethical discourse as Kant believed.

The discussion of special obligations between those enmeshed in close, personal relationships points to another pillar of care-based ethics: some duties simply cannot be understood via impartiality. In this way, an ethics of care stands in stark contrast to Kantian-based systems and utilitarianism. Recall that utilitarians take the utility principle and, upon impartially taking everyone's happiness or suffering into account, prescribe that act which maximizes utility. Consequently, the happiness or suffering of your child is no more or less important than any other sentient being. But it's clear that this kind of impartiality with respect

> "The game starts now. You have to score a thousand points. If you do that, you take home a tank with a big gun. . . . The one with the fewest points will have to wear a sign that says 'Jackass' on his back," *Life Is Beautiful,* scene 19

to morally significant action is contrary to the values inherent in our close, personal relationships. In fact, it is difficult to make sense of family interactions via impartiality at all. That utilitarian approaches fail to capture the importance of close personal relationships lends more intuitive support for an ethics of care. That both Kantian-based systems and utilitarian approaches fail to capture some of the most crucial aspects of the ethical life, argues care ethics sympathizers, is reason to rethink our overall approach to morally significant situations.

Perhaps the most fundamental difference between an ethics of care and other, more traditional approaches is the role of abstract, moral principles. In systems like Kantianism or utilitarianism, they are paramount, but in an ethics of care, they are downplayed as much as conceptually possible. This seemingly includes doubting the effectiveness of universalization, a hallmark of Kantian-based systems and utilitarianism. Noddings all but denies that agent B must also do action X in circumstances C because it's true that agent A ought to X in circumstances C. She believes that this assumes a kind of "sameness" between A and B as applied to C that simply isn't possible to achieve without destroying the specifics that gave rise to the ethical question in the first place. Moral judgments must be sensitive to our personal situation and the intention with which our acts are performed; thus, our moral judgments must depend primarily on these features and not on abstract principles. Furthermore, Noddings goes so far as to say that moral judgments are neither statements of fact nor true statements derived from general principles.[3] They are more akin to attitudes or stances taken given a more emotional approach to the world, and one grounded in caring for those we encounter. But she denies that

> "I think our son left us both with an emptiness that can't be filled." *I Want to Believe,* scene 8

this leads to any sort of ethical conventionalism because she affirms caring as a kind of universal ethical ideal. That ideal—maintenance of the caring relation—offers moral guidance at least in terms of what kind of person one should strive to become.

The most fundamental aspect of an ethics of care approach, then, is to recognize our being enmeshed in various relationships, recognizing how they (respectively) are most effectively maintained, and then attending to them via that knowledge as best we can. In this way, and even though care ethicists resist abstract principles, the moral standard for an ethics of care could be (roughly) articulated:

> Everyone ought to act in ways that promote the flourishing of reciprocally intimate, care-based relationships.

Meeting this standard (or something like it) will require us to develop a certain set of virtuous, or "caring-excellence," traits to keep the webs of our relationships strong. The specific set of virtues conducive to caring-excellence will vary somewhat with the relationship—moral excellence for a parent will no doubt be different than that between close friends—but, invariably, we should all strive to become loving, empathetic, kind, loyal, sympathetic, and nurturing. We might refer to the example of those who exemplify these traits in commendable ways for guidance in ethically significant situations. Consequently, and insofar as an ethics of care admits of an analysis of moral obligation, right actions are those that a "care-exemplar" would perform when acting in character.[4] Wrong actions are those that subvert or undermine intimate, caring relationships—those that no "care-exemplar" would perform when acting in character. Therefore, we ultimately ought to become a certain kind of person and once we begin approaching this (perhaps by keeping in mind distinctive caring-exemplars), then we will be better informed and sensitive to what we ought to do in specific situations. In this way, an ethics of care is plausibly interpreted as a variant or modification of virtue ethics, stressing characteristics germane to being enmeshed with those around us. If approaching *eudaimonia*—along with the character transformation necessary for it—is intrinsically valuable to virtue ethics, then reciprocally participating in intimate, care-based relationships—along with the character transformation necessary for such participation—is intrinsically valuable to an ethics of care.

The "Messiness" of Ethics

Because our relationships (respectively) are often uniquely complicated, which explains their being "messy," the ethics of care sympathizer holds that the content of our moral obligations is analogously "messy." This "messiness" is exacerbated by the fact that we are simultaneously parents and children, or friends and spouses (or combinations of these). So sometimes it can be difficult to know what to do. A parent may recognize that her caring-based obligations to her mother sometimes conflict with her obligations to her own children. A spouse might find himself in a similar situation with a close friend or sibling. True, some of this "messiness" could be alleviated by invoking an operative, abstract moral principle. Further, relying on such principles would no doubt deflect temptations to simply act from personal bias. However, recall that ethics of care sympathizers are suspicious of such principles. Even if they could be articulated, which they doubt, abstract principles invariably blind us to the richness and complexity—the "messiness"—that occasioned appealing to them in the first place. In this way, it is argued, invoking abstract general

Vera Drake, New Line Cinema, 2004. Vera (Imelda Staunton) and her family must come to grips with how she chooses to help young girls in trouble. (Moviegoods, Inc.)

principles for moral guidance becomes somewhat self-defeating. Rather, we are to do the best we can in the situations we face, noting our care-based successes and mistakes along the way, and learning from each as we go.

The beauty of film is that it effectively captures the messiness of life. First, note that Vera acts compassionately toward young girls in trouble who have nowhere else to turn, but in doing so, she remains secretive about her "procedures" to her family. So, in caring for pregnant women in the way she does, she seemingly acts in ways that separate her from her family. Does Vera act permissibly? She seems to think so, and presumably Noddings would agree, but Vera's son, Sid, disagrees because his "mum is killing little babies." But recall that Vera doesn't believe she is performing abortions—"that's not what she does dear, even if that's what you call it"—she is merely helping young girls out, and does so simply because they seek her help and she wishes to help them. Second, note that Mulder is a bit like Vera in that the FBI has no one else it can turn to in helping them relocate missing agent Bannon and solve the case. Only Mulder has the requisite expertise in dealing with cases involving psychics. That his help is required seemingly takes precedence over other concerns, including, perhaps, his well-being (he might be reapprehended for his past crimes) or even his relationship with Scully. However, third, note that "self-care" is still paramount, as Noddings is quick to point out. Scully ought not to stand idly by and watch Mulder's reignited passions again become obsessions. Even though she suggested that he help with the case, there comes a time when she may permissibly practice "tough-caring." Not wanting to become again subjected to the harms of "chasing monsters in the dark," she is firm with Mulder, but only because she intends to renew their reciprocal one-caring and one-cared-for loving friendship. That she is successful in this regard energizes her caring efforts with respect to young Christian Fearon.

> "Don't you be upset. I'm here to help you. And that's what I'm going to do." —*Vera Drake*, scene 6

Ethics of care defenders also believe that our interactions would become much less messy if we ceased standing on our rights. Making demands upon others via rights-based claims tend to divide us and create competition of interests. This competition tends to evoke antagonism toward others. Ethics of care defenders downplay the importance of rights and argue that we should be more cooperative, developing opportunities to help one another—perhaps in ways similar to Vera Drake. Due to our connectedness, our responsibilities to others should be emphasized, not our rights against others, which only serve to insulate us from them. Perhaps this is the pull that many feel about Vera's "procedures." She has made helping others part of her daily routine. An ethics of care person wouldn't expect others to act exactly as Vera does (and Noddings is clear about this), but, in many ways, Vera is an exemplar of caring. So perhaps the stigma of abortion should take a backseat to the motivations she has for performing them. By making this sort of cooperation paramount— by asking "how can I help you" instead of barking "you have no right"—care ethics offers a more harmonious, empathetic approach to our interactions with others and society generally. That this result seems so welcome is another intuitive strength of an ethics of care.[5]

> "Whatever she done, she done it out of the goodness of her heart!" —*Vera Drake*, scene 19

Mulder, Scully, Aristotle, and Friendship

An ethics of care is invariably developed around the relationship between mother and child. However, there are other close, personal relationships deserving of philosophical attention. At the forefront of these is friendship. In fact, the nature of friendship has long been a topic of philosophical discussion. At first this seems odd. Why would philosophers worry about something that is so obvious? We assume we know what friendship is, how to identify it, and how to judge its worthiness. For example, in *The X-Files: I Want to Believe*, it seems rather obvious that Assistant Director Walter Skinner acts as a worthy friend when he comes to Mulder's rescue at Scully's request, despite the risks to his personal safety and professional career, especially given the fact that Mulder and Scully are no longer FBI agents. But once we remind ourselves that we have different kinds of friends, and that our friendships come in varying degrees, we soon see that understanding the nature of friendship can get a bit tricky. Moreover, some people claim to be "the best of friends." But what does this actually mean? What kind of friendship is best, anyway? Aristotle tried to answer questions like these in books 8 and 9 of his *Nicomachean Ethics*. Among the various notable duos from popular culture, *The X-Files*'s Fox Mulder and Dana Scully rather uniquely capture Aristotle's highest form of friendship.[6] Fully appreciating this claim, however, requires us to first explore Aristotle's two lower forms of friendship.

The first of the lower forms of friendship is that based on pleasure. Friendships of this type are made and sustained because they "feel good" or are fun in some way—for example, a drinking buddy or tennis partner. Aristotle is certainly not claiming that true friendships shouldn't give us pleasure or that we shouldn't engage in fun activities with true friends. He is only claiming that friendships that are based primarily on pleasure are of a lower form. One reason for this is rather obvious: pleasure friendships tend not to last once the fun is gone or something better comes along. Aristotle writes, "This is why [young people] quickly become friends and quickly cease to be so; their friendship changes with the object that is found pleasant, and such pleasure alters quickly."[7] We can rather easily rule out pleasure friendship as the type that best describes the relationship between Scully and Mulder. Neither Scully nor Mulder seems to have much fun alone, much less together, and, in any event, there is clearly something deeper between them.

The second of the lower forms of friendship is that based on utility. Friendships of this type are made and sustained because they are useful or profitable to us in some way—for example, a business partnership. Aristotle writes, "Those who pursue utility . . . sometimes they do not even find each other pleasant; therefore they do not need such companionship unless they are useful to each other; for they are pleasant to each other only in so far as they rouse in each other hopes of something good to come" (1156a 27–30). Again, even true friendships can be useful to us, but here Aristotle has in mind those friendships based primarily on utility. As with pleasure friendships, utility friendships are easily dissolved once the other is no longer useful to us and, as such, constitutes a lower form of friendship. We might conceivably place Scully and Mulder in this category of friendship based on a few early episodes from season one of *The X-Files*—say, if Mulder merely relied on Scully's medical expertise in doing autopsies or Scully merely saw her partnership with Mulder as a steppingstone in her fledgling FBI career. However, their relationship clearly develops into something much more—even by the end of the first season we can see that they are more than mere partners in the FBI.

According to Aristotle, the best friendships are not based merely on pleasure or utility. True (or complete) friendship is a relationship between good people, each of whom recognizes the good character of the other, and each of whom desires to preserve and promote the other's virtue simply because it is good to do so. True friendship occurs between equals—a relationship in which one person is vastly superior to the other in moral virtue is more likely a paternalistic relationship than a true friendship. Aristotle writes, "Perfect friendship is of [those] who are good, and alike in virtue; for these wish each other well alike to each other qua good, and they are good in themselves. Now those who wish well to their friends for their sake are most truly friends" (1156b 7–10). Unlike pleasure and utility friendships, true friendships must involve a genuine caring for the well-being of the other person, not merely egoistic motives. Of course, that doesn't mean that one may not consider how the friendship affects one's own interests—Aristotle is not advocating slavishness or radical self-sacrifice. The idea is simply that one cares about the other person for his or her own sake and wants to see the other person flourish, regardless of any benefit that one might also receive as a result. Nevertheless, Aristotle does believe, as a matter of fact, that true friendships are beneficial to those involved. In that way, true friendship involves a happy convergence of self-interest and altruism and, as such, results in an ideal kind of moral motivation.

So, for Aristotle, the highest form of friendship occurs between persons of roughly equally good moral character (virtue) that is enhanced in various ways due to their interactions with each other. Such friendships are admittedly rare; however, when they do obtain, it is because the friends spend a great deal of time together, developing a secure mutual trust (1156b 24–26). Their relationship is fostered by participating in joint ventures, and engaging in activities that exercise their own virtues for the betterment of the other and the friendship. All of this is done primarily for the sake of the other person (and not for selfish purposes), even though their interests have grown so close together that it is difficult to separate one's good from that of the other (1157b 33–35 and 1166a 29–32). Fully appreciating how Mulder and Scully fit these criteria requires briefly revisiting the acclaimed FOX television series (1993–2002).

That the relationship between Mulder and Scully satisfies Aristotle's conditions for true friendship arguably begins with the season four episode "Memento Mori." The episode opens with Scully's voice-over; we are privileged to hear some of Scully's innermost thoughts and feelings as she faces the looming prospect of losing her battle with cancer. Much of her soliloquy concerns the issue we would expect—fear of death—but it's also revealing how her thoughts turn to Mulder. Scully thinks of Mulder as an equal partner together on an important journey; she trusts him as one can only trust the closest of confidantes, someone with shared values and a mutual concern for the other's well-being. Also note Mulder's resounding refusal to accept that Scully's cancer is terminal. Mulder goes to great lengths to find a cure and considers making a deal with the nefarious Cigarette Smoking Man (CSM). He expresses his passion and determination for Scully, not because he is merely fond of her phone voice (the iconic "Mulder, it's me") or fears that no one else will perform the copious autopsies he requests, but simply for her own sake. Scully reciprocates in the season seven episode "Sixth Extinction." Mulder has been beset by a mysterious and mentally debilitating illness after encountering an extraterrestrial artifact. Scully continues the investigation without him, in part for the hope of curing him and in part to continue his work, despite her own doubts. She perseveres for Mulder and utilizes her unique traits for their joint pursuit of "the truth." She does so on her own terms—as a scientist—because she believes that "in the source of every illness lies its cure." But she does this for Mulder's sake—not for any glory of discovering a cure to his fantastic illness. Indeed Mulder and Scully regularly act on the behalf of the other, thereby satisfying one of the conditions Aristotle requires for true friendship.

The intrepid *X-Files* heroes have also strengthened each other, shoring up their virtuous character traits. Recall that in the first motion picture, *Fight the Future,* Scully visits Mulder's apartment to tell him she has resigned from the FBI. In pleading for her not to quit, Mulder replies: "But you saved me! As difficult and as frustrating as it's been sometimes, your goddamned strict rationalism and science have saved me a thousand times over! You've kept me honest . . . you've made me a whole person." Mulder recognizes that he has gained a kind of temperance through his relationship with Scully and is a better investigator—and person—for it. But Mulder has also strengthened Scully. In the season eight episode "Empedocles," Scully confides in Mulder that the greatest gift he has given her is courage—courage to accept the possibility of unexplained phenomena. Before she met Mulder, she was afraid to reexamine her worldview and, thus, simply rejected any experience that didn't fit it. She eventually imparts Mulder's gift to her new X-Files partner, John Doggett. As a result of her relationship with Mulder, Scully is a better investigator—and person. Therefore, another of Aristotle's conditions is met.

Mulder and Scully's joint venture of seeking the truth "out there" has also led to the intertwining of their individual goods into one, unified good. Going back to *Fight the Future,* after Mulder suggests (near the end of the film) that she was right to quit, Scully replies, "I can't. I won't. Mulder, I'll be a doctor, but my work is here with you now. That virus that I was exposed to, whatever it is, it has a cure. You held it in your hand.

How many other lives can we save? Look . . . if I quit now, they win." Mulder's quest has become her work, too. Their work requires, and deserves, complete solidarity. This solidarity reaches its pinnacle in the season seven episode "Sixth Extinction: Amor Fati," and the penultimate scene is especially telling. Mulder is trapped in his own mind. Either as a result of the illness from which he suffers, or an insidious plan hatched by the CSM (or both), Mulder is tempted to give up his search for the truth in exchange for the (false) comforts of a "normal" suburban life, complete with Samantha, a wife, and children. Scully arrives and somehow taps into Mulder's psyche. She calls him a "traitor, deserter, and coward." She tells him to get up and continue his "true mission." He must "fight the fight." She soon becomes desperate and pleads with him: "No one can do it but you, Mulder. Mulder, help me." He finally regains consciousness, only to see Scully standing over him in a Department of Defense medical room, and hoarsely rasps, "You . . . help . . . me." The episode concludes with a shaken Scully visiting a mending Mulder. She is confused and uncertain of what exactly happened. She is no longer sure who to trust or, even, what the truth is. Mulder confides in her: "Scully, I was like you once. I didn't know who to trust. Then I . . . I chose another path . . . another life, another fate, where I found my sister. The end of my world was unrecognizable and upside down. There was one thing that remained the same. You were my friend, and you told me the truth. Even when the world was falling apart, you were my constant . . . my touchstone." She replies, "And you are mine." Thus it seems clear that the interests of these virtuous persons have become intricately linked, and their bond strengthens them.

Having established this sort of idyllic relationship, the early scenes of *I Want to Believe* come as a bit of a shock. Mulder and Scully's relationship seems far from idyllic. Strain on it is evident from their first scene together. In attempting to convince Mulder to help with the Monica Bannan case, Scully says, "Wouldn't you like to step out into the sunshine again, Mulder? Wouldn't it be nice if we *both* could? Together?" Mulder eventually responds, "I'm fine, Scully. Happy as a clam here." It seems that their interests are no longer closely intertwined. She spends her days at the hospital caring for children, but Mulder stays holed up in his makeshift office silently shaking his fist at the powers conspiring against him. Not surprisingly, Mulder doesn't seem to grasp the force of her question: togetherness. Furthermore, Scully approaches Mulder about the Bannan case apprehensively. She believes that searching for a missing agent is the right thing to do. She also believes that getting Mulder out of the house will be good for him. Being involved with a paranormal case may even reenergize him, bringing back some of the passion, courage, and determination that once defined him—the traits that she admired most about him. But she also fears that it isn't right for him to be out chasing monsters in the dark again. It may reignite his obsessive tendencies, especially with respect to the misguided notion of saving his lost (and presumed dead) sister Samantha.

> "The truth is I worry about you, Mulder, and the effects of long-term isolation." —*I Want to Believe*, scene 3

So Scully's choice is risky. Although she is deeply committed to Mulder, what of her new personal commitment to keep the darkness away from the home that they now share?

As it turned out, Mulder's obsessive tendencies became problematic as a result of his consulting on the Bannan case. It seemed as if he couldn't help but keep searching in the dark wherever Father Joe Crissman's psychic visions led. But this time, Scully didn't impart temperance to Mulder, as she had done so often in the past. Rather, she starkly tells him to leave the case; it is no longer his job to search out monsters in the dark. Maybe he could write a book about it? When Mulder gently scoffs at these suggestions—reminding Scully that seeking the truth wherever it might lead is part of who he is—she not-so-subtly threatens that she won't be coming home. It might be argued that Scully is practicing a form of "tough love" here; nevertheless, her behavior speaks to how difficult committed relationships can be. Many relationships face difficult forks in the road after traveling so long with the same companion. What should Mulder and Scully do? Should they give up?

Throughout the movie, it is never quite clear whether Father Joe's eerie "Don't give up" imperative refers to Scully's attempt to cure Christian Fearon or Mulder and Scully's involvement in the Bannan case. But it seems to equally apply to Mulder and Scully and their relationship. But perhaps all three threads weave together. Should Mulder decide to remain involved in the Bannan case—seeking again the "truth out there"—he must be mindful of Scully's concerns that the darkness seep into their home. In being reinvigorated by Mulder's passion, courage, and determination, Scully more effectively proceeds with Christian's treatments. As a result, their relationship is renewed, as intimated by the first signs of spring at the end of the movie. Mulder and Scully have made it past one of the darkest, coldest winters of their relationship and have found each other again. Their passing from the dark of winter to the renewal of spring is dramatized by (series creator and *I Want to Believe* director) Chris Carter's decision to include the rowboat scene after the credits. Because they didn't give up on each other, we see Mulder and Scully in the warm tropical sun, literally basking in their being away from the darkness (at least for a while).

Mulder's choice to escape the darkness with Scully is actually quite significant because it now seems that he can either "fight the fight" and continue his "true mission" of seeking the truth out there, or he can nurture his relationship with Scully, but no longer can he do both. Which personal commitment should he pursue? Note that his choice is not unlike Scully's hesitation to inform Mulder of the missing FBI agent in the first place. She misses the driven partner she fell in love with; Mulder has become someone else holed up in his makeshift office. But to find him again, she must risk facing all the psychological and physical perils of searching for monsters in the dark. It is interesting that both characters decided to pursue the truths of the heart—to nurture their Aristotelian friendship. Paradoxically, might the most elusive but important truths only be found by looking *within* oneself? Is this the truth "out there" that Mulder has finally found?

It's fairly easy to see, then, that the highest form of Aristotelian friendship, in terms of its ethical significance, is a form of care and, indeed, love (1157b 30–35). Perfect friendship is thus an ideal that those of equal virtue ought to aspire. This will require helping each other to develop and refine various characteristics conducive to care: empathy, loyalty, concern, and courage (among others). In Noddings's terms, the "one-caring" and the "cared-for" enter into a reciprocal relationship where the care they share reaches fruition, simultaneously, in each other. If this is roughly correct, then an ethics of care need not be singly modeled on a mother-child relationship, even if it often is. That is, Guido's relationship with his son Joshua seems to be an effective example of care ethics (especially given the boy's narration at the end of the film). The friendship expressed between the Drake brothers Stan and Frank also seems to be a paradigm of care ethics. Thus there is some evidence that an ethics of care, at its core, is best understood as a variant or subcategory of virtue ethics, although one rightly freed from Aristotle's cultural (and misogynistic) moorings.

Care Ethics: Strengths and Weaknesses

An ethics of care does well with respect to stressing how we are not solitary, autonomous agents, but rather human persons enmeshed in various relationships. These relationships undoubtedly impact our ethically significant interactions, which may account for the widespread belief in "special obligations." Aristotle concurs that our duties are shaped by our personal relationships; he writes: "The duties of parents to children and those of brothers to each other are not the same nor those of comrades and those of fellow-citizens, and so, too, with other kinds of friendship . . . and the injustice increases by being exhibited toward those who are friends in a fuller sense; e.g., it is a more terrible thing to defraud a comrade than a fellow-citizen, more terrible not to help a brother than a stranger, and more terrible to wound a father than anyone else" (1160a 1–6). Of course, feminists would be quick to point out (correctly) that injustices toward sisters are just as serious as injustice done to brothers, and wounding one's mother is at least as serious as wounding one's father. But Aristotle's basic point about special obligations remains. Our obligations, and the severity of breaking them, are defined by the closeness of our personal relationships. This intuition is a staple of commonsense morality, and an ethics of care provides its most solid foundation (as it is far from clear that utilitarians or even Kantians can adequately accommodate special obligations).

However, it is difficult to fully embrace an ethics of care because it seems that we do have at least minimal obligations to complete strangers. Care ethicists, like Noddings, anticipate this sort of objection and maintain that complete strangers are deserving of *some* moral attention. However, it's not clear how much conceptual room can be made for complete strangers on an ethics of care. After all, if our moral obligations are determined by the closeness of our personal connections, then it seems to follow that we have the slimmest of obligations with respect to complete strangers. This objection, if it cannot be adequately addressed, is evidence that an ethics of care has difficulty regarding the moral universe test. Recall that Kant is criticized for not allowing room for nonhuman animals in his moral universe because they are not autonomous. Analogously, an ethics of care defender, seemingly, can be criticized for not allowing room for complete strangers in her moral universe because these individuals are not enmeshed in relationship with us. This result may remind us that rights and justice remain important to moral discourse even if they are sometimes overemphasized. The fact that the moral universe has been *enlarged* over the centuries is evidence of moral progress; persons—regardless of gender, race, color, creed, or geography—have moral standing, which ought to be respected and never violated (at least not without due cause). But this progress is very difficult to make sense of without reference to rights and justice. Thus, an ethics of care can neither be interpreted in ways that cut against this moral progress, nor in ways that completely disregard the rights of persons. And all of this holds even if care ethics defenders are correct that the world would benefit from people not standing on their rights, creating adversarial social arrangements.

Finally, insofar as an ethics of care seems to be a variant of virtue ethics, it may inherit some of its shortcomings with respect to being action-guiding. In apparent conflict situations, it seems it can only offer this: do what the ideally caring person would do. (Note that if universalization is jettisoned, as Noddings suggests, it's not even clear if that much can be said.) But what is that? Does Vera act permissibly in helping girls "begin their bleeding again?" If this is the caring thing to do, why must she keep this a secret from her family? If Lily acts impermissibly in keeping the fee she charges a secret from Vera, why isn't Vera to be blamed for keeping her "procedures" a secret from her family? Apart from this case, what if caring for one person necessarily involves harming another? If you may only care for your mother in ways that will result in harming the relationship with your spouse, what should you do? For that matter, what constitutes properly caring for another in the first place? If caring can sometimes be harmful, then more needs to be said about ethically significant harms and benefits. This isn't to say that those who defend an ethics of care cannot answer questions like these. But it is to say that if questions like these are not properly answered, then an ethics of care fares poorly regarding the completeness and action-guiding tests.

Perhaps further study about an ethics of care will show that the problematic issues associated with it can be resolved. However, it is clear that they must be resolved before an ethics of care can completely supplant more traditional approaches to ethics. Even if all of the potentially problematic implications of an ethics of care cannot be resolved, this does not diminish its attempt to revise (a) Aristotle's traditional virtue theory (insofar as it is somewhat misogynistic) or (b) moral philosophy generally. As it was argued with virtue ethics, it seems likely that an ethics of care approach could be melded with other approaches so as to retain its conceptual strengths regarding special obligations and friendship, but bolster its (alleged) shortcomings regarding completeness and being sufficiently action-guiding.

11.4. TWO ADDITIONAL FILMS

The X-Files: I Want to Believe (2008)

Director: Chris Carter
Screenwriters: Chris Carter and Frank Spotnitz

Plot Summary

> These people need my help. . . . And I can really use yours.

Fox Mulder was once a brilliant young psychological profiler with the FBI's violent crimes division. But the hazy memories of his sister's abduction never left him. Her mysterious disappearance fueled his interest in unexplained phenomena, which, in turn, led to his request to be transferred to the X-Files, that office dedicated to solving cases that resist conventional explanations. His FBI colleagues soon began calling him "Spooky" Mulder, which resulted in his being more or less ostracized from the rest of the bureau (a result he didn't discourage).

Dana Scully was fresh out of medical school. Ahead of her lay a bright and rewarding future in medicine; however, against her father's wishes, she entered the FBI. Her unflinching rationalism and dedication to scientific and bureau procedure was in stark contrast to "Spooky" Mulder. In 1993, they became partners. Their FBI supervisors believed that Mulder has gone overboard, obsessed with his work. Her job was to make regular field reports of X-Files cases, thereby reining Mulder back into the FBI mainstream.

Their first meeting was less than amiable. Mulder suspected that Scully has been assigned to spy on him; his conspiracy radar is blinking. He isn't about to reform. Noting

Scully's extensive scientific background—she also has an undergraduate physics degree—Mulder smugly quips that in his line of work, the laws of physics rarely apply. As if testing her, and citing the unexplained phenomena the X-Files explores, he further chides, "When convention and science offer us no answers, might we not finally turn to the fantastic as a plausibility?" Scully, the scientist, remains steadfast; without hesitation, she retorts: "What I find fantastic is any notion that there are answers beyond the realm of science. The answers are there. You just have to know where to look."

And look they did, for more than eight years they chased monsters, together, flashlight in hand peering into the dark. Their professional association quickly became a partnership, which in turn blossomed into a companionship—platonic at first and, later, something more. They survived her abduction, which seemingly led to her contracting cancer. They survived his abduction, presumably also at the hands of extraterrestrial factions (perhaps facilitated by a governmental shadow group known as the Syndicate). They both lost their fathers. They lost their son—a child that was supposed to be medically impossible, the unfortunate aftereffects of Scully's cancer. This they did in their joint pursuit of the "truth out there." They pursued it differently, in their own ways, but they did it together and for each other. In the process, Scully became open to extreme possibilities and Mulder learned temperance and discipline. Not all of their investigations fit rational, conventional paradigms, but some did. As a result, they grew together and became more complete individuals.

For their efforts, they—but particularly Mulder—were vilified by the FBI. After Mulder was found guilty at a military-style tribunal, they escaped from the facility, together. Six years later, they are no longer on the lam. They now live together in a modest home outside of Richmond, Virginia. Scully practices pediatric medicine at Our Lady of Sorrows Hospital in urban Richmond. Mulder remains interested in the paranormal, albeit exclusively from his makeshift home office. Rather than gallivanting across the continental United States chasing leads about unexplained phenomena, he has become a recluse, incessantly combing through newspapers and magazines for glimpses of his former life's work.

One day the FBI visit Scully at the hospital. Desperate, they seek Mulder's expertise for an unusual case, and are willing to offer him a reprieve for his services. Scully is hesitant to have Mulder involved in the case. It might reinvigorate him, sparking the passion that once burned within him. But it might also bring his obsessive tendencies back to the surface. Scully shares the message, but Mulder is skeptical; it smells like a trap. However, he agrees to pursue the opportunity—but only if Scully joins him.

Arriving in Quantico, Mulder and Scully learn that a young agent, Monica Bannan, has gone missing. Father Joseph Crissman cold-called the FBI, claiming to have information about the case—through psychic visions. Cue Mulder. But "Father Joe" is also a convicted pedophile, molesting thirty-seven altar boys. Yet he seems truly penitent for his past crimes. Decades ago, he castrated himself at twenty-six. He now lives voluntarily with other sex offenders in a dormitory-type compound where the residents police each other. Father Joe says of his neighbors, "We hate each other as we hate ourselves for our sickening appetites." Agent Dakota Whitney, the agent-in-charge is thus stuck between trusting Father Joe and his visions or believing that Father Joe is simply on *another* public relations attempt to reconcile with the church (he's been writing letters of expiation to the Vatican for years). Whitney is in over her head, and this is why she has called in Mulder. As she puts it, she is "not the most popular girl at the bureau" for bringing Mulder in on the case.

Scully soon regrets her decision to involve Mulder in his old profession. He cannot help himself from following Father Joe into the darkness. His obsessive tendencies return, including his nonrational desire to save his sister. Furthermore, Scully's attention has been diverted to Christian Fearon, a ten-year-old boy suffering from a rare and fatal brain condition. She simply cannot follow Mulder into the darkness again, and she's no longer inclined to even if she could. She tells him, "That's not my life anymore. . . . I can't look into the darkness with you anymore, Mulder. I can't stand what it does to you or to me . . . I'm asking you to look at yourself . . . We're not FBI anymore, Mulder. We are two people who come home at night, to a home now. I don't want that darkness in my house." Mulder, interjecting where he could, finally responds, "Are you asking me to give up?" Scully, crestfallen, replies, "No. I can't tell you to do that, Mulder. But I can tell you that I'm not coming home." They wish each other luck on their current, separate projects.

Mulder and the FBI, and although other women are abducted, eventually discover Crissman's connection to the case. One of the men responsible for the kidnappings was one of the altar boys Father Joe molested. Father Joe believes this can only be God's work—God is providing him the opportunity to, perhaps, redeem himself by helping the FBI solve the case. Scully's medical care plan for Christian is just as trying. Father Ybarra, the hospital chief of staff, disagrees with her about what is best for the boy. He urges for palliative care. She refuses to accept that. With Father Joe's eerie "Don't give up" imperative echoing in her head, she wishes to explore a cutting-edge, untested, but painful series of surgeries.

Mulder, not surprisingly, rushes headlong to solve the case at any and all costs. Scully, between surgeries, rushes to save him. She cannot do it alone, however, and calls upon their old boss, Assistant Director Walter Skinner, for help. Scully and Skinner rescue Mulder and apprehend the kidnappers. Almost simultaneously, Father Joe dies. Reunited, Mulder and Scully discuss the deceased Father Joe. Mulder asks Scully: "What if Father Joe's prayers were answered after all? What if he were forgiven? Because he didn't give up? . . . Maybe that's the answer. You know, the larger answer?" Still in his embrace, Scully inquires, "What do you mean?" He lovingly looks into her eyes, "Don't give up." This suggestion renews Scully's faith in herself to cure Christian and her faith in her relationship with Mulder. Scully proceeds with Christian's surgeries, and Mulder and Scully escape the darkness (by finding the warm, tropical sun)—at least for a while.

Discussion Questions

1. When, if at all, is it acceptable to give up on something? Is it ever not acceptable to give up? Explain.
2. Compare and contrast the ways Scully cares for Christian, on the one hand, but Mulder on the other. What are the morally significant similarities and differences?
3. In what does Mulder and Scully's friendship consist?
4. Why did Scully demur from telling Mulder to "give up"?
5. Does Father Joe deserve to be forgiven for his past heinous deeds? Explain.

Life Is Beautiful (1997)

Director: Roberto Benigni
Screenwriters: Roberto Benigni and Vincenzo Cerami

Plot Summary

> How ridiculous. . . . There are wood ovens, but there are no people ovens—putting people in ovens creates too much smoke.

In 1939, Guido, a vivacious, young Italian man decides to move from the country to the big city. He will live with his uncle, working as a waiter in a hotel, until he can save enough money to open a bookstore. During his journey, Guido charismatically introduces himself as the "prince of this principality" to a beautiful young lady. In a not-so-subtle attempt to impress her, he announces that he will replace all the cows and chickens with camels and ostriches. Moreover, luckily for the woman, just stung by a wasp, Guido is knowledgeable in the healing arts. Guido confidently "teaches" her about the dangers of wasp venom. Such wounds are "treated" by quickly removing all the wasp poison. Although he informs her that the treatment may last up to half an hour, he finishes sucking on her leg in only a minute or two. He departs, but they fortuitously meet again in the city. Guido calls out to her as his "princess." Recognizing Guido (and rather happy to see him again) she proclaims that he has "this amusing habit of appearing out of nowhere."

At the hotel, Guido often waits on a physician, Dr. Lessing, who is obsessed with riddles. They develop a rapport with one another, bordering on friendship. The doctor quizzes Guido: "The more of it there is, the more difficult it is to see; what is it?" Returning with Lessing's meal, Guido triumphantly announces: "Darkness!" Lessing is amazed; it took him days to decipher the riddle, but Guido was able to solve it in minutes. He claims that Guido is a genius and retires to his room for the evening.

But Lessing is not Guido's most interesting customer this evening. A government official—some sort of school or education inspector—from Rome is in town to speak with local schoolchildren. Having found out from their last fortuitous meeting that his "princess" is a schoolteacher, Guido schemes to pose as the inspector, and arrives prior to the scheduled appointment. All of this for the sole purpose of getting another glimpse of his "princess." Although he is asked to lecture the children on the superiority of the Aryan race, he learns that his wasp-stung princess will be later attending an opera in Venice. After the real inspector arrives, Guido quickly scuttles through an open window, but not before he devises a ruse to steal his princess away after the opera. After her initial shock and despite an inconvenient rainstorm that evening, the princess opens up to Guido, sharing with him her name and more importantly her hopes, dreams, and fears.

Guido is working an engagement party at the hotel. To his horror, his princess—his Dora—is the bride to be. Guido finds this unbearable; he must speak with Dora. He "accidentally" spills a serving tray near her table. After Guido ducks under the table to "clean up his mess," Dora quickly does the same. There they kiss and she whispers, "take me away from all of this." He grins and quickly disappears from the banquet hall. In moments, he reappears, riding his uncle's horse. Guido kindly presents the bridegroom a bottle of champagne and then steals his bride to be. They ride off together.

Five years later, Guido and his son, Joshua, are forced onto the back of a covered, military truck and whisked away to the train station. When Dora discovers this, she rushes to speak with the local Nazi authorities. She claims there was a mistake. But when the SS officer assures her that no mistake has been made, Dora insists upon boarding the train—even though she is not Jewish and she is uncertain of its destination. The young lieutenant hesitatingly acquiesces and the train leaves the station with Dora on it. The train pulls into the concentration camp that night. The next morning, its Jewish passengers are unloaded with the women exiting to the left and the men to the right. Joshua is confused and wants to know where his mother is. Guido spontaneously tells his son that they are about to play a game that might take a long time to complete. The men play the game in one area and the women play in another, so Joshua must stay with his dad for a while. Guido also reports that the game will be very organized, with some people dressed like soldiers barking orders from time to time. Those that do not follow the rules of the game very carefully will be sent home. But those that do follow the rules and orders will win first prize. First prize just happens to be what Joshua has always wanted—a real army tank for his very own.

Inside the barracks, Joshua is already tired of the game. The room is too crowded and it smells bad. Joshua again calls out for his mother. As Guido is attempting to comfort him by again explaining the importance of the game, Nazi officers barge into the barracks. One of them abruptly (and awkwardly) asks whether anyone speaks German in order to convey the camp regulations. Guido immediately raises his hand, although he speaks no German. He makes his way toward the front of the room and stands next to the ranking officer. The officer speaks and Guido seems to translate, but actually Guido is speaking only to his son, unbeknownst to Joshua. Guido listens and then "repeats": "The game starts now . . . Each day we will announce the scores from a loudspeaker . . . The one that has the fewest points will have to wear a sign that says 'Jackass' . . . There are three ways to lose points . . . One, turning into a big cry-baby . . . Two, telling us you want to see your mamma . . . Three, saying you're hungry and want something to eat."

At the end of the first day, Guido returns to the barracks after grueling foundry work. Joshua is waiting for him in the bunk they share. Guido reassures him that the game is going well but tells him there was almost a mix-up. They were about to be sent home, but then Joshua could not win the tank. Guido cleared up the error and to make sure it does not happen again, he had the soldiers put his reservation number on his "costume" and he even went so far as to have the reservation number tattooed on his arm. That way, if his shirt is ever lost, they merely need to check the number on his arm so that they are not sent home by mistake.

One day, Joshua searches for the foundry; he needs to speak with his father. The mean soldiers wanted him to take a "shower" with the other children and elderly "game-players." But it was not Friday—Joshua only bathes on Friday—so he ran away. Soon Joshua is more confused than ever because he never sees his playmates (or his Great Uncle Leo) again. From that day forth, Guido tells Joshua that the rules have changed. Joshua is to hide from all the mean people in the uniforms; they must never see him.

With the constant watchful eye of his father, Joshua is successful. A year passes. The game is nearly over now; they only need forty more points to win first place. But they must make it through one more night. Guido tells Joshua to hide in a very secret place. Joshua must stay there until it is completely quiet and there is no one around, especially the mean people in uniform. With Joshua carefully hidden away, Guido searches for Dora. He is unsuccessful in his search and is caught by a Nazi soldier. However, while he is being led away, Guido spies Joshua, smiles and winks at his son, in effect, reassuring him that the game will soon be over with Joshua the winner. The next morning, Joshua wins first place, as demonstrated by his first ride in his green tank with the white star on the front. He triumphantly rides out of the camp.

Discussion Questions

1. Throughout the film, Guido chooses to purposely hide the truths about World War II from his son. Is this morally acceptable? Explain.
2. Had the story revolved around Dora and Joshua, do you think Dora would have acted any differently? Do you think, generally speaking, that men and women approach ethical decision making differently?
3. Compare and contrast the ways Uncle Leo cared for Guido with the ways Guido cared for Joshua. What are the morally significant similarities and differences?
4. At the very end of the film, Joshua states, "this was my father's gift." What might he mean by this?
5. What would make life beautiful, morally speaking?

11.5. REVIEWING THROUGH THE THREE MOVIES

1. Reconsider *Vera Drake*, *Life Is Beautiful*, and *I Want to Believe*, examining each film for examples of impermissible behavior. How does an ethics of care approach explain the wrongfulness of each? How, if at all, does its interpretation differ from other ethical systems?
2. Is Vera, as portrayed in *Vera Drake*, or Guido, as portrayed in *Life Is Beautiful*, a better exemplar for an ethics of care? Explain.
3. Compare and contrast the way Guido cares for Joshua from the way Scully cares for Christian. Are there any morally significant differences?
4. Compare and contrast the friendships of Stan and his brother Frank from Mulder and Scully. Are there any morally significant differences? Explain.
5. Reconsider the six movie quotes from the chapter and explain whether each, given the adjacent paragraphs, *illustrates* a point the author is making, *supplements* (or extends) a point the author is making, or *contrasts* (for emphasis) a point the author is making. Explain your answers.

NOTES

1. Nel Noddings, *Caring: A Feminine Approach to Ethics and Moral Education* (Berkeley: University of California Press, 1984), 80, 84–89, 95, 101–2. Section headings have been added to aid reading comprehension.

2. Mencius's example of seeing a child about to mortally fall into a well is widely known: "My reason for saying no man is devoid of a heart sensitive to the suffering of others is this. Suppose a man were, all of a sudden, to see a young child on the verge of falling into a well. He would certainly be moved to compassion, not because he wanted to get in the good graces of the parents, nor because he wished to win the praise of his fellow villagers or friends. . . ." This is quoted in *Mencius*, trans. D. C. Lau (London: Penguin Books, 1970), 82.

3. See Noddings, *Caring*, 94–95.

4. Noddings's views about moral rightness and wrongness are rather nuanced. For example, see *Caring*, 90–94. To be clear, the discussion of an ethics of care offered here should not be interpreted as a strict exegesis of Noddings's views. Furthermore, Noddings would probably object to the implied role of care-exemplars, as this kind of abstraction takes agents too far away from individual situations. She might prefer that right action be interpreted as what, given your circumstances, most effectively represents your "best-self" under the caring ideal.

5. Of course, unbridled attempts at caring for those in our close, personal circles still might be discouraged. After all, the Russians from *I Want to Believe*, arguably, attempted to care for the cancer victim among them in a bizarre Dr. Frankenstein sort of way by abducting local females. It is simply implausible to believe that one can permissibly care for a loved one by kidnapping, terrorizing, and killing innocent women.

6. The analysis of Aristotelian friendship via *The X-Files* characters of Fox Mulder and Dana Scully draws heavily on Dean A. Kowalski and S. Evan Kreider, "*I Want to Believe* . . . But Now What?" in *The Philosophy of* The X-Files, ed. Dean A. Kowalski (Lexington: University Press of Kentucky, 2009), 241–61.

7. The quote is taken from Aristotle, *Nicomachean Ethics*, trans. W. D. Ross (Oxford: Oxford University Press, 1925), 1156a 34–35. Note that Aristotle refers explicitly to young people in this passage, but his basic point applies to people of all ages; if the friendship develops merely because two people find each other pleasant (and Aristotle also uses the example of finding the other witty—he or she makes you laugh), then the friendship will easily dissolve when the association is no longer mutually pleasant (say, when the person no longer makes you laugh).

CHAPTER 12

Plato and Being Good

THE EMPEROR'S CLUB (2002)
Director: Michael Hoffman
Screenwriter: Neil Tolkin

PLOT SUMMARY

Yes, but at what cost? Remember Socrates? It is not living that is important, but living rightly.

William Hundert, longtime teacher of Classics and History of Western Civilization at St. Benedict's Preparatory School for Boys, reminisces about the first time he met the freshman class of 1972. He recalls introducing them to Shutruk-Nahhunte, King of Elam, circa 1,000 BCE. He asks his students if any have ever heard of this ancient king. Not surprisingly, none have. Hundert informs them that this king does not appear in any of the history books. This sets up his very first lesson: "conquest without contribution is without significance." Unlike other kings, emperors, and philosophers—those like Caesar, Plato, and Aristotle—Nahhunte left no indelible mark on history. Mr. Hundert asks his students what they will contribute to history and society. He invites his students to "follow the path—walk where the great men before them have walked," in order to determine what their contributions might be.

Sedgewick Bell soon joins the class. Bell is the son of the senior senator from West Virginia, Hiram Bell. Sedgewick is also unlike the other boys in other ways. He has little respect for his studies, or even Mr. Hundert. Sedgewick immediately makes himself a problem. Hundert makes an appointment to see Senator Bell. Hundert informs the senator that Sedgewick is neither applying himself nor learning the material. Unmoved, the senator asks Hundert: "What's the good of what you're teaching those boys?" Hundert solemnly answers: "The Greeks and Romans provided a model of democracy which the framers of our own Constitution used as their inspiration. But more to the point, when the boys read Plato, Aristotle, Cicero, Julius Caesar, even, they're put into contact with men who in their own age exemplified the highest standards of statesmanship, of civic virtue, of character, conviction." Senator Bell is near flabbergasted. Hundert continues, "Sir, it is my job to mold your son's character." Bell interjects: "Mold him!? Your job is to teach him. I will mold him." Hundert leaves Bell's office discouraged but determined.

Hundert makes a surprise visit to Sedgewick's dorm room. Hoping to inspire the boy, Hundert presents him his old high school textbook. Hundert suggests that it might be helpful with the upcoming Mr. Julius Caesar competition. On the first written exam, Sedgewick receives a C-. Happily surprised that he passed, Sedgewick studies earnestly for the second exam. Hundert's plan is seemingly working. Sedgewick slowly climbs up the class rankings. The top three will compete in the oral competition, answering questions in front of family, friends, and classmates. Sedgewick attempts to check out a reference book from the school library. The librarian refuses, saying that it would be unfair to the other students. But the library closes in minutes, and Sedgewick is the only patron present. Mr. Hundert happens by and vouches for Sedgewick's character. The librarian acquiesces—if Sedgewick promises to return the book first thing in the morning.

BOX 12A: INSIDE *THE EMPEROR'S CLUB*

The Emperor's Club conveys intriguing issues about character, vice, and virtue. For example, does nonvirtuous action only result from ignorance (as Socrates more or less believed)? Moreover, can the virtues be taught by learning about great figures from history? And what is the proper relationship between teacher and student, and what is proper education in the first place?

The movie as a whole is helpful in better understanding the alleged tension between ethics and self-interest, especially as Plato understood it. A few segments are particularly noteworthy for their connections to ethics, self-interest, and Plato. The first segment consists of scenes 3, 4, and part of 5; we meet Mr. Hundert, his 1972 class, and its new arrival Sedgewick Bell. Scene 3 begins at 7:18 with a shot of Mr. Hundert learning his students' names, and the segment ends at 21:30 with a shot of Hundert looking out a window after dismissing his class. The second segment consists of scenes 12 and 13. Scene 12 begins at 53:38 with a shot of the campus; continue watching into scene 13 until 1:03:35 to view Bell's first Julius Caesar contest and Hundert confronting him about cheating. This segment ends with a shot of Hundert leaving Bell's dorm room. The third segment begins with scene 17 at 1:23:06 with a shot of a dinner reception. An adult Sedgewick re-creates the Julius Caesar contest from twenty-five years ago. Continue watching into scene 18 until 1:36:10 to witness the intricacies of the revisited contest. The segment ends with a shot of Hundert's back as he sits on a couch, but pay particularly close attention to the restroom conversation between Hundert and Sedge-wick from 1:32:35 to 1:35:43. If time permits, continue watching until the end of the film, making particular note of what Sedgewick says to the television cameras in the beginning of scene 19 (1:38:33–1:39:40), and Hundert's interactions with his other students later in scene 19 (1:39:40–1:42:18).

This is truly a quality film, and a full viewing is highly recommended. If you do watch the film in its entirety, then you should be able to answer the trivia questions from box 12B.

Sedgewick takes the full three hours to carefully finish the last written exam. Sedgewick's hard work pays dividends; Hundert scores his exam as an A–. However, Sedgewick finishes in fourth place, one point behind the third place student, Martin Blythe. Hundert thoughtfully peruses the standings, pauses for a moment, and decides to reevaluate Sedgewick's exam. Hundert subsequently rescores Bell's exam as an A+, which provides Sedgewick the points necessary to overtake Martin for third place. Sedgewick will compete for the Julius Caesar award after all.

Mr. Hundert emcees the Julius Caesar oral examination. If a boy cannot answer a question, he is disqualified. The last boy standing is crowned Mr. Julius Caesar. Sedgewick struggles with many of the questions. Hundert begins to suspect that Sedgewick is cheating. In a sidebar, the headmaster surprises Hundert by telling him to ignore it. Hundert, now crestfallen with Sedgewick, asks a question not from his prepared list. Sedgewick misses it, but the other remaining boy does not. After the competition, Hundert visits Sedgewick to ask why he cheated. Sedgewick simply answers, "Why not?" Sedgewick then asks Hundert: "Why didn't you call me out? It wasn't because of my father was it?" Sedgewick's academic career subsequently returns to its unimpressive beginnings. He manages to graduate from St. Benedict's in 1976, and his father's connections gain him entrance to Yale. Hundert remains crestfallen.

In 2001, Hundert is ready to become St. Benedict's new headmaster. However, the board has different ideas; they have hired a younger faculty member, James Ellerby. The board reassures Hundert that Ellerby is a forward thinking man. He has reached out to the community and built relationships with some of the school's most important alumni. Although the board maintains that Ellerby "is a wonderful communicator with impeccable moral standing and an unwavering commitment" to St. Benedict's, it is pretty clear that Hundert is being passed over because he seems to lack the worldly penchants for marketing and fund-raising. Hundert promptly resigns. The board is horrified. One member begs him to reconsider, pleading, "You are the finest teacher the school has ever had!"

BOX 12B: *THE EMPEROR'S CLUB* TRIVIA

If your instructor assigns the film to be watched outside of class, you should be able to answer the following questions:

1. What is Hundert's favorite morning activity?
2. What out-of-the-ordinary garment do Hundert's students wear on Sedgewick's first day of class?
3. What game does Hundert play with the boys in the quad?
4. How many brothers and sisters does Hundert have?
5. What does Senator Bell attempt to give Hundert as a gift?
6. By what means does (young) Sedgewick cheat at the first Julius Caesar contest?
7. What project does Hundert attempt to finish once he retires?
8. What does grown Sedgewick return to Mr. Hundert at the hotel?
9. What two items do his past students present Hundert just before he leaves the resort hotel?
10. Whose son does Hundert meet at the very end of the movie?

Sedgewick, now a wealthy and powerful businessman, subsequently contacts St. Benedict's. He informs Headmaster Ellerby that he will make a sizable donation only if a rematch for the Mr. Julius Caesar contest is arranged—complete with Mr. Hundert as the master of ceremonies. Hundert agrees (but not before he points out the irony to Ellerby—he is the lynchpin in the school's largest ever donation). Sedgewick flies out his old classmates and Mr. Hundert to his private estate. In a quiet moment before the competition, Hundert confides in Martin Blythe, "I never gave you your due." Martin kindly rebuffs his teacher, replying, "Of course you gave me my due, Mr. Hundert. That recommendation you wrote for me to the academy was glowing." Sedgewick later visits Hundert in his hotel room. Sedgewick politely asks why Hundert put up with him. Hundert confides in him, "I saw a young man under a lot of pressure; I, too, had a 'very busy' father."

The rematch begins. It goes much the same way it did twenty-five years ago. Hundert soon realizes that the contest is going too much like the first contest. He suspects that Sedgewick is cheating again. This time, Hundert spies a small earpiece in Bell's ear. Hundert turns around and sees an awkward looking young man in the corner of the room. He is standing in front of a computer with books scattered about. Once again, Hundert puts down his index cards. He slowly looks at Bell and asks, "Who is Shutruk-Nahhunte?" His classmates giggle. Why would Mr. Hundert ask such an easy question so deep into the competition? Martin yells out, "Come on, Bell, it was on the plaque above the damn door!" But Sedgewick wasn't present the first day of class. Bell's accomplice cannot find Nahhunte in any of the history books. Sedgewick fails to answer. Bell's classmate recites the answer, thereby winning the competition (again). Bell admits defeat, but reassures his guests that there is no shame in losing to the brightest minds of their generation. Upon asserting that education must be a priority in this country again, he thanks Mr. Hundert, saying, "Your virtue is a beacon of light." He then announces his bid for the Senate following in his father's footsteps. His classmates congratulate him and many quickly offer donations to his campaign fund.

After the competition, Hundert and Bell meet. Again, Hundert wants to know why Bell cheated. He looks Hundert in the eye, saying, "I trust you will keep this between us, as always." Hundert is again crestfallen. He admits to Bell, "I have failed you, as a teacher. But I will give you one last lecture. All of us, at some point, are forced to look at ourselves in the mirror and see who we really are. When that day comes for you, Sedgewick, you will be confronted with a life lived without virtue, without principle, and for that I pity you." Unmoved, Sedgewick responds: "Who out there gives a shit about your principles and your virtues? I mean, look at you. What do you have to show for yourself? I live in the real world where people do what they need to do to get what they want. If it's lying and if it's cheating, then so be it."

12.1. THINKING THROUGH THE MOVIE

Discussion Starter Questions

1. Why did Hundert take such an interest in young Sedgewick Bell?
2. Why did the headmaster tell Hundert to ignore the fact the Sedgewick was cheating on the Julius Caesar oral exam? Was the headmaster's choice permissible?
3. Why did Hundert decide to rescore Bell's last exam? Was this permissible?
4. Why is it so important to live a life of "virtue and principles"?

5. Who leads the better life, Mr. Hundert or Sedgewick Bell? Which life would you rather lead? Defend your answers.

Questions for Further Thought

1. Is William Hundert correct in that a person can become virtuous by examining the past lives of exemplary people from history? What is the moral significance of this?
2. One predominant idea from the film is: "Great ambition and conquest without contribution is without significance." What does this mean? Does this idea carry any moral significance?
3. Is Hundert's decision to retire after being passed over for headmaster (scene 14 beginning at 1:08:00) the act of a virtuous person? What, then, might this say about the relationship between being and acting virtuous?
4. During scene 18 (about 1:30:42) a grown Sedgewick Bell proclaims of Mr. Hundert, "Your virtue is a beacon of light." What does this mean? What is its moral import?
5. Was Hundert morally required to inform Martin that he gave Martin's Julius Caesar spot away to Sedgewick all those years ago (scene 18 beginning 1:36:42 into the movie)? If not, then why did he do so? Why was Martin so uncomfortable in learning this fact?

12.2. HISTORICAL SETTING

Republic (excerpt)[1]

The passage below is taken from Plato's great work, the *Republic*. (For a biographic synopsis of Plato, please see chapter 1.) The excerpt contains a discussion between Socrates and Plato's brother Glaucon about the nature of justice (a topic raised earlier in the dialogue by Thrasymachus). At this stage of Plato's literary career, however, scholars tend to believe that he is primarily expressing his own views through the Socrates character.

Preparing to Read

A. How do Sedgewick Bell, William Hundert, and Justin McLeod (*The Man without a Face*) respectively exemplify Socrates's (Plato's) ideas in the excerpt below?

B. How does the ring of power (the "one ring") from *Lord of the Rings* compare to the ring of Gyges? How do the two differ?

[Three Types of Goods]

Socrates: With these words I was thinking that I had made an end of the discussion; but the end, in truth, proved to be only a beginning. For Glaucon, who is always the most contentious of men, was dissatisfied at Thrasymachus's retirement; he wanted to have the discussion continue.

Glaucon: Socrates, do you wish really to persuade us, or only to seem to have persuaded us, that to be just is always better than to be unjust?

Soc: I should wish really to persuade you, if I could.

Glau: Then you certainly have not succeeded. Let me ask you now—How would you arrange goods—are there not some which we welcome for their own sakes, and independently of their consequences, as, for example, harmless pleasures and enjoyments which delight us at the time, although nothing follows from them?

Soc: I agree in thinking that there is such a class.

Glau: Is there not also a second class of goods, such as knowledge, sight, health, which are desirable not only in themselves, but also for their results?

Soc: Certainly.

Glau: And would you not recognize a third class, such as gymnastics, and the care of the sick, and the physician's art; also the various ways of money-making—these do us good but we regard them as disagreeable; and no one would choose them for their own sakes, but only for the sake of some reward or result which flows from them?

Soc: There is this third class also. But why do you ask?

Glau: Because I want to know in which of the three classes you would place justice?

Soc: In the highest class, among those goods that he who would be happy desires both for their own sake and for the sake of their results.

[Justice Reexamined]

Glau: The many are of another mind; they think that justice is to be reckoned in the troublesome class, among goods which are to be pursued for the sake of rewards and of reputation, but in themselves are disagreeable and rather to be avoided. . . .

. . . If you please, then, I will revive the argument of Thrasymachus. And first I will speak of the nature and origin of justice according to the common view of them. Secondly, I will show that all who practice justice do so against their will, out of necessity, but not as a good. And thirdly, I will argue that there is reason in this view, for the life of the unjust is after all far better than the life of the just—if what they say is true, Socrates, since I myself am not of their opinion. But still I acknowledge that I am perplexed when I hear the voices of Thrasymachus and myriads of others dinning in my ears; . . .

They say that to do injustice is, by nature, good; to suffer injustice, evil; but that the evil is greater than the good. And so when men have both done and suffered injustice and have had experience of both, not being able to avoid the one and obtain the other, they think that they had better agree among themselves to have neither; hence, there arise laws and mutual covenants; and that which is ordained by law is termed by them lawful and just. This they affirm to be the origin and nature of justice: it is a compromise between the best of all, which is to do injustice and not be punished, and the worst of all, which is to suffer injustice without the power of retaliation; and justice, being at a middle point between the two, is tolerated not as a good, but as the lesser evil, and honored by reason of the inability of men to do injustice. For no man who is worthy to be called a man would ever submit to such an agreement if he were able to resist; he would be mad if he did. Such is the received account, Socrates, of the nature and origin of justice.

[The Ring of Invisibility]

Glau: That those who practice justice do so unwillingly is clearest if we imagine something of this kind: having given both to the just and the unjust power to do what they will, let us watch and see how desire will lead them; then we shall discover in the very act the just and unjust man to be proceeding along the same road, following their interests . . . and are only diverted into the path of justice by the force of law.

[Socrates, consider] . . . Gyges . . . the Lydian. According to the tradition, Gyges [who found a mysterious ring] was a shepherd in the service of the king of Lydia; . . . Now the shepherds met together . . . and as [Gyges] was sitting among them he chanced to turn the face of the ring inside his hand, when instantly he became invisible to the rest of the company and they began to speak of him as if he were no longer present. He was astonished at this, and again touching the ring he turned the face outwards and reappeared; he made several trials of the ring, and always with the same result—when he turned the face inwards he became invisible, when turning it outwards he reappeared. He then contrived to be chosen one of the messengers sent to the court; as soon as he arrived he seduced the queen, and with her help conspired against the king and slew him, and took the kingdom.

Suppose now that there were two such magic rings, and the just [man] put on one of them and the unjust [man] the other; no man can be imagined to be of such an iron nature that he would stand fast in justice. No man would keep his hands off what was not his own when he could safely take what he liked out of the market, or go into houses and lie with any one at his pleasure, or kill or release from prison whom he would, and in all respects be like a god among men. Then the actions of the just would be as the actions of the unjust; they would both come at last to the same point. And this we may truly affirm to be a great proof that a man is just, not willingly or because he thinks that justice is any good to him individually, but of necessity, for wherever anyone thinks that he can safely be unjust, there he is unjust. For all men believe in their hearts that injustice is far more profitable than justice, and he who argues as I have been supposing, will say that they are right. If you could imagine any one obtaining this power of becoming invisible, and never doing any wrong or touching what was another's, he would be thought by the lookers-on to be most foolish. . . .

[Appearing Just versus Being Just]

Glau: Now [Socrates] . . . let the unjust man be entirely unjust, and the just man be entirely just; nothing is to be taken away from either of them, and both are to be perfectly furnished for the work of their respective lives. First, let the unjust be like other distinguished masters of craft; like the skillful pilot or physician, who knows intuitively his own powers and keeps within their limits, and who, if he fails at any point, is able to recover himself. So let the unjust make his unjust attempts in the right way, and lie hidden if he means to be great in his injustice (he who is found out is nobody): for the highest reach of injustice is to be deemed just when you are not. Therefore I say that in the perfectly unjust man we must assume the most perfect injustice; there is to be no deduction, but we must allow him, while doing the most unjust acts, to have acquired the greatest reputation for justice. If he has taken a false step he must be able to recover himself; he must be one who can speak with effect, if any of his deeds come to light, and who can force his way where force is required by his courage and strength, and command of money and friends.

At his side let us place the just man in his nobleness and simplicity, wishing, as Aeschylus says, to be and not to seem good. There must be no seeming, for if he seems to be just he will be honored and rewarded, and then we shall not know whether he is just for the sake of justice or for the sake of honors and rewards; therefore, let him be clothed in justice only and have no other covering; and he must be imagined in a state of life the opposite of the former. Let him be the best of men, and let him be thought the worst; then he will have been put to the proof; and we shall see whether he will be affected by the tear of infamy and its consequences. And let him continue thus to the hour of death; being just and seeming to be unjust. When both have reached the uttermost extreme, the one of justice and the other of injustice, let judgment be given which of them is the happier of the two. . . .

. . . And now that we know what they are like there is no difficulty in tracing out the sort of life that awaits either of them. . . . The praisers of injustice . . . will tell you that the just man who is thought unjust will be scourged, racked, bound—will have his eyes burnt out; and, at last, after suffering every kind of evil, he will be impaled: Then he will understand that he ought to seem only, and not to be, just; the words of Aeschylus may be more truly spoken of the unjust than of the just. For the unjust is pursuing a reality; he does not live with a view to appearances—he wants to be really unjust and not to seem only. . . . In the first place, he is thought just, and therefore bears rule in the city; he can marry whom he will, and give in marriage to whom he will; also he can trade and deal where he likes, and always to his own advantage, because he has no misgivings about injustice; and at every contest, whether in public or private, he gets the better of his antagonists, and gains at their expense, and is rich, and out of his gains he can benefit his friends, and harm his enemies; moreover, he can offer sacrifices, and dedicate gifts to the gods abundantly and magnificently, and can honor the gods or any man whom he wants to honor in a far better style than the just, and therefore he is likely to be dearer than they are to the gods. And thus, Socrates, gods and men are said to unite in making the life of the unjust better than the life of the just. . . .

Soc: Well, . . . now having arrived at this stage of the argument, we may revert to the words which brought us: Was someone saying that injustice was a gain to the perfectly unjust who was reputed to be just?

Glau: Yes, that was said.

Soc: Now then, having determined the power and quality of justice and injustice, let us have a little [hypothetical] conversation with him.

Glau: What shall we say to him?

[The Three Parts of the Soul]

Soc: Let us make an image of the soul, that he may have his words presented before his eyes.

Glau: Of what sort?

Soc: An ideal image of the soul, like the composite creations of ancient mythology, such as the Chimera or Scylla or Cerberus, and there are many others in which two or more different natures are said to grow into one.

Glau: There are said to have been such unions.

Soc: . . . Envision the form of a . . . many-headed monster, having a ring of heads of all manner of beasts, tame and wild, which it is able to generate and metamorphose at will.

Glau: You suppose marvelous powers of the imagination; but . . . let there be a model as you propose.

Soc: Now imagine a second form as of a lion, and a third of a man, the second smaller than the first [the many-headed monster], and the third smaller than the second.

Glau: That is an easier task; I have imagined them as you say.

Soc: Now join them, and let the three [forms] grow into one. . . . Next fashion the outside of them into a single image, as of a man, so that he who is not able to look within, and sees only the outer hull, may believe the beast to be a single human creature.

Glau: I have done so.

Soc: To him who maintains that it is profitable for a man to be unjust, and unprofitable to be just, let us reply that, if he be right, it is profitable for this creature to feed the [many-headed] monster and strengthen the lion and the lion-like qualities, but to starve and weaken the man, who is consequently liable to be dragged about at the mercy of either of the other two; and he is not to attempt to familiarize or harmonize them with each other—he ought rather to suffer them to fight and bite and devour another.

Glau: Certainly, that is what the praiser of injustice says.

Soc: The praiser of justice replies that one should always speak and act as to give the man within him in some way or other the most complete mastery over the entire human creature. He should watch over the many-headed monster like a good husbandman [farmer], fostering and cultivating the gentle qualities, and preventing the wild ones from growing; he should be making the lion-heart his ally, and . . . should be uniting the several parts with one another and with himself.

Glau: Yes, that is quite what the praiser of justice will say.

Soc: And so from every point of view, whether of pleasure, honor, or advantage, the praiser of justice is right and speaks the truth, and the disapprover [of justice] is wrong and false and ignorant?

Glau: Yes, from every point of view.

[An Unbalanced Soul Leads to Unhappiness]

Soc: Come, now, and let us gently reason with the praiser of injustice, who is not intentionally in error. We will say to him, "What think you of things esteemed noble and ignoble? Is not the noble that which subjects the beast to the man . . . ; and the ignoble that which subjects the man to the beast?" He can hardly avoid saying yes—can he now?

Glau: Not if he has any regard for my opinion.

Soc: But, if he agrees so far, we may ask him to answer another question: "Then how would a man profit if he received gold and silver on the condition that he was to enslave the noblest part of him to the worst?" . . .

Has not the intemperate been censured of old, because in him the huge [many-headed] monster is allowed . . . too much [freedom]?

Glau: Clearly.

Soc: And men are blamed for pride and bad temper when the lion . . . element in them disproportionately grows and gains strength?

Glau: Yes.

Soc: And luxury and softness are blamed, because they relax and weaken this same creature, and make a coward of him?

Glau: Very true.

Soc: And is not a man reproached for flattery and meanness who subordinates the [lion] to the unruly monster, and, for the sake of money, of which he can never have enough . . . ?

Glau: True. . . .

Soc: From what point of view, then, and on what ground can we say that a man is profited by injustice or intemperance or other baseness, which will make him a worse man, even though he acquires money or power by his wickedness?

Glau: From no point of view at all.

Soc: What shall he profit, if his injustice be undetected and unpunished? He who is undetected only gets worse, whereas he who is detected and punished has the brutal part of his nature silenced and humanized; the gentler element in him is liberated, and his whole person is perfected and ennobled by the acquirement of justice and temperance and wisdom, more than one ever is by receiving gifts of beauty, strength and health, in proportion as the [inner person] is more honorable than the body [alone].

Glau: Certainly, he said. . . .

Review Questions

1. What are the three types of goods Socrates describes? How does Socrates's description of these shape his view of justice?
2. What is the point of Glaucon's making the unjust man seem (thoroughly) just and the just man seem (thoroughly) unjust?
3. What is Socrates's (that is, Plato's) view of the inner person (that is, human nature)? How does it relate to his view of (true) happiness?

12.3. DISCUSSION AND ANALYSIS

The various moral theories discussed in this text offer intriguing advice: work to reduce suffering globally; do not treat persons as mere things; abide by the agreements that you knowingly make; develop character traits conducive to human excellence; foster and maintain close, personal, and enriching relationships. To these could be added the more general claims of do not cause unnecessary harm; treat equals equally; it is wrong to punish

The Emperor's Club, Universal Pictures, 2002. Professor William Hundert (Kevin Kline, left) strives to impart life-long lessons on troubled student Sedgewick Bell (Emile Hirsch). (Moviegoods, Inc.)

someone for circumstances beyond her control; and take stock of what and who you are when deciding appropriate courses of action. Perhaps you are becoming convinced that some of these insights serve as plausible candidates for ethically significant truths of reason. Consequently, you might be warming to the idea that some behaviors are simply obligatory or permissible despite the fact that their moral status is not a matter of human convention or divine legislation. Yet, perhaps, one question still lingers: Why should moral agents act on these insights? *Why* should one "do the right thing," as Spike Lee advises? What if doing the right thing requires me to forego something I really want—perhaps great wealth or fame?

William Hundert's answer to this question, not surprisingly, harkens back to the ancient Greeks: A life without principle is not truly living. Moreover, chapter 10 discussed (in part) how Aristotelians have an easier time than most addressing this perennial question: A life without virtue is not in one's best interest. But this basic approach cannot be properly explored without discussing Socrates and Plato.

Plato's *Republic* is incredibly expansive in its philosophical scope. Among his projects is convincing the reader to *not* lead a life like Sedgewick Bell from *The Emperor's Club* or Henry Hill from *GoodFellas*. Plato wishes to establish that it's always better to be (morally) good than not. If he is correct, then one always has sufficient reason to "do the right thing." Plato concurs with William Hundert (or Hundert concurs with Plato) that one should *always* abide by those insights that approach the status of ethically significant truths of reason. Indeed, one cannot lead a good life without doing the right thing. This position entails that Plato (like Socrates before him and Aristotle after him) is ultimately concerned with articulating the necessary and sufficient conditions for leading the good life. Although influential, Plato's ideas about this are controversial, as Glaucon (Plato's brother) immediately points out to him. By revisiting the dialogue between Glaucon and Socrates, one achieves deeper insights into the complex relationship between moral goodness, happiness, and the good life that, in turn, sheds light on Aristotle's position as well as more contemporary approaches.

Glaucon, Gyges, and Plato

Glaucon is troubled. *He* doesn't believe that a person benefits more by becoming unjust (immoral) rather than just (moral), but he is aware of many who do believe this. In fact, we might call it the "majority view" about justice. A holder of the majority view believes that no one does the morally correct thing for its own sake; rather, a person acts justly only because acting unjustly invariably has consequences that are so much worse. Unfortunately, Glaucon has never heard the majority view sufficiently refuted; he hopes that Socrates can provide the refutation he seeks. But before he can be convinced of Socrates's success, he must present the majority view as strenuously as he can.

Glaucon begins espousing the majority view by questioning whether people really want to become morally good. Rather, it seems that we choose to do good acts only because it is, proverbially, the lesser of two evils. Often doing the right thing inconveniences us, but if we were to ignore our duties and act immorally, we would certainly be censured. Acting unjustly invariably means having to pay for the consequences of our moral indiscretions. This is much worse than putting up with the minor inconveniences of acting morally. Thus, although doing the morally correct thing is not ideal for us, it is better than going to jail or acquiring a bad reputation. This is how doing the right thing is the lesser of two evils.[2]

But what if the more worrisome of the two evils was no longer a factor? Consider the following analogy with visiting the dentist: leading the life of a morally good person seems comparable to making regular trips to the dentist's office. Imagine if you or I could eat and drink whatever we wanted without ever needing to brush, floss, or *especially* sit in the dentist's chair? In a world without tooth decay, cavities, or gum disease, dentistry is a very lonely occupation. This plausible intuition opens the door for the majority view about justice to make the following analogy: just as no one goes to the dentist for its own sake,

---

BOX 12C: LEARNING OUTCOMES

Upon carefully studying this chapter, students should better comprehend and be able to explain

- Why the question of whether one has adequate reason to lead the good life arises.
- Plato's classic answer to this question, including its strengths and weaknesses, but also how it informs Aristotle's position.
- Some non-Platonic strategies at answering this sort of question.
- How themes expressed in *The Emperor's Club*, *GoodFellas*, and *The Man without a Face* are conducive to better understanding ethical issues pertinent to debates about moral goodness, happiness, and leading the good life.

no one does the morally correct thing for its own sake. If you or I could lead an unjust (immoral) life without ever having to worry about paying the price for our misdeeds, it would seem irrational for us to behave justly. If we enjoyed the kind of freedom Henry Hill enjoyed, why not lie, steal, and cheat? Glaucon didn't know about modern dentistry or mafiosos, but he knows enough to realize that the majority view seems plausible. If there are no prospects of going to jail or being executed, it certainly seems that our best interests are served by doing *whatever* is required to satisfy our wildest desires.

Glaucon further develops the majority view with the mythical story of Gyges, a shepherd who finds a gold ring. Donning it, he soon discovers that turning the band one way makes him invisible, but turning it back makes him visible again. Gyges straightaway seduces the queen, kills the king (with her help), assumes the throne, and thereby gains immediate access to great wealth and fame. He is apparently able to accomplish this without damaging his reputation. In fact, Gyges has every appearance of being noble, generous, and kind.

> "Those goody, good people who worked crappy jobs for bum paychecks . . . and worried about bills . . . were suckers. If we wanted something, we just took it. If anybody complained about it, they got hit so bad, they never complained again." —*GoodFellas*, scene 9

Glaucon next has us imagine *two* invisibility rings. One ring is given to a morally good person and the other to an immoral person. Glaucon contends that we would (very) soon have two unjust persons because "no one, it seems, would be so incorruptible that he would stay on the path of justice, or bring himself to keep away from other people's possessions . . . when he could take whatever he wanted with impunity."[3] So, on behalf of the majority view, Glaucon concludes: "No one is [morally good] willingly but only when compelled. No one believes justice to be a good thing when it is kept private, since whenever either person [possessing an invisibility ring] thinks he can do injustice with impunity, he does it" (360c).

Glaucon offers one more thought-experiment on behalf of the majority view. It has two interlocking, main features. First, Glaucon proposes the possibility of a completely immoral person who is so resourceful and connected that he is able to deceive everyone into believing that he is thoroughly morally good. Sedgewick Bell is a prime example of the kind of person Glaucon intends. As a wealthy soon-to-be senator with many influential contacts, he maneuvers himself to appear as a paragon of virtue and education. Moreover, he has a loving wife and two beautiful children. Yet he also cunningly cheats, cuts corners, and subtly uses people like William Hundert to further his self-serving ends. Second, Glaucon proposes the possibility of a thoroughly morally good man who has been completely misunderstood by society. He has the (false) reputation of being completely immoral. Justin McLeod from *The Man without a Face* comes close to such an example. He is a skilled teacher like William Hundert, believing that a student's character can be positively transformed by studying important figures from history. Also like Hundert, he strives mightily to positively transform the characters of his students, and (unlike Sedgewick) actually *is* a paragon of virtue and education. However, McLeod is forced into seclusion due

> "Do you like living alone?" "It likes me." —*The Man without a Face*, scene 24

to a misunderstood past event. This tragedy left him disfigured and (falsely) earned him a reputation of being a pedophile. This (obviously) makes it difficult to practice his one true love: teaching.

The main point of Glaucon's last thought-experiment is simply this: Who lives the more desirable life? Which person would you choose to be—Sedgewick Bell or Justin McLeod? Glaucon fears that the answer is clear: No one would choose to live a life like McLeod's (let alone the kind of dreadful life Glaucon actually describes for the misunderstood virtuous person in the *Republic*). If so, then Glaucon—perhaps to his own dismay—has gone a long way to establish the majority view. If we could get away with being like Bell, our best interests are served by not acting in morally good ways.

Glaucon's thought-experiments support the following argument for the majority view: either we act justly for its own sake, such that becoming a morally good person is its own unique reward, or we act justly only because of the negative consequences of not acting justly.[4] If being a morally good person is its own reward and pursued for its own sake, then regardless of the negative consequences associated with leading such a life, we still have sufficient reason to act justly. But Glaucon's interlocking thought-experiments seemingly show that the benefits of being a thoroughly unjust person who is believed to be just (Sedgewick Bell) are too attractive to pass up, and the negative consequences of being a thoroughly just person who is believed to be unjust (Justin McLeod) are too severe to endure (361d–362d). If so, then justice is not its own unique reward or sought for its own sake. Therefore, we act justly only because of the negative consequences of acting unjustly. Consequently, perhaps the majority view is correct and Plato is mistaken. Without having to worry about getting caught, we would all act like Sedgewick Bell or Henry Hill; our lives would be better and we would be far happier.

The Just State and the Just Person

Socrates—that is, Plato—attempts to answer Glaucon's challenge by constructing an elaborate analogy between the perfectly just state (or commonwealth) and the thoroughly just person (368e–369a). Plato believes that the ideal society is made up of three societal classes or factions: producers, guardians, and rulers.[5] Each faction has a distinctive role to play in society. When each faction successfully fulfills its role, the state is well-ordered, harmonious, and justice prevails. When justice prevails, happiness obtains. But if any faction fails to fulfill its distinctive role, then the state is not well-ordered. It is disharmonious and neither justice nor happiness prevails. Analogously, Plato believes that there is a threefold division within the self or person. This division corresponds to his belief that there are three interrelated elements of human nature: appetitive, spirited, and rational. When each of these elements exhibits the characteristic it is fittest to exemplify, then the person is well-ordered. Analogous to the just state, someone who enjoys harmony among her three basic elements is a perfectly just—or morally good—person. She is also truly happy. Disharmonious persons cannot be truly happy. Therefore, just as the citizens of a commonwealth have sufficient reason to work toward living in a well-ordered commonwealth, individual persons have sufficient reason to work toward becoming well-ordered and harmonious.[6]

Plato initially discusses the appetitive and rational elements in conjunction. The appetitive element corresponds to one's basic desires for water, food, and sex, among others. This element drives one toward physical gratification and worldly possessions. Indeed, it motivates one to act at all. The appetitive element is thus analogous to a person's engine; it keeps one moving throughout the day. The analogy with the producers in Plato's ideal society is this: Just as the producers (laborers, doctors, merchants) provide the commonwealth with its daily necessities and services, the person would not do anything, let alone survive, without the appetitive element. Consequently, Plato's analogy between the rulers and the rational element is straightforward: Just as the rulers enjoin judicious policies for the well-being of the state, one's rational element is to determine sensible courses of action that individuals ought to follow. The rational element ("small man") keeps the appetitive element ("many-headed beast") in check by issuing sound policies; a person should seek neither too much (lest one becomes a lazy glutton) nor too little (lest one become an out-of-touch ascetic). Therefore, these two elements function properly when the appetitive exemplifies moderation (or temperance) and the rational exemplifies wisdom (439d–e).

Plato believes that the third element of human nature is analogous to the guardian faction of the commonwealth. He calls this the spirited element ("the lion"). Plato holds that it cannot be reduced to either the appetitive or rational elements (440b–441b). Plato's analogy between the guardians and the spirited element is this: Just as the guardians (police, national guard, army) are to act as the brave and loyal agents of the rulers, the spirited element is to provide us the courage to do as reason demands. It also explains the personal pride and satisfaction we experience when utilizing our courage successfully. It further explains why we become angry or disappointed with ourselves when we cave to the appetitive element and act contrary to what our reason demands. Therefore, this element functions properly when it exemplifies courage (which involves loyalty to oneself).

In some ways, Hundert serves as an example of a person whose spirited element regularly aids the rational element to keep his appetitive element in check. There seems to be an amorous attraction between Hundert and his colleague Elizabeth; however, she is married to another academic. Both resist the temptation to pursue a romantic relationship, at least until Elizabeth becomes divorced. But even someone like Hundert may occasionally stumble. Hundert, at the last minute, decides to rescore young Sedgewick's exam for the Mr. Julius Caesar contest, propelling him into the finals. In this case, perhaps his spirited element ran ahead of his rational element. Had Hundert known all the relevant facts, it seems unlikely that he would have given Martin Blythe's spot away to Sedgewick. This is supported by Hundert's later regret about this decision. The fact that Hundert felt regret about this is evidence (according to Plato) that his three elements were not (always) acting harmoniously when it came to Sedgewick.

But when harmony is achieved—the appetitive element functions properly manifesting temperance, the spirited element functions properly manifesting courage (and loyalty), and the rational element functions properly manifesting wisdom—a person becomes well-ordered and thereby functions optimally. According to Plato, anything that functions optimally in this sense achieves the best overall state of affairs it can; it reaches the pinnacle of its existence. Persons who reach their pinnacle by becoming (regularly) well-ordered thereby become truly happy. But the fact that a person is temperate, courageous, and wise also means that she has become a just or morally good person. Thus, a just or morally good person is also truly happy. Furthermore, because reaching our pinnacle of (human) existence is in our all-around best interest, each of us has good reason to become a morally good person. Anything short of (regular) harmony between the three elements thus means that the person cannot be truly happy. Thus anything short of *being* a just or morally good person is not in our best interests. So unjust persons like Sedgewick Bell or Henry Hill cannot be truly happy. Consequently, it's not in one's best interest to merely appear to be just, but actually be thoroughly unjust or immoral "on the inside." This is the heart of Plato's response to the "majority view" challenge Glaucon espouses.

The ramifications of Plato's view are controversial. It seems that Plato is committed to the view that persons like William Hundert or Justin McLeod lead among the best sorts of life possible even though neither man is all that wealthy, well-known, or even joyful. The idea is that both men possess (primarily) harmonious souls and thus approach the pinnacle of human existence. In this way, they lead optimally desirable lives. But Hundert is often overlooked by others; he was passed over for headmaster at St. Benedict's even though he was assistant headmaster for seventeen years. He possesses a Platonic harmonious soul, but he lacks certain "worldly virtues" associated with fund-raising and schmoozing wealthy alumni. McLeod is friendless, and is largely shunned as a result of the car accident involving a past student. He suffers for an undeserved reputation as a pedophile with no one to turn to for comfort. It's tempting to say that these men are *eventually* compensated for their hardships, making their lives more desirable. Hundert's grown students recognize his efforts on their behalf by the end of *The Emperor's Club*, and do in ways that are truly moving (especially to a teacher). McLeod manages to follow (and perhaps guide) young Charles Norstadt from a distance. We feel relief for McLeod as he attends Norstadt's graduation and are gladdened when the two men wave at each other across the quad. But Plato would have us resist this temptation. Hundert and McLeod live the best sort of life apart from these joyful moments; in fact, Plato believes that they lead the best sort of life even if they experience no joyful moments, and no Hollywood "happy endings" with their respective students. This is perhaps the most controversial implication of Plato's view: possessing a harmonious soul is *sufficient* for leading the good life and being truly happy.

> "The worth of a life is not determined by a single failure or a solitary success." —*The Emperor's Club*, scene 19

The Unbalanced Self

Plato attempts to reinforce how the malfunctioning of oneself leads to unhappiness with the following dramatic metaphor. Plato has us imagine a kind of mythical creature formed by combining different parts of familiar animals. For example, centaurs are the combination of a human torso with the lower half of a horse. But Plato's mythical creature is less familiar. He combines a beast with several tame and savage heads, a lion, and a human being smaller than the first two. Upon combining these "so that they somehow grow together," they are to be mentally encompassed in a large human being so that from the outside it looks "like a single creature, a human being" (588e–589a).

The multifarious beast with the several heads is the appetitive element, with each head representing a different bodily desire or need. The lion, of course, is the spirited element. The small human being is the rational element—the proverbial "voice of reason." According to Plato, for anyone who may merely appear just on the outside but actually be unjust on the inside, the appetitive and spirited elements have become dominant. Thus, the rational element—the element that is most closely associated with who we are as *rational* animals—has become enslaved. The person has become more like an animal and, in effect, has lost rational control of his or her own actions. One's voice of reason loses all of its import. Sometimes the appetitive element wins out, leading to accumulating greater wealth, pleasure, or power. Occasionally, the spirited element wins out by infusing sufficient disgust, shame, or anger to sway the person from feeding his overrun appetites. But because the person is malfunctioning, the element that wins out—and it may be a classic psychological struggle—is not up to him. In fact, nothing is up to him in the sense of being in rational control of what he does next.

It's also tempting to argue on Plato's behalf that the disharmonious person suffers from some sort of psychological turmoil created by the appetitive and spirited elements overstepping their proper place (444b). The voice of reason goes all but ignored by the other two more powerful elements. Plato might thereby be interpreted as holding that the unjust person is always conflicted in his actions. The rational element knows what ought to be done and wishes to accomplish it, but cannot because the appetitive and spirited elements have grown beyond its control. Suffering from such psychological conflict, the unjust person cannot be truly happy.

Henry Hill provides stunning examples of the appetitive element overexerting itself, especially as *GoodFellas* turns to the 1980s. Henry and his wife, Karen, now live in a lavishly extravagant home. Their luxuries are the result of Henry's booming drug trade. His drug operation has become so incredibly large and complex that, along with Karen, he enlists the help of fellow mobsters Jimmy Conway and Tommy DeVito. He further employs his mistress Sandy and his old babysitter Lois. But Henry snorts nearly as much cocaine as he sells. His cocaine addiction and the pressures of running his drug operation make Henry incredibly anxious and paranoid. He never sleeps and is constantly worried that someone is following him, including police helicopters. As Plato would say, Henry's appetitive element has overtaken his rational element. Henry's lifestyle is evidence that he suffers from an internal imbalance. This would probably lead Plato to conclude that Henry is not happy, even though, akin to Gyges, he enjoys many material luxuries and relative freedom from legal prosecution.

The Tommy DeVito character from *GoodFellas* is an effective example of someone whose spirited element is out of control. Tommy's spirited element tends to overexert itself but not (obviously) for the sake of acquiring further monetary or otherwise appetitive ends (unlike Henry or Jimmy). Consider the scene where Tommy meets Billy Batts in Henry's Suite Lounge nightclub. Batts, recently released from prison after serving a six-year term, reminds everyone in the club that Tommy used to shine his shoes. Tommy reminds him that he isn't that little kid anymore. He now deserves Billy's respect. Sensing that Tommy is becoming unnerved, Batts throws more barbs Tommy's way. The bravado of the two Sicilians gets the better of them. In fact, Tommy becomes enraged. Although Henry convinces Tommy to "get some air," Tommy tells Jimmy, "Keep him here; I'll be back." When he returns, Tommy savagely beats Billy to a bloody pulp simply out of spite. He later kills Billy with his mother's kitchen knife.[7]

Plato would conclude that each *GoodFellas* character is unjust and, thus, none of them is leading the good life or is truly happy. However, the "goodfellas" ironically seem to also represent a worrisome objection to Plato's view. In fact, the problem may appear to be rather obvious: none of them seems all that obviously unhappy. Furthermore, as demonstrated by Henry's soliloquy at the end of the film, Henry detests leading a life that is more just; he was clearly happier when he was living the unjust life of a gangster. Moreover, none of these characters seem all that psychologically conflicted about his behavior. It wasn't the case that any of them suffered from some sort of conscious turmoil as they conducted their "business." There is no evidence that any of them desired to act justly but couldn't due to being enslaved by their respective appetitive or spirited elements. Rather, Henry seemingly wanted to sell drugs, Jimmy seemingly loved to steal, and Tommy seemingly reveled in being hot-tempered. Because it seems that imbalanced persons (in Plato's sense of the term) do not necessarily suffer from psychological conflict or turmoil, it is not necessarily the case that they are any less happy than Plato's perfectly harmonious and just person. Therefore, the objection concludes, it is not necessarily in one's best interest to lead a just life. If so, then Plato's answer to Glaucon's "majority view" challenge seems to be in jeopardy.

> "You see, the hardest thing for me was leaving the life. I still love the life. We were treated like movie stars with muscle. We had it all, just for the asking. . . . And now it's all over. . . . I'm an average nobody."
> —*GoodFellas*, scene 34

The objection to Plato's view being developed here might manifest most clearly in the cases of Paul Cicero from *GoodFellas* and Sedgewick Bell from *The Emperor's Club*. Both became powerful and wealthy men. As the Lucchese crime boss, Paulie was virtually untouchable. But as the boss, Paulie is akin to Plato's ruler. Paulie invariably made careful decisions and laid down policies that he believed would best benefit himself and his "family." Paulie was never psychologically conflicted; he always seemed cool and collected. Nevertheless, Paulie willfully participated in unlawful and immoral behaviors. Perhaps the most striking example of this is when he becomes partners with Sonny the restaurateur. Paulie ran the restaurant into the ground, bankrupted Sonny, and then set Sonny's place ablaze for the insurance money. Sedgewick was properly educated at St. Benedict's and then later at Yale. Mr. Hundert afforded the future US senator every opportunity to learn from great citizens and statesmen of the past. But calmly and coolly, Sedgewick concludes that he is better off without Hundert's principles and virtues, turning his back forever on his teacher's lessons.

> "I live in the real world, where people do what they need to do to get what they want, and, if it's lying or cheating, so be it. . . . And I'll worry about my 'contribution' later." —*The Emperor's Club*, scene 18

Health and Happiness

Plato might respond to this objection by saying that, for all organisms, including the commonwealth and the human being, happiness is a matter of being optimally healthy. An organism's being optimally healthy, in turn, is a matter of its varied functions being brought into harmony or attunement with one another. So, for a biological organism, the heart must pump blood at the correct rate, neither too fast nor too slow. The kidneys must clean the blood at the rate it circulates and the lungs must oxygenate it accordingly. Analogously, the state is healthiest when its "organs"—producers, guardians, and rulers—have achieved a harmonious arrangement. Just so, a person is healthiest when the appetitive, spirited, and rational elements achieve harmonious interaction. Therefore, although it is a bit strange to say that a commonwealth or animal can be happy in this sense, Plato is clearly committed to holding that a person cannot be truly happy unless she is optimally healthy.

Accordingly, perhaps the best response Plato can make to the objection posed by the *GoodFellas* characters or Sedgewick Bell is to reinforce his analogy between health and justice. It is clearly not in one's best interests to lead a life that continuously harms the body. This remains true even if the harm inflicted is due to pleasurable activities. One should not unceasingly smoke cigarettes or eat greasy cheeseburgers (even in paradise) despite any great pleasures of doing so. But if this is true of the body, why can't it be true of one's soul or inner self? If so, then it is clearly not in one's best interests to lead a life that continuously harms (or distorts) the inner self. And this is so even if the harm inflicted is somehow enjoyable. One should not allow the appetitive element to satiate itself even if it brings you great pleasure to do so. Thus, to ask whether it is in one's best interest to be a morally good person is like asking whether one desires a healthy body rather than one riddled with cancer. In many ways, Plato would say that the *GoodFellas* characters or Sedgewick Bell suffer from "cancer of the soul." Henry's appetitive element grew out of control, enfeebling the other two elements. Tommy's spirited element is the cancerous culprit. Arguably, Paulie, and Sedgewick, are beset with both forms of the psychological "disease." If no one would willingly choose to suffer from bodily cancer, no one would willingly choose to suffer from "soul cancer." In fact, merely raising the question seems, as Plato claims, "ridiculous" (445a–b).

The plausibility of Plato's analogy may ultimately rest on his distinction between *feeling* happy and *being* happy. Plato seemingly held that the former does not entail the latter and vice versa. One can feel happy without thereby being happy, and one can be happy without thereby feeling happy. The *GoodFellas* characters (including Paulie) are examples of the former, and Glaucon's thoroughly just man who seems unjust (like Justin McLeod) is an example of the latter. Consequently, Plato is committed to the position that one can be mistaken about being happy. The possibility of error here is grounded in Plato's belief that genuine happiness is a state of being and not necessarily a psychological state. Plato doesn't argue that being optimally healthy necessarily produces more pleasure than a life of pleasure seeking. Rather, he argues that being optimally healthy is *better* or more *valuable* than any pleasurable psychological state. Therefore, insofar as being optimally healthy is to be just, a person is happier being just rather than not because he or she achieves an optimally best state of being.

Whether Plato's rejoinder suffices may depend on his implicit interpretation of psychological turmoil. Plato seemingly holds that a person's *being* psychologically conflicted does not require him to *feel* psychologically conflicted. Some might find this suggestion even more outlandish than Plato's contention that a person can be mistaken about what makes him or her truly happy. Someone may ask: How can I possibly not be consciously aware that I am psychologically conflicted? But recall that Plato's sense of psychological conflict refers to one's inner being or person and how it is malfunctioning. So, just as a person might be unaware that they are neurotic—she may enjoy washing her hands with a new bar of soap every time—a person can be unaware that her three elements are not in harmonious attunement. If so, then although Sedgewick or the *GoodFellas* characters don't *feel* inner conflict in that they are not consciously aware of it, they have *become* conflicted in the sense of failing to fully grasp what leading the good life requires of them. Becoming conflicted entails a kind of malfunction, but, by definition, this cannot be as good or valuable as functioning properly. So, if Plato's rejoinders hold up, even Sedgewick and the *GoodFellas* characters—like the rest of us—have sufficient reason to be more like William Hundert and Justin McLeod: leaders of the good life.[8]

Beyond Plato

Plato's influential answer to the "Why should I be moral" question nevertheless remains controversial. The problematic issue is that, for Plato, nothing else but possessing a "balanced soul" is required for the good life. This is initially difficult to accept. Is it plausible to hold that a person can lead the good life without *ever* feeling happy? Doesn't it seem plain that one's well-being is nontrivially benefited if she, in addition to possessing a balanced soul, also experienced moments of joy? Furthermore, it seems Aristotle is correct that, insofar as we are rational, *social* beings, the good (human) life cannot be led in complete isolation; one's welfare is significantly enhanced by experiencing love or (true) friendship.

Nevertheless, perhaps part of Plato's enduring legacy is that he provides an effective case for believing that a life led by Mr. Hundert–like "virtue and principles"—thereby keeping the appetites at bay—is a *necessary* component for the good life. Plato seems correct that practicing naive hedonism makes one a slave to his or her desires and passions. It is difficult to hold that one leads the good life in slavery. Furthermore, recall Nozick's "experience machine" challenge (chapter 7). If feeling happy is the only truly worthy pursuit in life, then there is no reason to not enter the experience machine. But plausible reasons not to enter remain—many having to do with autonomous existence, genuine character formation, and cultivating significant relationships.[9] If so, these pursuits are just as worthy as feeling happy. That is, being a certain way is just as (morally) valuable as feeling a certain way.

Plato's implicit distinction between instrumental and intrinsic goods is also relevant here. An instrumental good is valuable only because of its ability to secure a further desire. Money is a prime example. Money itself is merely ink on paper; its value lies with the (other) things it can get us. But if there are instrumental goods, then it seems that there must also be intrinsic goods. An intrinsic good is valuable for its own sake. There is something about it that, when considered properly, makes it desirable, even if possessing it doesn't lead to any (obvious) further good. Some examples are autonomous agency, character formation, significant relationships—those candidates for not entering the experience machine. It thereby seems that one's well-being is significantly enhanced if they are possessed; thus, one cannot lead the good life without possessing a significant degree or level of these sorts of goods. In a way, then, Plato is correct that possessing them is uniquely rewarding. They thus represent some of the most important goods one can achieve or aspire to.

But note that the various moral theories offer guidelines about how to lead one's life in accordance with these intrinsic values. Kantianism stresses autonomous agency. Virtue ethics stresses character formation; care ethics (as a contemporary variant of virtue ethics) stresses being in intimate relationship with others. Consequently, it seems that the good life cannot be led without one's taking the moral point of view. This conclusion is bolstered by the premise that if it is bad to be the last human being on earth (because humans are essentially rational, *social* beings), then it is bad to live as if you are the only person on earth. Your welfare is significantly improved by entering into communion with others. But accomplishing this requires the insight that you are one person among many. Other persons do not exist simply to be exploited by you; treating others like mere objects or things is not entering into communion with them. This is merely a different way to live alone. But community also achieves the further insight that if it is bad for you to suffer, it is bad for others to suffer. This spurs us to work toward the reduction of suffering, which the utilitarian stresses. Therefore, the various moral theories all propose suggestions about how to lead the good life; it furthermore seems that the good life cannot be achieved without them.

Accordingly, the good life seemingly includes—necessarily—leading one's life in ways that are conducive to possessing intrinsic goods: autonomous agency, character formation, significant relationships, and happiness (joyful experiences). This conclusion sufficiently solidifies an objectivist-type answer about what kind of life is best or at least good: one that contains rich levels of intrinsic goods. Of course, because conflicts among these goods are always looming, it's natural to seek more specific strategies about how to live, or guiding principles recommending what to do in conflict situations. Multiple plausible strategies present themselves; this text has explored the more influential attempts. Perhaps some of these strategies are less plausible than others. Yet the goal is to learn from each, thereby improving one's systematic approach to ethics. This is an ongoing process. Any interesting approach will invariably remain somewhat controversial, which explains the enduringness of the questions: What ought I to do? How ought I to be? How ought I to live? Moral philosophy, therefore, (in part) attempts to coherently and consistently answer these three interlocking questions in systematic and fruitful ways, allowing each of us to fully and equally (inasmuch as we can) participate in the good life.

In some ways, this text challenges the reader to glean insights from the various traditional moral theories and then begin constructing a moral theory of one's own. If the good life cannot be led without possessing a significant degree of intrinsic goods, then this project is valuable for its own sake. However, it is also personally valuable insofar as conflicts about competing goods are bound to arise. Working out informative, action-guiding strategies about what to do in these situations thereby engages one in moral philosophy. As you begin articulating and defending your views, and the moral principles upon which they depend, be aware of the criteria for assessing moral theories. Take care that your theory is free of internal contradiction and that it doesn't suffer from conceptual incompleteness. Take care that it is sufficiently action-guiding and avoids prescribing a moral universe that is too large or too small. And always be aware of potential counterexamples to your view. Many of these are bound to arise as you face new and difficult situations. Do your best to explain them away, but be prepared to revise your view if they cannot be suitably addressed.

Plato's approach to moral philosophy was rather rigid, at least in that individuals have *no* significant say about of what the good life consists. For Plato, leading the good life is merely a matter of following moral principles implicit in our common human essence and becoming a certain kind of person as a result. Aristotle both agreed and disagreed with his teacher. Human nature is indeed important in determining (moral) goodness, but Plato seemingly overlooked (or underestimated) the importance of our sociability and the role of external goods, including close friendships and experiencing simple joys. The truly good life is a *desirable* life; thus, true happiness is not strictly equivalent to the moral life, grounded exclusively in a life of principle. This allows each of us some input into what makes one's life go best. Choosing to become a teacher like McLeod or Hundert, or a doctor, or a law enforcement official are all plausible facets of leading the good life. Arguably, this extends to McLeod's artwork or Hundert's mornings on the lake. Yet our individual preferences must not lead us to ignore the moral point of view, which explains why Paulie's "business transactions" are not conducive to the good life. Indeed, there seem to be defensible constraints on what choices are good, bad, right, and wrong, Plato is correct that the moral life is *necessary* for the good life (even if it is not sufficient). Furthermore, Aristotle is correct that some choices are better or worse than others (even if not,

The Man without a Face, Warner Brothers Pictures, 1993. Retired prep school teacher Justin McLeod (Mel Gibson), now a recluse, must come to terms with a tragic accident from his past. (Moviegoods, Inc.)

strictly speaking, wrong); leading the moral life requires that one be able to discern the difference, and regularly act upon this knowledge. Achieving this requires one to articulate and defend plausible moral principles and internalize them so as to transform one's character. Clearly, then, inquiring about what makes one's life go best "is no unimportant question." In fact, it may be the most important of all questions. Answering it requires us to do some philosophy.

> "Take some responsibility for what you want." —*The Man without a Face*, scene 16

Discovering insights into Plato's "not unimportant question" is the charge left to the "fledgling philosopher" at the end of this book. If Mr. Hundert, paraphrasing Socrates, is correct that living *well*—and not merely living—is truly important, how will you do that? It is almost—almost—as if Mr. Hundert is asking *you*: What path will you walk? What will be your contribution? How will history remember you?

12.4. TWO ADDITIONAL FILMS

GoodFellas (1990)

Director: Martin Scorsese
Screenwriters: Nicholas Pileggi and Martin Scorsese

Plot Summary

> As far back as I can remember I always wanted to be a gangster. Being a gangster was better than being President of the United States.

Thirteen-year-old Henry Hill longingly peers across the street at the local cabstand, a legitimate front for the Cicero crime family. He doesn't go unnoticed for long. The Ciceros soon employ Henry to run errands. But Henry begins to spend all of his time at the local cabstand; his part-time afterschool job had become an all-day obsession. When Henry's father learns of his son's truancy, he savagely beats the boy. Henry shows up at the cabstand the next day with a black eye. He informs Tuddy Cicero, younger brother of patriarch Paulie Cicero, that he can no longer run errands, lest his father kill him next time. Tuddy and his crew immediately find the Hills' postman. As Cicero henchmen shove the man's head in a pizza oven, Tuddy demands that no more letters from Henry's school be delivered to the Hill residence. Henry's family ties with the Ciceros soon become stronger than those with his biological family. Henry would later reminisce: "People looked at me differently. They knew I was with somebody. . . . At thirteen, I made more money than most grown-ups in the neighborhood. . . . I had it all."

Jimmy "The Gent" Conway becomes a mentor of sorts to Henry. Henry's first arrest is for selling Jimmy's bootleg cigarettes. Immediately after Henry's court appearance, Jimmy is there to congratulate him because, as Jimmy states: "You took your first pinch like a man, and learned the two greatest things in life: Never rat on your friends, and always keep your mouth shut." Jimmy then leads Hill into the hallway where all of Henry's "family" is there to congratulate him. In fact, Paulie exclaims, "You broke your cherry!" Henry is now a full member of the Cicero family.

Henry turns twenty-one in 1963; he is handsome, well dressed, affluent, and respected. He simply relishes the life of a gangster. Now inseparable from Jimmy and Jimmy's other protégé, Tommy DeVito, Henry again reminisces: "For us to live any other way was nuts. To us, those goody, good people who worked . . . for bum paychecks and took the subway to work every day and worried about bills, were dead. They were suckers. . . . If we wanted something, we just took it." Soon after Jimmy, Tommy, and Henry steal $420,000 from Air France (without brandishing a gun), Henry meets Karen. Initially, she was not impressed with Henry. However, his connections, charm, and money win her over. Flashing rolls of bills, Henry and Karen never wait for a table, no matter how crowded the restaurant. One night at a show, Bobby Vinton sends a bottle of champagne to their table. Karen tells us, "There was nothing like it. I didn't think there was anything strange in all of this—you know, a twenty-one-year-old kid with such connections. He was an exciting guy." Henry and Karen are soon married. Both his birth and mob families attend. Members of the latter present the newlyweds envelopes stuffed with one hundred dollar bills.

Henry and Karen are surrounded by the extended Cicero family; those outside of the family are never allowed in. Henry's family and Jimmy's family regularly take vacations together. The wives go shopping together—after spending all morning at the hair salon. The husbands take their mistresses out every Saturday night (only Friday is reserved for the wives). As Karen recalls, "We were all so very close. . . . And being together all the time made everything seem all the more normal." Karen even came to accept the Ciceros' "business dealings." In fact, she eventually becomes "proud that she had a husband who was willing to risk his neck to get us a little extra" cash. But what Karen never got used to was Henry's taking a mistress. One morning, she straddled Henry, placed a loaded revolver in his face and waited for him to awake. She wants to know who his "whore" is. But she is still smitten with him and loves him dearly. She cannot harm him. She slinks to the floor in tears.

The one time Henry is actually convicted and sent to prison, he serves his time with Paulie and other gangsters. They enjoy separate quarters, home cooked meals, wine with dinner, and scotch and brandy to wash it all down afterward. Henry tells us, "When you think of prison, you get pictures in your mind from the old movies of rows of guys behind bars. But it wasn't like that for wiseguys. It really wasn't that bad. . . . Everybody else in the joint was doin' real time all mixed together living like pigs, but we lived alone. We owned the joint." There doesn't seem to be any real consequences for Henry's behavior. In fact, Henry begins selling drugs in prison. He is thus able to send some money home to Karen, at least after he bribes the guards for looking the other way and provides Paulie his cut.

However, Henry deliberately disobeys Paulie by continuing his drug trade. Dealing drugs in prison is one thing, believes Paulie, but "on the outside," he will not allow it. But it is the late 1970s, and the drug business is booming. He can make so much more money now that he's out. Henry and Karen purchase an extravagant home, complete with an imported, black marble table and a custom, remote controlled wall-sized entertainment center. Henry's drug operation becomes so incredibly large and complex that he enlists the help of Jimmy, Tommy, Karen, Sandy, his current mistress, and Lois, his old babysitter. But Henry also snorts almost as much cocaine as he sells. With his cocaine addiction and the pressures of running his drug operation, Henry becomes incredibly anxious and paranoid. He never sleeps and is constantly worried that someone is following him, including police helicopters.

Henry's paranoia turns out to be well-founded as narcotics officers arrest Henry in 1980 after Lois makes a drug-related call from Henry's house. After making bail, Henry meets Jimmy at a diner to allegedly discuss Hill's case. Jimmy then asks Henry to help with a hit in Florida; however, Jimmy has never before made this request. Henry knows that if he travels to Florida with Jimmy, he will be the one getting whacked. Henry thus becomes aware of the fact that Jimmy and presumably others in the mob want him dead because they fear that he will "rat them out." Fearful for his life, Henry indeed turns on his mafia family. He is granted clemency for doing so, and he, Karen, and his children enter the federal witness protection program. Henry laments: "I get to live the rest of my life like a schnook."

Discussion Questions

1. Would you lead a life like Henry's if you could? Why or why not?
2. Is it ever morally permissible for a parent to punish a child in the way that Mr. Hill did early in the film? Defend your answer.
3. Should Karen be proud of Henry for his industrious "business dealings"? Explain.
4. In what sense are the "goodfellas" good? Explain.

5. Are Henry, Jimmy, Tommy, and Paulie—especially prior to 1980—unhappy? What might make them happier? Explain your answers.

The Man without a Face (1993)

Director: Mel Gibson
Screenwriter: Malcolm MacRury (based on an Isabelle Holland novel)

Plot Summary

Is it this? . . . But if that is all you see, then you don't see me—you can't see me.

A single mother and her three children (from three different husbands) are traveling on the Boston ferry. The Norstadt children, Gloria, Charles, and Meg, are typical siblings and their mother Kitty struggles to keep the peace. Charles—"Chuck"—once again approaches his mother about attending Holyfield Military Academy, his father's alma mater. After being discouraged by his mother about this—again—he takes out his pre-pubescent angst on the family car. He believes he is alone when wreaking this havoc; however, he is not. A man and his dog witness Chuck's frustration. We don't see the man's face, but Chuck recognizes the man's truck and his "hound from hell."

Chuck enjoys the long summer days by spending time with his friends. One day they go for a boat ride, winding up at "Freak Beach," a landing near the home of recluse Mr. Justin McLeod—the same man who saw Chuck vandalize his mother's car. The children call him "Hamburger Head," and gossip about the secretive owner of the nearby beach house. McLeod's dog startles the young trespassers. Chuck unfortunately leaves his books behind. He fears that without them, he'll never get into Holyfield. He pleads with his friends to turn the boat around to retrieve them, but they refuse.

Chuck rides his bike back to McLeod's property only to find pages strewn in the water. Dejected, he sits on the rocks staring aimlessly into the sea. He seemingly shuts down, remaining motionless for hours. McLeod eventually approaches him on horseback, and begrudgingly invites the boy into his home to warm up by the fire. As McLeod prepares him a cup of hot chocolate, Chuck spies a plaque from Barrett Academy. "Hamburger Head" was once a prep school teacher! On his way out, Chuck gathers the courage to ask McLeod if he still teaches and whether he would be interested in doing any tutoring.

The next day Norstadt again rides his bike to McLeod's house. Chuck reminds him about the tutoring he requires to finally pass the Holyfield entrance exam. Still very distant and cold, McLeod tells Norstadt to dig a hole where he stands; it should be three feet cubed. Chuck sighs deeply and begins digging. Once finished, he enters McLeod's home. McLeod informs him that their policy shall be: "learn or leave." Norstadt agrees. McLeod commands that Chuck address him as "Sir"; Norstadt again agrees. McLeod next commands that Chuck write an essay. But this is too much. Norstadt lashes out at McLeod, shouting that there are no required essays on the entrance exam. McLeod tells Chuck that he can leave now.

The local townsfolk never tire of gossiping about McLeod and his solitary lifestyle. And, of course, they simply must know how the right side of his face was scarred so badly. Two friends of the police chief assert, "Nobody lives like that unless they've got history!"

Throughout all the gossip, Chuck remains silent. He doesn't want anyone—especially his family—knowing that he visits McLeod for tutoring sessions. What if his mother decided that he couldn't see McLeod? How would he pass the Holyfield exam then? No, McLeod is a resource he cannot miss. Further, "Sir" is now in full-swing with his lessons; Chuck is learning Latin, geometry, and even Shakespeare.

Both of his sisters soon learn that Chuck is visiting McLeod. Meg, his younger sister, can be trusted, but his older sister, Gloria, cannot be. Chuck quickly returns a book of sonnets McLeod lent him. McLeod is a bit surprised; he asks Chuck why he is returning the book so soon. He informs his tutor that Gloria found the book. McLeod is confused. He asks whether Norstadt has his mother's full permission to visit him. The boy shakes his head no. McLeod again becomes gruff; he refuses to see the boy again until Chuck receives permission to continue.

Chuck returns the next day and allows McLeod to believe that his mother has consented to the tutoring sessions. McLeod subsequently becomes a mentor to Chuck; their teacher-student relationship transforms into friendship. Norstadt begins asking McLeod rather personal questions about life and love. McLeod wistfully shares that he was married once, but that was a long time ago. McLeod shows Norstadt some artwork that has appeared on magazine covers like *Harper's*. This is how McLeod earns his living, because "tutoring doesn't pay what it used to." Chuck finally asks McLeod how he received his scars. He informs Chuck that his scars are from being burned in a car crash. The worst part, however, was that a boy, a past student of his, died in the crash. Charles tries to comfort McLeod, but the teacher quickly rebuffs the boy and leaves the room. Charles is confused and angry; he was only trying to comfort his new friend.

The tutoring session nevertheless continue. McLeod surprises Chuck by announcing that there will be a practice test tomorrow. Norstadt is alarmed. He nervously objects that he isn't ready. McLeod will have none of it. The next morning Chuck arrives donning a jacket and tie. After the test is finished, McLeod excitedly grades it. Norstadt scored an 84 percent! Both teacher and student are elated. McLeod congratulates Chuck by arranging a twin-engine plane ride for the boy. His father was apparently a pilot and it is Chuck's dream to follow in his footsteps (or flight path).

Later, McLeod drops Chuck off at his house. But neither his mother nor younger sister is at home. They've gone looking for a new house. Chuck finds Gloria and her new boyfriend in bed together. Gloria is petrified. Chuck will most certainly tattle on her. In a rage, she tells Chuck the truth about his father. She divulges the location of their mother's letters, so he can learn all of it firsthand. With letters strewn everywhere, Chuck is simply beside himself. The image of his father has been shattered. Not knowing where to turn, but needing someone to turn to, he mindlessly travels to McLeod's house. It is very late and Chuck is almost in shock. McLeod takes him in (again) and warms him with a blanket. They will tackle this problem in the morning. The boy sleeps.

Police Chief Stark knocks on McLeod's door early the next morning, inquiring whether Charles is present. McLeod immediately assures the chief that he is. Relieved, the chief requests permission to go get him; his mother will be arriving soon. Charles comes down the steps in his briefs and a T-shirt. Stark and McLeod share uncomfortably glances. Norstadt wants to know what's wrong. McLeod again becomes gruff and distant, telling Chuck that he must go home with the chief immediately. Later that evening, McLeod gathers the courage to visit Norstadt. Chuck's mother answers the door. She doesn't let McLeod inside. Rather, she simply asserts that he has a lot of nerve being on her doorstep after what he has done to her son. McLeod reassures her that he simply is interested in Charles's well-being. The mother does not believe him. He demands that McLeod have no further contact with her son.

Discussion Questions

1. Did McLeod, given his Barrett Academy experiences, act immorally or irresponsibly by agreeing to tutor Norstadt? Should he have ensured that Norstadt had his mother's permission to be tutored?
2. Why does McLeod require Charles to dig holes in the yard only to have him fill them in again?
3. McLeod confides in Norstadt that he considered having plastic surgery done on his scars, but he decided against it (scene 26, 1:17: 45 into the movie). Why?
4. Why did McLeod not directly answer Norstadt's question about whether he molested his Barrett Academy student (scene 31, 1:36:05 to 1:38:00)?
5. Why does McLeod agree to never contact Norstadt again even though he was innocent of any wrongdoing? Evaluate his decision.

12.5. REVIEWING THROUGH THE THREE MOVIES

1. Rewatch scenes 18 (from 1:32:35 to 1:36:10) and 19 (from 1:38:33 to 1:39:40) of *The Emperor's Club*, paying close attention to Sedgewick's dialogue. How would Henry Hill and Justin McLeod respond? How would Plato respond? Is Plato's evaluation plausible? Explain.
2. As Plato understands the term "happiness" who is the "happier" man—William Hundert or Justin McLeod? Who is the "unhappiest" man on Platonic grounds—Sedgewick Bell, Henry Hill, or Paulie Cicero? Assess Plato's answers to these questions.
3. Hundert asserts in the closing voice-over (scene 19 beginning 1:41:36 into the movie) that "the worth of a life is not determined by a single failure or a solitary success." What has Hundert and/or McLeod learned (or relearned) about a worthy life? What makes a life worthy for Plato? How would Henry Hill or Jimmy Conway answer this question?
4. Compare and contrast William Hundert and Justin McLeod as teachers and as men. Compare and contrast Sedgewick Bell and Charles Norstadt as students and as young men. What important ethical insights does this exercise uncover?
5. Reconsider the six movie quotes from the chapter and explain whether each, given the adjacent paragraphs, *illustrates* a point the author is making, *supplements* (or extends) a point the author is making, or *contrasts* (for emphasis) a point the author is making. Explain your answers.

NOTES

1. Excerpted from *The Dialogues of Plato*, trans. Benjamin Jowett (New York: Oxford University Press, 1920). Section headings and slight emendations added for reading comprehension.

2. Glaucon also places his arguments in terms of living under a powerful despot similar to High Chancellor Sutler from *V for Vendetta*, one who has all the means necessary to do whatever he or she wishes. It certainly seems attractive to live as that powerful person. However, very few of us ever

will. Furthermore, it is not at all attractive to live under a powerful despot, especially if there was no recourse to recoup injustices or injuries. Therefore, because it is so much worse to suffer (without recourse) at the hands of the despot than it is beneficial to enjoy the privileges of being the despot, we agree to not act despotically. This is one way in which Plato espouses a social contract type view of acting justly (or properly). However, Plato goes on in the *Republic* to argue that leading the morally good life is not merely pragmatically beneficial, but also intrinsically better (or valuable).

3. The passages quoted from the *Republic* are taken from either C. D. C. Reeve's new translation (Indianapolis: Hackett Press, 2004), or Francis MacDonald Cornford's translation (Oxford: Oxford University Press, 1945). Furthermore, I will keep with the standard practice of referring to Platonic passages via the margin page numbers, added by the Stephanus family, early editors of Plato's work. This passage can be found at 360b.

4. Plato was aware that the argument, to be as strong as possible, must somehow address concerns about the afterlife. After all, some (like Adeimantus, Plato's other brother) might counter that if the just person was rewarded in heaven, as the saying goes, then the just person could still benefit in the long run by remaining perfectly just until the day he dies. As such, the perfectly just person, although he suffers on earth, will be rewarded with the everlasting bliss of heaven, and the perfectly unjust person, although he benefits for a while on earth, will be sent to hell everlastingly. Plato's rejoinder (via Adeimantus) to this, in part, is that it seems possible that the Greek gods could be persuaded or bribed into not punishing the perfectly unjust person in the afterlife (365b–365d). As such, the perfectly just person still loses out because he foregoes the benefits of being unjust on this earth. After all, he could also bribe the gods. It is a bit more difficult to apply this line of argument to monotheism because it is believed that an omnicompetent God could not be bribed. However, note that if one leads a morally good life only because of the expected reward of heaven, and not because she believes that leading a morally good life is its own reward, then she is still acting from self-serving motives. Thus, we cannot answer Glaucon by merely saying that we will go to hell if we become the perfectly unjust person.

5. Plato's three societal classes are often translated as producers, auxiliaries, and guardians. For familiarity sake, however, the auxiliaries will be called "guardians" and the guardians "rulers." This usage seemingly better captures the role Plato intended for each faction.

6. When discussing justice among or within individual persons, Plato tended to use the Greek word *psyche*, and this has traditionally been interpreted as "soul." Because the word "soul" now invariably carries religious import that Plato did not intend, most commentators urge that Plato's "psyche" be interpreted as "self" or "person."

7. Henry's spirited element also seemingly causes disharmony. He continues his drug operation, even though crime boss Paulie has directly ordered him to stop. He apparently believes that he can traffic drugs without Paulie's knowledge or permission. Henry also attempts to spend time with his brother Michael. Arguably, Henry is moved by the pangs of not spending enough time with his paraplegic younger brother, even though doing so further complicates his drug operations. It seems Henry's (emotionally driven) choice to juggle one more thing is additional evidence that Henry's voice of reason goes almost completely unheard. Consequently, Henry's life at the beginning of 1980 is *completely* out of control. He has become a slave to both his appetitive and spirited elements. As such, Plato would ask: How can Henry be serving his best interests, even if he continues to go undetected by the authorities?

8. The discussion of Plato that appears in this section (and the plot summary of *GoodFellas* in the subsequent one) is adapted from Dean A. Kowalski, "*Goodfellas*, Gyges, and the Good Life," in *The Philosophy of Martin Scorsese*, ed. Mark Conard (Lexington: University of Kentucky Press, 2007), 31–52.

9. Louis Pojman develops this sort of argument by asserting that if what is lacking in the experience machine—autonomous agency, character formation, significant relationships—are also lacking in one's actual life, then one is not currently leading the good life, even if one is blissfully happy. See Louis Pojman, *Ethics: Discovering Right and Wrong* (Belmont, CA: Wadsworth, 2002), 76–78.

Index

abductive arguments, 14, 16
abortion, 20, 24; *The Cider House Rules* and, 115–19, 125–26; doctrine of double effect and, 162; ethic of care and, 303–4, 312; moral relativism and, 80; *Vera Drake* and, 297–301
absolutism, moral, 162, 218–19
Academy (Plato), 5
accountability, 130, 139n5
action-guiding test, 153; and ethical egoism, 159; and ethic of care, 317–18; and Kantian ethics, 217, 228; and moral absolutism, 162; and virtue ethics, 284–89
act utilitarianism, 186–89; as controversial, 189–92
Adams, Robert M., 114n6
ad hominem fallacy, 18–19
adultery: divine command theory and, 100; natural law and, 164
afterlife, Plato on, 352n4
Albert the Great, 147
Alexander the Great, 273
Allen, Woody, 49–53
altruism, 156
Amistad, 215–16, 219, 222–23, 225–26, 231–33
analogy, arguments by, 16
anarchy, 265n8
animals: ethic of care and, 303; and harm, 21; speciesism and, 188, 203n6
antecedent: denying, 17–18; term, 34n3
Aquinas, Thomas, 28, 147–50, 161, 165, 172n10
arbitrariness objection, and divine command theory, 102–6
arguments, 13–16; fallacious, 16–20
Aristotle, 28, 235n12, 269–95; on friendship, 312–16; on good life, 345; and Plato, 273, 287, 344; on special obligation, 317

As Good As It Gets, 278, 282, 284, 289, 291–93
atheism, 75, 165
autonomy, 227; ethic of care on, 307–10

backward-looking theories of justice, 25–26
bad, term, 22–24
balance: Aristotle on, 276–77, 280–83; Plato on, 333–34, 339–42
beliefs, 46
Benedict, Ruth, 74
benefits, 152
Bentham, Jeremy, 177, 183, 185
biology: analogies from, Reid on, 123–24; and ethical theory, 143–72
The Boondock Saints, 99, 101, 103–4, 110–12
Boys Don't Cry, 151, 163–66, 169–70
Buddhism, 52, 63n8, 82

capital punishment, 20
care, ethic of, 297–324; evaluation of, 317–18
Caring (Noddings), 301–6
Cast Away, 143–47, 157, 161
categorical imperative(s), 212–14, 217; combination of, 224–25
The Cider House Rules, 115–19, 124–26, 133
civil rights movement, 226; moral relativism and, 82–83
common sense: and Kantian ethics, 220; Reid on, 119–20; and utilitarianism, 191; and virtue ethics, 283–84
completeness test, 153; and Kantian ethics, 228; and natural law, 165–66; and virtue ethics, 288–89
conflict situations, 151, 153, 345; doctrine of double effect and, 163; ethical egoism and, 159; Kantian ethics and, 219, 224, 227–28; moral absolutism and, 162; utilitarianism and, 187, 193; virtue ethics and, 283, 286

consensus, 79–80

consequentialism, 183

considered moral judgments, 171n4

contraception: doctrine of double effect and, 162–63; natural law and, 162

contracts: Hobbes on, 242–44, 247; social contract theory, 237–65

contradiction, 12

contradiction test, 153; and virtue ethics, 287

counterexample test, 154–55; and Kantian ethics, 227; and natural law, 163–65; and utilitarianism, 191

Crimes and Misdemeanors, 40, 124–25, 131, 133–36

cultural imperialism, 73

cultural relativism, 74–76

culture, issues in, 78–80

Darwin, Charles, 69

DCT. *See* divine command theory

Decalogue, 99, 103

deductive arguments, 14–15

definitional statements, 128

demonic voices objection, and divine command theory, 104–5

denying the antecedent, 17–18

Descartes, Rene, 307

descriptive claims, 44–45, 50

dilemmas. *See* moral dilemmas

divine command theory (DCT), 89–114, 171n3; contemporary, 99–102; critique of, 102–6; modified, 106–7; versus virtue ethics, 294n5

Dr. Horrible's Sing-Along Blog, 20–21, 24–25, 28–29, 32–33

Do the Right Thing, 73–74, 76–77, 80, 86–87

double effect, doctrine of, 162–63

duty: and actions, 215–16; conflicts among, 224; Kant on, 210; Ross on, 302

education: *The Emperor's Club* and, 325–29; *The Man without a Face* and, 337, 349–51

egoism: ethical, 156–60; psychological, 156

emotions: Hume on, 44–46; Kant on, 214; simple ethical subjectivism and, 53–57

emotivism, 63n3

The Emperor's Club, 325–29, 335, 340, 342

The Emperor's New Groove, 50–51, 53–55, 57–60

ends, persons as, 214, 221, 223

equivocation, 18

essence, term, 161

Eternal Sunshine of the Spotless Mind, 183–85, 196–97, 200–202

ethical egoism, 156–58; evaluation of, 158–60

ethical judgments: considered, 171n4; nature of, 20–22

ethical objectivism, 115–40

ethics, 12, 334–35; biology and psychology and, 143–72; Hume on, 43–46; messiness of, 310–12; standards in, 24–27; terminology in, 22–24

ethnocentrism: and moral relativism, 73–74; Sumner on, 70–71

eudaimonia, 280, 283, 294n4

euthanasia, 20

Euthyphro (Plato), 93–97

Evan Almighty, 100, 102, 104, 106, 108–10

evil, Hume on, 44

excellence, 280–83; Aristotle on, 274–75, 278–80

exemplars, virtue ethics and, 284, 286

experience machine thought experiment, 197, 344

Extreme Measures, 173–77, 187–90, 192–93

facts, 24–27; Hume on, 128; moral, 131–33

fallacies, 16–20

feminist theory, ethic of care and, 297–324

fidelity: gods and, 98–99; natural law and, 164

Firefly, 248, 250, 255–59, 264n3, 265n7

first principles, Reid on, 119–24

Folkways (Sumner), 69–72

formal fallacies, 17–18

forward-looking theories of justice, 25–26

The Foundations of the Metaphysics of Morals (Kant), 209–14

Foy, Joseph J., 265n10

Frailty, 89–93, 100–101, 104–5

freedom, and moral responsibility, 35n11

friendship: Aristotle on, 312–16; ethic of care and, 297–324

genocide, *Hotel Rwanda* and, 65–69, 73, 78–80

God(s): and divine command theory, 89–114; existence of, 51–52, 75; Kant on, 234n6; Plato on, 93–97

golden mean, 276–77, 280–83

good: God and, 105–6; Hume on, 44; Plato and, 325–52; term, 22–24

GoodFellas, 335, 337, 341–42, 347–49

good life: elements of, 345; Plato on, 335–36, 340–41, 343–45

goods, types of, 329–30, 344
Gorgias (Plato), 5–12
greatest happiness, principle of, 177, 180
Groundhog Day, 269–73, 277–83
Gyges, ring of, 329–34, 336–38

habit, Aristotle on, 274–75
happiness: Aristotle on, 273–74, 278–80; complexity of, 181–82; feeling versus being, 279–80, 341–43; health and, 342–43; Hobbes on, 241; of others, 180; personal, 180; Plato on, 341–43; soul and, 333–34
harm, 20–22, 152
health, and happiness, 342–43
hedon: existence of, 189, 195; term, 186
hedonism, 183; versus Platonic ethics, 344
heroism, 220–21, 223–24
higher pleasures, 178–80
Hinduism, 52, 63n8
Hobbes, Thomas, 240–45, 247–50; evaluation of, 254–55
Holocaust: Kantian ethics and, 234n5; moral relativism and, 77, 83; *Schindler's List* on, 124, 129, 132, 136–38
homosexuality, 163–66; *Boys Don't Cry* and, 151, 163–66, 169–70; *V for Vendetta* on, 250–52
honesty: divine command theory and, 100; Kant and, 216–21, 235n9; *Life Is Beautiful* and, 308–9
Horton Hears a Who!, 205–9, 215, 220, 223, 225–26, 228
Hotel Rwanda, 65–69, 73, 78–80
House M.D., 193
human condition, 166
human rights, and utilitarianism, 192
Hume, David, 43–46, 49–53, 119, 128
Hume's fork, 51
hypothetical imperatives, 212, 216–17

immoral, term, Sumner on, 72
impartiality, ethic of care on, 307–10
imperialism, cultural, 73
inductive arguments, 14–16
informal fallacies, 17–18
instrumental goods, 329–30, 344
intellectual pleasures, 185
intractable disagreement objection, 127–28
intrinsic goods, 329–30, 344
intrinsic value, 152
invisibility, ring of, 329–34, 336–38
Isaac, sacrifice of, 103, 113n2

is statements, 50; and human condition, 166; Hume on, 44–45

Joe Dirt, 193
The Joy Luck Club, 72–73, 76, 80–82, 84–85
justice: appearance versus reality of, 331–32; Hobbes on, 244, 255; majority view on, 336–38; Plato on, 9–11, 15, 329–34; Rawls on, 256; Rosenstand on, 25–26
justification, ethic of care on, 304–5
just person, 338–40
just state, 338–40

Kant, Immanuel, 28, 205–35
karma, 52, 63n8
King, Martin Luther, Jr., 82
kingdom of ends, 214
knowledge: *Gorgias* on, 8–9; obligation to, 225–26; of self, 282, 343

The Last Samurai, 278–80, 282, 286–87, 289–91
law(s): Aquinas on, 147–50; Kant on, 212; of nature, versus natural law, 172n8; nature of, 101–2
Leibniz, Gottfried, 106
Leviathan (Hobbes), 240–45
Life Is Beautiful, 308–9, 320–23
Locke, John, 250–53, 265n6; evaluation of, 254–55
logic, 14; fallacies in, 16–20
logical positivism, 139n2
Lord of the Flies, 245–48, 259–61
lower pleasures, 178–80
luck: Aristotle and, 294n4; existence of, 51–52

majority rule, 79–80; Locke on, 255
The Man without a Face, 337–38, 346, 349–51
Match Point, 39–43, 51, 53–54
math analogies, Reid on, 123–24
maxim, term, 217
Mencius, 306, 323n2
metaethics, 27; divine command theory, 89–114; ethical objectivism, 115–40; moral relativism, 65–88; simple ethical subjectivism, 39–63
metaphysics, 35n10
Mill, John Stuart, 28, 177–85
Minority Report, 14–15, 17–18, 21, 25–27, 29–31
monotheism, 98–99, 352n4
moral absolutism, 162, 218; critique of, 219

moral dilemmas, 151, 153, 345; doctrine of double effect and, 163; ethical egoism and, 159; Kantian ethics and, 219, 224, 227–28; moral absolutism and, 162; utilitarianism and, 187, 193; virtue ethics and, 283, 286

moral judgments: considered, 171n4; nature of, 20–22

moral obligation: ethic of care on, 302–3; *Life Is Beautiful* and, 308–9; to strangers, 305, 317; and utilitarianism, 191, 194

moral point of view, 23, 28, 34n7; importance of, 344

moral principles, 131–33; ethic of care on, 309; term, 140n6

moral progress, 80–83; ethic of care and, 317

moral realism. *See* ethical objectivism

moral reasoning, 1–35; terminology in, 22–24

moral relativism (MR), 65–88, 171n3; cultural differences and, 74–76; versus ethical objectivism, 125; ethnocentrism and, 73–74; versus simple ethical subjectivism, 75, 83; tolerance and, 76–78

moral rules: *The Cider House Rules* and, 115–19, 124–26, 133; negative versus positive, 227; virtue ethics and, 283

moral standards, 24–27, 151–52; Sumner on, 71–72; universal, 73, 149–50

moral theories, 334–35; anatomy of, 151–52; as controversial, 155; evaluation of, 152–55; term, 151

moral universe test, 154; and ethical egoism, 159; and Kantian ethics, 227

mores, Sumner on, 71–72

MR. *See* moral relativism

multiculturalism, 78–80

natural law(s), 160–63; Aquinas on, 147–50; evaluation of, 163–66; Hobbes on, 242–45, 247–48; versus laws of nature, 172n8; rules in, 235n11

natural rights, Locke on, 250–52, 255

nature: state of, 241, 245–47; term, 161

Nazis. *See* Holocaust

negative hedon, definition of, 186

negative moral rules, 227

negligence, 23

Nicomachean Ethics (Aristotle), 273–77, 294n4

Noddings, Nel, 301–6, 309, 323n4

nondeductive arguments, 14–16

no rest objection, and utilitarianism, 190–91, 194

normative claims, 44–45, 50

normative theory, 151

Nozick, Robert, 197, 344

objectivism, ethical, 115–40

objectivity, 47–48; and well-being, 27–29

omnibenevolence, 105

omnipotence, 101

original position, Rawls on, 256

ought statements, 50; and human condition, 166; Hume on, 44–45; Sumner on, 71

pain, utilitarianism on, 177, 183–85

persons, respect for, 221–23; evaluation of, 226–29; Kantian ethics and, 205–35

persuasion: *Gorgias* on, 8–9; rational, 14–16

philosophy, 1–35; and rhetoric, 13; and sophistry, 13–14, 19

piety: Plato on, 93–97; virtue ethics and, 287

Plato, 15, 325–52; and Aristotle, 273, 287, 344; as controversial, 344–46; *Euthyphro,* 93–97; *Gorgias,* 5–12; *Republic,* 5, 329–40

pleasure: and friendship, 312–13; versus happiness, 279–80, 341–43; utilitarianism on, 177–79, 183–85

Pojman, Louis, 134, 352n9

polytheism, 98–99

positive hedon, definition of, 186

positive moral rules, 227

positivism, logical, 139n2

practice, Aristotle on, 274–75

prima facie duty, doctrine of, 302

principles: first, 119–24; moral, 131–33, 140n6, 309

property, Locke on, 252–53

psychological egoism, 156

psychology, and ethical theory, 143–72

rational persuasion, 14–16

Rawls, John, 171n4, 256–59

realism. *See* ethical objectivism

reason: Aristotle on, 279; versus ethic of care, 306–7; Plato on, 339–42; truths of, 128–30. *See also* moral reasoning

red herring fallacy, 18

Reid, Thomas, 119–24, 130, 132

relation: ethic of care on, 302–4, 307–10; Kantian ethics and, 308 relativism: cultural, 74–76; moral, 65–88, 125, 171n3

Republic (Plato), 5, 329–40

respect for persons ethics, 205–35

rhetoric, 1–35; *Gorgias* on, 6–11

right: ethic of care and, 323n4; Reid on, 120–23; Sumner on, 69–70; term, 22–24

rights: civil, 82–83, 226; ethic of care and, 312; natural, Locke on, 250–52, 255; Sumner on, 69–70; utilitarianism and, 192

Rosenstand, Nina, 25–26, 35n9

Ross, W. D., 302

rules: *The Cider House Rules* and, 115–19, 124–26, 133; negative versus positive, 227; virtue ethics and, 283

rule utilitarianism, 186, 192–95; as controversial, 195–96

Rusesabagina, Paul, 66, 82

Russell, Bruce, 134

Rwanda, 65–69, 73, 78–80

Saving Private Ryan, 183, 187, 189–90, 193, 197–200

Schindler's List, 124, 126, 129, 133, 136–38

science: analogies from, Reid on, 123–24; and ethical theory, 143–72; and objectivity, 126

scripture, 101, 113n2

self-defeating claims, 127–28

self-interest, 156–58

self-knowledge: Aristotle and, 282; Plato and, 343

sentiment, Hume on, 43–46

Serenity, 254–59, 261–64, 264n3, 265n7

SES. *See* simple ethical subjectivism

sexuality: natural law on, 163–66, 172n10. *See also* homosexuality

Shafer-Landau, Russ, 259, 294n5

The Shape of Things, 48, 50, 55–57, 60–62

simple ethical subjectivism (SES), 39–63; argument for, 53–54; case against, 54–57; versus ethical objectivism, 125; versus moral relativism, 75, 83; and self-defeating claims, 127–28. *See also* subjectivism

Singer, Peter, 203n6

Smith, Adam, 119

Smith, Michael, 132–33

Sober, Elliot, 140n11

social codes, Sumner on, 71–72

social contract theory, 237–65; critique of, 257–58

Socrates, 5, 13, 15

sophistry, 13–15, 19

soul: parts of, 332–33; term, 352n6

sovereign, Hobbes on, 245, 247–50, 255, 265n5

special obligation: ethic of care on, 302–3, 317; *Life Is Beautiful* and, 308–9; and utilitarianism, 191, 194

speciesism, 188, 203n6

Spider-Man 2, 151–52, 157–58, 160, 166–69

standards. *See* moral standards

Star Trek II: The Wrath of Khan, 183

state of nature, 245–47; Hobbes on, 241

Stocker, Michael, 235n13

strangers, obligations to, 305, 317

straw man fallacy, 19

subjectivism: argument for, 48–49; and self-defeating claims, 127–28. *See also* simple ethical subjectivism

subjectivity, 47–48

suicide, 22, 171n6; *Cast Away* and, 146; ethical egoism and, 157; Hobbes on, 265n5; Kantian ethics and, 217; natural law and, 162

Summa Theologica (Aquinas), 147–50

Sumner, William Graham, 69–72

Ten Commandments, 99, 103

Thank You for Smoking, 1–5, 16, 18, 22

theists, 101

3:10 to Yuma, 215, 220–21, 229–31

tolerance, and moral relativism, 76–78

true, Sumner on, 69–70

truth(s), 47; ethical objectivism and, 130–31; objective versus subjective, 47–49; of reason, 128–30

tu quoque fallacy, 19

tyranny: Hobbes on, 240–45; Locke on, 252–53; Plato on, 351n2

universal moral standards, 73; Aquinas on, 149–50; ethic of care on, 302, 309; Kant on, 210–12, 217; virtue ethics and, 288

utilitarianism, 173–203; conceptual framework of, 183–86; definition of, 177–78; versus ethic of care, 309

utility, and friendship, 313

utility principle, 181, 185

value(s): intrinsic, 152; and utilitarianism, 196–97

veil of ignorance, Rawls on, 256, 258–59

Vera Drake, 297–301, 311–12

V for Vendetta, 237–40, 245–46, 248–54

vice, Reid on, 120–23

virtue: Aquinas on, 149; Aristotle on, 274–77; definition of, 276–77; as difficult, 277; ethic of care and, 310; and friendship, 313–14; importance of, 275–76; Reid on, 120–23

virtue ethics, 269–95; evaluation of, 283–85

virtuous person, 284–85; Aristotle on, 279–80; and justice, 338–40

war, Hobbes on, 241–42

well-being, 20–22; and objectivity, 27–29

Whedon, Joss, 254–59, 261–64, 264n3, 265n7

White, Alan V., 139n5

women: Aristotle and Plato on, 287; ethic of care and, 297–324

wrong: ethic of care and, 323n4; Reid on, 120–23; term, 22–24

The X-Files: I Want to Believe, 310–16, 318–20

About the Author

Dean A. Kowalski is associate professor and UW-Colleges Philosophy Department Chair at the University of Wisconsin–Waukesha. He is the author of *Classic Questions and Contemporary Film: An Introduction to Philosophy*. He is the editor of *"The Big Bang Theory" and Philosophy* and the coeditor of *The Philosophy of Joss Whedon*, *The Philosophy of "The X-Files,"* and *Steven Spielberg and Philosophy*.